Fodor's

SEATTLE

5th Edition

Fodor's Travel Publications   New York, Toronto, London, Sydney, Auckland
www.fodors.com

Be a Fodor's Correspondent

Your opinion matters. It matters to us. It matters to your fellow Fodor's travelers, too. And we'd like to hear it. In fact, we *need* to hear it.

When you share your experiences and opinions, you become an active member of the Fodor's community. That means we'll not only use your feedback to make our books better, but we'll publish your names and comments whenever possible. Throughout our guides, look for "Word of Mouth," excerpts of your unvarnished feedback.

Here's how you can help improve Fodor's for all of us.

Tell us when we're right. We rely on local writers to give you an insider's perspective. But our writers and staff editors—who are the best in the business—depend on you. Your positive feedback is a vote to renew our recommendations for the next edition.

Tell us when we're wrong. We're proud that we update most of our guides every year. But we're not perfect. Things change. Hotels cut services. Museums change hours. Charming cafés lose charm. If our writer didn't quite capture the essence of a place, tell us how you'd do it differently. If any of our descriptions are inaccurate or inadequate, we'll incorporate your changes in the next edition and will correct factual errors at fodors.com *immediately.*

Tell us what to include. You probably have had fantastic travel experiences that aren't yet in Fodor's. Why not share them with a community of like-minded travelers? Maybe you chanced upon a beach or bistro or bed-and-breakfast that you don't want to keep to yourself. Tell us why we should include it. And share your discoveries and experiences with everyone directly at fodors.com. Your input may lead us to add a new listing or highlight a place we cover with a "Highly Recommended" star or with our highest rating, "Fodor's Choice."

Give us your opinion instantly at our feedback center at www.fodors.com/feedback. You may also e-mail editors@fodors.com with the subject line "Seattle Editor." Or send your nominations, comments, and complaints by mail to Seattle Editor, Fodor's, 1745 Broadway, New York, NY 10019.

You and travelers like you are the heart of the Fodor's community. Make our community richer by sharing your experiences. Be a Fodor's correspondent.

Happy traveling!

Tim Jarrell, Publisher

FODOR'S SEATTLE

Editors: Heidi Leigh Johansen, Eric Wechter

Editorial Contributors: Carissa Bluestone, Cedar Burnett, Nick Horton, Heidi Leigh Johansen, Holly S. Smith

Production Editor: Jennifer DePrima
Maps & Illustrations: David Lindroth and Mark Stroud, *cartographers;* Bob Blake, Rebecca Baer, *map editors;* William Wu, *information graphics*
Design: Fabrizio La Rocca, *creative director*; Guido Caroti, Siobhan O'Hare, *art directors*; Tina Malaney, Nora Rosansky, Chie Ushio, Jessica Walsh, Ann McBride, *designers*; Melanie Marin, *senior picture editor*
Cover Photo: (Pike Place Market): Hal Bergman/iStockphoto
Production Manager: Steve Slawsky

5th Edition

ISBN 978-1-4000-0494-2

ISSN 1531-3417

SPECIAL SALES

This book is available at special discounts for bulk purchases for sales promotions or premiums. Special editions, including personalized covers, excerpts of existing books, and corporate imprints, can be created in large quantities for special needs. For more information, write to Special Markets/Premium Sales, 1745 Broadway, MD 6-2, New York, New York 10019, or e-mail specialmarkets@randomhouse.com.

AN IMPORTANT TIP & AN INVITATION

Although all prices, opening times, and other details in this book are based on information supplied to us at press time, changes occur all the time in the travel world, and Fodor's cannot accept responsibility for facts that become outdated or for inadvertent errors or omissions. So **always confirm information when it matters**, especially if you're making a detour to visit a specific place. Your experiences—positive and negative—matter to us. If we have missed or misstated something, **please write to us.** We follow up on all suggestions. Contact the Seattle editor at editors@fodors.com or c/o Fodor's at 1745 Broadway, New York, NY 10019.

PRINTED IN SINGAPORE

10 9 8 7 6 5 4 3 2 1

CONTENTS

Fodor's Features

MAPS

ABOUT
THIS BOOK

Our Ratings

Sometimes you find terrific travel experiences and sometimes they just find you. But usually the burden is on you to select the right combination of experiences. That's where our ratings come in.

As travelers we've all discovered a place so wonderful that its worthiness is obvious. And sometimes that place is so unique that superlatives don't do it justice: you just have to be there to know. These sights, properties, and experiences get our highest rating, **Fodor's Choice**, indicated by orange stars throughout this book.

Black stars highlight sights and properties we deem **Highly Recommended**, places that our writers, editors, and readers praise again and again for consistency and excellence.

By default, there's another category: any place we include in this book is by definition worth your time, unless we say otherwise. And we will.

Disagree with any of our choices? Care to nominate a place or suggest that we rate one more highly? Visit our feedback center at www.fodors.com/feedback.

Budget Well

Hotel and restaurant price categories from ¢ to $$$$ are defined in the opening pages of the Where to Eat and Where to Stay chapters. For attractions, we always give standard adult admission fees; reductions are usually available for children, students, and senior citizens. Want to pay with plastic? **AE, D, DC, MC, V** following restaurant and hotel listings indicate whether American Express, Discover, Diners Club, MasterCard, and Visa are accepted.

Restaurants

Unless we state otherwise, restaurants are open for lunch and dinner daily. We mention dress only when there's a specific requirement and reservations only when they're essential or not accepted—it's always best to book ahead.

Hotels

Hotels have private bath, phone, TV, and air-conditioning and operate on the European Plan (aka EP, meaning without meals), unless we specify that they use the Continental Plan (CP, with a Continental breakfast), Breakfast Plan (BP, with a full breakfast), or Modified American Plan (MAP, with breakfast and dinner) or are all-inclusive (including all meals and

most activities). We always list facilities but not whether you'll be charged an extra fee to use them, so when pricing accommodations, find out what's included.

Listings	
★	Fodor's Choice
★	Highly recommended
✉	Physical address
↔	Directions or Map coordinates
🕮	Mailing address
☎	Telephone
🖷	Fax
⊕	On the Web
✎	E-mail
💳	Admission fee
☉	Open/closed times
Ⓜ	Metro stations
▭	Credit cards
Hotels & Restaurants	
🏠	Hotel
⊐	Number of rooms
♨	Facilities
❍|	Meal plans
✕	Restaurant
☟	Reservations
🎩	Dress code
⌇	Smoking
🍸	BYOB
Outdoors	
🏌	Golf
⛺	Camping
Other	
℃	Family-friendly
⇨	See also
✉	Branch address
☞	Take note

Experience
Seattle

WHAT'S WHERE

1 Downtown. This part of town is easy to pick out—it's the only part of the Seattle with skyscrapers. Seattle's governmental buildings are here, along with most of the city's hotels and many popular tourist spots, including the waterfront, Pike Place Market, and Seattle Art Museum. Just north of Downtown, Belltown is home to the Olympic Sculpture Park, as well as boutiques and nightlife.

2 Seattle Center, South Lake Union, and Queen Anne. Queen Anne, north of Belltown, rises up from Denny Way to the Lake Washington Ship Canal. At the bottom are the Space Needle, the Seattle Center, and the Experience Music Project museum. South Lake Union—a neighborhood in transition—has the REI superstore, lakefront, and some eateries and hotels.

3 Pioneer Square. Seattle's oldest neighborhood has lovely redbrick and sandstone buildings, plus numerous galleries and antiques shops, though it also has a shabbiness that clashes with the carefully maintained facades.

4 International District. Once called Chinatown, the I.D. is a fun place to shop and eat. The stunning Wing Luke Asian Museum and Uwajimaya shopping center anchor the neighborhood.

5 First Hill and the Central District. Nicknamed "Pill Hill" for its abundance of hospitals, the First Hill neighborhood has only one must-see: the Frye Art Museum. Farther east is the Central District, which is way off the tourist track, but has some beautiful churches and street art.

6 Capitol Hill. The Hill has two faces: On one side, it's young and sassy, full of artists, musicians, and students. On the other side, it's elegant and upscale, with tree-lined streets, 19th-century mansions, and John Charles Olmsted's Volunteer Park. It has fantastic restaurants and nightlife.

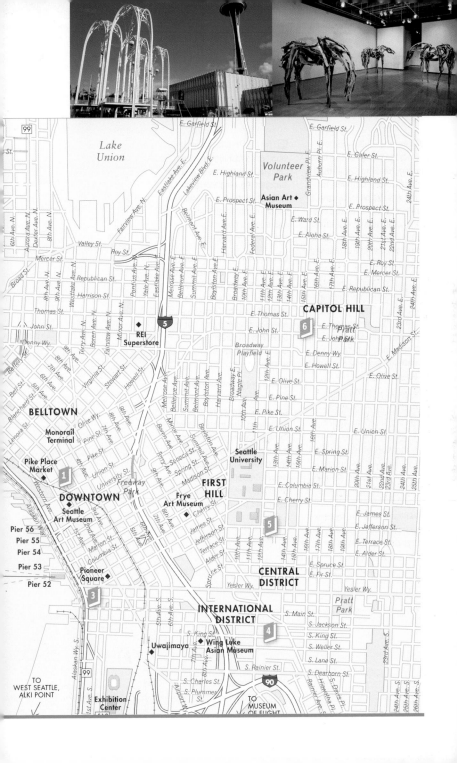

Lake Union

E. Garfield St.

99

E. Garfield St.

6th Ave. N.
Aurora Ave. N.
Dexter Ave. N.
8th Ave. N.

Fairview Ave. N.
Eastlake Ave. E.
Lakeview Blvd. E.

Volunteer Park

E. Galer St.

Grandview Pl. E.
Auburn Pl. E.

E. Highland St.

E. Highland St.

Belmont Ave. E.

Melrose Ave. E.
Bellevue Ave. E.
Boylston Ave. E.
Harvard Ave. E.
Broadway

E. Prospect St.

Asian Art Museum ◆

E. Prospect St.

Valley St.

Roy St.

Westlake Ave. N.
Pontius Ave. N.
Yale Ave. N.
Eastlake Ave. N.

Mercer St.

8th Ave. N.

Republican St.

Broad St.

Harrison St.

Thomas St.

Terry Ave. N.
Boren Ave. N.
Fairview Ave. N.
Minor Ave. N.
9th Ave. N.

John St.

Denny Wy.

5

REI Superstore ◆

E. Ward St.

Federal Ave. E.

E. Aloha St.

16th Ave. E.
18th Ave. E.
19th Ave. E.
20th Ave. E.
21st Ave. E.
22nd Ave. E.

E. Roy St.
E. Mercer St.

11th Ave. E.
12th Ave. E.
14th Ave. E.

E. Republican St.

23rd Ave. E.
24th Ave. E.

CAPITOL HILL

E. Thomas St.

6

E. Thomas St.
E. John St.

Pratt Park

E. John St.

Broadway Playfield

E. Denny Wy.

E. Howell St.

E. Madison St.

Battery St.
8th Ave.
7th Ave.
6th Ave.
5th Ave.
Bell St.
Blanchard St.
Lenora St.

Virginia St.

Stewart St.

Howell St.

Melrose Ave.
Bellevue Ave.
Boylston Ave.
Summit Ave.
Harvard Ave.

Broadway E.
Maple Pl.

10th Ave.
11th
12th Ave. E.

E. Olive St.

E. Olive St.

E. Pine St.

E. Pike St.

13th Ave.
14th Ave.
15th Ave.

16th Ave.

E. Union St.

E. Union St.

BELLTOWN

Olive Wy.

Pine St.
7th Ave.
4th Ave.
Terry Ave.
Boren Ave.
Minor Ave.
Summit Ave.
Boylston Ave.

Monorail Terminal

Pike St.

8th Ave.

Union St.

Seneca St.
Spring St.
University St.

Freeway Park

Madison St.

Seattle University

E. Spring St.

E. Marion St.

17th Ave.
18th Ave.
19th Ave.
20th Ave.
21st Ave.
22nd Ave.
23rd Ave.
24th Ave.
25th Ave.

Pike Place Market ◆

1

DOWNTOWN

Western Ave.

Alaskan Way.

Seattle Art Museum ◆

1st Ave.
2nd Ave.
3rd Ave.
4th Ave.
5th Ave.
6th Ave.

Marion St.

Columbia St.

12th Ave.

Cherry St.

FIRST HILL

Frye Art Museum ◆

E. Columbia St.

E. Cherry St.

E. James St.
E. Jefferson St.

E. Terrace St.
E. Alder St.

Pier 56
Pier 55
Pier 54
Pier 53

James St.

Jefferson St.

Terrace St.

Alder St.

5

10th Ave.
11th Ave.
12th Ave.
14th Ave.
15th Ave.
16th Ave.

CENTRAL DISTRICT

E. Spruce St.
E. Fir St.

Pier 52

Pioneer Square ◆

Spruce St.

Yesler Wy.

Yesler Wy.

3

INTERNATIONAL DISTRICT

5th Ave. S.
6th Ave. S.

S. Main St.

Pratt Park

S. Jackson St.

17th Ave.
18th Ave.
19th Ave.

S. King St.

4

S. King St.

S. Weller St.

Uwajimaya ◆

Wing Luke Asian Museum ◆

7th Ave.
8th Ave.

S. Lane St.

23rd Ave. S.

Alaskan Wy. S.

99

S. Rainier St.

S. Dearborn St.

S. Charles St.

S. Plummer St.

TO WEST SEATTLE, ALKI POINT

1st Ave. S.

Exhibition Center

90

TO MUSEUM OF FLIGHT

Rainier Ave. S.
Hiawatha Pl. S.
24th Ave. S.
25th Ave. S.
26th Ave. S.

WHAT'S WHERE

7 Fremont. This 'hood on the northern side of the Lake Washington Ship Canal used to be *the* neighborhood for artists and hippies; it's now an interesting mix of pricey boutiques and yummy restaurants. Up the hill, residential Phinney Ridge includes the Woodland Park Zoo.

8 Ballard. Skirting the mouth of Shilshole Bay, Ballard's main attraction is the Hiram M. Chittenden Locks. This historically Scandinavian neighborhood is beloved for its eateries, trendy shops, and farmers market.

9 Wallingford. A large residential neighborhood that keeps a low profile, Wallingford starts at the ship canal with the wonderful waterfront Gas Works Park. Its booming commercial strip along N. 45th Street has a few excellent restaurants. Directly north of Wallingford is Green Lake, whose park has a paved path that circles the lake.

10 The "U District." The University of Washington's vast campus is truly lovely, and the surrounding neighborhood can be both gritty and charming. Loads of ethnic restaurants and a large student population keep things lively.

11 West Seattle. On a peninsula west of the city proper, West Seattle's California Avenue has some lovely shops and restaurants. Gorgeous Alki Beach offers views of the Seattle skyline. Lincoln Park is a fantastic place to hike or relax on the beach.

12 Eastside. East of Lake Washington, the Eastside suburbs are home to Microsoft. Bellevue is the most citylike, with its own skyline, an art museum, and high-end shops and restaurants. You can also visit Redmond, Woodinville wineries, Marymoor Park, or head into the mountains.

Shilshole Bay

West Point

Discovery Park

W. Emerson S

34th Ave. W.

MAGNOLIA

Magnolia Blvd. W.

TO
WINSLOW
ON BAINBRIDGE ISLAND

TO
BREMERTON

Alki Beach Park

Alki Point

Alki Av.

63rd Ave. SW

Beach Dr. SW

0   1 mile

0   1 km

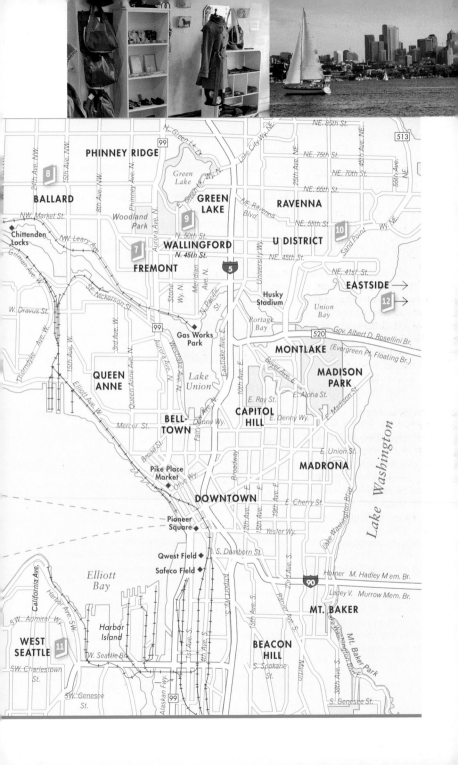

PHINNEY RIDGE

BALLARD

Chittenden
Locks

GREEN
LAKE

Green
Lake

Woodland
Park

RAVENNA

WALLINGFORD

U DISTRICT

FREMONT

EASTSIDE →

Gas Works
Park

Husky
Stadium

Portage
Bay

Union
Bay

MONTLAKE

(Evergreen Pt. Floating Br.)

QUEEN
ANNE

Lake
Union

MADISON
PARK

BELL-
TOWN

CAPITOL
HILL

MADRONA

Pike Place
Market

Lake Washington

DOWNTOWN

Pioneer
Square

Qwest Field

Safeco Field

Homer M. Hadley Mem. Br.

Elliott
Bay

Laney V. Murrow Mem. Br.

Harbor
Island

MT. BAKER

WEST
SEATTLE

BEACON
HILL

SEATTLE PLANNER

Airport Ease

Your can take Sound Transit's **Central Link Light Rail** (⊕ www.soundtransit.org) from Sea-Tac to Downtown. The train runs every 10 to 15 minutes from 5 AM to 1 AM weekdays and Saturday, and every 15 minutes from 6 AM to midnight on Sunday. The Downtown terminus is Westlake Station, which is convenient to many hotels. The Sound Transit Central Link fare is $2.50 one-way. (⇨ For more airport transfer options, see Travel Smart Seattle.)

Visitor Information

Contact the **Seattle Visitors Bureau and Convention Center** (⊕ www.visitseattle.org ☎ 206/461–5800) for help with everything from sightseeing to booking spa services. You can also follow their Twitter feed (⊕ twitter.com/seattlemaven). The main visitor information center is Downtown, at the Washington State Convention and Trade Center on 8th Avenue and Pike Street; it has a full-service concierge desk open daily 9 to 5 (in summer; weekdays only in winter). There's also an info booth at Pike Place Market.

Getting Around

(⇨ For detailed fare and schedule information, see Travel Smart.)

By Biking and Walking: Bicycling is popular but still somewhat of a cult endeavor thanks to a shortage of safe bike routes and some daunting hills. Check out ⊕ www.ridethecity.com/seattle. Walking is fun, though distances and rain can sometimes get in the way. Several neighborhoods—from Pioneer Square to Downtown, or from Belltown to Queen Anne, for example—are close enough to each other that even hills and moisture can't stop walkers.

By Bus: The bus system will get you anywhere you need to go, although some routes require a time commitment and several transfers. Within the downtown core, however, the bus is efficient—and, most of the time, it won't cost you a dime, thanks to the Ride-Free Area. The trip Planner (⊕ tripplanner.kingcounty.gov) is a useful resource. (Fare: $2.25)

By Light Rail: Sound Transit's Central Link Light Rail (⊕ www.soundtransit.org)—the first link of which was completed in 2009—will eventually accomplish what the buses can't: an efficient way to go north–south in this vertically oriented city. (Fare: $2.50)

By Monorail: Built for the 1962 World's Fair, the monorail (⊕ www.seattlemonorail.com) is the shortest transportation system in the city. It runs from Westlake Center (on 5th and Pine) to Seattle Center. But this is great for visitors who plan to spend a day at the Space Needle and the Seattle Center's museums. (Fare: $2.00)

By Seattle Streetcar: The second-shortest system in the city (⊕ www.seattlestreetcar.org) was built to connect Downtown to South Lake Union (directly east of Seattle Center). It runs from Westlake and Olive to the southern shore of Lake Union. (Fare: $2.25)

By Taxi: Seattle's taxi fleet is small, but you can sometimes hail a cab, especially Downtown. Most of the time you must call for one. Except on Friday and Saturday nights, you rarely have to wait more than a few minutes. Cabs can be pricey but useful, especially late at night when buses run infrequently. Two major cab companies are **Yellow Cab** (☎ 206/622–6500) and **Farwest** (☎ 206/622–1717).

Plan Ahead

Hotel reservations. If you're arriving during high season or around major festivals and events, book as far in advance as possible. This extends past city limits—accommodations go fast (including campsites) on the San Juan Islands and the Olympic Peninsula. Waterfront or water-view hotels, like the Edgewater and the Inn at the Market, see their best rooms booked six months in advance.

Restaurant reservations. Seattle's latest (and certainly not greatest) dining trend is the two-hour wait at places that don't take reservations. It never hurts to ask if you can reserve, and you should definitely lock down your table at splurge restaurants. If you have a large party, a reservation is even more important and may be easier to come by.

Tickets. Nearly any act that makes it to Key Arena is going to sell out the show. National touring acts at smaller rock clubs like Neumos, Showbox, Triple Door, and the Crocodile also play to full houses. Tickets for the most buzzed-about movies at the Seattle International Film Festival should be purchased as soon as they go on sale. Visits to the Bloedel Reserve on Bainbridge Island are by appointment only, and booking well in advance on summer weekends is advised. Tickets for major-league sports—such as Sounders and Mariners games—should be booked online in advance.

Car rentals. Though the parking lot that is Interstate 5 (I-5) may suggest otherwise, quite a few Seattleites don't own cars. On summer weekends, you'll be competing not only with the thousands of other visitors in town but also with residents making an exodus toward the mountains. If you find a good rate, book it immediately, especially at the few downtown rental offices. (Remember: you'll find better rates—and no airport tax—if you book in town.)

Train tickets. Amtrak tickets to Portland and Vancouver, B.C. sell out on summer weekends, and last-minute fares can be quite expensive.

Ferries. Whale-watching/ferry ride vacation packages like those offered by the *Victoria Clipper* can be booked in advance. The Washington State Ferries rarely accepts reservations (only on international sailings to Sidney, B.C., for example), so be sure to plan island travel thoughtfully: leave enough time in your schedule to arrive at the piers early—and to wait for the next ferry if you're last on line.

When to Go

Seattle is most enjoyable May through October. July through September is mostly dry, with warm days reaching into the mid-70s and 80s, with cooler nights. Although the weather can be dodgy, spring and fall are also excellent times to visit, as lodging and tour costs are usually much lower (and the crowds much smaller). In winter, the weather can be dreary, but temperatures rarely dip below the low 40s; days are short, as well, because of Seattle's far-north location.

Festivals

■TIP→ The Seattle Convention and Visitors Bureau has a full calendar of events at ⊕ www.visitseattle.org/cultural. Foodies will want to hit up **Taste of Washington** (spring; ⊕ *www. tastewashington.org*) and **Bite of Seattle** (July; ⊕ *www. biteofseattle.com*). The **Seattle International Film Festival** presents more than 200 features (May–June; ⊕ *www. siff.net*). **Bumbershoot** (September; ⊕ *www.bumbershoot. org*) is SIFF's musical equivalent and includes dance and theater performances. The **Seattle Pride Festival** (June; ⊕ www.seattlepride.org) has the Northwest's biggest gay, lesbian, and transgender pride parade. **Seafair** (July–August; ⊕ www.seafair.com) is the biggest summer festival; hydroplane races are just one major event.

QUINTESSENTIAL SEATTLE

Coffee

It may be a cliché, but coffee is a huge part of Seattle's cultural identity. Starbucks has enough local fans to be a presence here, but to understand the coffee culture—and to get a great cup of coffee—visit one of the numerous independent shops and local mini-chains, several of which manage to roast their own beans on-site without burning them. A Seattleite's relationship with coffee ranges from grabbing the daily quick fix in the morning to spending half the day at a local shop where every barista knows their name (and coffee order), reading, chatting with friends, or tapping away on a laptop. Many coffee shops pull double duty as art galleries, and some of them even pull double duty as *good* art galleries. Occasionally, shops feature hard-to-get coffees at special "cupping" events, which take on the structure and feel of wine tastings.

Music

It's mystifying that many people still persist in describing all manner of the city's carefully disheveled indie rockers as grunge. Today you're more likely to catch alt-country bands, post-emo song-writers, or eclectic folk-pop like the Fleet Foxes than anything resembling grunge. The city's love of music is demonstrated more outside of its clubs than in them. You can see it in the independent record shops, where staff members handwrite poetic recommendations; in the continued success of local label Sub Pop Records; in the fanatical support for local radio station KEXP; in the health of midsize venues that can draw national acts; and the tendency of coffeehouse baristas to treat their shifts like DJ sessions.

If you want to savor the Emerald City like a local, start by familiarizing yourself with some of its passions.

Pacific Northwest Cuisine

With such an active population, and easy access to the best the sea and the land have to offer, it's no wonder that eating well is so important to Seattleites. Pacific Northwest dishes emphasize fresh, locally produced ingredients; even some of the fanciest restaurants get their raw materials from the city's farmers' markets, Pike Place Market, and in some cases from their chef's own organic farms. These fresh, seasonal goods can be combined in straightforward ways—inventive takes on American comfort food is a recent trend—or fused with European and Asian influences. Many of Seattle's chefs have gained their fame through their ambitious takes on Pacific Northwest cuisine, but you don't have to spend big bucks for a taste: many bistros, bakeries, and cafés use local and organic ingredients as a matter of principle.

The Great Outdoors

Yeah, it rains a lot . . . in winter. But summers are gorgeous (as are most falls and springs), and with a major mountain range on each side and Mt. Rainier rising to the south, it's no wonder that Seattleites are obsessed with the outdoors. The best adventures—heading east to hike in the Cascade range; south to hike in Mt. Rainier or Mt. St. Helens national parks; west to camp, hike, and spot wildlife in Olympic National Park; or across the Sound to explore one of many nearby islands on foot or by canoe or kayak—involve leaving the city, but even within Seattle proper, there's plenty to do. Kayaking is one of the easiest sports to try, thanks to the abundance of water; many people paddle around Portage Bay. Favorite urban parks include Discovery Park, Washington Park Arboretum, and Seward Park. Enjoying an outdoor adventure is easy and memorable here.

IF YOU LIKE

Arts and Culture

The Great Outdoors gets so much attention it's easy to overlook Seattle's Great Indoors—its myriad galleries, museums, and cinemas. The city teems with visual artists and sculptors; several excellent film festivals attest to the number of resident cinephiles. Nearly every local coffee shop (and many restaurants, bars, and stores) serves as an impromptu art gallery; some even hold official openings with food, drinks, and music when exhibits change.

A great way to get an overview of Seattle's art scene—and do some socializing in the process—is to participate in one of the city's many **art walks**, which include stops at galleries, coffeehouses that have rotating art exhibits, restaurants, shops, and public works of art in all their quirky glory. The biggest walk is the First Thursday Art Walk in Pioneer Square (first Thursday of every month from noon to 8 PM ⊕ *www. firstthursdayseattle.com*), which starts at Main Street and Occidental and takes you through the city's gallery district, as well as to some Downtown spots. There are also smaller, though no less interesting, walks in Capitol Hill (*second* Thursdays from 5 PM to 8 PM ⊕ *www.blitzcapitolhill. com*), Fremont (first Fridays from 6 PM to 9 PM ⊕ *www.fremontfirstfriday.blogspot. com*), and Ballard (second Saturdays from 6 PM to 9 PM ⊕ *www.ballardchamber. com*).

Check out what local writers are up to at readings at the **Richard Hugo House, Open Books,** and **Pilot Books.**

The *grande dame* of the art scene, the **Seattle Art Museum** has rotating exhibitions and a lovely permanent collection; SAM's outdoor branch, **Olympic Sculpture Park,** is where striking sculptures compete with views of the Puget Sound. Other favorite museums include the **Wing Luke Asian Museum** and the **Frye Art Museum,** among others.

A nonprofit that aids Seattle's budding filmmakers, the **Northwest Film Forum** (⊕ *www.nwfilmforum.org*) has the scoop on independent film in the Northwest and worldwide. At NWFF's hip screening room, film geeks can catch hard-to-find documentaries and feature films or just revisit classic films from masters like Jean Renoir and Akira Kurosawa.

Water

No, not the kind of water that falls from the winter sky. Seattle is bounded and sliced by impressive stretches of blue. Even longtime residents can be found gawking at the mountain-backed Puget Sound and its bays.

A must-see on any itinerary, the **Seattle Aquarium** shows you what's going on underneath the surface, with special exhibits concerning the marine and river ecosystems of the Pacific Northwest. Get an up-close look at all sorts of craft, from research boats to posh yachts as they navigate the Lake Washington Ship Canal and the **Hiram M. Chittenden (aka "Ballard") Locks.**

If you're not content with views alone, **rent a canoe or kayak** from Agua Verde Paddle Club and tool around the ship canal; head into Lake Union to see Seattle's famous houseboats.

On hot days, the swimming rafts in **Lake Washington** beckon. Several beaches along the western shore of this massive lake have lifeguards and other amenities. The eastern shore of **Green Lake** also has a beach and swimming raft and offers a more subdued dip—a good way to cool off after you join Seattleites in a jog around the lake's nearly-3-mi pedestrian path.

To experience a little taste of California in Seattle, take the **West Seattle water taxi** (⊕ *www.kingcounty.gov*) across Elliott Bay. Stroll or bike along Alki Beach, dip a toe or a kayak in the water, and enjoy a great panorama of city skyline, mountains, and sea. Riding a **Washington State ferry**—such as the trip from Downtown Seattle to Bainbridge Island—is a true joy.

Lazy Days

Despite all the activities they enjoy, Seattleites appreciate the beauty of slowing the pace and spending a few quiet hours away from distractions.

Grab a few books, **find a coffee shop**, and spend a couple of hours reading and writing postcards. The porch of Fremont Coffee Company is particularly conducive to chilling out, as are Caffé Vita and Victrola on Capitol Hill, and the Panama Hotel Tea and Coffee House in the International District.

Instead of jostling with joggers around Green Lake or power walking in Discovery Park, head to **Gasworks Park** and stake out a piece of green. From the park's hill you can idly watch the boats in Lake Union or even fly a kite—the Gasworks Park Kite Shop is right around the corner at Stone Way and N. 34th Street.

Take the ferry to nearby islands **Vashon or Bainbridge**. Rent a bike and tool around past parkland, farmland, and orchards; then pop into galleries and crafts shops if you feel so inclined. Or just find a piece of beach and relax for a few hours.

Wining and Dining

It's no secret that Seattle has excellent restaurants as well as an obsession with wine (both Northwest and international varieties) that is second only to its obsession with coffee. A wine list is never an afterthought at the city's best restaurants, and it's never difficult to find a place that does food and drink equally well.

Purple Café and Wine Bar is the first stop for the indecisive. You can get anything from baked Brie with apricot preserves to short rib sandwich. You can also order flights of three or four different wines, paired with cheeses, if you have trouble choosing from the wine list, which is so long it has a table of contents. **106 Pine**, a wine shop with a tasting bar run by a very knowledgeable staff, will also provide crash courses in notable Northwest wines.

Out of all of the city's current favorite restaurants, **Café Juanita, Joule, Poppy, Spring Hill, Anchovies & Olives, Matt's in the Market,** and **Lark** are just a few that get a special nod for excellent food and wine choices that never disappoint. **The Herbfarm**, in the city's eastern suburbs, and the **Corson Building**, in the southern city limits, both take special-occasion dining to a whole new level. At the Herbfarm you'll get no fewer than nine courses and five or six paired wines, along with commentary from the chef and owners. The Corson Building serves Saturday family-style meals determined by the seasonal bounty of local producers.

To indulge during daylight hours, **create the perfect picnic** with food from Salumi in Pioneer Square or DeLaurenti's at Pike Place Market (be sure to grab a few choice bottles from the Pike & Western Wine Shop nearby).

SEATTLE'S TOP ATTRACTIONS

The World of SAM

(A) Downtown's Seattle Art Museum (SAM) is known for its collection of modern and Native American art; a sleek addition to the original building—complete with a stylish café and gift shop—created the proper modern aesthetics for Picasso and Warhol. SAM'S Olympic Sculpture Park, in Belltown, overlooks Puget Sound and the Olympic Mountains and showcases works by Calder and Serra amidst green space. On Capitol Hill, peruse the Seattle Asian Art Museum's fascinating collection of Chinese, Japanese, and Korean art before venturing into surrounding Volunteer Park.

Seattle Aquarium

(B) Seattle's homage to its marine habitats and inhabitants sits, fittingly, on one of its piers. This small but delightful aquarium has a well-rounded selection of Northwest-focused exhibits, from river otters to a salmon ladder. Watch divers feed fish in a replica of Neah Bay, then pay a visit to a Giant Pacific Octopus.

Discovery Park

(C) Well off the radar, on a peninsula in a residential neighborhood, this park always feels like a serendipitous discovery. Though the city has many other impressive green spaces, none has such variety: densely forested trails spill out onto beaches with jaw-dropping vistas of Puget Sound.

Seattle Center, the Space Needle, and EMP

(D) Almost every trip, especially an inaugural one, includes a stop at Seattle Center, which was built for the 1962 World's Fair and is home to the Space Needle, museums, and performance halls. There's something for everyone: Pacific Science Center and Children's Museum; Experience Music Project/Science Fiction

Museum; a brand-new Seattle Center Skatepark; and the SIFF Film Center. You can catch opera or ballet at McCaw Hall and theater performances at Intiman Theatre.

Local Farmers' Markets

(E) A tour of the Northwest's seasonal bounty should start at glorious Pike Place Market. Then visit smaller neighborhood markets in the University District, West Seattle, Columbia City, and along historic Ballard Avenue, and Broadway on Capitol Hill.

The Burke-Gilman Trail

(F) This major cycling corridor stretches from Ballard all the way around the northern tip of Lake Washington into the Eastside suburbs. Along the way it skirts the canal and Lake Union, goes through the UW campus, passes lakeside Magnuson Park, and spends its last leg along the shore of Lake Washington.

Washington Park Arboretum

(G) From autumn's effulgent colors to the tiny pink petals of spring, the arboretum is a 230-acre reminder that Seattle is a city with seasons. Easy-to-navigate paths include the Shoreline Trail. One of the many highlights is the beautiful Japanese Garden.

Hiram M. Chittenden Locks

Also called the Ballard Locks, this attraction is an important passage within the Lake Washington Ship canal, connecting Puget Sound to Lake Washington. To learn more, see the feature on Seattle's waterways in Chapter 7.

GREAT ITINERARIES

Seattle Highlights

Though Seattle's not always the easiest city to navigate, it's small enough that you can see a great deal of it in a week. If you've only got a long weekend here, you can easily mix and match any of the days in this itinerary. Before you explore, you'll need three things: comfortable walking shoes, layered clothing, and a flexible mind-set: it's easy and advisable to meander off-track.

Day 1: Pike Place Market and Downtown's Major Sights

Spend the first day seeing some of the major sights around Downtown. Get up early and stroll to Pike Place Market. Grab a latte or have a hearty breakfast at a café, then spend the morning wandering through the fish, fruit, flower, and crafts stalls. When you've had your fill, head a bit south to the Seattle Art Museum; take the steps down to the docks and visit the Seattle Aquarium; or stroll to Belltown to take in the views at the Olympic Sculpture Park. Stop for a simple lunch at El Puerco Lloron or Macrina Bakery. If you're not too tired, head to 1st Avenue in Belltown or to Downtown's Nordstrom and environs for some late-afternoon shopping. Have dinner and drinks in either Belltown or Downtown—both have terrific restaurants that will give you a first taste of that famous Pacific Northwest cuisine.

Day 2: Seattle Center or Pioneer Square

Take the two-minute monorail ride from Downtown's Westlake Center to the Seattle Center. Travel up the Space Needle for 360-degree city views. Then take in one of Seattle Center's many ground-level attractions: the Pacific Science Center, the Children's Museum, and the Experience Music Project/Science Fiction Museum.

If you didn't visit it the day before, walk southwest down Broad Street to the Olympic Sculpture Park. From there, cab or take the bus to the International District. Visit the Uwajimaya superstore, stroll the streets, and have dinner in one of the neighborhood's many restaurants.

If you can do without the Space Needle, skip Seattle Center and start your day in Pioneer Square. Tour a few galleries (most of which open late-morning), peek into some shops, and then head to nearby International District for more exploring—don't miss the Wing Luke Asian Museum. If you still want to see the Space Needle, you can go after dinner; the observation deck is open until 11 PM most nights.

Day 3: Side Trips from the City

Now that you've seen a little bit of the city, it's time to leave and get closer to nature. Start the day early and get outside. Hikers almost have too many options, but know that Mt. Rainier National Park never disappoints. Plan a whole day for any hiking excursion—between hiking time and driving time, you'll probably need it. When you return to the city, tired and probably ravenous, grab a hearty, casual meal and maybe an art flick—Capitol Hill is a great neighborhood for both, as is Wallingford.

If you'd rather take to the water, get on a ferry and check out either Bainbridge or Vashon islands. Bainbridge is more developed, but it's pretty and has large swaths of protected land with trails. The Bloedel Reserve is a major attraction, with trails passing through a bird refuge, second-growth forest, and themed gardens (a Japanese garden and a moss garden are just two). It's always serene, thanks to a limit on the number of daily visitors

(make reservations). Vashon is decidedly more agricultural and low-key. The most popular way to explore either island is by bicycle, though note that Bainbridge has some hills. Both islands have beach strolls. Bainbridge also has many shops and good restaurants, so it's easy to grab a bite before heading back into the city. You'll need less time to explore the islands than you'll need to do a hiking excursion, so you can probably see one or two sights Downtown before going to the pier. If you haven't made it to the aquarium yet, its proximity to the ferry makes it a great option.

Day 4: Stepping Off the Tourist Trail

Since you covered Downtown on Days 1 and 2, today you can sleep in a bit and explore the vastly differing residential neighborhoods. Visit Capitol Hill for great shopping, strolling, café culture, and people-watching. Or head north of the Lake Washington Ship Canal to Fremont and Ballard. Wherever you end up, you can start your day by having a leisurely breakfast or coffee fix at an independent coffee shop. To stretch your legs, make the rounds at Volunteer Park in Capitol Hill or follow the Burke-Gilman Trail from Fremont Center to Gasworks Park. Both the Woodland Park Zoo (slightly north of Fremont) and the Hiram M. Chittenden Locks ("Ballard" Locks) are captivating. In Capitol Hill or in the northern neighborhoods, you'll have no problem rounding out the day by ducking into shops and grabbing a great meal. If you're looking for late-night entertainment, you'll find plenty of nightlife options in both areas, too.

TIPS

■ Pike Place Market and waterfront attractions are open daily all year.

■ The ride to the top of the Needle is not worth the charge if the day is overcast or rainy.

■ Remember that Pioneer Square's galleries may not be open on Monday. They do, however, have late hours on the first Thursday of every month.

■ When leaving the city for an all-day hiking trip, try to time things so that you're not hitting I-5 during evening rush hour. Unless you get a very early start—or don't leave until 9:30 AM or 10 AM—you probably won't be able to avoid sitting in some morning rush-hour traffic.

Day 5: Last Rays of Sun and Loose Ends

Spend at least half of your last day in Seattle outdoors exploring Discovery Park or in the University District to rent kayaks from Agua Verde Paddle Club for a trip around Portage Bay or into Lake Washington. Linger in your favorite neighborhood (you'll have one by now). Note that you can combine a park visit with kayaking if you head to the Washington Park Arboretum and Japanese Garden first. From there, it's a quick trip to the U-District.

SEATTLE THEN AND NOW

The Early Days

"There is plenty of room for one thousand settlers. Come at once." Upon receiving his brother's note, Arthur Denny set out from Portland on the schooner *Exact* with two dozen settlers. It landed at Alki Point on November 13, 1851.

The Denny party wasn't the first to arrive at the wild land that would become the Emerald City. British explorers surveyed the same spot in 1792, and the Duwamish tribe had been living there for millennia. But Arthur Denny was the first of Seattle's many mad visionaries. He dreamed of creating a future endpoint for the transcontinental railroad, one to rival the already steadily developing Portland. The party moved to Elliot Bay's eastern shore in 1852; in 1853, the first boundaries of the city were marked on present-day Pioneer Square and Belltown, and Seattle—named after Chief Seattle (Si'ahl) of the Duwamish and Suquamish tribes—was born.

Despite a few interruptions, including an 1856 attack on the settlement by displaced Native Americans, Seattle's rise was inevitable. Before the city was named, Denny had persuaded Henry Yesler to build a steam-powered sawmill here, which quickly turned the city into a major lumber producer. Even being snubbed by the Northern Pacific Railroad (which chose Tacoma for its western terminus) couldn't deter the founders: they built their own small rail lines from the city to outlying coal deposits and watched their city boom while Tacoma waited for its rail link.

The Gold Rush

Amidst all that growth came a series of disasters. In 1889, the Great Fire burned 64 acres. Then the "Panic of 1893" stock-market crash crippled the local economy. Seattle seemed down on its luck until in 1897 a boat docked carrying gold from the Klondike, heralding the last Gold Rush.

The city quickly repositioned itself as the "Gateway to Alaska" (Alaska being the preferred point of entry into the Klondike) with the help of Erastus Brainerd, an early public-relations genius who convinced friends at East Coast papers to run with the story. The assay office Brainerd convinced the federal government to open was just part of the city's Gold Rush revenue—Canada's Northwest Mounted Police required that each prospector show up with a year's worth of supplies, and Seattle merchants profited heavily from the edict.

Floatplanes and Post-War Prosperity

William E. Boeing launched his first floatplane from Lake Union in 1916. This marked the start of an industry that would define the city and would long outlast timber. World War I bolstered aircraft manufacturing enough that Boeing moved south to a former shipyard.

Seattle was devastated by the Great Depression, with its only growth the result of New Deal programs that built parks, housing, and roads, including the floating bridge that links Seattle and Mercer Island. But entry into World War II again buoyed shipbuilding and aircraft industries. Boeing produced the B-29 bomber, the aircraft used to drop atomic bombs on Hiroshima and Nagasaki.

Seattle's renewed prosperity, which prompted it to host the 1962 World's Fair, remained tethered to Boeing, and the early '70s "Boeing Bust," when loss of federal funding caused Boeing to lay off tens of thousands of employees, sunk the city back into recession. After that, although Boeing would remain an influential

employer, new industries would start to take its place. In 1963, Seattle had spent $100 million to upgrade its port in a successful bid to lure cargo traffic from Asia away from Portland and San Francisco. In 1970, six Japanese shipping lines started calling at Seattle.

The Tech Boom and Today's Seattle

The tech boom may have defined the '90s, but it planted its roots in Seattle in the '70s. In 1978, Microsoft moved from Albuquerque to the Eastside suburb of Bellevue, bringing the first influx of tech money—even today "Microsoft money" is shorthand for wealthy techies (Microsoft moved to its current Redmond campus in 1986). In 1994, Amazon.com became incorporated in the State of Washington; it retains its company headquarters in Seattle proper. Although the dot-com bust temporarily took the wind out of Seattle's entrepreneurial sails, Google's decision to open offices in Seattle and Kirkland shows that Seattle is still seen as a place where great ideas germinate.

Today, the city of more than 600,000 holds a diverse portfolio: one part of the port is dominated by container ships while the other side welcomes Alaska-bound ships to Smith Cove Cruise Terminal. The University of Washington is a national leader in medical research, and a biotech hub is rising in the city center. Money still flows in from Boeing, Microsoft, Amazon, and, of course, Starbucks.

Important Dates

1851 Denny party arrives in Seattle.

1853 Washington Territory formed; Seattle loses out to Olympia for state capital.

1861 University of Washington is established.

1889 Seattle's Great Fire destroys the commercial core.

1889 Washington becomes the 42nd state.

1903 John C. Olmsted arrives; his master plan creates most of the city's parks.

1907 The city annexes Ballard, West Seattle, and Southeast Seattle, doubling its size.

1910 Washington women get the vote, 10 years before the rest of the nation.

1911 Port of Seattle created, awarding public control of waterfront.

1919 Port workers initiate first general strike in the nation.

1941 Eight thousand Japanese immigrants sent to internment camps after Pearl Harbor is attacked.

1951 First Seafair festival commemorates the centennial.

1962 The World's Fair opens and runs for six months.

1982 Visitors Bureau starts using nickname "Emerald City." Seattle's also been called Queen City, Jet City, and, of course, Rain City.

1999 World Trade Organization protests occur in Seattle.

2001 Sesquicentennial coincides with a 6.8 earthquake that causes more than $1 billion in damage.

2004 The Central Library opens, the crown jewel in the city's massive "Libraries for All" project.

2009 Sound Transit completes its first light rail project, the Central Link, connecting Downtown to Sea-Tac.

WITH KIDS

Seattle is great for kids. After all, a place where floatplanes take off a few feet from houseboats, and harbor seals might be spotted on a routine ferry ride, doesn't have to try too hard to feel like a wonderland. And if the rains fall, there are plenty of great museums to keep the kiddos occupied. A lot of child-centric sights are easily reached via public transportation, and the piers and the Aquarium can be explored on foot from most Downtown hotels. A few spots (Woodland Park Zoo, and Discovery and Gas Works parks) are easier to visit by car, especially if you're schlepping a lot of supplies.

Museums

Several museums cater specifically to kids, and many are conveniently clustered at the Seattle Center. The Center's winning trio is the **Pacific Science Center**, which has interactive exhibits and IMAX theaters; the **Children's Museum**, which has exhibits on Washington State and foreign cultures plus plenty of interactive art spaces; and, of course, the **Space Needle.** For older, hipper siblings there's a skatepark; the Vera Project, a teen music and art space; and the Experience Music Project/Science Fiction Museum.

Downtown there are miles of waterfront to explore along the piers. The **Seattle Aquarium** is here and has touch pools and otters—what more could you want?

Parks and Outdoor Attractions

Discovery Park has an interpretive center, a Native American cultural center, easy forest trails, and accessible beaches. **Alki Beach** in West Seattle is lively and fun; a wide paved path is the perfect surface for wheels of all kinds—you can rent bikes and scooters, or take to the water on rented paddleboats and kayaks. **Gas Works Park** has great views of the skyline and floatplanes over Lake Union, along with the rusty remnants of the old machinery. **Volunteer Park** has a shallow pool made for splashing toddlers and wide lawns.

The **Woodland Park Zoo** is easy to explore and has 300 different species of animals, from jaguars to mountain goats; cheap paid parking and stroller rentals are available. Watching an astonishing variety of boats navigate the ship canal at the **Ballard Locks** will entertain visitors of any age. The **Northwest Puppet Center** has a museum and weekend marionette plays.

Hotels

Downtown, the **Hotel Monaco** offers a happy medium between sophisticated and family-friendly. The colorful, eccentric decor will appeal to kids but remind adults that they're in a boutique property. Fun amenities abound, like optional goldfish in the rooms, and lobby events featuring tarot card readers and Guitar Hero showdowns. Surprisingly, one of the city's most high-end historic properties, the **Fairmont Olympic**, is also kid-friendly. The hotel's decor is a little fussy, but the grand staircases in the lobby will awe most little ones, and there's a great indoor pool area. In addition, it offers babysitting, a kids' room-service menu, as well as toys and board games.

Several properties offer kitchenette suites that help families save some money on food costs. The **Silver Cloud Inn**, Lake Union, has suites with kitchens. It's north of Downtown on Lake Union, which is slightly out of Downtown, but the South Lake Union streetcar is across the street and gets you into Downtown and to bus connections quickly.

FREE AND ALMOST FREE

Free Art

The Olympic Sculpture Park has installations from sculptors like Alexander Calder set against the backdrop of the sparkling waters of the Sound.

Pioneer Square has the largest concentration of art galleries in the city, all of which are free. Elsewhere in the city, Belltown and Capitol Hill also have free galleries.

The Frye Art Museum is always free.

Free Music

Unless it's a major ticketed venue, cover charges at small music venues are always cheap ($5–$7), and often free.

Throughout the year, City Hall hosts free lunchtime concerts, mostly jazz and world music (⊕ *www.seattle.gov/arts/community/seattle_presents.asp*).

Local indie music station KEXP and Seattle Center host the Concerts at the Mural series at the Mural Amphitheatre lawn in late July and August (⊕ *www.kexp.org/events*).

All shows at the four-day (Memorial Day weekend) **Northwest Folklife Festival** (⊕ *www.nwfolklife.org*) are free.

Free Words

Only residents can check out materials, but the gorgeous main branch of the Rem Koolhaas– and Joshua Ramus–designed Seattle Public Library is open to everyone—check e-mail, listen to a CD from the music library, or catch up on reading in one of the many lounges and study areas.

Seattle's favorite independent bookstore, **Elliott Bay Book Company** (⊕ *www.elliottbaybook.com*), often has free readings by well-known authors. **Third Place Books** (⊕ *www.ravenna.thirdplacebooks.com*) and **Open Books** (⊕ *www.openpoetrybooks.com*) are also beloved local bookstores that have author nights.

Town Hall, the city's premier venue for lectures, sometimes has free series—tickets to most lectures, even for heavy hitters, are only $5 (⊕ *www.townhallseattle.org*).

Free Buses

Seattle Metro Transit's Ride-Free Area covers most of Downtown. From 6th Avenue to the waterfront, and Battery Street in Belltown down to S. Jackson Street in Pioneer Square, you can hop on and off city buses for free from 6 AM to 7 PM daily.

Free Museum Days

ALWAYS FREE

Frye Art Museum

Klondike Gold Rush Museum

FIRST THURSDAY

Asian Art Museum

Burke Museum

Experience Music Project (5 PM–8 PM)

Henry Art Gallery

Museum of Flight (5 PM–9 PM)

Museum of History and Industry

Science Fiction Hall of Fame (5 PM–8 PM)

Seattle Art Museum

Wing Luke Asian Museum

SATURDAY

Asian Art Museum (1st Sat. of month; families only)

Wing Luke Asian Museum (3rd Sat. of month)

SEATTLE'S BEST PARKS

Mountain ranges, ocean waters, and islands may surround the city, but Seattleites are often content to stay put on sunny weekends. Why? Because the incredible park system makes for fantastic outdoor adventures, offering everything from throwing beach rocks into the ocean against the backdrop of the Olympics to hiking under canopies of old growth, and from eating ice cream next to gurgling fountains in the center of town to wandering pathways of traditional Japanese gardens.

Luckily for today's residents, more than a century ago, the city's Board of Commissioners had the wisdom to hire the Olmsted Brothers (who had inherited the firm from Frederick Law Olmsted, designer of New York's Central Park) of Brookline, Massachusetts, to conduct a survey of the potential for a park system. J.C. Olmsted's visionary plan not only placed a park, playground, or playing field within walking distance of most homes in Seattle, it also created a 20-mile greenway connecting many of the urban parks, starting at Seward Park on Lake Washington and traveling across the city to Woodland Park and Discovery Park. Later the architect created plans for the campus of the University of Washington and the Washington Park Arboretum.

What follows are our top picks for best parks in the city *(see also the Neighborhoods chapter for more in-depth reviews of top parks).*

Best for Families and Picnics

Cal Anderson Park. An urban park in every sense, this Capitol Hill expanse has a lovely water sculpture, a playing field, and green space. Grab an ice cream at nearby **Molly Moon's** (⊠ *917 E. Pine St.*) and enjoy. ⊠ *1635 11th Ave., Capitol Hill*

Gas Works Park. Reachable by the Burke-Gilman Trail, this Wallingford park gets its name from the remains of an old gasification plant. Twenty acres of rolling green space look out over Lake Union and the city skyline. ⊠ *North end of Lake Union at N. Northlake Way and Meridian Ave. N, Wallingford*

Volunteer Park. Capitol Hill's best green spot houses a plant conservatory, the Asian branch of the Seattle Art Museum, a water tower, paths, and an Isamu Noguchi sculpture (along with a great view). ⊠ *14th Ave. E at Prospect St., Capitol Hill*

(See also Carkeek Park, Marymoor Park, Olympic Sculpture Park, and Warren Magnuson Park.)

Best for Seasonal Blooms

Kubota Garden. It may be far south, but Kubota Garden is striking, with 20 acres of landscaped gardens blending Japanese and native plants and techniques. ⊠ *817 55th Ave. S, South Seattle*

Washington Park Arboretum. The park system's crown jewel may well be this 230-acre expanse, with flowering fruit trees in early spring; vibrant rhododendrons and azaleas in late spring and early summer; and brightly hued trees and shrubs in fall. ⊠ *2300 Arboretum Dr. E, Washington Park*

(See also Bellevue Botanical Gardens.)

Best Views

Alki Point. West Seattle comes to life in summer, and there's no better way to enjoy it than walking along this beachfront path to enjoy the sparkling views of Puget Sound, the Seattle skyline, and the Olympics. ⊠ *1702 Alki Ave. SW, West Seattle*

Carkeek Park. North of Ballard, Carkeek has awe-inspiring views of Puget Sound and the Olympics. Its Pipers Creek, playgrounds, picnic areas, and forest trails make this a fun family spot. ⊠ *950 NW Carkeek Park Rd., Broadview*

Discovery Park. Seattle's largest park, in Magnolia, is all about variety, with shaded forest, open meadows, pebbled beach stretches, and even sand dunes. A lighthouse, plus sweeping views of Puget Sound and the mountains make this an extremely picturesque spot. ⊠ *3801 W. Government Way, Magnolia*

Golden Gardens. This Ballard park, perched on Puget Sound, is the best place for beachcombers. Loads of facilities and a pretty pathway make this spot even more special. ⊠ *8498 Seaview Pl. NW, Ballard*

Myrtle Edwards. Adjacent to the Olympic Sculpture Park, Myrtle Edwards has a short bike-and-pedestrian path along Elliott Bay, with vistas of the Sound and the mountains. ⊠ *3130 Alaskan Way W, Downtown*

Olympic Sculpture Park. The Seattle Art Museum's 9-acre outdoor playground, located in Belltown, has fabulous views of Elliot Bay and the Olympics, complemented by huge works of art by the likes of Alexander Calder. ⊠ *Western Ave. at Broad St., Belltown*

(See also Gas Works Park.)

Best Walking Trails
Seward Park. Old-growth forest, views of the mountains and Lake Washington, and a very fun walking loop make this a beloved spot at the southwest side of Lake Washington. ⊠ *5902 Lake Washington Blvd.*

Green Lake. The 2.8-mi loop around the lake is a favorite spot for joggers, bikers, kids, and dog walkers alike. You can rent a paddleboat and explore the waters. ⊠ *E. Green Lake Dr. N and W. Green Lake Dr. N, Green Lake*

Warren Magnuson Park. Northeast of University District, this large green space has great playgrounds, walkable trails, and one of the largest off-leash dog parks in the city. ⊠ *Sand Point Way NE at 65th St., Sand Point*

(See also Discovery Park.)

Best Oceanside Parks
Lincoln Park. With old-growth forest and rocky beaches, as well as facilities like a pool and tennis courts, this is a West Seattle favorite. ⊠ *5551 SW Admiral Way, West Seattle*

(See also Alki Point, Discovery Park, Golden Gardens Park, Lincoln Park, and Myrtle Edwards Park.)

Best Parks on the Eastside
Bellevue Botanical Gardens. Perennial borders, colorful rhododendron, rock gardens, and the lovely Lost Meadow Trail fill the 36 acres of this spot in Bellevue. ⊠ *510 Bellevue Way NE, Bellevue, Eastside*

Marymoor Park. Six hundred and forty acres of fun can be found at this huge Redmond green space, including a climbing rock, tennis courts, game fields, an off-leash dog area, and a path along the Sammamish River. ⊠ *6046 W. Lake Sammamish Pkwy. NE, Redmond, Eastside*

SEATTLE'S SIPPING CULTURE
ARTISAN COFFEES, CRAFT MICROBREWS, AND BOUTIQUE WINES

by Carissa Bluestone

Seattle's beverage obsession only *begins* with coffee. Whether you're into hoppy microbrews, premium wines, or expertly crafted cappuccinos, prepare to devote much of your visit to sipping the best Seattle and Washington State have to offer.

Seattle may forever be known as the birthplace of Starbucks, but nowadays foodies are just as likely to talk about Washington state's wine industry as the city's coffeehouses. Not to pronounce coffee dead, however. After a few years of inertia, the coffee scene is growing again with more independent roasters and shops than ever.

In fact, in the past few years the city's seen a profusion of potables: New microbreweries and wineries are opening, and hip new bars, taprooms, and tasting rooms are thriving more than ever. Like its sister city, Portland, Seattle is a hotspot for entrepreneurial spirit—it's this energy, mixed with a passion for local and organic ingredients, that has raised the bar on everything artisan.

COFFEE

Although Seattle owes much of its coffee legacy to Starbucks, the city's independent coffee shops rule the roast here. Their ardent commitment to creating premium artisanal blends from small batches of beans is what truly defines the scene. The moment you take your first sip of an expertly executed cappuccino at a coffeehouse such as **Caffé Vita** or **Espresso Vivace** you realize that the drink is never an afterthought here. Perfectly roasted beans ground to specification and pulled into espresso shots using dual-boiler machines and velvety steamed milk are de rigueur. In most restaurants, your coffee is likely to be a personal French press filled with a brew roasted just a few blocks away.

LATTE ART

Latte art is a given in Seattle. Designs vary by barista, but the most common flourish is the rosetta, which resembles a delicate fern. Here's how it's done:

1. THE BASE. A latte consists of a shot (or two) of espresso and hot, frothy milk.

2. THE POUR. First the shot is poured. The milk pitcher gets a few gentle swirls and taps (to burst the largest bubbles), then the milk is poured at a steady pace into the center of the tilted cup.

3. THE SHAKE. When the cup's about three-quarters full, the milk is streamed with tiny side-to-side strokes up and down the cup's center line. The "leaves" will start to fan out.

4. THE TOP. When the cup's almost full, the milk is drawn towards the bottom. With the last stroke the "stem" is drawn through the center of the leaves.

The "rosetta," a common latte design.

BEST COFFEEHOUSES

Many Seattle roasters obtain their beans through Direct Trade, sourcing directly from growers rather than brokers. They travel across the globe to meet with farmers, often paying them well above Fair Trade prices to ensure the highest-quality beans. Local roasters are also intensely community-minded: Caffé Vita, for example, recently partnered with the much-loved local chocolate factory Theo to produce sublime espresso-flavored chocolate bars.

Stumptown

CAFFÉ VITA. Though now a mini-chain (with locations in Fremont, Queen Anne, Pioneer Square, and Seward Park), Vita's roasting operations (and heart and soul) are in Capitol Hill. ✉ *1005 E. Pike St., Capitol Hill* ☎ *206/709–4440* ⊕ *www.caffevita.com*

Caffé Vita

ESPRESSO VIVACE. A top roaster, Vivace has two tidy coffee shops (the other's by REI in South Lake Union), and a sidewalk espresso stand at Broadway and Harrison. ✉ *532 Broadway Ave E, Capitol Hill* ☎ *206/860–2722* ⊕ *www.espressovivace.com*

FREMONT COFFEE COMPANY. Known for its awesome wraparound porch and exceptional brews, this friendly shop is the city's latest small-batch roaster. ✉ *459 N. 36th St., Fremont* ☎ *206/632–3633* ⊕ *www.fremontcoffee.net*

HERKIMER. This cheerful small-batch roaster is a northern neighborhoods favorite. ✉ *7320 Greenwood Ave. N, Phinney Ridge* ☎ *206/784–0202* ⊕ *www.herkimercoffee.com*

STUMPTOWN. This hip Portland powerhouse has two branches (the other is on Pine and Boylston). The 12th Ave. branch has the roasting facility. ✉ *1115 12th Ave., Capitol Hill* ☎ *206/323–1544* ⊕ *www.stumptowncoffee.com*

VICTROLA COFFEE. The original branch on 15th Avenue is a favorite standby, but the newer branch at 310 E. Pike St. in the Pike-Pine Corridor has a great view of the roasting room from its cafe tables. ✉ *310 E. Pike St., Capitol Hill* ☎ *206/624–1725* ⊕ *www.victrolacoffee.com*

Victrola Coffee

BEER

Craft brews have fewer ingredients than you might think.

Next time you drink a beer, thank the state of Washington. More than 70% of the nation's hops is grown in the Yakima Valley, and Washington is the fourth-largest producer of malting barley. The state's 80-plus breweries combine top-notch ingredients with crystal-clear snowpack waters to make high-quality craft beers. Seattle has at least a dozen breweries within its city limits, plus many fine gastropubs with standout locals on tap.

GREAT BREWERIES

ELLIOTT BAY BREWING. A dozen of Elliott Bay's beers are certified organic. The pub is a neighborhood favorite for its good, locally sourced food. ⊠ *4720 California Ave NW, West Seattle* ☎ *206/932–8695* ⊕ *www.elliottbaybrewing.com*

PIKE PUB. The most touristy of the local breweries, Pike Pub also has a small microbrewery museum. The pale ale and the Kilt Lifter Scottish ale have been local favorites for two decades. There's a full pub menu. ⊠ *1415 1st Ave, Down-town* ☎ *206/622–6044* ⊕ *www.pikebrewing.com*

ELYSIAN BREWING COMPANY. Known for its Immortal IPA and good seasonal brews and pub grub, Elysian has three branches, in Capitol Hill, Green Lake, and across from Qwest Field. ⊠ *1221 E. Pike St., Capitol Hill* ☎ *206/860–1920* ⊕ *www.elysianbrewing.com*

FREMONT BREWING. This newcomer (2008) makes small-batch pale ales using organic hops. The Urban Beer Garden is open Thurs.–Sat. 4–8:30.

Elysian Brewing Company

Hale's beer

✉ *3409 Woodland Park Avenue N, Fremont* ☎ *206/420-2407* ⊕ *www.fremont-brewing.com*

GEORGETOWN BREWING CO. This brewery offers a very small list, including Manny's Pale Ale and a special namesake porter for neighborhood bar the Nine Pound Hammer. Visit the store to pick up souvenirs or a growler of beer. Open weekdays 10–6 and Sat. 9–noon. ✉ *5200 Denver Ave. S., Georgetown* ☎ *206/766–8055* ⊕ *www.georgetownbeer.com*

HALE'S ALES. One of the city's oldest craft breweries (1983), Hale's does cask-conditioned ales and nitrogen-conditioned cream ales. The Mongoose IPA is also popular. The pub serves a full menu and has a great view of the fermenting room. ✉ *4301 Leary Way NW, Fremont* ☎ *206/706–1544* ⊕ *www.halesbrewery.com*

REDHOOK. This brewery specializes in amber ales—their ESB is an award-winner. The Forecaster's Pub has a full menu. It's open Mon.–Thurs. 11–10, Fri. and Sat. 11–midnight, and Sun. 11–9. ✉ *14300 NE 145th St, Woodinville* ☎ *425/483–3232* ⊕ *www.redhook.com.*

TWO BEERS BREWING CO. A small list of ales and IPAs, and interesting seasonal experiments—such as a summer ale with coriander and sweet orange peel. Tasting room open Thurs. and Fri. 3–7. No food. ✉ *4700 Ohio Ave. S., SoDo* ☎ *206/414–2224* ⊕ *www.twobeersbrewery.com*

BEER FESTIVALS

Washington Brewers Festival (⊕ www.washingtonbeer.com/festival_cask.htm; June/Father's Day weekend).

Fremont Oktoberfest (⊕ www.fremont-oktoberfest.com; September).

Tacoma Craft Beer Festival (⊕ www.tacomacraftbeerfest.com; October).

Washington Cask Beer Festival (⊕ www.washingtonbeer.com/cbf.htm; end of March).

Fremont Oktoberfest

Pike Pub

WASHINGTON STATE WINE REGIONS

Second only to California in U.S. wine production, Washington has more than 500 wineries and 11 official American Viticultural Areas. The state is increasingly becoming known for its fine cabernet sauvignons after decades-strong on its crisp chardonnays and complex merlots. Here's a sampling of some of the state's best grape varieties.

Orchards and vineyard near Wishram, WA

WHITE WINES

CHARDONNAY. The French grape widely planted in eastern Washington, where the wines range from light to big and complex.

GEWÜRTZ-TRAMINER. A German-Alsatian grape in the Columbia Gorge and the Yakima Valley that produces a spicy, aromatic wine.

RIESLING. A German grape that makes a delicate, floral wine.

Chateau Ste. Michelle

SAUVIGNON BLANC. Herbal, dry wine from this Bordeaux grape, fermented in oak, is sold as fumé blanc.

VIOGNIER. A Rhône Valley grape that in eastern Washington makes fragrant wine with a good acid content.

WINERY SAMPLING

Amavi Cellars (🌐 www.amavicellars.com)

Chateau Ste. Michelle (🌐 www.ste-michelle.com)

Columbia Crest (🌐 www.columbiacrest.com)

Cote Bonneville (🌐 www.cotebonneville.com)

DeLille (🌐 www.delillecellars.com)

Gramercy Cellars (🌐 www.gramercycellars.com)

L'Ecole no. 41 (🌐 www.lecole.com)

Leonetti Cellar (🌐 www.leonetticellar.com)

Long Shadows (🌐 www.longshadows.com)

Mark Ryan (🌐 www.markryanwinery.com)

Maryhill (🌐 www.maryhillwinery.com)

àMaurice (🌐 www.amaurice.com)

RED WINES
CABERNET FRANC. A Bordeaux grape that produces well-balanced wine in the Walla Walla and Yakima Valleys and Columbia Gorge.

CABERNET SAUVIGNON. The famed Bordeaux grape grows well in the Columbia Valley and makes deeply tannic wines in Walla Walla and Yakima.

MERLOT. A black grape yielding a softer, more supple wine than cabernet sauvignon, merlot has recently experienced a boom, especially in the Walla Walla Valley.

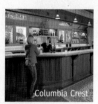
Columbia Crest

SYRAH. A Rhône grape that produces complex, big-bodied wines; increasingly planted in the Yakima and Walla Walla Valleys.

ZINFANDEL. A hot-climate grape that in the Yakima Valley and the Columbia Gorge makes big, powerful wines.

BEST TASTING ROOMS AND WINE BARS

Almost every wine list in Seattle includes at least some regional choices, even when the cuisine has origins far from the Pacific Northwest.

106 PINE. Part wine bar, part wine shop, and part gourmet market, 106 Pine sells only Northwest wines. Weekly Urban Wine Tours (reservations essential) are fun. ✉ *106 Pine St, Downtown* ☏ *206/443–1106* 🌐 *www.106pine.com.*

BRICCO DELLA REGINA ANNA. Less comprehensive on the Northwest selections than some of its peers, Bricco compensates with a good list of Italian wines. ✉ *1525 Queen Anne Ave N, Queen Anne* ☏ *206/285–4900* 🌐 *www.briccoseattle.com*

LOCAL VINE. An ultrasleek lounge with a stunning wine menu featuring many Washington reds. ✉ *2520 2nd Ave, Belltown* ☏ *206/441–6000* 🌐 *www.thelocalvine.com*

PIKE & WESTERN. This well-respected wine shop holds weekly tastings—limited-production bottles are sampled Wed. 4–6 PM ($5); new arrivals are tested Fri. 3–6 PM. ✉ *1934 Pike Pl., Downtown* 🌐 *www.pikeandwestern.com*

POCO WINE ROOM. Feels like both a date spot and a friendly neighborhood hangout. Reasonably priced Pacific Northwest wines are the focus. ✉ *1408 E. Pine St., Capitol Hill* ☏ *206/322–9463* 🌐 *www.pocowineroom.com*

PORTALIS. A cozy wine bar and well-stocked shop, Portalis has happy hours, prix-fixe dinners, and regular thematic tastings. ✉ *5205 Ballard Ave NW, Ballard* 🌐 *www.portaliswines.com*

THE TASTING ROOM. Wine shop and tasting bar with hard-to-find boutique Washington wines. *Tastings range from $2 to $6.* ✉ *1924 Post Alley, Downtown* 🌐 *www.tastingroomseattle.com*

Cabernet Sauvignon, Chateau Ste. Michelle

Seattle Neighborhoods

WORD OF MOUTH

"If ideal weather was a given (laugh), I would include a round-trip, walk-on ferry ride to Bainbridge Island for mountain, water, and skyline views. Then lunch on the Seattle waterfront, shopping in Pioneer Square, or a walk around Olympic Sculpture Park. Take the bus to Broadway [on Capitol Hill] for interesting shopping, people-watching, and burgers at Dick's Drive-In."

—NorthwestMale

Updated
by Carissa
Bluestone

Seattle isn't just a city—it's a feat of environmental engineering. When the Denny party arrived on its shores, "Seattle" was a series of densely forested valleys covered by Douglas fir, Western hemlock, and red cedar; ridges that were far steeper than its current leg-burning hills surrounded it. Where SoDo (the stadium district south of Downtown) currently is was nothing but mudflats. Pioneer Square was actually an island of sorts where Duwamish tribespeople crossed to the mainland over sandbars.

Once Seattle started to grow, its residents literally changed the city's geography. Massive Denny Hill once occupied the Belltown neighborhood—it simply had to go. The multi-stage "regrade" started in 1899 and was completed 32 years later. Dirt from the project helped fill in the tidelands, creating new land that supports what is now the entire waterfront district.

The Denny Hill Regrade was just one of dozens of projects; other equally ambitious earth-moving missions created the city you see today. One of the largest was the digging of the canal that links Lake Washington to Puget Sound, which required, in addition to the carving of the canal itself, the construction of large fixed bridges with drawbridges. Today, construction of a new light rail line plus a replacement of the viaduct are examples of how the city is once again moving a lot of earth around.

It's hard to think of Seattle as anything but natural, though. After all, the city owes much of its appeal to its natural features—the myriad hills that did survive settlement offer views of mountain ranges and water, water, water. Outside of Downtown and other smaller commercial cores, Seattle's neighborhoods fan out in tangles of tree-lined streets. Massive parks like Discovery, Magnuson, and Washington Park Arboretum make Seattle one of the greenest and most livable cities in the nation. From the peaks of the Olympics or Cascades to an artistically landscaped garden in front of a classic Northwest bungalow, nature is in full effect every time you turn your head.

Each of Seattle's neighborhoods is distinctive in personality, and taking a stroll, browsing a bookstore, or enjoying a cup of coffee can feel different in every one. It's the adventure of exploring these vibrant neighborhoods that will really introduce you to the character of Seattle.

Major Bus Routes in Central Seattle

KEY

46 Bus Terminals
46 Bus Route

Downtown Seattle (3rd Ave.) Transit Tunnel

5am–1am Monday through Saturday; 6am–midnight Sunday

Used by ST Link Light Rail and the following bus routes:
41, 71, 72, 73, 101, 106, 150; rush hour only: 74E, 76, 77, 102, 212, 216, 217, 218, 225, 229, 256, 301, 316

Ride Free Area (6am–7pm)

QUEEN ANNE

SEATTLE CENTER

Space Needle

Seattle Center Monorail

South Lake Union Streetcar

Lake Union Park

BELLTOWN

DOWNTOWN

Westlake Station

Convention Place Station

University St. Station

Pioneer Sq. Station

PIONEER SQUARE

INTERNATIONAL DISTRICT

International District/Chinatown Station

Qwest Field

CAPITOL HILL

FIRST HILL

Seattle University

CENTRAL DISTRICT

Elliott Bay

Cal Anderson Park

Edwin T. Pratt Park

1/2 mi

1/2 km

DOWNTOWN AND BELLTOWN

Sightseeing
★★★★★

Dining
★★★★

Lodging
★★★★★

Shopping
★★★★★

Nightlife
★★★★

Downtown Seattle may not be the soul of the city, but it's certainly the heart. There's big-city skyline, as well as plenty of marvelous things to see and do in the Downtown area: the city's premier art museum, the eye-popping Rem Koolhaus–designed Central Library, lively Pike Place Market, and a major shopping corridor along 5th Avenue and down Pine Street. And, of course, there's the water: Elliott Bay beckons from every crested hill.

Downtown is one of the most difficult areas of the city to sum up—in sharp contrast to the residential neighborhoods, it doesn't really have a personality of its own. Although developers are starting to build luxury condos here, the neighborhood is still mostly a business hub. Except for the busy areas around the Market and the piers, and the always-frenetic shopping district, a lot of Downtown can often seem deserted.

Within the core of Downtown—which is bounded on the west by Elliott Bay and on the east by I–5, stretching from Virginia Street to Yesler Way—are several different experiences. The waterfront and much of 1st Avenue are lively and at times touristy, thanks to Pike Place Market, the Seattle Art Museum, and the piers, which have several kid-friendly sights as well as ferries to West Seattle and to Bainbridge Island. As you head east from Pike Place Market, you soon hit Downtown's shopping and entertainment district. You won't find anything particularly "Seattle" here, except for the fantastic flagship Nordstrom department store—this is where big chains like Banana Republic, Sephora, H&M, and the Gap are concentrated. You will find a lot of activity, though. In addition to the shopping, there are multiplex movie theaters, a multistory arcade, and a few popular chain restaurants.

Heading south of Pike Street toward Yesler Way, Downtown gets a little quieter. This area is also referred to as the Central Business District and

A steel sculpture by Richard Serra at the Olympic Sculpture Park

holds mostly office and municipal buildings. There are a few sights scattered about, however, including the remarkable Central Library and a few art galleries; the tail-end of the 5th Avenue corridor has a few higher-end shops. There are a few major cultural sights, too, including the Seattle Symphony's elegant concert venue, Benaroya Hall, and a few of the city's major theaters.

Belltown is Downtown's younger sibling, just north of Virginia Street (up to Denny Way) and stretching from Elliott Bay to 6th Avenue. Not too long ago, Belltown was home to some of the most unwanted real estate in the city; the only scenesters around were starving artists. Today, Belltown is increasingly hip, with luxury condos, trendy restaurants, swanky bars, and an ever-increasing number of boutiques. (Most of the action happens between 1st and 4th avenues and between Bell and Virginia streets.) You can still find plenty of evidence of its edgy past—including a gallery exhibiting urban street art, a punk-rock vinyl shop, and a major indie rock music venue that was a cornerstone of the grunge scene—but today Belltown is almost unrecognizable to long-term residents. Except for the stunning Olympic Sculpture Park, the area doesn't have much in terms of traditional sights, but it's an interesting and characterful extension of Downtown. Though the number of homeless people in the neighborhood can be off-putting, Belltown is generally safe during the day and is very pleasant to explore.

TOP ATTRACTIONS

Fodor's Choice ★ **Olympic Sculpture Park.** This 9-acre open-air park is the spectacular outdoor branch of the Seattle Art Museum. Since opening in 2007, the Sculpture Park has become a favorite destination for picnics, strolls,

GETTING ORIENTED

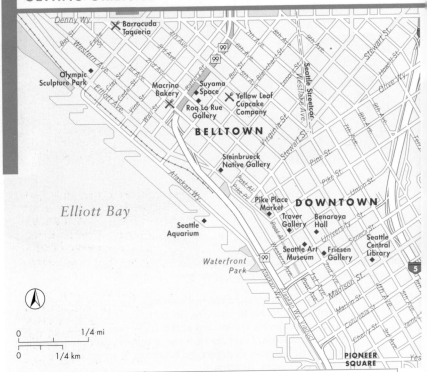

Denny Wy.
Barracuda Taqueria
Olympic Sculpture Park
Macrina Bakery
Suyama Space
Yellow Leaf Cupcake Company
Roq La Rue Gallery
BELLTOWN
Steinbrueck Native Gallery
Elliott Bay
Pike Place Market
DOWNTOWN
Traver Gallery
Benaroya Hall
Seattle Aquarium
Seattle Art Museum
Friesen Gallery
Seattle Central Library
Waterfront Park
1/4 mi
1/4 km
PIONEER SQUARE

GETTING AROUND

Both Downtown and Belltown are very easy to explore on foot—walking from one neighborhood to the other is easy, too—but if you head down to the waterfront, be prepared for some major hills on the way back up toward your hotel or the main shopping area. Both neighborhoods are part of the "Ride Free Area," which means you can hop on and off the bus for free from 6 AM to 7 PM. Cabs are relatively easy to flag down, too.

PLANNING YOUR TIME

A Downtown day can have a variety of combinations. All itineraries should include a stop at Pike Place Market. Two other can't-miss sights are the Olympic Sculpture Park in Belltown and the Seattle Art Museum. If you have children in tow, you'll definitely want to see the aquarium, along the waterfront close to Pioneer Square.

Try to arrive at Pike Place Market in the morning when it's a bit calmer (before cruise ships have docked). The aquarium gets crowded midday, but it's a happy kind of chaos and likely preferable to getting stuck negotiating the midday Market crowds.

Even though the shops in both neighborhoods are concentrated in small areas, doing a comprehensive shopping tour will take all day and you shouldn't try to schedule much sightseeing—just plan to hit Belltown when you start to get tired, as there are good cafés along 1st and 2nd avenues.

QUICK BITES

The best place for a quick snack is **Pike Place Market** (⇨ *See the highlighted feature in Chapter 6*). You can get anything from chowder and pierogi to gourmet tea and decadent desserts.

A good stop on the way to the Olympic Sculpture Park or Seattle Center is **Barracuda Taquería** (⊠ *159 Denny Way, at 2nd Ave.* ☎ *206/448–2062*), with fresh, traditional ingredients, and good prices ($3 per taco or torta).

Macrina Bakery (⊠ *2408 1st Ave.* ☎ *206/448–4032*), also close to the Olympic Sculpture Park, is famous for its delicious breads, sandwiches, cookies, and coffee cakes.

Seattle's still in the throes of a cupcake obsession and **The Yellow Leaf Cupcake Company** (⊠ *2209 4th Ave.* ☎ *206/441–4240*) turns out very inventive flavors (Pancakes 'n' Bacon and White Chocolate Wasabi, for example).

TOP REASONS TO GO

Find your perfect souvenir—along with yummy breakfast or lunch—at **Pike Place Market**.

Visit the **Seattle Art Museum**—consider doing it on a First Thursday or during a Remix event.

Hit all the **shopping areas**: On Pike and Pine between 4th and 6th avenues are favorite chains, department stores, and high-end labels. Belltown has boutiques, design stores, and a big branch of Patagonia. Western Avenue on the waterside of the market has upscale furniture stores that are fun to browse.

Make time for a stroll in the **Olympic Sculpture Park**, or, if you're traveling with kids, make a beeline for the **Seattle Aquarium** to watch sea otters frolic.

Attend a concert at **Benaroya Hall**. The home of the Seattle Symphony is renowned for its near-perfect acoustics. The hall is stunning, and tours are available.

and quiet contemplation. Nestled between Belltown and Elliott Bay, this gently sloping green space is planted with native shrubs and plants and is crisscrossed with walking paths. On sunny days, the park flaunts an astounding panorama of the Olympic Mountain Range, but even the grayest afternoon casts a favorable light on the site's sculptures. The grounds are home to works by such artists as Richard Serra, Roy McMakin, Lou-

> ### ARCHITECT'S TOUR
>
> Within a few blocks on 4th Avenue (between University and Madison), you'll find two very different iconic buildings: the historic Fairmont Olympic Hotel (go inside for a look at the grand staircase or to have afternoon tea) and the ultramodern, Rem Koolhaus–designed Central Library.

ise Bourgeois, Mark di Suvero, and Alexander Calder, whose bright-red steel "Eagle" sculpture is a local favorite—indeed, you may even see a real bald eagle passing by overhead. The PACCAR Pavilion has a gift shop, café, and more information about the park. ⊠ *2901 Western Ave., between Broad and Bay Sts., Belltown* ☎ *206/654–3100* ⊕ *www.seattleartmuseum.org/visit/osp* 🎟 *Free* ⊗ *Park open daily sunrise–sunset. PACCAR Pavilion open May–Labor Day, Tues.–Sun. 10–5; Sept.–Apr., Tues.–Sun. 10–4.*

☾ **Pike Place Market.** ⇨ *For an in-depth description of the Market, see the*
Fodor'sChoice *highlighted feature in Chapter 6.* Pike Place Market, one of the nation's
★ largest and oldest public markets, plays host to happy, hungry crowds all year round, but summer is when things really start to heat up. Strap on some walking shoes and enjoy its many corridors: shops and stalls provide a pleasant sensory overload—stroll among the colorful flower, produce, and fish displays, plus bustling shops and lunch counters. Specialty-food items, tea, honey, jams, comic books, beads, and cookware—you'll find it all here. ⊠ *Pike Pl. at Pike St., west of 1st Ave., Downtown* ☎ *206/682–7453* ⊕ *www.pikeplacemarket.org* ⊗ *Stall hrs vary: 1st-level shops Mon.–Sat. 10–6, Sun. 11–5; underground shops daily 11–5.*

A GOOD COMBO
If you plan to spend the morning exploring Pike Place Market or the Seattle Art Museum, but still have energy for a walk, head north into the Belltown neighborhood, grab lunch to go at Macrina Bakery, and stroll down to the Olympic Sculpture Park: Views, works of art, and chairs aplenty await.

☾ **Seattle Aquarium.** The city's renovated aquarium is more popular than
Fodor'sChoice ever. Among its most engaging residents are the sea otters—kids,
★ especially, seem able to spend hours watching the delightful antics of these creatures and their river cousins. In the Puget Sound Great Hall, "Window on Washington Waters," a slice of Neah Bay life, is presented in a 20-foot-tall tank holding 120,000 gallons of water. The aquarium's darkened rooms and large, lighted tanks brilliantly display Pacific Northwest marine life. The "Life on the Edge" tide pools recreate Washington's rocky coast and sandy beaches. Huge glass windows provide underwater views of seals and sea otters; go up top to watch them play in their pools. Kids love the Discovery Lab, where they can touch starfish, sea urchins, and sponges, then examine baby

SEATTLE ART MUSEUM

✉ *1300 1st Ave., Downtown*
☎ *206/654–3100* ⊕ *www.
seattleartmuseum.org* 🎟 *$15,
free 1st Thurs. of month*
🕑 *Wed. and weekends 10–5,
Thurs. and Fri. 10–9, 1st Thurs.
until midnight.*

TIPS

■ SAM's free floors have the best attractions for kids, including an installation of cars hanging upside down from the ceiling and the WaMu OpenStudio. Select second Saturdays are Family Fun days, with kid-focused tours, performances, and workshops from 10 am to noon.

■ You can download SAM Audio—podcasts about the museum's collection—to your iPod or smart phone.

■ For the full scope of SAM's Asian-art collection—one of the best in the country—be sure to visit the Seattle Asian Art Museum in Volunteer Park—the collection here is just a sampling.

■ TASTE (www.tastesam.com), the museum's stylish restaurant, has good weekday happy hour deals and a solid wine and beer list. It's a pleasant spot for a sit-down meal, too, but it's a bit pricey for food that is consistently good but not outstanding. Remember, Pike Place Market is only a block away.

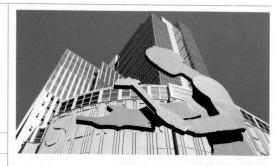

Fodor's Choice ★ Long the pride of the city's art scene, SAM is now better than ever after a massive expansion that connects the iconic old building on University Street (where sculptor Jonathan Borofsky's several-stories-high *Hammering Man* still pounds away) to a sleek, light-filled high-rise adjacent space, on 1st Avenue and Union Street. Wander two floors of free public space. The 1st floor includes the museum's fantastic shop, a café that focuses on local ingredients, and drop-in workshops where the whole family can get creative. The second floor features free exhibitions, including awesome large-scale installations.

HIGHLIGHTS

SAM's permanent collection surveys American, Asian, Native American, African, Oceanic, and pre-Columbian art. Check out Jackson Pollock's *Sea Change* and the anonymous 14th-century Buddhist masterwork *Monk at the Moment of Enlightenment* (note that this is often on view at the Seattle Asian Art Museum branch, on Capitol Hill). Collections of African dance masks and Native American carvings are both strong. Kanye Quaye's *Mercedes Benz Coffin* installation and the Italian Room, a reproduction of typical Lombard Renaissance–era room, are also favorites.

The grand staircase in the original South Building, with its imposing Chinese funerary statues, has always been fun to climb. As part of the renovation, SAM added murals and interactive installations.

Arty film series, from British noir festivals to Andy Warhol retrospectives, take place monthly in the Plestcheeff Auditorium; tickets are $7. Second Thursdays feature jazz ensembles from 5:30 to 7:30. The real party, however, is SAM Remix, which happens on select Fridays (8–midnight). The exhibits are open and complemented by live music and DJ sets, talks, and wacky performance art.

The stunning Seattle Central Library

barnacles and jellyfish. Nearby, cylindrical tanks hold a fascinating octopus. ■ TIP→ Spend a few minutes in front of the octopus tank even if you don't detect any movement. Your patience will be rewarded if you get to see this amazing creature shimmy up the side of the tank. If you're visiting in fall or winter, dress warmly—the Marine Mammal area is on the waterfront and catches all of those chilly Puget Sound breezes. The café serves Ivar's chowder and kid-friendly food like burgers and chicken fingers; a balcony has views of Elliott Bay. ⊠ *1483 Alaskan Way, at Pier 59, Downtown* ☎ *206/386–4300* ⊕ *www.seattleaquarium.org* ⊠ *$17* ⊙ *Daily 9:30–6 (last entry at 5).*

Fodor's Choice
★

Seattle Art Museum. *See highlighted listing in this chapter.*

Fodor's Choice
★

Seattle Central Library. The hub of Seattle's 25-branch library system, the Central Library, is a stunning jewel of a building that stands out against the concrete jungle of Downtown. The bold construction brings to mind a futuristic, multifaceted gemstone covered in steel webbing— perched right on 4th Avenue. Designed by renowned Dutch architect Rem Koolhaas and Joshua Ramus, this 11-story structure houses 1.45 million books—plus more than 400 computers with Internet access, an auditorium, a "mixing chamber" floor of information desks, an area with materials in foreign languages, and a café. The building's floor plan is anything but simple; standing outside the beveled glass-and-metal facade of the building, you can see the library's floors zigzagging upward. Tours focusing on the building's architecture are offered several times a week on a first-come, first-served basis; call for a current schedule. The reading room on the 10th floor has unbeatable views of the city and the water, and the building has Wi-Fi throughout. Readings and free film screenings happen on a regular basis; check the Web site for more information. ⊠ *1000 4th Ave., Downtown* ☎ *206/386–4636* ⊕ *www.spl.org* ⊗ *Mon.–Thurs. 10–8, Fri. and Sat. 10–6, Sun. noon–6.*

WORTH NOTING

Friesen Gallery. This small, sophisticated gallery on the ground floor of a large office building is one of the more respected fine-art spaces in the city. You won't necessarily find the cutting edge here, but you will find paintings, sculpture, and colorful glass pieces from talented international artists. ⊠ *1210 2nd Ave., Downtown* ☎ *206/628–9501* ⊕ *www.friesengallery.com* ⊠ *Free* ⊗ *Tues.–Fri. 10–6, Sat. 11–5.*

★ **Roq La Rue Gallery.** Cheeky surrealist pop art hangs in Roq La Rue, whose "emphasis is on art that embodies technical craftsmanship blended with fantastical imagery and visually dynamic narratives." Owner Kirsten Anderson is well known for injecting some much-needed life into the city's gallery scene by exhibiting work that often gets ignored by traditional venues, in spaces that are as professional as all the rest. ⊠ *Roq La Rue, 2312 2nd Ave., Belltown* ☎ *206/374–8977* ⊕ *www.roqlarue.com* ⊠ *Free* ⊗ *Wed.–Sat. 1–6.*

Steinbrueck Native Gallery. Prints, masks, drums, sculptures, baskets, and jewelry by local Native artists fill the space of this elegant Belltown gallery near Pike Place Market. Alaskan and Arctic art is also on display, including pieces carved from ivory and soapstone. ⊠ *2030 Western Ave., Belltown* ☎ *206/441–3821* ⊕ *www.steinbruecknativegallery.com* ⊠ *Free* ⊗ *Mon.–Sat. 10–5, Sun. 11–5.*

Suyama Space. The brainchild of art advocate and noted local architect George Suyama, this gallery exhibits large-scale, site-specific installations. A recent exhibit entitled "Grotesque Arabesque: Dan Corson" referenced the topographical intricacies of the interior of a Yucatan cave, complete with turquoise-colored electroluminescent on steel and a reflecting pool. Unlike many of Seattle's galleries, this is not a commercial venue—its programming is made possible through grants and donations—which is just another reason to stroll through the lofty space. ⊠ *2324 2nd Ave., Belltown* ☎ *206/256–0809* ⊕ *www.suyamapetersondeguchi.com/art* ⊠ *Free* ⊗ *Weekdays 9–5.*

Traver Gallery. A classic gallery space with white walls and creaky, uneven wood floors, Traver Gallery is like a little slice of SoHo in Seattle—without the attitude. Light pours in from large picture windows. The focus is on high-price (tens of thousands of dollars) glass art from local and international artists. Pieces are exquisite—never too whimsical or gaudy—and the staff is extremely courteous. After you're done tiptoeing around the gallery, head back downstairs and around the corner to **Vetri** (⊠ *1404 1st Ave.*), which sells glass art and objects from emerging artists at much more reasonable prices. ⊠ *110 Union St., Downtown* ☎ *206/587–6501* ⊕ *www.travergallery.com* ⊠ *Free* ⊗ *Tues.–Fri. 10–6, Sat. 10–5, Sun. noon–5.*

SEATTLE CENTER, SOUTH LAKE UNION, AND QUEEN ANNE

Sightseeing
★★★★
Dining
★★★
Lodging
★★
Shopping
★★
Nightlife
★

Seattle Center is the home to Seattle's version of the Eiffel Tower—the Space Needle—and is anchored by Frank Gehry's wild Experience Music Project building. Almost all visitors make their way here at least once, whether to visit the museums or catch a show at one of the many performing arts venues. The neighborhoods that bookend Seattle Center couldn't be more different: Queen Anne is all residential elegance (especially on top of the hill), while South Lake Union, once completely industrial, is becoming Seattle's next hot neighborhood.

Seattle Center's 74-acre complex was built for the 1962 World's Fair. A rolling green campus is organized around the massive International Fountain. Among the arts groups based here are the Seattle Repertory Theatre, Intiman Theatre, the Seattle Opera, and the Pacific Northwest Ballet. It's also the site of three of summer's largest festivals—Northwest Folklife Festival, Bite of Seattle, and Bumbershoot. Seattle International Film Festival's Cinema is also here.

Just west of the Seattle Center is the intersection of Queen Anne Avenue N and Denny Way. This marks the start of the Queen Anne neighborhood, which stretches all the way up formidable Queen Anne Hill to the ship canal on the other side. The neighborhood is split into Upper and Lower Queen Anne, and the two are quite different: Lower Queen Anne is a mixed-income neighborhood that has a small, interesting mix of independent record shops and bookstores, laid-back pubs, as well as a few up-market restaurants and bars. Past Aloha Street, the neighborhood starts to look more upscale, with the snazzy Galer Street commercial strip marking the heart of Upper Queen Anne. Queen Anne doesn't have many sights, but the residential streets west of Queen Anne Avenue in Upper Queen Anne are fun to stroll, and sunny days offer gorgeous views. This ribbon of residential turf extends to the Magnolia neighborhood. There's only one sight to see in off-the-beaten-path Magnolia, but it's a terrific one: Discovery Park.

South Lake Union, on the east side of Seattle Center, will soon be a destination in itself. Though it's currently a bit of a ghost town, Amazon's new headquarters here will bring more and more amenities—famed restaurateur Tom Douglas even has plans to open two new eateries here. For now, the biggest attraction is Lake Union itself, as well as the incredible REI megastore.

TOP ATTRACTIONS

The Children's Museum. This colorful, spacious museum is located just off the Center House's food court, in the heart of Seattle Center. Enter through a Northwest wilderness setting, with winding trails, hollow logs, and a waterfall. From there, you can explore a global village where rooms with kid-friendly props show everyday life in Ghana, the Philippines, and Japan. The "Go Figure!" exhibit allows children to step inside the pages of their favorite storybooks. Cog City is a giant game of pipes, pulleys, and balls; and kids can also test their talent in a mock recording studio. There's a small play area for toddlers and lots of crafts to help kids learn more about the exhibits. ⊠ *305 Harrison St., Seattle Center* ☎ *206/441–1768* ⊕ *www.thechildrensmuseum.org* ⊠ *$7.50* ⊙ *Weekdays 10–5, weekends 10–6.*

★ **Experience Music Project/Science Fiction Museum.** *See the highlighted listing in this chapter.*

Pacific Science Center. Located on the Seattle Center campus, the Science Center has been a destination for families, school groups, and curious tourists since the 1962 World's Fair. Much has changed since then: the center now has more than 200 indoor and outdoor hands-on exhibits and a state-of-the-art planetarium. The dinosaur exhibit—complete with moving robotic reproductions—is a kid's favorite, while Tech Zones has robots and virtual-reality games that captivate visitors of all ages. Machines analyze human physiology in the *Body Works* exhibit. The tropical butterfly house is stocked with new chrysalides weekly; other creatures live in the Insect Village and saltwater tide-pool areas. Next door, IMAX movies and laser rock shows run daily. Outdoor attractions include a giant water wheel that kids can play in and Northwest-focused exhibits like a Puget Sound tide pool. ■TIP➔ The center holds after-hours cocktail parties once a month, usually to celebrate a new IMAX release. ⊠ *200 2nd Ave. N, Queen Anne* ☎ *206/443–2001* ⊕ *www. pacsci.org* ⊠ *Center $14, IMAX $9, light shows $5–$8.50, combined museum/IMAX $18* ⊙ *Weekdays 10–4, weekends 10–6.*

Space Needle. Almost 50 years old, Seattle's most iconic building is as quirky and beloved as ever. The distinctive, towering structure of the 605-foot-high Space Needle is visible throughout much of Seattle—but the view from the inside out is even better. A less-than-one-minute ride up to the observation deck yields 360-degree vistas of Downtown Seattle, the Olympic Mountains, Elliott Bay, Queen Anne Hill, Lake Union, and

GETTING ORIENTED

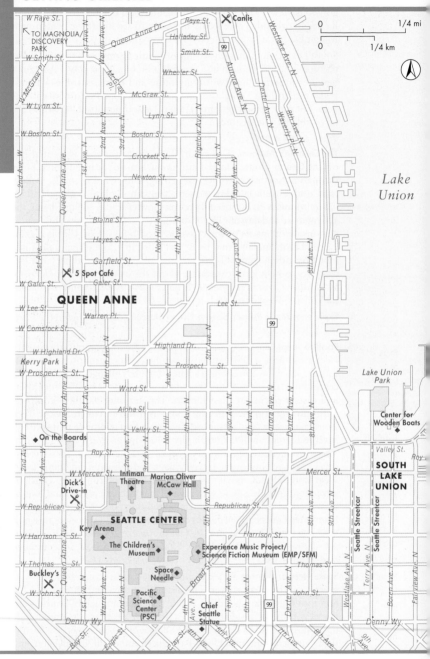

0 _____ 1/4 mi

0 _____ 1/4 km

W Raye St.

Raye St. ✕ Canlis

TO MAGNOLIA/
DISCOVERY
PARK

Queen Anne Dr.

Halladay St.

99

Smith St.

W Smith St.

Wheeler St.

Westlake Ave. N.

W McGraw Pl.

Warren Ave. N.

McGraw Pl.

McGraw St.

Bigelow Ave. N.

Dexter Ave. N.

Warren Pl. N.

8th Ave. N.

Aurora Ave. N.

W Lynn St.

Lynn St.

1st Ave. N.

2nd Ave. N.

3rd Ave. N.

W Boston St.

Boston St.

Queen Anne Ave.

Crockett St.

Newton St.

Taylor Ave. N.

5th Ave. N.

Lake
Union

Howe St.

Queen Anne Dr. N.

Blaine St.

Nob Hill Ave. N.

4th Ave. N.

Hayes St.

8th Ave. N.

Garfield St.

✕ 5 Spot Café

W Galer St.

Galer St.

QUEEN ANNE

Lee St.

W Lee St.

1st Ave. W.

Warren Pl.

W Comstock St.

99

W Highland Dr.

Warren Ave. N.

Highland Dr.

5th Ave. N.

Kerry Park

W Prospect St.

Prospect   St.

Queen Anne Ave. N.

1st Ave. N.

Aurora Ave. N.

Dexter Ave. N.

8th Ave. N.

Lake Union
Park

Ward St.

Aloha St.

Nob Hill

4th Ave. N.

Taylor Ave. N.

6th Ave. N.

Center for
Wooden Boats

Valley St.

♦ On the Boards

2nd Ave. W.

1st Ave. W.

Roy St.

Valley St.   Roy

W Mercer St.

Intiman
Theatre

Marion Oliver
McCaw Hall

3rd Ave. N.

Mercer St.

**SOUTH
LAKE
UNION**

Dick's
Drive-in ✕

W Republican   St.

Republican St.

8th Ave. N.

9th Ave. N.

Seattle Streetcar

Seattle Streetcar

SEATTLE CENTER

Key Arena

Queen Anne Ave. N.

1st Ave. N.

2nd Ave. N.

Harrison St.

W Harrison St.

5th Ave. N.

The Children's
Museum

Experience Music Project/
Science Fiction Museum (EMP/SFM)

Westlake Ave. N.

Terry Ave. N.

Boren Ave. N.

Fairview Ave. N.

W Thomas   St.

Thomas St.

Buckley's
✕

Space
Needle

Broad St.

W John St.

Pacific
Science
Center
(PSC)

Chief
Seattle
Statue

4th Ave.

6th Ave.

99

John St.

Denny Wy.

Bay St.

Eagle St.

Clay St.

5th Ave.

8th Ave.

9th Ave.

Denny Wy.

GETTING HERE AND AROUND

The monorail runs from Westlake Center (5th Avenue and Pine Street) and makes getting here easy from Downtown. It runs daily from 9 AM to 11 PM (with slightly shorter hours in winter), with departures every 10 minutes. Traffic and parking around the Center can be nightmarish during special events and festivals, so try to walk or take public transportation. Walking to Seattle Center from the Olympic Sculpture Park is a ½ mi (about 15 minutes strolling) northeast on Broad Street.

From Downtown, multiple bus lines run up 3rd and 1st avenues to Seattle Center. Buses also climb Queen Anne Avenue, making the commercial districts easy to reach from Downtown or Seattle Center; the rest of that neighborhood will require a car to tour.

From Downtown, South Lake Union is served by the Seattle Streetcar (⊕ *www.seattlestreetcar.org*). The #30 bus connects Lake Union to Seattle Center.

TOP REASONS TO GO

Visit the **Space Needle** and rock out at the **EMP/SFM**, but leave an hour to tour the **Seattle Center**, as well.

Kerry Park at 211 West Highland Drive has outstanding views of the city skyline and Elliott Bay. It's an all-time favorite spot for snapshots. If you're heading north on Queen Anne Avenue North, turn left onto West Highland Drive.

Be a **culture vulture:** Seattle Center houses the city's opera and ballet companies and the new SIFF cinema. And don't overlook **On the Boards** (⊕ *www.ontheboards.org*), a smaller but important performing-arts space in Queen Anne.

Reserve the ultimate restaurant splurge for **Canlis**, which is shorthand in this town for "special occasion."

Rent a small boat at the **Center for Wooden Boats** and tour the lower part of Lake Union. Or just gaze at the water from Lake Union Park.

PLANNING YOUR TIME

You can combine a visit to the Space Needle with one museum visit before exhaustion may set in. Schedule more time for the Pacific Science Center (PSC) and Experience Music Project/ Science Fiction Museum (EMP/ SFM) than other sights—both have a lot of interactive exhibits. Seattle Center has evening attractions, too—the Space Needle is open late, and PSC has an IMAX theater. When you get hungry, both Queen Anne and South Lake Union have a few notable dinner spots.

QUICK BITES

Queen Anne has quite a few sports bars and pubs. **Buckley's** (✉ *232 1st Ave. W* ☎ *206/691–0232*) stands above the rest— wash down a delish burger or sandwich with a pint.

You won't find a quicker or more affordable snack than a few burgers and a milkshake at **Dick's Drive-In** (✉ *500 Queen Anne Ave. N* ☎ *206/285–5155*).

Skillet Street Food (⊕ *www. skilletstreetfood.com*) is a mobile food cart in a converted airstream trailer. It is often in the South Lake Union area for lunch. This gourmet street food, such as duck tacos, grass-fed beef burgers, is worth seeking out. The Web site lists the coming week's locations.

The **5 Spot Café** (✉ *1502 Queen Anne Ave. N* ☎ *206/285–7768*) in Upper Queen Anne serves breakfast and lunch daily and is popular with families.

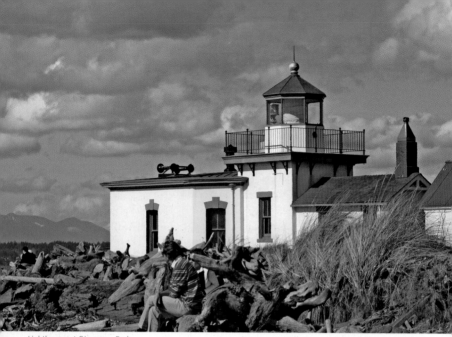

Lighthouse at Discovery Park

the Cascade Range. The Needle was built just in time for the World's Fair in 1962, but has since been refurbished with educational kiosks, interactive trivia game stations for kids, and the glass-enclosed SpaceBase store and Pavilion spiraling around the base of the tower. The top-floor SkyCity restaurant is better known for its revolving floor than its cuisine, but the menu has improved markedly in the last few years. ■TIP→ Don't bother doing the trip to the top of the Needle on rainy days—the view just isn't the same. If you can't decide whether you want the daytime or nighttime view, for $17 you can buy a ticket that allows you to visit twice in one day. ✉ *5th Ave. and Broad St., Seattle Center* ☎ *206/905–2100* ⊕ *www.spaceneedle.com* ✆ *$16 Mon.–Thurs. 10 AM–9:30 PM; Fri.– Sat. 9:30 AM–10:30 PM; Sun. 9 AM–9:30 PM.*

WORTH NOTING

Center for Wooden Boats. Though it used be considered an off-the-beaten-path gem, the Center for Wooden Boats is now a major feature of Lake Union Park. The center gives free boat rides on the lake every Sunday; they sail at 1:30 and 2:30, but the first-come, first-served slots go fast, so you should stop by

CHIEF SEATTLE

At the southeast side of Seattle Center (on the corner of 5th Avenue and Denny Way) stands a statue of Chief Seattle (originally Si'ahl), of the Duwamish tribe. The chief was among the first Native Americans to have contact with the white explorers who came to the region. His fellow tribesmen considered him to be a great leader and peacemaker. The sculpture was created by local artist James Wehn in 1912 and dedicated by the chief's great-great granddaughter, Myrtle Loughery.

the center to sign up as soon as it opens. You may also rent a variety of small craft—pedal-boats, rowboats, and small sailboats—to explore the lake on your own (lessons are available if you don't have much experience). Rates are $25–$50 per hour. The Center largely functions as a school and most courses span several weeks and are not practical for visitors; check out the events calendar anyway, as you might get to watch the staff at work on a restoration if there's a boat-building class in session. Plus there are occasional carving demonstrations by master boat-builders that are free and open to the public. ⊠ *1010 Valley St., South Lake Union* ☎ *206/382-2628* ⊕ *www.cwb.org* ⊠ *Free* ☉ *Center and library Oct.–Apr., Tues.–Sun. 10–5; May–Sept. Tues.–Sun. 10–8. Boat rentals start at 12:30 most days; call to confirm hrs.*

Lake Union Park. Before this park at the foot of Lake Union was completed, you had to travel up to Wallingford's Gas Works Park to enjoy Lake Union from the vantage of a park. Now the southern shore is much more accessible and vibrant than ever—the 12-acre park includes a model boat pond, a boardwalk, a beach where you can launch small craft like kayaks and rowboats to paddle past the houseboats, and a Historic Ships Wharf. In addition, the Center for Wooden Boats (⇨ *see listing above*) is in the park, and in 2012 the Museum of History & Industry will relocate to the refurbished Naval Reserve Armory. ⊠ *860 Terry Ave. N, South Lake Union* ☎ *206/684-7254* ⊕ *www. atlakeunionpark.org* ⊠ *Free.*

OFF THE
BEATEN
PATH

Fodor's Choice
★

Discovery Park. Discovery Park is Seattle's largest park, and it has an amazing variety of terrain: shaded, secluded forest trails lead to meadows, saltwater beaches, sand dunes, a lighthouse, and views that include Puget Sound, the Cascades, and the Olympics. There are 2.8 mi of trails through this urban wilderness, but the North Beach Trail, which takes you along the shore to the lighthouse, is a must-see. Head to the South Bluff Trail to get a view of Mt. Rainier. The park has several entrances—if you want to stop at the visitor center to pick up a trail map before exploring, use the main entrance at Government Way. The North Parking Lot is much closer to the North Beach Trail and to Ballard and Fremont, if you're coming from that direction. ■TIP→ Note that the park is easily reached from Ballard and Fremont. It's easier to combine a park day with an exploration of those neighborhoods than with a busy Downtown itinerary. ⊠ *3801 W. Government Way, Magnolia* ⊹ *From Downtown, take Elliot Ave. W (which turns into 15th Ave. W), and get off at the Emerson St. exit and turn left onto W. Emerson. Make a right onto Gilman Ave. W (which eventually becomes W. Government Way). As you enter the park, the road becomes Washington Ave.; turn left on Utah Ave.* ☎ *206/386-4236* ⊕ *www.cityofseattle.net/parks* ⊠ *Free* ☉ *Park daily 6 AM–11 PM, visitor center Tues.–Sun. 8:30–5.*

EXPERIENCE MUSIC PROJECT/SCIENCE FICTION MUSEUM

✉ *325 5th Ave. N, between Broad and Thomas Sts., Seattle Center* ☎ *877/367–7361* ⊕ *www.empsfm.org* 💲 *$15* ⊙ *Sept.–May, daily 10–5; rest of yr, daily 10–7.*

TIPS

■ At one time, the two museums were considered separate entities and each charged admission. Those days are gone—your ticket is good for both.

■ EMP/SFM participates in First Thursdays; admission is free those days from 5 to 8 pm.

■ EMP is a great place for teenagers. It regularly holds After Hours events that are all-ages rock shows and dance parties in the Sky Church auditorium.

■ As with most Seattle museums, EMP/SFM is least crowded early in the morning (before 11 am) and after 4 pm. You'll need more time to see EMP than SFM, so plan accordingly. It may be best to see SFM first and then leave more time to play with the interactive exhibits at EMP. There's a café onsite, so you'll be able to take a break in between the two experiences.

🐾 Seattle's most controversial architectural statement is the 140,000-square-foot complex designed by architect Frank Gehry, who drew inspiration from electric guitars to achieve the building's curvy metallic design. (Some say, however, that it looks more like robot open-heart surgery than a musical instrument.) Regardless, the building stands out among the city's cookie-cutter high-rises, and therefore it's a fitting backdrop for rock memorabilia from the likes of Bob Dylan and the grunge-scene heavies. The Science Fiction Museum (SFM) has its own wing and tackles the major themes of the genre in a way that's both smart and fun.

HIGHLIGHTS

Complementing the amazing "Roots and Branches" installation, a 35-foot tower made of guitars, this beautiful collection, starting with a model from the 1770s and leading up to the Gibsons, Fenders, and Les Pauls of today, traces the history of guitar amplification.

Two permanent exhibits provide a primer on the evolution of Seattle's music scene. In "Northwest Passage," instruments, costumes, concert photos, and testimonials give all major moments from "Louie Louie" to Nirvana's rise to fame. Some Northwest musicians show up in "Sound and Vision," a collection of videotaped oral histories.

EMP's interactive space has 12 mini-studios, where you can learn simple licks or jam with friends on real or MIDI-compatible instruments. You can also record a CD of your playing or singing in the Jam Studio.

Homeworld is the sci-fi novice's introduction to the genre, with a hall of fame and timeline, plus crowd-pleasing memorabilia like authentic *Star Trek* uniforms. Brave New Worlds is the intermediate course, exploring the different visions science fiction has produced regarding our future.

2

PIONEER SQUARE

Sightseeing
★ ★ ★

Dining
★

Lodging
★

Shopping
★ ★ ★

Nightlife
★ ★ ★

The Pioneer Square district, directly south of Downtown, is Seattle's oldest neighborhood. It attracts visitors for its elegantly renovated (or in some cases replica) turn-of-the-20th-century redbrick buildings and its art galleries. It's undeniably the center of Seattle's arts scene—there are more galleries in this small neighborhood than we have room to list, and they make up the majority of its sights.

Today's Yesler Way was the original "Skid Road," where, in the 1880s, timber was sent to the sawmill on a skid of small logs laid crossways and greased so that the cut trees would slide down to the mill. The area later grew into Seattle's first center of commerce. Many of the buildings you see today are replicas of the wood-frame structures destroyed by fire in 1889.

Nowadays, the role Pioneer Square plays in the city today is harder to define. Despite the concentration of galleries, the neighborhood is no longer a center for artists per se, as rents have risen considerably; only established gallery owners can rent loftlike spaces in heavily trafficked areas. The neighborhood had begun to go upscale before the dot-com bust, and developers are again eyeballing the area, ready to make it another Belltown. So far, rising rents have only succeeded in creating too many empty storefronts.

By day, you'll see a mix of Downtown workers and tourists strolling the area. The local parks are, sadly, mainly inhabited by homeless people. Pioneer Square has a well-known nightlife scene, but these days it's a much-derided one, thanks to the meat-market vibe of many of the clubs. If you want classier venues, you'll be smart to head north up 1st Avenue to Belltown.

When Seattleites speak of Pioneer Square, they usually speak of the love they have for certain unique neighborhood spots—the original Grand Central Bakery in the historic Grand Central Arcade, Zeitgeist

GETTING ORIENTED

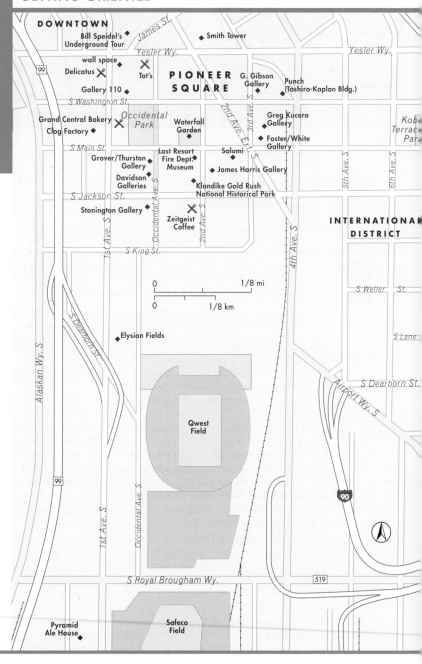

DOWNTOWN

Bill Speidel's
Underground Tour

James St.

Smith Tower

Yesler Wy.

Yesler Wy.

wall space

99

Delicatus

Tat's

PIONEER

SQUARE

G. Gibson
Gallery

Punch
(Tashiro-Kaplan Bldg.)

Gallery 110

S Washington St.

Occidental
Park

Greg Kucera
Gallery

Kob
Terrac
Par

Grand Central Bakery

Clog Factory

Waterfall
Garden

Foster/White
Gallery

S Main St.

2nd Ave. Ext. S

3rd Ave. S

Grover/Thurston
Gallery

Last Resort
Fire Dept.
Museum

Salumi

James Harris Gallery

5th Ave. S

6th Ave. S

Davidson
Galleries

Klondike Gold Rush
National Historical Park

S Jackson St.

Stonington Gallery

Zeitgeist
Coffee

2nd Ave. S

INTERNATIONAL

DISTRICT

1st Ave. S

Occidental Ave. S

S King St.

4th Ave. S

0   1/8 mi

0   1/8 km

S Weller St.

Elysian Fields

S Lane

Alaskan Wy. S

S Dearborn St.

Airport Wy. S

S Dearborn St.

Qwest
Field

99

I-90

Occidental Ave. S

1st Ave. S

S Royal Brougham Wy.

519

Pyramid
Ale House

Safeco
Field

GETTING HERE AND AROUND

Pioneer Square is directly south of Downtown, which means you can easily walk here. However, the stretch between the two neighborhoods is not the most scenic trip, so you can also hop on the bus—Pioneer Square is within the Ride Free Area, so during the day it won't cost you anything to catch one of the buses heading south on 1st Avenue.

Pioneer Square itself is pretty small; you'll easily be able to walk to all the galleries. If you've driven in from a more distant neighborhood, most of the pay parking lots and garages are on S. Jackson Street.

Most people combine Pioneer Square with a trip to the International District, which together would make a full day of sightseeing. Pioneer Square is also the closest neighborhood to Qwest Field and Safeco Field, so it also makes sense to end a touring day here before heading to a game.

TOP REASONS TO GO

Leave the Space Needle to the masses and check out the observation deck at 42-story **Smith Tower** at 506 2nd Avenue and Yesler Way.

Gallery hop on First Thursday art walks—perhaps the best time to see Pioneer Square, when animated crowds walk from gallery to gallery, viewing the new exhibitions. Or tour on your own: Greg Kucera, G. Gibson, James Harris, and the Tashiro-Kaplan Building are must-sees.

Soak up some weird and wonderful historic Seattle tidbits on the zany **Bill Speidel's Underground Tour.**

Buy some quintessential Northwest footwear at the **Clog Factory.** (⇨ See Chapter 6, Shopping).

Catch your reflection in the hood of an antique fire truck at **Last Resort Fire Department Museum.**

Cheer for one of the home teams at Qwest or Safeco Field. (⇨ See Chapter 7, Sports and Activities).

TOURS

At a kiosk on Occidental between Main and Jackson streets, you can pick up a booklet that outlines three walking tours around the historic buildings of Pioneer Square.

The Underground Tour shows you the remnants of passageways and buildings buried when the city regraded the streets in the 1880s. The tour is fun and full of Seattle-history tidbits.

QUICK BITES

Delicatus (✉ 103 1st Ave. S ☎ 206/623–3780) is an ambitious sandwich shop with selections like pulled lamb shank with chive aioli.

An outpost of the **Grand Central Bakery** (✉ 214 1st Ave. S ☎ 206/622–3644) is in one of the square's historic redbrick buildings. Along with fresh pastries, it serves panini, soups, and salads.

Salumi (✉ 309 3rd Ave. S ☎ 206/621–8772) is something of a pilgrimage site. Sample its artisanal cured meats in a heavenly sandwich. Call ahead, as the store keeps odd hours.

Tat's (✉ 159 Yesler Way ☎ 206/264–8287) has a large selection of New York–style deli sandwiches and subs.

Zeitgeist Coffee (✉ 171 S. Jackson St. ☎ 206/583–0497) is the best-loved coffee shop in the neighborhood.

2

coffeehouse, a certain art gallery, a friend's loft apartment, a great store—than the love they have for the neighborhood as a whole. (Indeed the major store on that list would have been Elliott Bay Bookstore, which moved to its new home on Capitol Hill in 2010.) Pioneer Square is always worth a visit, but reactions do vary. Anyone seriously interested in doing the gallery circuit will be thrilled. Anyone looking for a vibrant, picture-perfect historic district that invites hours of contented strolling will be underwhelmed.

Pioneer Square is a gateway of sorts to the stadium district, which segues into Sodo (South of Downtown). First comes Qwest Field, where the Seahawks and the Sounders play. Directly south of that is Safeco Field, where the Mariners play. There's not much to see in this industrial area, but if you're a sports fan you can easily make a run from Pioneer Square to one of the stadiums' pro shops. There are also a few good brewpubs close to the stadiums.

TOP ATTRACTIONS

Bill Speidel's Underground Tour. Present-day Pioneer Square is actually one story higher than it used to be. After the Great Seattle Fire of 1889, Seattle's planners regraded the neighborhood's streets one level higher. The result: there is now an intricate and expansive array of subterranean passageways and basements beneath Pioneer Square, and Bill Speidel's Underground Tour is the only way to explore them. Speidel was an irreverent historian, PR man, and former *Seattle Times* reporter who took it upon himself to preserve historic Seattle, and this tour is packed with his sardonic wit and playful humor. It's very informative, too—if you're interested in the general history of the city or anecdotes about the city's early politicians and residents, you'll appreciate it that much more. Kids will probably be bored, as there's not much to see at the specific sites, which are more used as launching points for the stories. ■ TIP➔ Comfortable shoes, a love for quirky historical anecdotes, and an appreciation of bad puns are musts. Several tours are offered daily, and schedules change month to month: call or visit the Web site for a full list of tour times. ⊠ *608 1st Ave., Pioneer Square* 🕾 *206/682–4646* ⊕ *www. undergroundtour.com* 🖃 *$15* ⊘ *Tours daily; call for schedules.*

Smith Tower. New York tycoon Lyman Cornelius Smith had big plans for Seattle in 1909—in the form of blueprints for a 14-story building. Turns out his son, Burns Lyman Smith, had even bigger plans, for a 21-story structure with an additional 21-story tower, topped by a pyramid-shaped Gothic cap. The building opened on July 4, 1914, and was the tallest office building outside New York City and the fourth tallest building in the world. (It remained the tallest building west of the Mississippi for nearly 50 years.) The Smith Tower Observation Deck on the 35th floor is an open-air wrap-around deck providing panoramic views of the surrounding historic neighborhood, the city skyline, and the mountains on clear days. ⊠ *506 2nd Ave. S, Pioneer Square* 🕾 *206/622–4004* ⊕ *www.smithtower.com/Observation.html* 🖃 *$7.50* ⊘ *May–Sept., daily 10–sunset; Apr. and Oct., daily 10–5; Nov.–Mar., weekends only 10–4.*

The Pioneer Square skyline is dominated by historic Smith Tower.

OFF THE
BEATEN
PATH
Qwest Field. Located directly south of Pioneer Square, Qwest Field hosts two professional teams, the Seattle Seahawks (football) and the Seattle Sounders FC (soccer). The open-air stadium has 67,000 seats; sightlines are excellent, thanks to a cantilevered design and the close placement of lower sections—some seats are only 40 feet from the end zones. Tours start at the pro shop (be sure to arrive at least 30 minutes prior to purchase tickets) and last an hour and a half. ✉ *800 Occidental Ave. S, Sodo* ☎ *206/381–7555* ⊕ *www.qwestfield.com* 🖃 *$7* ⊙ *Sept.–May, Fri. and Sat. at 12:30 and 2:30; June–Aug., daily at 12:30 and 2:30.*

OFF THE
BEATEN
PATH
Safeco Field. This 47,000-seat, grass turf, open-air baseball stadium with a retractable roof is the home of the Seattle Mariners. If you want to see the stadium in all its glory, take the one-hour tour, which brings you onto the field, into the dugouts, back to the press and locker rooms, and up to the posh box seats. Wear comfortable shoes. Tours depart from the Team Store on 1st Avenue, and you purchase your tickets here, too. Afterward, head across the street to the Pyramid Alehouse for a brew. ✉ *1st Ave. S, Sodo* ☎ *206/622–4487* ⊕ *www.mariners.mlb. com* 🖃 *$7* ⊙ *Apr.–Oct. nongame-day tours at 10:30, 12:30, and 2:30, game-day tours at 10:30 and 12:30; Nov.–Mar. tours Tues.–Sun. at 12:30 and 2:30.*

WORTH NOTING

Klondike Gold Rush National Historical Park. A redbrick building with wooden floors and soaring ceilings contains a small museum illustrating Seattle's role in the 1897–98 Gold Rush in the Klondike region. Antique equipment is on display, and the walls are lined with photos of gold miners, explorers, and the hopeful families who followed them.

Film presentations, gold-panning demonstrations (daily in summer, at 10 and 3), and rotating exhibits are scheduled throughout the year. Other sectors of this park are in southeast Alaska. ⊠ *319 2nd Ave. S, Pioneer Square* ☎ *206/220–4240* ⊕ *www.nps.gov/klse/index.htm* ▣ *Free* ⊘ *Daily 9–5.*

> ### GALLERY WALKS
>
> It's fun to simply walk around Pioneer Square and pop into galleries. South Jackson Street to Yesler between Western and 4th Avenue South is a good area. Visit ⊕ *www.artguidenw.com*.

Last Resort Fire Department Museum. Occupying the bottom floor of the Seattle Fire Department's headquarters, the museum includes eight historic rigs dating from the 19th and early 20th centuries, as well as artifacts (vintage helmets and uniforms, hose nozzles, and other equipment) and photos, logs, and newspaper clippings recording historic fires. ⊠ *301 2nd Ave. S, Pioneer Square* ☎ *206/783–4474* ⊕ *www.lastresortfd.org* ▣ *Free* ⊘ *June–Aug., Wed. and Thurs. 11–3; Sept.–May, Wed. 11–3.*

Occidental Park. This picturesque cobblestone "park" and the ivy-covered wall on its western boundary show up in a lot of brochures. It's the geographical heart of the historic neighborhood—too bad its current layout is not that historic at all. Though it once was the site of the Savoy Hotel, the park actually spent a lot of time as a parking lot before the restoration of the neighborhood started in the late 1960s and early '70s. It can be lovely on sunny days, and there's a small outdoor café in seasonal weather. Note, however, that this square is a spot where homeless people congregate; depending on how intense the panhandling activity is, it may be more of a stroll-through than a sit-down-and-linger affair. The square is best avoided at night. ⊠ *Occidental Ave. S and S. Main St., Pioneer Square.*

Waterfall Garden. You can find a fun spot to take a break in this small garden surrounding a 22-foot (artificial) waterfall that cascades over large granite stones. There are a few café tables; before heading over, grab some lunch to go from Grand Central Baking Company in the Grand Central Arcade on 1st Avenue S and Washington Street. ⊠ *Corner of S. Main St. and 2nd Ave. S, Pioneer Square.*

GALLERIES

Davidson Galleries. Davidson has several different departments in one building: the Contemporary Print & Drawing Center, which holds the portfolios of 40 print artists; the Antique Print Department, and the Painting, Sculpture & Multimedia Department. Though the antique print department is more of a specialized interest, the contemporary print exhibits are always interesting and worth a look. ⊠ *313 Occidental Ave. S, Pioneer Square* ☎ *Contemporary prints 206/624–1324, antique prints 206/624–6700, painting and sculpture 206/624–7684* ⊕ *www.davidsongalleries.com* ▣ *Free* ⊘ *Tues.–Sat. 10–5:30.*

★ **Foster/White Gallery.** One of the Seattle art scene's heaviest hitters, Foster/White has digs as impressive as the works it shows: a century-old building with high ceilings and 7,000 square feet of exhibition space.

A striking show at Greg Kucera Gallery

Works by internationally acclaimed glass artist Dale Chihuly, and paintings, sculpture, and drawings by Northwest masters Kenneth Callahan, Mark Tobey, and George Tsutakawa are on permanent display. ⊠ *220 3rd Ave. S, Pioneer Square* ☏ *206/622–2833* ⊕ *www.fosterwhite.com* 🖃 *Free* ⊙ *Tues.–Sat. 10–6.*

Gallery 110. Gallery 110 works with a collective of 31 artists, showing pieces in its small space that are edgy, energetic, and sometimes just plain weird. Occasionally, special exhibits will involve work from outside the collective and its affiliates—a recent show spotlighted the best work from a collective in Portland. ⊠ *110 3rd Ave. S, Pioneer Square* ☏ *206/624–9336* ⊕ *www.gallery110.com* 🖃 *Free* ⊙ *Wed.–Sat. noon–5.*

Fodor'sChoice
★ **G. Gibson Gallery.** Vintage and contemporary photography is on exhibit in this elegant corner space, including shows by the likes of Michael Kenna as well as retrospectives of the works of Walker Evans and Berenice Abbott. The savvy gallery owner also shows contemporary paintings, sculpture, and mixed-media pieces. This is another institution of the Seattle art scene, and the gallery's taste is always impeccable. ⊠ *300 S. Washington St., Pioneer Square* ☏ *206/587–4033* ⊕ *www. ggibsongallery.com* 🖃 *Free* ⊙ *Tues.–Sat. 11–5.*

Fodor'sChoice
★ **Greg Kucera Gallery.** One of the most important destinations on the First Thursday gallery walk, this gorgeous space is a top venue for national and regional artists. Be sure to check out the outdoor sculpture deck on the second level. If you have time for only one gallery visit, this is the place to go. You'll see big names that you might recognize along with newer artists, and the thematic group shows are

consistently well thought out and well presented. ⊠ *212 3rd Ave. S, Pioneer Square* ☎ *206/624–0770* ⊕ *www.gregkucera.com* 🎫 *Free* ⊙ *Tues.– Sat. 10:30–5:30.*

Grover/Thurston Gallery. Twenty Northwest artists are represented in this historic space. Shows, which can be either solo or group exhibitions, are often fun, as many of the artists create wry pieces, many of which seem more like fine art imitating folk art. ⊠ *309 Occidental Ave. S, Pioneer Square* ☎ *206/223–0816* ⊕ *www.groverthurston.com* 🎫 *Free* ⊙ *Tues.–Sat. 11–5.*

James Harris. One of Seattle's oldest and most respected galleries, Harris is known for creating small shows that selectively and impeccably survey both local and international work. This strength is well showcased in the gallery's multiple tiny exhibition rooms, which provide intimacy and connectivity to tightly curated group shows, for example Alexander Kroll with Jason Hirata, or solo shows such as Margot Quan Knight, who is a regular. ⊠ *312 2nd Ave. S, Pioneer Square* ☎ *206/903–6220* ⊕ *www.jamesharrisgallery.org* 🎫 *Free* ⊙ *Tues.–Sat. 11–5.*

Punch. This small artist-run gallery has been a critical favorite since opening in 2006. Its eclectic shows combine the many mediums of its founding members—painting, digital media, sculpture, and collage. ■TIP➔ Punch is just one of a handful of artist collectives in the Tashiro Kaplan Building at 3rd Ave. S and Washington St. SOIL and Platform are also worth checking out in this complex; there are also open studios (make the rounds on First Thursdays) and a great café. ⊠ *119 Prefontaine Pl. S, Pioneer Square* ☎ *206/621–1945* ⊕ *www.punchgallery.org* 🎫 *Free* ⊙ *Thurs.–Sat. 12–5.*

★ **Stonington Gallery.** You'll see plenty of cheesy tribal art knockoffs in tourist-trap shops, but this elegant gallery will give you a real look at the best contemporary work of Northwest Coast and Alaska tribal members (and artists from these regions working in the native style). Three floors exhibit wood carvings, paintings, sculpture, and mixed-media pieces. ⊠ *119 S. Jackson St., Pioneer Square* ☎ *206/405–4040* ⊕ *www.stoningtongallery.com* 🎫 *Free* ⊙ *Weekdays 10–6, Sat. 10–5:30, Sun. noon–5.*

wall space. Seattle doesn't have many spaces devoted solely to photography, which makes wall space notable among Pioneer Square's umpteen galleries. Equal attention is giving to Ansel Adams–style black-and-white prints and to the new possibilities and genres that are emerging through digital technologies. ⊠ *600 1st Ave., Suite 623, Pioneer Square* ☎ *206/330–9137* ⊕ *www.wall-spacegallery.com* 🎫 *Free* ⊙ *Tues.–Sat. 10:30–5:30.*

2

INTERNATIONAL DISTRICT

Sightseeing
★★
Dining
★★★★
Lodging
★
Shopping
★★★
Nightlife
★

Bright welcome banners, 12-foot fiberglass dragons clinging to lamp posts, and a traditional Chinese gate confirm you're in the International District. The I.D., as it's locally known, is synonymous with delectable dining—it has many cheap Chinese restaurants (this is the neighborhood for barbecued duck), but the best eateries reflect its Pan-Asian spirit: Vietnamese, Japanese, Malay, Cambodian. With the endlessly fun Uwajimaya shopping center, the gorgeously redesigned Wing Luke Asian Museum, and two up-and-coming galleries, you now have something to do in between bites.

The I.D. used to be called Chinatown; it began as a haven for Chinese workers who came to the United States to work on the transcontinental railroad. It was later a hub for Seattle's growing Japanese population, and now one of the biggest presences is Vietnamese, both in the center of the I.D. and in "Little Saigon," directly east of the neighborhood. Though the neighborhood has weathered the anti-Chinese riots and the forced eviction of Chinese residents during the 1880s and the internment of Japanese-Americans during World War II, it's become increasingly less vital to its communities. Many of the people who actually live in the neighborhood are older—the northern and southern suburbs of the city are where the newer generations are being raised (though young people still often make the I.D. an obligatory snack stop before heading home after a night out in Seattle).

The I.D. stretches from 4th Avenue to 12th Avenue and between Yesler Way and S. Dearborn Street. The main business anchor is the Uwajimaya superstore, and there are other small businesses scattered among the restaurants, including herbalists, acupuncturists, antiques shops, and private clubs for gambling and socializing. Note that the area is

GETTING ORIENTED

DOWNTOWN

Yesler Wy.
8th Ave.
Broadway
10th Ave.
E Yesler Wy.

Washington St.
10th Ave. S
S Washington St.

Kobe
Terrace Park

0   1/8 mi
0   1/8 km

5th Ave. S
S Main St.
S Main St.

◆ Panama Hotel

Saigon Deli

◆ Kobo at Higo

S Jackson St.
S Jackson St.
12th Ave. S

Jade
Garden
Szechuan
Noodle Bowl

Kau Kau
✕
✕
✕

S King St.
S King St.

6th Ave. S
Maynard Ave. S
Maynard Al. S
Canton Al. S
◆ Wing Luke
Asian Museum
10th Ave. S

S Weller St.
S Weller St.

◆
Uwajimaya
INTERNATIONAL

DISTRICT

S Lane St.
7th Ave. S
8th Ave. S

← TO QWEST FIELD
0.1 mi./1 min.

S Dearborn St.

◆ Lawrimore Project/
Ohge Ltd.
9th Ave. S

S Charles St.

90

90

S Plummer St.

Dr. Jose
Rizal Park

TO
SAFECO FIELD
←
12th Ave. S

5

S Royal Brougham Way   519

Airport Way S

S Judkins St.

GETTING AROUND

The I.D. is southeast of Pioneer Square, and the neighborhoods are often combined in one visit—you may find yourself wandering into the I.D. anyway, along South Jackson Street, which is the main thoroughfare connecting the two neighborhoods.

From the center of Downtown, walking to the I.D. takes about 20 minutes. However, it's not a scenic route, so unless you need the leg stretch, take a bus or hail a cab. Buses 7, 14, and 36 pick up on Pine (at 3rd or 4th avenues). Bus 99 picks up by each of the major piers and travels along Alaskan Way.

TOP REASONS TO GO

Browse for unique gifts, souvenirs, and trinkets at **Uwajimaya** and **Kobo at Higo.** Uwajimaya has an amazing selection of Asian foods, plus a great bookstore and home section. Kobo, a gallery for local artists, is the spot for classy mementos.

See the modern side of the I.D. at the avant-garde gallery **Lawrimore Project,** which is the talk of the gallery scene and specializes in large-scale installations.

Get a history lesson with your tea at the **Panama Hotel.** Although not one of our top choices for lodging, this hotel is a must-see for its lovely ground-floor teahouse.

Tour the neighborhood with docents from the **Wing Luke Asian Museum.** The museum casts a no-nonsense eye on the story of Seattle's Asian and Pacific Islander communities, and guided tours point out the living history in the neighborhood, which is getting harder and harder to find.

Sample something from **every major Asian cuisine.** The Quick Bites section below barely covers what can be found in one block.

PLANNING YOUR TIME

The I.D. is a very popular lunchtime spot with Downtown office workers and a popular dinner spot with many Seattleites. You should definitely make a meal here part of your visit. You'll need at least an hour at the Wing Luke Asian museum. A stop at Uwajimaya is essential. Don't plan on spending a full day here—a morning or an afternoon will suffice. And be forewarned that, as in adjacent Pioneer Square, Seattle's homelessness problem is quite visible here.

QUICK BITES

Jade Garden (✉ 704 S. King St. ☎ 206/622–8181) is the go-to place for dim sum. Note that it gets very crowded at lunch.

Kau Kau (✉ 656 S. King St. ☎ 206/682–4006) is a simple spot serving arguably the best Chinese barbecue in the I.D.— try the duck and the spareribs.

Also a sight to see, **Uwajimaya** (✉ 600 5th Ave. S ☎ 206/624–6248) is an Asian supermarket with a full food court.

Bánh mi (Vietnamese sandwiches on French rolls) are great for refueling, and **Saigon Deli** (✉ 1237 S. Jackson St. ☎ 206/322–3700) has the best in the neighborhood.

The debate regarding the I.D.'s best noodle shop is unending, but **Szechuan Noodle Bowl** (✉ 420 8th Ave. S ☎ 206/623–4198) gets a lot of votes.

more diffuse than similar communities in larger cities like San Francisco and New York. You *won't* find the densely packed streets chockablock with tiny storefronts and markets that spill out onto the sidewalk—scenes that have become synonymous with the word "Chinatown."

When the Wing Luke Asian Museum moved from its tiny cluttered home to a refurbished historic building on one of the main drags here, it refocused the city's attention on the I.D. as more than a collection of restaurants. There are indeed signs of further improvement, which the neighborhood sorely needs. (As with Pioneer Square, the I.D. is interesting and fun, but can be sorely rough around the edges: it's in these two adjacent neighborhoods that Seattle's horrible homeless problem is most visible.) The I.D. does have more energy these days: students crowd bubble tea parlors, and the community has been holding more special events like parades and periodic night markets and movie nights in Hing Hay Park.

WHAT TO SEE

Kobe Terrace park. Seattle's sister city of Kobe, Japan, donated a 200-year-old stone lantern to adorn this small hillside park. Despite being so close to I–5, the terrace is a peaceful place to stroll through and enjoy views of the city, the water, and, if you're lucky, Mt. Rainier; a few benches line the gravel paths. The herb gardens you see are part of the Danny Woo Community Gardens, tended to by the neighborhood's residents. ⊠ *Main St. between 6th Ave. S and 7th Ave. S, International District* ⚒ *Free* ☉ *Daily dawn–dusk.*

★ **Lawrimore Project/Ohge Ltd.** The talk of the contemporary art scene, Lawrimore represents some of the hottest visual artists around, including large-scale installation provocateurs SuttonBeresCuller and Lead Pencil Studio. Lawrimore's former manager Alex Ohge opened his own gallery in the same building. Though much smaller in scope and size, Ohge Ltd. has already had some impressive shows including a solo show of Nicholas Nyland's paintings and ceramics. ⊠ *831 Airport Way S, International District* ☎ *206/501–1231 Lawrimore; 206/261–2315 Ohge* ⊕ *www.lawrimoreproject.com; www.ohgeltd.com* ⚒ *Free* ☉ *Lawrimore: Tues.–Sat. 10–5:30. Ohge: Fri. and Sat. 11–6.*

A GOOD COMBO

For a great day of walking and exploring, start your day with breakfast at Pike Place Market, then bus, cab, or stroll down 1st Avenue to Pioneer Square (you'll pass SAM en route—another option!). After visiting some art galleries (which generally open between 10:30 and noon) and stopping at any of the neighborhood's coffee shops, walk southeast to the International District for some retail therapy at Uwajimaya and a visit to the Wing Luke Asian Museum. Then cab it back to your hotel.

Fodor's Choice **Uwajimaya.** This huge, fascinating Japanese supermarket is a feast for
★ the senses. A 30-foot-long red Chinese dragon stretches above colorful mounds of fresh produce and aisles of delicious packaged goods—including spicy peas, sweet crackers, gummy candies, nut mixes, rice snacks, and colorful sweets—from countries throughout Asia. A busy food court serves sushi, Japanese bento-box meals, Chinese stir-fry

Roasted nuts for sale right outside the delightful Uwajimaya superstore

combos, Korean barbecue, Hawaiian dishes, Vietnamese spring rolls, and an assortment of teas and tapioca drinks. This is the best place to pick up all sorts of snacks; dessert lovers won't know which way to turn first. The housewares section is well stocked with dishes, cookware, appliances, textiles, and gifts. There's also a card section, a Hello Kitty corner, and Yuriko's cosmetics, where you can find Shiseido products that are usually available only in Japan. Last but not least, there's a small branch of the famous Kinokuniya bookstore chain, selling paper goods, pens, stickers, gift items, and many Asian-language books. The large parking lot is free for one hour with a minimum $5 purchase (which will be no problem) or two hours with a minimum $10 purchase—don't forget to have your ticket validated by the cashiers. ⊠ *600 5th Ave. S, International District* ☎ *206/624–6248* ⊕ *www.uwajimaya. com* ♡ *Mon.–Sat.* 7 AM–10 PM, *Sun.* 9–9.

Wing Luke Asian Museum. *See the highlighted listing in this chapter.*

WING LUKE ASIAN MUSEUM

✉ *719 S. King St., International District* ☎ *206/623–5124* ⊕ *www.wingluke.org* 🎫 *$12.95, free 1st Thurs. and 3rd Sat. of month* ⊙ *Tues.–Sun. 10–5.*

TIPS

■ The museum is a great place to start your tour of the I.D., as it will provide a context to the neighborhood and the communities living here that you won't get by simply wandering around.

■ Parts of the historic building can only be visited on the Museum Experience tour.

■ Note that in addition to participating in First Thursdays, the museum is also free on the third Saturday of each month. The museum is open until 8 pm both days.

■ Parking in the I.D. is sometimes tricky. The closest public lots are behind the museum on Weller Street, one block south of King Street.

■ Be sure to check out what's going on in the Tateuchi Story Theater. The museum has long supported Asian-American playwrights, musicians, and artists, and its cultural offerings keep getting better. Shows range from concerts of traditional instruments to avant-garde theater to documentary film screenings.

Named for the Northwest's first Asian-American elected official, this gorgeous museum is in a renovated 1910 hotel and commercial building that once was the first home for many new immigrants. The museum surveys the history and cultures of people from Asia and the Pacific islands who settled in the Pacific Northwest. It provides a sophisticated and often somber look at how immigrants and their descendants have transformed (and been transformed by) American culture. The evolution of the museum has been driven by community participation—the museum's library has an oral history lab, and many of the rotating exhibits are focused around stories from longtime residents and their descendants.

HIGHLIGHTS

The backdrop in the Tateuchi Story Theater is restored scrim from historic Nippon Kan Theater. The museum includes re-creations of typical early-20th-century one-room apartments, a communal kitchen, and the Yick Fung Company store.

A Seattle-born sculptor and painter, George Tsutakawa is best known for his bronze fountains. This gallery named in his honor presents group shows of established and up-and-coming Asian-Pacific-American artists.

The museum offers two tours. The "Museum Experience" includes the current exhibits and the 1910 Historic Hotel and Yick Fung Company buildings. Tours start in the museum's lobby at 10:30, 11:30, 1:30, 2:30, and 3:30. The second, "Touch of Chinatown," is a 90-minute guided stroll around the I.D. Tours depart Tuesday–Friday at 10:15 and 2, and Saturday at 10:15, 1, and 3. Tickets are $17 and include admission to the museum.

2

FIRST HILL AND THE CENTRAL DISTRICT

Sightseeing
★★
Dining
★★
Lodging
★
Shopping
★
Nightlife
★

The little-visited neighborhoods of First Hill and the Central District are nonetheless important pieces of the city's fabric. First Hill is an eastern extension of Downtown, and one tree-lined street has something truly spectacular: the Frye Art Museum. The Central District, mostly residential and off the beaten path, is the historic hub of Seattle's African-American community. It has a few monuments honoring this community, as well as some good restaurants and a few landmarks that provide a fairly good survey of architectural trends throughout the decades.

Smack between Downtown and Capitol Hill, First Hill is an odd mix of sterile-looking medical facility buildings (earning it the nickname "Pill Hill"), old brick buildings that look like they belong on a college campus, and newer residential towers. There are a few businesses along Boren Avenue, but they're mostly unremarkable. The main draws of the neighborhood are the Frye Art Museum, which is well worth a detour, and the fantastic historic Sorrento Hotel.

The Central District, or the "C.D.," lies south of Capitol Hill

CENTRAL DISTRICT LANDMARKS

■ Immaculate Conception Church (1904) at 820 18th Avenue

■ Old Firehouse #23 (1909) at 722 18th Avenue

■ Victorian House (1900) at 1414 S. Washington Street

■ Langston Hughes Cultural Arts Center (built in 1912 as the Bikur Cholim Synagogue) at 104 17th Avenue

■ James Washington Jr. Home and Studio (1918) at 1816 26th Avenue

■ First African Methodist Episcopal Church (1912) at 14th Avenue and Pine Street

GETTING ORIENTED

GETTING AROUND

Because the sights are so spread out here, having a car is essential. This is especially true if you want to tool around the Central District to see the landmark buildings and houses, or if you want to visit the Northwest African American Museum, which is far south of everything else, in the Rainier Valley area. If you're bussing it to the Northwest African American Museum from Downtown, take Bus 7 to Rainier Avenue South and South State Street. From Capitol Hill take Bus 48 from 23rd Avenue and E. Madison Street to 23rd Avenue and S. Massachusetts Street, which is right in front of the museum. If you're just visiting the Frye and the Sorrento Hotel, you can walk from either Downtown or Capitol Hill. By bus, take the 2, 10, 11, or 14 from Downtown.

TOP REASONS TO GO

Spend a quiet, art-filled afternoon at the **Frye Art Museum**, the only real attraction in First Hill, and one of Seattle's best museums. The Frye mixes representational art with rotating exhibits of folk and pop art, so there's something for everyone.

Settle into an overstuffed chair for a drink at the Sorrento Hotel's delightfully fussy **Fireside Room**. This is an especially pleasant stop on a chilly, rainy day—a few leather easy chairs are parked in front of a crackling fireplace.

Redefine dinner theater at **Central Cinema**. This off-the-beaten-path movie house serves beer, wine, burgers, pizzas, and salads. Screenings are a mix of classics (*The Shining, Animal House*) and small independent films.

QUICK BITES

Katy's Corner Café (⊠ *2000 E. Union St.* ☎ *206/329–0121*) is a tiny, friendly neighborhood spot with homemade pastries, quiches, sandwiches and soup.

Ezell's (⊠ *501 23rd Ave.* ☎ *206/ 324–4141*), a Seattle institution, does one thing to perfection: crispy, juicy fried chicken with all the fixings.

If you're driving to the Northwest African American Museum, you can stop at **Charlie's Flame-Broiled Burgers** (⊠ *2608 S. Judkins* ☎ *206/322–1091*). The Kitchen Sink burger is a favorite—it's piled with cheese, bacon, and hot pastrami.

SoHo Coffee Company (⊠ *1918 E. Yesler Way* ☎ *206/322–0807*) serves Stumptown coffee, bagels, and salads.

PLANNING YOUR TIME

Both of these neighborhoods are best as detours from other itineraries. First Hill is adjacent to Downtown, and the C.D. is close to the International District. Both areas also can feel like extensions of Capitol Hill. There's no good way to tour this large, mostly residential area—you'll have to make targeted trips to sights of interest. The Northwest African American Museum requires at least an hour. A visit to the small but captivating Frye Art Museum could take anywhere from one to three hours.

and northeast of the International District. Its boundaries are roughly 12th Avenue on the west, Martin Luther King Jr. Boulevard on the east, E. Madison to the north, and S. Jackson Street to the south. As Downtown Seattle rapidly develops, the C.D. is facing a transitional period. Community groups are working hard to ensure that the "revitalization" of the area doesn't come at the expense of stripping the city's oldest residential neighborhood of its history or breaking up and pricing out the community that's hung in there during years of economic blight.

JAZZY SCHOOL

Garfield High School (⊠ *400 23rd Ave.*) is one of the Central District's historic landmarks. Alumni include Quincy Jones and Jimi Hendrix; today the school enjoys national attention for its jazz program. The 30-piece ensemble often performs at local festivals, including Earshot Jazz Festival in October and Folk Life in May.

WHAT TO SEE

Crespinel Martin Luther King Jr. Mural. Heading west on Cherry Street in the Central Area, you'll see a 17-foot-tall mural of Dr. Martin Luther King Jr. Pacific Northwest artist James Crespinel painted the mural in the summer of 1995 on the eastern face of the building that houses Catfish Corner, a soul-food take-out place. ⊠ *Corner of Martin Luther King Jr. Way and Cherry St., Central District.*

Frye Art Museum. *See the highlighted listing in this chapter.*

OFF THE BEATEN PATH

Northwest African American Museum. Focusing on the history of African Americans in the Northwest, this museum traces their journeys through a combination of photos, art, and historical timelines. Past exhibits have covered the civil-rights movement in Washington State, the Northwest jazz scene—which flourished from the 1930s to the 1960s—and spotlights on the particular cultures that make up modern-day Seattle, like its large Ethiopian community. One gallery is dedicated to the work of local artists.⊠ *2300 S. Massachusetts St., Leschi* ☎ *206/518–6000* ⊕ *www.naamnw.org* ⊡ *$6* ⊙ *Wed. and Fri. 11–4:30, Thurs. 11–7. Sat. 11–4, Sun. 12–4.*

OFF THE BEATEN PATH

Seward Park (⊠ *5895 Lake Washington Blvd. S, Columbia City–Seward Park*), 20 minutes south of Downtown, is a relatively undiscovered gem. The 300-acre park includes trails through old-growth forest, mountain views, and a small swimming beach complete with a swimming raft. Though you feel very far away from the city here, the park sits on the shores of Lake Washington. There are restrooms, picnic tables, and lifeguards on duty in summer. A large paved path circles the edge of the park, along Lake Washington, making for a lovely stroll.

FRYE ART MUSEUM

✉ *704 Terry Ave., First Hill*
☎ *206/622–9250* ⊕ *www.*
fryemuseum.org 🏷 *Free*
🕐 *Tues.–Sat. 10–5 (Thurs. until*
8), Sun. noon–5.

2

TIPS

■ The museum is small enough that you can move through it in an hour, but you could easily spend more time here, too.

■ The café, which has a small courtyard and larger entrées in addition to sandwiches and sweets, is a local favorite. It has free Wi-Fi access.

■ The Frye is best midweek. Because of its size, weekend crowds can overwhelm the space and detract from its charm.

■ The museum store carries clever and arty itemsdesigned and crafted by students from The Center School, a public high school in Queen Anne with an arts-focused curriculum.

■ Public and private tours are available, including "Tea and Tours" every Tuesday during the first four weeks of a new show, in which visitors can discuss what they've seen over tea in the café with Frye curators. And Art Talks is a popular lecture series led by curators and artists.

■ Download podcasts on exhibits past and present at fryemuseum.org/podcasts.

The Frye was a forgotten museum for a while, frequented only by Seattleites who would come to visit their favorite paintings from the permanent collection—mostly 19th- and 20th-century pastoral scenes. But a new curator shook the Frye out of its torpor, and now, in addition to its beloved permanent collection, this elegant building hosts eclectic and often avant-garde rotating exhibits. Past shows have included "The Old, Weird America: Folk Themes in Contemporary Art," surveying folk themes in recent art; a large collection of pieces from illustrator Henry Darger's mad-genius, 15,000-page, unpublished manuscript; an exhibition exploring the imagery of puppets through the work of 29 artists; and a retrospective of works from the Leipzeig Art Academy. No matter what's going on in the stark, brightly lighted back galleries, it always seems to blend well with the permanent collection, which occupies two hushed and elegant galleries with velvet couches and dark-blue and purple walls.

HIGHLIGHTS

Charles and Emma Frye amassed a huge collection of late-19th- and early-20th-century European, particularly German, paintings. Their core collection is particularly strong on the Munich Secession artists and includes Sin by Franz von Stuck. There isn't nearly enough room for all 232 paintings, so the founding collection is rotated regularly.

In addition, the Frye's permanent collection features paintings by American artists, including Albert Bierstadt, William Merritt Chase, and John H. Twachtman. One of the Frye's most successful shows linked the German Secession to its American counterparts.

Perhaps because of the challenges of integrating such a conservative collection with avant-garde contemporary works, the Frye excels at providing context for its shows. Supplemental materials are clear and accessible.

CAPITOL HILL

Sightseeing
★★★
Dining
★★★★★
Lodging
★★★
Shopping
★★★★
Nightlife
★★★★★

With its mix of theaters and churches, quiet parks and night-clubs, stately homes and student apartments, Capitol Hill still deserves its reputation as Seattle's most eclectic neighborhood. Old brick buildings, modern apartment high-rises, colorfully painted two-story homes, and old-school mansions all occupy the same area. There are plenty of cute, quirky shops to browse and quite a few fantastic coffee shops.

The Pike–Pine Corridor—Pike and Pine streets running from Melrose Avenue to 15th Avenue—is the heart of the Hill. Pine Street is a slightly more pleasant walk, but Pike Street has more stores—and unless you're here in the evening (when the area's restaurants come to life), it's the stores that will be the main draw. The architecture along both streets is a mix of older buildings with small storefronts, a few taller buildings that have lofts and office spaces, and garages and warehouses (some converted, some not). Pine skirts Cal Anderson Park—a small, pleasant park with an unusual conic fountain and reflecting pool—it's a lovely place to take a break after walking and shopping. The park can be either very quiet or filled with all kinds of activities from softball games to impromptu concerts from a neighborhood marching band.

The Hill's other main drag is Broadway E (a north–south avenue that crosses both Pike and Pine). Seattle's youth culture, old money, gay scene, and everything in between all converge on Broadway's lively if somewhat seedy stretch between E. Denny Way and E. Roy Street. Broadway is undergoing a renaissance, thanks to a few new high-profile condo buildings and some mass demolitions to make way for a future Light Rail station. Although it's got a few new landmarks of note (Jerry Traunfeld's excellent restaurant, Poppy, for one), it's still mostly a cluttered stretch of cheap restaurants, even cheaper clothing stores, and a few bars. Many people still find the area compelling because of its human parade. If you really want to see Seattle in all its quirky glory, head to Dick's Drive-In around midnight on a weekend night.

Capitol Hill's old-money, fancy side quickly becomes noticeable as you head east and north of this neighborhood core, but new money is starting to change the neighborhood, too. Though this has some longtime residents on edge, the neighborhood's reputation as one of the city's hippest and most vibrant is bringing some good developments, too—in 2010 Seattle's beloved Elliott Bay Book Company relocated here in the hopes that the constant street traffic and focus on the arts would revitalize its business, which had been dwindling in Pioneer Square.

WHAT TO SEE

Fetherston Gallery. As you make your way down the Pike–Pine Corridor, this airy, contemporary space is a great diversion, especially if you want to feel like you've done more with the day than shop or people-watch. The bright abstract works (mainly paintings) will pop out enough to beckon you in, even amid all the activity on this stretch of the road. High-quality shows present thought-provoking yet often playful and humorous works from nationally known names as well as local talent—often done in striking, saturated colors. ⊠ *818 E. Pike St., Capitol Hill* ☎ *206/322–9440* ⊕ *www.fetherstongallery.com* ✆ *Free* ⊗ *Tues.–Sat. 11–5.*

Lakeview Cemetery. One of the area's most beautiful cemeteries looks east toward Lake Washington from its elevated hillside directly north of Volunteer Park. Bruce Lee's grave and that of his son Brandon are the most visited sites. Several of Seattle's founding families are also interred here (their bodies were moved from a pioneer cemetery when Denny Hill was leveled to make room for the motels, car dealerships, and parking lots of the Denny Regrade south of Lake Union). Ask for a map at the cemetery office. ⊠ *1554 15th Ave. E, Capitol Hill* ☎ *206/322–1582* ✆ *Free* ⊗ *Daily 9–dusk.*

Martin-Zambito Fine Art. If you're interested in Northwest regional art, this gallery is a must. But don't expect a "greatest hits" collection here—David Martin and Dominic Zambito are well known in Seattle's art scene for expanding the study of regional Northwest art namely by uncovering little-known, unknown, or long-forgotten artists, many of them women. Their research has extended the history of the genre to the late 1800s (before they started digging, most collections started in the 1940s). Their exhibits consist of mostly paintings and photographs and tend to focus on WPA and Depression-era works. ⊠ *721 E. Pike St., Capitol Hill* ☎ *206/726–9509* ⊕ *www.martin-zambito.com* ✆ *Free* ⊗ *Tues.–Sat. 11–6.*

Photographic Center Northwest. A small, starkly attractive gallery space occupies the front of this photo education center. Student work is often on display, but this gallery is not just a repository for end-of-workshop projects. Curated shows often feature well-respected photographers,

GETTING ORIENTED

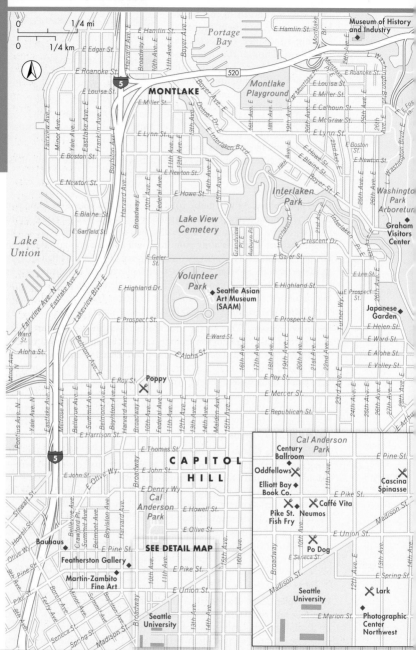

TOP REASONS TO GO

Rock out at **Neumos,** to anything from indie music to national touring acts.

Browse the stacks at **Elliott Bay Book Company,** Seattle's biggest independent bookstore. Then find a sunny reading spot in **Cal Anderson Park,** a block away.

Browse the art collection at the **Seattle Asian Art Museum,** then relax in the surrounding **Volunteer Park.**

Salsa or swing dance at the **Century Ballroom,** where instructors give free lessons before the party begins.

Sample the amazing restaurants and coffeehouses, including **Poppy, Anchovies & Olives, Cascina Spinasse,** and **Lark** (for food); and **Bauhaus, Stumptown, Espresso Vivace,** and **Caffé Vita** (for caffeine).

See the season's colors at nearby **Washington Park Arboretum**—cherry blossoms in spring, fiery leaves in autumn.

QUICK BITES

Pike Street Fish Fry (⊠ 925 E. Pike St. ☎ 206/329–7453) has perfectly fried cod, halibut, salmon, and calamari, served with chips or on a fresh baguette.

Baguette Box (⊠ 1203 Pine St. ☎ 206/332–0220) serves tasty sandwiches and salads. Favorites include the drunken chicken and Serrano ham with manchego.

The hot dogs at **Po Dog** (⊠ 1009 E. Union St. ☎ 206/325–6055) are dressed according to themes (the Morning Glory comes with scrambled eggs, cheddar, and bacon). You can also choose a field-roast dog or a sausage.

Grab a premade sandwich to go or kick back in **Oddfellows** (⊠ 1525 12th Ave. ☎ 206/325–0807) lively café while you wait for some pulled pork. The pastries, cookies, and cupcakes here are delicious. There's a full espresso bar plus beer and wine.

GETTING HERE AND AROUND

You can walk from Downtown, taking Pine or Pike Street across I–5 to Melrose Avenue, but keep in mind that touring the neighborhood itself will require a lot of walking, and it's uphill from Downtown.

Buses 10, 11, and 49 all pick up on Pike Street downtown and travel up Pine Street after crossing I–5. This is the easiest crosstown route to Capitol Hill's Pike–Pine Corridor. The 10 and the 49 continue up toward Volunteer Park. The 8 connects Seattle Center to Capitol Hill via Denny Way. The 11 and the 43 (the latter also picks up on Pike Street downtown) will get you the closest to the Washington Park Arboretum, which is technically several neighborhoods out of Capitol Hill (most people usually drive or bike there).

Street parking here is difficult. Keep an eye out for pay lots, which are numerous.

PLANNING YOUR TIME

Not much gets going on the Hill until after lunch, so spend the morning at Volunteer Park and the Seattle Asian Art Museum or at nearby Washington Park Arboretum. Be sure to stop for coffee first—this neighborhood has many great coffeehouses to choose from. If you save your visit for the afternoon, do some strolling and shopping, pep up with a coffee stop, then stick around for dinner and barhopping—these are the Hill's real attractions.

2

LAKESIDE BEACHES NEARBY

Madison Park (✉ *2300 43rd Ave. E, Madison Park*). This sandy Lake Washington beach—with its easy access to the water, sloping lawns, playgrounds, and tennis courts—fills quickly on sunny days. There are coffee shops, restaurants, and other amenities nearby; the beach has drinking water, picnic tables, phones, restrooms, and showers. From Downtown, go east on Madison Street for about 3 mi, turn right on E. Howe Street and then turn left to head north on 43rd Avenue.

Madrona Park (✉ *853 Lake Washington Blvd., Madrona*). Several beach parks and green spaces front the lake along Lake Washington Boulevard; Madrona Park is one of the largest. Young swimmers stay in the roped-in area while teens and adults swim out to a floating raft with a diving board. Joggers follow the mile-long trail along the shore. Kids clamber about the sculpted-sand garden and climb on rocks and logs. Grassy areas encourage picnicking; there are grills, picnic tables, phones, restrooms, and showers. A barbecue stand is open seasonally. From Downtown, go east on Yesler Way about 2 mi to 32nd Avenue. Turn left onto Lake Dell Avenue and then right; go to Lake Washington Boulevard and take a left.

whose work ranges from journalistic to fantastical. The gallery is convenient to the Pike–Pine Corridor—it's a few blocks south of Pike. ✉ *900 12th Ave., Capitol Hill* ⊕ *www.pcnw.org* ☎ *206/720–7222* ✆ *Free* ☾ *Mon. and Fri. noon–9:30, Tues.–Thurs. 9–9:30, weekends 11–5.*

Seattle Asian Art Museum. *See the highlighted listing in this chapter.*

Volunteer Park. *See the highlighted listing in this chapter.*

OFF THE BEATEN PATH ☾
Fodor's Choice
★

Washington Park Arboretum. As far as Seattle's green spaces go, this 230-acre arboretum is arguably the most beautiful. On calm weekdays, the place feels really secluded; though there are trails, you feel like you're freer to roam here than at Discovery Park. The seasons are always on full display: in warm winters, flowering cherries and plums bloom in its protected valleys as early as late February, while the flowering shrubs in Rhododendron Glen and Azalea Way are in full bloom March through June. In autumn, trees and shrubs glow in hues of crimson, pumpkin, and lemon; in winter, plantings chosen specially for their stark and colorful branches dominate the landscape. From March through October, visit the peaceful **Japanese Garden**, a compressed world of mountains, forests, rivers, lakes, and tablelands. The pond, lined with blooming water irises in spring, has turtles and brightly colored koi. An authentic Japanese teahouse is reserved for tea ceremonies and instruction on the art of serving tea. The Graham Visitors Center at the park's north end has descriptions of the arboretum's flora and fauna (which include 130 endangered plants), as well as brochures, a garden gift shop, and walking-tour maps. ✉ *2300 Arboretum Dr. E, Capitol Hill* ☎ *206/543–8800 arboretum, 206/684–4725 Japanese garden* ⊕ *depts.washington. edu/uwbg/index.php* ✆ *Free, Japanese garden $5* ☾ *Park open daily 7 AM–sunset, visitor center daily 10–4. Japanese garden May–Aug., daily 10–8, hrs vary seasonally, call to confirm.*

VOLUNTEER PARK AND THE SEATTLE ASIAN ART MUSEUM

⊠ *Park entrance: 14th Ave. E at Prospect St., Capitol Hill*
⊕ *www.seattleartmuseum.org*
☎ *Museum 206/654–3100, conservatory 206/684–4743*
🎫 *Park free; museum $7, free 1st Thurs. (all day) and 2nd Thurs. (5–9)* ⊙ *Park daily sunrise–sunset; museum Wed.–Sun. 10–5, Thurs. until 9; conservatory Tues.–Sun. 10–4.*

2

TIPS

■ SAAM is small: you could hit the museum and conservatory and sunbathe on the lawn, and still leave the park by lunchtime.

■ Climbing the 108 steps of the park's old water tower yields some decent views of the city.

■ The conservatory is, surprisingly, not a great place for kids, mostly because of its narrow paths—tough to navigate even without a stroller. But there are plenty of kid-friendly attractions in the park. A wading pool is extremely popular on hot summer days. SAAM has crafts tables related to current exhibits, and admission for families is free on every first Saturday.

■ SAAM has a café, which is a smaller version of TASTE at the Seattle Art Museum. Volunteer Park Café, just east of the northeastern corner of the park on Galer Street, is an excellent stop for sandwiches, sweets, and coffee. Just be aware that on pleasant weekends, half of the neighborhood has the same idea.

High above the mansions of North Capitol Hill sits 45-acre Volunteer Park, a grassy expanse perfect for picnicking, sunbathing, reading, and strolling. You can tell this is one of the city's older parks by the size of the trees and the rhododendrons, many of which were planted more than a hundred years ago. The Olmsted Brothers, the premier landscape architects of the day, helped with the final design in 1904; the park has changed surprisingly little since then. The manicured look of the park is a sharp contrast to the wilds of Discovery Park, but the design suits the needs of the densely populated neighborhood well—after all, Capitol Hill residents need someplace to set up Ultimate Frisbee games. In the center of the park is the **Seattle Asian Art Museum (SAAM, a branch of the Seattle Art Museum),** housed in a 1933 art moderne–style edifice. It fits surprisingly well with the stark plaza stretching from the front door to the edge of a bluff, and with the lush plants of Volunteer Park. The museum's collections include thousands of paintings, sculptures, pottery, and textiles from China, Japan, India, Korea, and several Southeast Asian countries.

HIGHLIGHTS

The Victorian-style Volunteer Park Conservatory greenhouse, across from the museum, has a magnificent (if cramped) collection of tropical plants. The Anna Clise Orchid Collection, begun in 1919, is at its most spectacular in late fall and early winter, when most of the flowers are in full bloom. Admission is free.

A focal point of the park, at the western edge of the 445-foot-high hill and in front of the Asian Art Museum, is Isamu Noguchi's sculpture *Black Sun*, carved from a 30-ton block of black granite.

FREMONT AND PHINNEY RIDGE

Sightseeing
★★

Dining
★★★★

Lodging
★

Shopping
★★★★★

Nightlife
★★★

If you ever wondered where the center of the universe is, look no further—the self-styled "Republic of Fremont" was declared just this by its residents in the 1960s. This pretty neighborhood isn't as eccentric as it used to be, but it's a great side trip when you're done sightseeing and want to do some shopping or strolling along the canal or sample artisan goodies (the neighborhood has both a chocolate factory and a craft brewery).

For many years, Fremont enjoyed its reputation as Seattle's weirdest neighborhood, home to hippies, artists, bikers, and rat-race dropouts. But Fremont has lost most of its artist cache as the stores along its main strip turned more upscale, luxury condos and town houses appeared above the neighborhood's warren of small houses, and rising rents sent many longtime residents reluctantly packing (many to nearby Ballard). On weekend nights, the downtown strip sometimes looks like one big party, as a bunch of new bars draw in a very young crowd from Downtown, the University District, and the city's suburbs.

The mixed bag of "quintessential sights" in this neighborhood reflects the intersection of past and present. Most of them, like Seattle's favorite photo stop, the Fremont Troll, are works of public art created in the 1980s and '90s. Others, like Theo Chocolate and Fremont Brewing, celebrate the independent spirit of the neighborhood but suggest a much different lifestyle than the founders of the "republic" espoused. Still others are neutral and timeless, like a particularly lovely section of the Burke Gilman Trail along the Lake Washington Ship Canal.

Phinney Ridge, above Fremont, is almost entirely residential, though it shares the booming commercial street of Greenwood Avenue North with its neighbor to the north, Greenwood. Although not as strollable as similar districts in Fremont or Ballard, Greenwood Avenue has a lot of boutiques, coffee shops, and restaurants that range from go-to diner food to pricey Pacific Northwest.

The welcoming interior of Theo Chocolate in Fremont

WHAT TO SEE

Francine Seders Gallery. It's the only major gallery in this neck of the woods, and it's run by a legend. Francine Seders has been in the business for 40 years, and her space—a converted house with art on every floor, including the basement—is just as unusual as her business practices, which eschew the wheeling and dealing with museums and patrons that tend to short-change the artists. The gallery shows paintings and prints from established regional artists—her collection also includes Northwest icons like Guy Anderson and Morris Graves. ⊠ *6701 Greenwood Ave. N, Phinney Ridge* ☏ *206/782–0355* ⊕ *www.sedersgallery. com* ☞ *Free* ☉ *Tues.–Sat. 11–5, Sun. 1–5.*

History House of Greater Seattle. This small museum celebrates the history of Seattle's neighborhoods, mostly through displays of old photographs. ■ TIP→ It's a fun way to get a small glimpse of the Seattle of yesteryear. The museum's entrance is bound to grab your eye as you walk by: the wrought-iron gates look like tree branches sprouting colorful houses, butterflies, and the Space Needle; behind them is a fun sculpture garden. ⊠ *790 N. 34th St., Fremont* ☏ *206/675–8875* ⊕ *www.historyhouse.org* ☞ *1$* ☉ *Wed.–Sun., noon–5.*

Ⓒ
Fodor's Choice
★
Theo Chocolate. If it weren't for a small sign on the sidewalk pointing the way, you'd never know that Fremont has its own chocolate factory. Theo has helped to boost the Northwest's growing artisan chocolate scene and has already taken the city by storm, thanks to high-quality chocolate creations. Theo uses only organic, Fair Trade cocoa beans, usually in high percentages—yielding darker, less-sweet, and more complex flavors than some of their competitors. You'll see Theo chocolate bars for sale

GETTING ORIENTED

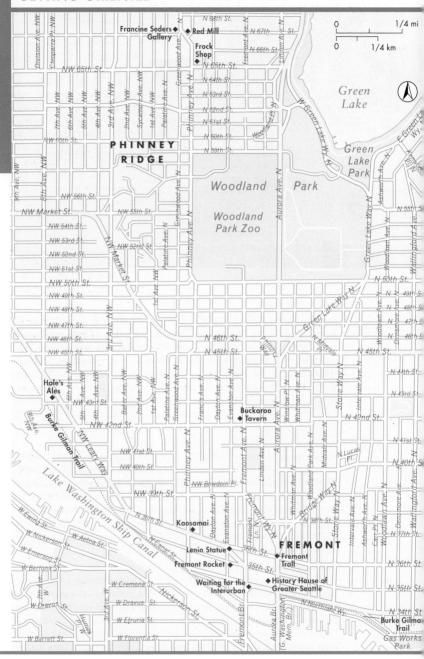

2

FREMONT SOLSTICE PARADE

If you want to know where all of Fremont's legendary weird-ness has retreated, look no further than the Fremont Arts Council's warehouse on Fremont Avenue N. For months leading up to the Fremont Solstice Parade (held on the summer solstice weekend in June), half-finished parade floats spill out of the workshop. The parade is Seattle's most notorious summer event—some of the floats and costumes are political (mostly pleading for the legalization of marijuana) and/or wacky (a brass band playing in drag), and the "highlight" is a stream of naked bicyclists, only some of which don elaborate body paint. And the professionally built floats and puppets are truly spectacular: past participants have included giant robots and a papier-mâché Flying Spaghetti Monster.

QUICK BITES

People line up out the door at **Red Mill** (✉ 312 N. 67th St. ☎ 206/783–6362) for juicy burgers and milkshakes in yummy flavors like mandarin-chocolate and butterscotch.

PCC Natural Markets (✉ 600 N. 34th St. ☎ 206/632–6811), an upscale food co-op, has all the fixings you need for a picnic along the canal, including sandwiches and salads.

Royal Grinders (✉ 3526 Fremont Pl. N ☎ 206/545–7560) serves hearty hot subs on soft crusty rolls. The Crown and the Italian are the best.

"I can't believe this is vegan!" is a common reaction to the delicious pastries, cookies, and muffins made by the **Flying Apron Baking Company** (✉ 3510 Fremont Ave. N ☎ 206/442–1115). All items are also gluten- and wheat-free.

GETTING HERE AND AROUND

Buses 26, 28, and 5 will drop you in Fremont center. Driving, take either Aurora Avenue N (Route 99) and exit right after you cross the bridge, or take Westlake Avenue N and cross the Fremont Bridge into the neighborhood's core. Phinney is at the top of a big hill. If you want to walk it, the best strategy is to thread your way up through the charming residential streets. If not, take the number 5 bus up Fremont Avenue.

TOP REASONS TO GO

Follow the **Burke-Gilman Trail** along the Fremont section of the Lake Washington Ship Canal.

Bring your credit card for some retail therapy at the area's **boutiques.** Mandatory stops on the shopping tour include Les Amis and Burnt Sugar in Fremont and the Frock Shop in Phinney Ridge.

Sip some brews at a **neighborhood tap house.**

Take a spin on a historic wooden carousel, then hang out with Sumatran tigers, snow leopards, Asian elephants, and grizzly bears at the nearby **Woodland Park Zoo.**

Tour an artisan chocolate factory: **Theo Chocolate's** inventive, rich confections are best sampled after seeing the cocoa roasters and chocolate makers at work.

CLOSE UP

Three Hours Like a Local

Check out the neighborhood's Web site (⊕ *www.fremont.com*) for more information.

WACKY PUBLIC ART

Kick-start your tour under the north end of the Aurora Bridge at N. 36th Street, where you'll find the **Fremont Troll** (⊠ *N. 36th St. at Troll Ave.*), a two-ton, 18-foot-tall concrete troll clutching a real Volkswagen beetle in his massive hand. The troll appeared in 1991, commissioned by the Fremont Arts Council. Pose for a shot atop his head or pretending to pull his beard.

Next, head west down the hill to the statue of **Lenin** (⊠ *N. 36th St. at Fremont Place and Evanston Ave. N*). Constructed by Bulgarian sculptor Emil Venkov for the Soviets in 1988, the 16-foot, 7-ton statue was removed shortly after the Velvet Revolution and eventually made its way to Seattle. Visitors here during Gay Pride Week might catch a glimpse of him in drag.

A few blocks away you'll find the **Fremont Rocket** (⊠ *N. 35th St. and Evanston Ave. N*), a 53-foot Cold War–era rocket nonchalantly strapped to the side of a retail store—which just may mark the official center of the "center of the universe." This Seattle landmark was rescued from a surplus store in 1991 and successfully erected on its current locale in '94, when neon lights were added, along with the crest "De Libertas Quirkas," meaning "Freedom to Be Peculiar."

Walk along the water toward the Fremont Bridge, past the offices of Adobe, Getty Images, and Google (among others) to visit the cast-aluminum sculpture **Waiting for the Interurban** (⊠ *N. 34th St. and Fremont*

Ave. N). Artist Richard Beyer created this depiction of six people and a dog waiting for a trolley in 1979. Observe that the dog's face is actually that of a man—story goes this is the face of recycling pioneer (and onetime honorary mayor of Fremont) Armen Stepanian, who may have made disparaging remarks about the statue. It's been a long local tradition to "vandalize" the sculpture with anything from brightly colored umbrellas to signs congratulating newlyweds.

THAI FOOD AND CHOCOLATES AND T-SHIRTS, OH MY!

If the comrades are hungry, opt for Thai food. On sunny days, choose **Kaosamai** (⊠ *404 N. 36th St.* ☎ *206/925–4657* ⊕ *www.kaosamai. com*), a crowd-pleasing eatery with a large deck. On rainy days, you might prefer cozy **Kwanjai Thai** (⊠ *469 N. 36th St.* ☎ *206/632–3656*) across the street, where you can dive into homestyle Thai curries in a cramped blue house.

After you've had your fill of spicy food, peruse nearby **Destee-Nation** (⊠ *3412 Evanston Ave. N* ☎ *888/332–6437* ⊕ *www.desteenation.com*), a fun little shop that sells vintage-looking T-shirts from independent restaurants and establishments across Seattle and the country.

Next stop is **Theo Chocolate Factory** (⊠ *3400 Phinney Ave. N* ☎ *206/632–5100* ⊕ *www.theochocolate.com*), an organic and Fair Trade chocolate factory offering tours through its redbrick factory. You'll learn all about the chocolate-making process and get to sample some of Theo's favorites. Be sure to try the Coconut Curry bar!

—Cedar Burnett

2

A resident tiger at the Woodland Park Zoo

in many local businesses, from coffee shops to grocery stores. Stop by the factory to buy exquisite "confection" truffles—made daily in small batches—with unusual flavors like basil-ganache, lemon, fig-fennel, and burnt sugar. The super-friendly staff is known to be generous with samples. ■TIP➜ You can go behind the scenes as well: informative, yummy tours are offered daily; reservations aren't always necessary, but it's a good idea to call and make sure there's a spot, particularly on weekends. ✉ *3400 Phinney Ave. N, Fremont* ☎ *206/632–5100* ⊕ *www.theochocolate.com* ✉ *Tour $6* ☉ *Store daily 10–6. Tours Mon.–Thurs. at 2 and 4; Fri. at 10, noon, 2, and 4; weekends at 10, 10:30, noon, 2, and 4.*

☾ **Woodland Park Zoo.** Many of the 300 species of animals in this 92-acre
★ botanical garden roam freely in habitat areas. A jaguar exhibit is the center of the Tropical Rain Forest area, where rare cats, frogs, and birds evoke South American jungles. The Humboldt penguin exhibit is environmentally sound—it uses geothermal heating and cooling to mimic the climes of the penguins native home, the coastal areas of Peru. With authentic thatch-roof buildings, the African Village has a replica schoolroom overlooking animals roaming the savanna; the Asian Elephant Forest Trail takes you through a Thai village; and the Northern Trail winds past rocky habitats where brown bears, wolves, mountain goats, and otters scramble and play. The terrain is mostly flat, making it easy for wheelchairs and strollers (which can be rented) to negotiate. The zoo has parking for $5; it's a small price to pay to avoid the headache of searching for a space on the street. ✉ *5500 Phinney Ave. N, Phinney Ridge* ☎ *206/684–4800* ⊕ *www.zoo.org* ✉ *Oct.–Apr. $11, May–Sept. $16.50* ☉ *Oct.–Apr., daily 9:30–4; May–Sept., daily 9:30–6.*

BALLARD

Sightseeing
★★

Dining
★★★★★

Lodging
★

Shopping
★★★★★

Nightlife
★★★★

Ballard is Seattle's sweetheart. Locals of all stripes can't help but hold some affection for this neighborhood, even as it gets farther away from its humble beginnings. Ballard doesn't have many sights outside of the Hiram M. Chittenden Locks (⇨ *aka "Ballard Locks"—see highlighted feature in Chapter 7)*; you'll spend more time strolling, shopping, and hanging out than crossing attractions off your list. It's got a great little nightlife, shopping, and restaurant scene on Ballard Avenue.

Ballard used to be almost exclusively Scandinavian and working class; it was the logical home for the Swedish and Norwegian immigrants who worked in the area's fishing, shipbuilding, and lumber industries. Reminders of its origins still exist—most literally in the Nordic Heritage Museum—but the neighborhood is undergoing inevitable changes as the number of artists, hipsters, and young professionals (many of whom have been priced out of Fremont and Capitol Hill) increases. Trendy restaurants, upscale furniture stores, and quirky boutiques have popped up all along NW Market Street and Ballard Avenue, the neighborhood's main commercial strips. But no matter how tidy it gets, Ballard doesn't feel as gentrified as Fremont or as taken with its own coolness as Capitol Hill—Ballard still stands apart from the rest of the city.

Ballard used to be its own city: It wasn't a part of Seattle until 1907 when Ballard residents voted to be "annexed" by the city. The citizens of Ballard were responding to a water crisis—which would be solved by becoming part of Seattle—as well as to myriad promises of new and better public services made by Seattle's mayor. Today Ballard residents old and new adopt the "Free Ballard" slogan for many reasons. Although a few people would like to see Ballard revert to being its own city, many simply see it as a way to express neighborhood pride—a way

GETTING ORIENTED

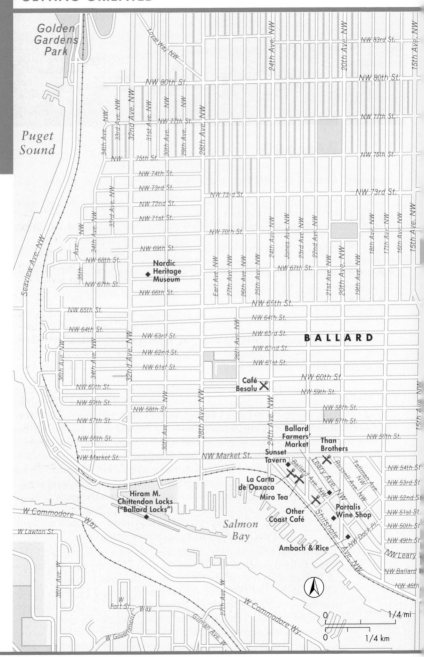

Golden Gardens Park

Puget Sound

Loyal Way NW

NW 83rd St.

24th Ave. NW

20th Ave. NW

15th Ave. NW

NW 80th St.

NW 80th St.

34th Ave. NW

33rd Ave. NW

32nd Ave. NW

31st Ave. NW

30th Ave. NW

29th Ave. NW

28th Ave. NW

NW 77th St.

NW 77th St.

NW 75th St.

NW 75th St.

NW 74th St.

NW 73rd St.

NW 73rd St.

NW 73rd St.

NW 72nd St.

NW 71st St.

33rd Ave. NW

NW 70th St.

24th Ave. NW

Jones Ave. NW

23rd Ave. NW

22nd Ave. NW

21st Ave. NW

20th Ave. NW

19th Ave. NW

18th Ave. NW

17th Ave. NW

16th Ave. NW

15th Ave. NW

Seaview Ave. NW

NW 69th St.

35th Ave. NW

NW 68th St.

Nordic Heritage Museum ◆

NW 67th St.

NW 67th St.

NW 67th St.

NW 66th St.

Earl Ave. NW

27th Ave. NW

26th Ave. NW

25th Ave. NW

NW 65th St.

NW 65th St.

NW 64th St.

NW 64th St.

32nd Ave. NW

NW 63rd St.

NW 63rd St.

BALLARD

26th Ave. NW

NW 62nd St.

NW 62nd St.

NW 61st St.

NW 61st St.

36th Ave. NW

NW 60th St.

NW 60th St.

Café Besalu ✕

NW 59th St.

15th Ave.

NW 59th St.

28th Ave. NW

NW 58th St.

NW 58th St.

NW 57th St.

NW 57th St.

NW 56th St.

30th Ave. NW

Ballard Farmers' Market

Than Brothers ✕

NW 56th St.

NW 54th St

Sunset Tavern ✕ ✕

24th Ave. NW

Leary Ave. NW

Ballard Ave. NW

Russell Ave. NW

Vernon Pl. NW

Tallman Ave. NW

15th Ave. NW

NW Market St.

NW Market St.

La Carta de Oaxaca

Miro Tea ✕

NW 53rd St

NW 52nd St

NW 51st St

Hiram M. Chittendon Locks ("Ballard Locks") ◆

W Commodore Way

Other Coast Café ✕

Partalis Wine Shop ◆

Shilshole Ave. NW

NW 50th St

NW 49th St

W Lawton St.

Salmon Bay

Ambach & Rice ◆

NW Dock Pl.

NW Leary

38th Ave. W

NW Ballard

NW 46th

W Fort St. Way

22nd Ave. W

W Commodore Wy.

0 ___ 1/4 mi

0 ___ 1/4 km

Gilman Ave. W

W Government Way

TOP REASONS TO GO

Dip your toes in the water at **Golden Gardens Park.** Here, kids splash in a designated swim area, while windsurfers wade in on rockier parts of the shore.

The **Ballard Farmers' Market,** on Ballard Avenue every Sunday from 10 to 3 (rain or shine, year-round), is one of the city's best farmers' markets.

See a show at the **Sunset Tavern.** Ballard has its own music scene, with several small clubs on Ballard Avenue; The Tractor is a small venue with a big reputation.

Imbibe by the glass and buy by the bottle at **Portalis Wine Shop.** This swanky spot also has welcoming lounge.

Get some **retail therapy,** Ballard-style: the area's artsy galleries and many boutiques, shoe, and clothing stores offer some very fine reasons to drop some dough.

GETTING HERE AND AROUND

Ballard's main drags are NW Market Street and Ballard Avenue. If you're driving from Downtown, the easiest way to reach Ballard's center is to take Western Avenue and follow it as it turns into Elliott Avenue W and then 15th Avenue NW. Cross the bridge and make a left onto NW Market Street.

By bus, the 15, 17, and 18 will get you from Downtown to NW Market Street. Ballard is well connected to Phinney Ridge, Wallingford, and the U-District—the 44 and 46 buses pick up on NW Market Street and make their way to the other northern neighborhoods. Bus 28 connects Fremont's center to NW Market Street.

Note that the neighborhood is more spread out than it appears on a map. For example, walking west from the heart of Market Street to the Locks and back is long. Golden Gardens Park may not be worth the effort if you don't have a car.

PLANNING YOUR TIME

Set aside an hour or two to visit the Ballard Locks. After that, you can spend your afternoon one of three ways before having dinner in the neighborhood: stroll and shop on Ballard Avenue; relax on the sand at Golden Gardens Park; or visit the Nordic Heritage Museum and area art galleries.

QUICK BITES

Than Brothers (⌧ *2021 NW Market St.* ☎ *206/782–5715*) serves consistently good Vietnamese *pho* in all varieties. Save room for some cream puffs or a coffee sweetened with condensed milk.

Café Besalu (⌧ *5909 24th Ave. NW* ☎ *206/789–1463*) is possibly the city's best French bakery. This is best as an afternoon stop, as long morning lines form for croissants.

Good, simple, and filling deli sandwiches (think turkey and Swiss on rye or a standard Italian sub) are the specialty of **Other Coast Café** (⌧ *5315 Ballard Ave. NW* ☎ *206/789–0936*).

Miro Tea (⌧ *5405 Ballard Ave. NW* ☎ *206/782–6832*) has catalog of teas, plus amazing pastries.

La Carta de Oaxaca (⌧ *5431 Ballard Ave. NW* ☎ *206/782–8722*) is one of Ballard's favorite restaurants, serving traditional Mexican favorites in a lively, packed space on Ballard Avenue. The margaritas are outstanding.

Colorful clogs on display at the Nordic Heritage Museum

to remind them and the rest of Seattle that Ballard's unique heritage and way of life must be preserved as it becomes one of the city's hippest neighborhoods.

WHAT TO SEE

Ambach & Rice. What started out as OKOK—part gallery, part store, part rocket-ship ride into pop surrealism—settled down into a respectable and respected gallery focusing on painting and installations. Ambach & Rice, which occupies a great space in a converted garage, represents both regional and international artists, including Seattle hotshot, not-so-functional furniture designer Roy McMakin and Dutch bas-relief sculptor Ron Van Der Ende. ⊠ *5107 Ballard Ave. NW, Ballard* ☎ *206/789–6242* ⊕ *www.ambachandrice.com* ✉ *Free* ☉ *Tues.–Sat. noon–6, Sun. 11–5.*

Golden Gardens Park. The waters of Puget Sound may be bone-chilling cold, but that doesn't stop folks from jumping in to cool off. Besides brave swimmers, who congregate on the small strip of sand between the parking lot and the canteen, this Ballard-area park is packed with sunbathers in summer. In other seasons, beachcombers explore during low tide, and groups gather around bonfires to socialize and watch the glorious Seattle sunsets. The park has drinking water, grills, picnic tables, phones, and restrooms. It also has two wetlands, a short loop trail, and unbelievable views

WORD OF MOUTH

"If you are at the locks on a weekend, there will be lots more boat traffic. It is entertainment in itself! Took the grandchildren there on a Sunday afternoon in the winter and it was a riot!"   · —Jean

of the Olympic Mountains. From Downtown, take Elliott Avenue N, which becomes 15th Avenue W, and cross the Ballard Bridge. Turn left to head west on Market Street and follow signs to the Ballard Locks; continue about another mile to the park. Note that even though the park has two dedicated parking lots, these quickly fill up on weekends, so be prepared to circle. ✉ *8498 Seaview Pl. NW (near N.W. 85th St.), Ballard* ☎ *206/684–4075* ⎘ *Free* ⊗ *Daily 6* AM–*11:30* PM.

⊙ **Hiram M. Chittenden Locks ("Ballard**
Fodor'sChoice **Locks").** ⇨ *For an in-depth look at*
★ *the Locks, flip to the highlighted feature in Chapter 7.* The locks are an important passage in the 8-mi Lake Washington Ship Canal that connects Puget Sound to freshwater Lake Washington and Lake Union—and, on a sunny day, this is a great place to visit. In addition to boat traffic, the Locks see an estimated half-million salmon and trout make the journey from saltwater to fresh each summer, with the help of a fish ladder. ✉ *3015 NW 54th St., Ballard* ✛ *From Fremont, head north on Leary Way NW, west on N.W. Market St., and south on 54th St.* ☎ *206/783–7059* ⎘ *Free* ⊗ *Locks daily 7* AM–*9* PM; *visitor center Thurs.–Mon. 10–4; call for tour information and reservations.*

⊙ **Nordic Heritage Museum.** The only educational institute in the country to focus solely on Nordic cultures, this museum in a massive 1900s schoolhouse traces Scandinavian art, artifacts, and heritage all the way from Viking times. Behind the redbrick walls, nine permanent galleries on three floors give an in-depth look at how immigrants from Denmark, Finland, Iceland, Norway, and Sweden came to America and settled in the Pacific Northwest. Among the finds are textiles, china, books, tools, and photographs. Delve into Nordic history in the library; learn a few phrases at the on-site Scandinavian Language Institute; or join in a class or children's program on Nordic arts and crafts. The temporary galleries display paintings, sculpture, and photography by contemporary artists. ✉ *3014 NW 67th St., Ballard* ☎ *206/789–5707* ⊕ *www.nordicmuseum. org* ⎘ *$6* ⊗ *Tues.–Sat. 10–4, Sun. noon–4.*

WALLINGFORD AND GREEN LAKE

Sightseeing
★★
Dining
★★★★
Lodging
★
Shopping
★★
Nightlife
★★★

Wallingford's even more laid-back and low-profile than Fremont or Ballard, and outside of a few parks it has no sights per se. But 45th Street NW has an eclectic group of shops, from a gourmet beer store to an erotic bakery to a Hawaiian merchant, along with a few great coffeehouses, and several notable restaurants. There's not as much to do in Green Lake either, besides strolling around the lovely lake—though the lake is worth a detour to see a terrific cross section of Seattleites.

Wallingford is directly east of Fremont—the boundaries actually blur quite a bit— and is full of colorful Craftsman houses. In the 1920s, Wallingford was one of the city's most important neighborhoods. It went from forest and cow pasture (one of which, incidentally, hosted Seattle's first golf course for a very short time) to a densely populated neighborhood of 50,000 in less than two decades. The game changer was a trolley line from the University District to Fremont—once the tracks were laid, the bungalow-building frenzy started. Although the initial hoopla died down after a major commercial district on Stone Way never materialized, the neighborhood grew steadily, if quietly. In the past five years, however, it's been on everyone's radar again, as some of Seattle's most celebrated chefs—Maria Hines of Tilth and Rachel Yang of Joule, in particular—have chosen the neighborhood for their distinctive and highly praised restaurants. Other eateries and shops have filled in around 45th's other big draw, a popular two-screen movie theater. By the time the fabulous restaurant Cantinetta opened far off the main drag, it came as no surprise to anyone that Wallingford could be a place where you wait two hours for a table.

The neighborhood of Green Lake surrounds the eponymous lake, which is 50,000 years old. It was formed by the Vashon Glacial Ice Sheet, which also gave Seattle, among other things, Puget Sound. Green Lake (the neighborhood) is pleasant bordering on bland and not as easy to stroll in as Wallingford. It has a few mostly unremarkable shops and eateries along the lake, and one stand-out B&B, if you're looking to be far from Downtown's busy streets.

WHAT TO SEE

Gas Works Park. The park gets its name from the hulking remains of an old 1907 gas plant, which, far from being an eyesore, actually lends quirky character to the otherwise open, hilly, 20-acre park. Get a great view of Downtown Seattle while seaplanes rise up from the far shore of the lake; the best vantage point is from the zodiac sculpture at the top of the hill. The sand-bottom playground has monkey bars, wooden platforms, and a spinning metal merry-go-round. Crowds throng to picnic and enjoy outdoor summer concerts, movies, and the July 4th fireworks display over Lake Union. ■TIP➡ This lovely park can easily be reached from Fremont Center, via the waterfront Burke-Gilman Trail— remember to stay in the clearly designated pedestrian lane, as you'll be sharing the trail with many other walkers, joggers, and speed-demon bicyclists. ⊠ *2101 N. Northlake Way, at Meridian Ave. N (the north end of Lake Union) Wallingford* ☉ *Daily 4 AM–11:30 PM.*

Fodor'sChoice ★

Green Lake Park. This beautiful 342-acre park is a favorite of Seattleites, who jog, blade, bike, and walk their dogs along the 2.8-mi paved path that surrounds the lake. Beaches on both the east and west sides (around 72nd Street) have lifeguards and swimming rafts. Boats, canoes, kayaks, and paddleboats can be rented at Green Lake Boat Rental on the eastern side of the lake. There are also basketball and tennis courts and baseball and soccer fields. A first-rate play area includes a giant sandbox, swings, slides, and all the climbing equipment a child could ever dream of—plus lots of grassy areas and benches where adults can take a break. The park is generally packed, especially on weekends. And you'd better love dogs: the canine-to-human ratio here is just about even. Surrounding the park are lovely homes, plus a compact commercial district where you can grab some snacks after your walk. ⊠ *7201 E. Green Lake Dr. N, Green Lake* ☎ *206/684–4075 general info, 206/527–0171 Greenlake Boat Rental* ⊕ *www.seattle.gov/parks.*

A GOOD COMBO

A trip to Woodland Park Zoo (on the border of Phinney Ridge and Green Lake), a stroll around (or boat ride on) adjacent Green Lake, and then exploring Wallingford's main drag (⊠ *45th Ave. NW*) is a great way to spend a sunny day. Or, instead of Wallingford, you could drive to Ballard and peruse its many shops and restaurants.

GETTING ORIENTED

2

GETTING HERE AND AROUND

Bus 16 connects Downtown to N. 45th Street in Wallingford (the neighborhood's main drag) and continues north to the east (and main) entrance of Green Lake Park (get out at 71st and E. Green Lake Way). From Downtown it takes about a half hour to reach the lake; the trip between the lake and N. 45th Street takes about 10 minutes.

To reach Green Lake by car, take either Aurora Avenue N (Route 99) to W. Green Lake Way or I-5 to 50th Street (go west back over the highway at that exit). There are parking lots at both Green Lake Park and Woodland Park; lots at the latter are generally less full. Wallingford is a five-minute drive from Green Lake—if there's no traffic.

QUICK BITES

Hiroki (✉ 2224 N. 56th St. ☎ 206/547–4128), in the Tangletown area of Green Lake, makes wonderful Japanese desserts, along with some standard European ones like tiramisu.

One of three pubs owned by the Elysian Brewing Company, **Tangletown** (✉ 2106 N. 55th St. ☎ 206/547–5929) has microbrews on tap and good burgers, sandwiches, and vegetarian dishes.

Two of the city's best ice cream parlors are across the street from each other. **Molly Moon's** (✉ 1622 N. 45th St. ☎ 206/547–5105) makes rich, delicious ice creams with local ingredients. **Fainting Goat Gelato** (✉ 1903 N. 45th St. ☎ 206/327–9459) makes gelato in ever-changing seasonal flavors like honey-lavender and grapefruit.

Rancho Bravo (✉ 211 N.E. 45th St. ☎ No phone) has a Capitol Hill storefront, but it started with this humble taco truck in a parking lot by a Jiffy Lube. Pork tacos (*carnitas* or *al pastor* style) are favorites.

Family-friendly **Tutta Bella** (✉ 4411 Stone Way N ☎ 206/633–3800) makes delicious and filling Neapolitan pizza and salads.

PLANNING YOUR TIME

Green Lake is adjacent to Woodland Park Zoo. You could spend an entire day outside touring the zoo, then strolling around the lake—or floating in a rented rowboat or paddleboat. The Tangletown area of Green Lake can be reached on foot (follow N. 55th Street east to the "K" streets of Kenwood, Keystone, Kirkwood, and Kensington) and has a few great casual eateries. Some of the city's best chefs have put down roots in Wallingford, making the neighborhood a good place to end the day.

TOP REASONS TO GO

Enjoy the definitive north-shore view of Lake Union from **Gas Works Park**, which incorporates the rusting remnants of the historic gas works plant.

Go souvenir hunting at **Archie McPhee**, a shrine to irreverence. You'll find great Seattle-themed items here, like Tofu Mints and librarian and barista action figures, amidst tons of assorted weirdness and fun (⇨ *See Chapter 6*).

Visit the "poem emporium"—**Open Books** is one of two poetry-only bookstores in the country.

Stroll or jog around **Green Lake's** loop. If your running shoes are a little ragged, stop at Super Jock 'n' Jill (✉ 7210 E. Green Lake Dr. N ☎ 206/522–7711) for a new pair.

UNIVERSITY DISTRICT

Sightseeing
★★

Dining
★★★★

Lodging
★★★

Shopping
★

Nightlife
★★

The U-District, as everyone calls it, is the neighborhood surrounding the University of Washington (UW or "U-Dub" to locals). The campus is extraordinarily beautiful (especially in springtime, when the cherry blossoms are flowering), and the Henry Art Gallery, on its western edge, is one of the city's best small museums. Beyond that, the appeal of the neighborhood lies in its variety of cheap, delicious ethnic eateries, its proximity to the waters of Portage and Union Bays and Lake Washington, and its youthful energy.

The U-District isn't everyone's cup of chai. Almost all businesses are geared toward students, and the area has its own transient population. The U-District often feels like it's separate from the city—and that's no accident. The university was founded in 1861 and was constructed on newly clear-cut land long before there were any convenient ways to get to the city that was growing Downtown. More so than any other northern neighborhood, the U-District had to have it all. Nowadays that's still true—at least until the Light Rail links the neighborhood with Capitol Hill and Downtown in 2016. Residents don't even have to travel to Downtown to get their shopping done: they have their own megamall, University Village ("U Village"), an elegant outdoor shopping center with an Apple store, chain stores (including H&M, Gap, Eddie Bauer, Crate & Barrel, and Banana Republic), as well as restaurants, boutiques, and a large grocery store.

WHAT TO SEE

⟳ **Burke Museum of Natural History and Culture.** Totem poles mark the entrance to this museum, where exhibits survey the land and cultures of the Pacific Northwest. Highlights include artifacts from Washington's 35 Native American tribes, dinosaur skeletons, and dioramas depicting the traditions of Pacific Rim cultures. An adjacent ethnobotanical

Fascinating exhibits fill the Burke Museum of Natural History and Culture.

garden is planted with species that were important to the region's Native American communities. For $1 more on the admission price, you get same-day admission to the Henry Art Gallery. ⊠ *University of Washington campus, 17th Ave. NE and NE 45th St., University District* ☎ *206/543–5590* ⊕ *www.burkemuseum.org* ✉ *$9.50, free 1st Thurs. of month* ☽ *Daily 10–5, 1st Thurs. of each month 10–8.*

A GOOD COMBO

The Henry Art Gallery (open Thurs.–Sun.) is well worth the trip. Stroll around the UW campus in the morning, pay a visit to the Henry when it opens at 11 AM, then enjoy spicy Vietnamese pho or Thai curry for lunch on The Ave—the U-District's main drag. If you still have energy, stroll from there to the Montlake Bridge; part of your walk can be along the Burke Gilman Trail. The bridge is a fun place to watch passing boats and kayakers in summer. You can end your journey on the other side at the Museum of History & Industry, which is also very close to the Washington Park Arboretum.

Fodor's Choice ★ **Henry Art Gallery.** The Henry is perhaps the best reason to take a side trip to the U-District. The large gallery consistently presents sophisticated and thought-provoking work. Notable recent examples: large-scale installations by environmental artist Maya Lin, photography by Kiki Smith, and a comprehensive survey of the multimedia works of William Kentridge. Exhibits pull from many different genres and include mixed media, photography, 19th- and 20th-century paintings, and textiles from the permanent collection. Its permanent installation, *Light Reign,* is a "Skyspace" from artist James Turrell—an elliptical chamber that allows visitors to view the sky (more than a few people have used this

GETTING ORIENTED

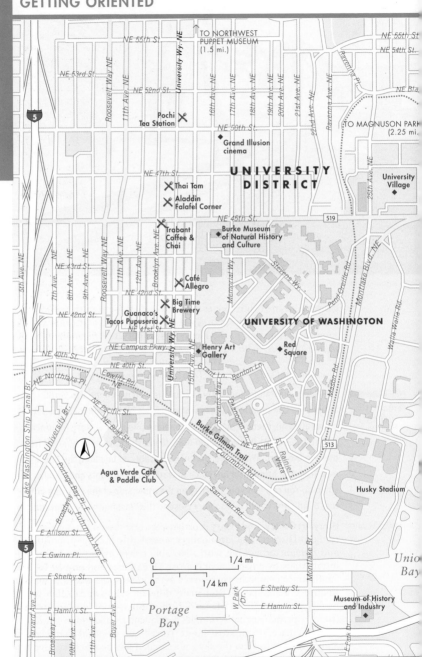

NE 55th St.
TO NORTHWEST
PUPPET MUSEUM
(1.5 mi.)

NE 55th St

NE 54th St.

NE 53rd St.

Roosevelt Way NE

University Wy. NE

11th Ave. NE

NE 52nd St.

16th Ave. NE

17th Ave. NE

18th Ave. NE

19th Ave. NE

20th Ave. NE

21st Ave. NE

22nd Ave. NE

Ravenna Ave. NE

Ravenna Pl.

NE Bta

Pochi
Tea Station ✕

NE 50th St.

TO MAGNUSON PARK
(2.25 mi.)

Grand Illusion
cinema

**UNIVERSITY
DISTRICT**

25th Ave. NE

University
Village

NE 47th St.

✕ Thai Tom

✕ Aladdin
Falafel Corner

NE 45th St.

519

5th Ave. NE

7th Ave. NE

8th Ave. NE

9th Ave. NE

Roosevelt Way NE

11th Ave. NE

12th Ave. NE

Brooklyn Ave. NE

✕ Trabant
Coffee &
Chai

◆ Burke Museum
of Natural History
and Culture

Montlake Blvd NE

Penny Drette Rd

NE 43rd St.

NE 42nd St.

✕ Café
Allegro

Memorial Wy.

Stevens Wy.

Walla Walla Rd.

NE 42nd St.

Guanaco's ✕
Tacos Pupuseria ✕

✕ Big Time
Brewery

UNIVERSITY OF WASHINGTON

NE 41st St.

NE Campus Pkwy.

NE 40th St.

University Wy. N

◆ Henry Art
Gallery

Grant Ln.

Benton Ln.

Red
Square

Mason Rd.

NE 40th St.

Cowlitz Rd.
NE

15th Ave. N

Stevens Way

Okanogan Ln.

NE Pacific St.

NE Northlake Pl.

University Br.

NE Pacific St.

NE Blvd. St.

Portage Bay Pl. E

Burke Gilman Trail

Columbia Rd.

NE Pacific Pl.

Rainier
Vista

513

Lake Washington Ship Canal Br.

Agua Verde Café ✕
& Paddle Club

San Juan Rd.

Husky Stadium

5

E Allison St.

E Gwinn Pl.

E Shelby St.

Broadway

40th Ave. E

Furhman Ave. E

NE

0   1/4 mi

0   1/4 km

Montlake Br.

Unio
Bay

E Hamlin St.

Harvard Ave. E

Boyer Ave. E

11th Ave. E

W Park
Dr.

*Portage
Bay*

E Shelby St.

E Hamlin St.

◆ Museum of History
and Industry

E Park Dr.

GETTING HERE AND AROUND

One day, getting to the U-District from Downtown will be a breeze—but until the Light Rail line is completed in 2016, getting here requires a car or a long bus ride. Driving is technically the easiest solution; unless you hit traffic, taking I-5 north to 45th Street takes only 10 minutes from Downtown. However, driving around the area is a headache, and parking is really hard to come by, especially on weekends.

The bus takes longer—45 minutes depending on the route—but it has its perks. The number 43 bus, which you can catch Downtown along Pike Street, takes a pleasant route through Capitol Hill, over the Montlake Bridge, and stops on the western side of the campus in front of the Henry Art Gallery.

Getting around the U-District is fairly easy. The major action happens on "The Ave" (University Way NE), between 42nd and 50th streets. Getting to the other northern neighborhoods of Wallingford, Fremont, and Ballard is easy, too. The only thing not convenient is the University Village shopping center, which is a long walk.

TOP REASONS TO GO

See the other **Red Square**, UW's lovely main plaza, named after its brick paving. Stop here for views of both college life and, on sunny days, Mt. Rainier. Then check out the well-curated exhibits at the **Henry Art Gallery.**

Paddle around **Portage Bay** from Agua Verde Café & Paddle Club, on the southwest end of the campus. They can set you up with a kayak—and a margarita and Mexican grub when you return.

Make a detour to the **Museum of History and Industry,** which is right across the Montlake Bridge from the southern end of the campus. Seattle's history is on display, along with cool iconic artifacts like a 1953 analog computer from Boeing.

PLANNING YOUR TIME

The few sights the neighborhood has are helpfully grouped close together. The Henry Art Gallery and the Burke Museum are on the lovely UW campus. You can combine a museum stop with a campus stroll and then hit The Ave (the area's main drag) for lunch. Alternatively, plan your campus and museum visit for later in the afternoon, have dinner on The Ave, and cap off the day with a movie at one of the neighborhood's theaters.

QUICK BITES

Lamb gyros, falafel sandwiches, and hummus platters are all excellent at **Aladdin Falafel Corner** (⌧ *4541 University Way NE* ☎ *206/548-9539*), which has, according to many, the city's best tzatziki sauce.

Along with bubble tea (tapioca pearls in sweet milky tea), **Pochi Tea Station** (⌧ *5014 University Way NE* ☎ *206/529-8388*) has terrific frozen yogurt (try the taro flavor) and crepes.

Salvadoran eatery **Guanaco's Tacos Pupusería** (⌧ *4106 Brooklyn Ave. NE* ☎ *206/547-2369*) has items you won't find at most taco stands, including fried plantains and *pupusas* (corn pancakes stuffed with meats, veggies, or beans).

Close to the Henry Art Gallery old-school Seattle coffeehouse **Café Allegro** (⌧ *4214 University Way NE* ☎ *206/633-3030*) makes a mean latte.

The outdoor space of the Henry Art Gallery

as a meditation spot); at night the chamber is illuminated by thousands of LED lights. ✉ *University of Washington campus, 15th Ave. NE and NE 41st St., University District* ☎ *206/543–2280* ⊕ *www.henryart.org* 🎫 *$10* ⏱ *Thurs. and Fri. 11–9, weekends 11–4.*

🧒
★ **Museum of History & Industry.** Just across the Montlake Cut (the bridge between the U-District and the nearby Montlake neighborhood, which crosses one area of the Lake Washington Ship Canal), but still close enough to be quite walkable from the university campus, this museum can help you really get a handle on the history of the Pacific Northwest. Since 1952 this museum has collected objects (some dating to 1780) that chronicle the region's economic, social, and cultural history. Factory and mining equipment, gramophones, clothing, newspapers, and everyday items from yesteryear are all on display, many along the re-created Seattle street from the 1880s. The interactive exhibits encourage kids to have fun and learn. On weekends look for educational presentations, family workshops, and historical walks. Students, teachers, and history buffs are always roaming the vast museum library. The museum will be moving into the converted Naval Reserve Building in Lake Union Park in 2012. ✉ *2700 24th Ave. E, across Montlake Bridge from University, on south side of Union Bay, University District* ☎ *206/324–1126* ⊕ *www.seattlehistory.org* 🎫 *$8, free 1st Thurs. of month* ⏱ *Daily 10–6, 1st Thurs. of month 10–8.*

OFF THE
BEATEN
PATH 🧒

Northwest Puppet Museum. In a renovated church in the Maple Leaf neighborhood, the only puppet center in the Northwest highlights the renowned marionettes of the Carter family, professional puppeteers trained by masters from Italy, Romania, and China. For their talents they have received a Fulbright Award and a UNIMA/USA Citation of Excellence, the highest award in American puppet theater. Performances are open to the public on weekends. Recent shows include *The Nutcracker, The Travels of Babar,* and *The Adventures of Sinbad.* Also on-site are a museum, theater, research library, picnic area, playground, and shop where puppet-making workshops and marionette classes are held. ✉ *9123 15th Ave. NE, University District* ✛ *Take I–5 north, Exit 171 to Lake City Way, turn left on 15th Ave. NE and continue to 92nd St.* ☎ *206/523–2579* ⊕ *www.nwpuppet.org* ✎ *Varies by performance* ☉ *Call for performance and workshop schedules.*

OFF THE BEATEN PATH

Warren G. Magnuson Park. Also called Sand Point–Magnuson Park and most often simply Magnuson Park, this 350-acre space was once a naval air base, so it's not surprising that this park northeast of the University District (U-District) is flat and open. The paved trails are wonderful for cycling, jogging, and pushing a stroller. Leashed dogs are welcome on the trails; a gigantic off-leash area includes one of the few public beaches where pooches can swim. Farther south, on the mile-long shore, there's a swimming beach, a seasonal wading pool, and a boat launch. The beachside park juts into Lake Washington northeast of the University District. Innovative art is threaded through the grounds, including *Soundgarden,* a series of aluminum tubes mounted to catch the wind and create flutelike music. (Yes, Seattle's famous band named itself after this sculpture.) Morning walkers and joggers often rest on the whale-shape benches to watch the sun rise over Lake Washington—a spectacle that's especially lovely when accompanied by this gentle sound track. The sculpture is in the northern part of the park, through the turnstile and across *Moby Dick* Bridge (embedded with quotes from Melville's novel). To get here from the U-District, you can follow 45th Street east past the University Village shopping center until it turns into Sand Point Way, and then follow Sand Point until you reach the park. If you're coming from Downtown, take 1–5 to the 65th Street exit and head east on 65th until you reach the park. Note that traffic around University Village is usually pretty slow, especially on weekends. ✉ *Park entrance: Sand Point Way NE at 65th St., Sand Point* ☎ *206/684–4946* ⊕ *www. seattle.gov/parks/magnuson.*

WEST SEATTLE

Sightseeing
★★
Dining
★★★★
Lodging
★
Shopping
★★
Nightlife
★

Cross the bridge to West Seattle and it's another world altogether. Jutting out into Elliott Bay and Puget Sound, separated from the city by the Duwamish waterway, this out-of-the-way neighborhood covers most of the city's western peninsula—and, indeed, it has an .identity of its own. In summer, throngs of people hang out at Alki Beach—Seattle's taste of California—while others head for the trails and playgrounds of Lincoln Park to the west.

The first white settlers parked their boat at Alki Point in 1851, planning to build a major city here until they discovered a deeper logging port at today's Pioneer Square. This makes West Seattle technically the city's oldest neighborhood. West Seattle is huge, and within it are more than a dozen neighborhoods. The two most visitors will see are Alki and West Seattle Junction—the former includes the shoreline and Alki Point; the Alki Point Lighthouse sits on the peninsula's northwest tip, a place for classic sunset views. The main shopping and dining areas line Alki Avenue, next to the beach, and California and Fauntleroy avenues on the way to the ferry docks. The latter neighborhood, named for a spot where old streetcar lines crisscrossed, is the fastest-growing part of West Seattle and has its own dining scene that is giving Seattle's city center a run for its money. It also has most of the area's good shopping and ArtsWest, a community theater and gallery.

The Admiral neighborhood, on the northern bluff, is less vital, but it does have an important old movie house that is one of the venues for the Seattle International Film Festival. Fauntleroy has two main attractions: the lovely Lincoln Park and a ferry terminal with service to Vashon Island and Southworth on the Kitsap Peninsula.

Seattle skyline views from Alki Beach in West Seattle

WHAT TO SEE

Fodor's Choice
★ **Alki Point and Beach.** In summer, West Seattle's Alki Beach is as close to California as Seattle gets—and some hardy residents even swim in the cold, salty waters of Puget Sound here (water temperature ranges from 46 to 56 degrees F). This 2½-mi stretch of sand has views of the Seattle skyline and the Olympic Mountains, and the beachfront promenade is especially popular with skaters, joggers, and cyclists. Year-round, Seattleites come to build sand castles, beachcomb, and fly kites; in winter, storm-watchers come to see the crashing waves. Facilities include drinking water, grills, picnic tables, phones, and restrooms; restaurants line the street across from the beach. ■ TIP→ To get here from Downtown, take either I–5 south or Highway 99 south to the West Seattle Bridge (keep an eye out, as this exit is easy to miss) and exit onto Harbor Avenue SW, turning right at the stoplight. Alki Point is the place where David Denny, John Low, and Lee Terry arrived in September 1851, ready to found a city. One of 195 Lady Liberty replicas found around the country lives near the 2700 block of Alki Avenue SW; it was erected by Boy Scouts in 1952 as part of their national "Strengthening the Arm of Liberty" campaign. The so-called Miss Liberty (or Little Liberty) is a popular meeting point for beachfront picnics and dates.

OFF THE
BEATEN
PATH

Museum of Flight. Boeing, the world's largest builder of aircraft, was founded in Seattle in 1916. So it's not surprising that this facility at Boeing Field, south of the International District, is one of the city's best museums. It's especially fun for kids, who can climb in many of the aircraft and pretend to fly, make flight-related crafts, or attend special programs. The Red Barn, Boeing's original airplane factory, houses an

GETTING ORIENTED

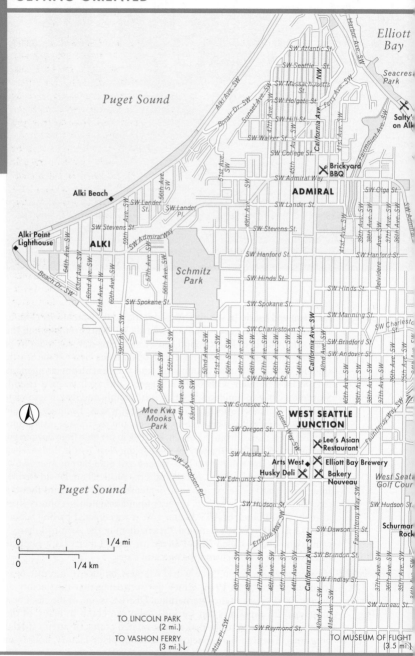

Puget Sound

Elliott Bay

Seacrest Park

Salty's on Alki

Alki Ave. SW

Bonair Dr. SW

Sunset Ave. SW

SW Atlantic St.

SW Seattle St.

SW Massachusetts St.

SW Halgate St.

SW Hill St.

SW Walker St.

SW College St.

SW Admiral Way

Harbor Ave. SW

Ferry Ave. SW

California Ave. SW

41st Ave. SW

Brickyard BBQ

ADMIRAL

SW Olga St.

SW Lander St.

Alki Beach

SW Lander St.

SW Lander Pl.

SW Stevens St.

ALKI

Alki Point Lighthouse

Beach Dr. SW

64th Ave. SW

63rd Ave. SW

62nd Ave. SW

61st Ave. SW

60th Ave. SW

59th Ave. SW

58th Ave. SW

56th Ave. SW

55th Ave. SW

53rd Ave. SW

54th Ave. SW

52nd Ave. SW

51st Ave. SW

50th Ave. SW

48th Ave. SW

47th Ave. SW

46th Ave. SW

45th Ave. SW

California Ave. SW

42nd Ave. SW

40th Ave. SW

39th Ave. SW

38th Ave. SW

37th Ave. SW

36th Ave. SW

SW Admiral Way

SW Stevens St.

SW Hanford St.

SW Hanford St.

Belvidere

Schmitz Park

SW Hinds St.

SW Hinds St.

SW Spokane St.

SW Spokane St.

SW Manning St.

SW Charlestown St.

SW Charlestown St.

SW Bradford St.

SW Andover St.

SW Dakota St.

SW Genesee St.

Mee Kwa Mooks Park

WEST SEATTLE JUNCTION

SW Oregon St.

Glenn Way SW

SW Alaska St.

Lee's Asian Restaurant

Arts West

Husky Deli

Elliott Bay Brewery

Bakery Nouveau

SW Edmunds St.

Faunleroy Way SW

West Seattle Golf Course

Puget Sound

SW Hudson St.

SW Hudson St.

Erskine Way SW

SW Dawson St.

Schurman Rock

49th Ave. SW

48th Ave. SW

46th Ave. SW

45th Ave. SW

44th Ave. SW

SW Brandon St.

California Ave. SW

42nd Ave. SW

41st Ave. SW

37th Ave. SW

36th Ave. SW

SW Findlay St.

SW Juneau St.

SW Jacobsen Rd.

Atlas Pl. SW

SW Raymond St.

0   1/4 mi

0   1/4 km

TO LINCOLN PARK (2 mi.)

TO VASHON FERRY (3 mi.)↓

TO MUSEUM OF FLIGHT (3.5 mi.)

2

GETTING HERE AND AROUND

Driving south on I–5, take the West Seattle Bridge. The Harbor Avenue SW exit will take you to Alki Beach; SW Admiral Way will get you to California Avenue. By bus, take Bus 22, 56, or 57 from Downtown; all travel along 1st Avenue, cross the West Seattle Bridge, and stop at California Avenue. Buses 56 and 57 continue on to the western edge of Alki Beach.

West Seattle is huge and easiest to traverse by car. However, if you arrived by West Seattle Water Taxi (a passenger- and bicycle-only ferry that travels from Pier 50, along the waterfront Downtown, to Seacrest Park at the peninsula's eastern shore), you have several other transit options: You can rent a bicycle at Seacrest, which will get you around the beach areas and up to the restaurants on California Avenue. Or you can take Bus 54 to California Avenue, or hop on Bus number 37, which travels around the peninsula almost as far as Lincoln Park.

QUICK BITES

Brickyard BBQ (✉ *2310 California Ave. SW* ☎ *206/933–3109*) serves up great Texas-style barbecue.

Grab an ice cream cone at **Husky Deli** (✉ *4721 California Ave. SW* ☎ *206/937–2810*).

One of Seattle's best bakeries, **Bakery Nouveau** (✉ *4737 California Ave. SW* ☎ *206/923–0534*) has a lunch menu that includes sandwiches on their fresh-made croissants and baguettes.

The pub at **Elliott Bay Brewery** (✉ *4720 California Ave. SW* ☎ *206/932–8695*) serves craft beers and sandwiches and salads made with fresh Pacific Northwest ingredients.

Salty's on Alki (✉ *1936 Harbor Ave. SW* ☎ *206/937–1600*) is a well-known seafood restaurant with unbeatable views of the skyline. Go for lunch and ask to sit on the patio. Happy-hour deals include fish tacos with a glass of Washington State wine for under $20.

PLANNING YOUR TIME

Head to Alki Beach and follow a path around the peninsula, enjoying the shoreline, Alki Point Lighthouse, and Lincoln Park. This is easiest to do by car. If you arrived by water taxi from Downtown, however, you can rent a bicycle by the terminal and bike the same route; the trip by bike takes roughly 35 minutes. California Avenue, which is in the center of the peninsula, can be your last stop, for sustenance.

TOP REASONS TO GO

See where it all started at **Alki Point.** Any trip to West Seattle should include some beach time on Alki Beach. But be sure to make it around the western edge of the peninsula to see the lighthouse and the spot where the first settlers landed.

Dine on **California Avenue SW.** The stretch between SW Genesee and SW Edmonds streets has most of West Seattle's notable eateries, from hip coffee shops to destination restaurant Spring Hill.

Cool off after a beach stroll in the saltwater swimming pool at **Lincoln Park.**

Catch the ferry to **Vashon Island.** The Fauntleroy terminal is the launching point for ferries to Vashon, where you can visit orchards, farms, and wineries. ⇨ *See also Chapter 8.*

Climb **Schurman Rock,** an outdoor climbing gym next to the West Seattle Golf Course.

exhibit on the history of flight. The Great Gallery, a dramatic structure designed by Ibsen Nelson, contains more than 20 vintage airplanes. The Personal Courage Wing showcases World War I and World War II fighter planes. ■ TIP➜ West Seattle is a good jumping-off point for a side trip to the Museum of Flight, which is farther south, close to Sea-Tac airport. Take the West Seattle Bridge back toward I–5, and then head south on I–5. At Exit 158, merge right onto S. Boeing Access Road. Turn right at the first stoplight (E. Marginal Way S); the museum is on the right after ½ mi. ⊠ 9404 E. Marginal Way S, Tukwila ✛ Take I–5 south to Exit 158, turn right on Marginal Way S ☎ 206/764–5720 ⊕ www.museumofflight.org ⊆ $15 ⊗ Daily 10–5, 1st Thurs. of every month until 9 PM.

PARKS CLOSE TO ALKI

Marvel at the lustrous 50 acres of rugged old-growth forest at **Schmitz Park** (⊠ *5551 S.W. Admiral Way, West Seattle*), steps from Alki Beach.Along the neighborhood's southwest edge, near the Fauntleroy ferry terminal, **Lincoln Park** (⊠ *5551 S.W. Admiral Way, West Seattle*) sets acres of old forests, rocky beaches, and such recreational facilities as a playground, a pool, and tennis courts, against views of Puget Sound. ⊠ *1702 Alki Ave. SW, West Seattle.*

West Seattle Junction art. Walk through West Seattle's business district, amid the small restaurants, shops, and businesses, and you'll come across works of art depicting scenes from local history. A few play tricks with perspective, reminiscent of the paintings Wile E. Coyote used in his attempts to trick the Roadrunner. *The Junction* is a perfect example: If not for the row of neatly trimmed laurel bushes just beneath the wall upon which it's painted, you might be tempted to walk right into the picture's 1918 street scene, painted from the perspective of a streetcar. Another mural is taken from a postcard of 1920s Alki. The most colorful, however, is the *The Hi-Yu Parade*, with its rendition of a *Wizard of Oz*–theme float reminding locals of a 1973 summer celebration. ⊠ *Along California Ave. SW and Fauntleroy Way SW (between 44th and 47th Aves.), West Seattle.*

THE EASTSIDE

Sightseeing
★★
Dining
★★★
Lodging
★★★
Shopping
★★★★
Nightlife
★★★

The suburbs east of Lake Washington can easily supplement any Seattle itinerary. The center of East King County is Bellevue, a fast-growing city with its own downtown core, high-end shopping, and a notable dining scene. Kirkland, north of Bellevue, has a few shops and restaurants (including fabulous Café Juanita) plus lakefront promenades. Redmond and Issaquah, to the northeast and southeast respectively, are gateways to greenery. Woodinville, north of Redmond, is the ambassador for Washington State's wine industry, with many wineries and tasting rooms.

Three-quarters of a century ago, Bellevue was a pleasant little town in the country, with rows of shops along Main Street serving the farmers who grew strawberries. Today it's fast becoming a destination in itself, with snazzy shopping malls, restaurants, and a strong art museum.

Kirkland's business district, along the Lake Street waterfront, is lined with shops, restaurants, pubs, and parks, though it lacks a certain soul. At the height of summer, it's often warm enough to swim in the sheltered waters of Lake Washington; Juanita Beach Park is a popular spot with an enclosed swimming area.

A string of pretty parks makes Redmond an inviting place to experience the outdoors, and the 13-mi Sammamish River Trail is an attraction for locals and tourists alike. The rapidly expanding city is today one of the country's most powerful business capitals, thanks to the presence of such companies as Microsoft, Nintendo, and Eddie Bauer. Although there are several good malls and a lot of generic strip-mall stores, this isn't a place to shop—locals come here either to work or to play.

Issaquah is experiencing rapid (and not terribly attractive) development, but it's what lies beyond the subdivisions that counts. The surrounding

Cougar, Tiger, and Squak mountain foothills—dubbed the Issaquah Alps—are older than the Cascade Range and pocketed with caves, parks, and trails. This area has some of the most accessible hiking and mountain biking in the Seattle area; Seattleites often use these trails to train on in early spring before the more arduous trails in the Cascades and Olympics open for hiking season.

Woodinville is perhaps the Eastside's most popular day trip. It's the home of Chateau Ste. Michelle and dozens of other wineries plus destination restaurant The Herbfarm. Additionally, luxurious Willows Lodge is just down the road from the main attractions, making Woodinville a great place for a romantic getaway. ⇨ *See Chapter 8 for more information on Woodinville's wineries.*

TOP ATTRACTIONS

Bellevue Arts Museum. A real feather in Bellevue's cap, this museum presents sophisticated exhibits on craft and design, with a focus on regional artists. Past exhibitions have included glass art from the Pilchuck Glass School Gallery, a raku ceramics exhibit by Judy Hill entitled "The Self Transparent," mixed media from Thomas Mann made from objects and debris found in New Orleans post-Katrina, zany shoes designed by Beth Levine, and a collection of contemporary tapestries. The dramatic puzzle piece–looking building, which really stands out in Bellevue's somewhat uninspired core, is worth the trip alone. In late July, the museum hosts the Bellevue Arts and Crafts Fair, which involves more than 300 local artists and craftspeople. ⊠ *510 Bellevue Way NE, Bellevue* ☎ *425/519–0770* ⊕ *www.bellevuearts.org* ⌷ *$10* ☉ *Tues.–Thurs. 11–5, Fri. 11–8, weekends noon–5.*

Bellevue Botanical Gardens. This beautiful, 36-acre public area in the middle of Wilburton Hill Park is encircled by spectacular perennial borders, brilliant rhododendron displays, and patches of alpine and rock gardens. ■TIP→ Docents lead tours of the gardens Saturdays and Sundays (April through October), beginning at the visitor center at 2 PM. The Yao Japanese garden is beautiful in fall, when the leaves change color. One of the most interesting features of the park is the Waterwise Garden, which was planted with greenery that needs little water in summer to demonstrate that not all great gardens require wasteful daily drenchings with a hose or sprinkler system. When you're tired of manicured gardens, take the Lost Meadow Trail, which winds through a heavily forested area, to see nature's disorganized beauty. The gardens are a short drive from Bellevue's core. ⊠ *12001 Main St., Bellevue* ☎ *425/452–2750* ⊕ *www.bellevuebotanical.org* ⌷ *Free* ☉ *Gardens daily dawn–dusk, visitor center daily 9–4.*

Chateau Ste. Michelle Winery. ⇨ *For more information on Washington wine, see the "Sipping" feature in Chapter 1.* One of the state's oldest wineries is 15 mi northeast of Seattle on 87 wooded acres. Once part of the estate of lumber baron Fred Stimson, it includes the original trout ponds, a carriage house, a caretaker's cottage, formal gardens, and the 1912 family manor house (which is on the National Register of Historic Places). Complimentary wine tastings and cellar tours run throughout the day. ■TIP→ Reservations are required for private tours, one week

GETTING ORIENTED

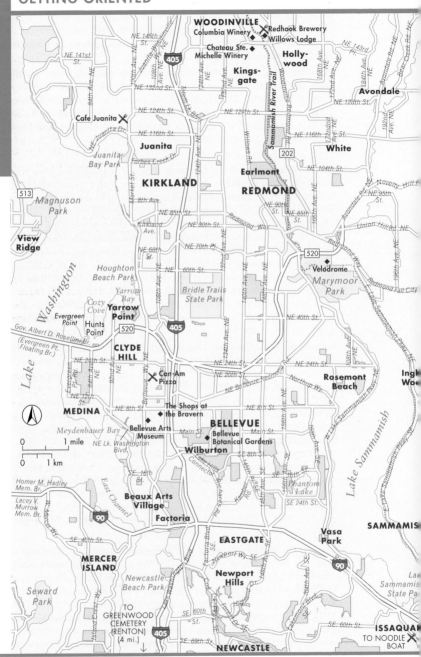

PLANNING YOUR TIME

There are quite a few hotels on the Eastside, mainly in Bellevue, Kirkland, and Woodinville, but unless you're planning an overnight at Willows Lodge after touring Woodinville's wineries, it's not worth staying here. You won't save any money—Bellevue's hotels are just as pricey as and far less interesting than Seattle's—and no local would recommend a daily commute to or from Seattle.

Instead, plan targeted day trips to the Eastside: a shopping excursion to Bellevue followed by a meal at one of the city's hot new restaurants; a winery or brewery crawl in Woodinville; or a day of hiking, biking or horseback riding that ends in time to return to Seattle for a shower and a nap before a night out.

TOP REASONS TO GO

Explore **Tiger Mountain,** the most popular hiking (and biking) spot a hop, skip, and jump from Seattle, with a large trail system and something for everyone, from grandparents to trail runners.

Feel the wind on your face in the **Velodrome:** Marymoor Park's bicycle racing track is open to the public, and although track bikes are given right of way, you can take a spin on any road bike. If you'd rather be a spectator, races are held weekly in summer.

Visit the **Bellevue Botanical Gardens,** a 36-acre park with colorful gardens and trails.

Splurge at the **Shops at the Bravern** in Bellevue. The city has many malls, but the Bravern is the ritziest—one-stop shopping for major international labels like Jimmy Choo, Ferragamo, and Hermès.

Sample Northwest wines in **Woodinville.** The town has more than 45 wineries (many with tasting rooms), all within easy reach of each other.

GETTING HERE AND AROUND

Buses run to the Eastside, but it's easier to get here by car. The most direct route to most of the Eastside is across the 520 floating bridge, though rush-hour traffic is a nightmare. The other route to the Eastside is I–5 South to I–90 East. Bellevue is the most accessible town by public transportation (⊕ *www.soundtransit.org*). It has a bus hub that's within walking distance of the art museum. The most bus direct route to central Bellevue is the number 550.

QUICK BITES

The **Redhook Brewery** (✉ *14300 NE 145th St., Woodinville* ☎ *425/483–3232* ⊕ *www.redhook.com*) is a popular side trip—it has a pleasant, family-friendly brewpub that serves food.

Can-Am Pizza (✉ *15400 NE 20th St., Bellevue* ☎ *425/747–7777* ⊕ *www.canampizza.com*) is known for garnishing its pies with East Indian flavors.

If you're craving Thai food, try delicious **Noodle Boat** (✉ *700 NW Gilman Blvd., Issaquah* ☎ *425/391–8096* ⊕ *www.noodleboat.com*), which serves lunch weekdays and dinner daily.

Elegant, modern interiors at the Bellevue Arts Museum

in advance. You're also invited to picnic and explore the grounds on your own; the wine shop sells delicatessen items. In summer Chateau Ste. Michelle hosts nationally known performers and arts events in its amphitheater. ✉ *14111 N.E. 145th St., Woodinville* ✛ *From Downtown Seattle take I–90 east to north I–405; take Exit 23 east (Hwy. 522) to Woodinville exit* ☎ *425/415–3300* ⊕ *www.ste-michelle.com* 🎟 *Free* ☉ *Daily 10–5.*

☺ **Marymoor Park.** This 640-acre park has the famous Marymoor Velo-
★ drome—the Pacific Northwest's sole cycling arena—a 45-foot-high climbing rock, game fields, tennis courts, a model airplane launching area, off-leash dog space, and the Pea Patch community garden. You can row on Lake Sammamish, fish off a pier, or head straight to the picnic grounds or to the Willowmoor Farm, an estate in the park. It has a Dutch-style windmill and the historic Clise Mansion, which contains the Marymoor Museum of Eastside History.

Marymoor has some of the best bird-watching in this largely urban area. It's possible to spot some 24 resident species, including great blue herons, belted kingfishers, buffleheads, short-eared and barn owls, and red-tailed hawks. Occasionally, bald eagles soar past the lakefront. The Sammamish River, which flows through the western section of the park, is an important salmon spawning stream. King County Parks naturalists periodically give guided wildlife tours. With all these attractions, it's no wonder the park has more than 1 million visitors annually.

Ambitious hikers can follow the Burke-Gilman/Sammamish River Trail to access the park on foot. ✉ *6046 W. Lake Sammamish Pkwy. NE, Redmond* ✛ *Take Rte. 520 east to the West Lake Sammamish Pkwy.*

exit. Turn right (southbound) on W. Lake Sammamish Pkwy. NE. Turn left at the traffic light ⊕ www.metrokc.gov/parks/marymoor ⊗ Daily 8 AM–dusk.

WORTH NOTING

Burke-Gilman/Sammamish River Trail. The 27-mi-long, paved Burke-Gilman Trail runs from Seattle's Gas Works Park, on Lake Union, east along an old railroad right-of-way along the ship canal, and then north along Lake Washington's western shore. At Blyth Park in Bothell, the trail becomes the Sammamish River Trail and continues for 10 mi to Marymoor Park, in Redmond. Energetic Seattleites take the trail to Marymoor for the annual Heritage Festival and Fourth of July Fireworks. Except for a stretch of the Sammamish River Trail between Woodinville and Marymoor Park, where horses are permitted on a parallel trail, the path is limited to walkers, runners, and bicyclists. ⊹ *Take I–90 east to north I–405, then Exit 23 east (Hwy. 522) to Woodinville.*

Columbia Winery. A group of UW professors founded this winery in 1962, making it the state's oldest. Using only European vinifera-style grapes grown in eastern Washington, the founders' aim was to take advantage of the fact that the vineyards share the same latitude as the best wine-producing areas of France. Complimentary wine tastings are held daily; cellar tours are on weekends. The gift shop is open year-round and sells wines and wine-related merchandise. Columbia hosts special food-and-wine events throughout the year. ⊠ *14030 N.E. 145th St., Woodinville ⊹ From Downtown Seattle take I–90 east to north I–405; take Exit 23 east (Hwy. 522) to Woodinville exit, go right. Go right again on 175th St., and left on Hwy. 202* ☎ *425/488–2776 or 800/488–2347* ⊕ *www.columbiawinery.com* ☞ *Free* ⊗ *Winery daily 10–6. Tours weekdays at 3:30; Sat. at 11, noon, 3, 4, and 5; Sun. at 11, 2, 3, 4, and 5.*

Houghton Beach Park (⊠ *5811 Lake Washington Blvd., Kirkland* ☎ *425/828–1217*). On hot days, sun-worshippers, swimmers, and the beach-volleyball crowd flock to this beach south of downtown Kirkland on the Lake Washington waterfront. The rest of the year, the playground attracts families, and the fishing pier stays busy with anglers. Facilities include drinking water, picnic tables, a beach volleyball court, phones, and restrooms. Head to the north end of the beach if you want some distance between you and the playground.

OFF THE BEATEN PATH

Jimi Hendrix Grave Site. Since his death in 1970, the famed guitarist has rested in Greenwood Cemetery. The site includes a memorial with a domed roof and granite columns. ⊠ *3rd and Monroe Sts., Renton* ⊹ *Take I–5 south to I–405 north and the WA–169 south (S.E. Maple Valley Hwy.) exit, keeping left at the fork in the ramp. Merge onto S.E. Maple Valley Hwy./WA–169 north. Take a right on Sunset Blvd. N, then a right at N.E. 3rd St. Continue 1 mi, as N.E. 3rd St. becomes N.E. 4th St. Turn right at the 3rd light* ⊕ *www.jimihendrixmemorial. com* ⊗ *Daily sunrise–sunset.*

Juanita Beach Park (⊠ *9703 N.E. Juanita Dr., Kirkland* ☎ *425/828–1217*). Directly across Juanita Bay from peaceful wetlands, this Kirkland beach

Biking along the Burke-Gilman Trail is a quintessential Seattle activity.

hops: children playing in the sand, sunbathers on the quarter-mile-long dock, swimmers in the closed-in swimming area, and picnickers in the park. There are grills, picnic shelters, phones, restrooms, drinking water, and a snack bar (seasonal). The beach has had problems with water quality in recent years, but a multiyear plan by the city of Kirkland is under way to revitalize the park and remedy its water quality issues.

Lake Sammamish State Park. East-siders flock to this day-use park in summer to soak up the sunshine on the sandy beach, then to cool off in the lake waters. Speedboats and kayaks zip through the waves out past the swimming float; hikers follow trails behind the shore. Picnic tables are crowded on weekends—and it's best to bring your own basket rather than test the concessions. ⊠ *Off I–90W, Issaquah* ☎ *425/455–7010 or 800/233–0321* ⊕ *www. parks.wa.gov* ✉ *Free* ☉ *Daily dawn–dusk.*

Where to Eat

WORD OF MOUTH

"Some of my favorite restaurants (other than Tom Douglas's places, which are definitely on my list, including his Serious Pie pizza place) include Lark, Matt's in the Market, Steelhead Diner, and Restaurant Zoë."

—NWWanderer

Updated
by Heidi
Johansen

Thanks to inventive chefs, first-rate local produce, adventurous diners, and a bold entrepreneurial spirit, Seattle has become one of the culinary capitals of the nation. Fearless young chefs have stepped in and raised the bar. Nowadays, fresh and often foraged produce, local seafood, and imaginative techniques make the quality of local cuisine even higher.

Seattle's dining scene has been stoked like a wildfire by culinary rock stars who make cameos on shows like *Top Chef* and regular appearances on "best of" lists. Among the 2010 James Beard nominees were Matt Dillon of the Corson Building; Jerry Traunfeld of Poppy; Rachel Yang of Joule; Mark Fuller of Spring Hill; and Ethan Stowell of Anchovies & Olives, How to Cook a Wolf, and Tavolàta. The winner? Jason Wilson of Crush restaurant won the "Best Chef Northwest" award.

The city is particularly strong on New American, French, and Asian cuisines. Chefs continuously fine-tune what can best be called Pacific Northwest cuisine, which features fresh, local ingredients, including anything from nettles and mushrooms foraged in nearby forests; colorful berries, apples, and cherries grown by Washington State farmers; and outstanding seafood from the cold northern waters of the Pacific Ocean, including wild salmon, halibut, oysters, Dungeness crab, and geoduck. Seattle boasts quite a few outstanding bakeries, too, whose breads and desserts you'll see touted on many menus.

Seattle is also seeing a resurgence in American comfort food, often with a gourmet twist, as well as gastropub fare, which can mean anything from divine burgers on locally baked ciabatta rolls to grilled foie gras with brioche toast. But innovation still reigns supreme: local salmon cooked *sous vide* and accompanied with pickled *kimchi* or fresh-picked peas can be just as common as aspic spiked with sake and reindeer meat. Many menus feature fusion cuisine or pages of small-plate offerings. One thing's for sure: chefs are highlighting their inventions with the top-notch ingredients that makes Pacific Northwest cooking famous.

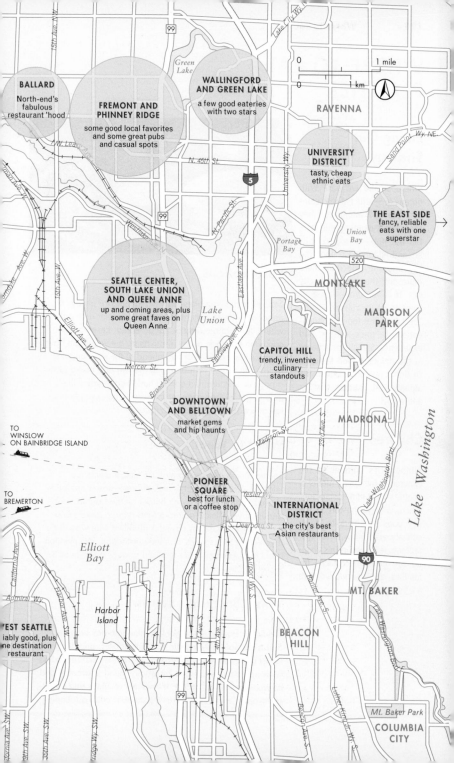

BALLARD
North-end's fabulous restaurant 'hood

FREMONT AND PHINNEY RIDGE
some good local favorites and some great pubs and casual spots

Green Lake

WALLINGFORD AND GREEN LAKE
a few good eateries with two stars

RAVENNA

0   1 mile
0   1 km

UNIVERSITY DISTRICT
tasty, cheap ethnic eats

99

N. 45th St.

I-5

THE EAST SIDE
fancy, reliable eats with one superstar

Union Bay

Portage Bay

99

SEATTLE CENTER, SOUTH LAKE UNION AND QUEEN ANNE
up and coming areas, plus some great faves on Queen Anne

Lake Union

Mercer St.

MONTLAKE

520

MADISON PARK

CAPITOL HILL
trendy, inventive culinary standouts

Elliott Ave W

Broad St.

DOWNTOWN AND BELLTOWN
market gems and hip haunts

TO WINSLOW ON BAINBRIDGE ISLAND

Madison St.

MADRONA

Lake Washington

TO BREMERTON

PIONEER SQUARE
best for lunch or a coffee stop

Yesler Wy

INTERNATIONAL DISTRICT
the city's best Asian restaurants

S. Dearborn St.

90

MT. BAKER

Elliott Bay

Harbor Island

Airport Wy S

WEST SEATTLE
reliably good, plus one destination restaurant

Admiral Wy

99

BEACON HILL

Mt. Baker Park

COLUMBIA CITY

WHERE TO EAT PLANNER

Eating-Out Strategy

Where should we eat? With dozens of Seattle eateries competing for your attention, it may seem like a daunting question. But fret not—our expert writers and editors have done the legwork. The selections here represent the best this city has to offer—from fish-and-chips to haute cuisine. Search "Best Bets" for top recommendations by price, cuisine, and experience. Sample local flavor in the neighborhood features. Or find a review quickly in the alphabetical listings. Dive in and enjoy!

Reservations

Seattleites dine out often, so reservations are always a good idea. Restaurant reviews in this chapter note only where they are required or not accepted. Reservations can often be made a day in advance, but you might have to make them a week or two ahead at the most popular restaurants. If you've just arrived in town and heard about a popular restaurant, it doesn't hurt to call—you'll likely be able to get a reservation for midweek when even hot restaurants don't always reach capacity.

Children

Although it's unusual to see children in the dining rooms of Seattle's most elite restaurants, dining with youngsters in the city does not have to mean culinary exile. Many of the restaurants reviewed in this chapter are excellent choices for families, and are marked with a ☺ symbol.

What to Wear

Seattle dining is very informal. It's almost a little too informal—though the city's lack of pretension is one of its charms, residents are trying harder on the fashion front, and it shows. Almost no restaurants require jackets and ties; however, business casual is usually a safe way to go if you're off to a spendy or trendy restaurant. We mention dress only when men are required to wear a jacket or a jacket and tie.

Wine, Beer, and Spirits

The liquor laws in the state of Washington are stringent. Spirits are sold only in state-run liquor stores, and liquor stores are closed Sunday. The laws are less strict regarding wine and beer, which can be readily found in grocery and convenience stores; in fact, the variety of wines and specialty beers sold in most grocery stores is quite astounding.

Mealtimes

Many of Seattle's better restaurants serve only dinner and are closed Sunday; quite a few are closed Monday. Many that serve lunch during the week do not do so on weekends, though they may offer brunch, which is an increasingly popular activity in Seattle. Unless otherwise noted, the restaurants listed are open daily for lunch and dinner. Seattle restaurants generally serve food until 10 or 11 PM on weekdays and often much later on Friday and Saturday. Great breakfast menus are easier to come by on weekends than midweek; consequently, most coffeehouses carry terrific pastries and breads—and, of course, amazing coffee.

Prices

If you're watching your budget, be sure to ask the price of daily specials recited by the waiter. The charge for specials at some restaurants can be noticeably out of line with the other prices on the menu. Beware of the $10 bottle of water; ask for tap water instead.

Many restaurants offer great lunch deals with special menus at lower prices designed to give customers a true taste of the place. Eateries are also featuring early-evening and late-night happy hours, complete with cheap drinks and satisfying food offerings.

Credit cards are widely accepted, but some restaurants (particularly smaller ones) accept only cash. If you plan to use a credit card, double-check its acceptability when making reservations or before sitting down to eat.

Some restaurants are marked with a price range ($$–$$$, for example). This indicates one of two things: either the average cost straddles two categories, or if you order strategically, you can get out for less than what most diners spend.

WHAT IT COSTS AT DINNER

¢	$	$$	$$$	$$$$
under $8	$8–$16	$17–$24	$25–$32	over $32

Price per person for a median main course or equivalent combination of smaller dishes. Note: if a restaurant offers only prix-fixe (set-price) meals, it has been given the price category that reflects the full prix-fixe price.

In This Chapter

3

Orientation

Throughout the chapter, you'll see mapping symbols and coordinates (⊹ 3:F2) after property names or reviews. To locate the property on a map, turn to the Seattle Dining and Lodging Atlas at the end of this chapter. The first number after the ⊹ symbol indicates the map number. Following that is the property's coordinate on the map grid.

Smoking

Smoking in restaurants and bars is prohibited in Washington State.

Tipping

Most Seattleites tip around 15%. You should leave 20% if the service was outstanding, or the server or kitchen fulfilled special requests. A 16%–18% gratuity will automatically be added to bills for larger parties—be sure to check your receipt before adding a tip, or to be certain ask your server.

SEATTLE'S BEST FARMERS' MARKETS

If you've been to Pike Place Market in the summer and walked its colorful, aromatic stalls of fresh flowers, berries, and peaches, and if you've had a great meal at a top-rated restaurant, then you know how obsessive Seattle is about its produce and ingredients.

(Above and opposite page bottom) West Seattle Farmers' Market (Opposite page top) Wild mushrooms

The many neighborhood farmers' markets throughout the city are helping to shape and define how Seattle-ites eat—from Ballard's year-round colorful and quirky bonanza on Ballard Avenue and Capitol Hill's miniature gem just off Broadway, to West Seattle's weekly bounty and Columbia City's midweek fresh fest. Check out the three Web sites listed below for more information about neighborhood markets, and definitely save an hour or two to peruse the produce—especially if you're here in the glorious summer months. You'll get a unique sense of each individual neighborhood, and be able to interact with some colorful local characters, as well as some of the best local suppliers and farmers. Children have a blast at farmers' markets, too—there's often a bluegrass band playing, cooking demonstrations, and samples galore.

HELPFUL HINTS

Be sure to check the Web ahead of time to find out about the particular farmers' market you'd like to visit—there are more than we have room to list here, and each one offers a special slice of neighborhood life and character. Dogs are allowed only at some of the markets; check the Web ahead of time, or assume your canine pal isn't invited. It's smart to bring a large basket to carry your goods, or at least a few reusable bags.

FAVORITE MARKETS

The **Ballard Farmers' Market** is open every Sunday year-round, rain or shine, from 10 AM to 3 PM at Ballard Avenue, between 20th Avenue NW and 22nd Avenue NW. Loads of vendors—selling anything from eggs, apples, and greens to candles and hats—set up colorful, welcoming tents and stands.

The **University District Market Farmers' Market** is open every Saturday year-round from 9 AM to 2 PM, at the corner of University Way and N.E. 50th Street, in the playground of the University Heights Center for the Community. An understated elegance pervades here, with loads of flowers and fine cheeses and meats. Come summertime, more than 60 farmers and vendors set up their goods, including a small food court with a yummy selection of ready-to-eat foods.

The **West Seattle Farmers' Market** is open every Sunday year-round from 10 AM to 2 PM, and is located in the heart of the "West Seattle Junction" at California Avenue SW and S.W. Alaska Street. Going south on I-5, take the West Seattle Bridge exit, then continue to Fauntleroy Way. At the fourth light (S.W. Alaska), take a right. Fruit, vegetables, herbs, greens, cheeses, free-range chicken, cut flowers, and plant starts fill the tents here.

The **Columbia City Farmers' Market** is open on Wednesday, April 28th through October 20th, from 3 PM to 7 PM, at Rainier Ave South and South Edmunds. This southern neighborhood is absolutely darling—hit up the market for eggs, nuts, grains, poultry, berries, jams and much, much more.

The **Broadway Farmers' Market** on Capitol Hill is open every Sunday, May 9th through December 19th, from 11 AM to 3 PM, at 10th Avenue East and East Thomas Street. This small and lively market filling up a parking lot is set one block east of Broadway; there's fresh produce galore, plus music, samples, and plenty of cut flowers.

PARKING AND PLANNING

It's a good idea to arrive at any neighborhood farmers' market prepared to deal with lots of people. That said, many of the best markets in the city are set in calm areas that have plenty of residential streets nearby that have free parking. Be sure to check street signs, though, as even some residential areas are seeing pay machines (though parking is always free on Sundays). Check online at the Websites listed here to find the market that is closest to you—part of the fun can be arriving on foot, as so many locals do. If you're staying Downtown, and have already hit up Pike Place Market, we recommend taking a bus up to Capitol Hill (such as Bus 10, 11 or 12), and making your way on foot to the Broadway Farmers' Market—then you can wind your way back downhill to the Downtown core, or jump on the bus or into a cab. Cal Anderson Park, between Pine and Denny at 11th, is a good place to eat your berries and plan the rest of the day.

BEST BETS FOR SEATTLE DINING

With so many restaurants to choose from, how to decide where to eat? Fodor's writers and editors have selected their favorite restaurants by price, cuisine, and experience in the Best Bets lists below. In the first column, Fodor's Choice properties represent the "best of the best" in every price category. Other favorites are listed by price category, cuisine, and experience.

Fodor'sChoice ★

Anchovies & Olives, p. 140

Boat Street Café & Kitchen, p. 131

Café Campagne, p. 126

Café Juanita, p. 161

Cascina Spinasse, p. 143

Joule, p. 156

La Carta de Oaxaca, p. 153

Lark, p. 145

Lola, p. 132

Matt's in the Market, p. 128

Poppy, p. 146

Salumi, p. 137

Shiro's Sushi, p. 133

Spring Hill, p. 160

Best By Price

¢

El Puerco Lloron, p. 127

Dick's Drive-In, p. 144

Green Leaf, p. 138

Macrina Bakery, p. 132

Samurai Noodle, p. 139

$

Baguette Box, p. 141

Barrio, p. 142

Delancey, p. 152

Maneki, p. 139

Salumi, p. 137

Tamarind Tree, p. 140

$$

Café Presse, p. 142

Cantinetta, p. 155

How to Cook a Wolf, p. 137

Joule, p. 156

Le Pichet, p. 127

Serious Pie, p. 133

Tavolàta, p. 134

$$$

Boat Street Café & Kitchen, p. 131

Café Juanita, p. 161

Crush, p. 144

Kisaku, p. 157

Lark, p. 145

Lola, p. 132

Monsoon, p. 145
Spring Hill, p. 160

$$$$

Canlis, p. 136
The Corson Building,
p. 126
Matt's in the Market,
p. 128
Rover's, p. 147

Best By Cuisine

ASIAN

Joule, p. 156
Monsoon, p. 145
Samurai Noodle,
p. 139
Tamarind Tree, p. 140

FRENCH

Bastille, p. 152
Café Campagne,
p. 126
Le Gourmand, p. 153
Le Pichet, p. 127
Rover's, p. 147

ITALIAN

Café Juanita, p. 161
Cantinetta, p. 155
Cascina Spinasse,
p. 143
Tavolàta, p. 134

JAPANESE

Kisaku, p. 157
Maneki, p. 139
Shiro's Sushi, p. 133

LATIN

Barrio, p. 142
La Carta de Oaxaca,
p. 153
Paseo, p. 150

MEDITERRANEAN

Harvest Vine, p. 145
Lola, p. 132
Vios, p. 149

NEW AMERICAN

Boat Street Café &
Kitchen, p. 131
The Corson Building,
p. 126
Crush, p. 144
Lark, p. 145
Poppy, p. 146
Spring Hill, p. 160

PACIFIC NORTHWEST

Matt's in the Market,
p. 128
Palace Kitchen, p. 132
Canlis, p. 136

SEAFOOD

Anchovies & Olives,
p. 140
Etta's, p. 127
Flying Fish, p. 135

STEAK HOUSE

El Gaucho, p. 132

John Howie Steak,
p. 162
Metropolitan Grill,
p. 129

Best by Experience

BAKERY

Bakery Nouveau,
p. 159
Café Besalu, p. 152
Macrina Bakery, p. 132

BRUNCH

Café Campagne,
p. 126
Café Presse, p. 142
Lola, p. 132
Monsoon, p. 145

BUSINESS DINING

Assaggio Ristorante,
p. 131
Il Terrazzo Carmine,
p. 137
Metropolitan Grill,
p. 129

CHILD-FRIENDLY

Café Flora, p. 142
Ivar's Salmon House,
p. 156
Tutta Bella, p. 157
Vios, p. 149

COFFEEHOUSE

Bauhaus Books and
Coffee, p. 142
Caffé Vita, p. 143
Stumptown Coffee
Roasters, p. 148
Victrola Coffee, p. 149
Vivace Espresso,
p. 149

GOOD FOR GROUPS

Bastille, p. 152
Steelhead Diner,
p. 130
Tutta Bella, p. 157

GREAT VIEW

Agua Verde, p. 158
Canlis, p. 136
Maximilien, p. 128
Ray's Boathouse,
p. 154

LATE-NIGHT DINING

Oddfellows, p. 146
Palace Kitchen, p. 132
Smith, p. 148
Tavolàta, p. 134

MOST ROMANTIC

Boat Street Café &
Kitchen, p. 131
Canlis, p. 136
Lark, p. 145
Serafina, p. 147

WINE LIST

Canlis, p. 136
Crush, p. 144
Rover's, p. 147

RESTAURANT AND COFFEEHOUSE REVIEWS

Listed alphabetically within neighborhoods.

DOWNTOWN AND BELLTOWN

After a day of exploring the shopping, museums, sights, galleries, and parks in these two adjacent neighborhoods, what could be better than a perfect meal? Luckily, this area is filled with a wide range of eateries, from a charming French bistro near Pike Place Market called Le Pichet and old-school Seattle sushi spot Shiro's to rustic-chic Italian at Tavolàta, plus plenty of favorites from local star-chef Tom Douglas, including his acclaimed Lola, Serious Pie, and Palace Kitchen eateries.

DOWNTOWN

$$$
FRENCH
Fodor's Choice
★

✕ **Café Campagne/Campagne.** The white walls, picture windows, pressed linens, fresh flowers, and candles at charming French restaurant Campagne—which overlooks Pike Place Market and Elliott Bay—evoke Provence. So does the robust French country fare, with starters such as grilled housemade merguez sausage, pork rillettes, and potato gnocchi with braised artichokes and black truffle butter. Main plates include pork short ribs with onion, raisin, and tomato compote; steamed mussels with expertly prepared *pommes frites*; and Oregon beef rib-eye with parsley-crusted marrow bones. ■ **TIP→ Campagne is open only for dinner, but downstairs, the equally charming (some would say even more lovely and authentic) Café Campagne serves breakfast, lunch, and dinner daily.** The café is an exceptional place for a satisfying weekend brunch before hitting Pike Place Market on foot. Try the impeccable quiche du jour with green salad; poached eggs with pearl onions, bacon, and champignons; or Brioche French toast—plus a big bowl of *café au lait*. ✉ *Inn at the Market, 86 Pine St., Downtown* ☎ *206/728–2800* ∰ *www.campagnerestaurant.com* ⊟ *AE, DC, MC, V* ✛ *1:D2.*

$$$$
NEW AMERICAN

✕ **The Corson Building.** Nestled in a diminutive, sweet old building south of Downtown that brings Italy to mind (albeit amidst train tracks and soccer fields) in the industrial Georgetown neighborhood, the Corson Building is feeding happy foodies while garnering major accolades across the nation. Chef Matt Dillon is inventive and curious, and serves up fearless meals that usually satisfy—and may include raw oysters, handmade pasta with anything from a rich ragu to sautéed mushrooms foraged from local forests, leg of lamb with roasted radicchio, fresh scallops with citrus sauce, and duck-leg confit. The menu changes constantly, and so does the restaurant's schedule; be sure call ahead to find out what's on the menu, and to make reservations. Saturday evening sees one dinner seating at family-style tables, which is intimate and interesting—spring for the amazing wine pairings (it's already going to be pricy, we promise). Sunday brunches are downright divine. Dillon is absolutely helping to push the culinary envelope in Seattle, and Corson Building is a memorable Seattle dining experience that will do nothing short of amaze you. ✉ *5609 Corson Ave. S, Downtown* ☎ *206/762–3330* ∰ *www.thecorsonbuilding.com* ⚑ *Reservations essential* ⊟ *DC, MC, V* ☺ *No dinner Sun.–Wed. No lunch* ✛ *1:H6.*

Matt's in the Market

¢ ✕ **El Puerco Lloron.** This funky, cafeteria-style diner perched on the Pike
MEXICAN   Place Market "Hillclimb" (a flight of stairs between Pike Place Market
and the piers along Elliott Bay) has delightful open-air terrace seating
perfect for sunny days. It's also got some of Seattle's best and most
authentic Mexican cooking—simple, tasty, and inexpensive. Try fresh
tacos filled with pork, chicken, or beef and spiked with cilantro and
salsa. More ambitious highlights include perfect *chiles rellenos* (mild
green peppers that are breaded, stuffed with cheese, and fried) and a
flavorful guacamole. ■ TIP→ This is a fantastic spot for a casual lunch after
a morning stroll at Pike Place Market. ⊠ *501 Western Ave., Downtown*
☎ *206/624–0541* ▭ *AE, MC, V* ✛ *1:D3.*

$$$ ✕ **Etta's Seafood.** Tom Douglas's restaurant perched next to Pike Place
SEAFOOD   Market has views of Victor Steinbrueck Park, which he is working to
clean up and revivify. Etta's is the happy medium between the pricey,
sleek Downtown restaurants and the established yet lovable standards.
The Dungeness crab cakes have always been one of Douglas's specialties
and they are a must, as are the various Washington oysters on the half
shell or the Coho salmon with Douglas's signature "Rub With Love"
seasoning. Leave room for a slice of heavenly banana cream pie. Brunch,
served weekends, is perhaps the best meal to enjoy here—it always
includes zesty seafood omelets, but the chef also does justice to French
toast, eggs and bacon, and Mexican-influenced breakfast dishes such as
huevos rancheros. ⊠ *2020 Western Ave., Downtown* ☎ *206/443–6000*
⊕ *www.tomdouglas.com* ▭ *AE, D, DC, MC, V* ✛ *1:C2.*

$$ ✕ **Le Pichet.** Are you missing Paris? Slate tabletops, tile floor, and a
FRENCH   rolled-zinc bar transport you out of Downtown Seattle and into the
charming 6th arrondissement. Blackboards spell out the specials, and

WATERSIDE RESTAURANTS

✕ Ivar's Acres of Clams (Pier 54). ✉ 1001 Alaskan Way, Pier 54, Downtown ☎ 206/624–6852 ⊕ www.ivars. net ▬ AE, DC, MC, V.

✕ Elliott's Oyster House (Pier 56). ✉ 1201 Alaskan Way, at Pier 56, Downtown ☎ 206/623–4340 ⊕ www.elliottsoysterhouse.com ▬ AE, DC, MC, V.

✕ Steamer's (Pier 56). ✉ 1201 Alaskan Way, at Pier 56, Downtown ☎ 206/623–2066 ⎙ Reservations not accepted ▬ D, MC, V.

✕ Anthony's (Pier 66). ✉ 2201 Alaskan Way (Bell St./Pier 66), Downtown ☎ 206/448–6688 ⊕ www.anthonys. com ▬ AE, D, MC, V.

✕ Six Seven (Pier 67). ✉ In Edgewater Hotel, 2411 Alaskan Way, Pier 67, Downtown ☎ 206/728–7000 ⊕ www.edgewaterhotel.com ▬ AE, DC, MC, V.

wines are served from the earthenware *pichets* that inspired the brasserie's name. The menu is heartbreakingly French: at lunch there are rustic pâtés and *jambon et fromage* (ham-and-cheese) sandwiches on crusty baguettes; dinner sees homemade sausages, daily fish specials, and steak tartare. The roast chicken (for two) takes an hour to prepare and is worth every second that you'll wait. Dinner reservations are recommended. ✉ 1933 1st Ave., Downtown ☎ 206/256–1499 ⊕ www. lepichetseattle.com ▬ MC, V ✛ 1:D2.

$$$$ ✕ **Matt's in the Market.** Your first dinner at Matt's is like a first date you
PACIFIC hope will never end. One of the most beloved of Pike Place Market's
NORTHWEST restaurants, Matt's is now owned by Dan Bugge, who continues to
Fodor's Choice value intimate dining, fresh ingredients, and superb service. An expan-
★ sion nearly doubled the number of seats, all the better to enjoy old
favorites—and some new dishes, as well. Perch at the bar for pints and
a delicious pulled pork or hot grilled-tuna sandwich or cup of gumbo,
or be seated at a table—complete with vases filled with flowers from
the market—for a seasonal menu that synthesizes the best picks from
the restaurant's produce vendors and an excellent wine list. At dinner,
starters might include such delectable items as Manila clams steamed
in beer with herbs and chilies; entrées always include at least one catch
of the day—such as whole fish in saffron broth or Alaskan halibut with
pea vines—as well as such delectable entrées as seafood stew, beef short
ribs, or braised lamb shank with ancho chili. Locals and visitors alike
keep this low-key but special spot humming. ✉ 94 Pike St., Suite 32,
Downtown ☎ 206/467–7909 ⊕ www.mattsinthemarket.com ⎙ Reservations essential ▬ MC, V ⊙ Closed Sun. ✛ 1:D3.

$$$ ✕ **Maximilien.** Despite its dramatic views of the Sound and the Olympic
FRENCH Mountains, romantic Maximilien remains a well-kept secret. That's
because it's tucked away in Pike Place Market behind the Market Spice
tea shop and a butcher shop, and it's not easy to find unless you know
the way. Persevere—you'll be delighted. The bistro-style food is quite
good, and the mood is very French. Start with foie gras and then try the
pan-seared Oregon beef tenderloin with mashed potatoes, a white-bean

cassoulet with sausage, salmon baked in puff pastry with goat cheese and spinach, or the fresh fish of the day. Just be sure to save room for *profiteroles au chocolat*. The happy hour here (5 to 7 during the week) is rightfully popular. ✉ *81-A Pike St., Downtown* ☎ *206/682–7270* ⊕ *www.maximilienrestaurant.com* ⊟ *AE, D, DC, MC, V* ✛ *1:D3.*

$$
SEAFOOD
✗ **McCormick's Fish House & Bar.** Evening happy hours (Monday to Friday 3:30–6 and 9:30–11:30) at this restaurant are popular with the after-work crowd; prices are very reasonable (there's a $2 bar menu), and the rotating selection is satisfying—burgers, spring rolls, taquitos, oysters, and more. The dining room specializes in typical steak and seafood fare. The raw bar has a huge selection of oysters; in summer, you can enjoy the bounty in the open-air dining area out front. The food and good times are good enough here that even some chain-hating Seattleites don't mind patronizing the place. Don't expect much in the way of atmosphere; come for the fresh fish. ✉ *722 4th Ave., Downtown* ☎ *206/682–3900* ⊕ *www.mccormickandschmicks.com* ⊟ *AE, D, DC, MC, V* ⊗ *No lunch weekends* ✛ *1:F4.*

$$$$
STEAK HOUSE
✗ **Metropolitan Grill.** This favorite lunch spot of the white-collar crowd is not for timid eaters: custom-aged mesquite-broiled steaks—arguably the best in Seattle—are huge and come with baked potatoes or pasta. Even the veal chop is extra thick. Expertly prepared lamb, chicken, and seafood entrées are also on the menu. The Met's take on a steak house is either "classic" or a caricature, depending on how you take to the cigar-and-cognac vibe: waiters wear tuxes, fixtures are made of brass, the bar is made of black marble, and the crowd is composed of Seattle's relatively small population of movers and shakers. ✉ *820 2nd Ave., Downtown* ☎ *206/624–3287* ⊕ *www.themetropolitangrill.com* ⊟ *AE, D, DC, MC, V* ⊗ *No lunch weekends* ✛ *1:E4.*

$$$$
NEW AMERICAN
✗ **Mistral Kitchen.** Chef William Belickis brought what he learned at New York's Bouley to this chic industrial space, and the results are getting better and better as the restaurant settles into its über-posh digs. Two sections of this large Downtown restaurant—sleekly designed by Tom Kundig—offer separate dining experiences: one is much fancier, while the bar setting has a more approachable and low-key vibe. A hip crowd shows up for good happy-hour deals (and dynamite cocktails, such as the "Arsenic & Old Lace" gin-infused version) in a decidedly stark-swank atmosphere. A diverse, open kitchen churns out interesting results, thanks to a bold mix of technique: conduction electric stovetops are used alongside sous-vide preparations and rustic wood-burning ovens. You can also skip the fire and order hamachi, tuna crudo, and raw oysters. Rabbit loin with foie gras, warm endive salad with a soft-poached egg, seared scallop with sun choke, or tender leg of lamb are all standouts. It may be pricey, but it sure does look and taste good. ✉ *2020 Westlake Ave., Downtown* ☎ *206/623–1922* ⊕ *www.mistral-kitchen.com* ⊟ *D, MC, V* ✛ *1:E2.*

¢–$
COFFEEHOUSE
✗ **Monorail Espresso.** More walk-up coffee window than actual coffeehouse, this is a good spot for a surprisingly good latte when you're shopping Downtown, waiting for the bus to take you up to Capitol Hill, or have just seen one too many Starbucks. A few blocks from the Convention Center, this casual spot frequented by bike messengers also

serves up famous "Chubby" chocolate-chip cookies with a genuine smile. This place deserves its loyal following—Monorail Espresso just turned 30 years old! ⊠ *520 Pike St., Downtown* ☎ *206/625–0449* ⊟ *No credit cards* ✛ *2:D6.*

$$ ✕**The Pink Door.** With its Post Alley
ITALIAN entrance and meager signage, The Pink Door's speakeasy quality draws Pike Place Market regulars almost as much as its savory Italian food does. ■TIP➔ In warm months, outdoor dining in Seattle doesn't get much better than the ample deck

WORD OF MOUTH

"For Italian, two reliable places are Assaggio and Il Terrazzo Carmine, in the Downtown and Pioneer Square areas respectively. Assaggio is noisy and fun, with the host, Mauro, filling the room with an excess of personality. Il Terrazzo is also wonderful (in an alley—not all that easy to find the first time) but more a power-lunch kind of place."   —Gardyloo

here, with its shaded grape arbor and views of Elliott Bay. The roasted garlic and tapenade are eminently shareable appetizers, pappardelle *al ràgu Bolognese* (with slow-simmered meat sauce), linguine *alle vongole* (with fresh baby clams, pancetta, and white wine), and cioppino are standout entrées, though nothing stands too far out—people come here mostly for the atmosphere. The whimsical bar is often crowded, the staff is saucy and irreverent, and cabaret acts regularly perform on a small corner stage. There's no place quite like it. The happy hour on weekdays from 3 to 5 and 10 to closing is festive and worth seeking out. ⊠ *1919 Post Alley, Downtown* ☎ *206/443–3241* ⊕ *www.thepinkdoor. net* ⩾ *Reservations essential* ⊟ *AE, MC, V* ◯ *No lunch Sun.* ✛ *1:D2.*

$$$ ✕**Place Pigalle.** Large windows look out on Elliott Bay in this cozy spot
NEW AMERICAN tucked behind a meat vendor in Pike Place Market's main arcade. In nice weather, open windows let in the fresh salt breeze. Flowers brighten each table, and the staff is warm and welcoming. Despite its name, this restaurant has only a few French flourishes on an otherwise American/Pacific Northwest menu. Go for the rich oyster stew, the sea scallops with rosé champagne beurre blanc, Dungeness crab (in season), poussin with barley risotto, or the fish of the day. Local microbrews are on tap, and the wine list is thoughtfully compact. Sip a Pastis as you gaze out the window. ⊠ *81 Pike St., Downtown* ☎ *206/624–1756* ⊟ *AE, MC, V* ◯ *No dinner Sun.* ✛ *1:D3.*

¢–$ ✕**Stella Caffé.** We love a coffee shop with a glossy bar. Think Rome! This
COFFEEHOUSE warm, inviting brick-exposed spot with expertly pulled espresso (beans are roasted in-house) is close to the Seattle Art Museum on 1st Avenue. ■TIP➔ Look for Seattle Art Museum's Hammering Man statue; Stella is just across the street. You can also order a yummy panino sandwich and enjoy it in the large Diller Room in the back. Free Wi-Fi and exceptionally talented and friendly baristas make this a go-to spot for many Downtown workers and visitors alike. ⊠ *1224 1st Ave., Downtown* ☎ *206/624–1299* ⊕ *www.stellacoffees.com* ⊟ *D, MC, V* ✛ *1:E4.*

$$ ✕**Steelhead Diner.** New Jersey Diner–variety meets Seattle seafood flair—
AMERICAN with an amazing Washington wine menu, to boot. Fresh fish is expertly prepared here, such as olive-crusted Bristol Bay sockeye salmon with spinach. And the fried chicken simply can't be beat. Other fine favorites

include the beef-brisket sandwich, rainbow trout with crispy sage, and "jumbo lump" crab cakes. But blaring music, odd lighting, and touristy crowds may make the steep prices seem less than worth it. It's the price you pay for being right smack in the heart of Pike Place Market. ⊠ *95 Pine St., Downtown* ☎ *206/625–0129* ⊕ *www.steelheaddiner.com* ▤ *D, MC, V* ✚ *1:D2.*

> ### GOOD TO-GO LUNCH
>
> Dahlia's bakery shop (right next to its restaurant) offers up delicious lunches daily: soups, sandwiches, cookies, salads, and espresso beverages are available.

3

BELLTOWN

$$ ╳ **Assaggio Ristorante.** Suited-up Downtown lunch and after-work
ITALIAN crowds love this straightforward Italian eatery for its elegant, white-table-clothed aesthetic; very reliable dishes; extensive (if expensive) wine list; and welcoming, sometime loud, ambience. It's not the super trendy spot that many of its neighbors tend to be, so this bustling, upscale-without-being-overly-uptight eatery is a great spot for a business lunch. Start with tender calamari or prosciutto with fresh melon; the *papparadelle cinghial* (wild boar ragu served over wide, flat noodles) is popular, as is the housemade gnocchi Gorgonzola. Pizzas and salads are also on the menu, as well as a well-executed tiramisu. ⊠ *2010 4th Ave., Belltown* ☎ *206/441–1399* ⊕ *www.assaggioseattle.com* ▤ *D, MC, V* ⊘ *Closed Sun. No weekend lunch* ✚ *1:D1.*

$$$ ╳ **Boat Street Café & Kitchen.** Two rooms decorated in a French bistro–
NEW AMERICAN meets–Nantucket decor have a scattering of casual tables with fresh
Fodor's Choice flowers and candles. Tables often fill up with couples at night, but
★ the lunchtime scene runs the gamut from Downtown office workers to tourists. Food is understated, fresh, and divine: start with raw oysters and a crisp glass of white wine. Next up, sautéed Medjool dates sprinkled with *fleur de sel* and olive oil, a radish salad with pine nuts, or a plate of the famous housemade pickles. Entrées, too, take advantage of whatever is in season, so expect anything from Oregon hanger steak with olive tapenade to spring-onion flan and Alaskan halibut with cauliflower. Though it's housed in the ground floor of an odd office building (just north of the Olympic Sculpture Park), Boat Street positively blooms in the quirky space, and the food and dining experience are memorable and uniquely Seattle. Save room for desserts: wild blackberry clafouti, honey ice cream, and vanilla bean *pot de crème* are just a few toothsome examples. Monday through Sunday, brunch and lunch is served from 10:30 to 2:30. ⊠ *3131 Western Ave., Belltown* ☎ *206/632–4602* ⊕ *www.boatstreetcafe.com* ▤ *D, MC, V* ⊘ *No dinner Sun.–Mon.* ✚ *2:A5.*

$$$–$$$$ ╳ **Dahlia Lounge.** Romantic Dahlia Lounge has the valentine-red walls
PACIFIC and deep booths you may be looking for—it's been working its magic
NORTHWEST on Seattle since 1980, though it does feel to many like the menu hasn't changed since then. It's cozy and then some, but the food plays its part, too: Chef Tom Douglas's famous crab cakes, served as an appetizer or an entrée, lead a regionally oriented menu. Other standouts are the grilled-bread salad with pesto, delicious lamb with smashed English peas, seared ahi tuna, near-perfect gnocchi, and such desserts

as blissful triple-coconut cream pie and fresh doughnuts. ✉ *2001 4th Ave., Belltown* ☎ *206/682–4142* ⊕ *www.tomdouglas.com* ▭ *AE, D, DC, MC, V* ✆ *No lunch weekends* ✛ *1:D1.*

$$$$
STEAK HOUSE

✕ **El Gaucho.** Waistcoated waitstaff coolly navigate the packed floor of this retro steak house serving up satisfying fare in a swanky, expansive room. Flaming lamb shish kebab, double-thick venison chops, King crab legs, crispy seared chicken, and cool Caesar salads (possibly the city's best) all tantalize, but the eatery is best known for perfectly cooked steaks—and the virtuoso presentation seems to make everything taste better. Ritzy yet comfortable, El Gaucho makes you relax no matter how stressful your day. Of course, you may get heart palpitations once again when you see the prices—just sit back, enjoy your luscious cut of meat, and listen to the live piano music. ✉ *2505 1st Ave., Belltown* ☎ *206/728–1337* ⊕ *www.elgaucho.com* ▭ *AE, MC, V* ✆ *No lunch* ✛ *1:B1.*

$$$
MEDITERRANEAN
Fodor'sChoice
★

✕ **Lola.** Tom Douglas dishes out his signature Northwest style, spiked with Greek and Mediterranean touches here—another huge success for the local celebrity chef, if not his best. Try a glorious tagine of goat meat with mustard and rosemary; grape leaf–wrapped trout; lamb burgers with chickpea fries; and scrumptious spreads including hummus, tzatziki, and *harissa* (a red-pepper concoction). Booths are usually full at this bustling, dimly lighted restaurant, which anchors the Hotel Ändra. The fabulous weekend brunches are inventive: try Tom's Big Breakfast—octopus, mustard greens, cumin-spiced yogurt, bacon, and an egg. If you still have room, there are made-to-order doughnuts, too. ✉ *2000 4th Ave., Belltown* ☎ *206/441–1430* ⊕ *www.tomdouglas.com* ▭ *D, MC, V* ✛ *1:D1.*

¢–$
BAKERY

✕ **Macrina Bakery.** One of Seattle's favorite bakeries is also popular for breakfast and brunch. With its perfectly executed breads and pastries—from Nutella brioche and ginger cookies to almond croissants and dark-chocolate sugar-dusted brownies—it has become a true Belltown institution, even if this small spot is usually too frenzied to invite the hours of idleness that other coffee shops may inspire. ■ TIP→ Macrina is an excellent place to take a delicious break on your way to or from the Olympic Sculpture Park. You can also wait for a table and have a larger breakfast or lunch—sandwiches, quiches, and salads are all yummy and fresh. ✉ *2408 1st Ave., Belltown* ☎ *206/448–4032* ⊕ *www.macrinabakery. com* ✛ *1:B1.*

$$
PACIFIC
NORTHWEST

✕ **Palace Kitchen.** The star of this chic yet convivial Tom Douglas eatery (he's also responsible for Dahlia Lounge, Etta's, Lola, and Serious Pie) may be the 45-foot bar, but the real show takes place in the giant open kitchen at the back. Sausages, wood-grilled chicken wings, olive poppers, Penn Cove mussels, roast-pork ravioli, and a nightly selection of cheeses vie for your attention on the ever-changing menu of small plates. There are always a few entrées, mouthwatering desserts, and a rotisserie special from the apple-wood grill—always the best bet here. ✉ *2030 5th*

Ave., Belltown ☎ *206/448–2001* ⊕ *www.tomdouglas.com* ▭ *AE, D, DC, MC, V* ☺ *No lunch* ✢ *1:D1.*

$$$
NEW AMERICAN

✗ **Restaurant Zoë.** Reservations are sought after at this chic eatery on a high-traffic corner. Its tall windows, lively bar scene, and charming waitstaff add to the popularity, which comes mainly from its inspired

kitchen. The talents of chef-owner Scott Staples can be seen in his Painted Hills beef short rib served with roasted potatoes and blue cheese, and his roasted halibut served with English-pea puree and artichoke-butter sauce. Salmon is prepared *sous vide* and accompanied by corn hash. Zoë is a great representative of the kind of fine dining experience that Seattle excels at, wherein a sleek urban space, upscale cooking, and a hip crowd that enjoys people-watching come together to create not a pretentious, overblown, and overpriced spectacle, but a place that is unfailingly laid-back, comfortable, and satisfying. Reservations are recommended. ⊠ *2137 2nd Ave., Belltown* ☎ *206/256–2060* ⊕ *www. restaurantzoe.com* ▭ *AE, D, MC, V* ☺ *No lunch* ✢ *1:C1.*

$$
PIZZA

✗ **Serious Pie.** Seriously yummy artisan pizzas are worth the wait—and you will wait, as this teeny-tiny, hole-in-the-wall Belltown restaurant doesn't take reservations. Tom Douglas (of Etta's, Dahlia Lounge, and Lola) recognized before many others that Seattle was missing a dynamite pizza spot and he delivered: chewy, substantial, buttery crusts anchor such toppings as fresh arugula, *guanciale* (cured pork jowl), and a soft egg; or Meyer lemon, chili, and buffalo mozzarella. Make a true meal of it and start with an elegant bean-and-anchovy salad. Wash it down with a local brew, a glass of local wine, or some bubbly. High seats and communal tables crowd this tiny, loud space, but we find ourselves going back for more, again and again. ⊠ *316 Virginia Ave., Belltown* ☎ *206/838–7388* ⊕ *www.tomdouglas.com* ⊘ *No reservations* ▭ *D, MC, V* ✢ *1:D1.*

$$$
JAPANESE
Fodor's Choice
★

✗ **Shiro's Sushi Restaurant.** Shiro Kashiba is the most famous sushi chef in Seattle; he's been in town for more than 40 years, and he still sometimes takes time to helm the sushi bar at his popular restaurant. ■ TIP➔ **If you get a seat at the sushi bar, in front of Shiro, don't be shy—this is one place where ordering omakase (chef's choice) is a must.** Willfully unconcerned with atmosphere, this simple spot is a real curiosity amid Belltown's chic establishments, though it does seem to be charging Belltown prices for simpler pleasures like teriyaki and tempura dinners. Be forewarned that the place has a reputation for spotty table service. ⊠ *2401 2nd Ave., Belltown* ☎ *206/443–9844* ⊕ *www.shiros.com* ▭ *AE, MC, V* ☺ *No lunch* ✢ *1:C1.*

$$
SPANISH

✗ **Taberna del Alabardero.** Flavorful tapas and Spanish favorites are all the rage at this intimate, warm space in Belltown. Start with a house sangria, then order to your heart's content from the tapas list: mini lamb burgers, Penn Cove mussels with white wine, Serrano ham, a traditional egg "tortilla," and gazpacho. Larger dishes include paella, rack of lamb with rosemary, and grilled duck breast with fried polenta. Happy hour,

Tavolàta

desserts, and brunch all receive very high marks from happy locals—
as does the attentive service. A real slice of Madrid in Belltown—*olé!*
⊠ *2328 1st Ave., Belltown* ☎ *206/448–8884* ⊕ *www.alabardero.com*
⊟ *MC, V* ✛ *1:C1.*

$$ ✕ **Tavolàta.** This Belltown favorite is helmed by superstar-chef Ethan
ITALIAN Stowell (also of Anchovies & Olives and How to Cook a Wolf). Serving
up Italian goodness by the plateful in an industrial-chic bi-level space,
Tavolàta is a decidedly lively, loud, and delicious night out on the town.
Skinny-jeaned young things mingle with families here—and everyone
has fun. The long bar serves up simple, elegant cocktails (Campari or
Cynar with soda never fails). Start with a chickpea salad, buffalo moz-
zarella, or chilled heirloom tomato soup. Homemade pasta is the main
draw here, such as fresh campanelle with mussels, squash, preserved
lemon and pesto, or linguine with clams, garlic, and chili. Meat offer-
ings are traditional with flair: pork chop is vivified with currants and
grilled radicchio; fresh halibut is poached in olive oil with escarole
and mushrooms. ⊠ *2323 2nd Ave., Belltown* ☎ *206/838–8008* ⊕ *www.*
tavolata.com ⊟ *D, MC, V* ✛ *1:C1.*

SEATTLE CENTER, SOUTH LAKE UNION, AND QUEEN ANNE

The areas north of Downtown and Belltown are poised on the brink
of becoming culinary destinations. You certainly won't go hungry after
rocking out at the Experience Music Project, ascending the Space Nee-
dle, or shopping at the REI megastore. This is a very large area, so keep
that in mind when you're planning your mealtimes. On Queen Anne,
friendly neighborhood haunts are the norm, but a few standouts, such as

How to Cook a Wolf and destination-restaurant Canlis, up the ante. South Lake Union is still in transition from industrial neighborhood to rising star, with a few dynamite selections on a roster that's sure to grow with the neighborhood.

SOUTH LAKE UNION

$ ✕ **Feierabend.** There still isn't much
GERMAN in the South Lake Union neighborhood in terms of restaurants, but that's changing. This German pub is an exception, though, and it's a fun spot after you've had your fill of tents, tarps, hiking boots, canteens, and snow axes at the nearby REI superstore. How about a cold beer? Spaten pils, Dunkel weisse, Munich lager, and Kostritzer come in enormous steins—but be sure to also sample regional food, such as bratwurst with sauerkraut, pork schnitzel, and housemade spätzle topped with cheese. ✉ *422 Yale Ave. N, South Lake Union* ☎ *206/340–2528* ⊕ *www.feierabendseattle.com* ▭ *MC, V* ✛ *2:E4.*

$$$–$$$$ ✕ **Flying Fish.** Chef-owner Christine Keff got the idea for Flying Fish on
SEAFOOD a trip to Thailand; she was impressed by the simplicity and quality of the seafood dishes grilled up in beachside restaurants. Even after almost 15 years, Flying Fish has stayed true to its inspiration: the fish is some of the freshest you'll find in Seattle, every ingredient is organic, and the dishes, while inventive, never get too busy. The menu changes daily, but you'll often find seafood and shellfish prepared with Thai curries and seasonings, and you'll always have the option of the delicious no-nonsense fried chicken. This joint is always jumping; dinner reservations are strongly recommended. ✉ *300 Westlake Ave. N, South Lake Union* ☎ *206/728–8595* ⊕ *www.flyingfishrestaurant.com* ▭ *AE, DC, MC, V* ⊙ *No lunch weekends* ✛ *2:D5.*

$$$ ✕ **Seastar Restaurant and Raw Bar.** Nestled in the Pan Pacific Hotel com-
SEAFOOD plex on the southern edge of South Lake Union, this sleek and spacious restaurant is known for its extensive happy hour. The raw bar features sushi and such delicacies as Thai seafood salad, giant black tiger prawns, ceviche, and a Northwest oyster sampler. Delicious tempura rolls, hamburger sliders, and cedar-plank salmon are all popular. Order a chilled white wine and get comfortable in a well-spaced booth. ✉ *2121 Terry Ave., South Lake Union* ☎ *206/462–4364* ⊕ *www.seastarrestaurant. com* ▭ *AE, MC, V* ⊙ *No lunch weekends* ✛ *2:D5.*

$ ✕ **Tutta Bella Neapolitan Pizzeria.** An extensive menu of freshly prepared,
PIZZA satisfying pizzas keeps visitors, locals, families, and couples alike com-
ⓒ ing back to this sophisticated space in a mall-like complex that also houses the Pan Pacific Hotel and an enormous Whole Foods. Authentic Neapolitan-style pizzas are made in a wood-fired oven; deliciously fresh salads and a good wine selection round out the meal. Takeout is available, but many people opt to enjoy this spacious eatery, which has decent views of the surrounding up-and-coming neighborhood of South Lake Union, and nearby Space Needle, too. Happy hour here is

> **GOOD FOR TO-GO LUNCH**
>
> A huge **Whole Foods Market** (✉ *2210 Westlake Ave.* ☎ *206/621–9700*) dominates the Pan Pacific Hotel complex at Westlake and Denny: premade sandwiches, soups, sushi, and the like are available to go.

3

fun and a great deal, with drink specials and happy-hour nibbles for $2 to $6—and Margherita pizza for $6 (Monday to Friday, 3–6). ✉ *2200 Westlake Ave., Suite 112, South Lake Union* ☎ *206/624–4422* ⊕ *www. tuttabella.com* ⊟ *AE, DC, MC, V* ✛ *2:D5.*

¢   ✕ **Vivace Espresso.** A cozy and large outpost of this famed Capitol Hill
COFFEEHOUSE   roaster, the Vivace coffee shrine in South Lake Union is housed right across from the REI megastore and amidst a growing number of hip boutiques and design shops. Grab a seat, order an expertly prepared espresso beverage, and munch on a small variety of snacks—this is a perfect stop after an exhausting jaunt through REI before you head to the next adventure. ✉ *227 Yale Ave. N, South Lake Union* ☎ *206/388–5164* ⊕ *www.espressovivace.com* ⊟ *AE, MC, V* ✛ *2:E5.*

QUEEN ANNE

$$$$ ✕ **Canlis.** Canlis has been setting the standard for opulent dining in
PACIFIC   Seattle since the 1950s. And although there are no longer kimono-
NORTHWEST   clad waitresses, the food and the views overlooking Lake Union are still remarkable. Executive chef Jason Franey (formerly of Manhattan's acclaimed Eleven Madison Park) has retained the restaurant's signature insistence on the finest cuts of meat and the freshest produce. To start, try fresh braised veal cheek with lemon confit, fresh carrot soup, foie gras terrine, or a Dungeness crab cake with Granny Smith apple. The famous Canlis Salad boasts romaine, bacon, Romano cheese, and mint, in a dressing of fresh lemon, olive oil, and coddled egg—always a crowd-pleaser. But the entrées are the stars here: King salmon with lentils, Muscovy duck with hedgehog mushrooms, and Wagyu tenderloin served atop shallots and potatoes. ■ **TIP→ The only way to wash this divine food down is with a bottle from one of the finest—if not the finest— wine cellars in town.** A banana-spiked *mille-feuille* or a "chocolate covered chocolate" molten creation should send you on your way happily. Canlis never fails to feel like a special-occasion splurge—make reservations well in advance, and request a table with a view. ✉ *2576 Aurora Ave. N, Queen Anne* ☎ *206/283–3313* ⊕ *www.canlis.com* ⌕ *Reservations essential; jacket required* ⊟ *AE, DC, MC, V* ☾ *Closed Sun. No lunch* ✛ *3:E6.*

$$ ✕ **Crow.** Inhabiting a converted warehouse space complete with art-
NEW AMERICAN   fully exposed ductwork, a modern comfort-food menu, and a list of shareable small plates, Crow feels very of-the-moment in Seattle. But this bistro has proved it has staying power and has become a Queen Anne institution. The food is the main component of locals' loyalty; share some appetizers and then move on to the pan-roasted chicken wrapped in prosciutto, portabella mushroom risotto, or the wonderful house lasagna with Italian sausage. Satisfy your sweet tooth with lavender crème brulée. Service is good, even on busy nights. ✉ *823 5th Ave. N, Queen Anne* ☎ *206/283–8800* ⊕ *www.eatatcrow.com* ⊟ *MC, V* ☾ *No lunch* ✛ *2:B4.*

¢   ✕ **El Diablo Coffee Co.** El Diablo is a Latin coffeehouse that serves Cuban-
COFFEEHOUSE   style coffee and delicious, authentic Mexican hot chocolate. If you don't want coffee, you can get a *batido*, a Cuban shake made with fresh fruit. El Diablo's interior is splashed with bright yellows, reds, blues, and purples, and most surfaces are covered with murals. It's a bit loud,

both in appearance and in noise level—but it's fun and certainly unique among Seattle's java stops. El Diablo is open late (until 11 on Friday and Saturday) and has live music several nights a week. ✉ *1811 Queen Anne Ave. N, Queen Anne* ☏ *206/285–0693* ⊕ *www.eldiablocoffee. com* ▭ *MC, V* ⊕ *2:A2.*

$$–$$$ ✕ **How to Cook a Wolf.** This sleek eatery—complete with curving-wood
ITALIAN ceiling and loads of trendy young couples perched at its tables—"pays homage to MFK Fisher and her philosophy of taking simple ingredients and transforming them into culinary splendor." Fresh, artisanal ingredients are the major draws, with starters such as cured-meat platters, roasted almonds, pork terrine, chicken-liver mousse, and arugula salad, and tasty main dishes focused on handmade pastas—the *casarecce* features bacon, onion, and black pepper. Fresh skate with brown butter and capers or quail with saffron aioli are examples of the rustic-chic Italian-inspired dishes chef Ethan Stowell has perfected in his various eateries around town. This restaurant is worth the trip even if you're far from Queen Anne. ✉ *2208 Queen Anne Ave. N, Queen Anne* ☏ *206/838–8090* ⊕ *www.howtocookawolf.com* ▭ *MC, V* ⊕ *2:A1.*

PIONEER SQUARE

Pioneer Square isn't the culinary destination that its neighbors International District and Downtown are. That said, there are some quirky and reliable lunch spots here, as well as some top-notch, authentic coffeehouses. There are also several old-school Italian eateries that Seattle locals still love, especially Carmine's.

¢ ✕ **Grand Central Bakery.** Housed in one of Pioneer Square's beautiful
BAKERY/DELI old redbrick buildings, Grand Central has been churning out loaves of fragrant bread, sandwiches, soups, and cinnamon rolls to Seattleites for decades. The spring chicken salad sandwich is loaded with house-roasted chicken, fresh herbs, asparagus, and lettuce on potato bread; the grilled ham and cheese comes with sweet mustard on delicious marbled rye. This is a fun stop before an afternoon of touring the area's art galleries, but be sure to grab a cinnamon roll or triple-chocolate cookie for the road. ✉ *214 1st Ave. S, Pioneer Square* ☏ *206/622–3644* ⊕ *www. grandcentralbakery.com* ▭ *DC, MC, V* ⊕ *1:E5.*

$$$ ✕ **Il Terrazzo Carmine.** Ceiling-to-floor draperies lend the dining room
ITALIAN understated dignity, and intoxicating aromas waft from the kitchen. Seattleites still love this Pioneer Square institution and flock here for special-occasion lunches, especially. The chef blends Tuscan-style and regional southern Italian cooking to create soul-satisfying dishes such as veal osso buco, homemade ravioli, linguine alle vongole, and roast duck with wild cherry sauce. Reservations are recommended. ✉ *411 1st Ave. S, Pioneer Square* ☏ *206/467–7797* ⊕ *www.ilterrazzocarmine.com* ▭ *AE, D, DC, MC, V* ⊗ *Closed Sun. No lunch Sat.* ⊕ *1:E6.*

$ ✕ **Salumi.** The chef-owner Armandino Batali (father of famed New
ITALIAN York chef Mario Batali) makes superior cured meats for this miniature
Fodor's Choice lunch spot run by his daughter, who serves up hearty, unforgettable
★ sandwiches filled with all sorts of goodies. Order a salami, bresaola, porchetta, meatball, oxtail, sausage, or lamb prosciutto sandwich with

onions, peppers, cheese, and olive oil. Most people do opt for takeout, though; be prepared for a long line, which most likely will be stretching well beyond the front door. ■TIP→ Note that Salumi is open only Tuesday–Friday from 11 AM to 4 PM. ✉ *309 3rd Ave. S, Pioneer Square* ☎ *206/621–8772* ⊕ *www.salumicuredmeats.com* ➡ *AE, D, DC, MC, V* ☾ *Closed Sat.–Mon.* ✛ *1:F5.*

¢   ✗ **Tat's East Coast Delicatessen.** Cheesesteaks, chop salads, chicken strips,
DELI   buffalo wings, egg-salad sandwiches, and hot roast beef are just a few of the many popular items on this weekday-only lunch menu. Lines form for their hoagies, and game days for the Sounders bring out even more lines, but it's all good fun. Where else in Seattle can you get an authentic East Coast–style sub or cheesesteak piled high with all the fixins? ✉ *159 Yesler Way, Pioneer Square* ☎ *206/264–8287* ⊕ *www. tatsdeli.com* ➡ *MC, V* ☾ *Closed Sun.* ✛ *1:F5.*

¢–$ ✗ **Zeitgeist Coffee.** Not only is Zeitgeist one of the best coffee shops in
COFFEEHOUSE   the southern part of the city, it is also a colorful local favorite. Even Seattleites who don't haunt Pioneer Square will happily hunt for parking to spend a few hours here. Housed in one of Pioneer Square's great brick buildings, with high ceilings and a few artfully exposed ducts and pipes, Zeitgeist has a simple, classy look that's the perfect backdrop for the frequent art shows held here. You'll feel smarter just sitting in here while you watch the parade of gallery-goers, locals, tourists, and Pioneer Square characters pass through. Plus, the sandwiches and pastries rival the fantastic espresso beverages. ✉ *171 S. Jackson St., Pioneer Square* ☎ *206/583–0497* ⊕ *www.zeitgeistcoffee.com* ✛ *1:F6.*

INTERNATIONAL DISTRICT

A favorite culinary destination for its many varied Asian restaurants— from dim sum palaces to hole-in-the-wall noodle shops, the International District (I.D.) is also coming into its own as a cultural destination. The Uwajimaya superstore and the Wing Luke Museum both warrant a visit before you settle in for an amazing—and spicy—meal here.

¢–$ ✗ **Green Leaf.** Locals pack this friendly café for an expansive menu of
VIETNAMESE   fresh, well-prepared Vietnamese staples. The quality of the food—the *pho*, spring rolls, *báhn xèo* (the Vietnamese version of an omelet), and lemongrass chicken are just a few standouts—and reasonable prices would be enough to make it an instant I.D. favorite. But Green Leaf also proves you don't have to sacrifice ambience to get cheap, authentic Asian food in Seattle: the walls are painted a soft yellow; you'll find bamboo embellishments on lighting fixtures, tables, and chairs; and instead of glaring fluorescents, you'll get dim mood lighting in the evening. The staff greets everyone as though they're regulars. And there are plenty of regulars, enough to fill the small space, so reservations for dinner are recommended. ✉ *418 8th Ave. S, International District* ☎ *206/340–1388* ⊕ *www.greenleaftaste.com* ➡ *MC, V* ✛ *1:H6.*

$ ✗ **Jade Garden.** Dim sum enthusiasts, take note: this is the spot in the
DIM SUM   I.D. for spongy BBQ pork buns, walnut shrimp, chive dumplings, congee, and sticky rice. There's no doubt that the waits are long and the atmosphere is lacking, but when you are craving dim sum, this is the

place to go. Avoid the mad rush at lunchtime and go to the Wing Luke museum while everyone else is eating, then try for a table closer to 2 PM. ⊠ *704 S. King St., International District* ☎ *206/622–8181* ▤ *MC, V* ✛ *1:E1.*

$ ✕ **Malay Satay Hut.** Grilled flat breads, called *roti canai* (unstuffed) and
MALAYSIAN *roti relur* (stuffed with egg, green onion, and red pepper), are a specialty here. The roti are served with a curry dipping sauce studded with chunks of chicken and potato. Other menu favorites include Buddhist Yam Pot (scallops and prawns served in a ring of cooked shredded yam), Belachan string beans (string beans and prawns tossed in a spicy sauce), mango chicken, any of the curries, and the banana pancakes. ⊠ *212 12th Ave. S, International District* ☎ *206/324–4091* ⊕ *www. malaysatayhut.com* ▤ *MC, V* ✛ *1:H6.*

$ ✕ **Maneki.** The oldest Japanese restaurant in Seattle, Maneki is no longer
JAPANESE a hidden gem that caters to in-the-know locals and chefs from other Japanese restaurants in the area, but the food isn't any less authentic. Though the restaurant serves decent sushi, its better known for its home-style Japanese, which can be ordered as small plates—often enjoyed with copious amounts of sake. Try the miso black cod collar, a rice bowl with your choice of meat and greens, and any of the delicious daily fish specials. Rice-paper lamps and screens add a little bit of old Japan to the otherwise uninspiring space. Larger parties can reserve a tatami room. Maneki is a mob scene on weekends—so don't even think about coming here without a reservation. ⊠ *304 6th Ave. S, International District* ☎ *206/622–2631* ⊕ *www.manekirestaurant.com* ▤ *V* ⊙ *Closed Mon. No lunch* ✛ *1:G6.*

¢ ✕ **Panama Hotel Tea and Coffee Shop.** On the ground floor of the historic
TEAHOUSE Panama Hotel is a serene teahouse with tons of personality and a subtle Asian flair that reflects its former life as a Japanese bathhouse. The space is lovely, with exposed-brick walls, shiny, hardwood floors, and black-and-white photos of old Seattle (many of them relating to the history of the city's Japanese immigrants). Kick back with an individual pot of tea—there are dozens of varieties—or an espresso. This is a good place to bring a book, as it's usually calm and quiet. ⊠ *607 S. Main St., International District* ☎ *206/515–4000* ⊕ *www.panamahotelseattle. com/teahouse.htm* ▤ *No credit cards* ✛ *1:G5.*

¢ ✕ **Samurai Noodle.** A teeny-tiny space on the outside area of the Uwa-
JAPANESE jimaya superstore, Samurai is definitely worth seeking out for its large bowls of authentic Japanese ramen soup, many of which are super-spicy and come served with a slice of tender pork and a hard-boiled egg. Try the spicy Chili Green Onion variety, which is deep red and flavorful. ■ TIP➡ Waits can be excruciatingly long during the workweek, so try to arrive early (11:30) or after the lunch crowds. ⊠ *606 5th Ave. S, International District* ☎ *206/624–9321* ▤ *MC, V* ⊙ *Dinner served until 8:15 PM* ✛ *1:G6.*

¢ ✕ **Sichuanese Cuisine.** For cheap and greasy but oh-so-good Szechuan
CHINESE cooking, head to this hole-in-the-wall in the Asian Plaza strip mall east of I–5. The atmosphere is forgettable, and the surroundings are downright shabby, but the service is friendly, and this is just about as authentic as it gets. Dry-cooked string beans (available with a variety of

meats), Kung Pao chicken, delicious dumplings, spicy Sichuanese ravioli, and the *ma po tofu* (a spicy combination of tofu and minced pork) are favorites; the sizzling hot pot is popular and good, but whether it's the best in town is still passionately debated. ⌧ *1048 S. Jackson St., International District* ☎ *206/720–1690* ⊕ *sichuan.cwok.com* ⊟ *AE, MC, V* ✣ *1:H6.*

$ ✕ **Tamarind Tree.** Wildly popular with savvy diners from across the city,
VIETNAMESE this Vietnamese haunt on the eastern side of the I.D. *really* doesn't look like much from the outside: you'll enter through a grungy parking lot (which it shares with Sichuanese Cuisine restaurant). But once you're inside, a simple, large, and warm space welcomes you. The food is the real draw—try the Tamarind Tree spring rolls, which are stuffed with fresh herbs, fried tofu, peanuts, coconut, jicama, and carrots; authentic *bánh xèo*; spicy, authentic pho; various satisfying rice-and-chicken dishes; spicy-beef noodle soup; and, to finish, grilled banana cake with warm coconut milk. Service is attentive, but the waits can be long, even with reservations—proof that Seattleites have indeed discovered this festive spot. ⌧ *1036 S. Jackson St., International District* ☎ *206/860–1404* ⊕ *www.tamarindtreerestaurant.com* ⌲ *Reservations essential* ⊟ *MC, V* ✣ *1:H6.*

$ ✕ **Uwajimaya Village Food Court.** Not only an outstanding grocery and
ASIAN gift shop, Uwajimaya also has a hoppin' food court offering a quick tour of Asian cuisines at lunch-counter prices. For Japanese or Chinese, the deli offers sushi, teriyaki, and barbecued duck. For Vietnamese food, try the fresh spring rolls, served with hot chili sauce, at Saigon Bistro. Shilla has Korean grilled beef and *kimchi* stew, and there are Filipino *lumpia* (spring rolls) to be found at Inay's Kitchen. Finish your meal with some cream puffs at Beard Papa's or simply stroll the aisles in Uwajimaya to find fun snacks like rice candy, gummy delicacies, and mochi ice cream. ⌧ *600 5th Ave. S, International District* ☎ *206/624–6248* ⊟ *MC, V* ✣ *1:G6.*

CAPITOL HILL

Capitol Hill has become Seattle's major culinary destination. The greatest concentration of restaurants is in and around the Pike–Pine Corridor—Pike and Pine streets running from Melrose Avenue to 15th Avenue. Gastropub food served up in über-hip spaces at Quinn's, Smith, and Oddfellows is all the rage, as are smaller, posh New American and Italian-inspired eateries like Lark, Anchovies & Olives, and Cascina Spinasse. On the northern end of Broadway, Poppy is a delicious departure from standard menus, with its Indian-inspired *thali* (small amounts of different dish preparations served in small compartments on a large platter), while a wide variety of coffeehouses make the Hill downright destination-worthy. Chef Jason Wilson of local darling Crush won a 2010 James Beard Awards for "Best Chef Northwest."

$$$ ✕ **Anchovies & Olives.** A sleek, sophisticated space serves an equally posh
SEAFOOD clientele. An utterly exposed, simple kitchen set-up anchors this spot
Fodor's Choice in the ground floor of a residential high-rise at the eastern end of the
★ Pike–Pine Corridor. The food at this Ethan Stowell eatery is downright tantalizing, and the young line chefs and waitstaff are charming.

Anchovies & Olives

Modern bent-wood wall coverings, artful lighting, a well-edited Italian wine list, and a lively small bar create the backdrop for some of the best, and most elegant, seafood dishes in the city, including mackerel with cauliflower and radicchio; skate wing with asparagus and saffron leeks; clams with pine nuts and hot pepper; and octopus with corona beans and fennel. Seafood is lovingly prepared and never overdone: the inherent texture and flavor of each fresh piece of fish is respected, and the Mediterranean-inspired garnishes, sauces, and accompaniments that go with them are nothing if not graceful. A small *crudo* selection and salads such as golden beets with almonds and endive will get the meal started. Plates are smaller and are easily shared. A tiny selection of desserts is equally sublime. Reservations are highly recommended. ⊠ *1550 15th Ave., at Pine St., Capitol Hill* ☎ *206/838–8080* ⊕ *www. anchoviesandolives.com* ⊟ *AE, MC, V* ✛ *2:H6.*

$ ✕ **Baguette Box.** A short walk up the hill from Downtown, perched
DELI on the western edge of Capitol Hill, this relaxed lunch (or early-dinner) spot serves Vietnamese-inspired sandwiches on crusty baguettes. You can eat at one of the simple tables here or take your meal to go. ■ TIP➜ This is one of our favorite casual lunch options on Capitol Hill, especially if you're making your way to the Hill on foot after a morning Downtown. Simply start walking up Pine Street—Baguette Box will be on the right-hand side after you cross over I–5. Standout sandwiches include roasted leg of lamb with cucumber yogurt; habit-forming crispy drunken chicken with tangy sauce; braised Berkshire pork belly; and grilled Asian eggplant with feta cheese and tomato. Truffle fries are also fantastic. Its big-sister restaurant, Monsoon, is also divine. ⊠ *1203 Pine*

St., Capitol Hill ☎ *206/332–0220* ⊕ *www.baguettebox.com* ⊘ *Closes at 8 PM* ▭ *AE, MC, V* ✛ *2:E6.*

$ ✕ **Barrio.** This festive Mexican eatery is perfect if you're looking for a
MEXICAN strong cocktail and some tasty Mexican nibbles—such as chips with dynamite salsa, smoky pork-shoulder tacos, or roasted poblano quesadillas. The Mexican chop-chop salad is also a huge hit. Barrio is nestled in the trendy Pike–Pine Corridor. The food isn't transcendent, but the hip (if noisy) ambience, attentive service, and more than 200 candles hand-lit every night make for a cool scene. Wash it all down with a salted-rim margarita—and top it off with homemade churros. Barrio serves lunch, weekend brunch, and "half-off Tequila" on Mondays. Hit up the very popular happy hour from 3 to 6 PM. ✉ *1420 12th Ave., Capitol Hill* ☎ *206/588–8105* ⊕ *www.barriorestaurant.com* ▭ *AE, MC, V* ✛ *2:G6.*

¢ ✕ **Bauhaus Books and Coffee.** This is a wonderful place to people-watch—
COFFEEHOUSE from punk rockers to hip moms to professors—while you enjoy a delectable espresso beverage and perhaps a Ding Dong (a signature item here) or a pastry. Scenesters aside, the coffee's great, the baristas are pleasant, and the airy, bi-level space is big enough that you won't have to fight for room. The bookshelf-lined walls (which are chock-full of art and architecture books) make the interior of this café more interesting than most. ✉ *301 E. Pine St., Capitol Hill* ☎ *206/625–1600* ⊕ *www. bauhauscoffee.net* ▭ *AE, MC, V* ✛ *2:E6.*

$–$$ ✕ **Boom Noodle.** Long family-style tables, modern-graphic decor, tall
ASIAN ceilings, and casual service set the scene at this Asian eatery in the Pike-Pine Corridor. Expect quick service and good, spicy food, not a romantic experience. Ingredients are fresh and bright, and the quality is consistently high. Deep bowls of steaming soup are all the rage, including Tokyo ramen with braised pork, tamago, and bamboo shoots; and spicy beef udon with mushrooms and sprouts. The Vietnamese rice noodle salad comes with grilled pork, crispy shallots, and flavorful fresh herbs; a mochi trio is a lovely way to end the meal. ✉ *1121 E. Pike St., Capitol Hill* ☎ *206/701–9130* ⊕ *www.boomnoodle.com* ▭ *AE, MC, V* ✛ *2:G6.*

$$ ✕ **Café Flora.** This sweet, off-the-beaten-path (from Capitol Hill) restau-
VEGETARIAN rant offers vegetarian and vegan food for grown-ups who want more
⏲ than grilled tofu. The menu changes frequently, though the chefs tend to keep things simple, offering dishes like black-bean burgers with spicy aioli, polenta with leeks and spinach, and the very popular "Oaxaca tacos" (corn tortillas filled with potatoes and four types of cheese) at both lunch and dinner. Request a table in the Atrium, which has a stone fountain, skylight, slate floors, and garden-style café tables and chairs. Brunch is very popular, too—try the fantastic waffles served with fresh seasonal fruits, hoppin' john fritters, and the addictive cheesy grits—but the scene can get a bit hectic with the mass of families. This spot is a short walk or cab ride down Madison Street from the top of Capitol Hill, toward Lake Washington. ✉ *2901 E. Madison St., Capitol Hill* ☎ *206/325–9100* ⊕ *www.cafeflora.com* ▭ *MC, V* ✛ *2:H5.*

$$ ✕ **Café Presse.** Two distinct rooms create plenty of space in this French
FRENCH bistro just off the Pike–Pine Corridor, where you can get such Parisian

Cascina Spinasse

grub as pressed chicken with greens; a *croque madame*; *moules frites* (mussels with french fries); pan-roasted quail with sautéed potatoes and apples; and simple cheese platters with slices of baguette. This is the spot to order some red table wine and people-watch. Come weekend, a popular brunch keeps things lively. A quirky, low-key vibe pervades this beloved Capitol Hill haunt, thanks in part to Seattle University, which is just steps away. ✉ *1117 12th Ave., Capitol Hill* ☎ *206/709–7674* ⊕ *www.cafepresseseattle.com* ▭ *AE, MC, V* ✛ *2:G6.*

¢ ✕ **Caffè Vita.** Though now a certifiable mini-chain (with locations in
COFFEEHOUSE Fremont, Queen Anne, Pioneer Square, and Seward Park—check their Web site for more details), Caffè Vita's roasting operations, and indeed its heart and soul, are located right in Capitol Hill's Pike–Pine Corridor. The super-savvy owner also owns Via Tribunali pizzeria and several other hot locales on Capitol Hill—and there's no doubt he knows how to tap into that gritty Seattle energy. This flagship coffee shop—with its friendly, tattooed baristas; local artwork; dog-walking regulars; and laptop-toting freelance crowd sipping on Americanos—has everything a Seattle coffee shop should, plus dynamite coffee (roasted on-site; take a peek through the doors in the back), pastries, and yummy pressed sandwiches. ✉ *1005 E. Pike St., Capitol Hill* ☎ *206/709–4440* ⊕ *www. caffevita.com* ▭ *AE, MC, V* ✛ *2:G6.*

$$$ ✕ **Cascina Spinasse.** A postage stamp–size eatery with cream-colored
ITALIAN lace curtains and true Italian soul has bar seating and communal tables.
Fodor's Choice Squeeze in, and come hungry, because chef Jason Stratton knows how
★ to make pasta. It's made fresh daily and comes with such sauces and fillings as lamb or rabbit ragu, roasted carrot and goat cheese, or duck confit. Brussels sprouts and kale are vivified with pine nuts and aged

balsamic; the melt-in-your-mouth gnocchi nearly floats off the plate. *Secondi* options can range from braised pork belly with cabbage to stewed venison served over polenta. The dessert selections are lovely; two favorites are *panna cotta* with cardoon flower honey and delectable *gianduja* semifreddo. With the friendly service and dynamite grappa, amaro, and wine selection, you likely won't mind paying the price, even if it is loud and small. It's a night on the town to remember, and a perfect way to experience Capitol Hill's flourishing restaurant scene. ⊠ *1531 14th Ave., Capitol Hill* ☎ *206/251–7673* ⊕ *www.spinasse.com* ⊟ *AE, MC, V* ⊙ *No lunch* ✢ *2:G6*.

$$$–$$$$

NEW AMERICAN

✕ **Crush.** Chef Jason Wilson added a respectable feather to his cap in 2010, when he won a James Beard award for Best Chef Northwest. Occupying a converted two-story house (with dining rooms on both levels), with a sleek beige-and-brown palette and mod 1960s gleaming-white chairs, Crush may convince you that you're Downtown, not on the southeastern edge of Capitol Hill. The food is always very tasty (and often sublime): braised short ribs are Crush's signature dish, and they're so good that the menu could begin and end right there. However, seafood dishes are also superbly executed, such as crusted Neah Bay black cod with Wagyu beef broth and salsify. Start the meal with crispy sautéed veal sweetbreads or roasted beet salad with chevre. The desserts—such as lemon olive oil cake, housemade doughnuts with berry sauce, or molten chocolate cake—are very ambitious and sometimes quite good. The place doesn't seem to have one particular demographic—you'll see gourmands, couples, local families, Capitol Hill hipsters, and more. Despite the clamor for a table on the weekend, friendly servers remain serene and you'll never be rushed out the door. ⊠ *2319 E. Madison St., Madison Park* ☎ *206/302–7874* ⊕ *www.chefjasonwilson.com* ⌫ *Reservations essential* ⊟ *AE, MC, V* ⊙ *Closed Mon. No lunch* ✢ *2:H5*.

¢

BURGERS

✕ **Dick's Drive-In.** This local chain of hamburger drive-ins with iconic orange signage has changed little since the 1950s. The fries are hand-cut, the shakes are hand-dipped (made with hard ice cream), and the burgers hit the spot on a late weekend night. The most popular burger, Dick's Deluxe ($2.50), has two beef patties, American cheese, lettuce, and onions, and is slathered in their special tartar sauce, but many folks swear by the frill-free plain cheeseburger ($1.40). Open until 2 AM daily, these drive-ins are particularly popular among students and late-night bar-hoppers. The original Dick's is the Wallingford branch, but the Capitol Hill one is more of a local landmark. ⊠ *115 Broadway E, Capitol Hill* ☎ *206/323–1300* ⊕ *www.ddir.com* ⊟ *No credit cards* ✢ *2:F5*.

$$

NEW AMERICAN

✕ **Dinette.** Dinette's main claim to fame is fancy toast, which is served up with anything from radishes and egg salad to smoked salmon with herbed mascarpone or rapini pesto with salami. Larger dishes include clams with chorizo, Alaskan halibut with tomato-fennel broth, gnocchi, and daily seafood specials. A focus on seasonal ingredients means that the menu offerings change regularly but they're often mouthwatering. The space, on the western edge of Capitol Hill, just up from South Lake Union, couldn't be cozier. Dimly lighted but not dark and brooding, Dinette is all soft blues and creams and gold-foil details. Hip couples fill the space on weekends before heading out to nearby clubs. ⊠ *1514*

E. Olive Way, Capitol Hill ☎ *206/328–2282* ⊕ *www.dinetteseattle.com* ⌂ *Reservations not accepted* ═ *MC, V* ⊘ *Closed Sun. and Mon. No lunch* ⊹ *2:F5.*

$$$ ✕ **Harvest Vine.** A tiny tapas-and-wine bar close to Capitol Hill, Harvest
SPANISH Vine has limited seating (they hold only a few tables each night for reservations), so you might be waiting a while when you get here. Try to arrive early for a perch at the upstairs kitchen-side bar, because the downstairs room isn't nearly as atmospheric. Regulars have grumbled lately over changes in the quality after a management shake-up, but this sweet spot remains a cheerful place to enjoy often-delicious Basque tapas, including chorizo with grilled bread, pan-seared tuna belly with vanilla bean–infused oil, grilled sardines, or duck confit. There is an impressive wine and sherry list that focuses on Basque-region wines. Come early to score a table outside in summer. ⊠ *2701 E. Madison St., Capitol Hill* ☎ *206/320–9771* ⊕ *www.harvestvine.com* ═ *MC, V* ⊘ *No lunch* ⊹ *2:H5.*

$$$–$$$$ ✕ **Lark.** Just off the Pike–Pine Corridor in a converted garage with
NEW AMERICAN exposed beams and gauzy curtain dividers, Lark was one of the first
Fodor'sChoice restaurants to kick-start the small-plate trend in Seattle. And small
★ plates often don't feel like enough, as the food is so mouth-wateringly delicious—the idea is to order several and enjoy to your heart's content. You can always order more, and the expert servers can help you choose from an impressive wine list, and will happily offer up their opinions of the long menu, which is divided into cheese; vegetables and grains; charcuterie; fish; meat; and, of course, dessert. Seasonally inspired dishes include chicken-liver parfait with grilled ramps; pork rillettes with bright radishes; carpaccio of yellowtail with preserved lemons; veal sweetbreads with black truffle; and poached organic egg with chorizo. For dessert try the Theo-chocolate madeleines (lots of them!), which come wrapped in a white napkin with a small pot of dipping chocolate. ■ TIP➔ Reservations are recommended; if you do have to wait for a table, hop next door to Licorous (which also serves an abbreviated menu) for a distinctly cool libation. ⊠ *926 12th Ave., Capitol Hill* ☎ *206/323–5275* ⊕ *www.larkseattle.com* ═ *MC, V AE* ⊹ *2:G6.*

$$ ✕ **Monsoon.** A small, serene space decorated with simple woven hats
VIETNAMESE hanging graphically on a bright wall and black-and-white photographs, Monsoon serves delicious, upscale Vietnamese food to happy Capitol Hill locals—but you should definitely make the short trek here. Favorites, blending Vietnamese and Pacific Northwest elements, include wild gulf prawns with lemongrass, catfish clay pot with fresh coconut juice and green onion, and lamb with fermented soybeans and sweet onions. Homemade ice creams include lychee and mango, but the restaurant's most famous dessert is the coconut crème caramel. The wine cellar has nearly 250 varieties, including many French selections. Reservations are recommended. ■ TIP➔ The weekend brunch—which serves traditional Vietnamese offerings, dim sum, and "colonial" favorites like French toast and eggs en cocotte—is divine, elegant, and more than worth the trip to this tree-lined residential stretch of Capitol Hill. ⊠ *615 19th Ave. E, Capitol Hill* ☎ *206/325–2111* ⊕ *www.monsoonrestaurants.com* ═ *MC, V* ⊘ *No lunch* ⊹ *2:H4.*

Poppy

$–$$
NEW AMERICAN

✕ **Oddfellows Café and Bar.** A huge, ultra-hip space anchoring the Oddfellows Building, across from Cal Anderson Park and smack in the center of the Pike–Pine universe, serves up good (and sometimes inspired) American food, including a pulled-pork sandwich; buffalo-fried chicken livers; meatballs with pine nuts; lamb ragout with mint and goat cheese; fried quail; and seasonal fruit crisps. Service is a little bit lacking, but the huge communal-style seating, Capitol Hill–hipster-chic vibe, cold brews, and festive music make this a fun evening out. ✉ *1525 10th Ave., Capitol Hill* ☎ *206/325–0807* ⊕ *www.oddfellowscafe.com* ▭ *AE, MC, V* ✛ *2:F6.*

$$$$
NEW AMERICAN
Fodor's Choice
★

✕ **Poppy.** Jerry Traunfeld's bright, airy restaurant on the northern end of Broadway is a feast for the senses. Deep-red walls, high-design lighting fixtures, friendly staff, and a happening bar area welcome you to this hip eatery with floor-to-ceiling windows. Start with one of the many interesting cocktails and eggplant fries with sea salt and honey; then you can peruse the interesting menu, which offers thali (and cleverly named "smalli")—inspired by an Indian meal of the same name in which a selection of different dishes is served in small compartments on a large platter. The inspired New American cuisine is completely dependent on seasonal bounty—you'll enjoy anything from stinging nettle soup, braised Wagyu beef cheek with ginger; rhubarb pickles; onion-poppy naan; and roasted halibut with saffron leeks. Gimmicky, some say— we disagree. Somehow each small-portioned delight is better than the last, and your senses will be pulled happily in a variety of Asian- and Northwest-inspired directions. ■ TIP→ Fantastic vegetarian and standard thali-style menus change regularly to reflect whatever is in season. It's a fun way to dine—make reservations, and come hungry and ready to be delighted. ⊠ *622 Broadway E, Capitol Hill* ☎ *206/324–1108* ⊕ *www. poppyseattle.com* ⊟ *AE, MC, V* ⊗ *No lunch* ✛ *2:F4.*

$–$$ ✕ **Quinn's.** Capitol Hill's coolest gastropub has friendly bartenders, an
GASTROPUB *amazing* selection of beers from all over the world on tap (with the West
Fodor'sChoice Coast and Belgium heavily represented), an extensive list of whiskey,
★ and an edgy menu of quite good food, which you can enjoy at the long
bar or at a table on either of the two floors of the industrial-chic space.
Spicy fried peanuts, baby lettuces in sherry vinaigrette, and country-style
rabbit pâté are good ways to start—then you can choose from Painted
Hills beef tartare with pumpernickel crisps, a delicious beef burger with
cheddar and bacon, perfect marrow bones with baguette and citrus jam,
or a cheese and mostarda plate. The folks here take their libations seriously, so feel free to chat up the bartenders about their favorite whiskey
or brew. ⊠ *1001 E. Pike St., Capitol Hill* ☎ *206/325–7711* ⊕ *www.
quinnspubseattle.com* ⊟ *AE, MC, V* ⊗ *No lunch* ✛ *2:G6.*

$$$$ ✕ **Rover's.** The restaurant of Thierry Rautureau (dubbed the "chef in the
FRENCH hat" for his fondness for Panama-style hats), one of the Northwest's
most imaginative chefs, is an essential Seattle foodie destination. Sea
scallops, venison, squab, lobster, and rabbit are frequent offerings (vegetarian items are also available) on the prix-fixe menu (though items are
also available à la carte). Traditional accoutrements such as foie gras
and truffles pay homage to Rautureau's French roots, but bold combinations of local ingredients are evidence of his wanderlust. The service at
Rover's is downright excellent—friendly but unobtrusive—the setting
romantic, and the presentation stunning. Rover's is a short cab ride
from the center of Capitol Hill, in the Madison Valley neighborhood.
■TIP➔ **Much to the surrounding neighborhood's delight, Rautureau opened
adorable Luc (**⊠ *2800 E. Madison* ☎ *206/328–6645***), a casual French bistro, just next door.** ⊠ *2808 E. Madison St., Capitol Hill* ☎ *206/325–7442*
⊕ *www.thechefinthehat.com* ⌖ *Reservations essential* ⊟ *AE, MC, V*
⊗ *Closed Mon. No lunch Sat.–Thurs.* ✛ *2:H5.*

$$$ ✕ **Serafina.** To many loyal patrons, Serafina is *the* perfect neighborhood
ITALIAN restaurant. And then there's the romance: burnt-sienna walls topped by
a forest-green ceiling convey the feeling of a lush garden villa—a sense
heightened by the small sheltered courtyard out back. Menu highlights
(some available in small and large portions) include grilled eggplant
rolled with ricotta and basil; asparagus with an egg and truffle oil; gnoc-
chi with rotating ingredients such as mushrooms, nettle, or beef cheeks;
and seared sea scallops with baby turnips, pine nuts, and golden raisins.
Live jazz every Friday through Sunday (and occasionally on Wednesday
and Thursday, too) should be considered a plus, but be forewarned that
it can be kind of difficult to hold a conversation while the band is play-
ing. Note that Serafina is close to Capitol Hill, in the Eastlake neighbor-
hood, so definitely spring for the short cab ride here. ■TIP➔ **Cicchetti
Kitchen, by the same proprietors, is around the corner (**⊠ *121 E. Boston St.*
☎ *206/859–4155***); it's a delightful spot to enjoy Mediterranean small plates
and inventive cocktails around the flicker of a wood-fired hearth.** ⊠ *2043
Eastlake Ave. E, Capitol Hill* ☎ *206/323–0807* ⊕ *www.serafinaseattle.
com* ⊟ *AE, DC, MC, V* ⊗ *No lunch Sat.* ✛ *2:F1.*

$$$
NEW AMERICAN

✕ **Sitka & Spruce.** Anchoring the hot Melrose Project (between Pike and Pine) that houses a cool clothing shop, a hip bar, a cheesemonger, and a butcher, Sitka & Spruce is the Capitol Hill eatery of Corson Building chef Matthew Dillon. Romantic, chic, friendly, and cutting edge all at once, S&S is a heaven for foodies—try to snag a table at the large butcher block that extends from the chef's kitchen. Smelt with lemon and beans, Serrano ham with cured olives, halibut with fennel, deliciously tender chicken. ⊠ 1531 Melrose Ave. E, #6 *Capitol Hill* ☎ 206/324–0662 ⊕ *www.sitkaandspruce.com* ▭ AE, MC, V ⊗ *No lunch* ✛ 2:E6.

$–$$
GASTROPUB

✕ **Smith.** Hunting lodge–meets–prep school–meets–Capitol Hill hip at Linda Derschang's (of Oddfellows and Linda's) always-busy eatery on 15th Avenue E, a short walk northeast of the Pike–Pine corridor. Taxidermied birds and cheeky oil portraits of ex-presidents fill the walls, and dark booths invite lingering and sipping. Flank steak here is expertly prepared—substitute sweet-potato fries for the regular ones. A grilled Gruyère with onion-jam sandwich is best washed down with a cold IPA, while a house cocktail goes well with any of the daily specials, which often feature fresh local produce. The burgers are most popular though (with good reason), as are the weekend brunch items. ⊠ 332 15th Ave. E, Capitol Hill ☎ 206/709–1900 ⊕ *www.smithpub.com* ▭ AE, MC, V ⊗ *No lunch* ✛ 2:H5.

¢
COFFEEHOUSE

✕ **Stumptown Coffee Roasters.** This hip Portland powerhouse is quickly becoming one of the West Coast's most well-known coffee-roasting operations. And Seattle simply loves the stuff. There's good reason: the coffee is hands-down divine, and the vibe, while über-hip, isn't too-cool-for-school. Plus, the roasting operation and mini-empire is backed by some very sound practices, including "direct trade," which means they source directly from growers, usually paying well above fair trade prices. The original Seattle location is a small, airy space with a lively bar area, plus simple open-booth seating, which is often filled with Seattle University hipsters and tattooed locals. ■ TIP➜ The other Stumptown branch (⊠ 616 E. Pine at Boylston ☎ 206/329–0115 ✛ 1:H1), in the Pike–Pine Corridor, is just as stylish, with more seating. ⊠ 1115 12th Ave., Capitol Hill ☎ 206/323–1544 ⊕ *www.stumptowncoffee.com* ▭ AE, MC, V ✛ 2:G6.

$
PIZZA

✕ **Via Tribunali.** This dark, moody, and very happenin' pizza spot on Pike Street is a reliable spot for a fun pizza feast—they churn Napolitano-style pizzas from the wood-burning stove so quickly that it may take you by surprise—so take your time ordering. Fresh, large salads—such as the di Parma, with arugula and Parmigiano reggiano, a standard Caprese, and the di Tonno, with mozzarella, cherry tomatoes, tuna, and olives—and a huge amount of pizza toppings make this a crowd-pleaser. We love the *funghi* pizza with pomodoro, mozzarella, mushroom, and basil, as well as the Spaccanapoli, with smoked mozzarella, ricotta, olive, basil, and arugula or prosciutto di parma. A carafe of the house red wine goes well, but save room for their amazingly delicious tiramisu—very authentic. ⊠ 913 Pike St., Capitol Hill ☎ 206/322–9234 ⊕ *www.viatribunali.com* ▭ AE, MC, V ⊗ *No lunch* ✛ 2:F6.

¢ **Victrola Coffee.** Victrola is probably the most loved of Capitol Hill's
COFFEEHOUSE many coffeehouses, and it's easy to see why: The space is lovely—
its walls feature constantly changing artwork from local painters and
photographers—and the coffee, pastries, and sandwiches (especially the
"Duke Ellington" version, with fresh basil, cheese, and turkey) are fantastic, the baristas are skillful, and everyone, from soccer moms to indie
rockers, is made to feel like this neighborhood spot exists just for them.
Unfortunately, it can be hard to score a table here, especially if you have
a big group. If 15th Avenue E is too far off the beaten path for you,
there's a branch at 310 East Pike Street (☎ 206/462–6259), between
Melrose and Bellevue. ✉ *411 15th Ave. E, Capitol Hill* ☎ *206/429–
6269* ⊕ *www.victrolacoffee.com* ▭ *AE, MC, V* ✛ *2:G4.*

$ ✕ **Vios.** This family favorite is set in a leafy, residential part of Capitol
GREEK Hill near Volunteer Park. Juicy lamb burgers, hummus plates, dolmas,
☾ Greek salad, orzo with eggplant, and toothsome moussaka have locals
coming back for more. Sure, there's a children's corner, and lots of the
seating is communal, but there's also a sweet, warm feeling of community here—the chef-owner is a well-loved fixture on the restaurant
scene. ■ TIP➜ It's a great place to stroll for a satisfying lunch after a morning at the Seattle Asian Art Museum and Volunteer Park. ✉ *903 19th Ave.
E, Capitol Hill* ☎ *206/329–3236* ⊕ *www.vioscafe.com* ▭ *AE, MC, V*
☾ *Closed Sun. and Mon.* ✛ *2:H4.*

¢ **Vivace Espresso Bar at Brix.** Vivace is considered by many (including us)
COFFEEHOUSE to be the home of Seattle's finest espresso. A long, curving bar and a
colorful mural add some character to a space that might otherwise
feel ho-hum in Vivace's new home on the ground floor of the upscale
Brix condo complex on Broadway (it was relocated out of its old digs
due to construction of the future Light Rail station farther south on
Broadway). The place has great energy—lively and bustling, where Hill
residents tippity-tap on laptops and students hold study groups—but it's
not necessarily a good spot for a quiet read. Pastries are a bit lackluster,
but the espresso beverages more than make up for it. There's another
branch right across the way from REI in South Lake Union, at 227 Yale
Avenue North (☎ *206/388–5164*). ■ TIP➜ We're not the only ones who
consider this the best espresso on Capitol Hill; if the weekend line is too
long, there's also a Vivace sidewalk stand south of here at Broadway and
Harrison Street (☎ *206/324–8861*). ✉ *532 Broadway Ave. E, Capitol Hill*
☎ *206/860–2722* ⊕ *www.espressovivace.com* ▭ *AE, MC, V* ✛ *2:F4.*

$$ ✕ **Volunteer Park Café.** Cute as a button, and completely beloved by the
AMERICAN locals who flock here, VPC couldn't have chosen a better Web site name:
AlwaysFreshGoodness.com. Indeed! It's got a general-store farmhouse
feeling to it, and wholesome, decadent pastries, cookies, and cakes
are piled high at the counter. Dinners manage to feel both handmade
and elegant, with very good pastas, risottos, fresh fish, and fine cuts
of meat complemented by a dynamite, small selection of Washington
wines. Our favorite time to come, though, is for weekend brunch: the
pastries are simply divine, as are sandwiches, quiches, and larger egg
dishes. Be prepared for weekend crowds. ✉ *1501 17th Ave. E, Capitol
Hill* ☎ *206/328–3155* ⊕ *www.alwaysfreshgoodness.com* ▭ *AE, MC, V*
☾ *Closed Mon. No dinner Sun.* ✛ *2:H2.*

FREMONT AND PHINNEY RIDGE

Friendly neighborhood joints, Thai restaurants, good pubs, and a few swankier eateries worth making the trek to the northern part of the city round out the options in these quirky adjacent neighborhoods. Fremont, in particular, has a bumpin' evening scene, with scenesters filling the tables. Phinney Ridge, farther up the hill, is more laid-back and quiet, with mostly family-friendly spots and a few beloved gems.

FREMONT

$ ✗ **El Camino.** Loose, loud, and funky, this Fremont restaurant gives its
MEXICAN own irreverent Northwest interpretation of Mexican cuisine. Rock-shrimp quesadillas, chipotle-pepper and garlic sea bass, and duck with a spicy green sauce are typical of the kitchen's spin. Even a green salad becomes transformed with toasted pumpkin seeds on crispy romaine with a cool garlic, lime juice, and cilantro dressing. Most people come for fried plantains with fantastic guacamole and strong drinks. Weekend brunches are also excellent—everything from standard scrambled eggs and bacon to Mexican favorites like *chilaquiles* is done well. ⊠ *607 N. 35th St., Fremont* ☎ *206/632–7303* ⊕ *www.elcaminorestaurant.com* ▤ *AE, DC, MC, V* ✆ *Closed Mon. No lunch weekdays* ✛ *3:D5.*

¢ ✗ **Lighthouse Roasters.** Since 1994, Lighthouse has been roasting small
COFFEEHOUSE batches of quality coffee in vintage cast-iron roasters each day. Their blends are used in many restaurants and cafés, and this popular neighborhood spot (which is off the tourist track) is a great place to sample their handiwork. Every day of the week, you'll find folks gathered on the wooden benches outside the cheery yellow storefront or on the set of concrete steps adjacent to the building. There's no Wi-Fi here, and the food is only so-so, but neighborhood crowds still show up for the expert espressos. ⊠ *400 N. 43rd St., Fremont* ☎ *206/634–3140* ⊕ *www. lighthouseroasters.com* ▤ *MC, V* ✛ *3:D4.*

$ ✗ **Paseo.** The centerpiece of Lorenzo Lorenzo's slim, Cuban-influenced
CUBAN menu is the mouthwatering Midnight Cuban sandwich: The marinated pork sandwich, topped with sautéed onions and served on a chewy baguette, is doused with an amazing sauce (the ingredients of which are known only by Lorenzo) that keeps folks coming back for more. The entrées are also delicious, from fresh fish in garlic tapenade to prawns in a spicy red sauce. This place is so small, it's more like a glorified lunch truck than a sit-down eatery. There are a few tables, but don't count on getting a seat without a wait—Paseo gets so busy the line usually snakes way out the door, and most people opt for takeout. ⊠ *4225 Fremont Ave. N, Fremont* ☎ *206/545–7440* ⊕ *www.paseoseattle.com* ▤ *No credit cards* ✆ *Closed Sun. and Mon.* ✛ *3:D4.*

$$ ✗ **35th Street Bistro.** The 35th Street Bistro replaced the vaunted Still
BISTRO Life Café, which was the epitome of all things Fremont back when the hood was more hippie than yuppie. Although the white tablecloths, good wine list, and the generic bistro-ness of the place suggest that Downtown has moved in uptown, the ghosts of the Still Life must still linger—this place is as casual as some of Fremont's less-flashy eateries, service goes beyond warm into personable, and organic foods populate the menu. The menu is seasonal, but roasted chicken, lamb,

porterhouse, and fresh seafood are usually on it. The weekend brunch serves up a popular brioche French toast with mascarpone cream and fruit and croque madame and monsieur sandwiches. ✉ *709 N. 35th St., Fremont* ☎ *206/547–9850* ⊕ *www.35bistro.com* ▭ V ☺ *No lunch Mon.* ✛ *3:D5.*

PHINNEY RIDGE

$ ✕**Carmelita.** One of the best of Seattle's upscale vegetarian spots, Carmelita could convert a carnivore with the smells emanating from the kitchen alone. Everything on the menu is fresh and well prepared: from the sweet potato gnocchi and beet ravioli to crusty pizza topped with nettle-spinach pesto and root-vegetable potpie. Note that the menu changes constantly to take advantage of whatever is in season. This is a popular place, so reservations are recommended. The dining room is lovely, paying homage to the natural world with lots of wood, oil paintings, and leaf shapes on the ceiling, but if the weather's nice, request a spot on the garden-shrouded patio. ✉ *7314 Greenwood Ave., Phinney Ridge* ☎ *206/706–7703* ⊕ *www.carmelita.net* ▭ MC, V ☺ *Closed Mon. No lunch* ✛ *3:D1.*

VEGETARIAN

$ ✕**Red Mill.** *"Gimme a Red Mill Double Deluxe with Cheese"*—those words will get you two quarter-pound patties, lettuce, tomato, pickle, red onion, a slice of cheese, and a special sauce. Burgers here are superbly crafted by a quick assembly-line staff. You can order one dressed simply, with lettuce and smoky Mill Sauce mayo, or more elaborately, with menu combinations of luscious roasted Anaheim peppers, blue cheese, red onion jam, or Tillamook cheddar. Vegetarians note: you can order meatless patties as substitutions on the regular burger menu. Fries and delicious shakes are on offer, as well. ✉ *312 N. 67th St., Phinney Ridge* ☎ *206/783–6362* ⊕ *www.redmillburgers.com* ▭ *No credit cards* ✛ *3:D2.*

BURGERS
☺

$$$ ✕**Stumbling Goat.** Having cranked out delicious regional fare for years, the Stumbling Goat sure knows its way around a farmers' market— you'll find the freshest organic ingredients here and no missteps in the presentation, which is kept simple to let those fresh flavors shine. The menu changes frequently, but you'll find hearty dishes like risottos made with seasonal vegetables, mini–Waygu beef burgers, and in-season fish served with greens and potatoes. Though it's a bit spendy for this neck of the woods, the Stumbling Goat definitely belongs in Phinney Ridge. The place has enough quirks to fit in, from its name (surely an ode to the excellent wine and cheese offerings) to the red walls and velvet accents in its dining room to its peach-hue happy-hour den. ✉ *6722 Greenwood Ave., Phinney Ridge* ☎ *206/784–3535* ⊕ *www.stumblinggoatbistro.com* ▭ MC, V ☺ *Closed Mon. No lunch* ✛ *3:D1.*

PACIFIC
NORTHWEST

BALLARD

Ballard is the north end's answer to Capitol Hill when it comes to edgy, innovative, and delicious dining. Restaurants have taken a cue from the beloved year-round farmers' market (held every Sunday, rain or shine, from 10 to 3 along historic Ballard Avenue NW), and fresh produce, local ingredients, and top-notch quality are de rigueur here. There's sure a lot to choose from—savor anything from chewy slices at local pizza darling Delancey to French elegance at Le Gourmand.

$$$
SEAFOOD

✕ **Anthony's Homeport at Shilshole Bay.** Anthony's isn't a culinary destination by any stretch of the imagination, but it's a Seattle institution, and this Ballard branch has marvelous views out over the Shilshole marina. It's a comfortable waterfront restaurant with ample outside dining in protected nooks, allowing you a sea breeze and great views without getting blasted by gales. The seafood preparations are simple and as good as those of the more upscale Ray's, next door. ✉ *6135 Seaview Ave. NW (at Shilshole Marina), Ballard* ☎ *206/783–0780* ▭ *AE, MC, V* ✛ *3:A2.*

$$
FRENCH

✕ **Bastille.** A trendy, high-design French brasserie-mecca for hip folks seeking out reliably delicious French cuisine, Bastille is one of the more popular spots in Ballard. Some high tables have flickering hearths, casting shadows on the vast, often-packed interior with booths, shared tables, and ample high-gloss counter space. A lovely outdoor area is perfect for satisfying summer brunches. Snazzy diners munch on lamb burgers, delicious steak frites, duck confit salad, leek flan, braised pork cheek, and well-executed fish of the day. Chocolate mousse, salted peanut butter ice cream, and simple house cocktails are all popular. ✉ *5307 Ballard Ave. NW, Ballard* ☎ *206/453–5014* ⊕ *www.bastilleseattle.com* ▭ *AE, MC, V* ✛ *3:A3.*

$
BAKERY

✕ **Café Besalu.** A true slice of France right in Ballard, this casual, small bakery sees patrons from across the entire city, thanks to its *I-swear-I'm-in-Paris* croissants—buttery, flaky perfection. Weekend lines are long, but if you score a table, you'll be in heaven. You can also, of course, take pastries to go if you're en route to Golden Gardens or are exploring Ballard on foot. Apple turnovers, *pain au chocolat,* breads, cookies, decent espresso drinks, quiches, and sandwiches round out the rest of the offerings. Note that Besalu is a bit north of downtown Ballard on 24th, but the walk is worth it. ✉ *5909 24th Ave. NW, Ballard* ☎ *206/789–1463* ▭ *AE, MC, V* ☾ *Closed Mon. and Tues.* ✛ *3:A2*

¢
COFFEEHOUSE

✕ **Café Fiore.** A superb neighborhood café in an old brick building with lots of seating (including a gigantic communal table in one corner of the room), Fiore's baristas make a mean Americano to go with the various pastries, including Mighty-O doughnuts. The vibe here is definitely neighborly, laidback, and comfortably hip. On sunny days, grab a chair out front to enjoy the sunshine. ✉ *5405 Leary Ave. NW, Ballard* ☎ *206/706–0421* ▭ *AE, MC, V* ✛ *3:A3.*

$
PIZZA

✕ **Delancey.** Ballard's most adorable pizza spot is run by "Orangette" food blogger Molly Wizenberg and her husband. The signature quirky-sweet appeal she brings to her blog comes through at this tiny eatery north of downtown Ballard. Fresh, local ingredients reign supreme on the itsy-bitsy menu: Thin-but-chewy artisan crusts are topped with anything from fresh cheeses, local clams, tangy housemade tomato sauce, pork fennel sausage, prosciutto, nettles, and crimini mushrooms. The small wine list is well edited and elegant; desserts are simple but inspired—the homemade chocolate chip cookie with sea salt is delish. Charming service and quirky mismatched tables and lighting make this a true Ballard experience to remember. ✉ *1415 N.W. 70th St.,*

Ballard ☎ *206/838–1960* ⊕ *www. delanceyseattle.com* ▤ *AE, DC, MC, V* ⊗ *Closed Mon. and Tues.* ⊹ *3:B1.*

$ ✕ **The Hi-Life.** The Hi-Life is Ballard's go-to brunch spot. In a converted firehouse, the echo-y space has the familiar feeling of a TGI Friday's, which makes it a safe bet for families, but it also has personality enough to appeal to anyone needing some French toast. From morning until night, the Hi-Life has something to satisfy—you can get small plates, full entrées, wood-fired pizzas, breakfast until 3 PM, and so on. The standards, such as burgers and salads, are done well, and the kitchen also tries its hand

AMERICAN ☺

WORD OF MOUTH

"Delancey is really good, though I was surprised to find that it was thin-crust pizza. If you go, be prepared for a wait, since they only take reservations for 6 or more. One could easily get a seat at the bar immediately (though the "bar" is really in the entryway of the restaurant), but waiting for a table can take easily an hour. There's a small dive bar across the street where you can wait with a drink—the folks at Delancey will call you when your table is ready."
—beanweb24

at creative dishes paprika-rubbed lamb chops, goat cheese ravioli with artichoke hearts, and salmon cakes with fennel salad. ⊠ *5425 Russell Ave. NW, Ballard* ☎ *206/784–7272* ⊕ *www.chowfoods.com/hilife* ▤ *MC, V* ⊹ *3:A3.*

$ ✕ **La Carta de Oaxaca.** True to its name, this low-key, bustling Ballard favorite serves traditional Mexican cooking with Oaxacan accents. The *mole negro* is a must, served with chicken or pork; another standout is the *albondigas* (a spicy vegetable soup with meatballs). Halibut tacos are served on fresh tortillas—and you can choose your spice at the salsa bar. The menu is mostly small plates, which works out to your advantage because you won't have to choose just one savory dish. The small, casual space has an open kitchen enclosed by a stainless-steel bar, the walls are covered in gorgeous black-and-white photos, and the light wood tables and black chairs and banquettes look more Scandinavian than Mexican. The place gets very crowded on weekends and stays busy until late, though if you have a small party you usually don't have to wait too long for a table. ⊠ *5431 Ballard Ave. NW, Ballard* ☎ *206/782–8722* ⊕ *www.lacartadeoaxaca.com* ▤ *AE, DC, MC, V* ⊗ *No lunch Sun. and Mon.* ⊹ *3:A3*

MEXICAN
Fodor's Choice
★

$$$$ ✕ **Le Gourmand.** On an unattractive corner somewhere halfway between Ballard and Fremont is a charming and innovative French restaurant. The intimate, rustic-chic spot is part unassuming bistro and part romantic, special-occasion dining room. The chef uses classic French techniques and locally grown ingredients to create stunning dishes such as ruby trout with mustard greens; roast guinea hen with housemade bacon; or poached line-caught halibut in dill sauce. The dessert menu might include a flourless chocolate cake, a berry crème brûlée, honey cake, or almond crème anglaise. Many patrons love the extensive (and pricey) tasting menus. ■TIP➜ You can also go next door to swanky Sambar to order from an abbreviated bar menu—cocktails and frites is a great way to end a night out in Ballard. ⊠ *425 N.W. Market St., Ballard*

FRENCH

☎ 206/784–3463 ⊕ *www.legourmandrestaurant.com* ⚄ *Reservations essential* ▭ *AE, MC, V* ✛ *3:C3*.

$–$$ ✕ **Moshi Moshi.** A huge faux cherry tree with sparkling pink lights vivifies
SUSHI   this sleek, urban Ballard Avenue sushi spot with high ceilings, glossy floors, and welcoming booths. Choose from a wide array of respectable rolls and sushi, as well as tempura, yakimono, miso soup, and salads. Regulars love the *nigiri* of seared salmon belly with yuzu juice and grated daikon. The main attraction is the über-chic bar, presided over by an exceptional mixologist. The "improved orchard" drink has apple-infused bourbon, amaro, absinthe, all-spice, and Peychaud's bitters, while the "buckshot" cocktail touts rum, housemade falernum, lime, bitters, and ginger brew. Try the daily happy hour from 4:30 to 6. ✉ *5324 Ballard Ave., Ballard* ☎ *206/971–7424* ⊕ *www.moshiseattle. com* ▭ *AE, MC, V* ✛ *3:A3*.

$$$ ✕ **Ray's Boathouse.** The view of Shilshole Bay might be the big draw
SEAFOOD   here, but the seafood is also fresh and well prepared. Perennial favorites include broiled salmon, Kasu sake–marinated cod, Dungeness crab, and regional oysters on the half shell. Ray's has a split personality: there's a fancy dining room downstairs (reservations essential) and a casual café and bar upstairs (reservations not accepted). In warm weather you can sit on the deck outside the café and watch fishing boats, tugs, and pleasure craft floating past. Be forewarned that during happy hour (or early-bird special time) in high season, the café's service can suffer greatly because of the crowds. ■ TIP→ Sure, it's touristy, but snagging a spot on the sun-drenched balcony here after an afternoon spent exploring the Ballard Locks is quintessential Seattle summertime fun. ✉ *6049 Seaview Ave. NW, Ballard* ☎ *206/789–3770* ⊕ *www.rays.com* ▭ *AE, DC, MC, V* ✛ *3:A2*.

WALLINGFORD AND GREEN LAKE

Wallingford has plenty of options for a casual meal. Along 45th Street, you'll also find quite a few cheap and decent (if not spectacular) sushi spots, several curry houses, and a few dinerlike establishments serving reliable comfort food. Take note that two restaurants along 45th have James Beard–quality chefs in the kitchen—Joule and Tilth—so make your reservations now. Green Lake has fewer spots of note, though Kisaku is quickly gaining recognition and popularity amongst Seattle's die-hard sushi fans.

WALLINGFORD

$$$$ ✕ **Art of the Table.** You'll be in good hands here: the chef is absolutely
NEW AMERICAN   obsessive about finding the perfect ingredients for his utterly inspired meals. The Supper Club (Thursday to Saturday) offers up a communal-dining experience with a prix-fixe menu highlighting local farmers' markets finds. Dinner is served at 7:30, and reservations are essential. "Happy Mondays" sees small plates, no reservations, and a more laid-back and affordable atmosphere. Fresh local organic ingredients are an absolute obsession. Small, pricey, but utterly unforgettable, Art of the Table is a constantly changing tour de force. Sitting at a communal table while listening to the chef speak about each course is de rigueur;

Regional Flavors of the Pacific Northwest

Seattle is a foodie's city, and enjoys easy access to an incredible bounty of foods from land and sea, from wild Dungeness crab and line-caught halibut to foraged stinging nettles and brightly colored apples. Many Seattleites tend kitchen gardens, hunt and fish, trap crabs, dig clams, harvest berries in season, and cross the mountains to pick fruit in the Wenatchee and Yakima valleys.

Gathering fresh foods at the source has honed local palates: Seattleites know—by taste, smell, and touch—when foods are fresh and at their peak. Wild salmon, in particular, has played an important role in local cuisine, as have halibut, oysters, Dungeness crab, prawns, mussels, scallops, geoduck and razor clams, as well as blackberries, huckleberries, fiddlehead ferns, chanterelle and morel mushrooms, and wild greens.

It is an absolute passion of Seattle's chefs to find and use organic ingredients from local farms, orchards, and dairies. Asparagus, tomatoes, and hot peppers arrive from Yakima Valley; sweet onions from Walla Walla; apricots and pears from Wenatchee; apples from Lake Chelan and beyond. Lamb and beef come from dryland pastures, while clams and oysters are harvested from tidal flats in Samish Bay, the Hood Canal, Totten Inlet, and Willapa Bay. Pike Place Market is a major meeting place for high-quality ingredients from across the state.

Local chefs' obsession with the freshest seasonal ingredients may make it difficult to get the same dish twice—especially at top-notch restaurants, where menus usually change seasonally, if not daily. No Northwest meal is complete, of course, without a bottle of wine from a regional winery or ale from a local microbrewery.

you'll enjoy anything from braised ox tail, caramelized Brussels sprouts with pistachios, and rockfish ceviche, to manila clams with cauliflower over pasta, halibut with asparagus and flavorful broth, and rhubarb soup with crème fraiche. The wine pairings are elegant and worth the splurge. ⊠ *1054 N. 39th St., Wallingford* ☎ *206/282–0942* ⊕ *www.artofthetable.net* ⊟ *AE, MC, V* ☺ *No lunch; no dinner Sun. or Tues.–Wed.* ✛ *3:E5.*

$$ ✕ **Cantinetta.** A large but welcoming candlelit space south of Wallingford's main drag in a residential area nevertheless gets loads of hungry
ITALIAN patrons night after night. They come for chic, delicious, romantic Italian dining, friendly service, and a certain rustic flair—there's certainly an undeniable soul to this place. Couples and small groups sip wine in the bustling bar area while waiting for a table to enjoy the housemade pastas—served with nettle and pine nuts; crème fraiche and a farm egg; baby carrots, ramps, and pork; or rabbit sugo and mushrooms. Risotto dishes are toothsome, and *secondi* offerings—from a sublime Painted Hills steak with polenta to locally made sausage with cassouletta—are memorable. A small wine list, simple cocktails, and tasty desserts (pumpkin panna cotta, orange zepoli) are also on offer. ⊠ *3650 Wallingford Ave., Wallingford* ☎ *206/632–1000* ⊕ *www.cantinettaseattle.com* ⊟ *AE, DC, MC, V* ✛ *3:F5.*

$$ ✕ **Ivar's Salmon House.** This long dining room facing Lake Union has
SEAFOOD original Northwest Indian artwork collected by the former owner. It's
🍃 touristy, often gimmicky, and always packed, but it's also great Seattle
fun—a real institution. Plus the views are terrific, and the building is a
loose replica of a traditional longhouse. You can dine inside (ask for a
window table), but you really want to snag a table on the deck for views
of Lake Union and Downtown. ■ TIP➔ It's all about the Sunday brunch
buffet here, though you pretty much can't go wrong with any salmon dish
for lunch or dinner. The views get even more spectacular at sunset. The
other Ivar's locations in town are uninspiring, but this one comes the
closest to living up to the hype. ⊠ *401 N.E. Northlake Way, Wallingford*
☎ *206/632–0767* ⊕ *www.ivars.net* ▭ *AE, DC, MC, V* ✛ *3:G5.*

$$ ✕ **Joule.** Set in an adorable Wallingford storefront with graphic decor
KOREAN-FRENCH and an open kitchen, Joule is a true feast for your senses. Happy, casual
Fodor'sChoice Wallingford diners fill this bright space to feast on Chefs Rachel Yang
★ and Seif Chirchi's exciting take on French-Korean fusion. The menu is
divided into playful sections, including *Simmered* (such as spicy beef
soup); *Tossed* (Japanese greens with Asian pear, Rogue blue cheese, and
walnut agrodolce); *Crisped* (including Kimchi and trotter dumplings or
braised cucumber, Chinese sausage, and shiitake); and *Sparked* (incredible whole branzino with salted shrimp fricasse; Kasu-brined pork chop;
and Bison hanger steak with preserved garlic). The best approach is to
order family-style so that you can try several dishes. You may not have
room, but desserts are equally fascinating, such as a "Joule" box with
tapioca pearls and ruby grapefruit brûlée. ⊠ *1913 N. 45th St., Wallingford* ☎ *206/632–1913* ⊕ *www.joulerestaurant.com* ▭ *AE, DC, MC, V*
◷ *No lunch; closed Mon.* ✛ *3:F4*

$ ✕ **May.** In a reconstructed traditional teak home on an otherwise unin-
THAI spiring strip in Wallingford, May's bar on the lower floor is sexy and
dim, with comfortable booths and candlelit corners. To focus on the
food, head up the curving staircase to the elegant dining room. The
pad Thai, often a flavorless mess at other places, is complex and comes
with some of its ingredients laid out in a banana leaf; you mix them in
as you see fit. The *grapao kaidow* (meat sautéed in a garlic basil sauce
accompanied by a fried egg over rice) is excellent; and the tart, spicy
tom ka soups, whether made with shrimp or chicken, are the best in the
city. Don't miss the specialty cocktails made with fresh juices. ⊠ *1612
N. 45th St., Wallingford* ☎ *206/675–0037* ⊕ *www.mayrestaurant.com*
▭ *AE, DC, MC, V* ◷ *No lunch* ✛ *3:E4.*

$$$ ✕ **Tilth.** A certified organic restaurant by the much-lauded Maria Hines,
NEW AMERICAN Tilth serves up wonderful, inventive dishes that can be had as small
plates or full entrées—the mini–duck burgers, seasonally inspired risot-
tos, and wild salmon deserve special mentions. It's not the sort of place
you'd expect to find on Wallingford's busy commercial strip: occupying
a Craftsman house, it has been lovingly spruced up with leafy green
paint and local artwork. The small, homey dining room—backed by an
open kitchen—occupies the main floor and has an accidental elegance.
Though overall dining here is a wonderful experience, Tilth has two
notable drawbacks: the service can be a bit snooty and the acoustics are
terrible (be prepared to shout across your tiny table if you dine during

Kisaku

peak hours). Tilth serves a delicious, busy brunch on weekends. ⊠ *1411 N. 45th St., Wallingford* ☎ *206/633–0801* ⊕ *www.tilthrestaurant.com* ⌂ *Reservations essential* ▭ *MC, V* ☽ *Closed Mon. No lunch* ✛ *3:E4.*

$ ✕ **Tutta Bella Neapolitan Pizzeria.** It's sometimes hard to find good pizza in
PIZZA Seattle, but Tutta Bella serves authentic Neapolitan-style pizzas that are
☺ made with organic local and imported ingredients and baked in a wood-fired oven. Crusts are thin but wonderfully chewy, and sauces are light and tangy. They go easy on the cheese, so be sure to order extra cheese if that's what you're craving. The salads are excellent, too. Takeout is available, but many people opt to sit down in the spacious dining room, which has more of a café vibe than that of a typical pizza house. Tutta Bella is very family-friendly, but as the evening progresses you'll see plenty of couples and groups, too. The place gets packed on weekends. ⊠ *4411 Stone Way N, Wallingford* ☎ *206/633–3800* ⊕ *www.tuttabella. com* ▭ *AE, DC, MC, V* ✛ *3:E4.*

GREEN LAKE

$$$ ✕ **Kisaku.** One of the most outstanding sushi restaurants in Seattle is
SUSHI quietly nestled in Green Lake—and the diners come flocking. Fresh sushi is served up happily, along with signature rolls—such as the Green Lake variety, with salmon, flying fish eggs, asparagus, avocado, and marinated seaweed, or the Wallingford, with yellowtail, green onion, cucumber, radish, sprouts, and flying fish eggs. Definitely spring for the *omakase* (chef's menu), which can mean anything from fatty tuna, shrimp, octopus, and albacore to salmon, yellow tail, hammer jack, and unagi. Straightforward decor and ambience means you can concentrate even more on the delicious food in front of you. Regulars swear by the

DINING WITH KIDS

Seattle is just as serious about its food as it is about ensuring that no visiting parent leaves town without knowing why. Here are some picks you and your kids will enjoy.

Anthony's Pier 66, Downtown. Children are welcome at the fish bar (where they mix a mean Shirley Temple) and in the more formal dining room. Kids love to watch the tugboats and ferries in the busy harbor.

Café Flora, Capitol Hill. Local families love this vegetarian spot a short drive from the top of Capitol Hill—brunches are particularly fun.

Etta's, Downtown. Tom Douglas named this restaurant, one of many he owns, after his daughter. The jovial staff will make you feel right at home with your own kiddos.

The Hi-Life, Ballard. Ballard families love this casual restaurant in a

converted firehouse. The menu is large; basics like great burgers are well represented, but fancier fusion dishes keep parents happy, too. The waitstaff is also very friendly.

Kidd Valley. Burgers, fries, shakes, and more in an indestructible fast-food restaurant that has branches in Queen Anne (on Queen Anne Avenue), Greenlake, and the University District.

Red Mill, Phinney Ridge. Some say the burgers here are the best in town, and this location is only a short walk north from the Woodland Park Zoo.

Tutta Bella, South Lake Union and Wallingford. Though Neapolitan pizza is a bit different from the classic slice, kids don't seem to mind. You won't be the only one with kids in tow if you're here on a weekend afternoon or early evening.

agedashi tofu. Non-sushi entrees are also on offer, including terikayi and a tempura dinner with prawns. ☒ *2101 N. 55th St., Green Lake* ☏ *206/545–9050* ⊕ *www.kisaku.com* ▤ *AE, MC, V* ✛ *3:F3.*

UNIVERSITY DISTRICT

The "U-District" is great for cheap ethnic eats but falls short on fine dining. It's worth strolling up and down The Ave (University Way NE) to see if anything beckons to you before settling on a spot. There are some popular brunch spots scattered about, too.

$ MEXICAN ✕ **Agua Verde Café and Paddle Club.** Baja California Mexican cuisine and a laid-back vibe define this casual spot that is done up in bright, beachy colors and has a lively deck come summertime. Regulars swear by the fresh fish tacos, black-bean cakes, and *mangodillas* (quesadillas with mango and poblano chilies). Be sure to pay a visit to the salsa bar. We like to wash it all down with a salt-rimmed margarita. ■TIP➔ In the warmer months, you can rent kayaks at Agua Verde and paddle around Portage Bay; Agua Verde is perched waterside on a street surrounded by quirky boat-repair shops. ☒ *1303 N.E. Boat St., University District* ☏ *206/545–8570* ⊕ *www.aguaverde.com* ▤ *MC, V* ☾ *Closed Sun.* ✛ *3:H5*

$$ BRAZILIAN ✕ **Tempero Do Brasil.** A festive taste of Brazil, Tempero serves up satisfying cod, prawn, and halibut dishes simmered in coconut-based sauces;

entrées arrive with moist, chewy, long-grain rice and black beans. For a larger meal, try *bife grelhado* (charbroiled Argentine steak). Finish with cold passion-fruit mousse or tangy guava paste served with farmer's cheese, and strong dark coffee. The outstanding food, attention to detail, and earnest staff make dining here a pleasure. The airy patio is perfect for icy Brazilian cocktails in summer. Note that this is at the north end of The Ave; it's a long walk from the campus. ⊠ *5628 University Way NE, University District* ☎ *206/523–6229* ⊕ *www.temperodobrasil.net* ⊟ *AE, DC, MC, V* ☺ *Closed Mon. No lunch* ✛ *3:H3.*

$ ✕ **Thai Tom.** This might be the cheapest Thai restaurant in town, but
THAI rock-bottom prices aren't the only reason this place is always packed— the food is delicious, authentic, and spicy (two stars is usually pretty hot). But be forewarned: the is a hole-in-the-wall if there ever was one. Nevertheless, students and foodies pack in for garlic chicken, spicy curries, Thai coconut soup with shrimp, and rich, flavorful pad Thai. Tables can be hard to come by during the dinner rush, but there's usually space at the counter that lines the open kitchen. ⊠ *4543 University Ave., University District* ☎ *206/548–9548* ⊟ *MC, V* ☺ *Closed Sun. No lunch Sat.* ✛ *3:H4.*

WEST SEATTLE

West Seattle is enough of a trek from Seattle's central neighborhoods that some restaurants historically have had a hard time filling their seats. Luckily, West Seattleites love to eat out, and a new culinary energy is taking hold, making even gourmands from Ballard make the trek. The real superstar here is Spring Hill, but plenty of other neighborhood joints are top-notch and inviting. A walk up and down California Avenue will offer up plenty of choices.

$ ✕ **Bakery Nouveau.** Widely considered one of the best bakeries in the city,
BAKERY Bakery Nouveau has perfected many things, including cakes, croissants, and tarts. The chocolate cake, in particular, makes us swoon, though twice-baked almond croissants aren't too shabby either—so good, in fact, that you'll be thinking of France while you're on California Avenue. Sandwiches, quiches, and pizzas are also on offer if you need something deliciously substantial before a lemon meringue tart, banana mousse, or chocolate éclair. Artisan breads and good coffee make locals even happier. ⊠ *4737 California Ave. SW, West Seattle* ☎ *206/923–0534* ⊕ *www.bakerynouveau.com* ⊟ *MC, V* ✛ *1:E6.*

$$ ✕ **Salty's on Alki.** It's undeniably touristy, but those views simply can't
SEAFOOD be beat on a summer afternoon. Famed for its Sunday and holiday brunches and said view of Seattle's skyline across the harbor, Salty's offers more in the way of quantity than quality—and a bit too much of its namesake ingredient. But it's a couple of steps up from the mainstream seafood chains. And, oh, that view. If you can get a table with a view, order a wine by the glass and a cup of chowder or some crab legs, and enjoy. ⊠ *1936 Harbor Ave. W (just past port complex), West Seattle* ☎ *206/937–1600* ⊟ *AE, MC, V* ✛ *1:E6.*

Spring Hill

$$$
NEW AMERICAN
Fodor's Choice
★

✕ **Spring Hill.** West Seattle's most exciting culinary beacon, Spring Hill takes quality and freshness seriously. A quietly hip vibe pervades this large eatery on California Avenue, with polished wood floors, simple seating, a huge bar surrounding an open kitchen, and gently mod wooden wall treatments. Diners of all stripes relish the Pacific Northwest bounty, which is the star here, with raw oysters served atop a bundle of fresh seaweed; Dungeness crab with melted butter; housemade tagliatelle with crispy pork shoulder and fried parsley; Painted Hills hanger steak with beef-fat fries; Manila clams with razor-clam sausage and herbed mayo; and fresh halibut prepared to perfection and accompanied by smoked clam crumbs, corn grits chowder, and pea tendrils. Chef Mark Fuller creates dish after dish that combines expert execution of favorites, the finest ingredients, and subdued yet innovative flourishes. Weekend brunches are hoppin' and also more than worth the trek. This is a Seattle meal to be relished. ⊠ *4437 California Ave. SW, West Seattle* ☎ *206/935–1075* ⊕ *www.springhillnorthwest.com* ▭ *AE, MC, V* ☺ *No dinner Sun.* ✣ *1:E6.*

THE EASTSIDE

Bellevue, Kirkland, and Woodinville are easy to get to from Downtown Seattle if you are traveling during off-peak hours: the 520 and I–90 bridges both are accessible from I–5. However, come rush hour, traffic grinds to a halt. Don't plan a culinary expedition unless you already plan to visit this side of things—unless, of course, you have reservations at Café Juanita or The Herbfarm, two beloved and critically acclaimed restaurants that are more than worth the trek.

Café Juanita

$$$
ITALIAN
Fodor's Choice
★

✗ **Café Juanita.** There are so many ways for a pricey "destination restaurant" to go overboard, making itself nothing more than a special-occasion spectacle, but Café Juanita manages to get everything just right. This Kirkland space is refined without being too design-y or too posh, and the food—much of which has a northern Italian influence—is also perfectly balanced: you won't find needlessly flashy fusion cooking or heavy sauces that obliterate subtle flavors. Chef Holly Smith (who won the "Best Chef Northwest" award from James Beard in 2008, among many other accolades) is a seasoned and elegant pro. One bite of the tender saddle of Oregon lamb with baby artichokes, fava beans, and lemon emulsion and you'll be sold. The daily fish specials are also worth the plunge, especially when the menu's featuring whole fish. Desserts are positively blissful, such as vanilla-bean panna cotta with honey and bittersweet chocolate torta with cherry-vinegar sauce and mint gelato. To top it all off, the restaurant has an *excellent* wine list. ⊠ *9702 N.E. 120th Pl., Eastside* ☎ *425/823–1505* ⊕ *www.cafejuanita.com* ▭ *MC, V* ☉ *Closed Mon. No lunch* ✛ *3:H6.*

$$$$
PACIFIC
NORTHWEST

✗ **The Herbfarm.** You may want to fast before dining at the Herbfarm. You'll get no fewer than nine courses here—"Dinner" takes at least four hours and includes five fine Northwest wines, so you may also want to arrange for transportation to and from the Woodinville-area restaurant. Before you tuck in, you'll be treated to a delightful tour of the herb garden. The dining room itself is in a century-old farmhouse and is reminiscent of a country estate. The set menus change weekly; if you have dietary restrictions, it's essential to call ahead. With all products coming from the farm, or other local growers and suppliers, you can always expect fresh seafood and shellfish, artisanal cheeses, and luscious seasonal fruits. Book a room at elegant Willows Lodge to make a true getaway of it (sometimes the hotel runs specials if you have reservations here, so do call ahead). ⊠ *14590 N.E. 145th St., Eastside* ☎ *425/485–5300* ⊕ *www.theherbfarm.com* ⟆ *Reservations essential* ▭ *AE, MC, V* ⊘ *No lunch* ✛ *3:H6.*

$$$$ ╳ **John Howie Steak.** An upscale Northwest steakhouse in the Shops at
STEAKHOUSE the Bravern, John Howie is well known for its USDA Prime 28-day and 42-day custom-aged, American Wagyu beef from Snake River Farms. Steaks are tender, juicy, and perfectly executed. Salmon, king crab legs, Maine lobster, ahi tuna, swordfish, and mahimahi are also on offer, and are deliciously prepared. Happy hours (from 3 to 6 and 9 to 11 most nights) see a huge amount of dressed-up Eastsiders and businesspeople, who come for the swank ambience and satisfying food. Save room for the dessert, especially the flourless chocolate volcano cake with warm caramel. ⊠ *11111 N.E. 8th St., Suite 125, Eastside* ☎ *425/440–0880* ⊕ *www.johnhowiesteak.com* ▭ *AE, MC, V* ✛ *3:H6.*

$$ ╳ **Monsoon East.** The Eastside sibling of Capitol Hill's darling Vietnam-
VIETNAMESE ese eatery is utterly polished and sleek—and much fancier than the original restaurant. Specialty cocktails (such as the White Lion, with chili-infused tequila, jicama juice, and a sweet-and-salty paprika rim) are served in the lounge, while the Ocean Bar serves fresh oysters and sashimi. The Vietnamese dishes are the favorites, though: Diners love the *bo la lot* beef, crispy drunken chicken, catfish clay pot, and barbequed hoisin pork ribs. The dishes are fresh and well executed, and may come with flourishes such as caramelized pineapple and crispy duck chips. In signature Bellevue style, diners dress up a bit more than, say, Capitol Hill or Ballard. Brunches are a bit hectic, but delicious. ⊠ *10245 Main St., Eastside* ☎ *425/635–1112* ⊕ *www.monsooneast. com* ▭ *AE, MC, V* ✛ *3:H6.*

$$ ╳ **Wild Ginger.** Housed in the swanky Shops at the Bravern, Wild Ginger
ASIAN mixes a Zenlike aesthetic with an upscale Bellevue vibe and touches of glass and steel; the eatery serves decent Asian fusion cuisine that is satisfying, especially if you come during the popular happy hour (daily from 3 to 6). Chefs reference Malaysian, Chinese, Vietnamese, and Indonesian culinary traditions. Rich, aromatic dishes include seven flavor beef (flank steak spiced with lemongrass, peanuts, hoisin, chilies, basil, garlic, and ginger); Mandarin chicken with sweet-and-sour sauce; and house-made egg noodles wok-fried in a Mongolian chili sauce. There's a vegetarian menu, and a tasty $2 satay menu at happy hour, too. ⊠ *11020 N.E. 6th St., Suite 90, Eastside* ☎ *425/495–8889* ⊕ *www. wildginger.net* ▭ *AE, MC, V* ⊘ *No lunch* ✛ *3:H6.*

Seattle Dining and Lodging Atlas

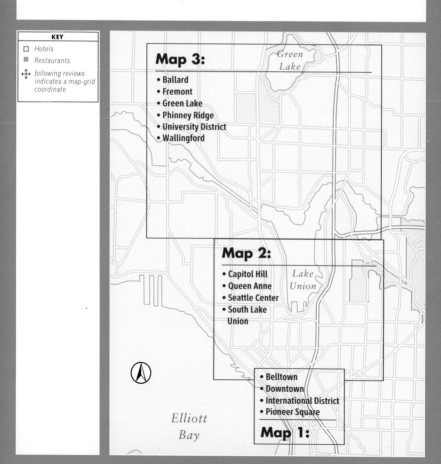

KEY	
☐	*Hotels*
■	*Restaurants*
⊕	*following reviews indicates a map-grid coordinate*

Map 3:
- Ballard
- Fremont
- Green Lake
- Phinney Ridge
- University District
- Wallingford

Green Lake

Map 2:
- Capitol Hill
- Queen Anne
- Seattle Center
- South Lake Union

Lake Union

- Belltown
- Downtown
- International District
- Pioneer Square

Map 1:

Elliott Bay

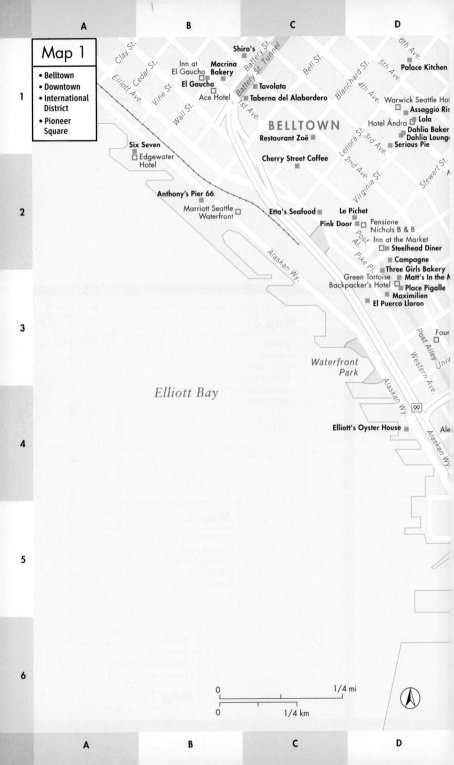

A **B** **C** **D**

W Smith St.

W McGraw Pl.

3rd Ave. W

W McGraw St.

McGraw Pl.

Wheeler St.

McGraw St.

Aurora Ave. N

Westlake Ave. N

8th Ave. N

Dexter Ave. N

1

How To Cook A Wolf

Boston St.

5th Ave. N

Crockett St.

Newton St.

Lake Union

2nd Ave. W

Queen Anne Ave. N

1st Ave. N

2nd Ave. N

3rd Ave. N

Howe St.

Blaine St.

Nob Hill Ave. N

4th Ave. N

Bigelow Ave. N

Tayor Ave. N

Queen Anne Dr. N

8th Ave. N

2

El Diablo

Galer St.

Caffe Fiore Five Spot

5th Ave. N

QUEEN ANNE

Lee St.

Nob Hill Ave. N

99

W Comstock St.

Kerry Park

W Highland Dr.

W Prospect St.

Queen Anne Ave.

Warren Ave. N

Highland Dr.

Prospect St.

5th Ave. N

*Lake Union
Park*

3

1st Ave. W

Queen Anne Ave.

3rd Ave. N

W Ward St.

Aloha St.

Valley St.

4th Ave. N

Crow

Tayor Ave. N

6th Ave. N

Aurora Ave. N

Dexter Ave. N

8th Ave. N

Valley St.

Roy St.

Maxwell
Hotel

MarQueen Hotel

Roy

4

W Mercer St.

Dick's Drive-In

Mercer St.

**SOUTH
LAKE UNION**

W. W.

3rd Ave. W

2nd Ave. W

1st Ave. W

Queen Anne Ave.

Republican St.

W Harrison St.

W Thomas St.

W John St.

SEATTLE CENTER

Republican St.

Harrison St.

5th Ave. N

Broad St.

1st Ave. N

Warren Ave. N

2nd Ave. N

4th Ave. N

Tayor Ave. N

6th Ave. N

Thomas St.

John St.

Dexter Ave. N

8th Ave. N

9th Ave. N

Westlake Ave. N

Flying
Fish

Terry Ave. N

Boren Ave. N

Fairview Ave. N

5

Denny Wy.

Bay St.

Boat Street Cafe

Eagle St.

Western Ave.

13 Coins

Pan Pacific
Hotel Seattle

Tutta Bella Neapolitan Pizza Seastar Seafood
Restaurant & Rav
Whole
Foods

7th Ave.

8th Ave.

Terry Ave.

9th Ave.

4th Ave.

3rd Ave.

99

Bell St.

6th Ave.

5th Ave.

Blanchard St.

Lenora St.

MistralKitchen

6

Clay St.

Cedar St.

Vine St.

Wall St.

Elliott Av

2nd Ave.

1st Ave.

Black
Bottle

Battery St.

Battery St. Tunnel

6th Ave.

Virginia St.

9th Ave.

8th A

BELLTOWN

0   1/4 mi

0   1/4 km

A **B** **C** **D**

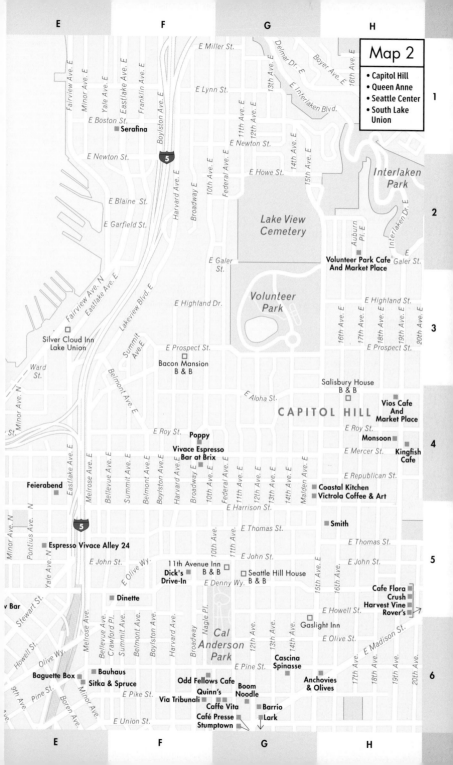

Map 2

- Capitol Hill
- Queen Anne
- Seattle Center
- South Lake Union

E Miller St.

E Lynn St.

E Boston St. Serafina

E Newton St.

E Newton St.

Fairview Ave. E Minor Ave. E Yale Ave. E Eastlake Ave. E Franklin Ave. E Boylston Ave. E Harvard Ave. E Broadway E 10th Ave. E Federal Ave. E 11th Ave. E 12th Ave. E

Delmar Dr. E Boyer Ave. E 13th Ave. E 16th Ave. E

E Interlaken Blvd.

E Howe St.

14th Ave. E 15th Ave. E

Interlaken Park

E Blaine St.

E Garfield St.

Interlaken Dr. E

Lake View Cemetery

Auburn Pl. E

Volunteer Park Cafe And Market Place

Galer St.

E Galer St.

E Highland Dr.

Volunteer Park

E Highland St.

16th Ave. E 17th Ave. E 18th Ave. E 19th Ave. E 20th Ave. E

Fairview Ave. N Eastlake Ave. E

Silver Cloud Inn Lake Union

Summit Ave. E Lakeview Blvd. E Belmont Ave. E

E Prospect St.

E Prospect St.

Bacon Mansion B & B

Ward St.

Salisbury House B & B

E Aloha St.

CAPITOL HILL

Vios Cafe And Market Place

Minor Ave. N

E Roy St. Poppy

Vivace Espresso Bar at Brix

E Roy St.

Monsoon

Eastlake Ave. E Melrose Ave. E Bellevue Ave. E Summit Ave. E Belmont Ave. E Boylston Ave. E Harvard Ave. E Broadway E 10th Ave. E Federal Ave. E 11th Ave. E 12th Ave. E 13th Ave. E 14th Ave. E Malden Ave. E

E Mercer St.

Kingfish Cafe

Feierabend

E Republican St.

Coastal Kitchen Victrola Coffee & Art

E Harrison St.

Minor Ave. N Pontius Ave. N

Smith

Espresso Vivace Alley 24

E Thomas St.

E Thomas St.

E John St.

11th Avenue Inn B & B Seattle Hill House B & B

E John St.

E John St.

15th Ave. E 16th Ave. E

Dick's Drive-In

Yale Ave. N Stewart St.

E Olive Wy.

Dinette

E Denny Wy.

Cafe Flora Crush Harvest Vine Rover's

Bellevue Ave. E Crawford Pl. Summit Ave. E Belmont Ave. E Boylston Ave. E Harvard Ave. Broadway Nagle Pl.

Bar

Howell St. Olive Wy.

Gaslight Inn

E Howell St.

E Olive St.

E Madison St.

Baguette Box Bauhaus

Sitka & Spruce

Cal Anderson Park

Cascina Spinasse

17th Ave. E 18th Ave. E 20th Ave. E

9th Ave. Boren Ave. Minor Ave. Pine St.

E Pike St.

E Pine St.

Odd Fellows Cafe

Quinn's

Via Tribunali

Boom Noodle

Anchovies & Olives

Caffe Vita

Café Presse Stumptown

Barrio

Lark

12th Ave. 13th Ave. 14th Ave. 15th Ave. 16th Ave.

E Union St.

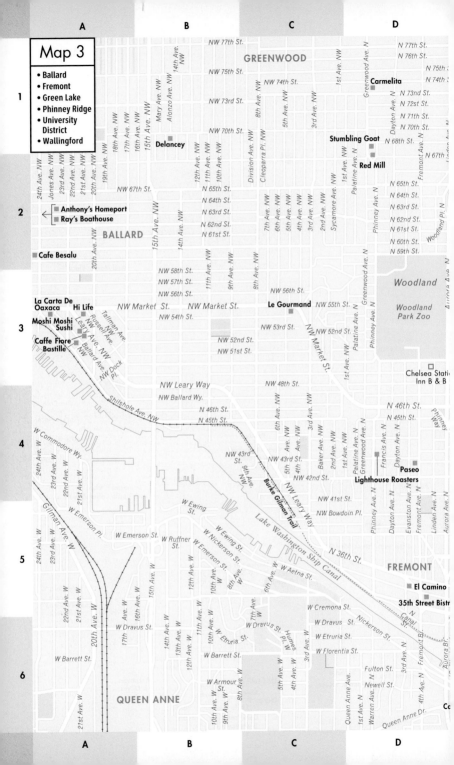

Map 3

- Ballard
- Fremont
- Green Lake
- Phinney Ridge
- University District
- Wallingford

A **B** **C** **D**

GREENWOOD

NW 77th St.
N 77th St.
N 76th St.
NW 75th St.
N 75th St.
NW 74th St.
Carmelita
N 73rd St.
NW 73rd St.
N 72nd St.
N 71st St.
N 70th St.
Delancey
NW 70th St.
Stumbling Goat
N 68th St.
N 67th St.
Red Mill
NW 67th St.
N 65th St.
N 65th St.
N 64th St.
N 64th St.
N 63rd St.
N 63rd St.
N 62nd St.
N 62nd St.
N 61st St.

BALLARD
◄— Anthony's Homeport
■ Ray's Boathouse
N 60th St.
N 59th St.

■ Cafe Besalu

NW 58th St.
NW 57th St.
NW 56th St.

Woodland

NW 56th St.

Woodland Park Zoo

La Carta De Oaxaca Hi Life
NW Market St. NW Market St.
Le Gourmand NW 55th St.
NW 54th St.
Moshi Moshi Sushi
NW 53rd St. NW 52nd St.
Caffe Fiore
Bastille
NW 52nd St.
NW 51st St.

□ Chelsea Station Inn B & B

NW Leary Way
NW 48th St.
NW Ballard Wy.
N 46th St. N 46th St.
N 45th St. N 45th St.

Shilshole Ave. NW

NW 43rd St. NW 43rd St.
Francis Ave. N
NW 42nd St.
Paseo
Lighthouse Roasters
NW 41st St. NW Bowdoin Pl.

W Commodore Wy.
Lake Washington Ship Canal
N 36th St.
FREMONT
W Emerson Pl.
■ El Camino
W Emerson St.
35th Street Bistro
W Emerson St.
W Ewing St.
W Ruffner St.
W Nickerson St.
W Aetna St.
W Cremona St.
Nickerson St.
W Dravus St.
W Dravus St.
W Dravus St.
W Etruria St.
W Etruria St.
W Barrett St.
W Florentia St.
W Barrett St.
Fulton St.
Newell St.
W Armour St.

QUEEN ANNE
Queen Anne Dr.

A **B** **C** **D**

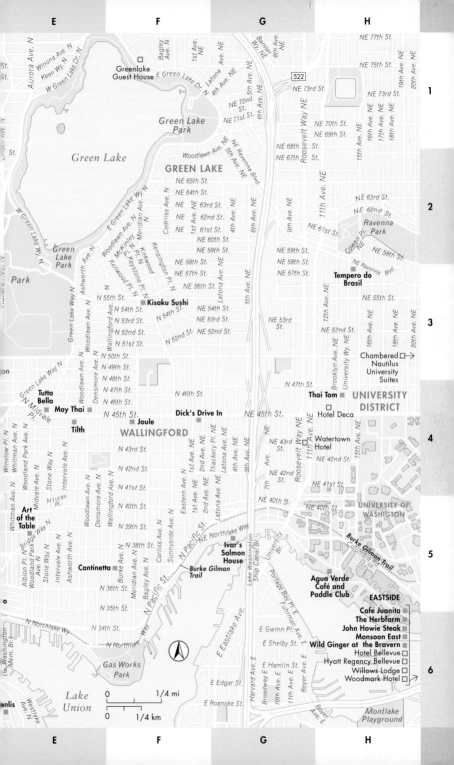

Restaurants

Where to Stay

WORD OF MOUTH

"The best hotel [in Seattle], if money is no object, is the new Four Seasons, hands down—get a bay view room. The Inn at the Market is also quite nice if you prefer a smaller boutique hotel; go for a partial water-view room. The Fairmont Olympic is a big, traditional hotel."

—NWWanderer

Updated by
Cedar Burnett

Much like its culture, food, and fashion, Seattle's lodging offers something for everyone. There are grand, awe-inspiring vintage hotels; sleek, elegant, modern properties; green hotels with yoga studios and enough bamboo for an army of pandas; and wee B&Bs with sweet bedspreads and home-cooked breakfasts.

Travelers who appreciate the anonymity of high-rise chains can comfortably stay here, while guests who want to feel like family can find the perfect boutique inn to lay their heads.

The newest properties on the scene are stunning: Four Seasons Hotel Seattle brings a modern, Northwest-infused take on the brand, while the Hyatt at Olive 8 offers luxurious green digs as the city's first LEED-certified hotel. The Maxwell Hotel is lower Queen Anne's chic new property with modern styling and great views of the Space Needle.

The budget-minded may notice that Seattle's typically grit-your-teeth-and-bear-it prices are a bit better than in recent years. As travelers have felt the squeeze, hotels have responded with lower prices and special packages. Also, you'll be able to enjoy sensible extras, like free parking or meal vouchers. Many hotel bars and restaurants are also offering happy hours, sometimes twice a day, with an emphasis on food as well as cocktails.

Lodging in Seattle is only getting more and more stylish. All the neighborhoods we list are great options, and prices are generally lower. What's the rub, you ask? *Parking*, particularly in Downtown, can be a major pain; also, "lower prices" does not translate into *low* prices. Some hotels charge for Wi-Fi, and, with all the convention and cruise travelers, high season can mean a scramble to find anything in the center of town. Never fear, though—most of the neighborhoods have relatively quick access to Downtown; a couple, like Queen Anne and Capitol Hill, are a quick walk away, and many hotels offer free shuttles to the core. Breathe deep, book ahead, and shoot for the stars—you never know what sort of deals you might find.

WHERE SHOULD I STAY?

	Neighborhood Vibe	Pros	Cons
Downtown and Belltown	Downtown is central, with the hottest hotels with water views. If you're a fan of galleries and bars, stay in Belltown.	A day in Downtown and Belltown can take you from the Seattle Art Museum to Pike Place Market.	Parking can be pricey and hard to come by. This is not your spot if you want quiet, relaxing respite.
Seattle Center, South Lake Union, and Queen Anne	Queen Anne boasts great water views and easy access to Downtown. South Lake Union can feel industrial.	Seattle Center's many festivals (such as Bumbershoot) means you'll have a ringside seat.	If you're mostly focused on seeing the key Downtown sights or have limited mobility, parking can be difficult.
Capitol Hill	One of Seattle's oldest and quirkiest neighborhoods, Capitol Hill has cozy accommodations.	A great place to stay if you want to mingle with creative locals in great bookstores and cafés.	If you're uncomfortable with the pierced, tattooed, or GLBT set, look elsewhere.
Fremont	From the Woodland Park Zoo to the Locks, funky Fremont is an excellent jumping-off point.	This quintessential Seattle 'hood is a short trek from Downtown and has restaurants and shops.	The only lodging to be found here are B&Bs—book ahead.
Green Lake	Laid back and wonderfully situated near the Woodland Park Zoo and Gas Works Park.	Outdoorsy types will love the proximity to Green Lake, a great place to stroll or jog.	You won't find anything trendy here, and, after a few days, you'll have seen everything.
University District	It offers everything you'd expect from a college area—from bookstores to ethnic food.	If you're renting a car, this area offers centrality with a lower price tag.	Homeless and college kids populate University Avenue ("The Ave"). Not much in the way of sightseeing.
West Seattle	In summer, West Seattle can feel a lot like Southern California: It's a fun place to stay.	Alki Beach and Lincoln Park are fun, plus great restaurants and shopping on California Ave.	You'll need a car to stay in this very removed 'hood. The only way in or out is over a bridge.
The Eastside	Proximity to high-end malls, Woodinville wineries, and Microsoft.	Woodinville is wine HQ; Kirkland offers cute boutiques; and Bellevue is a shopping mecca.	If you're here to experience Seattle, stick to the city. Traffic is a total nightmare.

4

WHERE TO STAY PLANNER

Lodging Strategy

Where should we stay? With so many Seattle hotels, it may seem like a daunting question. But fret not—our expert writers and editors have done most of the legwork. The selections here represent the best this city has to offer—from the best budget-friendly B&Bs to the sleekest designer hotels. Scan "Best Bets" on the following pages for top recommendations by price and experience. Or find a review quickly in the listings. Search by neighborhood, then alphabetically.

Need a Reservation?

It is imperative to book in advance for July and August, especially if you want to stay in one of the in-demand budget properties or at any bed-and-breakfast. Some B&Bs start to fill up their summer slots by March or April. The best water-view rooms in Downtown luxury hotels are often gone by mid-February. You aren't likely to have trouble booking a room the rest of the year as long as your visit doesn't coincide with major conventions or arts or sporting events.

B&Bs fill up quickly, but it's always worth giving them a call to see what's available. Because they encourage longer stays, you may be able to get a last-minute room for a night or two to bridge the gaps that pop up as long-term guests turn over. In this case, you're doing the B&B a favor and may get a discounted rate.

Smoking

The city has banned smoking in most public places, including all restaurants and bars, and the new and pervasive trend is for hotels to be completely smoke-free. It's now extremely difficult to find smoking rooms; puffers may want to reconsider upgrading to that balcony room.

Money-Saving Tips

The best way to save? Travel off-season. Amazing deals at the hottest properties can be had in spring (and sometimes even in early June). Weather is more hit or miss this time of year than in July or August, but there are often many beautiful dry days. Rates drop dramatically again once October rolls around. Mild, picture-perfect fall days are a well-kept secret here—hiking's often good until the end of the month and the Cascades get some beautiful fall colors.

But you probably want to see the city in its late-summer glory. In that case, good luck to you. Lodging-wise, there isn't much of an upside to Seattle's high season—the best you can do is book as far in advance as possible. Mid-week prices may be lower than weekend rates, but don't count on it. You'll always save more with multi-night stays, particularly at B&Bs, which often have unofficial policies of giving discounts to long-term guests. The best collection of good deals is on Capitol Hill because most of its properties are B&Bs; the Queen Anne and Lake Union neighborhoods also turn up some good deals and are much closer to Downtown than the U-District, which is the other neighborhood that has a decent selection of mid-range properties.

Parking

Parking in Seattle is expensive, particularly Downtown. Expect to pay between $15 and $45 a day, even at hotels that cost more than $300 a night. Many properties have a valet option, and a handful allow valet parking only. A few hotels offer complimentary parking—you'll find more options out of the city center. And street parking is de rigueur for much of the University District and Capitol Hill.

In This Chapter

Facilities

All hotels listed have a private bath, heat, air-conditioning, TV, and phone unless otherwise noted. In the past, air-conditioning was never a deal-breaker—mild summers and cool evenings made it unnecessary. However, recent heat waves have sent many an air-conditioning-hating resident running to the nearest movie theater for relief. If you require air-conditioning, make sure your room has it in summer.

Using the Maps

4

Throughout the chapter, you'll see mapping symbols and coordinates (✦ 3:F2) after property names or reviews. To locate the property on a map, turn to the Seattle Dining and Lodging Atlas. The first number after the ✦ symbol indicates the map number. Following that is the property's coordinate on the map grid.

Prices

Seattle's peak season is May through September, with August at the pinnacle. Prices throughout the city skyrocket then; some are nearly double what they are in low season.

The lodgings listed are the cream of the crop in each price category. Prices are based on the best high-season rates offered directly from the property; they do not take into account discounts or package deals you may find on consolidator Web sites. We list the facilities that are available—but we don't specify whether they cost extra.

Assume that hotels operate on the European Plan (EP, with no meals) unless specified that they use the All-inclusive (AI, with all meals and some drinks and activities), Continental Plan (CP, with a Continental breakfast), Modified American Plan (MAP, with breakfast and dinner), or the Full American Plan (FAP, with all meals).

Construction Concerns

Despite the recession, Seattle is still undergoing growth and development. Parts of the South Lake Union, the Eastside, and Downtown areas are seeing major construction, and projects in progress can be found throughout the metro area. It's worth inquiring about such things while booking and asking how local construction projects may affect the views, noise levels, and traffic situations around your hotel.

WHAT IT COSTS FOR TWO PEOPLE

¢	$	$$	$$$	$$$$
under $100	$100–$180	$181–$265	$266–$350	over $350

Prices reflect the rack rate of a standard double room for two people in high season, excluding the 12% (for hotels with fewer than 60 rooms) or 15.6% (for hotels with more than 60 rooms) city and state taxes. Check online for off-season rates and special deals or discounts.

BEST BETS FOR SEATTLE LODGING

Fodor's offers a selective listing of lodging experiences at every price range. Here, we've compiled our top recommendations by price and experience. The very best properties are designated in the listings with the Fodor's Choice logo.

Hyatt at Olive 8, p. 183

Fodor's Choice ★

Ace Hotel, p. 189

Chelsea Station Inn Bed & Breakfast, p. 197

Doubletree Arctic Club Hotel, p. 177

11th Avenue Inn Bed & Breakfast, p. 195

The Fairmont Olympic Hotel, p. 178

Four Seasons Hotel Seattle, p. 178

Greenlake Guest House, p. 198

Hotel 1000, p. 180

Hyatt at Olive 8, p. 183

Inn at El Gaucho, p. 191

Inn at the Market, p. 184

Pan Pacific Hotel Seattle, p. 192

Salisbury House Bed & Breakfast, p. 196

By Price

¢

11th Avenue Inn Bed & Breakfast, p. 195

Gaslight Inn, p. 196

Green Tortoise Backpacker's Hotel, p. 179

Pensione Nichols Bed & Breakfast, p. 185

$

Ace Hotel, p. 189

Greenlake Guest House, p. 198

Hotel Max, p. 180

Inn at El Gaucho, p. 191

Salisbury House Bed & Breakfast, p. 196

$$

Chelsea Station Inn Bed & Breakfast, p. 197

Doubletree Arctic Club Hotel, p. 177

Hyatt at Olive 8, p. 183

Hotel Vintage Park, p. 183

Inn at the Market, p. 184

Maxwell Hotel, p. 194

Pan Pacific Hotel Seattle, p. 192

$$$

Alexis Hotel, p. 177

Hotel Ändra, p. 190

Hotel Monaco, p. 180

Hotel 1000, p. 180

Sorrento Hotel, p. 187

W Seattle, p. 187

$$$$

The Fairmont Olympic Hotel, p. 178

Four Seasons Hotel Seattle, p. 178

By Experience

BEST VIEWS

Edgewater, p. 189

Four Seasons Hotel Seattle, p. 178

Inn at the Market, p. 184

Grand Hyatt Seattle, p. 179

GREEN FOCUS

The Fairmont Olympic Hotel, p. 178

Hotel Monaco, p. 180

Pan Pacific Hotel Seattle, p. 192

HOT SCENE

Four Seasons Hotel Seattle, p. 178

Hotel Ändra, p. 190

Hotel 1000, p. 180

Hyatt at Olive 8, p. 183

BEST SPA

Four Seasons Hotel Seattle, p. 178

Hyatt at Olive 8, p. 183

MOST KID-FRIENDLY

Chambered Nautilus University Suites, p. 199

The Fairmont Olympic Hotel, p. 178

Four Seasons Hotel Seattle, p. 178

Hotel Monaco, p. 180

Pan Pacific Hotel Seattle, p. 192

Silver Cloud Inn Lake Union, p. 194

DOWNTOWN AND BELLTOWN

Downtown has the greatest concentration of hotels, many of which are new or updated high-end high-rises, though there are also several boutique hotels and mid-range properties in historic buildings. There aren't many budget properties in the area. Belltown, slightly north and within walking distance of Downtown, has some of the city's trendiest hotels. It's a great place to stay if you plan to hit the bars and clubs in the neighborhood.

All Downtown and Belltown hotels are convenient (and within walking distance) to many major sights—including the Seattle Art Museum, Pike Place Market, and the Olympic Sculpture Park. Although the waterfront is an integral part of Downtown, there are surprisingly few hotels directly on the water. Many high-rises have water views, but make sure to specify that you want a room with a view.

4

DOWNTOWN

$$$–$$$$ ☒ **Alexis Hotel.** Aesthetes and modern romantics will adore the Alexis Hotel, which occupies two historic buildings near the waterfront. Using slate gray, soft blue, taupe, and white against exposed brick, walls of windows, and nouveau-baroque touches, the Alexis has updated its look while maintaining a classic feel—the palette may be modern, but the ornate leather chairs and wood-burning fireplaces recall a different era. The Alexis has always had a focus on art (including a rotating collection of artwork selected by a Seattle Art Museum curator in the corridor between wings), and that tradition continues in the rooms as well—all have unique works of art. The property has 10 different types of specialty rooms in addition to themed suites. The Alexis Suite is hard to ignore: it's a full-blown two-bedroom apartment with two baths, a skylight, and exposed-brick walls. Downstairs, the Library bistro is one of the city's favorite lunchtime hideaways and bars. **Pros:** beautifully refurbished rooms; in-room spa services; specialty suites aren't prohibitively expensive. **Cons:** small lobby; not entirely soundproofed; some rooms can be a bit dark. ☒ *1007 1st Ave., Downtown* ☎ *206/624–4844 or 888/850–1155* ⊕ *www.alexishotel.com* ➘ *88 rooms, 33 suites* ⌂ *In-room: refrigerator, safe, Wi-Fi. In-hotel: restaurant, room service, bar, gym, spa, laundry service, Wi-Fi hotspot, parking (paid), some pets allowed* ⊟ *AE, D, DC, MC, V* ✛ *1:B1.*

$$–$$$ ☒ **Doubletree Arctic Club Hotel.** Close to the stadiums and in the heart
Fodor's Choice of the financial district, this early-1900s landmark hotel was lovingly
★ restored from its gentlemen's club roots in 2006 to become a classy luxury hotel. From the Alaskan-marble-sheathed foyer and the antique walrus heads on the third floor, to the Northern Lights Dome room with its leaded glass ceiling and rococo touches, the Arctic Club pays homage to a different era of Gold Rush opulence. Guest rooms are done in earthy neutrals, with buttery leather chairs, and dark-wood crown molding. Fun touches like trunks for bedside tables and walrus bottle openers continue the arctic club theme. Choose from rooms with whirlpools or deluxe showers; some standard rooms (and all the suites) also have sofa beds for those traveling with children; a few rooms have outdoor terraces. Enjoy cocktails in their Polar Bar or sit for serious

noshing at the Northwest-influenced, urban-casual JUNO restaurant. **Pros:** cool, unique property; great staff; right on the bus line. **Cons:** fitness center is small; not in the absolute heart of Downtown; rooms are a bit dark. ⊠ *700 3rd Ave., Downtown* ☎ *206/340–0340* ⊕ *www. doubletree1.hilton.com* ⊅ *120 rooms* ⅗ *In-room: a/c, safe, refrigerator (some), DVD, Wi-Fi. In-hotel: restaurant, room service, 2 bars, gym, laundry service, Internet terminal, Wi-Fi hotspot, parking (paid), some pets allowed* ⊟ *AE, D, DC, MC, V* ✛ *1:F4.*

$$$$
☪
Fodor's Choice
★
The Fairmont Olympic Hotel. Grand and stately, the Fairmont Olympic transports travelers to another time. Between the marble floors, brocade chairs, silk wallpaper, Corinthian columns, massive chandeliers, and sweeping staircases worthy of Rhett Butler, this old-world hotel personifies class and elegance. It's no wonder that so many Seattleites get married in this Renaissance Revival hotel—it's as close to a princess palace as most of us will ever get to experience. Guest rooms are lovely and light, with French Country touches like pale yellow wallpaper and traditional floral patterns. The suites are a popular option for parents with kids—sofa beds are separated from the bedroom, and rollaway beds are available. The well-heeled leisure or business traveler will find everything he or she needs here: elegant dining and afternoon tea at the Georgian; an extensive fitness center with an indoor pool; a full-service business center; in-room massage; and a shopping arcade. Kids are even catered to, with child-size furniture and bathrobes, though wild tots might draw glances. **Pros:** elegant and spacious lobby; great location; excellent service; fabulous on-site dining. **Cons:** rooms are a bit small for the price; may be a little too old-school for trendy travelers. ⊠ *411 University St., Downtown* ☎ *206/621–1700 or 800/441–1414* ⊕ *www. fairmont.com/seattle* ⊅ *232 rooms, 218 suites* ⅗ *In-room: safe, DVD (some), Wi-Fi. In-hotel: 2 restaurants, room service, bar, pool, gym, children's programs, laundry service, Wi-Fi hotspot, parking (fee), some pets allowed* ⊟ *AE, D, DC, MC, V* ✛ *1:E3.*

$$$$
☪
Fodor's Choice
★
Four Seasons Hotel Seattle. The newest hotel jewel (or mega-diamond) in downtown Seattle gazes out over Elliott Bay. Just south of the Pike Place Market and steps from Benaroya Hall and the Seattle Art Museum, the hotel is polished and elegant, with Eastern accents and plush furnishings set against a definite modern-Northwest backdrop, in which materials, such as stone and fine hardwoods, take center stage, as seen in the sleek reception area. An extensive day spa and an infinity-pool terrace will help you relax after a day of exploring. Floor-to-ceiling windows in the guest rooms are unforgettable; lovely linens, comfortable living spaces, and sleek marble bathrooms with deep soaking tubs, luxurious rain showers, and TVs embedded in the mirrors are added bonuses. The vibe here isn't pretentious, but it's certainly not laid-back either: Guests seem to know that they are in for a real treat. ■ **TIP→** ART **Restaurant and Lounge, headed up by Kerry Sear, offers up fabulous cocktails and good Northwest cuisine, with stunning views.** A trip to the bar is a must if you're in the area for creative Northwest-inspired martinis and tapas menu; happy hour is 5 to 7 Sunday through Thursday. **Pros:** amazing views; wonderful aesthetics; large rooms with luxurious bathrooms; lovely spa. **Cons:** Four Seasons regulars might not click with

this modern take on the brand; some guests say service kinks need to be ironed out. ☒ *99 Union St., Downtown* ☎ *206/749–7000* ⊕ *www. fourseasons.com* ⇨ *134 rooms,13 suites* ⚇ *In-room: safe, refrigerator (some), DVD, Wi-Fi. In-hotel: restaurant, room service, bar, pool, gym, spa, children's programs, laundry service, parking (paid), some pets allowed* ⊟ *AE, D, DC, MC, V* ✛ *1:D3.*

$$–$$$ **Grand Hyatt Seattle.** Adjacent to the Washington State Convention Center, this view-centric hotel appeals to business travelers or conventioneers who want a dependable Hyatt-level stay in a great downtown location. The decor throughout is masculine-chic and not particularly imaginative but comfortably unobtrusive. Rooms, set upward from the 10th floor, are done in shades of brown with orange accents and enjoy vistas of Elliott Bay. Three types of large suites have separate sitting rooms, and executive quarters have refrigerators and wet bars. All bathrooms have marble floors, granite counters, and oversize soaking tubs. The famous Ruth's Chris Steak House and Cheesecake Factory restaurants are downstairs. **Pros:** spectacular views; central location; large bathrooms. **Cons:** some visitors complain of uninspiring amenities; there's no proper lounge. ☒ *721 Pine St., Downtown* ☎ *206/774–1234* ⊕ *www.grandseattle.hyatt.com* ⇨ *317 rooms, 108 suites* ⚇ *In-room: safe, refrigerator (some), Wi-Fi. In-hotel: 2 restaurants, room service, bar, gym, laundry service, Wi-Fi hotspot, parking (paid)* ⊟ *AE, D, DC, MC, V* ✛ *1:F2.*

¢ **Green Tortoise Backpacker's Hotel.** A Seattle institution, the Green Tortoise is still considered by many budget travelers to be the best deal in town. Even if you don't own a backpack and the word "hostel" gives you the heebie-jeebies, the impressive cleanliness here makes the Tortoise a viable option for all sorts of travelers who don't mind sacrificing a little comfort and privacy. Young (and young at heart) travelers might feel the most at home here, but anyone looking for a bargain is more than welcome. All rooms here share bathrooms, which are spacious, clean, and nicely tiled. Each bunk bed has its own locker, light, privacy curtains, four-plug outlet, and fan. The rate includes a fairly extensive breakfast buffet, and dinner Sunday, Tuesday, and Thursday nights. **Pros:** cheapest lodging in town; great place to make instant friends from around the globe; across the street from Pike Place Market. **Cons:** most guests are in their early twenties (and act like it); no frills rooms with shared bathrooms. ☒ *105½ Pike St., Downtown* ☎ *206/340–1222* ⊕ *www.greentortoise.net* ⇨ *30 rooms without private bath* ⚇ *In-room: no phone, no TV, Wi-Fi. In-hotel: laundry facilities, Wi-Fi hotspot* ⊟ *MC, V* ⏸*⊙* ⏸*BP* ✛ *1:D3.*

$$ **Hilton Seattle Hotel.** Just west of I–5, the Seattle Hilton is a popular site for meetings and conventions. The rooms are tasteful but nondescript—you'll be paying for a brand name here, reliable though it may be. Some rooms do have views over the city to Elliott Bay in the distance. Providing excellent views of the city, the Top of the Hilton bar-restaurant serves well-executed salmon dishes and other local specialties for breakfast or lunch. An underground passage connects the Hilton with the Rainier Square shopping concourse, the 5th Avenue Theatre, and the Convention Center. **Pros:** children up to age 8 stay

free; helpful staff; clean rooms; comfortable beds. **Cons:** overpriced for what you get; small bathrooms; hotel needs a renovation. ⊠ *1301 6th Ave., Downtown* ☎ *206/624–0500, 800/542–7700, or 800/426– 0535* ⊕ *www.seattlehilton.com* ➲ *237 rooms, 3 suites* ⚷ *In-room: safe, Wi-Fi. In-hotel: 2 restaurants, room service, bar, gym, laundry service, parking (paid)* ▭ *AE, D, DC, MC, V* ✥ *1:F3.*

$ ▦ **Hotel Max.** Sassy and art-forward, the Hotel Max blends artsy decor with punchy minimalism for an architect-office effect—one with cushy trimmings. Travelers interested in cutting-edge local artists, and anyone who wants to feel like a rock star, will be very happy with this super stylish hotel that swears it has created a new design aesthetic, "Maximalism." The hallway of each floor is dedicated to a different local photographer and giant black-and-white photos cover each door. A few paintings from local artists are all that decorate the gray walls of the guest rooms; a few carefully placed accent colors like an orange bedspread or a red cushion on a stool save the rooms from being drab. The beds are huge and heavenly. The only downside to the Max is that most of the rooms are quite small—owing more to the constraints of being in a historic building than to tenets of minimalism—and bathrooms have very little counter space. **Pros:** amazing beds; cool artwork; late checkout time available. **Cons:** small rooms; no views; older travelers may not be comfortable here. ⊠ *620 Stewart St., Downtown* ☎ *206/728–6299 or 866/833–6299* ⊕ *www.hotelmaxseattle.com* ➲ *163 rooms* ⚷ *In-room: safe, refrigerator, Wi-Fi. In-hotel: restaurant, room service, gym, laundry service, parking (paid), some pets allowed* ▭ *AE, D, DC, MC, V* ▯◎| *EP* ✥ *1:E1.*

$$$ ▦ **Hotel Monaco.** Travelers with a sense of whimsy and a penchant for
☺   fun will fall hard for the Hotel Monaco. With near-circus aesthetics— think bright raspberry-and-cream striped wallpaper, gold sunburst decorations, and animal prints—even the rainiest Seattle day seems bearable. All (and we do mean all) pets are welcome, or you can can opt to borrow a goldfish for your stay. The bright lobby is done up with hand-painted nautical murals, and serves as party headquarters: check out the nightly wine receptions in the lobby sometimes include chair fortune-telling services and Guitar Hero on Fridays. Amazingly, none of this fun feels too forced; guests wishing to have a more low-key experience will be able to do so. **Pros:** inviting lobby; fun and quirky decor and amenities; helpful staff. **Cons:** room decor may be too off-the-wall for some; rooms are a bit pricey for what you get; on-site restaurant is not notable. ⊠ *1101 4th Ave., Downtown* ☎ *206/621–1770 or 888/454– 8397* ⊕ *www.monaco-seattle.com* ➲ *144 rooms, 45 suites* ⚷ *In-room: refrigerator, DVD, Wi-Fi. In-hotel: restaurant, room service, bar, gym, laundry service, Wi-Fi hotspot, parking (paid), pets allowed* ▭ *AE, D, DC, MC, V* ✥ *1:E3.*

$$$ ▦ **Hotel 1000.** Chic and cosmopolitan, Hotel 1000 is luxe and decid-
Fodor's Choice   edly art-forward and modern—the centerpiece of the small lobby is
★   a dramatically lighted glass staircase and original artwork by Pacific Northwest artist J.P. Canlis. Studio 1000, the small sitting room off the lobby, pairs an elegant fire pit with mid-century modern swiveling leather chairs. The designers wanted the hotel to have a distinctly

CLOSE UP

Seattle Spas

Seattle's spa scene is on the rise, with several top-notch places and new organic options that offer everything from haircuts and pedicures to elaborate all-day massage and body-treatment packages. In addition to the independent choices listed here, there are several notable hotels spas in town, especially the **Spa at Four Seasons** and the **Elaia Spa at Hyatt at Olive 8.**

Gene Juarez Salon and Spa. With both a lively hair and nail salon and a more tranquil retreat for massage and skin treatments, Gene Juarez (in Downtown and Bellevue) offers one-stop shopping. The skin-care menu is long and inventive; massage techniques stick to the classics like deep tissue, shiatsu, and reflexology, with some Hawaiian hot-stone methods thrown in for good measure. The spa also offers a full menu of men's treatments, including hide-the-gray hair coloring and "sport" pedicures. ✉ *607 Pine St., Downtown* ☎ *206/326–6000* ✉ *Bellevue Galleria, 550 106th Ave. NE, Bellevue* ☎ *425/455–5511* ⊕ *www.genejuarez.com.*

Habitude Salon, Day Spa and Gallery. Beamed ceilings, polished wood floors, plush furnishings, and tropical scents relax you the moment you enter Habitude (in Ballard and Fremont). Indulge in a single treatment or in such packages as Beneath the Spring Thaw Falls (hydrating glow, massage, scalp treatment, sauna, and smoothie). Other offerings include the Hot Rocks detox sauna, Rainforest Steam Shower, delectable spa lunches, and door-to-door town-car service. It's the state's only Aveda Lifestyle spa. ✉ *2801 N.W. Market St., Ballard* ☎ *206/782–2898* ✉ *513 N. 36th St., Fremont* ☎ *206/633–1339* ⊕ *www.habitude.com.*

Spa Noir. If you're not into the new-age earth-tone vibe found in so many day spas, head to Spa Noir, a hip Belltown spot done in black, red, and gold. The spa specializes in facials, manicures and pedicures, and other beauty treatments, but it also offers a small menu of reasonably priced massage treatments. ✉ *2120 2nd Ave., Belltown* ☎ *206/448–7600* ⊕ *www.spanoir.net.*

Ummelina International Day Spa. Hand-carved Javanese doors open into this tranquil, luxurious, Asian-inspired Downtown spa. Relax beneath a warm waterfall, take a steamy, scented sauna, or submit to a mud wrap or smoothing body scrub. The three-hour Equator package for couples includes all this and more. Linger over the experience with a cup of delicately flavored tea. ✉ *1525 4th Ave., Downtown* ☎ *206/624–1370.*

4

Pacific Northwest feel, and they've succeeded without being campy. The whole hotel is done in dark woods and deep earth tones with an occasional blue accent. Rooms are full of surprising touches, including large tubs that fill from the ceiling. Hotel 1000 is without a doubt the most high-tech hotel in the city: Your phone will do everything from check the weather and airline schedules to give you restaurant suggestions; MP3 players and iPod docking stations are standard amenities. If you ever get tired of fiddling with the gadgets in your room, there's a state-of-the-art virtual golf club. **Pros:** lots of high-tech perks; guests feel pampered; hotel is hip without being alienating. **Cons:** rooms can

Fairmont Hotels & Resorts

Four Seasons Hotel

be dark; rooms without views look out on a cement wall; restaurant can be overpriced. ✉ *1000 1st Ave., Downtown* ☎ *206/957–1000* ⊕ *www.hotel1000seattle.com* ↵ *101 rooms, 19 suites* ♿ *In-room: safe, refrigerator, DVD, Wi-Fi. In-hotel: restaurant, room service, bar, gym, spa, laundry service, Wi-Fi hotspot, parking (paid), some pets allowed* ▭ *AE, MC, V* ✛ *1:E4.*

$$ 🛏 **Hotel Vintage Park.** Wine aficionados will be particularly taken with the Hotel Vintage Park, a charming boutique hotel, wonderfully situated near Downtown shopping, theaters, and the Convention Center. The Vintage Park's devotion to the Washington wine scene is as strong as ever. In addition to holding nightly receptions in the lobby where wine-makers are often present to discuss their products, the hotel can set up almost any wine-theme vacation you want. Each guest room is named for a Washington winery, has photographs and artwork donated by the winemakers, and features a color palette that includes all the hues you might encounter while walking among the vines. The best views offered here are of the Rem Koolhaas–designed public library. This is a smaller property with fewer facilities than some of the other nearby properties—the lobby's only interesting when the reception is in full swing. However, it's an updated place that's not another mid-century modern clone, which makes it a good choice for anyone looking for comfort, quiet, and coziness versus the latest trends and gadgets. **Pros:** wonderful service and friendly staff; great value; quiet rooms. **Cons:** small rooms; tiny gym; uninspiring on-site restaurant. ✉ *1100 5th Ave., Downtown* ☎ *206/624–8000 or 800/853–3914* ⊕ *www.hotelvintagepark.com* ↵ *124 rooms, 1 suite* ♿ *In-room: refrigerator, Wi-Fi. In-hotel: restaurant, room service, laundry service, Wi-Fi hotspot, parking (paid), some pets allowed* ▭ *AE, D, DC, MC, V* ✛ *1:F3.*

$$–$$$

Fodor's Choice

★

🛏 **Hyatt at Olive 8.** In a city that's known for environmental responsibility, being the greenest hotel in Seattle is no small feat, but the Hyatt at Olive 8 has achieved the honor by becoming the first LEED-certified hotel in the city, and environmentally friendly has rarely been this chic. The hotel manages to be modern and minimalist without being austere, with a warm blue-and-brown palette, tasteful metal accents, and dark- and light-wood interplay. Maybe it's the floor-to-ceiling windows flooding the place with light or extensive Elaia Spa, but the guests seem remarkably relaxed here. Middle-aged globe-trotters with sensible Euro shoes mix seamlessly with Tokyo hipsters and businessmen in the coffee and wine bar with (gasp) reasonable prices. Visitors also enjoy the on-site restaurant's extensive list of local wines and beer while seated around a reclaimed tree-turned-table that was downed by the '07 windstorm. Standard rooms are well appointed with fun enviro touches like dual-flush toilets, fresh-air vents, and low-flow showerheads. Allergy and asthma sufferers will also be happy with the complete lack of smell in the hotel—low VOC paint, wool carpeting, and natural materials were used throughout. From the green roof to the serene indoor pool and huge fitness center with yoga studio, this Hyatt proves that what's good for the planet can also be luxurious. **Pros:** central location; superb amenities; environmental responsibility; wonderful spa. **Cons:** standard rooms have showers only; fee for Wi-Fi use. ✉ *1635 8th Ave.,*

4

Downtown ☎ *206/695–1234* ⊕ *www.olive8.hyatt.com* ↪ *333 rooms, 13 suites* ⚴ *In-room: safe, refrigerator, Wi-Fi. In-hotel: restaurant, room service, bar, pool, gym, spa, laundry service, Internet terminal, Wi-Fi hotspot, parking (paid; discounts for hybrid vehicles)* ▤ *AE, D, DC, MC, V* ✛ *1:F1.*

\$\$ **Inn at Harbor Steps.** Just steps from the waterfront and Pike Place Mar-
☾   ket, this inn is sure to please those looking for a B&B feel with hotel amenities. Although it's on the lower floors of a modern high-rise residential building, the decor is quaint and country, with lots of florals in the guest rooms, country-manor plaid armchairs in the lobby, and wicker furniture in the library. Guest rooms are large, with high ceilings, gas fireplaces, and tidy kitchenettes. Bathrooms have large tubs and oversize shower stalls. The complimentary breakfast buffet is extensive and delicious. Hors d'oeuvres, wine, and tea are served each afternoon in the library. **Pros:** refrigerators come with complimentary water and soft drinks; good price for the location; spacious rooms; comfortable for families. **Cons:** in a condo complex so lacks the full "hotel experience"; not romantic or hip; no valet parking. ⊠ *1221 1st Ave., Downtown* ☎ *206/748–0973 or 888/728–8910* ⊕ *www.innatharborsteps. com* ↪ *30 rooms* ⚴ *In-room: refrigerator, Internet. In-hotel: 2 pools, 3 gyms, laundry service, parking (fee)* ▤ *AE, D, DC, MC, V* ❢◎❢ *BP* ✛ *1:E3.*

\$\$–\$\$\$\$ ⊡ **Inn at the Market.** From its heart-stopping views and comfortable
Fodor'sChoice   rooms to its fabulous location and amazing fifth-floor deck perched
★   above Puget Sound, the Inn at the Market is a place you'll want to visit again and again. The inn is well known locally and abroad for friendly, helpful service and excellent room service from French charmer Café Campagne and Northwest gastropub Bacco. Foodies, romantics, and nearly everyone in between will love the inn's prime location just off Pike Place Market, as well as the simple, sophisticated guest rooms with Tempur-Pedic beds, Northwest art, and bright, spacious bathrooms. Rooms are differentiated by the types of views they offer. You certainly won't be disappointed with the Partial Water View rooms—some have small sitting areas arranged in front of the windows. The four Deluxe Water View rooms—with glorious sundecks—are really spectacular, though. Even if you have to settle for a City Side room (a good deal even in high season), you can enjoy uninterrupted water views from the fifth-floor garden deck. **Pros:** outstanding views from most rooms and roof deck; steps from Pike Place Market; small and serene; complimentary town-car service for Downtown locations. **Cons:** little common space; not much in the way of amenities; a full renovation should take place in early 2011, so some rooms may be unavailable. ⊠ *86 Pine St., Downtown* ☎ *206/443–3600 or 800/446–4484* ⊕ *www.innatthemarket.com* ↪ *63 rooms, 7 suites* ⚴ *In-room: safe, refrigerator, Wi-Fi. In-hotel: 3 restaurants, room service, laundry service, Wi-Fi hotspot, parking (paid)* ▤ *AE, D, DC, MC, V* ✛ *1:D2.*

\$–\$\$ ⊡ **Mayflower Park Hotel.** Classic and comfortable, the Mayflower Park is unabashedly old school. Situated in a historic building, the hotel is decked out with sturdy antiques, Asian accents, brass fixtures, and florals. The standard rooms are on the small side, but all rooms have nice bathrooms with large mirrors and pedestal sinks. The main draw, however, is the location. The Mayflower Park is a quick walk from Pike Place Market and wonderfully central to Downtown shopping and Belltown sites. Despite its centrality, the hotel is so sturdily constructed that it's much quieter than many modern Downtown hotels. The Mayflower also boasts a star restaurant, Andaluca, as well as Oliver's, a well-known martini bar, which even locals flock to for its authentic cocktails. **Pros:** central Downtown location; access to spa next door; direct connection to the airport via Light Rail; excellent service. **Cons:** rooms are small; no pool. ⊠ *405 Olive Way, Downtown* ☎ *206/623–8700 or 800/426–5100* ⊕ *www.mayflowerpark.com* ⇥ *161 rooms, 29 suites* ♿ *In-room: safe, refrigerator, Wi-Fi. In-hotel: restaurant, room service, bar, gym, laundry service, Wi-Fi hotspot, parking (paid)* ▭ *AE, D, DC, MC, V* ✛ *1:E2.*

$–$$ 🏨 **The Paramount Hotel.** Good value meets great location with this solid midline boutique hotel. You won't find flashy amenities or an impressive lobby here, but the Paramount delivers on clean, tasteful rooms and easy access to theaters, the Convention Center, Downtown shopping, and the Pike Place Market. Dragonfish, the on-site Pan-Asian restaurant, has impressive happy-hour deals and fabulous sushi. The restaurant's decor is playful: dragon heads peer out over turquoise walls, lacquered red shutters, black furniture, and shoji screens, while the hum of locals and guests gives the place infectious energy. The hotel's guest rooms are done up in maroon, gold, and tan with a contemporary flare, and business travelers will enjoy the decent-size desks and in-room safes that can accommodate laptops. **Pros:** good value; excellent location; popular on-site restaurant. **Cons:** no view; not much in the way of amenities; tiny fitness center; thin walls. ⊠ *724 Pine St., Downtown* ☎ *206/292–9500* ⊕ *www.paramounthotelseattle.com* ⇥ *144 rooms, 2 suites* ♿ *In-room: safe, refrigerator (some), Internet, Wi-Fi. In-hotel: restaurant, room service, bar, gym, laundry facilities, laundry service, Internet terminal, Wi-Fi hotspot, parking (paid)* ▭ *AE, D, DC, MC, V* ✛ *1:E1.*

$–$$ 🏨 **Pensione Nichols Bed & Breakfast.** Once the favored lodging of Alan Ginsberg and a smattering of beat poets and artists throughout the years, Pensione Nichols offers one of the few affordable and unique options in Downtown Seattle. This is kind of like a hostel for grownups, or one for young people who want more privacy and style than a hostel can provide. The bed-and-breakfast is in a historic building, so the rooms are a mixed bag of sizes and layouts, but most have English antique furnishings, and all have newer beds. Some rooms have shared bathrooms (which are clean and spacious), and most of the rooms on the third floor have skylights instead of windows (because of the building's historic status, Nichols can't renovate to add windows). Second-floor suites have their own bathrooms, as well as full kitchens and large living rooms. The huge common room boasts spectacular views of Pike Place Market and Puget Sound. Breakfast is served in the light-filled common area. Ask for a skylight room for a quieter stay; the window rooms are noisier but provide a TV-like view of the bustle on 1st Avenue. **Pros:** unique layout; very different from typical hotel experience; great value for location. **Cons:** shared bathrooms; limited amenities; staff not always available. ⊠ *1923 1st Ave., Downtown* ☎ *206/441-7125* ⊕ *www.pensionenichols.com* ⇨ *8 rooms without bath, 2 suites* ⌂ *In-room: no phone, no TV, Wi-Fi. In-hotel: Wi-Fi hotspot, some pets allowed* ⊟ *AE, D, DC, MC, V* ⋓⊙⏐ *CP* ✛ *1:D2.*

$$ ⊞ **Red Lion Hotel on 5th Avenue.** Location is the major draw for this for-
℧   mer bank headquarters in the heart of Downtown. Convenient to the shopping and financial districts, as well as just about every other Downtown attraction, this traditional hotel offers casual comfort without a lot of fuss. The public spaces have high ceilings, tall windows, and dark-wood paneling. Guest rooms are midsize and are attractive enough, though decor in standard rooms is only a small step above a standard chain motel; they do, however, have pillow-top mattresses. Rooms on the executive floors (17–20) have exquisite views of Puget Sound or the city skyline. Definitely take advantage of the on-site bar and grill's huge outdoor patio. **Pros:** kids up to age 17 stay free; location; great water views from some rooms; free Wi-Fi. **Cons:** boutique prices for a chain hotel; readers complain about poor sound insulation between rooms; spotty service. ⊠ *1415 5th Ave., Downtown* ☎ *206/971–8000 or 800/733–5466* ⊕ *www.seattleredlionfifthavenue.com* ⇨ *287 rooms, 10 suites* ⌂ *In-room: refrigerator, Wi-Fi. In-hotel: restaurant, room service, gym, laundry service, Wi-Fi hotspot, parking (fee), some pets allowed* ⊟ *AE, D, DC, MC, V* ✛ *1:E2.*

$$ ⊞ **Renaissance Seattle.** After a $28 million renovation, this high-rise between Downtown and I–5 has a calm, woodsy feel to it, with lush green, burgundy, and brown decor, metal accents, and dark-wood furniture. The views from rooms above the 10th floor make it almost worth the proximity to the freeway, and exceptional views of Downtown, Elliott Bay, and the mountains can be enjoyed from rooms above the 20th floor. Traffic noise can be present throughout, so request a room on the west side for a quieter stay. The rooftop health club has a 40-foot pool. If you're willing to do a bit of extra walking, there are often great deals available for this dependably nice hotel. **Pros:** helpful staff; comfy beds; good deals are often available online. **Cons:** freeway noise; some visitors won't enjoy the walk uphill; not much happening in the area during the evening. ⊠ *515 Madison St., Downtown* ☎ *206/583–0300 or 800/546–9184* ⊕ *www.marriott.com/seam* ⇨ *465 rooms, 85 executive suites, 3 luxury suites* ⌂ *In-room: refrigerator, Wi-Fi. In-hotel: restaurant, room service, 2 bars, pool, gym, laundry service, Internet terminal, Wi-Fi hotspot, parking (paid), some pets allowed* ⊟ *AE, D, DC, MC, V* ✛ *1:F3.*

$$ 🏨 **Seattle Sheraton Hotel and Towers.** A favorite with conventioneers and ☾ those travelers selecting lodging based on location, this Sheraton is still not one of our favorites. It may have filled a luxury hotel void at one point, but as Seattle's hotel boom brings eye-popping new places like the Four Seasons, the Sheraton seems less and less worthy of the expense. That said, you could do worse: the large, quiet accommodations are decorated in warm, honey hues, with plush carpets and bright glass-art accents. The hotel charges for some amenities, like Wi-Fi, and the valet-only parking is a steep $40 a day. Overall, the hotel caters primarily to business travelers and people attending events at the nearby convention center. **Pros:** large rooms; great location. **Cons:** boring decor; subpar bed linens; spotty service. ✉ *1400 6th Ave., Downtown* ☎ *206/621–9000 or 800/325–3535* ⊕ *www.sheraton.com/seattle* ⟿ *1,248 rooms, 10 suites* � *In-room: safe. In-hotel: 3 restaurants, room service, bar, pool, gym, spa, laundry service, parking (paid)* ▭ *AE, D, DC, MC, V* ✛ *1:F2.*

$$$–$$$$ 🏨 **Sorrento Hotel.** If you're the type who owns a smoking jacket, names aged Scotch as your poison, or often just wants to pretend you're on the set of a period piece, look no further. Built in 1909, the Sorrento was designed to look like an Italian villa, with a dramatic circular driveway surrounding a palm-fringed fountain. The hotel is in between Downtown and Capitol Hill and convenient to both. Though its immediate area is not terribly attractive (a lot of hospital buildings nearby), walking a few blocks north takes you along tree-lined streets to the excellent Frye Art Museum. The rich wood-paneled lobby and adjacent Fireside Room—a perfect spot for a martini on a rainy night—are visions of old-world elegance. Guest rooms are as light as the common areas are dark and contemporary, with only a few tasseled pillows and antique furnishings to tie them to the decor downstairs. The largest are the corner suites. Italian marble bathrooms gleam, and day-of-the-week rugs in the elevators show that even those oft-neglected spaces get a daily once-over. The Hunt Club serves excellent Pacific Northwest dishes. Keep in mind that this property is a short hike uphill from the center of Downtown. **Pros:** serene and classy; great restaurant; fabulous beds with luxurious linens; free Downtown car service. **Cons:** odd location; rooms are a bit small; won't appeal to mod/trendy travelers. ✉ *900 Madison St., Downtown* ☎ *206/622–6400 or 800/426–1265* ⊕ *www.hotelsorrento.com* ⟿ *34 rooms, 42 suites* � *In-room: refrigerator, Wi-Fi. In-hotel: restaurant, room service, bar, gym, laundry service, Wi-Fi hotspot, parking (fee)* ▭ *AE, D, DC, MC, V* ✛ *1:G3.*

$$$–$$$$ 🏨 **W Seattle.** The W Seattle is like an aging hipster—it once set the bar for Seattle's trendy hotels, and, although its cool has been recently eclipsed by newer properties like Hotel 1000, it still thinks it can reel in the stylish with minimal effort. That being said, it's a decent choice for a boutique hotel with hip and reliable luxury. Custom-designed board games encourage lingering around the lobby fireplace on deep couches, and the hotel's bar is popular with guests and locals alike. A renovation to the fitness center will please exercise buffs. Decorated in black, brown, and French blue, guest rooms would almost be austere if they didn't have the occasional geometric print to lighten things up a bit. The beds are exceptionally comfortable with pillow-top mattresses

Inn at the Market

Pan Pacific Hotel

Hotel 1000

and 100% goose-down pillows and comforters (allergy sufferers may request hypoallergenic pillows). **Pros:** lively bar and restaurant; comfortable beds. **Cons:** unattractive (if central) location; self-consciously trendy; some folks complain about snotty staff members and poor concierge service. ✉ *1112 4th Ave., Downtown* ☎ *206/264–6000 or 877/946–8357* ⊕ *www.whotels.com/seattle* ⇥ *415 rooms, 9 suites* ♿ *In-room: safe, refrigerator, DVD, Wi-Fi. In-hotel: restaurant, room service, bar, gym, laundry service, Wi-Fi hotspot, parking (fee), some pets allowed* ▱ *AE, D, DC, MC, V* ✛ *1:F3.*

BELLTOWN

$–$$
Fodor's Choice
★

Ace Hotel. The Ace is a dream come true for both penny-pinching hipsters and creative folks who appreciate unique minimalist decor. Almost everything is white—even the wood floors and brick walls have been painted over—making organic elements like driftwood lamps and randomly placed tree stumps pop in this gallery-like space. Rooms continue the theme, with such touches as army-surplus blankets, industrial metal sinks, and street art, breaking up any notion of austerity. The cheapest rooms share bathrooms, which are clean and have enormous showers. Suites are larger and have full private bathrooms hidden behind cool rotating walls. A small dining room hosts a Continental breakfast and has a vending machine with unusual items like Japanese snacks and hangover cures. The Ace attracts guests of all ages (and levels of cool), but understand that this is a very specific experience and aesthetic: if you're not soothed (or stimulated) by the stripped-down quality of the rooms or not amused by finding a copy of the *Kama Sutra* where the Bible would be, you may want to stay elsewhere. **Pros:** ultratrendy spot with some the most affordable rates in town; cool art selection in rooms; good place to meet other travelers; free Wi-Fi. **Cons:** most rooms have shared bathrooms; not good for people who want pampering; neighborhood rife with panhandlers; lots of stairs to walk up to get to lobby. ✉ *2423 1st Ave., Belltown* ☎ *206/448–4721* ⊕ *www.acehotel. com* ⇥ *14 standard rooms, 14 deluxe rooms* ♿ *In-room: no a/c (some), refrigerator (some), Wi-Fi. In-hotel: laundry facilities, Wi-Fi hotspot, parking (paid), some pets allowed* ▱ *AE, D, DC, MC, V* ✛ *1:B1.*

$$$$

Edgewater. Perched over Elliott Bay—with the waves lapping right underneath it—the Edgewater affords spectacular west-facing views of ferries and sailboats, seals and seabirds, and the distant Olympic Mountains. The whole hotel has a rustic-chic, elegant hunting-lodge look, with plaid rugs and fabrics and peeled-log furnishings. Many rooms have gas fireplaces. All that being said, the hotel has fallen short on service and guest satisfaction of late, and guests looking for luxury should probably head to the Four Seasons or Hotel 1000. There is a significant price jump here between the waterfront rooms and the waterfront premium rooms—unless you want a little more space, save your money. City-view rooms are very expensive and probably not worth it unless you love the hotel's aesthetic or want to stay where the Beatles once slept in 1964. ■TIP➜ If you just want a taste of the hotel, stop into the elegant Six Seven restaurant for indoor-outdoor seating with a bay vista. **Pros:** amazing views; great upscale seafood restaurant; great public lounge area. **Cons:** overpriced for what you get; standard rooms

CLOSE UP

Staying with Kids

Traveling with kids can be a challenge, from hauling their gear to finding a spot for them to sleep in cramped hotel rooms. Don't let that stop you, though. Children are welcome at most Seattle hotels; some even cater to your munchkins with kid-friendly treats and amenities. While most hotels in Seattle allow children under a certain age to stay in their parents' room at no extra charge, others charge for them as extra adults, so be sure to find out the cutoff age for children's discounts. Cribs are also usually available upon request, and hotel staff can assist you in finding a reputable babysitter. Be sure to check the service information in individual hotel listings throughout this chapter for information on pools, gyms, and other kid-friendly activities; in-room refrigerators are also listed for those travelers whose children need refrigerated food or formula. And always let hotel staff know you'll be traveling with children when you book your room—most love the chance to treat your tots and will appreciate the advanced warning. Here are a few of our favorite kid-friendly hotels:

Tweens and teens will love the **Hotel Monaco's** whimsical decor and fun extras, like Guitar Hero, chair massage, and fortune-telling in the lobby. Smaller kids will be thrilled to have a pet goldfish on loan for the duration of their stay. (⇨ Downtown.)

For a family-friendly B&B stay, the **Chambered Nautilus University Suites** offers mini apartments with private entrances and kitchens in a residential part of the U-District. It's also just one block away from Ravenna Park, where families can picnic, play, or hike through the woods. (⇨ University District.)

The **Silver Cloud** hotels are all suitable for families, especially the one on Lake Union. (⇨ South Lake Union.)

The **Seattle Sheraton's** big rooms and rooftop pool make it popular with families. (⇨ Downtown.)

Some of the loveliest (and most expensive) hotels also cater to young ones:

The **Fairmont Olympic Hotel** has a swimming pool and offers outstanding children's treats, such as milk and cookies, kid-friendly movies (popcorn included!), and child-size furniture and bathrobes. (⇨ Downtown.)

Both the **Pan Pacific Hotel Seattle** in South Lake Union and downtown's **Four Seasons Hotel Seattle** greet small guests with a stuffed toy on their beds, while the Four Seasons also pampers kids with mini-robes, milk and cookies, and baby bath products. (⇨ South Lake Union and Downtown.)

---

are small; readers complain of poor service and thin walls. ✉ *Pier 67, 2411 Alaskan Way, Pier 67, Belltown* ☎ *206/728–7000 or 800/624–0670* ⊕ *www.edgewaterhotel.com* ⮒ *213 rooms, 10 suites* ⚵ *In-room: Wi-Fi. In-hotel: restaurant, room service, bar, gym, laundry service, Wi-Fi hotspot, parking (fee), some pets allowed* ▭ *AE, D, DC, MC, V* ⎪⌾⎪ *EP* ✛ *1:A2.*

$$$–$$$$ ⛾ **Hotel Ändra.** Scandinavian sensibility and clean, modern lines define this sophisticated hotel on the edge of Belltown. The lobby is fantastic,

with armchairs and couches arranged in front of a fireplace that's flanked by floor-to-ceiling bookcases. Rooms (most of which are suites) have khaki-color walls and dark fabrics and woods, with a few bright accents and geometric prints. Alpaca headboards and large wood-framed mirrors are interesting touches, and all the linens, towels (from Frette), and toiletries are high quality. The hotel is also smack in the middle of restaurateur Tom Douglas's many haunts (including on-site Lola, a delicious Mediterranean spot)—be sure to hit Serious Pie's happy hour for cheap gourmet pizza or Dahlia Lounge across the street for yummy crab cakes and coconut cream pie. **Pros:** great lobby lounge; hip and funky vibe; spacious rooms; upscale bathroom amenities. **Cons:** pricey valet parking; not family-friendly. ⊠ *2000 4th Ave., Belltown* ☎ *206/448–8600 or 877/448–8600* ⊕ *www.hotelandra.com* ➦ *23 rooms, 4 studios, 92 suites* ♿ *In-room: safe, Wi-Fi. In-hotel: restaurant, room service, bar, gym, laundry service* ⊟ *AE, D, MC, V* ✢ *1:D1.*

$–$$

Fodor's Choice

★

🛏 **Inn at El Gaucho.** Old Hollywood Rat Pack enthusiasts will want to move right in to this dark, swank, and sophisticated, retro-style inn. Upstairs from Belltown's beloved El Gaucho steak house and the Big Picture—a fabulous movie theater with a full bar—the Inn is hip and luxurious. Seventeen ultrachic suites have pale yellow walls, chocolate-color wood, workstations cleverly concealed in closets, and buttery leather furniture. They're filled with such goodies as feather beds, Egyptian linens, Reidel stemware, fresh flowers from Pike Place Market, and large-screen plasma TVs. The sleek bathrooms have rain-style showers as well as L'Occitane and Philip B bath products. Rooms face Puget Sound, the city, or the hotel's atrium; atrium rooms are quieter than those that face the street. Additional perks include room service from El Gaucho and in-room massages and spa services from the Hyatt's spa team. ■TIP➜ One major drawback: the flight of stairs you'll have to climb to get to the Inn—there's no passenger elevator because it's a historic property. **Pros:** beautiful rooms with upscale amenities; free long-distance calls from rooms; some great views; lovely location; warm, helpful staff. **Cons:** set of steep stairs with no elevator; some rooms only have showers; you have to go off-site for some amenities (such as a fitness center). ⊠ *2505 1st Ave., Belltown* ☎ *206/728–1133 or 866/354–2824* ⊕ *inn.elgaucho.com* ➦ *17 suites* ♿ *In-room: Wi-Fi. In-hotel: restaurant, room service, bar, Wi-Fi hotspot, parking (paid)* ⊟ *AE, MC, V* ✢ *1:B1.*

$$$

🛏 **Marriott Seattle Waterfront.** Business and leisure travelers who enjoy the dependability of a Marriott won't be disappointed by this waterfront hotel. With views of Elliott Bay from most rooms (half have small Juliet balconies), comfy beds, and a great location near the tourist spots and the financial district, this property delivers. The elegant and inviting lobby was renovated in 2009 and features cascading Italian chandeliers, walnut detailing, and glass-tile mosaic floors. The decor in the public spaces is warm, rich, and somewhat interesting, while guest rooms fall back on standard hotel decor with a vaguely dated feel. For the best views, book the north tower; non-waterside rooms have a less appealing view of the freeway and train tracks. The hotel's restaurant, 2100 Bistro and Bar, serves casual American fare with local and organic meats and produce. **Pros:** relaxing lobby invites lounging; great views from many of the rooms; elevator takes you directly to Pike Place Market. **Cons:** service isn't consistent; train noise; expensive restaurant and bar; you'll have to walk uphill to most sites. ✉ *2100 Alaskan Way (between Piers 62/63 and Pier 66), Belltown* ☎ *206/443–5000 or 800/455–8254* ⊕ *www.marriott.com/seawf* ✍ *345 rooms, 13 suites* ♿ *In-room: Internet. In-hotel: restaurant, room service, bar, pool, gym, laundry service, executive floor, Wi-Fi hotspot, parking (paid)* ⊟ *AE, D, DC, MC, V* ⏘ *EP* ✛ *1:B2.*

$$ ⊡ **Warwick Seattle Hotel.** Space Needle views and vintage charm abound at this classic, older hotel in Belltown. Service is friendly and leisurely; rooms are understated and traditional with beige carpets, mid-tone woods, and neutral furnishings. Bathrooms step it up with Italian marble and designer bath products. The rooms' best feature, however, is that most have sliding doors and small balconies providing Downtown views and fresh air. Brasserie Margeaux, the hotel's Northwest/French fusion restaurant-lounge, is a lovely retreat. A welcome remodel is afoot at this vintage property, so be sure to ask about construction when you book your room. **Pros:** great location and views; floor-to-ceiling sliding glass doors and Juliet balconies in most rooms; kid-friendly indoor pool. **Cons:** smoking rooms not segregated from nonsmoking rooms; no fans in bathrooms; guests complain of traffic noise. ✉ *401 Lenora St., Belltown* ☎ *206/443–4300 or 800/426–9280* ⊕ *www.warwickwa. com* ✍ *225 rooms, 4 suites* ♿ *In-room: refrigerator, safe, Wi-Fi. In-hotel: restaurant, room service, bar, pool, gym, Internet terminal, Wi-Fi hotspot, parking (paid)* ⊟ *AE, D, DC, MC, V* ✛ *1:D1.*

SEATTLE CENTER, SOUTH LAKE UNION, AND QUEEN ANNE

The South Lake Union area is going through a rather radical transformation. For years it was an industrial, forgotten part of town with few businesses or restaurants. With the introduction of several high-profile companies moving in, including Amazon, this neighborhood is rapidly becoming a hub of new condo, green space, and amenity development. Stay here and you'll be close to both Downtown and Capitol Hill.

Queen Anne is a large, mostly residential neighborhood spread out over a large hill just to the north of Belltown and close to Seattle Center. Upper Queen Anne is posh, quiet, and quite gorgeous. Lower Queen Anne, where all the lodging options lie, is very walkable to Belltown, Downtown, and Seattle Center—but it's considerably less elegant than the top of the hill. You can find better deals here than in most of Downtown—and you'll still be close to everything.

SEATTLE CENTER AND SOUTH LAKE UNION

$$–$$$ ⊡ **Pan Pacific Hotel Seattle.** Views of the Space Needle and Lake Union
☾ are one of the many perks at this stunning hotel. The lobby features a
Fodor's Choice dramatic staircase, a fireplace, and plush brown leather couches. The
★ color palette blends blond and light woods, tan marble, cinnamon accents—and the result is that the hotel feels full of light even during the gray Seattle winter. In the rooms large soaking tubs are shielded by elegant sliding shoji doors, and Hypnos beds and ergonomic Herman Miller chairs at the desks ensure further comfort. The curving shape of

CLOSE UP

Going Green

It takes much more than a recycling program to make a hotel "green," and although few properties in Seattle are doing everything right, a handful of local luxury hotels have expanded the industry's definition of eco-friendly.

Hyatt at Olive 8
The first LEED-certified (Leadership in Energy and Environmental Design) hotel in Seattle, the Hyatt at Olive 8 was built from the ground up with sustainability in mind. From the demolition of the previous building and the painstaking construction of a green roof to details like naturally anti-microbial wool carpeting and dual-flush toilets, this hotel and residence (the upper floors are condos) is healthier for the planet and guests alike. (⇨ Downtown)

Pan Pacific Hotel Seattle
Motion detectors make sure heating and a/c units don't run when there's no one in the room. All toilets are dual-flush European models that save on the hotel's water consumption. (⇨ South Lake Union)

The Fairmont Olympic Hotel
The Fairmont has a wide-reaching Green Partnership program in which all hotel employees are educated to help the hotel conserve water and energy. Initiatives range from recycling and composting programs to more inventive programs like capturing condensation from the hotel's steam heating to be used in the washing machines. Eco-friendly weddings and meetings are available. Guest's hybrid vehicles get free valet parking. (⇨ Downtown)

Kimpton Properties
Kimpton, whose Seattle hotels include Hotel Monaco, Hotel Vintage Park, and the Alexis Hotel, has a far-reaching approach. Recycling, towel and linen reuse, and energy conservation and water conservation schemes are standard here, and the company uses environmentally friendly cleaning products in all its properties, and all of its printed materials are printed on recycled paper with soy-based ink. (⇨ Downtown)

4

the hotel causes rooms to be interestingly asymmetrical and allows for fabulous views from many rooms. ■ TIP➔ The South Lake Union Streetcar has a dedicated stop out front that will whisk travelers right into the heart of Downtown. The Pan Pacific is part of a luxury condo development that includes a large fitness center (open to hotel guests), a spa, a courtyard of high-end specialty shops, a FedEx Office, a Starbucks, and an enormous Whole Foods with a fabulous outdoor dining area. Guests love the on-site restaurant and raw bar, and the delicious Tutta Bella pizzeria next door. **Pros:** warm, helpful staff; feels more luxurious than it costs; away from the tourist throngs. **Cons:** long walk to downtown sights if you don't take the streetcar; not many free amenities; shoji doors are pretty but cut down on bathroom privacy in smaller standard rooms. ⊠ *2125 Terry Ave., South Lake Union* ☎ *206/264–8111* ⊕ *seattle.panpacific. com* ⤳ *160 rooms, 1 suite* ⟁ *In-room: safe, refrigerator, DVD (some), Wi-Fi. In-hotel: restaurant, room service, bar, gym, laundry service, Wi-Fi hotspot, parking (fee)* ⊟ *AE, DC, MC, V* ⓘⓞⓘ *EP* ✛ *2:D5.*

$–$$ 🛏 **Silver Cloud Inn Lake Union.** With views of Lake Union, free parking, and family-friendly services, this property offers great value for guests looking to explore more of Seattle than just Downtown. Rooms are simply and adequately furnished; some of the larger water-view rooms have nice love seats and glass doors. The hotel is on the southeast corner of the lake, and dining options within easy walking distance are a bit better here than on the west side. Breakfasts are complimentary, and free wine and cheese await guests on Tuesday evenings. The hotel has a complimentary shuttle service to Downtown sights. Book early for summer, as weekends in August fill up quickly. **Pros:** pool; great value with free parking and Internet; yummy breakfast. **Cons:** not within walking distance of major sights; feels like a business hotel. ⊠ *1150 Fairview Ave. N, South Lake Union* ☎ *206/447–9500 or 800/330–5812* ⊕ *www.silvercloud.com* ↩ *184 rooms* ⚲ *In-room: refrigerator, Wi-Fi. In-hotel: pool, gym, Wi-Fi hotspot, parking (free)* ▭ *AE, D, DC, MC, V* ⦿I *CP* ✛ *2:E3.*

QUEEN ANNE

$$ 🛏 **MarQueen Hotel.** Fans of historic boutique hotels will love this 1918 brick property at the foot of Queen Anne Hill. Formerly an apartment building, the MarQueen greets guests with a dark and decadent lobby featuring marble floors, overstuffed furniture, Asian-style lacquered screens, and a grand staircase. The spacious guest rooms are furnished with reproduction antiques; most have kitchens and sitting areas. The hotel provides complimentary van shuttle service to Downtown locations, and it's a quick walk into Belltown from this part of Queen Anne. Patrons of the opera, ballet, and theater will also enjoy being just blocks away from Seattle Center and its lovely Marion Oliver McCaw Hall. Note that although the historic nature of the building gives the place a lot of character, it also means that it's not as sealed off from street noise. **Pros:** in-room kitchens and living room areas in many rooms; charming character; free Wi-Fi; proximity to Belltown. **Cons:** streetside rooms can be loud; housekeeping not always consistent; not a good place for travelers with special needs. ⊠ *600 Queen Anne Ave. N, Queen Anne* ☎ *206/282–7407 or 888/445–3076* ⊕ *www.marqueen.com* ↩ *51 rooms, 7 suites* ⚲ *In-room: kitchen (some), refrigerator (some), Wi-Fi. In-hotel: room service, laundry service, Wi-Fi hotspot, parking (paid)* ▭ *AE, D, DC, MC, V* ⦿I *CP* ✛ *2:A4.*

$$$ 🛏 **Maxwell Hotel.** Lower Queen Anne's newest hotel sits conveniently across from Seattle Center. This is *the* hotel for those visitors planning on frequenting Marion Oliver McCaw Hall for opera or performances by the Pacific Northwest Ballet company or for those going to Teatro Zinzanni, whose huge, colorful tent is just steps from the hotel's front door. Whimsical-but-functional decor is accented with art inspired by the performing arts. In the lively, open lobby area, take note of the tiled pineapple on the floor—this fruit is a theme here. Also at check-in are mini-cupcakes (pineapple-flavored, of course), a small latte counter, and a glittering bead-and-glass chandelier. Rooms have graphic bedspreads, colorful argyle-print chairs, outlines of chandeliers painted on the walls, and lovely (if small) bathrooms with black marble counters. Among the amazing room amenities are iPod docking station alarm clocks and Keurig coffee machines; and a microwave with a complimentary bag of popcorn upon arrival. **Pros:** jazzy rooms are clean and comfortable; some rooms have great views of the Space Needle; loads of free amenities. **Cons:** most rooms do not have bathtubs (showers only); hotel is on a busy street; pool and gym are tiny; neighborhood is a bit shabby. ⊠ *300 Roy St., Queen Anne* ☎ *206/286–0629 or 877/298–9728* ⊕ *www.themaxwellhotel.com* ↪ *139 rooms* ⚴ *In-room: safe, refrigerator, DVD, Internet, Wi-Fi. In-hotel: pool, gym, bicycles, laundry facilities, laundry service, Wi-Fi hotspot, parking (free), some pets allowed* ☰ *AE, D, DC, MC, V* ✛ *2:B4.*

CAPITOL HILL

4

For travelers looking to experience a real Seattle neighborhood, Capitol Hill is a terrific option. Close to Downtown, but with a unique scene of its own, "the Hill" offers character-rich bed-and-breakfasts in old mansions and oversized Craftsmans, run with flare by thoughtful proprietors. Though many of the Hill's residents appear to be hipsters, pierced and tattooed baristas, and intellectual dilettantes, anyone of any age or background is welcome here if you come with an open mind. Seattle's historically gay neighborhood is chock full of live music venues, true foodie establishments, and little retail gems. While the Pike/Pine corridor and much of Broadway are alive until the wee hours, most of the neighborhood's lodging spots are set in quiet, tree-lined side streets off the main drags.

$–$$ ▨ **Bacon Mansion Bed & Breakfast.** Lodging romanticists with children or pets, take heart—the Bacon Mansion offers two separate suites that welcome your knee-high companions. Serene and traditional, this 1909 Tudor is surrounded by opulent gardens and is near both Volunteer Park and Broadway. The first-floor living room is filled with comfortable furniture and lots of natural light; it also has a grand piano. Guest rooms are uniquely appointed with collectibles old and new; they feel homey, if a bit worn. Some rooms have views and hideaway beds in addition to the queen-size beds. **Pros:** quiet, relaxing retreat; knowledgeable owner; great location. **Cons:** no a/c; rooms could use updating; breakfasts are on the light side; low water pressure in shower. ⊠ *959 Broadway Ave. E (at E. Prospect St.), Capitol Hill* ☎ *206/329–1864 or 800/240–1864* ⊕ *www.baconmansion.com* ↪ *11 rooms, 9 with bath; 2 suites* ⚴ *In-room: refrigerator (some), Wi-Fi. In-hotel: Wi-Fi hotspot, some pets allowed* ☰ *AE, D, DC, MC, V* ⑩ *BP* ✛ *2:F3.*

¢–$ ▨ **11th Avenue Inn Bed & Breakfast.** The closest B&B to Downtown, the 11th Avenue Inn offers all the charm of a classic bed-and-breakfast with the convenience of being near the action. Exquisitely styled with antique beds, Oriental rugs, and a grand dining room table draped in a lace-edged tablecloth, the Inn positively oozes vintage charm. The owner has impeccable taste, and even the small den that holds two public computers and stacks of travel guides, brochures, and laminated menus from the best local restaurants is thoughtfully arranged and appointed. Modest-size guest rooms are on two floors. The second floor has five rooms; the Citrine is our favorite for its regal antique headboard, but the Opal is a very close second because of the amount of light it gets. A

Fodor's Choice
★

full breakfast is served in the elegant dining room, which is the show-piece of the house. Don't worry about using the wrong fork, though—despite its formal appearance, the inn is a warm and laid-back place. **Pros:** unpretentious take on classic B&B; friendly staff. **Cons:** no a/c; although most guests are courteous, sound does carry in old houses. ⊠ *121 11th Ave. E, Capitol Hill* ☎ *206/720–7161 or 800/720–7161* ⊕ *www.11thavenueinn.com* ☞ *8 rooms, 6 with bath* ⌂ *In-room: no phones, Wi-Fi. In-hotel: Wi-Fi hotspot, parking (paid), no kids under 12* ⊟ *AE, D, MC, V* |◯| *BP* ⊹ *2:G5.*

¢–$ ☷ **Gaslight Inn.** It's easy to imagine the splendor of this 1906 house when it was a single-family residence—the Gaslight retains much of the original charm, while offering contemporary and artistic touches not typically seen in B&Bs. Rooms here range from a crow's nest with peeled-log furniture and Navajo-print fabrics to a more traditional suite with Arts and Crafts–style furnishings, a fireplace, cloisonné vases, and stained-glass windows. The large common areas evoke a gentlemen's club, with deer mounts overlooking oak wainscoting, Oriental carpets, and leather chairs. There's room to move around in here, including a lovely backyard and a deck with fabulous views. The Gaslight also has something no other B&B can claim: a seasonal heated pool, nicely positioned in a private oasis of a backyard. **Pros:** great art collection; house and rooms are more spacious than at other B&Bs; heated pool. **Cons:** breakfast is unimpressive; some readers find staff standoffish. ⊠ *1727 15th Ave., Capitol Hill* ☎ *206/325–3654* ⊕ *www.gaslight-inn.com* ☞ *5 rooms with private bath; 3 rooms with shared bath* ⌂ *In-room: no a/c (some), refrigerator (some), Wi-Fi. In-hotel: pool, Wi-Fi hotspot, no kids under 16* ⊟ *AE, MC, V* |◯| *CP* ⊹ *2:G6.*

$–$$ ☷ **Salisbury House Bed & Breakfast.** If you like to start your mornings with
Fodor'sChoice   the *New York Times* and a full vegetarian breakfast with mouthwater-
★   ing choices like rhubarb coffee cake and fresh, fruit-laden huckleberry pancakes, look no further. Built in 1904, this large Craftsman sits on a wide, tree-lined street a few blocks south of Volunteer Park. The spacious rooms contain an eclectic collection of furniture. The decor isn't eye-popping, but travelers who prefer a simpler, country charm look will appreciate the B&B's restraint. The basement suite has a private entrance and phone line, a king-size bed, fireplace, and whirlpool bath. The Blue Room is the best of the rest, for its private deck overlooking the garden. One of the common areas is a sun porch with wicker furniture, where tea awaits guests each afternoon. A guest computer in the library is available to all, and free Wi-Fi throughout is a plus. The B&B is tucked away near the park and laidback 15th Avenue, which is lined with several great restaurants, bars, and coffee shops. A bus around the corner will take you straight to Downtown. Allergy sufferers take note: the owner has two cats. **Pros:** close to Volunteer Park; friendly innkeeper can help you plan your stay; porches to relax on. **Cons:** a bit far from Pike-Pine Corridor; some street noise. ⊠ *750 16th Ave. E, Capitol Hill* ☎ *206/328–8682* ⊕ *www.salisburyhouse.com* ☞ *4 rooms, 1 suite* ⌂ *In-room: no a/c (some), no TV (some), Wi-Fi. In-hotel: Wi-Fi hotspot, no kids under 12* ⊟ *AE, MC, V* |◯| *BP* ⊹ *2:H4.*

$ ☷ **Seattle Hill House Bed & Breakfast.** Twin Victorian houses built by two brothers in 1903 offer eight cheery rooms, lovely common areas, and gourmet breakfasts. The B&B is done up in shades of springy pastels, with romantic furnishings, antique touches, and floral accents for a casual, comfortable effect. The rooms, named for their color palettes, are unique, and include different amenities. The spacious Celadon room, for example, has hardwood floors and a queen bed. The Rose Room is small and cozy and best for singles. The Forget-Me-Not Room has its own private bath, and space enough for a small antique writing desk. The lovely deck off the dining room is open to all guests. **Pros:** free on-site parking in a neighborhood where parking is tough; great breakfasts; wonderful location. **Cons:** no a/c means it can be quite hot in summer; owners don't live on-site; readers say housekeeping is hit and miss. ⊠ *1113 E. John St., Capitol Hill* ☎ *206/323–4455 or 866/417–4455* ⊕ *www.seattlehillhouse.com* ⇄ *4 rooms with bath, 2 rooms with shared bath, 2 suites* ♿ *In-room: no phone, no a/c, no TV (some), refrigerator (some), Wi-Fi. In-hotel: Wi-Fi hotspot, parking (free), no kids under 11* ▭ *AE, D, DC, MC, V* ⦿|*BP* ✢ *2:G5.*

4

FREMONT

This charming north-end neighborhood is a short drive from Downtown. If you don't mind being in a self-contained spot far away from most attractions, this is a good bet, because there are restaurants, shops, and lovely walking galore. Fremont is close to Ballard, Phinney Ridge, and Green Lake; the closest attractions are the Ballard Locks, the Woodland Park Zoo, and Green Lake's lively park.

$$ ☷ **Chelsea Station Inn Bed & Breakfast.** Situated on the south end of the

Fodor's Choice Woodland Park Zoo, on the edge of Fremont and Phinney Ridge, this

★ 1920s brick colonial B&B was reopened in 2009 and offers a convenient jumping-off point for all the north end has to offer. Four beautifully styled, 900-square-foot suites feature distressed hardwood floors with colorful rugs, fireplaces, sleeper sofas, contemporary furnishings, and a soft, modern palette. Guests enjoy breakfast delivered to their private dining rooms and granite-counter kitchenettes stocked with local treats. Master bathrooms are large and sumptuous, with double walk-in rain showers and marble countertops, and each suite also boasts a separate powder room—a fabulous benefit for couples or families. There are several outdoor spaces for lounging, including a flower-filled patio and outdoor fire pit and hot tub areas. This is a truly luxurious property, suitable even for those who usually shy away from the B&B experience. It's far from Downtown, but the nearby bus line takes travelers directly to the core. **Pros:** great, unobtrusive host; 1½ bathrooms per suite; sweet location. **Cons:** far from Downtown; no TVs; no elevator. ⊠ *4915 Linden Ave. N, Fremont* ☎ *206/547–6077* ⊕ *www.chelseastationinn. com* ⇄ *4 suites* ♿ *In-room: no phone, no a/c, kitchen, refrigerator, no TV, Internet, Wi-Fi. In-hotel: laundry facilities, Wi-Fi hotspot, parking (free)* ▭ *MC, V* ⦿|*BP* ✢ *3:D3.*

LODGING ALTERNATIVES

B&BS AND HOME RENTALS

There are many tiny B&Bs scattered throughout Seattle—especially in northern areas such as Fremont, Ballard, Wallingford, Green Lake, and the University District. If you are looking for the micro-lodging experience, check out ⊕ www.seattlebedandbreakfast.com. Renting an apartment or a house will give you access to Seattle neighborhoods that don't have a lot of traditional accommodations. A furnished rental can save you money, especially if you're traveling with a group.

Sea to Sky Rentals (☎ 206/632–4210 ⊕ www.seatoskyrentals.com). **Seattle Bed and Breakfast** (☎ 206/439–7677 ⊕ www.seattlebedandbreakfast.com).

Vacation Rentals by Owner (⊕ www.vrbo.com).

HOSTELLING INTERNATIONAL

The clean, affordable **Hostelling International Seattle at American Hotel** (✉ 520 S. King St., International District, ⊕ www.hiusa.org/seattle) is a terrific choice if you're on a budget ($) and want to be in the center of things. The hostel is one block of Union Station, which is a Sound Transit Link Light Rail stop from SeaTac Airport. There are lots of great Asian eateries are nearby, as is Pioneer Square and, a bit farther, Downtown. This is a hostel, so expect bunkbeds and shared baths, though there are a handful of private rooms.

GREEN LAKE

An upbeat, leafy park with a walking loop around a lake, several small commercial stretches with cafés and restaurants, and a relaxed residential vibe make Green Lake a no-fuss option that is well out of the Downtown core.

$–$$

Fodor's Choice
★

Greenlake Guest House. Outdoorsy types, visitors who want to stay in a low-key residential area, and anyone who wants to feel pampered and refreshed will enjoy this charming B&B. The house is directly across the street from the eastern shore of beautiful Green Lake; it's a short walk from several restaurants and the devilishly good Chocolati. The romantic Parkview Suite is the pièce de résistance, with a full view of the park, and pale green walls that play off the green of the leaves just outside the windows. All rooms have private baths with jetted tubs (except the Ballard room), fluffy robes, and heated tile floors. A public computer with Internet is available in the living room; a communal minibar in the hall has sodas, water, fresh fruit, cookies, and other snacks; and bookshelves in the upstairs hallway have an extensive DVD collection of Oscar-winning movies. To keep things interesting, the full breakfast alternates between made-to-order savory (a spinach-and-feta omelet, for example) and sweet (such as Brie-and-apple French toast). **Pros:** views of and quick access to Green Lake; thoughtful amenities; can accommodate kids over 4 years old. **Cons:** 5 mi from Downtown; on a busy street. ✉ 7630 E. Green Lake Dr. N, Green Lake ☎ 206/729–8700 or 866/355–8700 ⊕ www.greenlakeguesthouse.com ⬖ 4 rooms

⛲ In-room: no phone, DVD, Wi-Fi. In-hotel: Internet terminal, Wi-Fi hotspot, no kids under 4 ⊟ DC, MC, V ⏃⏃| BP ✛ 3:F1.

UNIVERSITY DISTRICT

We have a love-hate relationship with the University District. On one hand, you'll find some reasonably priced, decent accommodations here, thanks to the many parents visiting their kids at the University of Washington (UW). On the other hand, the areas closest to the main drag, University Avenue (The Ave) can feel both college-y and gritty. One plus of staying close to The Ave is the plethora of cheap ethnic restaurants. The area on the other side of the campus, closest to the upscale open-air mall University Village, is nicer and more residential but inconvenient to the rest of the city. In terms of location, the U-District is more cut off from Downtown than its western neighbors of Wallingford, Fremont, and Ballard, though it's reasonably convenient to Capitol Hill.

$$ 🖩 **Chambered Nautilus University Suites.** Part of the Chambered Nautilus complex, these cozy mini-apartments are perfect for families, have access to all of the adjacent Chambered Nautilus facilities, and offer the same great gourmet breakfasts. Each suite is unique: for example, the Ravenna has hardwood floors, an antique cast-iron bed, and herb-print kitchen tiles. You can wander across the lawn to the Chambered Nautilus to enjoy its breakfast room, grab a few chocolates, or use the business center. Naturalists will love strolling through nearby Ravenna Park, and cyclists can ride the Burke Gilman Trail. ■ TIP➔ **The Chambered Nautilus hotel next door (in a 1915 Georgian Revival home) is a great choice in the same complex. Pros:** helpful staff; large suites; delicious food and snacks. **Cons:** steep walk up many steps; college housing nearby; can be hard to find. ⊠ *5005 22nd Ave. NE, University District* 🕾 *206/522–2536* ⊕ *www.chamberednautilus.com* ⤶ *4 suites ⛲ In-room: kitchen, refrigerator, DVD, Wi-Fi. In-hotel: Wi-Fi hotspot, some pets allowed* ⊟ *AE, MC, V ⏃⏃| BP ✛ 3:H3.*

$–$$ 🖩 **Hotel Deca.** Within blocks of UW, this 1931 property has been restored to its original art-deco elegance. Guest rooms are individually decorated in shades of brown with jewel-tone accents and striped window treatments. Beds have tall headboards done in vibrant colors and fabrics, and some rooms have blue velvet furniture and deep soaking tubs. Sky Level rooms have great views of the Cascades and the skyline to boot. The elegant District Lounge restaurant serves a mix of tasty comfort dishes, snacks, and upscale Pacific Northwest cuisine. A popular choice for Seattle International Film Festival participants, guests staying during the fest might even catch a glimpse of independent film stars at the bar. **Pros:** trendiest hotel in the U-District; inexpensive onsite parking; free shuttle rides, high-tech amenities. **Cons:** small bathrooms; expensive for the area; guests complain of disappointing room service and thin walls. ⊠ *4507 Brooklyn Ave. NE, University District* 🕾 *206/634–2000 or 800/899–0251* ⊕ *www.hoteldeca.com* ⤶ *158 rooms ⛲ In-room: Wi-Fi, DVD. In-hotel: restaurant, room service, bar, gym, laundry service, Wi-Fi hotspot, parking (paid)* ⊟ *AE, D, DC, MC, V ⏃⏃| EP ✛ 3:H4.*

$ ☷ **Watertown Hotel.** Free parking, freshly baked cookies, complimentary Wi-Fi, shuttle service to Downtown, and creative amenities make this University District Hotel a great deal. The developer of this property is a boater and an architect, and his predilection and profession are reflected in the exposed-concrete-and-metal construction, porthole windows in bathroom doors, and the clean lines of the fountains and pools. Guest quarters have attractive bathrooms, contemporary styling, space-saving closets accessible from two sides, and big operable windows that let in lots of light. One of the most unique features of the hotel is its "Ala Cart" menu, from which you can request a rolling cart filled with games or other goodies, depending on the theme; for example, the "Spa cart" indulges you with a foot spa, relaxing CDs, Tazo tea, and bath salts. **Pros:** fun amenities; free shuttle service to Downtown; hotel has free bicycles for guests to use; great value. **Cons:** street noise in some rooms; panhandlers in the area; breakfasts are nothing fancy. ■TIP→ Next door, the University Inn is a good value for a kid-friendly hotel. ⊠ *4242 Roosevelt Way NE, University District* ☎ *206/826–4242 or 800/944–4242* ⊕ *www.watertownseattle.com* ⇆ *100 rooms* ⟁ *In-room: safe, refrigerator (some), Wi-Fi. In-hotel: laundry facilities, laundry service, Internet terminal, Wi-Fi hotspot, parking (free)* ⊟ *AE, D, DC, MC, V* ⊺⊙⊺ *CP* ⊹ *3:G4.*

THE EASTSIDE

The Eastside suburbs have a few high-end properties of note, especially the fantastic Willows Lodge. There are also quite a few mid-priced chain hotels, but we don't list them—unless you have business in the area or plan to spend a lot of time out here, it's really not worth staying this far from Downtown Seattle.

$$–$$$ ☷ **Hotel Bellevue.** Fitness buffs will particularly enjoy the perks of this architectural jewel in downtown Bellevue. A 200,000-square-foot private athletic club is at guests' disposal, while luxurious rooms are sure to please even those travelers whose most strenuous form of exercise is lifting the remote. A warm plethora of browns and tans greets visitors in the common areas, while clever lighting and original oil paintings by local artist Mark Rediske brighten the rooms. Guest quarters have updated furniture and bedding; bathrooms have limestone tiles, some with deep-soak tubs. Deluxe rooms aren't terribly exciting, so upgrading is a good move here. Premium rooms have a fireplace and balcony; first-floor Club rooms have 20-foot ceilings, a CD player, and a pretty terra-cotta patio set amid landscaped gardens. Unfortunately, many guests have complained about rude and disorganized service here, so be prepared for hassles—hopefully, you'll be pleasantly surprised. **Pros:** amazing gym and pools; indoor and outdoor tennis courts; complimentary town-car service to area shopping; good on-site restaurant. **Cons:** readers complain of shoddy service; problems with the heat; irritating motion-sensitive lighting. ⊠ *11200 S.E. 6th St., Bellevue, Eastside* ☎ *425/454–4424 or 800/579–1110* ⊕ *www.bellevueclub.com* ⇆ *64 rooms, 3 suites* ⟁ *In-room: safe, Wi-Fi. In-hotel: 3 restaurants, room service, bar, tennis courts, 3 pools, gym, spa, laundry service, Internet*

CLOSE UP

Airport Hotels

There are very few reasons to stay near SEA-TAC International Airport. The airport may be close enough to the city to make getting back and forth relatively easy, but it's far enough away to make staying out here impractical for anyone who doesn't have business in the area or a particularly long layover. However, if you find yourself in need of an airport hotel, these are your best options.

Marriott Sea-Tac (✉ 3201 S. 176th St., Sea-Tac ☎ 206/241–2000 or 800/314–0925 ⊕ www.marriott.com). The luxurious Marriott has a five-story tropical atrium complete with a waterfall, a dining area, an indoor pool, and a lounge. If you must stay in

the airport environs, this is your most comfortable option.

Hilton Seattle Airport and Conference Center (✉ 17620 International Blvd. S, Sea-Tac ☎ 206/244–4800 ⊕ www.hilton.com). Directly across the street from the airport, this hotel was designed with the business traveler in mind and therefore has lots of extras. Rooms are spacious and cheery.

Radisson Gateway Hotel (✉ 18118 International Blvd., Sea-Tac ☎ 206/244–6666 ⊕ www. radissonhotels.com). This is perhaps the best mid-range option close to the airport. Rooms have large desks and comfortable chairs, and the hotel has plenty of amenities.

4

---

terminal, Wi-Fi hotspot, some pets allowed, parking (paid) ⊟ AE, DC, MC, V ⍩ EP ⊕ 3:H6.

$$ 🛏 **Hyatt Regency Bellevue.** Near Bellevue Square and other downtown Bellevue shopping centers, the Hyatt looks like any other sleek high-rise, but its interior is adorned with huge displays of fresh flowers and elegant touches such as antique Japanese chests. Rooms are understated, with dark wood and earth tones predominating. Deluxe suites include two bedrooms, bar facilities, and meeting rooms with desks and full-length tables. You'll have access to a health club and pool that share a courtyard with the hotel. The restaurant serves excellent and reasonably priced breakfast, lunch, and dinner; an English-style pub and sports bar serves lunch and dinner. **Pros:** helpful staff; free parking on weekends; great martini bar. **Cons:** readers complain of construction noise; thin walls; slow (and costly) Internet service. ✉ 900 Bellevue Way NE, Bellevue, Eastside ☎ 425/462–1234 ⊕ www.bellevue.hyatt. com ⇨ 353 rooms, 29 suites ⟁ In-room: safe, refrigerator, Wi-Fi. In-hotel: restaurant, room service, bar, laundry service, Internet terminal, Wi-Fi hotspot, parking (paid), no-smoking rooms ⊟ AE, D, DC, MC, V ⊕ 3:H6.

$$–$$$ 🛏 **Willows Lodge.** A dramatically lighted 1,600-year-old Douglas fir snag greets you at the entrance to this elegant spa hotel. Timbers salvaged from a 19th-century warehouse lend rustic counterpoints to the lodge's sleek, modern design. A stone fireplace dominates the lobby, and contemporary Native American prints and sculptures by area artists adorn the walls and gardens. Each large, elegant guest room—categorized by size and amenities as "Nice, Nicer, and Nicest"—has a gas-lighted stone

fireplace, oversize soaking tub, CD and DVD players, and bathroom with freestanding marble sinks. Nicer rooms overlook lovely court-yards; the Nicest rooms also have a jetted tub and heated towel racks. The famous spa provides beauty and rejuvenating treatments, and the Barking Frog restaurant is one of the Northwest's top dining venues. ■ TIP → It's pretty far from town, but is a favorite of visitors and Seattleites alike because of its proximity to 50 Woodinville-area wineries, including Chateau Ste. Michelle and Columbia Winery, as well as the RedHook Brewery. Along with trying the Barking Frog, a dinner at the equally famous and nearby Herbfarm restaurant is a must—book ahead as it can fill up fast. Or just linger in Fireside Cellars, their casual wine bar, after a day spent biking through the Eastside. **Pros:** a truly romantic getaway; great for foodies and wine people; great on-site spa. **Cons:** not the best place for families; far from Downtown Seattle; not much in the way of free perks. ⊠ *14580 N.E. 145th St., Woodinville, Eastside* ☎ *425/424–3900 or 877/424–3930* ⊕ *www.willowslodge.com* ⤴ *77 rooms, 7 suites* ⚃ *In-room: safe, DVD, Wi-Fi. In-hotel: restaurant, room service, bar, gym, spa, bicycles, laundry service, Wi-Fi hotspot, parking (free), some pets allowed* ☰ *AE, D, DC, MC, V* ⦿ *CP* ✠ *3:H6.*

\$\$–\$\$\$ ⊡ **Woodmark Hotel.** Daily boat tours, waterside views, and compli-mentary kayak usage make this Kirkland hotel on the shores of Lake Washington a great bet for a fun and relaxing retreat. Contemporary accommodations overlook the water, a courtyard, or the street and are done in shades of café au lait, taupe, and ecru. You'll pay more for the better views and rooms with balconies, but it's probably worth it. Great views can also be had from the upscale restaurant, where diners are treated to such tasty Pacific Rim eats as lamb spring rolls with currants, pears, and apples in a quince sauce. Get there for its twice-daily happy hours to take advantage of their extensive wine list. The Beach Cafe is equally good, and decidedly more casual. **Pros:** great staff; boat tours and kayak rentals; free late-night snacks. **Cons:** rooms not facing the water have a rotten view of an office park; gym closes early. ⊠ *1200 Carillon Pt., Kirkland, Eastside* ☎ *425/822–3700 or 800/822–3700* ⊕ *www.thewoodmark.com* ⤴ *79 rooms, 21 suites* ⚃ *In-room: safe, refrigerator. In-hotel: 2 restaurants, room service, 3 bars, gym, spa, laundry service, parking (fee)* ☰ *AE, MC, V* ⦿ *EP* ✠ *3:H6.*

Nightlife and the Arts

WORD OF MOUTH

"Zig Zag Café is known for having the best cocktails in town and is in a neat location on the Pike Place Market Hillclimb. If you are really a cocktail aficionado, go there and put yourself in the bartender's hands. And the Pink Door has a wonderful rooftop deck."

—christy1

NIGHTLIFE AND THE ARTS PLANNER

The City That Goes to Sleep Early

With very few exceptions, bars and clubs close at 2 AM. This means that last call can come as early as 1:30, which, depending on where you're from, may be the time you're used to *starting* your evening. Seattle-ites don't seem to mind this too much, but visitors may be disappointed if they don't start their evenings early enough. Early closing times also mean that it can be difficult to find a restaurant that serves later than midnight or 1 AM. So plan accordingly.

Smoke Won't Get in Your Eyes

Smoking is prohibited in restaurants, bars, and clubs (the smoking ban covers all public places and workplaces). You're not supposed to smoke within 25 feet of any door or window connected to a public place, although this is difficult to enforce in the more congested nightlife areas.

Getting Around

Program the numbers for the city's cab companies (⇨ *Travel Smart*) into your cell phone. Unless you have a designated driver or are not venturing too far from your hotel, you will need them. (Expect longer waits for pickups on Friday and Saturday nights.) Though you'll probably be able to hail cabs on the street in even the quieter sections of Downtown, you'll have trouble finding empty cabs in Capitol Hill, Belltown, and in north-end neighborhoods like Ballard and Fremont.

If you are driving around, exercise caution on the roads, especially when the bars start to let out. Unfortunately, drunk driving is far too common here, as so many people rely on their cars to get around and public transportation becomes even less frequent late at night.

Parking in Belltown is a nightmare on weekend nights. The neighborhood has ample pay lots, but even those fill up, and finding a space on the street requires either a miracle or a lot of circling. Capitol Hill and Ballard are also tough, though at least the former has a few parking garages and pay lots in the Pike–Pine Corridor.

Music Festivals

Ballard Jazz Festival (⊕ www.ballardjazzfestival.com; late April).

Bumbershoot (⊕ www.bumbershoot.org; September).

Capitol Hill Block Party (⊕ www.capitolhillblockparty.com; late July).

Decibel Festival (⊕ www.dbfestival.com; September).

Earshot Jazz Festival (⊕ www.earshot.org; mid-October to early November).

Noise for the Needy (⊕ www.noisefortheneedy.org; June).

Northwest Folklife (⊕ www.nwfolklife.org; June).

Seattle Chamber Music Society Concert Series (⊕ www.seattlechambermusic.org; July/January).

Seattle Improvised Music Festival (⊕ www.seattleimprovisedmusic.com/simf; February).

Best Bets: Music

Best Mid-Size Venues: The Crocodile (Belltown), Triple Door (Downtown)
Best Dives: The Comet (Capitol Hill), The Sunset (Ballard)
Unique Spaces: Gallery 1412 (Eastlake), Jewelbox Theater at the Rendezvous (Belltown)

The Best of Nightlife

BREWPUBS
Elysian Brewing Company, Capitol Hill
Naked City Taphouse, Phinney Ridge/Greenwood
DANCE CLUBS
Century Ballroom, Capitol Hill
Contour, Pioneer Square
Emerald City Soul Club, various locations
GAY and LESBIAN SPOTS
The Elite, Capitol Hill
Pony, Capitol Hill
Re-Bar, Capitol Hill
Wildrose, Capitol Hill
BEST HOTEL BARS
ART Lounge, Four Seasons Hotel, Downtown
BoKa, Hotel 1000, Downtown
Oliver's, Mayflower Hotel, Downtown
BEST DIVE BARS
Linda's, Capitol Hill
People's Pub, Ballard
Whisky Bar, Belltown
BEST COCKTAILS
Moshi Moshi, Ballard
Oliver's, Downtown
Sambar, Ballard
Tavern Law, Capitol Hill
Zig Zag Café, Downtown
BEST BEER LIST
Brouwer's, Fremont
Collins Pub, Pioneer Square
Quinn's, Capitol Hill

Information

For detailed music, art, and nightlife listings, as well as hot tips and suggestions for the week's events, check out *The Stranger* (⊕ www.thestranger. com) and *Seattle Weekly* (⊕ www.seattleweekly.com). Pick them up at delis and coffeehouses throughout the city. Friday editions of the *Seattle Times* include weekend pullout sections detailing arts and entertainment events.

Tickets and Cover Charges

Tickets for high-profile performances range from $15 to $125; fringe-theater plays and performance-art events range from $5 to $25. The Seattle Symphony offers half-price tickets to seniors and students one hour before scheduled performances. Cover charges at non-ticketed music venues range from $5 to $12. Pioneer Square dance clubs, like Trinity, charge $15 to $20. Tickets for major events can be purchased through a venue's Web site or at its box office; Sonic Boom record stores (⇨ *Shopping*) also sell tickets to select music venues like The Crocodile, Chop Suey, and Neumo's, as well as to some music festivals. ■TIP➔ **Major online ticket retailers are Ticketmaster** (⊕ *www.ticketmaster. com*) **and Brown Paper Tickets** (☎ *800/838–3006* ⊕ *www. brownpapertickets.com*).

Updated
by Carissa
Bluestone

Seattle's amazing musical legacy is well known, but there's more to the arts and nightlife scenes than live music. In fact, these days, there are far more swanky bars and inventive pubs than music venues in the city.

Seattle is, bluntly put, a great place to drink. You can sip overly ambitious and ridiculously named specialty cocktails in trendy lounges, get a lesson from an enthusiastic sommelier in a wine bar or restaurant, or swill cheap beer on the patio of a dive bar. Though some places have very specific demographics, most Seattle bars are egalitarian affairs, drawing loyal regulars of all ages.

The music scene is still kicking—there's something going on every night of the week in nearly every genre of music. And today, the city's dynamic theater scene is a highly regarded proving ground for Broadway, while the Seattle International Film Festival draws the finest in world cinema. The ethereal Marion Oliver McCaw Hall is a first-class venue for opera and ballet, and Benaroya Hall, with its outstanding acoustics, is an elegant premier symphony hall. Families enjoy the Children's Theatre, the Northwest Puppet Center, and the many summertime folk art and music festivals.

Use the coordinate (⊕ 1:B2) at the end of each listing to locate a site on the corresponding map at the end of the chapter.

NIGHTLIFE

Every neighborhood has a little bit of everything, save for dance clubs, which are in short supply and mostly concentrated in Pioneer Square and Belltown. The number of bars in each neighborhood increases greatly if you take into account all of the great restaurants that also have thriving bar scenes—in some cases the line between restaurant and nightspot is quite blurred. ■ TIP→ The happy-hour scene is positively bumpin' in Seattle; bars, lounges, gastropubs, breweries, sushi spots, hotel bars, and restaurants alike often have one, or even two, happy hours per night, often from 3 to 6 and again after 10. It's definitely worth calling to ask about happy-hour details. Also check out the *Where to Eat* chapter in this book; many favorite restaurants—especially those on Capitol

Hill and in Ballard and Belltown—have swanky bar areas that rival the most popular watering holes in the same locales.

DOWNTOWN AND BELLTOWN

Downtown is a great place for anyone looking to dress up a bit and hit swanky hotel bars, classy lounges, and wine bars where you don't have to be under the age of 30 to fit in. Downtown also has a smattering of pubs popular with the happy-hour crowd. Barhopping Downtown may require several taxi rides, as things can be a bit spread out, but cabs can actually be hailed on the street in this part of town.

Belltown can be a trendy madhouse on weekends. That said, there are some lovely spaces here, a few of which stay relatively low-key even during the Saturday-night crush, as well as some quirky old neighborhood dives left over from Belltown's former life.

In addition to its bars, Downtown and Belltown in particular have notable restaurants with separate bar areas. ■TIP→ Nearly all of Tom Douglas's restaurants (⇨ *Dining*) have lively after-work and weekend bar scenes, as do trendy hotel restaurants. Most restaurants have impressive bar menus, and food is often served until 11 PM, midnight, or even 1 AM in some spots.

BARS AND LOUNGES

Alibi Room (⊠ *85 Pike St., in Post Alley, Downtown* ☎ *206/623–3180* ⊕ *www.seattlealibi.com*), a wood-paneled bar in exquisitely hard-to-find Post Alley at Pike Place Market, is where well-dressed locals sip double martinis while taking in views of Elliott Bay or studying the scripts, handbills, and movie posters that line the walls. The lower level is more crowded and casual. It's an ever-cool yet low-key, intimate place. Stop by for a drink or a meal, or stay to listen and dance to live music. Happy hour from 3 to 6 is quiet and a good respite from the Market. ✤ *1:D3*

ART Lounge (⊠ *99 Union St., Downtown* ☎ *206/749–7000*), in the Four Seasons Hotel, is sleekly elegant, with amazing views. Drinks are pricey but quite delicious, and there's also plenty of food to choose from, including sushi and delectable sliders. Hip mood lighting and soft music hum while a really varied crowd enjoy the inventive cocktails—happy hour is your best bet, from 5 to 7. If you haven't had a drink while staring at water views, come here after a day at Pike Place Market. ✤ *1:D3*

The speakeasy trend has produced some lovely, intimate bars like **Bathtub Gin** (⊠ *2205 2nd Ave., Belltown* ☎ *206/728–6069*). It's reached via an alley next to the Humphrey Apartments—it's actually in the basement of the building. The tiny, shabby-chic bar is a very laid-back spot to settle into a couch for a few drinks. Note that despite being a pain in the neck to find, the bar still attracts the hard-partying Belltown crowd on weekends, so go midweek for maximum serenity. ✤ *1:C1*

Black Bottle (⊠ *2600 1st Ave., Belltown* ☎ *206/441–1500* ⊕ *www.blackbottleseattle.com*) is quite sleek and sexy, making the northern reaches of Belltown look good. The interior of this gastropub/wine bar is simple but very sleek, with black chairs and tables and shiny wood floors. It gets crowded with a chill but often dressed-up clientele on nights and weekends. A small selection of beers on tap and a solid wine list (with Washington, Oregon, California, and beyond well represented) will help you wash down the pub snacks, including wild boar ribs, grilled octopus, butter-bean salad, and seven-spice shrimp. ✛ *1:B1*

BoKa Kitchen and Bar (⊠ 1010 1st Ave., *Downtown* ☎ 206/357–9000), in Hotel 1000, has an all-afternoon happy hour (2:30 to 6), plus creative cocktails, addictive burgers, a posh clientele, and a sublimely sleek atmosphere: think mood lighting, graphic art pieces, and booth seating. Try a Spicy Chipotle Margarita, with chipotle-pepper puree, tequila, lime juice, and triple sec. ✛ *1:E4*

List (⊠ 2226 1st Ave., *Belltown* ☎ 206/441–1000 ⊕ *www.listbelltown. com*) is a Belltown favorite for great happy-hour deals. The hip, dimly lit space has a nice glow thanks to some red and white backlighting. An all-day happy hour on Sunday and Monday means you get half off the yummy food menu (mussels, angus beef burgers, rack of lamb, spicy calamari), plus $14 bottles of wine. ✛ *1:C1*

★ **Oliver's** (⊠ 405 Olive Way, *Downtown* ☎ 206/382–6995), in the Mayflower Park Hotel, is famous for its martinis. In fact, having a cocktail here is like having afternoon tea in some parts of the world. Wing chairs, low tables, and lots of natural light make it easy to relax after a hectic day. The likes of Frank Sinatra or Billie Holiday may be playing in the background; expect an unfussy crowd of regulars, hotel guests, and mature Manhattan-sippers who appreciate old-school elegance. ✛ *1:E2*

106 Pine (⊠ 106 Pine St., *Downtown* ☎ 206/443–1106 ⊕ *www.106pine. com*) is part wine bar, part wine shop, and part gourmet market. 106 Pine sells only Northwest wines and offers Weekly Urban Wine Tours (reservations essential) include an overview of the Washington wine scene plus visits to nearby wineries. The folks pouring here are super knowledgeable and charming. ✛ *1:D2*

Purple Café and Wine Bar (⊠ 1225 4th Ave., *Downtown* ☎ 206/829–2280 ⊕ *www.thepurplecafe.com*) is certainly the biggest wine bar in the city and possibly its most dramatic—despite the cavernous quality of the space and floor-to-ceiling windows, all eyes are immediately drawn to the 20-foot tower ringed by a spiral staircase that holds thousands of bottles. There are full lunch and dinner menus (American and Pacific Northwest fare), as well as tasting menus. Try the popular lobster mac and cheese or a yummy baked Brie. Though Purple is surprisingly unpretentious for a place in the financial district of Downtown, it's sophisticated enough that you'll want to dress up a bit. ✛ *1:E3*

Rendezvous (⊠ 2232 2nd Ave., *Belltown* ☎ 206/441–5823 ⊕ *www. rendevousseattle.com*) has been around since 1924, starting out as an elite screening room for film stars and moguls. It weathered some rough times as a porn theater and a much-loved dive bar, but it's been spruced up just enough to suit the new wave of wealthy locals without alienating everyone else. An old-time feel and the great calendar of events at the bar's Jewelbox Theater (live music, film, burlesque shows) set it apart from the neighborhood's string of cookie-cutter trendy spots. The food is nothing to write home about, but the atmosphere is chilled out and fun. ✛ *1:E3*

★ **Spur Gastropub** (✉ *113 Blanchard St., Belltown* ☎ *206/728–6706* ⊕ *www. spurseattle.com*) is a favorite among foodies. The inventive small plates and carefully curated drink menu (Spur is owned by the same folks who run Tavern Law on Capitol Hill), and stylish "pioneer-lite" space also make this a very popular nightspot. Sip a bourbon-infused cocktail and munch on stellar crostini with salmon, veal sweetbreads, or baby artichokes. Spur can be a bit spendy, so it may make sense to save your visit for happy hour (Sunday to Thursday 57) or for a late-night snack (it serves a special pairing menu from 11 to 1:30).✢ *1:C1*

Umi Sake House (✉ *2230 1st Ave., Belltown* ☎ *206/374–8717* ⊕ *www. umisakehouse.com*) offers a great selection of sake and sake-based cocktails in a space designed to look like someone shoehorned a real *izakaya* (a sake house that also serves substantial snacks) into a Belltown building—there's even an enclosed patio, which they refer to as the "porch," and a tatami room that can be reserved for larger parties. The sushi is good, and there's a very long happy hour offered at one of the bar areas. Despite its chic interior, Umi is less of a meat market than some Belltown spots—unless you're here late on a Friday or Saturday night. ✢ *1:C1*

★ **Vessel** (✉ *1312 5th Ave., Downtown* ☎ *206/652–5222* ⊕ *www. vesselseattle.com*) is the place to go Downtown for intricate and inventive cocktails. The specialty drinks are outstanding here, and you're bound to find a few concoctions that you won't find anywhere else. Service can be a bit slow on crowded weekends, but just spend the time people-watching in the attractive, supermodern bi-level space. The staircase leading to the mezzanine is backlighted in the type of unnatural yellow hue you'd expect to find in a cocktail with 10 ingredients—it's a surprisingly nice touch. This is a sophisticated place (leave the sport sandals at home) that knows it doesn't have to trade on pretension—it's all about the drinks, such as the Frick, with bourbon, Cinzano Rosso, peach bitters, and dried fig, or the Blueberry Flip, with brandy, crème de mûre, egg, and bitters. ✢ *1:F3*

Whisky Bar (✉ *2000 2nd Ave., Belltown* ☎ *206/443–4490*) is one of Belltown's reigning dive bars. Some of its elements seem a little self-conscious—punk-rock versions of cheesecake pinup girls decorate the walls—but this place still has more edge than the hipster watering holes of Capitol Hill. There is indeed a great selection of whiskey and bourbon, as well as the obligatory terrible beers (Miller, Pabst) at supercheap prices. ✢ *1:D2*

The W Hotel Bar (✉ *1112 4th Ave., Downtown* ☎ *206/264–6000*) allows you to enjoy the hotel's signature design style even if you haven't booked a room here. You will certainly feel fabulous sipping a well-poured—if pricey—martini among the beautiful, swank patrons—definitely dress up, and come prepared for a scene if it's a weekend night. There's a bar menu that will give you a taste of the hotel's restaurant, Earth and Ocean. ✢ *1:F3*

Fodor'sChoice **Zig Zag Café** (✉ *1501 Western Ave., Downtown* ☎ *206/625–1146*
★ ⊕ *zigzagseattle.com*) gives Oliver's at the Mayflower Hotel a run for its money when it comes to pouring perfect martinis—plus, it's much

more eclectic and laid-back here. A mixed crowd of mostly locals hunts out this unique spot at Pike Place Market's Hillclimb (a nearly hidden stairwell leading down to the piers). Several memorable cocktails include the Don't Give Up the Ship (gin, Dubonnet, Grand Marnier, and Fernet Branca), the One-Legged Duck (rye whiskey, Dubonnet, Mandarine Napoleon, and Fernet Branca), and Satan's Soulpatch (bourbon, sweet and dry vermouth, Grand Marnier, orange, and orange bitters). A very simple, ho-hum food menu includes cheese and meat plates, bruschetta, soup, salad, olives, and nuts. A small patio is the place to be on a summery happy-hour evening. Zig Zag is friendly; retro without being obnoxiously ironic; and very Seattle—with the occasional live music show, to boot. ✛ *1:D3*

BREWPUBS

Pike Pub and Brewery (✉ *1415 1st Ave., Downtown* ☎ *206/622–6044*) is a cavernous bar and restaurant operated by the brewers of the Pike Place Pale Ale. It also houses the Seattle Microbrewery Museum and an excellent shop with home-brewing supplies. True to its location, you might find more tourists than locals here, though it is popular with the Downtown after-work crowd. Pints of beer are cold and satisfying— the pale ale and the Kilt Lifter Scottish ale have been local favorites for two decades. ✛ *1:D3*

Pyramid Alehouse (✉ *1201 1st Ave. S, Downtown* ☎ *206/682–3377* ⊕ *www.pyramidbrew.com*), a loud, festive spot south of Pioneer Square and across from Safeco Field, brews the varied Pyramid line, including a top-notch Hefeweizen and an apricot ale that tastes much better than it sounds. Madhouse doesn't even begin to describe this place during games at Safeco Field, so if you're looking for quiet and immediate seating, make sure your visit doesn't coincide with one. The brewery offers tours daily. ✛ *1:E6*

COMEDY CLUBS

Unexpected Productions Improv (✉ *Market Theater, 1428 Post Alley, Downtown* ☎ *206/587–2414* ⊕ *www.unexpectedproductions.org*), adjacent to Pike Place Market, hosts tons of different improv events; shows may have holiday or seasonal themes or be done in the style of a certain TV or film genre like sci-fi or noir. On Friday and Saturday at 10:30, the troupe presents the long-running "TheatreSports" show, wherein skits are based entirely on audience suggestions. ✛ *1:D3*

SEATTLE CENTER, SOUTH LAKE UNION, AND QUEEN ANNE

Queen Anne is a diffuse and mostly residential neighborhood, so there's no real center to its nightlife. Pubs around Seattle Center cater to post-event crowds. Most of the bars are along Queen Anne Avenue North. Perhaps because a pub crawl isn't logistically easy, neighborhood favorites tend to be places you could easily settle into for the evening. Some of the bars we list here are on the top of Queen Anne's formidable hill, but most are on the lower reaches, near Seattle Center and Key Arena. Definitely check the map if you're on foot and planning an early-evening drink.

BARS AND LOUNGES

Bricco Della Regina Anna (⊠ *1525 Queen Anne Ave. N, Queen Anne* ☎ *206/285–4900* ⊕ *www.briccoseattle.com*) is a lovely candlelit wine bar on the top of Queen Anne Hill that serves a small menu of Italian snacks and entrées that change nightly. The wine list ranges all over the map, but Italian and Northwest wines are particularly well represented. Though it can get crowded on weekends, this place is unfailingly low key, despite the fact that it's popular with the upscale Upper Queen Anne set. ✛ *2:A2*

The Sitting Room (⊠ *108 W. Roy St., Queen Anne* ☎ *206/285–2830* ⊕ *www.the-sitting-room.com*) has a European-café vibe, excellent mixed drinks, and the hearts of residents of both the lower and upper parts of Queen Anne. It's quite an accomplishment to get those two very different demographics to agree on anything, but this sweet, relaxed little spot has done it with its eclectic, mismatched (but not shabby) furniture; zinc bar; sexy, dim lighting; and friendly staff. ✛ *2:A4*

Solo (⊠ *200 Roy St., Queen Anne* ☎ *206/213–0080* ⊕ *www.solo-bar. com*) has a lot going on: it's part tapas bar, part art gallery, part screening room, and part music venue, where up-and-coming indie musicians perform intimate sets on a small stage. The cutting-edge artwork and music bring in a lot of Seattle's hipsters, but the bar's location near the Seattle Center and its reputation for excellent, reasonably priced tapas mean that folks without tattoos often wander in, too. ✛ *2:B4*

BREWPUB

McMenamins (⊠ *200 Roy St., Queen Anne* ☎ *206/285–4722* ⊕ *www. mcmenamins.com*) is part of the same Portland-based brewpub chain as Six Arms on Capitol Hill, with the same brands on tap. It's a madhouse when Seattle Center events let out, but otherwise is a respectable watering hole. ✛ *2:B4*

DANCE CLUB

A regular venue for the **Emerald City Soul Club** (⊕ *www.myspace.com/ emeraldcitysoulclub*), a fun monthly dance party of classic funk and soul, **Lo-Fi Performance Space** (⊠ *920 Elliott Ave., South Lake Union* ⊕ *www.thelofi.net*) is a small, laid-back space that's a stark contrast to velvet-rope clubs. It's kind of divey—warehouse-chic, if you will—which makes it a favorite among Seattleites who don't enjoy the Pioneer Square experience. ✛ *2:E4*

PIONEER SQUARE

Pioneer Square is dance-club central; most places attract a very young crowd, many of whom come in from the suburbs. The scene here can get pretty obnoxious, so unless you really want to dance, there are better areas to go barhopping. The exception is First Thursdays, when the art walk attracts a more varied crowd, and galleries provide another focal point, and an additional reason beyond the occasional pub stop, to spend the evening here.

Pioneer Square is not Seattle's safest neighborhood even in daylight, and on weekends the typical problems with drug activity and transient population are complemented by additional disturbances from the hard-partying crowd.

BARS AND LOUNGES

Collins Pub (⊠ *526 2nd Ave., Pioneer Square* ☎ *206/623–1016* ⊕ *www. thecollinspub.com*) is the best beer bar in Pioneer Square. It has 22 rotating taps of Northwest (including Boundary Bay, Chuckanut, and Anacortes, among others) and California beers and a long list of bottles from the region. Its full menu of upscale pub grub features local and seasonal ingredients—try smoked pork tenderloin or seared duck breast with your pint. ✛ *1:F5*

For an introduction to, or an advanced course on, sake, visit **Sake Nomi** (⊠ *76 S. Washington St., Pioneer Square* ☎ *206/467–7253* ⊕ *www. sakenomi.us*) is a shop and tasting bar open until 10 PM Tuesday through Saturday and from noon to 6 on Sunday. Don't be shy—have a seat, try a few of the rotating samples, and ask a lot of questions. Sake can be served up in a variety of temperatures and it's fun to sample the sake-sipping tradition. ✛ *1:E5*

COMEDY CLUB

Comedy Underground (⊠ *109 S. Washington St., Pioneer Square* ☎ *206/ 628–0303* ⊕ *www.comedyunderground.com*) is literally underground, beneath Swannie's Sports Bar & Grill. Stand-up comedy, open-mike sessions, and comedy competitions are scheduled nightly at 8:30. Though it doesn't draw the big national names that Giggles does, it's a nicer venue. ✛ *1:F5*

DANCE CLUBS

Contour (⊠ *807 1st Ave., Pioneer Square* ☎ *206/447–7704* ⊕ *www. clubcontour.com*) is the place to go if you're not ready to quit partying when Seattle's bars shut at 2—this small club is famous for its after-hours events that keep the doors open until 7 AM. On weekends DJs spin mostly trance and deep house, hip-hop happens on Monday and Wednesday, and Sunday's all about break beats.

Trinity (⊠ *111 Yesler Way, Pioneer Square* ☎ *206/447–4140* ⊕ *www. trinitynightclub.com*) is a multilevel, multiroom club that offers hip-hop, reggae, disco, and Top 40. It gets packed on weekends—get there early to avoid lines or to snag a table for some late-night snacks. This is the most tasteful and interesting of the Pioneer Square megaclubs—in terms of decor, anyway. ✛ *1:F5*

CAPITOL HILL

Capitol Hill has a lot of music venues and interesting watering holes—it's one of the city's liveliest areas for nightlife. The Pike–Pine Corridor was always base camp for hipsters drinking Pabst out of the can, but the changing face of the neighborhood has brought some edgy, upscale gastropubs and appearance-conscious lounges. The Hill is also the center of the city's gay and lesbian community, with the majority of gay bars and dance clubs along Pike, Pine, and Broadway. A short stretch of 15th Avenue around East Republican Street is another mini–nightlife district, which is a bit more subdued.

As with Downtown, most of the neighborhood's restaurants double as nightspots. Quinn's on Pike Street and Smith on 15th Avenue, for example both get kudos for great food but are also notable as drinking spots (in Quinn's case for its excellent beer list).

BARS AND LOUNGES

Barca (✉ *1510 11th Ave., Capitol Hill* ☎ *206/325–8236* ⊕ *www.barcaseattle.com*) is a large space with chic decor of large tables and velvet-lined booths, dark lighting, and lots of mood. There is plenty of bar space early on in the evening and a mezzanine with ample seating, too. Because they can tout the largest vodka selection in the state at their Vodka Bar, as well as a renowned menu of mixed drinks, the bar fills up rather early with young patrons. As the evening unfolds, it becomes a frenzy of drinking, merrymaking, and people watching. ✛ *2:G6*

Capitol Club (✉ *414 E. Pine St., Capitol Hill* ☎ *206/325–2149* ⊕ *www.thecapitolclub.net*) is a sumptuous Moroccan-theme escape where you can sprawl upon tasseled floor cushions and dine on Mediterranean treats. Despite this being one of the neighborhood's see-and-be-seen spots, good attitudes prevail, and the waitresses are always affable and efficient, even during busy weekend nights. ✛ *1:G1*

Gallery 1412 (✉ *1412 18th Ave. E,Capitol Hill* ☎ *206/324–0671* ⊕ *www.gallery1412.org*) doesn't hold regular shows, but when this independent arts collective does host music, it's usually something unique: improvised music, homemade instruments, experimental classical pieces. The space is small, raw (not much more than concrete, walls, and a grand piano), and intimate.✛ *2:H6*

Hopvine (✉ *507 15th Ave. E, Capitol Hill* ☎ *206/328–3120*) is a neighborhood institution: a no-frills pub offering about a dozen local beers on tap and solid pub grub. This is a favorite spot for locals in this slightly-out-of-the-way neighborhood—it's not Pike–Pine central, but rather is on 15th, closer to Volunteer Park. It has open-mic night on Wednesday and trivia night on most Tuesdays. Note that it serves beer and wine only. ✛ *2:G4*

Fodor'sChoice ★ Licorous (✉ *928 12th Ave., Capitol Hill* ☎ *206/325–6947* ⊕ *www.licorous.com*) is Lark restaurant's attractive next-door bar, complete with a striking molded-tin ceiling, well-poured cocktails, and a dynamite whiskey list (be sure to ask about it). This has provided something that the Hill was once missing: a hip, well-designed space that attracts an eclectic clientele, from young couples to larger groups and local regulars—one where everyone can feel like a grown-up and enjoy a low-key evening sipping tasty specialty cocktails and munching tasty small dishes from an abbreviated Lark menu. ✛ *1:H2*

★ Linda's Tavern (✉ *707 E. Pine St., Capitol Hill* ☎ *206/325–1220*) is one of the Hill's iconic dives—and not just because it was allegedly the last place Kurt Cobain was seen alive. The interior has a vaguely Western theme, but the patrons are pure Capitol Hill indie-rockers and hipsters. The bartenders are friendly, the burgers are good (brunch is even better), and the always-packed patio is one of the liveliest places to grab a happy-hour drink. ✛ *1:H1*

Oddfellows (⊠ *1525 10th Ave., Capitol Hill* ☏ *206/325–0807* ⊕ *www. oddfellowscafe.com*) anchors a building of the same name that also houses the Century Ballroom, Tin Table, Elliott Bay Books, and more. This casual, hip eatery doubles as a bar on weekends, and there's a pleasant, small outdoor space, too. The vibe is hipster-chic; grab a seat at one of the large communal tables and hit up the small but quirky cocktail list. Burgers, pulled-pork sandwiches, soups, salads, chocolate pudding, and more are on offer, as well. ✛ *2:F6*

Poco Wine Room (⊠ *1408 E. Pine St., Capitol Hill* ☏ *206/322–9463* ⊕ *www.pocowineroom.com*) deserves accolades just for taking one of the least interesting architectural spaces out there—the oddly proportioned retail space of a condo complex—and making it into a sophisticated parallel universe where a friendly crowd lounges on couches and huddles around two small bars to enjoy a competent menu of artisan Northwest wines. A selection of subtle fruit wines is a nice surprise. ✛ *2:G6*

Fodor's Choice
★ **Quinn's** (⊠ *1001 E. Pike St., Capitol Hill* ☏ *206/325–7711* ⊕ *www. quinnspubseattle.com*) is our favorite go-to place for a dynamite beer at a laid-back but very cool bar. A friendly, knowledgeable staff tends the bar and the tables at the gastropub serving yummy food (especially the burgers) and even better beers. It can be very busy on weekends, but if you arrive in early evening on a weekday, you can sidle up to the bar, order some nibbles, and chat up the bartender about the numerous (rotating) brews on tap, including Belgian favorites, local IPAs, Russian River winners, and more. ✛ *2:G6*

★ **Smith** (⊠ *332 15th Ave. E, Capitol Hill* ☏ *206/709–1099* ⊕ *www. smithpub.com*), a bit outside the Pike–Pine heart, on 15th Avenue East, is a large, dark space with portraits of ex-presidents and taxidermied birds all over the walls, plus a mixture of booth seating and large communal tables. Filled to brimming with tattooed hipsters on weekends, this is actually a super-friendly and inviting space, with a very solid menu of food (including a top-notch burger and sweet-potato fries) and a full bar. Beer selection is small but good, and the cocktail list is decent. It's great people-watching and very Capitol Hill. ✛ *2:H5*

Tavern Law (⊠ *1406 12th Ave., Capitol Hill* ☏ *206/322–9734* ⊕ *www. tavernlaw.com*) celebrates the golden age of cocktails before Prohibition and the speakeasies that followed it. The space is dark and tucked away, and houses a "secret" upstairs area (accessed, if there's room available, by picking up the phone next to old bank-vault door). And the drinks are impeccably made, often with surprising ingredients like Earl Grey tea or maple syrup. ✛ *2:G6*

The Tin Table (⊠ *915 E. Pine St., Capitol Hill* ☏ *206/320–8458* ⊕ *www. thetintable.com*), upstairs from Oddfellows and across from Cal Anderson Park, is a welcoming little lounge with a shabby-chic aesthetic and a long, glossy bar. Its happy hour (3 to 6 and 11 to 1) is very popular: try the floozy burger (with roasted onion, bacon, cheese, and fries) and a creative cocktail. It's also beloved for its good food, like dynamite steak frites. Chimay and Peroni on tap make this even more popular. ✛ *2:F6*

Elysian Brewing Company

BILLIARDS

★ **Garage Billiards** (✉ *1130 E. Broadway, Capitol Hill* ☎ *206/322–2296* ⊕ *www.garagebilliards.com*), built in 1928 as an auto-repair shop, is now a large, happening, chrome-and-vinyl pool hall, restaurant, and bar. The large garage doors are thrown wide open on warm evenings, making this a pleasurable alternative to other cramped places. There are 18 tournament pool tables and a small bowling alley. The place is 21 and over only. ✛ *1:H2*

BREWPUBS

★ **Elysian Brewing Company** (✉ *1221 E. Pike St., Capitol Hill* ☎ *206/860–1920* ⊕ *www.elysianbrewing.com*) is a Capitol Hill mainstay with worn booths and tables scattered across a bi-level warehouse space and decent food (burgers, fish tacos, sandwiches, salads). The standouts here are the beers, which are a good representation of the thriving brewing scene in the Northwest. Seasonal brews are sometimes outstanding, with IPAs, lagers, and ales showcasing hops, spices, and even pumpkin flourishes. Always on tap are the hop-heavy Immortal IPA, the rich Perseus Porter, and the crisp Elysian Fields Pale Ale. This is a favorite of Seattleites and Capitol Hill residents and a good alternative to the hipster haunts and swanky lounges in the area. There's another branch in Wallingford near Green Lake on North 55th and Meridien, but it's a bit off the beaten path unless you're staying in that area. ✛ *2:G6*

Six Arms (✉ *300 E. Pike St., Capitol Hill* ☎ *206/223–1698* ⊕ *www. mcmenamins.com*), named for its six-armed Indian dancer logo, is a spacious and popular, two-story brewpub with 17 house and craft beers on tap. Two that stand out are the medium-bodied Hammerhead and the Terminator Stout. As you head back to the restrooms, note the fermenting tanks painted with amusing murals. ✛ *1:G1*

DANCE CLUBS

The Baltic Room (✉ *1207 E. Pine St., Capitol Hill* ☎ *206/625–4444* ⊕ *www.thebalticroom.net*), a classy piano bar–turned–art deco cocktail lounge, is the little dance club that could—it's still popular after quite a few years on the scene, and it still manages to get Seattleites of all stripes to take a few turns on the dance floor. Dress up a bit, but keep it comfortable. Along with top-notch DJs, skillful rock, acid jazz, and blues acts entertain from a small stage. The compact dance floor gets crowded—a little too crowded—on weekends. ✛ *1:G1*

★ **Century Ballroom** (✉ *915 E. Pine St., 2nd fl., Capitol Hill* ☎ *206/324–7263* ⊕ *www.centuryballroom.com*) is an elegant place for dinner and dancing, with a polished, 2,000-square-foot dance floor. Salsa and swing events often include lessons in the cover charge. The Tin Table, the restaurant/bar across the hall, is excellent. Additional (and all-ages) dance nights take place at Century's sister space HaLo, a loft a few blocks away at 500 East Pike Street. There's a bachata social on Wednesdays, salsa on Saturday, and swing on Sunday. See the Web site for a full calendar of what's on at both spaces. ✛ *2:F6*

GAY AND LESBIAN SPOTS

The Elite (✉ *1520 E. Olive Way, Capitol Hill* ☎ *206/860–0999* ⊕ *www. theeliteseattle.com*) technically the oldest gay bar on the Hill, has settled in well at its new location (it used to be on Broadway Avenue East). This laid-back pub and sports bar has a pool table, darts, and four TVs showing local sports. ✛ *2:F5*

Girl4Girl (⊕ *www.girl4girlseattle.com*) organizes the largest lesbian dance parties and events in the Pacific Northwest. The party has changed venues several times over the years, and recently it's been happening in city outskirts; check the Web site for more information. Events generally take place on the third Saturday of every month. Expect a lot of dancing and drinking, and the odd burlesque performance. The crowd is often very young, but all are welcome.

The newest addition to the Hill's gay and lesbian scene, **The Lobby Bar** (✉ *916 E. Pike St., Capitol Hill* ☎ *206/328–6703* ⊕ *www. thelobbyseattle.com*) is a chic space done in gray and white that, despite its location on one of the divier blocks of Pike, does a fairly good approximation of a hip hotel-lobby bar. It's a quiet, chill place to catch up with friends.✛ *2:F6*

Madison Pub (✉ *1315 E. Madison St., Capitol Hill* ☎ *206/325–6537* ⊕ *www.madisonpub.com*) is a laid-back place to grab a drink—leave your hair gel and dancing shoes at home. Regulars shoot pool, hang out with groups of friends, and chat up the friendly bartenders. This is the antithesis of the scenester spots. ✛ *2:G6*

Neighbours (✉ *1509 Broadway, Capitol Hill* ☎ *206/324–5358* ⊕ *www. neighboursnightclub.com*) is an institution thanks in part to its drag shows, great theme DJ nights, and relaxed atmosphere (everyone, including the straightest of the straights, seems to feel welcome here).

It's no longer the center of the gay and lesbian scene but the place is still usually packed Thursday through Saturday. ✛ *1:H1*

★ The original and short-lived **Pony** (✉ *1221 Madison St., Capitol Hill* ⊕ *www.ponyseattle.com*), which got bulldozed along with the rest of the 500 block of Pine Street, was notorious for wild fun. The newer, permanent incarnation is just a bit more polished and has an amazing patio, and retains some of the former space's decorating touches (vintage nude photos). There's a small dance floor and a mix of gays, lesbians, and hipsters. ✛ *2:G6*

Re-Bar (✉ *1114 Howell St., Capitol Hill* ☎ *206/233–9873* ⊕ *www. rebarseattle.com*) is a bar, theater, dance club, and art space that is extremely friendly to all persuasions—straight, gay, lesbian, transgender, whatever. A loyal following enjoys cabaret shows, weekend stage performances, and great DJs. The place has a reputation for playing good house music, but there are many different theme nights, including a rock-and-roll karaoke. Every fourth Saturday of the month Re-Bar hosts Cherry, a popular lesbian dance party. ✛ *2:E6*

Wildrose (✉ *1021 E. Pike St., Capitol Hill* ☎ *206/324–9210* ⊕ *www. thewildrosebar.com*) is Seattle's only dedicated lesbian bar, so expect a mob nearly every night. The crowd at weeknight karaoke is fun and good-natured, cheering for pretty much anyone. Weekends are raucous, so grab a window table early and settle in for perpetual ladies' night. ✛ *2:G6*

FREMONT AND PHINNEY RIDGE

Fremont has quite a few bars lining its main commercial drag of North 36th Street, including a few spots for live music. Unfortunately, Fremont suffers from a Dr. Jekyll and Mr. Hyde syndrome. During the week, almost any of its simple bars are fine places to grab a quiet drink with a friend. Come Friday night, however, the neighborhood can transform into an extended college party—so consider yourself warned.

BARS AND LOUNGES

★ **Brouwer's** (✉ *400 N. 35th St., Fremont* ☎ *206/267–2437* ⊕ *www. brouwerscafe.com*) is a Belgian-beer lover's heaven—even if it looks more like a trendy Gothic dungeon than a place with white clouds and harp-bearing angels. A converted warehouse provides an ample venue for a top selection of suds provided by the owners of Seattle's best specialty-beer shop, Bottleworks. There are plenty of German and American beers on offer, too, as well as English, Czech, and Polish selections. A menu of sandwiches, frites, and Belgian specialties help to lay a pre-imbibing foundation (remember that Belgian beers have a higher alcohol content). Before settling on a seat downstairs, check out the balcony and the cozy parlor room. ✛ *3:D5*

Fremont Brewing (✉ *3409 Woodland Park Ave. N, Fremont* ☎ *206/420– 2407* ⊕ *www.fremontbrewing.com*) is a relative Fremont newcomer making small-batch pale ales using organic hops. Locals (including their kids and dogs) crowd into the communal tables at the Urban Beer Garden, which is open Thursday to Saturday 4–8. ✛ *3:E5*

The George and Dragon (⊠ *206 N. 36th St., Fremont* ☎ *206/545–6864* ⊕ *www.georgeanddragonpub.com*), beloved of all Fremont residents, is a divey English pub that sees everything from grizzled old Brits watching soccer to hipsters looking for cheap beer and whiskey to the weekend frat crowd that clogs up the front patio area. Major soccer events like the World Cup bring in huge crowds. There's a popular quiz night on Tuesday. ✛ *3:D5*

Oliver's Twist (⊠ *6822 Greenwood Ave. N, Phinney Ridge* ☎ *206/706–6673* ⊕ *www.oliverstwistseattle.com*) is the right mix of trendy and adorable. The space is dark and mildly swanky, with quilted leather booths and dark wood. On the other hand, it's lively and noisy, especially on weekends, and accents like local artwork and a wall full of different size mirrors show that it doesn't take itself too seriously. The drinks, which are expertly poured and include en-vogue liqueurs like Cynar, are more impressive than the Pacific Northwest tapas and snacks (garlic truffled popcorn, mini soup and sandwich combos). But all together it makes for a fun evening slightly off the beaten path. ✛ *3:D1*

BREWPUBS

Hales Ales Brewery and Pub (⊠ *4301 Leary Way NW, Fremont* ☎ *206/706–1544* ⊕ *www.halesbrewery.com*) is one of the city's oldest craft breweries (1983). Hales produces unique English-style ales, cask-conditioned ales and nitrogen-conditioned cream ales, plus a popular Mongoose IPA. The pub serves a full menu and has a great view of the fermenting room. Order a taster's "flight" if you want to taste everything. ✛ *3:C4*

★ **Naked City Taphouse** (⊠ *8564 Greenwood Ave. N, Phinney Ridge* ☎ *206/838–6299* ⊕ *www.nakedcitybrewing.com*) has its own small brewery, so expect to see a few of its ales and stouts. The rest of the 24 taps are dedicated to their peers, including a few you won't find everywhere, like Lazy Boy, Roslyn, and Snipes. Pub grub is simple but local and organic. ✛ *3:D1*

BALLARD

On weekends, Ballard rivals Capitol Hill in popularity. There are at least a dozen bars and restaurants on Ballard Avenue alone. The neighborhood has quickly evolved from a few pubs full of old salts to a thriving nightlife district that has equal parts average-Joe bars, hipster haunts, music spots, wine bars, and Belltown-style lounges.

BARS AND LOUNGES

Balmar (⊠ *5449 Ballard Ave. NW, Ballard* ☎ *206/297–0500* ⊕ *www.balmar.com*) is one of Ballard's largest and most attractive bars—exposed-brick walls, hardwood floors, comfy cocoa-color couches and ottomans. The two-story space has areas to dine (serving a small-plates menu), drink, and shoot pool. It can be a bit of a fratty meat market on Saturday (it's definitely more New Ballard than Old Ballard), but other than that it's usually pretty mellow, and there's room enough to accommodate all the groups of friends and co-workers who enjoy having a slightly more upscale alternative to Ballard's neighborhood joints. ✛ *3:A3*

French bistro **Bastille** (✉ *5307 Ballard Ave. NW, Ballard* ☎ *206/453–5014* ⊕ *www.bastilleseattle.com*) is one of the neighborhood's most attractive spots to sip. First, there's the 45-foot zinc bar in the main dining room. Then there's the Back Bar, which is cozy, dimly lighted, with salvaged antique wood paneling and prints. On warm evenings, there's the partially enclosed patio that looks out onto Ballard Avenue. Specialty cocktails are popular, and the wine list is extensive (though a bit overpriced). The bar menu lets you sample favorites like the lamb burger and moules frites.✛ *3:A3*

The **Copper Gate Tavern** (✉ *6301 24th Ave. NW, Ballard* ☎ *206/706–3292* ⊕ *www.thecoppergate.com*) keeps Old Ballard's Scandinavian heritage alive. Antique bric-a-brac from the tavern's original owner shares the space with part of a hull from a replica Viking ship and many vintage black-and-white photos of bare-breasted Nordic babes. This may be the only bar in Seattle that serves aquavit as a mainstay, not a curiosity. Gravlax, pickled herring, and Swedish meatballs with lingonberry preserve lay the foundation for specialty cocktails like the Big Cucumber (Aalborg Akvavit, lemon, sugar, and cucumber).✛ *3:A2*

King's Hardware (✉ *5225 Ballard Ave. NW, Ballard* ☎ *206/782–0027* ⊕ *www.kingsballard.com*), brought to you by the owner of Linda's Tavern in Capitol Hill, has the same ironic rustic decor, the same great patio space, and the same caché with the hipster crowd. It also has great burgers. This place gets packed to the rafters on weekends—if you want the same scene with fewer crowds, go two doors down to Hattie's Hat, which was the reigning hipster spot until King's showed up. ✛ *3:A3*

★ Japanese restaurant **Moshi Moshi** (✉ *5324 Ballard Ave., Ballard* ☎ *206/971–7424* ⊕ *www.moshiseattle.com*) has a tree with lighted faux-cherry blossoms branching out over the bar, and the inventive cocktails are expertly poured beneath it. Unlike at most Japanese restaurants, the cocktail menu steers clear of sake-tinis—there are one or two sake concoctions, but you're more likely to find whiskey, gin, brandy, or even tequila put to good use, as in the Bella Donna (gin, black muscat, vermouth blanc, and lavender bitters) or the Sweet Savage (whiskey, Aperol, maple syrup, and grapefruit). There always seems to be a happy hour or nightly special at the bar, including the evening-long happy hour on Sunday.✛ *3:A3*

★ The **People's Pub** (✉ *5429 Ballard Ave. NW, Ballard* ☎ *206/783–6521*) is a Ballard institution and a great representative of what locals love about this unpretentious neighborhood. The pub (a dining room and a separate bar in the back) isn't much to look at—just a lot of wood paneling, simple wood tables and chairs, and some unfortunate floral upholstery—but it has a great selection of German beers and draws a true cross section of the neighborhood's denizens from hipsters to old-school fishermen. ✛ *3:A3*

Portalis (✉ *5205 Ballard Ave. NW, Ballard* ☎ *206/783–2007* ⊕ *www.portaliswines.com*) attracts serious oenophiles who gather around communal tables and at the long bar to sample wines from around the world in this cozy, brick-lined bar. It's a full-service retail shop as well, so you can pick up a few bottles to take home. Though it's a bit stuffy for Ballard, it's a nice alternative to the frenetic scene on the upper part of Ballard Avenue. ✣ *3:A3*

If you manage to score a table at **Sambar** (✉ *425 NW Market St., Ballard* ☎ *206/781–4883*), a teeny-tiny bar attached to French restaurant Le Gourmand, you probably won't leave for hours—there's nothing else like it in Seattle. Though it claims to have French flair, the only thing that cries corner café is its small size. The interior is modern in a way that would look pretentious and stark if translated into a bigger space. Excellent cocktails are mixed with panache and made with premium liquors—just try to walk a straight line out the door when you're done. A small menu offers delicious bites from Le Gourmand, from fresh salads to guilty pleasures like the *croque monsieur* and rich desserts. The crowd is mixed and different every night. A small patio adds some additional and highly coveted seating in summer. ✣ *3:C3*

UNIVERSITY DISTRICT

The U-District doesn't offer much of interest unless you're taking your new fake ID out for a spin. With the exception of jazz club Lucid *(⇨ Music Venues, below)* and the District Lounge in the Hotel Deca, most U-District haunts fall firmly in the pub category and are filled with students on weekends. If you don't want to drink, you'll have better luck: the neighborhood has a comedy club, a few theater troupes, and several good movie theaters, including beloved art house Grand Illusion Cinema *(⇨ Film, below)*.

BAR AND BREWPUB

Big Time Brewery (✉ *4133 University Way NE, University District* ☎ *206/545–4509* ⊕ *www.bigtimebrewery.com*), with its neat brick walls, polished wood floors, and vintage memorabilia, is one of the best places in the U-District for a quiet beer apart from the frenetic college scene. At least 10 beers—including pale ale, amber, and porter—are always on tap; tours of the adjacent brewery tell the whole story. Skip the mediocre pub grub. ✣ *3:H4*

COMEDY CLUBS

Giggles (✉ *5220 Roosevelt Way NE, University District* ☎ *206/526–5653* ⊕ *www.gigglescomedyclub.com*) hosts local comedians and open-mike events starting at 9 PM on Thursday and Sunday (free admission before 8:30). Nationally known comedians perform on Friday and Saturday at 8 and 10. Note that national acts draw big crowds, and the club gets insufferably packed. Bring cash or an ATM card—Giggles does not accept credit cards as payment for its overpriced drinks. ✣ *3:H3*

Jet City Improv (✉ *5510 University Way, University District* ☎ *206/781–3879* ⊕ *www.jetcityimprov.com*), Seattle's best improv group, fuses quick wit with music and games. The audience often provides input on what the improvisational skits should be. Shows, which are all ages, are on every Friday and Saturday at 10:30; there are also 8 shows on most Saturdays. ✣ *3:H3*

THE ARTS

The high-tech boom provided an enthusiastic and philanthropic audience for Seattle's arts community, which continues to grow. Gorgeous Benaroya Hall is a national benchmark for acoustic design. Its main tenant is the Seattle Symphony. At the Seattle Center, the ethereal Marion Oliver McCaw Hall combines Northwest hues and hanging screens in colorful light shows accompanying performances by the Seattle Opera and the Pacific Northwest Ballet.

Although the city's music scene has lost some of its shine as Portland has become the go-to city for indie rock, music is still a main form of entertainment here. This very literate city also supports a full calendar of readings, lectures, and writing workshops.

DANCE

Meany Hall for the Performing Arts (⊠ *15th Ave. NE and 41st Ave. NE, University District* ☎ *206/543–4880 ticket office* ⊕ *www.meany.org*), on the UW campus, hosts important national and international companies September through May. The emphasis is on modern and jazz dance. ✛ *3:H5*

On the Boards (⊠ *100 W. Roy St., Queen Anne* ☎ *206/217–9888* ⊕ *www.ontheboards.org*) presents contemporary dance performances, as well as theater, music, and multimedia events. The main subscription series runs from October through May, but events are scheduled nearly every weekend year-round. ✛ *2:A4*

Pacific Northwest Ballet (⊠ *Marion Oliver McCaw Hall at Seattle Center, 321 Mercer St., Queen Anne* ☎ *206/441–2424* ⊕ *www.pnb.org*), the resident Seattle company and school, has an elegant home at the Seattle Center. The season, which runs September through June, has traditionally included a mix of classic and international productions (think *Swan Lake* and *Carmina Burana*); however, Peter Boal, a well-known former New York City Ballet principal dancer, shook things up a bit when he took the reins as artistic director, and the lineup now includes works from celebrated contemporary choreographers like Christopher Wheeldon; a recent show featured three works by Ulysses Dove. Fans of *Swan Lake* and *The Nutcracker* can rest assured that those timeless productions are still part of the company's repertoire. ✛ *2:B4*

FILM

The Seattle International Film Festival gets a lot of attention, but the city also hosts numerous smaller festivals throughout the year. The most popular include **STIFF** (*Seattle's True Independent Film Festival;* ⊕ *www.trueindependent.org*) in June; the **Children's Film Festival** (⊕ *www.nwfilmforum.org/go/childrensfilmfest/cffseattle.htm*), held at the Northwest Film Forum in January; and the **Seattle Lesbian and Gay Film Festival** (⊕ *www.threedollarbillcinema.org*) in October.

Fodor's Choice ★ Seattle has several wonderful film festivals. The **Seattle International Film Festival** (☎ *206/324–9996* ⊕ *www.siff.net*) takes place over several

GLASS ART IN SEATTLE AND BEYOND

Dale Chihuly is an icon of glass art-work in the Northwest. His work can be found in more than 225 museums around the world, including numerous locations in and around Seattle.

■ In the lobby of **Benaroya Hall** (✉ *200 University St.* ☎ *206/215–4800* ⊕ *www.seattlesymphony.org*), the grand Downtown performing arts venue, are two stunning Chihuly chandeliers.

■ A Chihuly "Seaform" installation is on display at the **Seattle Aquarium** (✉ *1483 Alaskan Way,*

Pier 59 ☎ *206/386–4300* ⊕ *www.seattleaquarium.org*)

■ Chihuly, a University of Washington alum, created installation for the lobby of the University's **Meany Hall for the Performing Arts** (✉ *University of Washington Campus* ☎ *206/543–4882* ⊕ *www.meany.org*)

■ In Tacoma, the **Museum of Glass** (✉ *1801 E. Dock St., Tacoma* ☎ *253/396–1768* ⊕ *www.museumofglass.com*) and the adjacent Chihuly Bridge of Glass pay homage to their hometown hero.

weeks from mid-May to mid-June. Though some highly anticipated events sell out, last-minute and day-of tickets are usually available. The festival has grown so rapidly in the past five years that SIFF's organizers decided it needed a permanent home in the Seattle Center. The SIFF Film Center includes a cinema (✉ *Corner of 3rd Ave. N and Mercer St.* ☎ *206/633–7151*), lecture halls, and a reference library. Check SIFF's Web site or call for showtimes.

Enjoy the same first-run films that are playing down the street at the multiplex—minus the crowds, screaming kids, and sensory overload—at the **Big Picture** (✉ *2505 1st Ave., Belltown* ☎ *206/256–0572* ⊕ *www.thebigpicture.net*). This small, elegant theater has a full bar (you can order refills during the screening, so it's 21 and older only. ✛ *1:B1*

★ If you're tired of 40-ounce Cokes and $10 popcorn with neon-color butter, check out **Central Cinema** (✉ *1411 21st Ave., Central District* ☎ *206/686–6684* ⊕ *www.central-cinema.com*). The first few rows of this charming, friendly little theater consist of diner-style booths—before the movie starts a waiter takes orders for delicious pizzas, salads, and snacks (including real popcorn with inventive toppings like curry or dill); your food is delivered unobtrusively during the first few minutes of the movie. Wash it down with a normal-size soda, a cup of coffee, or better yet a glass of wine or beer. You won't find first-run films here, but the theater shows a great mix of favorites (*Hairspray* and *E.T.*) and local indie and experimental films. ✛ *2:H6*

Grand Illusion Cinema (✉ *1403 NE 50th St., at University Way, University District* ☎ *206/523–3935* ⊕ *www.grandillusioncinema.org*), Seattle's longest-running independent movie house, was a tiny screening room in the 1930s. It's still tiny, but it's an outstanding and unique home for independent and art films that feels as comfortable as a home theater. ✛ *3:H3*

★ The **Northwest Film Forum** (✉ *1515 12th Ave., Capitol Hill* ☎ *206/829–7863* ⊕ *www.nwfilmforum.org*) is the cornerstone of the city's independent film scene. Its hip headquarters has two screening rooms that show everything from classics like *East of Eden* to cult hits to experimental films and documentaries. ✛ *2:G6*

MUSIC

POPULAR MUSIC VENUES
FOLK AND COUNTRY
You might actually hear an Irish accent or two at **Conor Byrne Pub** (✉ *1540 Ballard Ave. NW, Ballard* ☎ *206/784–3640* ⊕ *www.conorbyrnepub.com*), along with live folk, roots, alt country, bluegrass, and traditional Irish music. There's live music almost every night of the week and great beer (including the obligatory Guinness on tap) at this laid-back pub. ✛ *3:A3*

The Little Red Hen (✉ *7115 Woodlawn Ave. NE, Green Lake* ☎ *206/522–1168* ⊕ *www.littleredhen.com*) is a country bar through and through. Bring your cowboy boots and hats to this divey honky-tonk, inexplicably located in one of Seattle's most gentrified and generic neighborhoods. Live country bands take the stage most nights; there are free country- and line-dancing classes on Sunday and Monday nights. Don't expect anything fancy—this place has not been sanitized for tourists. ✛ *3:G1*

Owl N' Thistle Irish Pub (✉ *808 Post Ave., Downtown* ☎ *206/621–7777*) presents acoustic folk music on a small stage in a cavernous room. It's an affable pub near Pike Place Market, and it's often loaded with regulars who appreciate both the well-drawn pints of Guinness and the troubadours. ✛ *1:E4*

Tractor Tavern (✉ *5213 Ballard Ave. NW, Ballard* ☎ *206/789–3599* ⊕ *www.tractortavern.com*) is Seattle's top spot to catch local and national acts that specialize in roots music and alternative country. The large, dimly lighted hall has all the right touches—wagon-wheel fixtures, exposed-brick walls, and a cheery staff. The sound system is outstanding. ✛ *3:A3*

JAZZ, BLUES, AND R&B
For a unique experience, check out the Seattle Jazz Vespers held every first Sunday at the Seattle First Baptist Church (corner of Harvard Avenue and Seneca Street) starting at 6 PM. The event lasts about an hour and a half, with outstanding musicians playing two sets; the church's pastor give a brief sermon between sets.

Dimitriou's Jazz Alley (✉ *2033 6th Ave., Downtown* ☎ *206/441–9729* ⊕ *www.jazzalley.com*) is where Seattleites dress up to see nationally known jazz artists. The cabaret-style theater, where intimate tables for two surround the stage, runs shows nightly. Those with reservations for cocktails or dinner, served during the first set, receive priority seating. ✛ *1:D1*

Egan's Jam House (✉ *1707 N.W. Market St., Ballard* ☎ *206/789–1621* ⊕ *www.ballardjamhouse.com*) has provided Seattle with a gift—another club devoted solely to jazz that's a neighborhood spot rather than an overpriced tourist trap. This small club and restaurant is devoted to jazz education for local high-schoolers during the day and performances from local and touring acts in the evenings. ✛ *3:B3*

The Crocodile

SeaMonster Lounge (✉ *2202 N. 45th St., Wallingford* ☎ *206/992–1120* ⊕ *www.seamonsterlounge.com*), with its low, low lighting and wall of very secluded booths, makes the tame Wallingford neighborhood just a little bit sexier. The space is tiny—the "stage" is more like a musician holding pen sandwiched between the bar and a few tables—but that just makes it all the more intimate and friendly. The bar presents high-quality local acts, mainly of the jazz and funk variety. ⊕ *3:F4*

ToST (✉ *513 N. 36th St., Fremont* ☎ *206/547–0240* ⊕ *www.tostlounge.com*), pronounced "toast," is a swank-looking but super-laid-back martini bar that just happens to have great live music many nights. This is a good place to catch a smokin' jazz, funk, or jazz-funk act, but the club also presents everything from spoken word to alt-country. Thursday nights host the popular improv soul-and-funk show Marmalade. ⊕ *3:D5*

Tula's (✉ *2214 2nd Ave., Belltown* ☎ *206/443–4221* ⊕ *www.tulas.com*) is less of a production (and expense) than Dimitriou's but still manages to offer a similar lineup of more traditional favorites as well as top-notch local and national acts. The intimate space hosts weekly Latin jazz and big-band jazz jams and often showcases vocal artists. ⊕ *1:C1*

ROCK AND POP

Fodor'sChoice ★ **The Crocodile** (✉ *2200 2nd Ave., Belltown* ☎ *206/441–7416* ⊕ *www.thecrocodile.com*) is one of the few places that can call itself "the heart and soul of Seattle" without raising many eyebrows. Indeed, it is—and has been since 1991—the heart and soul of Seattle's music scene. Nirvana, Pearl Jam, Mudhoney, and REM have all taken the stage here. Seattleites mourned the abrupt closing of this Belltown club in

2007, and rejoiced even harder when it reopened, fully renovated with much improved sightlines, in 2009. Nightly shows are complemented by cheap beer on tap and pizza right next door at Via Tribunali. All hail the Croc!⊹ *1:C1*

★ **Neumo's** (✉ *925 E. Pike St., Capitol Hill* ☎ *206/709–9467* ⊕ *www.neumos. com*) was one of the grunge era's iconic clubs (when it was Moe's), and it has managed to reclaim its status as a staple of the Seattle rock scene, despite being closed for a six-year stretch. And it is a great rock venue: acoustics are excellent and the roster of cutting-edge indie rock bands is the best in the city. Some lament that it's one of the most uncomfortable places in town to see a show (sightlines throughout the club can be terrible). It's also stuffy and hot during sold-out shows.⊹ *2:F6*

Showbox (✉ *1426 1st Ave., Downtown* ☎ *206/628–3151* ⊕ *www. showboxonline.com*), near Pike Place Market, presents locally and nationally acclaimed artists. This is a great place to see some pretty big-name acts—the acoustics are decent, the venue's small enough that you don't feel like you're miles away from the performers, and the bar areas flanking the main floor provide some relief if you don't want to join the crush in front of the stage. In 2007, Showbox opened another venue, **Showbox SoDo** (✉ *1700 1st Ave. S, SoDo*) not far from the stadiums in SoDo (south of Downtown). The converted warehouse is larger than the original venue and features big national acts from Nas to The Hives. ⊹ *1:D3*

Sunset Tavern (✉ *5433 Ballard Ave. NW, Ballard* ☎ *206/784–4880* ⊕ *www.sunsettavern.com*), a Chinese restaurant-turned-bar, attracts everyone from punks to college students to postgrad nomads and neighborhood old-timers. All come for the ever-changing eclectic music acts and a karaoke night backed by a band. ⊹ *3:A3*

The Triple Door (✉ *216 Union St., Downtown* ☎ *206/838–4333* ⊕ *www. thetripledoor.net*) has been referred to (perhaps not kindly) as a rock club for thirty- and fortysomethings. While it's true that you'll see more world music and jazz here than alternative music, and the half-moon booths that make up the majority of the seating in the main room are more cabaret than rock, the Triple Door has an interesting lineup that often appeals to younger patrons, too. ⊹ *1:E3*

OPERA AND SYMPHONY

Seattle Opera (✉ *Marion Oliver McCaw Hall at Seattle Center, 321 Mercer St., Queen Anne* ☎ *206/389–7676* ⊕ *www.seattleopera.org*), whose home is the beautiful Marion Oliver McCaw Hall, stages such productions as *Carmine, Ariadne auf Naxos,* and *The Girl of the Golden West* from August through May. Evening-event guests are treated to a light show from 30-foot hanging scrims above an outdoor piazza. Extra women's bathrooms and a soundproof baby "crying room" make the programs comfortable and family-friendly. ⊹ *2:B4*

Fodor'sChoice **Seattle Symphony** (✉ *Benaroya Hall, 200 University St., Downtown*
★ ☎ *206/215–4747* ⊕ *www.seattlesymphony.org*) performs from September through June in stunning, acoustically superior Benaroya Hall. The hall is so state of the art that the acoustics are pure in every one of the main hall's 2,500 seats. This exciting symphony has been nominated

Members of the Seattle Symphony on stage at Benaroya Hall

for numerous Grammy Awards and is well regarded nationally and internationally. ✛ *1:E3*

READINGS AND LECTURES

Elliot Bay Book Company (✉ *1521 10th Ave., Capitol Hill* ☎ *206/624– 6600* ⊕ *www.elliottbaybook.com*) presents a popular series of renowned local, national, and international author readings. Events are free, but tickets are often required. ✛ *2:F6*

Richard Hugo House (✉ *1634 11th Ave., Capitol Hill* ☎ *206/322–7030* ⊕ *www.hugohouse.org*) is a haven for writers, with classes, private work areas, and readings by Northwest luminaries and authors on their way up. As it's in a Victorian building that was once a residence, it's a warm, homey place. ✛ *2:G6*

Christian Scientists occupied the Roman-revival-style **Town Hall** (✉ *1119 8th Ave., Downtown* ☎ *206/652–4255* ⊕ *www.townhallseattle.org*) for decades, and attending lectures here does feel a bit like going to church, though the folks sharing the pews with you are liable to be among Seattle's most secular. Town Hall hosts scores of events in its spacious yet intimate Great Hall, chief among them talks and panel discussions with leading politicians, authors, scientists, and academics. ✛ *1:F3*

University Book Store (✉ *4326 University Way NE, University District* ☎ *206/634–3400* ⊕ *www.bookstore.washington.edu*), near the UW campus, schedules free readings by best-selling authors and academics. The second-floor space is rich with book stacks, perfect for browsing afterward. Tickets are required, and they go quickly. ✛ *3:H4*

THEATER

A Contemporary Theatre (*ACT;* ⊠ *700 Union St., Downtown* ☎ *206/292–7676* ⊕ *www.acttheatre.org*) launches exciting works by emerging dramatists. Four staging areas include a theater-in-the-round and an intimate downstairs space for small shows. ✛ *1:F2*

Balagan Theatre (⊠ *1117 E. Pike St., Capitol Hill* ☎ *206/718–3245* ⊕ *www.balagantheatre.org*) puts on small productions that are thought-provoking and intense, from a local playwright's passionate look at the world of roller derby to a staging of a classic like Sam Shepard's *True West.* ✛ *2:G6*

5th Avenue Theatre (⊠ *1308 5th Ave., Downtown* ☎ *206/625–1900* ⊕ *www.5thavenue.org*) opened in 1926 as a silent-movie house and vaudeville stage, complete with a giant pipe organ and ushers who dressed as cowboys and pirates. Today the chinoiserie landmark has its own theater company, which stages lavish productions October through May. At other times it hosts concerts, lectures, and films. It's worth a peek—it's one of the most beautiful venues in the city. ✛ *1:F3*

Intiman Theatre (⊠ *201 Mercer St., Queen Anne* ☎ *206/269–1900* ⊕ *www.intiman.org*), at the Seattle Center, presents important contemporary works and classics of the world stage from May through November in its 485-seat space. ✛ *2:B4*

Northwest Puppet Center (⊠ *9123 15th Ave. NE, University District* ☎ *206/523–2579* ⊕ *www.nwpuppet.org*) encourages kids to sprawl on the floor while folktales are told by marionettes. The troupe keeps the lively stories brief (45 minutes). Puppet workshops are available.

Seattle Children's Theatre (⊠ *Charlotte Martin Theatre at Seattle Center, 2nd Ave. N and Thomas St., Queen Anne* ☎ *206/441–3322* ⊕ *www.sct.org*) stages top-notch productions of new works as well as adaptations from classic children's literature. After the show, actors come out to answer questions and explain how the tricks are done. ✛ *2:B5*

Seattle Repertory Theater (⊠ *155 Mercer St., Queen Anne* ☎ *206/443–2222* ⊕ *www.seattlerep.org*) brings nine new and classic plays to life, split between Seattle Center's Bagley Wright and Leo K. theaters during its September–April season. Adoring fans flock to new takes on choice classics as well as those fresh from the New York stage. You can preorder a boxed dinner from the Café at the Rep before the show, or linger afterward over coffee and dessert. ✛ *2:B4*

Theater Schmeater (⊠ *1500 Summit Ave., Capitol Hill* ☎ *206/324–5801* ⊕ *www.schmeater.org*), as if you couldn't tell by the name, is one of Seattle's zanier fringe theaters. Productions—live reenactments of *Twilight Zone* episodes, radical reinterpretations of Chekov—at this tiny, no frills space are hit or miss, but there have been enough hits to garner the company a lot of respect. ✛ *1:G1*

Nightlife, the Arts, and Shopping Atlas

KEY

☐ Nightlife and the Arts

■ Shops

⊕ following reviews indicates a map-grid coordinate

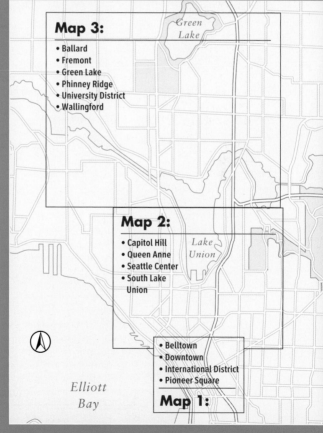

Map 3:
- Ballard
- Fremont
- Green Lake
- Phinney Ridge
- University District
- Wallingford

Green Lake

Map 2:
- Capitol Hill
- Queen Anne
- Seattle Center
- South Lake Union

Lake Union

- Belltown
- Downtown
- International District
- Pioneer Square

Map 1:

Elliott Bay

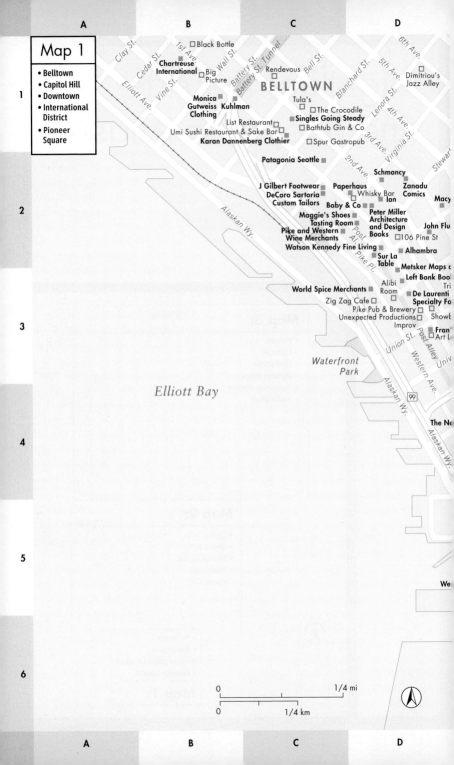

Map 1

- Belltown
- Capitol Hill
- Downtown
- International District
- Pioneer Square

BELLTOWN

Black Bottle

Chartreuse International

Big Picture

Rendevous

Tula's

The Crocodile

Monica

Gutweiss Clothing

Kuhlman

List Restaurant

Singles Going Steady

Bathtub Gin & Co

Umi Sushi Restaurant & Sake Bar

Karan Dannenberg Clothier

Spur Gastropub

Dimitriou's Jazz Alley

Patagonia Seattle

Schmancy

J Gilbert Footwear

Paperhaus

Zanadu Comics

DeCaro Sartoria Custom Tailors

Whisky Bar Ian

Macy

Baby & Co

Maggie's Shoes

Peter Miller Architecture and Design Books

John Flu

Tasting Room

Pike and Western Wine Merchants

106 Pine St

Watson Kennedy Fine Living

Sur La Table

Alhambra

Metsker Maps

Left Bank Book

World Spice Merchants

Alibi Room

Tri

De Laurenti Specialty Fo

Zig Zag Cafe

Pike Pub & Brewery

Unexpected Productions Improv

Showb

Fran

Art L

Waterfront Park

Elliott Bay

The N

We

0   1/4 mi

0   1/4 km

E · F · G · H

Westlake Ave. N

Stewart St.
9th Ave.
Howell St.
Olive Wy.
Pine St.
9th Ave.
8th Ave.

Melrose Ave.
Minor Ave.
Bellevue Ave.
Crawford Pl.
Summit Ave.
Belmont Ave.
Boylston Ave.
Harvard Ave.

□ The Capitol Club
E Pine St.
Le Frock Limited
Baltic Room □   ■■ **Edie's**
Sonic Boom Records ■   ■ **Area 51**
Six Arms □   **Wall of Sound**
Linda's
Tavern
Theater
Schmeater

Nube Green
Flora and Henri

Neighbours □

Broadway

1

E Union St.

**Bluebottle
Art Gallery
& Store**

CAPITOL HILL

Pacific Place
Nordstrom ■   **Flora & Henri**
□ Oliver's
Bar
■ **Barneys
New York**
**Sway
and
Cake**
Mario's

Boren Ave.
Terry Ave.
7th Ave.
Pike St.
St.
Pine St.

Summit Ave.
Boylston Ave.

Garage
Billiards □

□↗
Licorous

2

evog Shoes
Pike St.
Butch Blum ■

Turgeon Raine Jewellers ■

Seneca St.
Spring St.

f Seattle
ks Collective
ple Door
Nancy Meyer ■ □ Vessel
Fine Lingerie   5th Avenue Theatre
od & Wine
Purple Cafe
and Wine Bar
ox
□ Seattle   ■ **Clutch**
s Chocolates Symphony
ounge

□ Town Hall

Madison St.
Boren Ave.
Terry Ave.
9th Ave.
Minor Ave.

**FIRST
HILL**

Broadway
E James
Wy.

3

□ W Hotel Seattle

rsity St.
Seneca St.
1st Ave.
2nd Ave.
3rd Ave.
4th Ave.
5th Ave.
6th Ave.
8th Ave.
7th Ave.

🛡5

■ **A Mano**

rth Face ■
□ Boka Kitchen & Bar
■ **Arundel Books**

DOWNTOWN

James St.

James St.

Jefferson St.

Alder St.

Spruce St.

8th Ave.

4

Madison St.

Marion St.
Contour
Columbia St.
□   □
Owl'n Thistle
Irish Pub
Cherry St.

iaduct

Utilikilts Co ■
Ragazzi's Flying Shuttle ■   Trinity
Magic Mouse Toys ■   Nightclub
□ Collins Pub

Yesler Wy.

Agate Designs ■

Sake Nomi □

Synapse 206 ■
sel & Lieberman Booksellers ■ □
Clog Factory ■   Comedy
Underground

Occidental
Park

PIONEER SQUARE

■ **betty lin**

S Washington St.

S Main St.

3rd Ave.
4th Ave. S
5th Ave. S
6th Ave. S
7th Ave. S
8th Ave. S
Maynard Ave. S

**INTERNATIONAL
DISTRICT**

Kobe
Terrace
Park

5

Flury & Co ■   ■ **Glasshouse**
Chidori Asian Antiques ■   **Art Glass**
S Jackson St.

Momo ■
**Kobo Shop
&
Gallery** ■

S Jackson St.

Alaskan Wy. S
1st Ave.

■ **Northwest Fine
Woodworking**

S King St.

**Seattle Best
Tea Corporation** ■

6

■ **Kagedo Japanese Art**

Pyramid Alehouse □↓

Filson □↓

S Weller St.

Kinokuniya Book Store ■

S Lane St.

E · F · G · H

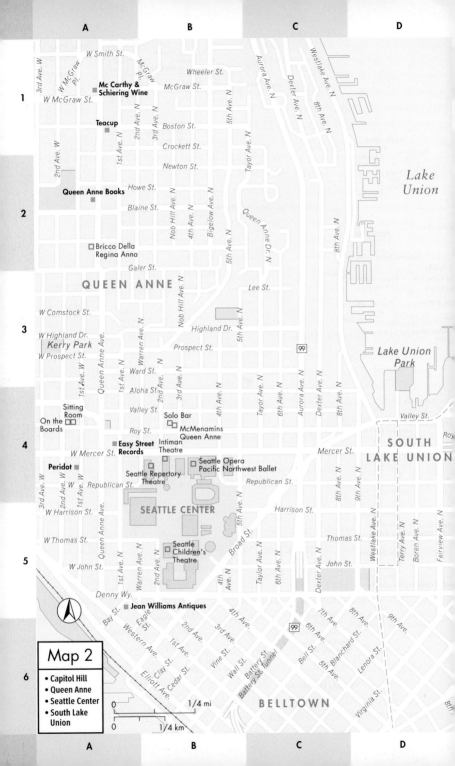

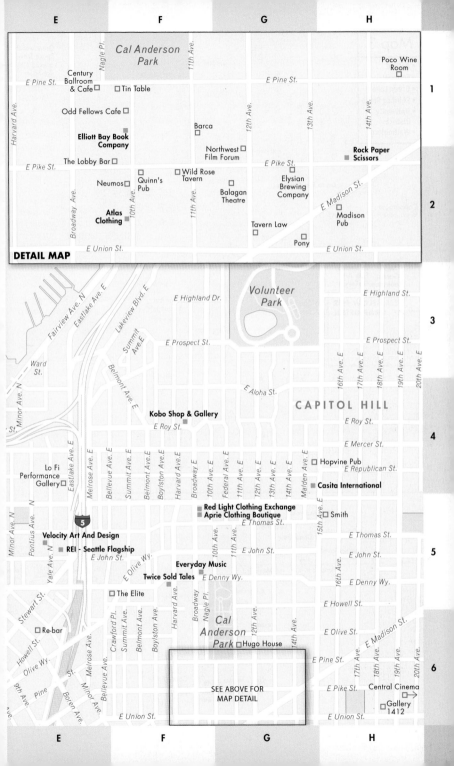

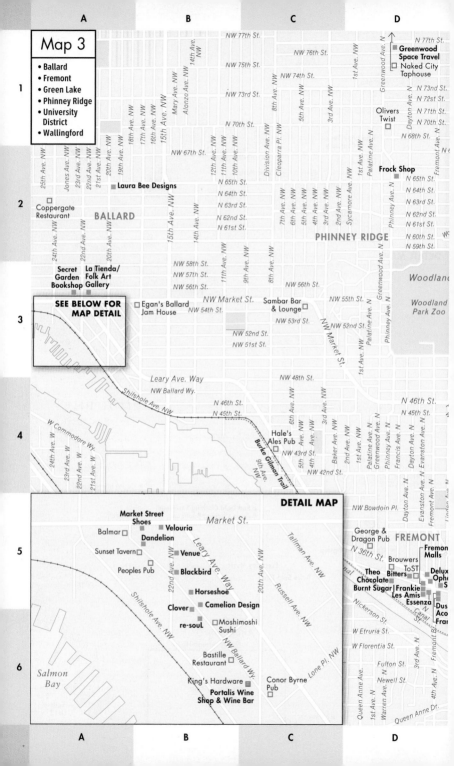

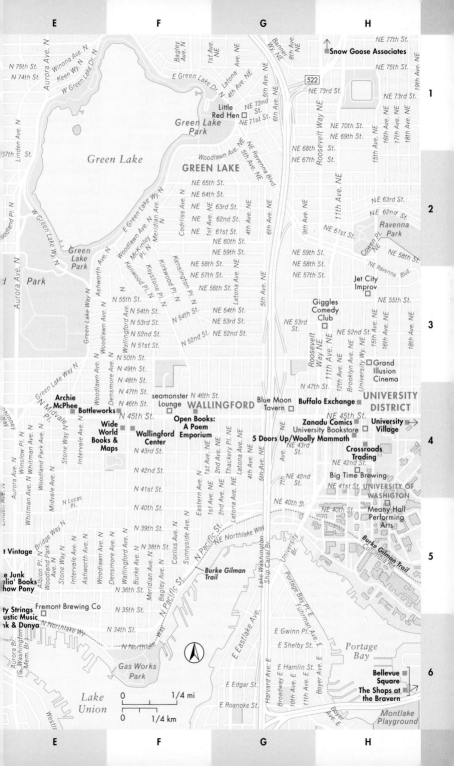

6

Shopping

WORD OF MOUTH

"[At Pike Place Market] we checked out the vendors: seafood, fruit, jams, spices, nuts, honey, pastas, candies, Seattle souvenirs, dry and fresh flowers. Our heads were in constant motion, swiveling back and forth at all the activity going on."

—LowCountryIslander

SHOPPING PLANNER

Business Hours	Top Spots to Shop

Business Hours

Malls and major national retailers keep pretty reliable hours, generally 9:30 AM–9 PM; with antiques shops and independent stores, however, anything goes. Many businesses close Monday; some close Sunday as well, and others may close for one day midweek. Small boutiques rarely open before 11 AM or noon and often close up shop by 5 or 6 PM. If you have your heart set on visiting a particular shop, call ahead to confirm its hours.

GO VINTAGE

Seattle boasts some of the best second-hand shopping in the country. There are plenty of trendy consignment and used-clothing shops like Atlas Clothing, Buffalo Exchange, and Crossroads Trading Co. on Capitol Hill and in the U-District, where each shirt and jacket has been carefully screened by the store's tastemakers; vintage shops like Red Light and the Fremont Antique Mall, where nearly every item is a one-of-a-kind find from the days of yore; and straight-up thrift shops like Goodwill and Salvation Army. If you're a fan of bargain prices and unique finds, and you enjoy the thrill of the hunt, take a chance on these shops. You never know what you might find.

Top Spots to Shop

The following areas have the greatest concentration of shops and the greatest variety.

5th and 6th Avenues, Downtown. Depending on where you're staying, you may not need to drive to this area, but if you do, the parking garage at Pacific Place mall (at 600 Pine) always seems to have a space somewhere (it also has valet parking). Tackling either Pacific Place or the four blocks of 5th and 6th avenues between Olive Way and University Street will keep you very busy for a day.

1st Avenue, Belltown. From Wall Street to Pine Street, you'll find clothing boutiques, shoe stores, and some sleek home and architectural design stores. 1st Avenue and Pike brings you to the Pike Place Market. There are numerous pay parking lots on both 1st and 2nd avenues.

Pioneer Square. Walk or bus here if you can. Art galleries are the main draw, along with some home decor and rug shops. If you do drive, many pay lots in the neighborhood participate in the "Parking Around the Square" program, which works with local businesses to offer shoppers validated parking; the Web site (⊕ www.pioneersquare.org) lists the lots and stores that offer it.

International District. Parking in the I.D. can be hit or miss depending on the time of day. It's best if you can walk here from Downtown or take a quick bus ride over. If you do drive, go directly to the Uwajimaya parking lot. They validate for purchases, and it's a safe bet you'll be buying something there. It's too fun to resist.

Pike–Pine Corridor, Capitol Hill. The best shopping in the Hill is on Pike and Pine streets between Melrose Avenue and 10th Avenue E. Most of the stores are on Pike Street; Pine's best offerings are clustered on the western end of the avenue between Melrose and Summit. There are pay lots on Pike Street (near Broadway) and one on Summit by E. Olive Way (next to the Starbucks).

Fremont and Ballard. Start in Fremont's small retail center, which is mostly along 36th Street. You may be able to snag street parking. After you've exhausted Fremont's shops, it's an easy drive over to Ballard. Ballard Avenue and NW Market Street are chockablock with great boutiques. Finding parking in Ballard can be tricky on weekends.

Updated by
Cedar Burnett

Seattleites are sometimes scorned for their fashion sense (polar fleece, sport sandals, and socks—oh my!), but as the city has grown and enough money has percolated through the ranks of retail, the city's style barometer has made a steady creep upward. Foodies, bibliophiles, wine aficionados, and design-centrists will find plenty of shopping opportunities—Seattle is a hotbed of unique, independent shops stocking one-of-a-kind treasures.

6

Shopping in Seattle is something best done gradually. Don't expect to find it all in one or two days worth of blitz shopping tours. Downtown is the only area that allows for easy daylong shopping excursions. Within a few blocks along 4th and 5th avenues, you'll find the standard chains (The Gap, Urban Outfitters, H&M, Anthropologie, Sephora, Old Navy), along with Nike's flagship store, and a few more glamorous high-end stores, some featuring well-known designers like Betsey Johnson. Downtown is also where you'll find department stores like Nordstrom, Macy's and Barneys New York. Belltown and Pioneer Square are also easy areas to patrol—most stores of note are within a few blocks.

To find many of the stores that are truly special to Seattle—such as boutiques featuring handmade frocks from local designers, independent record stores run by encyclopedic-minded music geeks, cozy used-book shops that smell of paper and worn wood shelves—you'll have to branch out to Capitol Hill, Queen Anne, and northern neighborhoods like Ballard. Shopping these areas will give you a better feel for the character of the city and its quirky inhabitants, all while you score that new dress or nab gifts for your friends.

Use the coordinate (✛ 1:B2) at the end of each listing to locate a site on the corresponding map preceding the chapter.

DOWNTOWN AND BELLTOWN

Where else can you shop with mountain and water views, serenading seagulls, and the low hum of ferries pulling into port? Shopping Seattle's core is as good as it gets, with high-end designers and tiny mom-and-pop shops, one of the oldest public markets in the country, and a seemingly endless supply of coffee shops.

(Above) Sundries from Watson Kennedy Fine Living (Opposite page bottom) Freshly made doughnuts (Opposite page top) Macrina Bakery

Put on some comfy shoes and get ready to explore. You could shop all day here and hit only a fraction of the stores. With no shortage of national chains and independent specialty shops, this area has a little something for everyone—from outdoor gear to imported perfume—all in a walkable area in the heart of the city. Start in Downtown to hit the high-end stores and the city's most beloved landmark—Pike Place Market. Browse the market stalls filled with local honey, flower bouquets, and fresh produce, then peruse the antique stores, jewelry boutiques, and gift shops in and around the market. After you've exhausted the Downtown core, head just north to Belltown, where you'll find clothiers and specialty shops tucked between art galleries and restaurants.

BEST TIME TO GO

The summer cruise season brings thousands of visitors to Downtown Seattle, so expect packed sidewalks in the warm months. Spring and fall are less crowded, and come winter it will mostly be you and the locals, if you're willing to brave the weather. Whatever the season, stick to daytime—Pike Place Market closes at 6 PM most days, and Belltown is choked with barhoppers when night falls.

BEST FOR...

CHIC CLOTHING

Baby and Co.: Edgy, pricey designs abound in this women's boutique. ✛ *1:D2*

Butch Blum: In this store will increase your style quotient. ✛ *1:E2*

Mario's of Seattle: Service is king, and the looks are classic at this high-end designer shop. ✛ *1:E2*

ITEMS FOR THE HOME

Sur La Table: Hard-to-find, special kitchen tools. ✛ *1:D2*

Watson Kennedy Fine Living: Lovely dishes, linens, bath soaps, and treasures galore. ✛ *1:D2*

TREATS AND WINE

DeLaurenti Specialty Food Markets: Nosh on panini or pizza while you browse the cheese, meat, and wine. ✛ *1:D3*

Fran's Chocolates: Salted caramels? Check. Raspberry-infused truffle? Check. A must–visit.✛ *1:D3*

Pike and Western Wine Shop or **The Tasting Room:** Choose a local wine for an in-room picnic, and be sure to get goodies from DeLaurenti. ✛ *1:C2*, ✛ *1:D2*

REFUELING

Caffe Senso Unico (✉ *622 Olive Way, at 6th Ave.* ☎ *206/264–7611*) has amazing sandwiches, croissants, and coffee.

Macrina Bakery (✉ *2408 1st Ave., between Wall St. and Battery St.* ☎ *206/448–4032*) is the spot to sit down with a slice of Sardinian flat bread, Nutella brioche, or a raisin twist—or more elaborate lunch options.

Stella Caffe (✉ *1224 1st Ave., at University St.* ☎ *206/624–1299*) is a great place for Italian espresso after a trip to SAM.

CAPITOL HILL

Like a rum-soaked tiramisu, Capitol Hill is wonderfully layered and steeped in both character and intrigue, you never know what you might encounter. Take a breath and bite into the Hill with an open mind and a sense of adventure. It's delicious.

(Above) Cupcake Royal (Opposite page bottom) Espresso Vivace (Opposite page top) Elliot Bay Book Company

Capitol Hill presents an interesting juxtaposition of old and new, rich and poor. Fabulous Edwardian mansions mingle with brick apartments and low-income housing for a blend of incomes and interests—and the shopping reflects this. You'll find dollar shops half a block from museum-quality antique galleries, and egalitarian bookstores next to hipster clothing boutiques. During the day, the Pike/Pine Corridor is a hotbed of great independent shopping and sleepy coffee shops, although at night this strip pulses with live music, dance clubs, street food, and high-end dining. Broadway is a mixed bag of cool shops and tacky stores—if time is limited, stick to Pike/Pine.

BEST TIME TO GO

It's best to wrap up before 5 PM if you're here only to shop. The Hill comes alive as night falls, and you'll have to push through dinner crowds.

If, however, you want to experience Pike/Pine in all its glory, stick around and take advantage of the late hours many stores keep in this strip—many stay open until 7 PM and some until midnight.

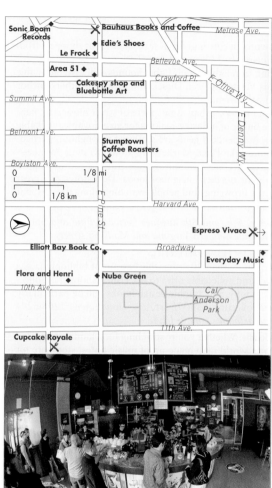

BEST FOR . . .

CLOTHES AND FOOTWEAR

Flora and Henri: Put your kids in gorgeous pieces that cost more than your outfit. ⊹ *1:F1*

Edie's Shoes: Comfy, trendy, get-you-noticed shoes for men and women. ⊹ *1:G1*

Le Frock: Vintage Chanel and new Gucci are packed into this classy consignment shop. ⊹ *1:G1*

QUIRKY GIFTS

Area 51: Score fun coffee mugs or mid-century side tables. ⊹ *1:G1*

Cakespy Shop and Bluebottle Art: Fans of indie craft fairs should check out the art, jewelry, and gifts here. ⊹ *1:G1*

NuBe Green: Environmentally friendly knickknacks and home goods. ⊹ *1:H1*

BOOKS AND MUSIC

Elliott Bay Book Company: Books and more books. If you want it, they probably have it. ⊹ *2:F6*

Everyday Music: A huge selection of used music in a store open until midnight. ⊹ *2:F5*

Sonic Boom Records: Indie rock, local music, and fun in-store events. ⊹ *1:G1*

REFUELING

Bauhaus Books and Coffee (⊠ *301 E. Pine St., at Melrose Ave.* ☎ *206/625–1600*) is a bi-level coffeehouse with floor-to-ceiling windows and tons of books.

Cupcake Royale (⊠ *1111 E. Pike St., between 11th Ave. and 12th Ave.* ☎ *206/328–6544*) offers up cupcakes and coffee—that should keep you going. Try flavors like salted caramel and lavender.

Espresso Vivace (⊠ *532 Broadway Ave. E, at E. Roy St.* ☎ *206/860–2722*) is one of Seattle's original kings of coffee. The espresso is as pretty as it is divine.

DOWNTOWN

Much of the Downtown core is given over to chains, but shoppers from towns without their own J.Crew and Ann Taylor will be pleased with the ample offering of reliable retail. Label hounds will also enjoy this corridor, as Louis Vuitton, Gucci, Diesel, and Brooks Brothers anchor the area around 5th Avenue. You'll find Nordstrom's lovely flagship store here, and an outdoor urban atmosphere of street musicians, panhandlers, and the bustle of industry, making for an enjoyable, walkable retail experience. Independent gems are scattered throughout, particularly in and around Pike Place Market and along Western Avenue—although for a greater concentration of indie stores, head to Capitol Hill, Belltown, or the northern neighborhoods. Downtown is a great area for wandering, browsing, and people-watching along the way, but we've listed the shops that are worth a special visit.

Best shopping: 4th, 5th, and 6th avenues between Pine and Spring streets, and 1st Avenue between Virginia and Madison streets.

BOOKS AND PRINTED MATERIAL

Arundel Books. For more than 20 years, this bastion of bibliophilia has offered new, used, and collectible titles to discerning shoppers. Collectors of art, photography, and graphic design books will be particularly interested in their collection. ⌧ *1001 1st Ave., Downtown* ☎ *206/624–4442* ⊕ *www.arundelbooks.com* ✛ *1:E4.*

Metsker Maps of Seattle. Whether you're searching for a laminated pocket map of Seattle or a world map made up of music notes, stop here for a massive selection of books, globes, charts, atlases, antique reproduction maps, and local satellite images. Don't let the store's location in the middle of the Pike Place Market melee fool you: this is a Seattle institution, not a tourist trap. ⌧ *1511 1st Ave., Downtown* ☎ *206/623–8747* ⊕ *www.metskers.com* ✛ *1:D3.*

Fodor's Choice ★ **Peter Miller Architectural & Design Books and Supplies.** Aesthetes and architects regularly haunt this floor-to-ceiling stocked shop for all things design. Rare, international architecture, art, and design books mingle with high-end products from Alessi and Iittala, while sleek notebooks, bags, portfolios, and drawing tools round out the collection. This is a great shop for quirky, unforgettable gifts, like a Black Dot sketchbook, and Arne Jacobsen wall clock, or an aerodynamic umbrella. ⌧ *1930 1st Ave., Downtown* ☎ *206/441–4114* ⊕ *www.petermiller.com* ✛ *1:D2.*

CHOCOLATE

Fodor's Choice ★ **Fran's Chocolates.** A Seattle institution, Fran's Chocolates (helmed by Fran Bigelow) has been making quality chocolates for decades. Their world-famous salted caramels are transcendent, as are delectable truffles, which are spiked with oolong tea, single malt whiskey, or raspberry, among other flavors. This shop is housed in the Four Seasons on 1st Avenue—how very elegant, indeed! ⌧ *1325 1st Ave., Downtown* ☎ *206/682–0168* ⊕ *www.franschocolates.com* ✛ *1:D3.*

CLOTHING

Alhambra. Sophisticated, casual, and devastatingly feminine, this pricey boutique delivers quality, European-style looks for women of all ages. Pop into the Moorish-inspired shop for a party dress, elegant jewelry, or separates, and be sure to check out their house line, designed by the owners. ✉ *101 Pine St., Downtown* ☎ *206/621–9571* ⊕ *www. alhambrastyle.com* ✛ *1:D2.*

> **FURNITURE ROW**
>
> You're probably not planning to browse for armchairs and coffee tables while on vacation, but if you're in the market for such things, Western Avenue between Union and Seneca streets has several high-end home-furnishings show-rooms, which make up an informal and stylish "Furniture Row."

Baby and Co. There's nothing child-ish about this sophisticated fashion house. A longtime Seattle favorite, Baby and Co. dresses women in urban lifestyle looks by designers such as Girbaud, Rundholz, High, and Lilith. Edgy, asymmetrical frocks, jackets, and sweaters with graphic prints come in butter-soft linens, wool, jersey, and crepe. You'll pay a lot for the privilege of being ahead of the trends. ✉ *1936 1st Ave., Downtown* ☎ *206/448–4077* ⊕ *www. babyandco.us* 2 ✛ *1:D2.*

Butch Blum. The attentive staff at this decidedly upscale retailer for men and women gives expert guidance on cultured creations by Giorgio Armani, Ermenegildo Zegna, Bluemarine, and Luciano Barbera—just to drop a few names. This is a fabulous spot for pricey but gorgeous men's suits—with a tailor on-site, too. ✉ *1408 5th Ave. N, Downtown* ☎ *206/622–5760* ⊕ *www.butchblum.com* ✛ *1:E2.*

Clutch. Handbag fanatics should scoot down 4th Avenue to this bag-only boutique stocked with trendy bags, hard-to-find designers, and classic looks you can sport season after season. Botkier hobos are dis-played next to CC Skye satchels and eco-friendly totes by Viaduct in this little shop. ✉ *1212 4th Ave., Downtown* ☎ *206/624–2362* ⊕ *www. clutchseattle.com* ✛ *1:E3.*

Ian. The hottest contemporary American sportswear and premium denim can be found at Ian, where the clientele is young and the clothes are very now. With the latest looks from J Brand, Rogues Gallery, Rxmance, RVCA, and Jack, and a service-oriented staff, this is a good bet for tidy hipsters who've moved beyond thrift-store finds. ✉ *1919 2nd Ave., Downtown* ☎ *206/441–4055* ✛ *1:D2.*

★ **Mario's of Seattle.** Known for fabulous service and designer labels, this high-end boutique treats every client like a superstar. Men shop the ground floor for Armani, Etro, and Zegna; women ascend the ornate staircase for Prada, Emilio Pucci, and Lanvin. A freestanding Hugo Boss boutique sells the sharpest tuxedos in town. ✉ *1513 6th Ave., Down-town* ☎ *206/223–1461* ⊕ *www.marios.com* ✛ *1:E2.*

Nancy Meyer Fine Lingerie. Elegant European lingerie designs by La Perla, Fleur of England, Sonia Rykiel, and others fill every nook and cranny of this tiny shop. The prices are sky high, but the goods are exquisite. ✉ *1318 5th Ave. N, Downtown* ☎ *206/625–9200* ⊕ *www.nancymeyer. com* ✛ *1:E2.*

6

Sway and Cake. Trendsetters who've graduated from H&M and Forever 21 will adore this body-conscious boutique full of colorful clothing with more fashion pedigree. The look is decidedly West Coast, with casual separates and dresses from Genetic Denim, Daftbird, Riller & Fount, and Frenzii. Prices are high, but not outrageous. ⊠ *1631 6th Ave., Downtown* ☎ *206/624–2699* ⊕ *www.swayandcake.com* ✛ *1:E2.*

DEPARTMENT STORES

Fodor'sChoice ★ **Barneys New York.** Anchoring Pacific Place Shopping Center, across from "Nordies," Barneys is a slice of the Big Apple in Seattle: über-trendy designer lines like 3.1 Philip Lim, Alexander Wang, Marc Jacobs, and Christian Louboutin fill two floors. Our favorite goods are right by the entryway: top-of-the-line make-up (by the likes of Shu Uemura), fragrances (Comme des Garçons never ceases to amaze), and baubles, including stackable rings encrusted with tiny gemstones. ⊠ *600 Pine St., Downtown* ☎ *206/622–6300* ⊕ *www.barneys.com* ✛ *1:E2.*

Macy's. This Downtown retail giant is a reliable source for clothing, housewares, cosmetics, and furniture. This centrally located superstore is a stone's throw from Nordstrom and Pacific Place. Every year, the store's entryway on 4th and Pine is bedecked with a giant retro star that lights up on Thanksgiving weekend and into the holidays. ⊠ *1601 3rd Ave., Downtown* ☎ *206/506–6000* ⊕ *www.macys.com* ✛ *1:D2.*

Fodor'sChoice ★ **Nordstrom.** Seattle's own retail giant sells quality clothing, accessories, cosmetics, jewelry, and lots of shoes—in keeping with its roots in foot-wear—including many hard-to-find sizes. Peruse the various floors for anything from trendy jeans to lingerie to goods for the home. A sky bridge on the store's fourth floor will take you to Pacific Place Shopping Center. Deservedly renowned for its impeccable customer service, the busy Downtown flagship has a concierge desk and valet parking. ■ TIP➔ The Nordstrom Rack store at 1st Avenue and Spring Street, close to Pike Place Market, has great deals on marked-down items. ⊠ *500 Pine St., Downtown* ☎ *206/628–2111* ⊕ *www.nordstrom.com* ✛ *1:E2.*

FOOTWEAR

A Mano. The store's name means "by hand," and that ethos of hand-made, high-quality craftsmanship seems soaked into the very (exposed brick) walls of this charming shop. A small selection of shoes from all over the world, along with some jewelry and handbags from local designers can be found here—all of it lovingly selected and much of it very unique. ⊠ *1115 1st Ave., Downtown* ☎ *206/292–1767* ⊕ *www. shopamano.com* ✛ *1:E4.*

John Fluevog Shoes. You'll find the store's own brand of fun, funky boots, chunky leather shoes, and urbanized wooden sandals here in men's and women's styles. ⊠ *205 Pine St., Downtown* ☎ *206/441–1065* ⊕ *www. fluevog.com* ✛ *1:D2.*

Maggie's Shoes. The owner makes twice-yearly trips to Milan to ensure she's stocking the best and most fashionable men's and women's shoes in fine Italian leather. You'll also find a few select pieces of women's Italian sportswear and purses. ⊠ *1927 1st Ave., Downtown* ☎ *206/728–5837* ⊕ *www.maggiesshoes.com* ✛ *1:D2.*

GIFTS AND HOME DECOR

Schmancy. Weird and wonderful, this toy store is more surreal art fun-

Fodor's Choice house than FAO Schwarz. Pick up a crocheted zombie (with a cute little
★ bow), a felted Ishmael's whale, your very own Hugh Hefner figurine—
or how about a pork-chop pillow? With collectibles from cult favorites
Plush You!, Kidrobot, and Lovemongers, kids of all ages will flip over
this quirky shop. Warning: Sense of humor required. ⊠ *1932 2nd Ave.,
Downtown* ☎ *206/728–8008* ⊕ *www.schmancytoys.com* ✛ *1:D2*.

★ **Sur La Table.** Need a brass-plated medieval French duck press? You've
come to the right place. Culinary artists and foodies have flocked to
this popular Pike Place Market destination since 1972. Sur La Table's
flagship shop is packed to the rafters with many thousands of kitchen
items, including an exclusive line of copper cookware, endless shelves of
baking equipment, tabletop accessories, cookbooks, and a formidable
display of knives. ⊠ *84 Pine St., Downtown* ☎ *206/448–2244* ⊕ *www.
surlatable.com* ✛ *1:D2*.

Watson Kennedy Fine Living. This jewel box of a store in the courtyard of
the Inn at the Market is worth a visit just for how heavenly it smells.
With a lovely line of artisan jewelry, luxurious bath products, and
enticing—and often aromatic—gifts, it makes for a relaxing stop in
the Pike Place tour. The sister store on 1st Avenue and Spring Street
(Watson Kennedy Fine Home) has vintage furniture, tableware, gourmet foods, and its own line of beeswax candles. ⊠ *86 Pine St., Downtown* ☎ *206/443–6281* ⊠ *1022 1st Ave.* ☎ *206/652–8350* ⊕ *www.
watsonkennedy.com* ✛ *1:D2*.

JEWELRY

Turgeon Raine Jewelers. Offering an art-forward take on gems and jewelry
in a spacious contemporary gallery, Turgeon Raine's employs only staff
with a design background—you can work with them to create a one-of-
a-kind piece, or pick from house-made items on display. It's also Washington's exclusive representative for Patek Philippe watches. ⊠ *1407 5th
Ave., Downtown* ☎ *206/447–9488* ⊕ *www.turgeonraine.com* ✛ *1:E2*.

MALL

★ **Pacific Place Shopping Center.** Shopping, dining, and an excellent movie
multiplex are wrapped around a four-story, light-filled atrium, making
this a cheerful destination even on a stormy day. The mostly high-end
shops include Tiffany & Co., MaxMara, Coach, and True Religion,
though there's also L'Occitane, Brookstone, Victoria's Secret, Ann Taylor, and J.Crew. A third-floor sky bridge provides a rainproof route to
neighboring Nordstrom. One of the best things about the mall is its
parking garage, which is surprisingly affordable, given its location, and
has valet parking for just a few bucks more. ⊠ *600 Pine St., Downtown*
☎ *206/405–2655* ⊕ *www.pacificplaceseattle.com* ✛ *1:E1*.

OUTDOOR CLOTHING AND EQUIPMENT

The North Face. This 1st Avenue location is one of the original stores by
the California outfitter, and it doesn't take a rocket scientist to figure
out why: You've probably heard about Seattle's often-dreary weather.
If you showed up with an optimistic suitcase full of shorts and shirts,
stop here for your requisite raincoat—an authentic souvenir if ever there

6

was one. ⊠ *1023 1st Ave., Downtown* ☎ *206/622–4111* ⊕ *www.thenorthface.com* ✛ *1:E4.*

WINE AND SPECIALTY FOODS

Fodor'sChoice ★ **DeLaurenti Specialty Food and Wine.** Attention foodies: clear out your hotel mini-bars and make room for delectable treats from DeLaurenti. And, if you're planning any picnics, swing by here first. Imported meats and cheeses crowd the deli cases, and packaged delicacies pack the aisles. Stock up on hard-to-find items like truffle-infused olive oil or excellent Italian vintages from the wine shop upstairs. Spring travelers will also want to stop by DeLaurenti's Pike Place nosh nirvana, called Cheesefest, in May. ⊠ *1435 1st Ave., Downtown* ☎ *206/622–0141* ⊕ *www.delaurenti.com* ✛ *1:D3.*

★ **Pike and Western Wine Shop.** The folks at Pike and Western have spent the last 35 years carving out the shop's reputation as one of the best wine shops in the city. With well over 1,000 wines personally selected from the Pacific Northwest and around the world—and expert advice from friendly salespeople to guide your choice—this shop offers taste-driven picks in a welcoming environment. ⊠ *1934 Pike Pl., Downtown* ☎ *206/441–1307* ⊕ *www.pikeandwestern.com* ✛ *1:C2.*

The Tasting Room. When you're ready for a break from sightseeing, make a detour into this relaxing little respite in the northern end of Post Alley. A handful of Washington State boutique wineries is represented at this tasting room and wine shop; most of the wines featured are handcrafted and/or reserve vintages. Taste the offerings, then purchase a bottle or two of your favorites—you can sit and enjoy your pick in the wine bar without a corking fee. ⊠ *1924 Post Alley, Downtown* ☎ *206/770–9463* ⊕ *www.winesofwashington.com* ✛ *1:D2.*

World Spice Merchants. If you're looking to shop where many of the city's best chefs get their spices, stop into World Spice Merchants for exotic and traditional spices, herbs, and tea. Tucked under Pike Place Market on Western Avenue, this aromatic shop stocks the best pure spices, flavorful salt varieties, and hand-ground spice blends you'll need to make just about any type of food authentically. ⊠ *1509 Western Ave., Downtown* ☎ *206/682–7274* ✛ *1:D3.*

> ### OUTDOOR NIRVANA
>
> If you are looking for more outdoor sportswear, or are in the market for a kayak, tent, snowshoes, or hiking boots—including weekend rentals—head to the nearby South Lake Union neighborhood for a visit to the memorable REI flagship store. For serious old-school anglers and mountain men, you can't miss the out-of-the-way Filson flagship store south of Downtown, for plaid vests, rugged pants, and coats that will last a lifetime.

BELLTOWN

Even though Belltown plays host to throngs of partying scenesters that descend on the area most evenings, the 'hood has a wide array of independent shops catering to all ages and aesthetic styles. Stroll along 1st Avenue to find an eclectic mix of high-end clothing boutiques, custom

CLOSE UP

Seattle Souvenirs

■TIP→ Find contact information for these shops in the Neighborhoods sections of this chapter, unless otherwise noted here.

FOOD AND DRINK
The Tasting Room in Pike Place Market's Post Alley is a great spot for Washington wines.

Pick up delectable fair-trade chocolates from **Theo Chocolate** in Fremont.

Visit Pike Place Market for a bag of famous chocolate-covered cherries by **Chukar Cherries** (✉ 1529 Pike Pl., Downtown ☎ 206/623–8043 ⊕ www.chukar.com), then stop into **Fran's Chocolates** on 1st Avenue for famous sea-salt caramels.

Seafood isn't the easiest thing to bring home, but if you go to **Pike Place Fish Market** (at Pike Place Market), the friendly, fish-flinging experts here can ship your purchase across the country for you.

Take home a Washington tea blend from the **Teacup** on Queen Anne—try Northwest Spearmint or Orcas Island Herbal Spice.

To bring home some coffee beans, pop into a coffee shop—most offer whole or ground coffee by the bag. Many coffee shops roast their own

brands, including **Caffe Vita, Victrola, Stumptown Coffee, Herkimer Coffee, Lighthouse Roasters, Neptune Coffee,** and **Caffe Fiore.**

MUSIC AND LITERATURE
Staff recommendations at **Sonic Boom Records** will help you discover the Northwest's up-and-coming musicians. **Elliott Bay Book Company** has a good, well-organized selection of local literature and history books, with handwritten staff recommendations to help you pick out the real gems.

SPORTS STUFF
At the **Seattle Team Shop** (✉ 1029 Occidental Ave. S, Sodo ☎ 206/621–1880 ⊕ www.seattleteams.com) you can kill three teams with one stone: the Seahawks, the Sounders, and the Mariners. **The Dawg Den** (✉ 4509 University Way NE, University District ☎ 206/547–6005 ⊕ www.thedawgden.com) has University of Washington Huskies jerseys.

T-SHIRTS
Before you buy a teenage relative— or anyone else for that matter—an oversize T-shirt that says "Seattle!" head up to Fremont's **Destee-Nation** (✉ 3412 Evanston Ave. N, Fremont ☎ 206/324–9403 ⊕ www.desteenation.com).

6

---

tailoring shops, artsy gift stores, and gritty standouts. Many local, independent designers are represented here, although the clothing tends to be more upmarket than the crafty, DIY goods offered in Capitol Hill or Ballard.

Best shopping: Along 1st Avenue between Cedar and Virginia streets.

CLOTHING
Gian DeCaro Sartoria. There is nothing quite like a custom-tailored suit to make a man look like a million bucks, and luckily, Gian DeCaro's offerings don't cost anywhere near that much. His custom suits may be pricey, but he's one of the best tailor/designers around, counting local

and visiting celebrities among his well-dressed clientele. For the rest of us, his shop is also stocked with elegant ties, cuff links, and other accessories, as well as some ready-to-wear clothing in luxurious fabrics. ✉ *2025 1st Ave., Belltown* ☎ *206/448–2812* ✢ *1:C2.*

Karan Dannenberg Clothier. A favorite of Seattle executives and sophisticates, this boutique stocks classy, modern clothing for women, but doesn't bow to useless trends. The staff is very knowledgeable, and offers wardrobe consulting for their customers—they'll even make house calls to critique your closets in a What Not to Wear–style evaluation. Shop here for perfect jeans, business attire, or glamorous formal wear. ✉ *2232 1st Ave., Belltown* ☎ *206/441–3442* ✢ *1:C1.*

Kuhlman. This tiny store on the same ultrahip block as the Ace Hotel has a careful selection of urban street wear that includes hard-to-find designers like Nudie Jeans Co., Barbour, and Fred Perry—it's sophisticated while still maintaining an edge. If you've got some time, Kuhlman is best known for creating bespoke clothing, often from superb European and Japanese fabrics. ✉ *2419 1st Ave., Belltown* ☎ *206/441–1999* ⊕ *www.kuhlmanseattle.com* ✢ *1:B1.*

Monica Gutweis. The dark side of couture can be oh-so-lovely, thanks to Monica Gutweis, who makes each one-of-a-kind garment in this tiny gallery. A little bit goth, a little bit punk, her highly wearable clothes, showcasing gorgeous fabrics and detailing, have earned her a cult following. She can even fit clothes to you while you wait. Creative handbags, belts, and accessories made by Gutweis and other local designers also line the walls of this Belltown boutique. ✉ *2405 1st Ave., Belltown* ☎ *206/956–4620* ✢ *1:B1.*

FOOTWEAR

★ **J. Gilbert Footwear.** Wrap your feet in comfort and European styling by designers Thierry Rabotin, Arche, Paul Green, and Robert Clergerie. Along with limited-edition handmade Western boots by Lucchese and Alden, you'll find glove-soft leather jackets and chic, casual clothing. ✉ *2025 1st Ave., Suite S, Belltown* ☎ *206/441–1182* ⊕ *www.jgilbertfootwear.com* ✢ *1:C2.*

GIFTS AND HOME DECOR

Chartreuse International. Savvy collectors shop here for authentic midcentury modern furniture and accessories by Harry Bertoia, Arne Jacobsen, Isamu Noguchi, and other design luminaries. The store also stocks new goods by Alessi, Kartell, and other modern designers. ✉ *2609 1st Ave., Belltown* ☎ *206/328–4844* ⊕ *www.modchartreuse.com* ✢ *1:B1.*

Jean Williams Antiques. If you have a thing for 18th- and 19th-century English and French furniture, you'll love Jean Williams. Even if you're not in the market for furniture, the showroom is fun to peruse, stocked as it is with decorative items from filigreed mirrors to enchanting chandeliers. ✉ *3025 1st Ave., Belltown* ☎ *206/622–1110* ⊕ *www.jeanwilliamsantiques.com* ✢ *2:A5.*

MUSIC

Singles Going Steady. If punk rock is more to you than anarchy symbols sewn on Target sweatshirts, you must stop at Singles Going Steady. Punk and its myriad subgenres on CD and vinyl are specialties, though they also stock rockabilly, indie rock, and hip-hop. It's a nice foil to the city's indie-rock-dominated record shops and a good reminder that Belltown is still more eclectic than its rising rents may indicate. ✉ 2219 2nd Ave., Belltown 🕾 206/441–7396 ⊕ www.singlesgoingsteady.com ✛ 1:C1.

OUTDOOR CLOTHING

Patagonia. If the person next to you on the bus isn't wearing North Face, he or she is probably clad in Patagonia. This popular and durable brand excels at functional outdoor wear—made with earth-friendly materials such as hemp and organic cotton—as well as technical clothing hip enough for mountaineers or urban hikers. The line of whimsically patterned fleece wear for children is particularly charming. Outdoor-chic trends of late have translated into seriously rising costs for a jacket here. ✉ 2100 1st Ave., Belltown 🕾 206/622–9700 ⊕ www.patagonia.com ✛ 1:C2.

PAPER GOODS

Paperhaus. Artists, designers, and writers should hightail it to Paperhaus to pick up professional portfolios and presentation materials. Lust-worthy notebooks from Moleskine, fancy-pants pens, home office materials, photo albums, and sleek attachés can also be found in this useful little shop. ✉ 2008 1st Ave., Belltown 🕾 206/374–8566 ⊕ www.paperhaus. com ✛ 1:D2.

SOUTH LAKE UNION

South Lake Union was once a forgotten industrial tract of land. Nowadays, cranes hover over new hotels, high-rise buildings, and Amazon's new campus, while design shops are popping up next to the enormous, trip-worthy flagship REI store. This neighborhood is just east of Seattle Center, whose Space Needle and Experience Music Project museum are on most visitors' itineraries; a walk (especially on a sunny day) from there to the REI store can be quite fun—then you can take the South Lake Union Streetcar (⊕ www.seattlestreetcar.org) back to the heart of Downtown.

GIFTS AND HOME DECOR

Velocity Art and Design. With treasures like white resin-cast incense holders, mod cufflinks, mid-century sunburst clocks, and sleek platform beds, design is at the forefront of this lifestyle shop. Velocity's showroom has a little bit of everything: furniture, bedding, lighting, accessories, clothing, gifts, and artwork from local artists. It all follows a modern organic esthetic, with pieces from luminaries Herman Miller, Blue Dot, Cul de Sac, and Kartell, among others. ✉ 251 Yale Ave. N, South Lake Union 🕾 206/749–9575 ⊕ www.velocityartanddesign.com ✛ 2:E5.

OUTDOOR CLOTHING AND EQUIPMENT

Fodor'sChoice ★

REI. Recreational Equipment, Inc. (REI) is Seattle's sports-equipment mega-mecca. The enormous flagship store in South Lake Union has an incredible selection of outdoor gear—from polar-fleece jackets and wool

The REI superstore in South Lake Union

socks to down vests, hiking boots, raingear, and much more—as well as its own 65-foot climbing wall. The staff is extremely knowledgeable; there always seems to be enough help on hand, even when the store is busy. You can test things out on the mountain-bike test trail or in the simulated rain booth. REI also rents gear such as tents, sleeping bags, skis, snowshoes, and backpacks. ⊠ *222 Yale Ave. N, South Lake Union* ☎ *206/223–1944* ⊕ *www.rei.com* ✢ *2:E5.*

QUEEN ANNE

There are actually two shopping areas in this hillside neighborhood—the more urban-feeling Lower Queen Anne, near the large Seattle Center campus and the more neighboorhoody Upper Queen Anne, along Queen Anne Avenue N at the top of the hill. West from the Seattle Center along Queen Anne and Mercer avenues are tiny cafés, antiques, and music stores. The cluster of businesses at the top of the hill includes a bookshop, gift stores, a tea emporium, and a heralded wine shop.

Best shopping: Along Queen Anne Avenue N between W. Harrison and Roy streets, and between W. Galer and McGraw streets.

BOOKS AND MUSIC

★ **Easy Street Records.** Hip and huge, this lively independent music store at the base of Queen Anne Hill has a well-earned reputation for its inventory of new releases, imports, used CDs, and rare finds. With in-store performances a few times a month, you may just be treated to live music while you shop. ⊠ *20 Mercer St., Queen Anne* ☎ *206/691–3279* ⊕ *www.easystreetonline.com* ✢ *2:A4.*

★ **Queen Anne Books.** One of the most
☺ beloved neighborhood bookstores in Seattle, Queen Anne Books is well known for their friendly, knowledgeable staff and extensive book selection. Pop in for their children's storytelling sessions on the third Sunday of every month, or browse at night and catch one of the many author events. After you grab your new books, slip into El Diablo, the incredibly cute coffee shop adjacent to the bookstore. ✉ *1811 Queen Anne Ave. N, Queen Anne* ☎ *206/283–5624* ⊕ *www.queenannebooks.com* ✛ *2:A2.*

> **NOVEL NEEDLE**
>
> The **SpaceBase Gift Shop** (✉ *400 Broad St., Queen Anne* ☎ *206/905–2100* ⊕ *www. spaceneedle.com*) has the city's ultimate icon, the Space Needle, rendered in endless ways. Among the officially licensed goods are bags of Space Needle Noodles, towering wooden pepper grinders, and artsy black T-shirts.

CLOTHING

Peridot Boutique. Strapless animal-print pocket dresses, retro gingham tops, and ruffly skirts abound in this contemporary women's boutique in lower Queen Anne. The prices are reasonable, the accessories are abundant, and local designers are represented as well. ✉ *523 1st Ave. W, Queen Anne* ☎ *206/284–3313* ⊕ *www.peridotboutique.blogspot. com* ✛ *2:A4.*

WINE AND SPECIALTY FOODS

★ **McCarthy & Schiering Wine Merchants.** One of the best wine shops in the city, this attitude-free store offers an amazing selection of wines from around the world in a range of prices. Check out their local specialty wines to experience the true flavor of the Northwest. ✉ *2401B Queen Anne Ave. N, Queen Anne* ☎ *206/282–8500* ⊕ *www.mccarthyandschiering. com* ✛ *2:A1.*

Teacup. Tea aficionados should not miss this aromatic shop on the top of Queen Anne. In a city full of coffee drinkers, Teacup boldly salutes the overlooked leaf with more than 150 varieties of tea sold loose by the pound. The excellent selection includes seasonal favorites and delicious blends like Provence Vanilla Rooibos and Elliott Bay Sunset. There are a few tables if you want to sample some tea in-house. ✉ *2128 Queen Anne Ave. N, Queen Anne* ☎ *206/283–5931* ⊕ *www.seattleteacup.com* ✛ *2:A1.*

PIONEER SQUARE

Gritty, eccentric, artsy, and fabulous, Pioneer Square is an eclectic blend of what makes Seattle . . . Seattle. Although this neighborhood has more than a few tourist traps hiding in its attractive brick buildings, it also has some wonderful clothiers, several bookstores, a few standouts we're positive you won't find anywhere else, plus many galleries and shops selling high-end furniture and collectibles. ■ TIP➜ Serious art collectors and gallery-hoppers should peruse the Neighborhoods chapter (⇨ Chapter 2) for a full list of galleries in Pioneer Square; here we've listed only the shops selling antiques and collectibles, not artwork.

Best shopping: 1st Avenue S between Yesler Way and S. Jackson Street, and Occidental Avenue S between S. Main and Jackson streets.

ANTIQUES AND COLLECTIBLES

Chidori Antiques. So packed full of stuff it looks more like a curio shop than a high-end antique seller, Chidori offers high-quality Asian antiques, pre-Columbian and primitive art, Japanese paintings, and antiquities from all over the world. ✉ *108 S. Jackson St., Pioneer Square* ☎ *206/343–7736* ✛ *1:E6.*

Flury and Company. View one of the largest collections of vintage photographs by Edward Curtis, along with Native American antiques, traditional carvings, baskets, jewelry, and tools in a historic space that's as interesting as the store's wares. ✉ *322 1st Ave. S, Pioneer Square* ☎ *206/587–0260* ⊕ *www.fluryco.com* ✛ *1:E6.*

★ **Kagedo Japanese Art and Antiques.** Museum quality works from the early 20th century and Japanese art in a variety of media are on display in this influential gallery. Among the treasures are intricately carved *okimono* sculptures, stone garden ornaments, and studio basketry. The gallery itself is worth a look—it's beautifully laid out, and includes a small rock garden and rice-paper screens that cover the storefront's picture windows. ✉ *520 1st Ave. S, Pioneer Square* ☎ *206/467–9077* ⊕ *www. kagedo.com* ✛ *1:E6.*

ART AND GIFTS

Agate Designs. Amateur geologists, curious kids, and anyone fascinated by fossils and gems should make a trip to Agate Designs, where there's no shortage of eye-popping items on display. Between the 500 million-year-old fossils and the 250-pound amethyst geodes, this store is almost like a museum (but a lot more fun). ✉ *120 1st Ave. S, Pioneer Square* ☎ *206/621–3063* ⊕ *www.agatedesigns.com* ✛ *1:E5.*

★ **Glass House Studio.** Seattle's oldest glassblowing studio and gallery lets you watch fearless artisans at work in the "hot shop." Some of the best glass artists in the country work out of this shop, and many of their impressive studio pieces are for sale, along with around 40 other Northwest artists represented by the shop. ✉ *311 Occidental Ave. S, Pioneer Square* ☎ *206/682–9939* ⊕ *www.glasshouse-studio.com* ✛ *1:F6.*

Northwest Fine Woodworking. For more than 30 years, this artist co-op has showcased a rotating cast of more than 20 Northwest craftspeople in a large, handsome showroom. Even if you're not in the market for new furniture, stop in for a reminder of how much personality wood pieces can have when they're not mass produced. The store also carries gifts like chess sets and ornate handcrafted kaleidoscopes and more practical household items like wooden bowls and utensils. ✉ *101 S. Jackson St., Pioneer Square* ☎ *206/625–0542* ⊕ *www.nwfinewoodworking.com* ✛ *1:E6.*

BOOKS AND TOYS

☺ **Magic Mouse Toys.** Since 1977, Magic Mouse has been supplying families
★ with games, toys, puzzles, tricks, candy, figurines, and more in their two-story, 7,000-square-foot shop in the heart of Pioneer Square. They claim a professional child runs the store—and it shows. The staff is friendly

and fun, and the shop will surely put a smile on your face. ⊠ *603 1st Ave., Pioneer Square* ☎ *206/682–8097* ⊕ *www.magicmousetoys. net* ✛ *1:E5.*

Wessel and Lieberman. Crammed with first editions, antiquarian materials, Pacific Northwest history and literature, Western Americana, book arts, poetry, and fine letterpress, this is a bookstore that smells exactly how a bookstore should—like books. There's nothing sterile about this handsomely fitted shop in a historic building. Come for the hard-to-find tomes, and stay for the small press, local material. ⊠ *208 1st Ave. S, Pioneer Square* ☎ *206/682–3545* ⊕ *www.wlbooks.com* ✛ *1:E5.*

CLOTHING

Betty Lin. Seattle's answer to the sample sale is found in this fashion-forward women's shop, where big-ticket designer labels at deep discount prices are snapped up quickly. You'll find last season's runway creations by Prada, Zac Posen, Driese Van Noten, Marni, Jil Sander, Michael Kors, Balenciaga, and many others. ⊠ *608 2nd Ave., Pioneer Square* ☎ *206/442–6888* ⊕ *www.shopbettylin.com* ✛ *1:F5.*

★ **Filson.** Seattle's flagship Filson store is a shrine to meticulously well-made outdoor wear for men and women. The hunting lodge–like decor of the space, paired with interesting memorabilia and pricey, made-on-site clothing, makes the drive south of Pioneer Square worth it (we recommend catching a cab, not hoofing it). The attention to detail paid to the plaid vests, oil-treated rain slickers, and fishing outfits is borderline fetishistic. ⊠ *1555 4th Ave. S, Pioneer Square* ☎ *206/622–3147* ⊕ *www. filson.com* ✛ *1:F6.*

Ragazzi's Flying Shuttle. For women of a certain age who want to add some whimsy and color to their wardrobe without veering into crazy cat-lady territory, Ragazzi's offers artisan-crafted, handwoven clothing in bold colors, as well as fun scarves and bold jewelry. Be sure to check out their travel line of washable easy-wear looks infused with a whole lot of moxie. ⊠ *607 1st Ave., Pioneer Square* ☎ *206/343–9762* ✛ *1:E5.*

Synapse 206. A near-seizure-inducing jumble of every imaginable fabric and color, Synapse 206 throws arty, innovative, and often audacious designs from local and international designers under one roof. Prices are actually reasonable, and whether or not you walk out with something, you'll have fun poking around in here. ⊠ *206 1st Ave. S, Pioneer Square* ☎ *206/447–7731* ⊕ *www.synapse206.com* ✛ *1:E5.*

Utilikilts. If you're a man burly enough to rock a skirt, then we've got the store for you. The flagship Utilikilts store stocks their own brand of utility-style "manskirts," which you'll see out and about often in Seattle, often paired with rugged combat boots—especially at such outdoor events as Bumbershoot. Pick up a workman's kilt, made from thick duckcloth, with a hammer loop and plenty of pockets for nails and screws; or snag a tuxedo kilt, for those formal occasions when you want to really make a statement. ⊠ *117 Occidental Ave. S, Pioneer Square* ☎ *206/691–9954* ⊕ *www.utilikilts.com* ✛ *1:E5.*

The Elliott Bay Book Company on Capitol Hill

FOOTWEAR

Clog Factory. There's a reason chefs wear them, and it's high time you knew why: clogs are ridiculously comfortable. If your stilettos are more foe than friend these days, pay a visit to the Clog Factory, where clogs of all sizes, shapes, and colors are lined up on high, exposed-brick walls. There's not much more to say: it's a store filled with clogs—it's fun, and though the fashion mags may not thank you, your feet probably will. ⊠ *217 1st Ave. S, Pioneer Square* ☎ *206/682–2564* ⊕ *www. clogheaven.com* ✛ *1:E5.*

INTERNATIONAL DISTRICT

This is a neighborhood meant for delicious exploring. Sample tea at Seattle Best Tea, leaf through books at Kinokuniya, check out Asian antiques, and stop for dim sum along the way. Megamarket Uwajimaya (⇨ *Neighborhoods chapter*) is the major shopping attraction of the International District, but the rest of the neighborhood is packed with shops worth visiting, too. Wander the neighborhood for bubble tea (milky tea with tapioca pearls), Chinese pastries, jade and gold jewelry, Asian produce, and Eastern herbs and tinctures. Little souvenir shops, dusty and deep, sell plants, Japanese kites, Vietnamese bowls, Chinese slippers, Korean art, and tea or dish sets. ■TIP➔ The International District is a very short walk from Pioneer Square. Simply walk east on Jackson Street from Pioneer Square (passing Amtrak's King Street Station), and you're well on your way.

Best shopping: S. Jackson Street to S. Lane Street, between 5th and 8th avenues S.

BOOKS

Kinokuniya Book Stores of America. Japanamaniacs, get thee to Kinokuniya, for their huge collection of Japanese books, magazines, office supplies, collectibles, clothes, and gifts. Their manga selection is particularly impressive—nearly every title you could want is represented, and they'll happily order anything you don't find in the store. ⊠ *525 S. Weller St., International District* ☎ *206/587–2477* ✣ *1:G6.*

GIFTS AND HOME DECOR

★ **Kobo at Higo.** Housed in what used to be a 75-year-old five-and-dime store, this distinctive gallery has fine ceramics, textiles, and exquisite crafts by Japanese and Northwest artists; you can also see artifacts from the old store. Items range from something as simple as incense from Kyoto to an enormous, painted antique chest. ⊠ *602 S. Jackson St., International District* ☎ *206/381–3000* ⊕ *www.koboseattle.com* ✣ *2:F4,* ✣ *1:G6.*

Momo. Right next door to Kobo is a perky little jewel with great gift options, including unique clothing, vials of perfume, plastic sushi magnets, coin purses with personality, canvas bags, quirky jewelry (such as a long chain necklace dangling a wee enamel cupcake at the end), and more. The owner is friendly and fun, and that comes through in this adorable shop. ⊠ *600 S. Jackson St., International District* ☎ *206/329–4736* ⊕ *www.momoseattle.com* ✣ *1:G5.*

SPECIALTY FOODS

Seattle Best Tea Corporation. If you haven't been introduced to the wonders of Asian tea, you need to make a trip to this tea nirvana, where the experience is as enriching as the tea itself. Palette pleasure abounds with their selection of oolong, pouchong, jasmine, and green teas. All the teas are available to try, and you can pick up a cute little teapot while you're at it. ⊠ *506 S. King St., International District* ☎ *206/749–9855* ✣ *1:G6.*

CAPITOL HILL

If you rock the skinny jeans, subscribe to *Dwell* magazine, embody the DIY ethos, or just like to people-watch, head to Capitol Hill for some of the best shopping in town. Broadway is popular among college students because of its cheap clothing stores, including standbys Urban Outfitters and American Apparel. The Pike–Pine Corridor holds the majority of the neighborhood's interesting and superhip shops.

Best shopping: E. Pike and E. Pine streets between Bellevue Avenue and Madison Avenue E, E. Olive Way between Bellevue Avenue E and Broadway E, and Broadway E between E. Denny Way and E. Roy Street.

BOOKS AND MUSIC

Fodor's Choice

★ **Elliott Bay Book Company.** After 36 years anchoring the Pioneer Square shopping district, Elliott Bay moved to new (but delightfully vintage) digs on Capitol Hill in 2010. Purist bibliophiles take heart: the new location is eerily like the old, as great pains were taken to move each and every massive cedar bookshelf onto the worn Douglas fir floors at

Continued on page 264

PIKE PLACE MARKET
Nine Acres of History & Quirky Charm

With more than a century of history tucked into every corner and plenty of local personality, the Market is one spot you can't miss. Office workers hustle past cruise-ship crowds to take a seat at lunch counters that serve anything from pizza to piroshkies to German sausage. Local chefs plan the evening's menu over stacks of fresh, colorful produce. At night, couples stroll in to canoodle by candlelight in tucked-away bars and restaurants. Sure, some residents may bemoan the hordes of visitors, and many Seattleites spend their dollars at a growing number of neighborhood farmers' markets. But the Market is still one of Seattle's best-loved attractions.

The Pike Place Market dates from 1907. In response to anger over rising food prices, the city issued permits for farmers to sell produce from wagons parked at Pike Place. The impromptu public market grew steadily, and in 1921 Frank Goodwin, a hotel owner who had been quietly buying up real estate around Pike Place for a decade, proposed to build a permanent space.

More than 250 businesses, including 70 eateries. Breathtaking views of Elliott Bay. A pedestrian-friendly central shopping arcade that buzzes to life each day beginning at 6:30 AM. Strumming street musicians. Cobblestones, flying fish, and the very first Starbucks. Pike Place Market—the oldest continuously operated public market in the United States and a beloved Seattle icon—covers all the bases.

The Market's vitality ebbed after World War II, with the exodus to the suburbs and the rise of large supermarkets. Both it and the surrounding neighborhoods began to deteriorate. But a group of dedicated residents, led by the late architect Victor Steinbrueck, rallied and voted the Market a Historical Asset in the early 1970s. Years of subsequent restoration turned the Market into what you see today.

Pike Place Market is many buildings built around a central arcade (which is distinguished by its huge red neon sign).

Shops and restaurants fill buildings on Pike Place and Western Avenue. In the main arcade, dozens of booths sell fresh produce, cheese, spices, coffee, crafts, and seafood—which can be packed in dry ice for flights home. Farmers sell high-quality produce that helps to set Seattle's rigorous dining standards. The shopkeepers who rent store spaces sell art, curios, clothing, beads, and more. Most shops cater to tourists, but there are gems to be found.

EXPLORING THE MARKET

TOP EATS

1 THE PINK DOOR. This adored (and adorable) Italian eatery is tucked into Post Alley. Whimsical decor, very good Italian food (such as the scrumptious *linguine alla vongole*), and weekend cabaret and burlesque make this gem a must-visit.

2 LE PANIER. It's a self-proclaimed "Very French Bakery" and another Seattle favorite. The pastries are the main draw, but sandwiches on fresh baguettes and stuffed croissants offer more substantial snacks.

3 PIROSHKY PIROSHKY. Authentic piroshky come in both standard varieties (beef and cheese) and Seattle-influenced ones (smoked salmon with cream cheese). There are plenty of sweet piroshky, too, if you need a sugar fix.

4 CAMPAGNE. This French favorite and its charming attached café have you covered, whether you want a quick Croque Madame for lunch, a leisurely and delicious weekend brunch, or a white-tablecloth dinner.

5 BEECHER'S. Artisanal cheeses—and mac-n-cheese to go—make this a spot Seattle-ites will brave the crowds for.

6 THREE GIRLS BAKERY. This tiny bakery turns out piles of pastries and sandwiches on their fresh-baked bread (the baked salmon is a favorite).

7 MATT'S IN THE MARKET. Matt's is the best restaurant in the Market, and one of the best in the city. Lunch is casual (try the catfish po'boy), and dinner is elegant, with fresh fish and local produce showcased on the small menu. Reservations are essential.

8 DAILY DOZEN DONUTS. Mini-donuts are made fresh before your eyes and are a great snack to pick up before you venture into the labyrinth.

9 MARKET GRILL. This no-frills counter serves up the market's best fish sandwiches and a great clam chowder.

10 CHUKAR CHERRIES. Look for handmade confections featuring—but not restricted to—local cherries dipped in all sorts of sweet, rich coatings.

TOP SHOPS

11 MARKET SPICE TEA. For a tin of the Market's signature tea, Market Spice Blend, which is infused with cinnamon and clove oils, seek out Market Spice shop on the south side of the main arcade.

12 PIKE & WESTERN WINE SHOP. The Tasting Room in Post Alley may be a lovely place to sample Washington wines, but Pike and Western is the place where serious oenophiles flock.

13 THE TASTING ROOM. With one of the top wine selections in town, the Tasting Room offers Washington wines for the casual collector and the experienced connoisseur. Stop by the bar for

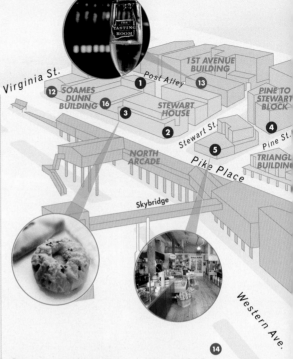

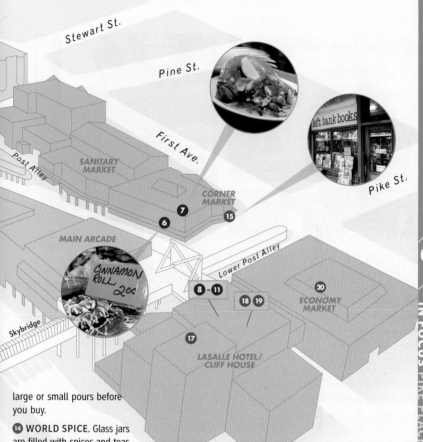

Stewart St.

Pine St.

First Ave.

Pike St.

Post Alley

SANITARY MARKET

CORNER MARKET

MAIN ARCADE

Lower Post Alley

CINNAMON ROLL 200

Skybridge

ECONOMY MARKET

LASALLE HOTEL/ CLIFF HOUSE

left bank books

6

large or small pours before you buy.

⓮ WORLD SPICE. Glass jars are filled with spices and teas from around the world here: Buy by the ounce or grab a pre-packaged gift set as a souvenir.

⓯ LEFT BANK BOOKS. A collective in operation since 1973, this tiny bookshop specializes in political and history titles and alternative literature.

⓰ THE ORIGINAL STARBUCKS. At 1912 Pike Place, you'll find the tiny store that opened in 1971 and started an empire. The shop is defi-

nitely more quaint and old-timey than its sleek younger siblings, and it features the original, uncensored (read: bare-breasted) version of the mermaid logo.

⓱ THE SPANISH TABLE. Though not technically in the Market, this amazing specialty store is nearby. It's the Spanish equivalent of DeLaurenti's, and carries hard-to-find cured meats and cheeses plus a nice stock of sweets and clay cookware like cazuelas.

⓲ TENZING MOMO. Your obligatory New Age stop, Tenzing sells high-quality essential oils, natural herbs, teas, tarot cards, incense, soaps, and much more.

⓳ PAPPARDELLE'S PASTA. There's no type of pasta you could dream up that isn't already in a bin at Pappardelle's.

⓴ DELAURENTI'S. This amazing Italian grocery has everything from fancy olive oil to digestifs and wine to meats and fine cheeses.

TOP EXPERIENCES

Pike Place Flowers

Pike Place Fish Co.

Market buskers

FISHMONGERS. There are four spots to visit if you want to see some serious fish: Pike Place Fish Co. (where the fish-throwers are—look for the awestruck crowds); City Fish (the place for fresh crab); Pure Food Fish Market (selling since 1911); and Jack's Fish Spot.

FLOWER STALLS. Flower growers, many of them Hmong immigrants, dot the main arcade. The gorgeous, seasonal bouquets are among the market's biggest draws.

PILES OF PRODUCE. The bounty of the agricultural valleys just outside Seattle is endless. In summer, seek out sweet peaches and Rainier cherries. In fall, look for cider made from Yakima Valley apples. There are dozens of produce vendors, but Sosio's and Manzo Brothers have been around the longest.

BUSKERS. The market has more than 240 street entertainers in any given year; the parade of Pacific Northwest hippie quirkitude is entertainment in itself.

POST ALLEY. There are some great finds in the alley that runs the length of the Market, paralleling First Avenue, from the highbrow (The Tasting Room) to the very lowbrow (the Gum Wall, a wall speckled with discarded gum supposedly left by people waiting in line at the Market Theater).

GHOSTS. If you listen to local lore, Pike Place Market may be the most haunted spot in Seattle. The epicenter seems to be 1921 First Avenue, where Butterworths & Sons Undertakers handled most of Seattle's dead in the early 1900s. You might see visitors sliding flowers into the building's old mail slot.

***SLEEPLESS IN SEATTLE* STOP.** Though it's been more than a decade since Rob Reiner and Tom Hanks discussed dating mores at the bar of The Athenian Inn, tourists still snap pictures of the corner they occupied. Look for the bright red plaque declaring: TOM HANKS SAT HERE.

A DAY AT THE MARKET

6:30 AM Delivery vans and trucks start to fill the narrow streets surrounding Pike Place Market. Vendors with permanent stalls arrive to stack produce, arrange flowers, and shovel ice into bins for displaying salmon, crab, octopus, and other delicacies.

7:30 AM Breakfast is served! ■TIP➔ For freshly made pastries head to Three Girls and Le Panier.

9 AM Craftspeople vying for day stalls sign in and are assigned spots based on seniority.

10 AM Craftspeople set up Down Under —the levels below the main arcade—as the main arcade officially opens. The Heritage Center on Western Avenue opens. Market tours ($10) start at the information booth. ■TIP➔ Make reservations for market tours at least a day in advance; call ☎ 206/774-5249.

11 AM The Market madness begins. In summer, midday crowds make it nearly impossible to walk through the street-level arcades. ■TIP➔ Head Down Under where things are often a bit quieter.

12 PM–2 PM Lunch counters at places like the Athenian Inn and the Market Grill fill up.

Pike Place Market

5 PM Down Under shops close and the cobblestones are hosed down. (The Market closes at 6 PM Mon.–Sat. and 5 PM on Sun.)

7 PM–2 AM Patrons fill the tables at the Alibi Room, Zig Zag Café, the Pink Door, Matt's at the Market, and Maximilien's.

RACHEL THE PIG

Rachel, the 550-lb bronze pig that greets marketgoers at the main entrance on Pike and 1st Avenue, is a popular photo stop. But she's also a giant piggy bank that contributes up to $9,000 per year to the Market Foundation. Rachel was sculpted by Georgia Gerber, of Whidbey Island, and was named for the 750-pound pig that won the 1985 Island County Fair.

PARKING

There are numerous garages in the area, including one affiliated with the market itself (the Public Market Parking Garage at 1531 Western Ave.), at which you can get validated parking from many merchants; some restaurants offer free parking at this garage after 5 PM. You'll also find several pay lots farther south on Western Ave. and north on 1st Ave. Street parking is next to impossible to find midday. From Downtown hotels, the Market is easy to reach on foot or on city buses in the "Ride Free Zone."

the new space. With an expanded bargain-books section, underground parking, lovely skylights, and a new café run by restaurateur Tamara Murphy, some might argue the store is even better. Elliott Bay hosts hundreds of author events every year, so nearly every day is an exciting one to visit the store, and the staff is as knowledgeable and clever as ever. As you enter, check out the great selection of Pacific Northwest history books and fiction titles by local authors, complete with handwritten recommendation cards from staff members. Probably the only downside of the move is that the store will no longer carry used books—a small sacrifice to pay to keep the literary heart of the city. ✉ *1521 10th Ave., Capitol Hill* ☎ *206/624–6600* ⊕ *www.elliottbaybook.com* ✛ *2:F6.*

Everyday Music. For a huge selection of used CDs and vinyl, wander over to Everyday Music, where you'll find more than 100,000 titles in stock. They're open until midnight, so you can join the late-night browsers clicking through the stacks after you've had dinner and a few drinks. Just don't blame us if you head home with a Milli Vanilli CD and can't remember why. ✉ *1521 10th Ave., Capitol Hill* ☎ *206/568–3321* ⊕ *www.everydaymusic.com* ✛ *2:F5.*

Sonic Boom Records Like the mothership store in Ballard, Sonic Boom on Capitol Hill is one of the best music shops around. It carries a little bit of everything, but the emphasis is definitely on indie releases. Handwritten recommendation cards from the staff help you find local artists and the best new releases from independent Northwest labels. Discover new bands in the handy listening stations and check out the small but fantastic collection of books, gifts, and other rockin' paraphernalia. ✉ *1525 Melrose Ave., Capitol Hill* ☎ *206/568–2666* ⊕ *www.sonicboomrecords.com* ✛ *1:G1.*

Twice Sold Tales. It's hard to miss this excellent used-book store—simply look for the 6-foot neon cat sign—he'll be waving his Cheshire tail. Inside, you'll find five more kitties (the oldest of which is 18) winding their way through the maze of stacks. Pick up a few tales and take advantage of the 25% discount offered the last two hours of the evening. Be sure to grab a map of all the used bookstores in the city if you're hungry for more. ✉ *1833 Harvard Ave., at Denny, Capitol Hill* ☎ *206/324–2421* ✛ *2:F5.*

Wall of Sound. If you're looking for Top 40 hits, this is not your record shop. If, however, you're on the hunt for Japanese avant-rock on LP, anti-war spoken word, spiritual reggae with Afro-jazz undertones, or old screen-printed show posters, you've found the place. Obscure, experimental, adventurous, and good? Wall of Sound probably has it. ✉ *315 E. Pine St., Capitol Hill* ☎ *206/441–9880* ⊕ *www.wosound.com* ✛ *1:G1.*

CLOTHING

Aprie. "Pretty" is the word that springs to mind when you visit Aprie—a contemporary young women's boutique with brands like Free People, Kensie Girl, Tulle, and Seychelles. Ultrafeminine frocks and fashion-forward shoes are the main attraction. A second location is in the U-District on University Way. ✉ *310 Broadway E, Capitol Hill* ☎ *206/324–1255* ⊕ *www.aprie.com* ✛ *2:F5.*

Atlas Clothing. Atlas is loaded with previously appreciated shirts, jackets, and tees; stacks of new and vintage denim; must-have sneakers from the '70s and '80s; and tons of accessories. This is not over-the-top costume vintage; visit Red Light Clothing Exchange for that. ⊠ *1419 10th Ave., Capitol Hill* ☏ *206/323–0960* ⊕ *www.atlasclothing.net* ✛ *2:F6.*

⟲ **Flora and Henri.** If you've ever lamented the lack of classic looks for your kids, or been tempted to steal the clothes off the backs of French toddlers, get thee to Flora and Henri for vintage-inspired, European-style children's wear. When you're done wishing the frocks also came in your size, take a gander at the new line of perfumes, linens, makeup, and chocolate for the decidedly grown-up. Everything in this shop is pricey, but these hand-stitched, quality garments should survive long enough to make gorgeous hand-me-downs. ⊠ *919 E. Pine St., Downtown* ☏ *206/749–9698* ⊕ *www.florahenri.com* ✛ *1:F1.*

★ **Le Frock.** It may look like just another overcrowded consignment shop, but Le Frock is Seattle's classiest vintage and consignment store. Among the racks, you'll find classic steals for men and women from Burberry, Fendi, Dior, Missoni, and the like, while contemporary looks from Prada, Gucci, and Chanel round out the collection. ⊠ *317 E. Pine St., Capitol Hill* ☏ *206/623–5339* ⊕ *www.lefrockonline.com* ✛ *1:G1.*

★ **Red Light Clothing Exchange.** Nostalgia rules in this cavernous space filled with well-organized, good-quality vintage clothing. Fantasy outfits from decades past are arranged by era or by genre. There's plenty of denim, leather, and disco threads alongside cowboy boots and eveningwear. There's a smaller branch in the University District. ⊠ *312 Broadway E, Capitol Hill* ☏ *206/329–2200* ⊕ *www.redlightvintage.com* ✛ *2:F5.*

FOOTWEAR

Edie's Shoes. Super-comfy, effortlessly cool shoes can be found at this small but carefully planned shop. Plop down on the big purple couch and try on trendy but sensible footwear by Camper, Onitsuka Tiger, Biviel, Tretorn, and Tsubo. You won't find any outrageous designs or one-of-a-kind items here, but it does have a great selection of favored brands in perhaps a few more styles than you'd find at Nordstrom. ⊠ *319 E. Pine St., Capitol Hill* ☏ *206/839–1111* ⊕ *www.ediesshoes. com* ✛ *1:G1.*

Rock Paper Scissors. Savvy "sneakerheads" come here to buy limited-edition Nikes, Pumas, Adidas, and New Balance kicks and reissued styles from the 1980s. Vintage shoes are also on sale at premium prices. This is one of the few stores in the neighborhood where you'll hear hip-hop playing instead of indie rock. ⊠ *1318 E. Pike, Capitol Hill* ☏ *206/322–2307* ⊕ *www.rpslife.com* ✛ *2:G6.*

GIFTS AND HOME DECOR

★ **Area 51.** Wander through this 10,000-square-foot temple of design and gape at the mix of retro-inspired new items and vintage, mid-century finds. Anything might materialize in this industrial space, from Eames replicas to clever coffee mugs, but it will all look like it's straight out of a handbook of the design trends from the middle of the last century. ⊠ *401 E. Pine St., Capitol Hill* ☏ *206/568–4782* ⊕ *www.area51seattle. com* ✛ *1:G1.*

6

CakeSpy Shop and Bluebottle Art. Etsy lovers and indie-craft-fair types should definitely make a trip to Bluebottle for affordable handmade art and gifts by mostly local artists. Much of the goods here are pastry- and cake-themed. ⊠ *415 E. Pine St., Capitol Hill* ☎ *206/325–1592* ⊕ *www. bluebottleart.com* ✛ *1:G1.*

Casita International. Brighten a rainy day with a trip to this sunny little boutique, where you'll find gorgeous treasures from Latin America, including Day of the Dead figurines, Frida Kahlo tote bags, handmade clothing, and lovely silver jewelry. ⊠ *423 15th Ave., Capitol Hill* ☎ *206/322–7800* ✛ *2:G4.*

Kobo. This lovely store sells artisan crafts from studios in Japan and in the Northwest. You'll find a similar stock here as in the International District branch: tasteful home wares, cute but functional gifts, and quirky pieces of furniture. After a long day of looking at retro and ironic items, this place will cleanse your palate. ⊠ *814 E. Roy St., Capitol Hill* ☎ *206/726–0704* ⊕ *www.koboseattle.com* ✛ *2:F4,* ✛ *1:G6.*

★ **NuBe Green.** An emphasis on recycled goods and sustainability is the mission of this well-presented store anchoring a corner of the Oddfellows Building. All items are sourced and made in the United States, including linens, candles, glass art, and even dog beds made from old jeans. Our favorite items are by local **Alchemy Goods** (⊕ *www.alchemygoods. com*), which recycles bicycle tubes, reclaimed vinyl mesh, and seatbelts into distinctively cool wallets and messenger bags. ⊠ *912 E. Pine St., Capitol Hill* ☎ *206/402–4515* ⊕ *www.nubegreen.com* ✛ *1:H1.*

FREMONT

Fremont is full of the sort of stores perfectly suited to browsing and window-shopping—lots of pretty, pricey nonessentials and fun junk shops, in a cute and quirky north-end neighborhood. The weekly summer Sunday market along the waterfront (with free parking nearby) is hit or miss, but worth a look if you're in the area.

Best shopping: Blocks bound by Fremont Place N and Evanston Avenue N to N. 34th Street and Aurora Avenue N.

ANTIQUES AND COLLECTIBLES

Deluxe Junk. Looking like an old Hollywood movie prop shop, this labyrinth of vintage furniture, retro cameras, turn-of-the-century photos, and racks of costume-ready clothing requires lots of time for worthwhile browsing. Snap up old typewriters, vintage jewelry, kitschy Seattle souvenirs, and abstract lamps before you go. ⊠ *3518 Fremont Pl. N, Fremont* ☎ *206/634–2733* ✛ *3:D5.*

Fremont Vintage Mall. Goods from about 25 vendors are crammed into every conceivable corner of this bi-level space, so, you'll likely score at least something to take home. Clothing, furniture, and collectible art are among the finds, and the dishes, toys, and other cool stuff are fun to look through whether you're a serious collector or just an innocent bystander. The Jive Time Records Annex is also a tenant. It's easy to walk right past this place—look carefully for the door and then proceed down the flight of stairs. ⊠ *3419 Fremont Pl. N, Fremont* ☎ *206/548–9140* ⊕ *www.fremontvintagemall.com* ✛ *3:D5.*

BOOKS AND MUSIC

★ **Dusty Strings.** A Seattle institution since 1979, Dusty Strings has long been delighting folk and roots music lovers with beautifully crafted hammered dulcimers, harps, guitars of all stripes, banjos, ukuleles, and mandolins. The relaxed shop invites hands-on browsing, and the lilting strains of traditional melodies often fill the space. The nonprofit group Victory Music frequently hosts acoustic concerts in the store—check ⊕ *www.victorymusic.org* for showtimes. ⊠ *3406 Fremont Ave. N, Fremont* ☎ *206/634–1662* ✛ *3:D5.*

Ophelia's Books. From the tiny spiral staircase leading to the basement, to the resident cats wandering through the tightly packed aisles, Ophelia's offers a classic used bookstore experience in an age when so many are disappearing. The owner is well known for her excellent taste in books and it shows—you'll find major titles from well-known authors as well as obscure works and poetry books. Be sure to ask for recommendations—she'll be happy to help. ⊠ *3504 Fremont Ave. N, Fremont* ☎ *206/632–3759* ✛ *3:D5.*

CHOCOLATE

Fodor'sChoice **Theo Chocolate.** Seattleites love their chocolate nearly as much as their
★ coffee (and preferably at the same time, thank you). This Fremont factory/storefront is one-stop fun, with factory tours on offer every day. Learn about the history of cacao, then stock up on free-trade organic tasty chocolate nibbles, such as spicy chile, cherry and almond, or coconut curry chocolate bars. ⊠ *3400 Phinney Ave. N, Fremont* ☎ *206/632–5100* ⊕ *www.theochocolate.com* ✛ *3:D5.*

CLOTHING

★ **Les Amis.** The most elegant boutique in Fremont, Les Amis is like a pop-up from a little girl's storybook set in a French country cottage. The over-35 set will breathe a sigh of relief when they see that the racks are not just filled with low-rise jeans: sophisticated dresses, gorgeous handknits, and the makings of great work outfits, much of it from Europe and Japan, fill the racks here. Younger fashionistas come here, too, for unique summer skirts and ultrasoft T-shirts. Everyone seems to love the whimsical lingerie collection. Les Amis carries some top designers such as Dosa, Rozae Nichols, and Nanette Lepore; accordingly, this is the most expensive store in Fremont. ⊠ *3420 Evanston Ave. N, Fremont* ☎ *206/632–2877* ⊕ *www.lesamis-inc.com* ✛ *3:D5.*

Show Pony. With a mix of new, used, and locally designed clothing, Show Pony is a great spot to grab reasonably priced girly frocks and fabulous accessories. Of particular pleasure is the used/vintage section upstairs, which mostly stocks designer labels. Jewelry, perfume, gifts, and home-decorating items round out the collection. ⊠ *702 N. 35th St., Fremont* ☎ *206/706–4188* ⊕ *www.showponyseattle.com* ✛ *3:D5.*

6

GIFTS AND HOME DECOR

Bitters Co. Filled with fair-trade treasures from around the world, this unique general store carries textiles, linens, tableware, and jewelry. There are handcrafted goods from Guatemala, Indonesia, and the Philippines; many items are made from reclaimed materials. ⊠ *513 N. 36th St., Fremont* ☎ *206/632–0886* ⊕ *www.bittersco.com* ✛ *3:D5.*

Burnt Sugar. If there's a rocket on the roof of the store, you've found Burnt Sugar—or you've gone too far and are in Cape Canaveral. This hip and funky shop offers a mélange of handbags, greeting cards, soaps, candles, jewelry, toys, children's gifts, and other eclectic baubles you never knew you needed. There's a makeup counter, and half the store is devoted to a small but ultracool selection of women's shoes. ⊠ *601 N. 35th St., Fremont* ☎ *206/545–0699* ⊕ *www.burntsugarfrankie.com* ✛ *3:D5.*

Essenza. A gurgling stone fountain stands in the center of this light-filled boutique, whose airy displays showcase delicately scented European bath products by Santa Maria Novella, Tocca, and Cote Bastide. You'll find the complete line of Fresh cosmetics, handmade bed linens, women's loungewear and lingerie, delicate jewelry, and exquisitely detailed children's clothing. ⊠ *615 N. 35th St., Fremont* ☎ *206/547–4895* ✛ *3:D5.*

Frank & Dunya. For cute, locally crafted art, head to Frank & Dunya. Functional gift items range from hand-painted switch-plate covers and elaborate nightlights to freestanding clocks, and coffee mugs. Although there's a lot of kitsch here, the paintings, prints, and mixed-media pieces displayed on the far wall are less whimsical and often very good. ⊠ *3418 Fremont Ave. N, Fremont* ☎ *206/547–6760* ⊕ *www.frankanddunya.com* ✛ *3:D5.*

PHINNEY RIDGE

Phinney Ridge and its nearby sister neighborhood of Greenwood are north of Fremont and east of Ballard. This is a great area for a fun couple of hours of browsing when you feel like strolling as much as shopping. You can park near the Woodland Park Zoo and walk the length of Phinney Avenue (which becomes Greenwood Avenue farther north). You'll be right near Greenlake and, on a clear day, will be looking out across at the Cascade Mountains to the east, and the Olympics to the west. It's not the most compact shopping district, but the stores, coffee shops, and restaurants on this 2-mi stretch are sweet and affordable, and make for a pleasant afternoon.

CLOTHING

Frock Shop. The clothing in this light-filled Phinney boutique is so creative and utterly unique looking, you'd swear it was vintage. Luckily, for those afraid of used clothes, everything here is new; much of it is locally designed. Anything purchased is sure to elicit lots of "where did you get that?" squeals. ⊠ *6500 Phinney Ave. N, Phinney Ridge* ☎ *206/297–1638* ✛ *3:D1.*

NOVELTIES AND GIFTS

🌀 **Greenwood Space Travel Supply Co.** The name of this shop baffled Greenwood residents for months until it was revealed as part of 826 Seattle, a branch of the amazing national creative-writing program for kids founded by novelist Dave Eggers and educator Nínive Calegari in 2002. The small store has kooky items purported to be space-travel essentials (freeze-dried meals), many of which are obvious nods to kitschy science-fiction movies (check out the ray guns). It also carries 826 clothing, and all of the proceeds go to the writing center. ■TIP→ While you're here, check the bulletin board for notices about upcoming events and single-session workshops. Note that this is not a full-blown toy store: go in with a sense of humor and an imagination because much of the cleverness is literary—standard toys and items given ridiculous new names to sound like important instruments of space travel. Everyone will enjoy filling out the hilarious space-traveler screening questionnaires and spaceship accident reports. ⊠ *8414 Greenwood Ave. N, Greenwood* ☎ *206/725–2625* ⊕ *www.greenwoodspacetravelsupply.com* ✛ *3:D1.*

GREENWOOD

If you really fall in love with this neighborhood just north of Phinney Ridge, **Greenwood Mail & Dispatch** (⊠ *8560 Greenwood Ave. N, Greenwood* ☎ *206/783–4299*), also known as the Sip & Ship, has T-shirts, hoodies, coffee mugs, and other hip accessories emblazoned with the neighborhood's name. Their sister store on Market St. has Ballard paraphernalia for diehard Scandinavians.

6

BALLARD

Ballard is the shining star of the north end when it comes to shopping. Packed with cute home stores, great clothing boutiques, locally made gifts, and just about every genre of store imaginable, this neighborhood is a must-visit locale. Their Saturday Farmers Market is one of the best in the city, and operates year-round for a dependably fun outing. Pick up smoked salmon, artisan cheese, and vegan baked goods, and pop into the shops listed here if the rain starts.

Best shopping: Ballard Avenue between 22nd Avenue NW and 20th Avenue NW; Northwest Market Street between 20th and 24th avenues.

BOOKS AND MUSIC

🌀 **Secret Garden Bookshop.** Named after the Francis Hodgson Burnett classic, Secret Garden Books has been delighting readers for 34 years in their cozy shop in downtown Ballard. A favorite of teachers, librarians, and parents, the store stocks a wide array of imaginative literature and thoughtful nonfiction for all ages; their children's section is particularly notable. ⊠ *2214 NW Market St., Ballard* ☎ *206/789–5006* ⊕ *www.secretgardenbooks.com* ✛ *2:A3.*

CLOTHING AND ACCESSORIES

Blackbird. Fashion-forward men are often sorely overlooked by retail, but this perfectly stocked store has become a favorite destination for hipsters and metrosexuals. With choice clothes from designers such as RVCA, KZO, and Obey, and sharp accessories like wrist cuffs and

Velouria in Ballard

fedoras, urban menfolk can finally kick their look up a notch. Ladies will be pleased to see accessories and makeup for women round out the store's collection. ✉ 5410 22nd Ave. NE, Ballard 🕾 206/547–2524 ⊕ www.blackbirdballard.com ✣ 3:A3.

⟳ ★ **Clover.** Easily the cutest children's store in town, the always-charming Clover carries wonderful handcrafted wooden toys, European figurines, works by local artists, and a variety of swoon-worthy, perfectly crafted little clothes. Even shoppers without children will be smitten—it's hard to resist their vintage French Tintin posters, knit-wool cow dolls, and classic Smurf figurines. ✉ 5335 Ballard Ave. NW, Ballard 🕾 206/782–0715 ⊕ www.clovertoys.com ✣ 3:A3.

Horseshoe. "A little bit country, a little bit rock and roll," Horseshoe offers girlie Western wear and hipster fare in its Ballard digs. Comfy, sassy shirts and dresses are available from designers like Kensie, Prairie Underground, Eva Franco, and Ella Moss. Premium denim, cowboy boots, unique jewelry, hot bags, and treats like Butter London nail polish are among the wares. ✉ 5344 Ballard Ave. NW, Ballard 🕾 206/547–9639 ✣ 3:A3.

Laura Bee Designs. If you have the design chops but can't find your way around a sewing machine, Laura Bee is the place for you. This fun studio shop gives creative types a chance to design their own handbags and wallets—pick the fabric, the bag type, embellishments like vintage buttons and ribbon trim, and extras like interior zip pockets and places to stash your cell phone. There are ready-made products, as well, if you'd rather leave the designs to the pros. ✉ 6418 20th Ave. NW, Ballard 🕾 206/782–0715 ⊕ www.laurabeedesigns.com ✣ 3:A2.

★ **Velouria.** The ultimate antidote to the mass-produced, unimaginative clothes choking much of the chains these days can be found at Velouria, where independent West Coast designers rule, and much on offer is one-of-a-kind. Step in to this exquisitely feminine shop to find handmade, '70s-inspired jumpsuits; romantic, demure eyelet dresses; and clever screen-printed tees. Superb bags, delicate jewelry, and fun cards and gifts are also on display. It's worth a look, just to check out all the wearable art. ⊠ *2205 NW Market St., Ballard* ☎ *206/788–0330* ⊕ *shopvelouria.tripod.com* ✛ *3:A3.*

FOOTWEAR

Market Street Shoes. One of the best shoe stores in town, Market Street stocks so many styles from so many designers for men, women, and kids, you're likely to find something. They skew on the end of Seattle-style comfort, so you'll see sensible picks from Dankso, Born, Camper, Clarks, and Doc Martins, but there are a plenty of fun options by Fluevog, Tsubo, Think!, and Frye, as well. Check out their sister store, Market Street Athlete, across the street for your sporty needs. ⊠ *2215 NW Market St., Ballard* ☎ *206/783–1670* ⊕ *www.marketstreetshoes. com* ✛ *3:A3.*

re-souL. Stocking cool but comfortable shoes from Biviel, MOMA, PF Flyers, Cydwoq, and the like, this hip space offers a small selection of crazy fashionable boots, shoes, sneaks, and high heels. In keeping with the "little bit of everything" trend so popular with Seattle boutiques, re-souL also sells great jewelry pieces, as well as usable art pieces from Alessi. They carry both men's and women's shoes and accessories. Everything is a bit pricey, but not excessively so. ⊠ *5319 Ballard Ave. NW, Ballard* ☎ *206/789–7312* ⊕ *www.resoul.com* ✛ *3:A3.*

GIFTS AND HOME ACCESSORIES

Camelion Design. This reasonably affordable, modern home-accessories store in Ballard is crammed, showroom-style, with furniture, accessories, and gift items that straddle the line between modern, arty, and organic-feeling. It's a good place to get living-room envy, order a custom-couch, or just pick up an area rug, vase, or picture frame. Camelion also sells jewelry, bath products, greeting cards, and stationery. ⊠ *5330 Ballard Ave. NW, Ballard* ☎ *206/783–7125* ⊕ *www.cameliondesign. com* ✛ *3:A3.*

Dandelion Botanical Company. "Apothecary" is the terms Dandelion uses to describe itself, and rightly so: the store's brick walls are lined with hundreds of jars of botanicals—bulk Chinese and Ayurvedic herbs, teas, and cooking spices among them. Essential oils, bath salts, and aromatherapy products are also on hand, and most of the items they sell are organic or made of all-natural materials. If you're picturing a claustrophobic Chinatown shop or dingy co-op, don't worry—the space is that of a high-end, if down-to-earth, boutique. ⊠ *5424 Ballard Ave. NW, Ballard* ☎ *206/545–8892* ⊕ *www.dandelionbotanical. com* ✛ *3:A3.*

Fodor'sChoice
★ **La Tienda.** Every item in La Tienda's showroom of handmade art from around the world was lovingly selected by the owners, who pride themselves on procuring art directly from craftspeople for a fair price. You'll

find delicate Chinese puppets, figurines from Peru, and Indonesian Buddha sculptures, but many American-made items are also among the collection. This store has been a favorite shopping destination since 1962. ✉ *2050 NW Market St., Ballard* ☎ *206/297–3605* ⊕ *www.latiendafolkart.com* ✢ *3:A3.*

Venue. Venue is the chic version of the Made In Washington stores: it stocks only goods made by local artists (some of whom have their studios in the sleek bi-level space), but you won't find anything resembling a tacky souvenir here. Watch the designers at work, chat with the staff (most are artists taking shifts), or just browse through artisan chocolates, custom handbags, handmade soaps, baby wear, and colorful prints and mosaics. ✉ *5408 22nd Ave. NW, Ballard* ☎ *206/789–3335* ⊕ *www.venueballard.com* ✢ *3:A3.*

WALLINGFORD

Wallingford offers a more grown-up selection of shopping than Fremont or Ballard. You won't find trendy clothing boutiques here, and the only scene you're likely to encounter is a pack of knitters congregating at Bad Women Yarn. But with a great selection of independent shops, specialty bookstores, fabulous gift-buying opportunities, and the best beer store in the city, you're likely to have a fun afternoon poking through this neighborhood.

Best shopping: 45th Street between Stone Way and Meridian.

BEER

Bottleworks. If you scoff at Bud Light and can name at least 10 microbrews without hesitation, make a pilgrimage to Bottleworks to peruse their massive collection of beer from around the world. With around 950 chilled varieties of malty goodness available, including seasonal varieties, vintage bottles, and global rarities, there's a beer for everyone here. Be sure to check out their sampling of mead and cider as well. ✉ *1710 N. 45th St., Wallingford* ☎ *206/633–2437* ⊕ *www.bottleworks. com* ✢ *3:F4.*

BOOKS AND PRINTED MATERIAL

Open Books. One of only a couple of poetry-only bookstores in the country, this serene space is conducive to hours of browsing; when you're ready to interact, the owners are always happy to answer your questions, make suggestions, or chat about the titles you've selected. There's also a good selection of magazines as well as chapbooks. ✉ *2414 N. 45th St., Wallingford* ☎ *206/633–0811* ⊕ *www.openpoetrybooks.com* ✢ *3:F4.*

Wide World Books and Maps. The first travel-only bookstore in the country, Wide World Books and Maps has been outfitting the adventurous for more than 34 years. This is a great place to grab hard-to-find travel guides to just about anywhere, along with trip essentials by Eagle Creek, Klean Kanteen, and more. From travel journals to sporks (a handy cross between spoons and forks), to voltage transformers for overseas trips, they'll either have it or know where to get it. ✉ *4411 Wallingford Ave. N, Wallingford* ☎ *206/634–3453* ⊕ *www.wideworldtravelstore. com* ✢ *3:F4.*

GIFTS AND HOME ACCESSORIES

Fodor'sChoice ★ **Archie McPhee.** If your life is seriously missing a punching-nun puppet, an Edgar Allen Poe action figure, or a bacon-scented air freshener, there's hope. Leave your cares and woes at the door and step into a warehouse of the weird and wonderful. It's nearly impossible to feel bad while perusing stacks of armadillo handbags, demon rubber duckies, handerpants (don't ask), and homicidal unicorn play sets. Grab a cat-in-a-can to keep you company, or leave with a dramatic chipmunk oil painting. You'll feel better. Trust us. ⊠ *1300 N. 45th St., Wallingford* ☏ *206/297–0240* ⊕ *www.archiemcpheeseattle.com* ✢ *3:E4.*

MALL

Wallingford Center. You won't find much in the way of chain stores in this charming shopping center in the heart of Wallingford. A converted 1904 schoolhouse hosts 15 resident shops—all independent minus, Pharmaca, an integrative pharmacy with on-site naturopaths. Start with a specialty cupcake from Trophy Cupcakes, then head to Yazdi for their flowy mix of ethnic and modern wear for women. If their colorful goods inspire your creative side, check out Bad Women Yarn for all your knitting needs. Browse through the unique handmade art at Crackerjack Contemporary Crafts, and grab a few games at local favorite Izilla Toys. Don't miss the tiny but well-stocked Amita for well-made, trendy bags and jewelry. May through September you'll also find a farmers' market in its parking lot on Wednesday afternoons. ⊠ *1815 N. 45th St., Wallingford* ⊕ *www.wallingfordcenter.com* ✢ *3:F4.*

6

UNIVERSITY DISTRICT

The "U-District" is packed with predictably college-friendly shopping— lots of used clothing and bookstores to trendy footwear and fun specialty shops. Meander down University Way (known to locals as "The Ave") to find the standout shops listed here, and stop at any of the numerous ethnic restaurants to refuel with cheap, decent eats. ■TIP→ If you're uncomfortable with panhandlers, skateboarding teens, and throngs of university students, bypass this area and head directly down the hill to outdoor shopping mall University Village.

Best shopping: University Way NE between NE 42nd and 47th streets, and University Village at 25th Avenue NE and N.E. 45th Street.

BOOKS

★ **University Book Store.** Campus bookstores are usually rip-offs to be endured only by students clutching syllabi, but the University of Washington's store is a big exception to that rule. This enormous resource has a well-stocked general book department in addition to the requisite textbooks. Author events are scheduled all year long. Check out the bargain-book tables and the basement crammed with every art supply imaginable. ⊠ *4326 University Way NE, University District* ☏ *206/634–3400* ⊕ *www.bookstore.washington.edu* ✢ *3:H4.*

Zanadu Comics. One of the oldest and best comic book stores in a city with close to 70 comic shops, Zanadu Comics specializes in "alternative," small-press, local, and self-published comics and graphic novels.

CLOSE UP

Native American Culture and Crafts

Looking at a map of the Seattle area, you're bound to encounter some unusual names. Enumclaw, for instance. Or Mukilteo, Puyallup, Snohomish, and Tukwila. As hard as they are to pronounce, these tongue-twisting words aren't intended to confuse you. In reality, these names are legacies of dozens of Native American tribes and nations that first occupied the region.

Seattle, in fact, is named after Chief Si'ahl, a leader of the Suquamish and Duwamish tribes. For many thousands of years, Native American tribes have called the Pacific Northwest home—from the salmon-packed waters of the Skagit River to the high country of the Cascade Mountains. The majority of these tribes were subgroups of the Coast Salish peoples, who historically inhabited the entire Puget Sound region from Olympia north to British Columbia.

Tribes residing in and around the Seattle area included Duwamish, Suquamish, Tulalip, Muckleshoot, and Snoqualmie. Each tribe developed complex cultural and artistic traditions, and a regional language—lushootseed—allowed tribes to trade resources. Today, members of many Seattle-area tribes are keeping their traditions alive: basketry, weaving, and sculpture—including totems—are traditional artistic media of the Coast Salish, and all three arts are still vibrant today. Contemporary Salish artists work in several modern media as well, including painting, studio glass, and printmaking.

Two top activities for experiencing Native culture up close and personal are:

■ On the campus of the University of Washington, the **Burke Museum of Natural History and Culture** houses

thousands of Coast Salish artifacts and artworks. The museum's exhibits also feature artwork from farther-flung native tribes, including the Tlingit and Haida of British Columbia and southeast Alaska. ⊠ *N.E. 45th St. and 17th Ave. NE, University District* ☎ *206/543–5590* ⊕ *www. burkemuseum.org.*

■ Located on Blake Island, 8 mi west of Seattle in Puget Sound, **Tillicum Village** offers a combination salmon bake and Native American stage show. Most visitors to the island travel aboard an Argosy Cruise ship; the four-hour tours are offered daily from May through September. Tours depart from Pier 55 on the Seattle waterfront. ☎ *206/933–8600* ⊕ *www. tillicumvillage.com* 🖃 *$79.95* ⊙ *Tours offered Sat. and Sun. Mar.–May and Sept.–Oct.; daily June– early Sept.*

Coast Salish arts and crafts can be found in many museums and galleries around Seattle. Some favorite sites for shopping include:

■ **Flury and Company** (⇨ *See listing in this chapter*).

■ **Seattle Art Museum Store** (⊠ *1300 1st Ave., Downtown 98101* ☎ *206/654–3100* ⊕ *www. seattleartmuseum.org*).

■ **Snow Goose Associates** (⇨ *See listing in this chapter*).

■ **Steinbrueck Native Gallery** (⊠ *2030 Western Ave., Belltown* ☎ *206/441–3821* ⊕ *www. steinbruecknativegallery.com*).

■ **Stonington Gallery** (⊠ *119 S. Jackson St., Pioneer Square* ☎ *206/405–4040* ⊕ *www. stoningtongallery.com*).

Superman fans will find their favorites as well—they carry mainstream titles alongside copies of harder-to-find titles like Joe Sacco's "Footnotes in Gaza." They have a second shop downtown on Third Avenue (✚ 1:D2). ✉ *1307 N.E. 45th St., University District* ☎ *206/632–0989* ⊕ *www.zanaducomics.com* ✚ *3:H4.*

CLOTHING

★ **Buffalo Exchange.** This big, bright shop of new and recycled fashions is always crowded—and it takes time to browse the stuffed racks—but the rewards are great: the latest looks from all the trend-heavy outfitters along with one-of-a-kind leather jackets and vintage dresses. As with all thrift stores, the selection can be hit or miss, but you can find some pretty great deals on high-quality clothing. Check out their smaller store in Ballard on N.W. Market Street. ✉ *4530 University Way NE, University District* ☎ *206/545–0175* ⊕ *www.buffaloexchange.com* ✚ *3:H4.*

Crossroads Trading Co. Another spot on the used-clothing-store offerings on The Ave, Crossroads Trading Co. carries dependably cute and trendy clothes, bags, and accessories. Their buyers screen each item, so you won't be stuck poring over a rack of stained T-shirts. This thrift store is clean, bright, and fun. A second location can be found on Broadway in Capitol Hill. ✉ *4300 University Way NE, University District* ☎ *206/632–3111* ⊕ *www.crossroadstrading.com* ✚ *3:H4.*

Red Light Clothing Exchange. Nostalgia rules in this cavernous space filled with well-organized, good-quality (if sometimes pricey) vintage and new clothing. Fantasy outfits from decades past—complete with accessories—adorn the dressing rooms, though you won't find the full-on costumes that the Capitol Hill branch has. ✉ *4560 University Way NE, University District* ☎ *206/545–4044* ⊕ *www.redlightvintage.com* ✚ *2:F5.*

FOOTWEAR

★ **5 Doors Up/Woolly Mammoth.** Fashion-forward shoe lovers of both sexes head to these sister stores that are five storefronts apart on a busy section of The Ave. Score some cool kicks from Vans, Converse, Blundstone, or Frye from 5 Doors Up, then head to Woolly Mammoth for more conservative, grown-up, comfy footwear by Naot, Dansko, La Canadienne, and the like. ✉ *4309 University Way NE, University District* ☎ *206/547–3192* ⊕ *www.5doorsup.com and www.woollymammothshoes.com* ✚ *3:H4.*

GIFTS AND HOME DECOR

Snow Goose Associates. Alaskan Eskimo, Canadian Inuit, and Northwest Coast Native American artists are represented through carvings, jewelry, baskets, masks, boxes, and prints. ✉ *8806 Roosevelt Way NE, University District* ☎ *206/523–6223* ✚ *3:H1.*

SHOPPING CENTER

★ **University Village.** Make a beeline here for fabulous upscale shopping and good restaurants in a pretty, outdoor, tree- and fountain-laden shopping "village." Be forewarned: Parking here is a nightmare, and the atmosphere is slightly snobby. ■ TIP➔ If you're in the mood to brave it, go immediately to the free parking garage, even if it means you have to walk farther. Once parked, you can have your fill of chains like Williams-

Sonoma, Banana Republic, L'Occitane, Hanna Andersson, Crate & Barrel, Sephora, Aveda, Restoration Hardware, H&M, Apple, Anthropologie, Coach, and Kiehl's. If you get enough of that at home, however, there are a few unique gems among the batch, including the excellent Village Maternity Store, candy wonderland The Confectionery, and local artsy chain Fireworks. ⊠ *N.E. 45th St. and 25th Ave. NE, University District* ☎ *206/523–0622* ⊕ *www.uvillage.com* ⊹ *3:H4.*

THE EASTSIDE

The core of Bellevue's growing shopping district is the Bellevue Collection (Bellevue Square Mall, Lincoln Center, and Bellevue Place) and the sparkling upscale mall called the Bravern. The community's retail strip stretches from Bellevue Square between N.E. 4th and 8th streets to the community-centered Crossroads Shopping Center several miles to the east.

Best shopping: Bellevue Square and The Shops at the Bravern.

CENTERS AND MALLS

☺ **The Bellevue Collection (Bellevue Square, Bellevue Place, and Lincoln Center).**
★ In this impressive trifecta of shopping centers, you'll find just about any chain store you've heard of (and some that you haven't). Bellevue Square alone has more than 200 stores, including Nordstrom, Macy's, Pottery Barn, Crate & Barrel, Aveda, Banana Republic, Coach, 7 For All Mankind, Build-a-Bear, and Helly Hansen. The Square's wide walkways and benches, many children's clothing stores, first-floor play area, and third-floor children's museum make this a great place for kids, too. You can park for free in the attached garage. Take the sky bridge to Lincoln Center, to catch a flick at their 16-screen cinema, organize your life at The Container Store, or sample an assortment of other retail and several popular chain restaurants. Bellevue Place, across from Lincoln Center, hosts a variety of retail along with the ever-popular Daniel's Broiler, STIR Martini & Wine Bar, and pickup-central Joey Bar. ⊠ *Bellevue Way, Bellevue* ☎ *425/454–8096* ⊕ *www.bellevuesquare. com* ⊹ *3:H6.*

The Shops at the Bravern. If you have some serious cash to burn, the sleek, upscale Bravern might be the Eastside spot for you. With über-high-end shops like Neiman Marcus, Hermes, Brooks Brothers, Jimmy Choo, Salvatore Ferragamo, and Louis Vuitton, it's tempting to empty your wallet—but save room for a spa treatment at the Elizabeth Arden Red Door Spa or a meal at Northwest favorite Wild Ginger. Valet and complimentary parking (with validation) are available. ⊠ *11111 N.E. 8th St., Bellevue* ☎ *425/456–8780* ⊕ *www.thebravern.com* ⊹ *3:H6.*

Sports and Activities

WORD OF MOUTH

"Take a look at a [Seattle] map and find Lake Washington. This large lake is great for boating—people use it for sailing, kayaking, waterskiing, rowing, fishing (not too successfully), jetskiing, and putzing around. There are a number of very livable communities around the lake, plus docks and boat ramps in many spots."

—enzian

Updated by
Nick Horton

The question in Seattle isn't "Do you exercise?" Rather, it's "How do you exercise?" Athleticism is a regular part of most people's lives here, whether it's an afternoon jog, a sunrise rowing session, a lunch-hour bike ride, or an evening game of Frisbee.

The Cascade Mountains, a 60-minute drive east, have trails and peaks for alpinists of all skill levels. Snoqualmie Pass attracts downhill skiers and snowboarders, and cross-country skiing and snowshoeing are excellent throughout the Cascades. To the west of the city is Puget Sound, where sailors, kayakers, and anglers practice their sports. Lake Union and Lake Washington also provide residents with plenty of boating, kayaking, fishing, and swimming opportunities. Farther west, the Olympic Mountains beckon adventure-seeking souls to their unspoiled wilderness.

Spectator sports are also appreciated here. To see how excited Seattle citizens can get about crew racing, stop by the Montlake Cut on the official opening day of the unofficial boating season. The University of Washington (UW) has been a rowing powerhouse since the 1930s, and tickets to Husky football games have been hot items for years. Attendance at Mariners games is at an all-time high, and the Seattle Sounders—a Major League Soccer (MLS) franchise—may be the best-loved team in town.

PARKS INFORMATION

King County Parks and Recreation (☎ *206/296–4232 for information and reservations ⊕ www.metrokc.gov/parks*) manages many of the parks outside city limits. To find out whether an in-town park baseball diamond or tennis court is available, contact the **Seattle Parks and Recreation Department** (☎ *206/684–4075 ⊕ www.seattle.gov/parks*), which is responsible for most of the parks, piers, beaches, playgrounds, and courts within city limits. The department issues permits for events, arranges reservations for facilities, and staffs visitor centers and naturalist programs. The state manages several parks and campgrounds in greater Seattle. For more information contact **Washington State Parks** (☎ *360/902–8844 for general information, 888/226–7688 for campsite* *reservations ⊕ www.parks.wa.gov/parkpage.asp).* ⇨ *For Parks and Beaches coverage, see Chapter 1 or specific neighborhoods throughout Chapter 2.*

BASEBALL

The **Seattle Mariners** play in the West Division of the American League, and their home is **Safeco Field** (✉ *1st Ave. S and Atlantic St., Sodo* ☎ *206/346–4000* ⊕ *seattle.mariners.mlb.com*), a retractable-roof stadium where there really isn't a bad seat in the house. One local sports columnist referred to the $656 million venue—which finished $100 million over budget—as "the guilty pleasure." You can purchase tickets through Ticketmaster or StubHub; online or by phone from Safeco Field (to be picked up at the Will Call); in person at Safeco's box office (no surcharges), which is open daily 10–6; or from the Mariners team store at 4th Avenue and Stewart Street in Downtown. The cheap seats cost $9; better seats cost $38–$98, and the best seats will cost you up to $300.

BASKETBALL

Following the departure of the Seattle SuperSonics after the 2007–2008 NBA season, Seattle was been in a period of basketball mourning. But thanks to the resurgence of local college teams—including the UW Huskies and the Seattle University Redhawks—the basketball clouds have lifted.

Now the city's only professional hoops team, the WNBA **Seattle Storm** (⊕ *www.wnba.com/storm*) has its season from mid-June to August. The Storm play at **Key Arena** (✉ *305 Harrison St., Downtown* ☎ *206/296–2835* ⊕ *www.goseattleu.com*), on the Seattle Center campus. Tickets cost $10–$47.

The **UW Huskies** represent Seattle basketball in the Pac-10 Conference. Under the guidance of coach Lorenzo Romar, the team has advanced to the NCAA Sweet Sixteen in 2005 and 2006 and captured the Pac-10 crown in 2009. The always-tough women's team—which also enjoys a very loyal (and loud) fan base—has also advanced to the NCAA tournament several times in recent years. **Bank of America Arena at Hec Edmundson Pavilion** (✉ *3870 Montlake Blvd. NE, University District* ☎ *206/543–2200* ⊕ *gohuskies.cstv.com*), known locally as "Hec Ed," is where the UW's men's and women's basketball teams play. Tickets are $6–$35.

BICYCLING

Biking is probably Seattle's most practiced sport. Thousands of Seattleites bike to work, and even more ride recreationally, especially on weekends. In the past, Seattle hasn't been a particularly bike-friendly city. But in 2007, city government adopted a sweeping Bicycle Master Plan, calling for 118 new miles of bike lanes, 19 mi of bike paths, and countless route signs and lane markings throughout the city by 2017. The plan can't erase the hills, though—Queen Anne Hill and Phinney

Bicyclists ride along Lake Washington in the Seattle-to-Portland (STP) event.

Ridge should be only attempted by sadists. Fortunately, all city buses have easy-to-use bike racks (on the front of the buses, below the windshield) and drivers are used to waiting for cyclists to load and unload their bikes. If you're not comfortable biking in urban traffic—and there is a lot of urban traffic to contend with here—you can do a combination bus-and-bike tour of the city or stick to the car-free Burke-Gilman Trail.

Seattle drivers are fairly used to sharing the road with cyclists. With the exception of the occasional road-rager or clueless cell-phone talker, drivers usually leave a generous amount of room when passing; however, there are biking fatalities every year, so be alert and cautious, especially when approaching blind intersections, of which Seattle has many. You must wear a helmet at all times (it's the law) and be sure to lock up your bike—though there are probably more car break-ins, bikes do get stolen, even in quiet residential neighborhoods.

The Seattle Parks Department sponsors Bicycle Sundays on various weekends from May through September. On these Sundays, a 4-mi stretch of Lake Washington Boulevard—from Mt. Baker Beach to Seward Park—is closed to motor vehicles. Many riders continue around the 2-mi loop at Seward Park and back to Mt. Baker Beach to complete a 10-mi, car-free ride. Check with the **Seattle Parks and Recreation Department** (☎ *206/684–4075* ⊕ *www.seattle.gov/parks/bicyclesunday*) for a complete schedule.

The trail that circles **Green Lake** is popular with cyclists, though runners and walkers can impede fast travel. The city-maintained **Burke-Gilman**

Trail, a slightly less congested path, follows an abandoned railroad line 14 mi roughly following Seattle's waterfront from Ballard to Kenmore, at the north end of Lake Washington. (From there, serious cyclists can continue on the Sammamish River Trail to Marymoor Park in Redmond; in all, the trail spans 42 mi between Seattle and Issaquah.) **Discovery Park** is a very tranquil place to tool around in. **Myrtle Edwards Park**, north of Pier 70, has a two-lane waterfront path for bicycling and running. The **islands of the Puget Sound** are also easily explored by bike (there are rental places by the ferry terminals), though be forewarned that Bainbridge, Whidbey, and the San Juans all have some tough hills.

King County has more than 100 mi of paved and nearly 70 mi of unpaved routes including the Sammamish River, Interurban, Green River, Cedar River, Snoqualmie Valley, and Soos Creek trails. For more information contact the **King County Parks and Recreation** office (☎ 206/296–8687).

The **Bicycle Alliance of Washington** (☎ 206/224–9252 ⊕ www. bicyclealliance.org), the state's largest cycling advocacy group, is a great source for information. The **Cascade Bicycle Club** (☎ 206/522–3222 ⊕ www.cascade.org) organizes more than 1,000 rides annually for recreational and hard-core bikers. The most famous of its events is the Seattle-to-Portland Bicycle Classic—or, as it's known around the state, the "STP." Cascade offers daily rides in Seattle and the Eastside that range from "superstrenuous" to leisurely, like relaxed rides to the Red Hook Brewery in Woodinville. Check out the Web site for a complete list of rides and contact information.

The **Seattle Bicycle Program** (☎ 206/684–7583 ⊕ www.seattle.gov/transportation/bikeprogram.htm) was responsible for the creation of the city's multiuse trails (aka bike routes) as well as pedestrian paths and roads with wide shoulders—things, in other words, that benefit bicyclists. The agency's Web site has downloadable route maps; you can also call the number above to request a printed version of the Seattle Bicycling Guide Map.

RENTALS

BikeStation. This Pioneer Square bike storage facility also offers perhaps the cheapest rentals in town. Though the selection is not terribly large, you can procure a regular, mountain, or electric bike for a mere $3 per hour ($15 per day). ⊠ 311 3rd Ave. S, Pioneer Square ☎ 206/332–9795 ⊕ www.bikestation.org/seattle.

Montlake Bicycle Shop (⊠ 2223 24th Ave. E, Montlake ☎ 206/329–7333 ⊕ www.montlakebike.com), located just one mile south of the University of Washington and within easy riding distance of the Burke-Gilman Trail, rents mountain bikes, road bikes, basic cruisers, and even tandems. Prices range from $25 to $85 for the day, with discounts for longer rentals. If you find yourself on the Eastside, rent a bike from their sister store, **Kirkland Bicycle Shop** (⊠ 208 Kirkland Ave., Kirkland ☎ 425/828–3800 ⊕ www.kirklandbikes.com).

BOATING AND KAYAKING

Fodor's Choice
★
Agua Verde Paddle Club and Café. Start out by renting a kayak and paddling along either the Lake Union shoreline, with its hodgepodge of funky-to-fabulous houseboats and dramatic Downtown vistas, or Union Bay on Lake Washington, with its marshes and cattails. Afterward, take in the lakefront as you wash down some Mexican food (halibut tacos, anyone?) with a margarita. Kayaks are available March through October and are rented by the hour—$15 for singles, $18 for doubles. It pays to paddle midweek: the third hour is free on weekdays. ⊠ *1303 NE Boat St., University District* ☎ *206/545–8570* ⊕ *www.aguaverde.com.*

★ **Alki Kayak Tours.** For a variety of day-long guided kayak outings—from a Seattle Sunset Sea Kayak Tour to an Alki Point Lighthouse Tour—led by experienced, fun staff, try this great outfitter in West Seattle. In addition to kayaks, you can also rent skates, fishing boats, and longboards here. Custom sea-kayaking adventures can be set up, so dream big! Note that to rent kayak without a guide, you must be an experienced kayaker; otherwise, sign up for a guided tour, which is memorable and fascinating. ⊠ *1660 Harbor Ave. SW, West Seattle* ☎ *206/953–0237* ⊕ *www.kayakalki.com.*

★ **The Center for Wooden Boats.** Located on the southern shore of Lake Union, Seattle's free maritime heritage museum is a bustling community hub. Thousands of Seattleites rent rowboats and small sailboats here every year; the Center also offers workshops, demonstrations, and classes. Rowboats are $20 an hour on weekdays and $25 an hour on weekends. There's a $10 skills-check fee. Free half-hour guided sails and steamboat rides are offered on Sunday from 2 to 4 (arrive an hour early to reserve a spot). ⊠ *1010 Valley St., Lake Union* ☎ *206/382–2628* ⊕ *www.cwb.org.*

Green Lake Boat Rental. This shop is the source for canoes, paddleboats, sailboats, kayaks, sailboards, and rowboats to ply Green Lake's calm waters. On beautiful summer afternoons, however, be prepared to spend most of your time negotiating other traffic on the water as well as in the parking lot. Fees are $15 an hour for paddleboats, single kayaks, rowboats, and sailboards, $20 an hour for sailboats. Don't confuse this place with the Green Lake Small Craft Center, which offers sailing programs but no rentals. ⊠ *7351 E. Green Lake Dr. N, Green Lake* ☎ *206/527–0171* ⊕ *www.greenlakeboatrentals.net.*

Moss Bay Rowing and Kayak Center. Moss Bay rents a variety of rowing craft—including Whitehall pulling boats, wherries, and sliding-seat rowboats. Single kayaks rent for $13 per hour, doubles go for $18. You can also rent kayaks to take with you on trips outside the city; daily rates are $55 for singles and $75 for doubles; weekly rates are $265 for singles and $345 for doubles. You can rent rowing shells or sailboats for $25–$35 depending on the type of craft; there is an additional $10 skills-check fee for renting these types of vessels. The center offers rowing and sailing lessons daily for $65 for a onetime private lesson; two- or four-lesson series cost $100 or $200, respectively. Lastly, the center also offers daily 2½-hour sailing tours of Lake Union as well as guided

Continued on page 290

THE BALLARD LOCKS AND SEATTLE'S MANY WATERWAYS

by Nick Horton

DID YOU KNOW?

More than 40,000 commercial vessels, private yachts, sail-boats, and even kayaks pass through the Ballard Locks each year.

SEATTLE'S WATERWAYS

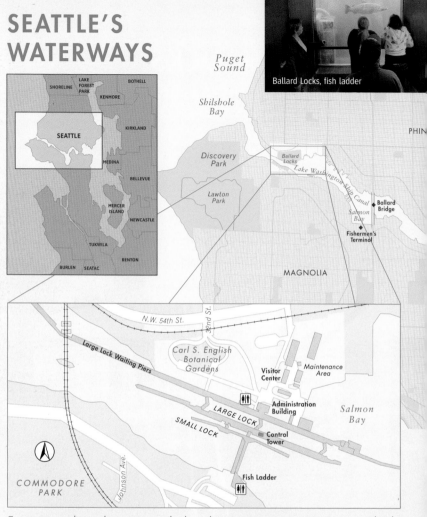

Puget Sound

Ballard Locks, fish ladder

Shilshole Bay

PHIN

SHORELINE **LAKE FOREST PARK** **BOTHELL**
KENMORE
KIRKLAND
SEATTLE
MEDINA
BELLEVUE
MERCER ISLAND
NEWCASTLE
TUKWILA
RENTON
BURLEN **SEATAC**

Discovery Park

Ballard Locks

Lake Washington Ship Canal

Lawton Park

Salmon Bay

Ballard Bridge

Fishermen's Terminal

MAGNOLIA

N.W. 54th St.

32nd St.

Large Lock Waiting Piers

Carl S. English Botanical Gardens

Visitor Center

Maintenance Area

Administration Building

Salmon Bay

LARGE LOCK

SMALL LOCK

Control Tower

Johnson Ave.

COMMODORE PARK

Fish Ladder

From its earliest days as a tribal settlement to its current status as high-tech hub, Seattle has been defined by its lakes, canals, and bays. Everywhere you look there is water: To the west is the deep, chilly saltwater of Puget Sound, and to the east are the welcoming, warmer waters of Lake Washington. Linking the two is the Lake Washington Ship Canal, a bustling marine thoroughfare. This astounding network of waterways plays a vital role in Seattle's daily life, whether it is for livelihood, transport, recreation, or sweet summertime relaxation.

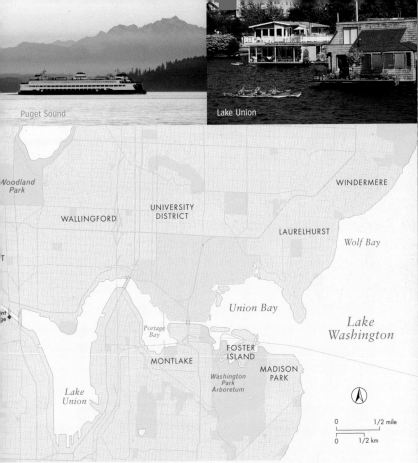

Puget Sound

Lake Union

Woodland Park

WINDERMERE

UNIVERSITY DISTRICT

WALLINGFORD

LAURELHURST

Wolf Bay

Union Bay

Lake Washington

Portage Bay

FOSTER ISLAND

MONTLAKE

MADISON PARK

Washington Park Arboretum

Lake Union

0   1/2 mile

0   1/2 km

Each of Seattle's bodies of water has a unique appeal. At 33 mi in length, **Lake Washington** is the city's largest lake. Come summer, it's a pleasure boater's paradise, often speckled with kayaks, motorboats, sailboats, and multimillion-dollar yachts. Its many beaches become crowded with sunbathers.

From Lake Washington, vessels may travel west via the Lake Washington Ship Canal toward **Lake Union**, a smaller, more urban lake that is the center of the city's maritime industry. The shoreline here is lined by yacht brokerages and shipyards, but Lake Union isn't all business. It hosts weekly sailing regattas and an annual Fourth of July fireworks

show. In addition, its northern shores are rife with houseboats—including the home made famous in the film *Sleepless in Seattle*. These live-aboard communities are the dwellings of well-off yuppies, eccentric sailors, and grizzled fishermen alike.

Traveling farther west, the Ship Canal leads vessels under the Fremont and Ballard bridges toward the bustling docks at **Fishermen's Terminal**, home to the city's vibrant fleet of commercial fishing boats. Finally, the canal leads through the **Ballard Locks**—the final step in a miles-long journey to **Puget Sound**, where oceangoing cargo ships sail in and out of Seattle's booming port.

THE BALLARD LOCKS

Hiram M. Chittenden

In the 1850s, when Seattle was founded, Lake Washington and Lake Union were inaccessible from the tantalizingly close Puget Sound. The city's founding fathers—most notably, Thomas Mercer in 1854—began dreaming of a canal that would connect the freshwater lakes and the Sound.

The lure of freshwater moorage and easier transport of timber and coal proved powerful, but it wasn't until 1917 that General Hiram M. Chittenden and the Army Corps of Engineers completed the Lake Washington Ship Canal and the locks that officially bear his name. More than 90 years later, the Ballard Locks, as they are more commonly known, are still going strong. Tens of thousands of boaters pass through the Locks each year, carrying over a million tons of commercial products—including seafood, fuel, and building materials.

THE LOCKS ESSENTIALS

- ✉ 3015 N.W. 54th St., Seattle, WA 98107
- ☎ 206/783-7059 (visitor center)
- 🌐 www.ci.seattle.wa.us/tour/locks.htm (City of Seattle)
- ⊙ Grounds are open 7 AM–9 PM year-round; fish ladder is open 7 AM–8:45 PM year-round; visitor center is open 10 AM–6 PM daily from May 1 through Sept. 30 and Thurs.–Mon. 10 AM–4 PM from Oct. 1 through April 30

The Locks are one of the city's most popular attractions, receiving more than one million visitors annually. Families picnic beneath oak trees in the adjacent 7-acre Carl S. English Botanical Gardens; jazz bands serenade visitors on summer Sundays; and steel-tinted salmon awe spectators as they climb a 21-step fish ladder en route to their freshwater spawning grounds—a heroic journey from the Pacific to the base of the Cascade Mountains. Hummingbirds flit from flower to flower in the nearby gardens, and the occasional sea lion can be spotted to the west of the Locks, snacking on unsuspecting salmon.

Best time to visit: The salmon runs and recreational boat traffic are most active from mid-June through mid-September.

Public transportation from downtown: Metro Route 17 runs from downtown Seattle to Ballard/Sunset Hill, and includes a stop at the Locks. Buses run approximately twice per hour from 5 AM–11 PM. The fare is $2.

Ample public parking ($2/hr) is available at the entrance to the Locks.

(top left) Tug boat going through the Locks, (top right) Children watching salmon swim the fish ladder.

FISH AT THE LOCKS

Chinook (king): Chinook tend to arrive at the locks in July, with late August being the best time to view them.

Coho (silver): Primetime coho viewing occurs in late September.

Sockeye (red): July is the peak time to view these fish, which gradually turn red as they migrate upstream.

Steelhead: Peak steelhead viewing occurs from mid-February through the end of March.

MIGRATING FISH

In a place where engineering has reshaped the natural landscape, it comes as a surprise that the most alluring and electrifying attraction at the Ballard Locks may be nature itself. Every summer, the fish ladder here flashes to life, and Seattle comes to watch.

Thousands upon thousands of migrating salmon pass through the ladder each year, making their way to freshwater spawning grounds in rivers and lakes throughout the region. They traverse the ladder's 21 steps, headed for the streams of their birth and distant gravel beds that will soon be their graves, as well. But their journey isn't in vain: The salmon carry with them the seeds of the next generation. It's a miraculous and mysterious voyage, and the fish ladder at the Locks is a wonderful place to witness it.

BEST BETS ON SEATTLE'S WATERS

LAKE WASHINGTON

BEACHES: The hands-down favorite sun-and-swim spots in Seattle are **Madison Park** (✉ E. Madison St. and E. Howe St. ☎ 206/684–4075) and **Matthews Beach** (✉ Sand Point Way NE and NE 93rd St. ☎ 206/684–4075).

BEACHSIDE PARK: Seward Park (✉ 5895 Lake Washington Blvd. S ☎ 206/684–4075) is a 300-acre piece of woodland along the Lake's western shore, and is a great spot for eagle-watching and trail walking.

CRUISE IT: Argosy Cruises (✉ 1101 Alaskan Way #201 ☎ 888/623–1445; ⊕ www. argosycruises.com) offers thrice-daily cruises of the lakes, including a peek at the lakeside estate of Microsoft co-founder Bill Gates.

SUMMER FEST: Every summer, Seattleites welcome **Seafair** (⊕ www.seafair.com), a monthlong celebration of the summer, water, and sun. Events include a triathlon, parades, an air show featuring the Blue Angels, and a hydroplane race.

LAKE UNION

LEARN TO PADDLE: South Lake Union's **Center for Wooden Boats** (✉ 1010 Valley Street ☎ 206/382–2628 ⊕ www.cwb.org) is a wonderful resource for all things maritime, including small-boat rental and tours.

RENT A BOAT: Northwest Outdoor Center (✉ 2100 Westlake Ave. N, Suite 101, on West Lake Union ☎ 206/281–9694 ⊕ www. nwoc.com) has a large fleet of rentable kayaks, wetsuits, paddleboards, and more.

QUACK: Ride the **Ducks of Seattle** (✉ 516 Broad St. ☎ 206/441–3825 ⊕ www. ridetheducksofseattle.com) offers 90-minute amphibian-vehicle tours around Seattle; the tour includes a brief cruise in Lake Union.

EAT AND PADDLE: Agua Verde Café and Paddle Club (✉ 1303 NE Boat St. ☎ 206/545–8570 ⊕ www. aguaverde.com), on Portage Bay, just west of Lake Union, rents kayaks by the hour; the upstairs café serves top-notch Mexican-American fare.

PUGET SOUND

RIDE A FERRY: Washington State Ferries (☎ 888/808–7977 ⊕ www.wsdot.wa.gov/ ferries) serves twenty ports of call around Puget Sound. The Seattle to Bainbridge Island round trip is a pleasant jaunt from the Downtown area.

CRUISE IT: Argosy Cruises (✉ 1101 Alaskan Way ☎ 888/623–1445 ⊕ www. argosycruises.com) offers sightseeing tours of Puget Sound; some include a trip through the Locks.

GO WEST: West Seattle's **Alki Beach** is a great summertime hangout. **Alki Kayak Tours** (✉ 1660 Harbor Ave SW ☎ 206/953–0237 ⊕ www.kayakalki.com) leads guided sunset tours for beginners and offers rentals to experienced paddlers.

EAT AT RAY'S: At the far western edge of Ballard is **Ray's Boathouse** (✉ 6049 Seaview Ave NW ☎ 206/789–3770 ⊕ www. rays.com). The food is worth the trip, but it's the water-front location and incredible sunsets that have made this place an institution.

(left) Seward Park, (center) kayaking in Lake Union, (right) Seattle Ferry in Puget Sound.

Agua Verde Paddle Club and Café

kayaking tours; prices start at $45 per person. ✉ *1001 Fairview Ave. N, Lake Union* ☎ *206/682–2031* ⊕ *www.mossbay.net.*

Northwest Outdoor Center. This center on Lake Union's west side rents one- or two-person kayaks (it also has a few triples) by the hour or day, including equipment and basic or advanced instruction. The hourly rate is $13 for a single and $18 for a double, with daily maximums of $65 and $90, respectively. Third and fourth hours are free during the week; a fourth hour is free on weekends. If you want to find your own water, NWOC offers "to-go" kayaks; the rate for a single is $65 first day, plus $35 each additional day. Doubles cost $90 the first day and $45 for each day thereafter. In summer, reserve at least three days ahead. NWOC also runs guided trips to the Nisqually Delta and Chuckanut Bay for $80 per person. Sunset tours to Golden Gardens Park ($55 per person) and moonlight tours of Portage Bay ($40 per person) are other options. Every May there are two overnight whale-watching trips to the San Juan Islands for $325 per person. ✉ *2100 Westlake Ave. N, Lake Union* ☎ *206/281–9694* ⊕ *www.nwoc.com.*

The **Seafair Hydroplane Races** (☎ *206/728–0123* ⊕ *www.seafair.com*) are a highlight of Seattle's rowdy Seafair festivities, which occur from mid-July through the first Sunday in August. Races are held on lake Washington near Seward Park. Tickets cost $25–$40. In summer, weekly sailing regattas take place on Lakes Union and Washington. Contact the **Seattle Yacht Club** (☎ *206/325–1000* ⊕ *www.seattleyachtclub.org*) for schedules.

Waterfront Activities Center. This center, located behind UW's Husky Stadium on Union Bay, rents three-person canoes and four-person rowboats for $8.50 an hour February through October. You can tour the Lake Washington shoreline or take the Montlake Cut portion of the ship canal and explore Lake Union. You can also row to nearby Foster Island and visit the Washington Park Arboretum. ✉ *3854 Montlake Blvd. NE, University District* ☎ *206/543–9433.*

Wind Works Sailing Center. Although members are given first picks at Wind Works, which is on Shilshole Bay in Ballard, nonmembers can arrange rentals. Experienced sailors are allowed to skipper their own boats after a brief qualifying process. Sailing a 25-foot Catalina will cost you $155 on weekdays and $194 on weekends; rates for a 30-foot Hunter are $277 on weekdays and $347 on weekends. ✉ *7001 Seaview Ave. NW, Suite 110, Ballard* ☎ *206/784–9386* ⊕ *www.windworkssailing.com.*

Yarrow Bay Marina. The marina rents 19- and 22-foot Bayliner runabouts for $60 an hour on weekdays and $65 an hour on weekends. There's a two-hour minimum; weekly rentals are also an option. ✉ *5207 Lake Washington Blvd. NE, Kirkland* ☎ *425/822–6066* ⊕ *www.yarrowbaymarina.com/boatrental.htm.*

FISHING

The Puget Sound region is an angler's paradise. Local salmon runs have been improving in recent years, and populations of pink (humpy) and coho (silver) salmon are actually booming. This translates to world-class saltwater fishing from July through September. Most salmon fishermen fish from small boats throughout the Sound, but shore fishing is also popular throughout the region. Seattle has public piers along Shilshole Bay in Ballard's Golden Gardens Park, and Elliott Bay has public piers at Waterfront Park, near Downtown and Pioneer Square. Shilshole Bay charter-fishing companies offer trips to fish for salmon, rockfish, cod, flounder, and sea bass.

Lake Washington has its share of parks department piers as well. You can fish year-round for rainbow trout, cutthroat trout, and large- and smallmouth bass. Chinook, coho, and steelhead salmon can also be fished, but often are subject to restrictions. Popular piers include the Reverend Murphy Fishing Pier, located at Seward Park, and the East Madison Street dock, located at the far eastern end of East Madison Street.

Additional freshwater fishing can be found at Green Lake, which is stocked with more than 10,000 legal-size rainbow trout each year. Anglers can also vie for brown trout, largemouth bass, yellow perch, and brown bullhead catfish. The parks department maintains three fishing piers along Green Lake's shores: East Green Lake Drive at Latona Avenue Northeast, West Green Lake Drive North and Stone Avenue North, and West Green Lake Way North, just north of the shell house.

All anglers age 15 and older are required to purchase licenses, which are sold at more than 600 locations throughout the state. Check regulations in the "Sport Fishing Rules" pamphlet (available at most sporting goods stores) when you buy your license. An annual freshwater license will cost you $21.90; a saltwater license is $20.26; and a combination license is $42.16. Visit ⊕ *fishhunt.dfw.wa.gov* for a list of locations.

Adventure Charters (⊠ *7001 Seaview Ave. NW, Ballard* ☎ *206/789–8245* ⊕ *www.seattlesalmoncharters.com*) takes private groups out on six-person troll boats to fish for salmon, bottom fish, and crab—depending on the season. The guided trips last for six or seven hours. The price per person is $160 September–July and $170 in August; a license, tackle, and bait are included, and your fish will be cleaned or filleted and bagged for free.

Fish Finders Private Charters (⊠ *6019 Seaview Ave. NW, Ballard* ☎ *206/632–2611* ⊕ *www.fishingseattle.com*) takes groups of two or more out on Puget Sound for guided salmon fishing trips. The cost is $175 per person and includes a fishing license. Morning trips last about six hours; afternoon trips are about five hours. All gear, bait, cleaning, and bagging are included in the fee.

FOOTBALL

The **Seattle Seahawks** play in the $430 million, state-of-the-art **Qwest Field** (⊠ *800 Occidental Ave. S, Sodo* ☎ *425/203–8000* ⊕ *www.seahawks.com*). Single-game tickets go on sale in late July or early August, and all home games sell out quickly. Tickets are expensive, with the cheapest seats, in the 300 section (where you actually get a really good view of the field), starting at $42. Note that traffic and parking are both nightmares on game days; try to take public transportation—or walk the 1 mi from Downtown—if possible.

Almost as popular as the Seahawks are the **UW Huskies.** The team plays at **Husky Stadium**, a U-shaped stadium that overlooks Lake Washington, so you can arrive by boat as well as by bike, bus, or car. Tickets are $30–$65 and go on sale at the end of July. ⊠ *University of Washington, 3800 Montlake Blvd. NE, University District* ☎ *206/543–2200* ⊕ *gohuskies.cstv.com.*

GOLF

★ **Gold Mountain Golf Complex.** Gold Mountain has two 18-hole courses, but most people make the trek to Bremerton to play the Olympic Course, a beautiful and challenging par 72 that is widely considered the best public course in Washington. The older, less-sculpted Cascade Course is also popular; it's better suited to those new to the game. There are four putting greens, a driving range, and a striking new clubhouse with views of the Belfair Valley. Prime-time greens fees are $27–$36 for the Cascade and $38–$49 for the Olympic. Carts are $32. You can drive all the way to Bremerton via I–5, or you can take the car ferry to Bremerton from Pier 52. The trip will take roughly an hour and a half no matter which way you do it, but the ferry ride (60 minutes) might be a more pleasant way to spend a large part of the journey. Note, however, that the earliest departure time for the ferry is 6 AM, so this option won't work for very early tee times. ✉ *7263 W. Belfair Valley Rd., Bremerton* ☎ *206/415–5432* ⊕ *www.goldmt.com.*

Golf Club at Newcastle. Probably the best option on the Eastside, this golf complex, which includes a pair of courses and an 18-hole putting green, has views, views, and more views. From the hilly greens you'll see Seattle, the Olympic Mountains, and Lake Washington. The 7,000-yard, par-72 Coal Creek course is

WORK ON YOUR SHORT GAME

If you don't want to set up a whole day of golfing, head to Hotel 1000 (✉ *1000 1st Ave., Downtown* ☎ *206/957–1000* ⊕ *www.hotel1000seattle.com*) to use their state-of-the-art virtual driving range. Choose from 50 of the world's best courses, including Pinehurst #2 and the Old Course at St. Andrews; private instruction is available. Rates are $30 per hour per person.

the more challenging of the two, though the China Creek course has its challenges and more sections of undisturbed natural areas. This is the Seattle area's most expensive golf club—greens fees for Coal Creek range from $125 to $160 depending on the season; fees for China Creek range from $80 to $110. Newcastle is about 35 minutes from Downtown—if you don't hit traffic. ✉ *15500 Six Penny La., Newcastle* ☎ *425/793–5566* ⊕ *www.newcastlegolf.com.*

★ **Harbour Pointe Golf Club.** Harbour Pointe is about 35 minutes north of Seattle in the town of Mukilteo. Its challenging 18-hole championship layout—with 6,800 yards of hilly terrain and wonderful Puget Sound views—is one of Washington's best. Greens fees range from $20 for twilight play to $49 for prime time on weekends. Carts cost $14 per person. There's also a driving range where you can get 65 balls for $5. Reserve your tee time online, up to 21 days in advance. Inquire about early-bird, twilight, off-season, and junior discounts. ✉ *11817 Harbour Pointe Blvd., Mukilteo* ☎ *425/355–6060* ⊕ *www.harbourpointegolf.com.*

Interbay Family Golf Center. Interbay has a wildly popular driving range ($7 for 68 balls, $9 for 102, $12 for 153), a 9-hole executive course ($15 on weekends, $13 on weekdays), and a miniature golf course ($7). The range and miniature golf course are open daily 7 AM–11 PM March–October and 7 AM–9 PM November–February; the executive course is open dawn to dusk year-round. Located within a 10-minute drive from Downtown, this is the city's most convenient course. ✉ *2501 15th Ave. W, Magnolia* ☎ *206/285–2200* ⊕ *www.seattlegolf.com.*

Jefferson Park. This golf complex—where the PGA Tour pro Fred Couples grew up golfing— has views of the city skyline *and* Mt. Rainier. The par-27, 9-hole course has a lighted driving range with heated stalls that's open from dusk until midnight. And the 18-hole, par-72 main course is one of the city's best. Greens fees are $35 on weekends and $30 on weekdays for the 18-hole course; you can play the 9-hole course for $8.50 daily. Carts are $26 and $17, and $2 buys you a bucket of 30 balls at the driving range. You can book tee times online up to 10 days in advance or by phone up to 7 days in advance. ⊠ *4101 Beacon Ave. S, Beacon Hill* ☎ *206/762–4513* ⊕ *www.seattlegolf.com.*

West Seattle Golf Course. This 18-hole course has a reputation for being tough but fair—and for offering up some excellent views of Downtown Seattle. Greens fees are $30 on weekdays, $35 on weekends. It's $26 for a cart. The front 9 will challenge you, while the back 9 will reward you with views of Elliott Bay and the skyline. ⊠ *4470 35th Ave. SW, West Seattle* ☎ *206/935–5187* ⊕ *www.seattlegolf.com.*

Willows Run Golf Course. Willows has it all: two 18-hole, links-style courses; a 9-hole, par-27 course; and a lighted, 18-hole putting course that's open until 11 PM. Thanks to an improved drainage system, Willows plays reasonably dry even in typically moist Seattle-area weather. Greens fees for 9 holes are $11 Monday through Thursday, $13 Friday through Sunday; fees for 18 holes are $42 or $55. Carts cost $10 per rider. There are also two pro shops and a driving range (75 balls cost $7; 35 balls cost $4). ⊠ *10402 Willows Rd. NE, Redmond* ☎ *425/883– 1200* ⊕ *www.willowsrun.com.*

HIKING

If there were ever a state sport of Washington, hiking would be it. The state is blessed with hundreds of miles of beautiful trails; Mt. Rainier National Park alone has enough to keep you busy (and awestruck) for months. If hiking is a high priority for you, and if you have more than a few days in town, your best bet is to grab a hiking book or check out the sites ⊕ *www.wta.org* and ⊕ *www.cooltrails.com,* rent a car, and head out to the Olympics or east to the Cascades *(⇨ Chapter 8 for more information on national parks and mountains near Seattle).* If you have to stay close to the city, don't despair: There are many beautiful walks within town and many gratifying hikes only an hour away.

■ TIP➜ Within Seattle city limits, the best nature trails can be found in Discovery Park, Lincoln Park, Seward Park, and at the Washington Park Arboretum. For farther-flung trips into the mountains, flip to the Side Trips chapter.

Walking the Burke-Gilman Trail from Fremont to its midway point at Matthews Beach Park (north of the U-District) would take several hours and cover more than 7 mi. You'll get a good glimpse of all sides of Seattle; the trail winds through both urban areas and leafier residential areas, and the first part of the walk takes you right along the Lake Washington Ship Canal.

OUTSIDE SEATTLE

Bridle Trails State Park. Though most of the travelers on the trails in this Bellevue park are on horseback, the 28 mi of paths are popular with hikers, too. The 500-acre park consists mostly of lowland forest, with Douglas firs, big-leaf maples, mushrooms, and abundant birdlife being just a few of its features. Note that horses are given the right of way on all trails; if you encounter riders, stop and stand to the side until the horses pass. ⊠ *Bridle Trails State Park., Bellevue* ✛ *From Downtown Seattle take I–90 or 520 East and get on I–405 North. Take Exit 17* *and turn right onto 116 Ave. NE. Follow that road to the park entrance* ⊙ *Daily 8* AM*–dusk*.

Cougar Mountain Regional Wildland Park. This spectacular park in the "Issaquah Alps" has more than 36 mi of hiking trails and 12 mi of bridle trails within its 3,000-plus acres. The Indian Trail, believed to date back 8,000 years, was part of a trade route that Native Americans used to reach North Bend and the Cascades. Thick pine forests rise to spectacular mountaintop views; there are waterfalls, deep caves, and the remnants of a former mining town. Local residents include deer, black bears, bobcats, bald eagles, and pileated woodpeckers, among many other woodland creatures. ⊠ *18201 S.E. Cougar Mountain Dr., Issaquah* ✛ *From Downtown Seattle take I–90 East; follow signs to park beyond Issaquah* ⊙ *Daily 8* AM*–dusk*.

★ **Larrabee State Park.** A favorite spot of the hippies and college students that call Bellingham home, Larrabee has two lakes, a coastline with tidal pools, and 15 mi of hiking trails. The Interurban Trail, which parallels an old railway line, is perfect for leisurely strolls or trail running. Head up Chuckanut Mountain to reach the lakes and to get great views of the San Juan Islands. ✛ *Take I–5 North to Exit 231. Turn right onto Chuckanut Dr. and follow that road to the park entrance.*

Mt. Si. A good place to cut your teeth before setting out on more-ambitious hikes—or a good place to just witness the local hiking and trail-running communities in all their weird and wonderful splendor—Mt. Si offers a challenging hike with views of a valley (slightly marred by the suburbs) and the Olympic Mountains in the distance. The main trail to Haystack Basin is 8 mi round-trip that climbs some 4,000 vertical feet, but there are several obvious places to rest or turn around if you'd like to keep the hike to 3 or 4 mi. Note that solitude is in short supply here—this is an extremely popular trail thanks to its proximity to Seattle. ✛ *Take I–90 East to Exit 31 (towards North Bend). Turn onto North Bend Way and then make a left onto Mt. Si Rd. and follow that road to the trailhead parking lot.*

Fodor'sChoice ★ **Snow Lake.** Washington State's most popular wilderness trail may be crowded at times, but the scenery and convenience of this hike make it a classic. The 8-mile roundtrip sports a relatively modest 1,300-foot elevation gain; the views of the Alpine Lakes Wilderness are well worth the sweat. The glimmering waters of Snow Lake await hikers at the trail's end; summer visitors will find abundant wildflowers, huckleberries, and wild birds. ✛ *Take I–90 East to Exit 52 (toward Snoqualmie Pass West). Turn left (north), cross under the freeway, and continue on to the trailhead, located in parking lot at the Alpental Ski Area.*

ROCK CLIMBING

The mountains of Washington have cut the teeth (among other body parts) of many a world-class climber. So it's only natural that there are several places to get in some practice.

★ **REI.** Every weekend more than 250 people have a go at REI's Pinnacle, a 65-foot indoor climbing rock. Climbing hours are Saturday 10–9 and

Sunday 10–7. The cost is $20 including equipment, but REI members pay only $7. Although reservations are a good idea, you can also schedule a climb in person. The wait can be anywhere from 30 minutes to four hours, but it's rare that you don't get to climb on the very day you sign up. ⊠ *222 Yale Ave. N, Downtown* ☎ *206/223–1944* ⊕ *www.rei.com.*

★ **Schurman Rock**. The nation's first man-made climbing rock was designed in the 1930s by local climbing expert Clark Schurman. Generations of climbers have practiced here, from beginners to rescue teams to such legendary mountaineers as Jim Whittaker, the first American to conquer Mt. Everest. Don't expect something grandiose—the rock is only 25 feet high. It's open for climbs Tuesday–Saturday 10–6. Rappelling classes for kids ($150 for 15 kids for two hours) are offered year-round at Camp Long, which is also the site of Seattle's only in-city campground, where cabins rent for $40 a night. ⊠ *Camp Long, 5200 35th Ave. SW, West Seattle* ☎ *206/684–7434* ⊕ *www.ci.seattle.wa.us/parks/environment/ camplong.htm.*

Stone Gardens Rock Gym. Beyond the trying-it-out phase? Head here and take a stab at the bouldering routes and top-rope faces. Although there's plenty to challenge the advanced climber, the mellow vibe is a big plus for families, part-timers, and the aspiring novice-to-intermediate crowd. The cost is $16; renting a full equipment package of shoes, harness, and chalk bag costs $9. There are "Climbing 101" classes most evenings for $50. ⊠ *2839 NW Market St., Ballard* ☎ *206/781–9828* ⊕ *www. stonegardens.com.*

SKIING AND SNOWBOARDING

Snow sports are one of the few reasons to look forward to winter in Seattle. Ski season usually lasts from late November until late March or early April. A one-day adult lift ticket at an area resort averages about $50, and most resorts rent equipment and have restaurants.

Cross-country trails range from undisturbed backcountry routes to groomed resort tracks. To ski on state park trails you must purchase a Sno-Park Pass, available at most sporting goods stores, ski shops, and forest service district offices. Always call ahead for road conditions, which might prevent trail access or require you to put chains on your tires.

Call for Snoqualmie Pass ski reports and news about **weather conditions** (☎ *206/634–0200 or 206/634–2754*) in the more distant White Pass, Crystal Mountain, and Stevens Pass. You can also do online research or listen to recorded messages about **road conditions** (☎ *800/695–7623* ⊕ *wsdot.wa.gov/traffic*). For information on cross-country trails and trail conditions, contact the **State Parks Information Center** (☎ *800/233–0321* ⊕ *www.parks.wa.gov/winter*).

Alpental at the Summit. Alpental, part of the Summit at Snoqualmie complex, attracts advanced skiers to its many long, steep runs. (Giant slalom gold medalist Debbie Armstrong trained here for the 1984 Olympics.) A one-day lift ticket will run you $38–$57; equipment is another $32–$38. The resort is 50 mi from Seattle, but it's right off the highway so

CLOSE UP

Major League, Seattle-Style

Seattleites love their sports teams, even if only two of Seattle's teams—the 1979 SuperSonics and the 2004 Storm—have ever captured championships. While the Mariners and Seahawks enjoyed some success in the last decade, neither team could bring home the proverbial bacon come championship time. Here's a breakdown of Seattle's major sports teams:

SEATTLE SEAHAWKS
Founded in 1976, Seattle's NFL franchise established a tradition of mediocrity during its first 20-odd seasons. That all began to change in 1997, when the team was purchased by local software and real-estate magnate Paul Allen, cofounder of Microsoft. A new stadium (Qwest Field) was erected in 2002, and a Super Bowl appearance followed in 2006. The fans remain passionate as ever: Qwest Field is frequently named the loudest stadium in football.

SEATTLE MARINERS
Seattle's best-loved sports team plays in Safeco Field, one of Major League Baseball's most beautiful ballparks. The team didn't always have such posh digs; the Mariners played in the now-demolished Kingdome from 1977 until 1999. The Mariners' fan base has hardly forgotten the glory days of the late 1990s and early 2000s, when the team made the postseason four times in seven years. With new management—and outstanding players, including Ichiro Suzuki—the Mariners seem poised to recapture their "SoDo Mojo."

SEATTLE SOUNDERS FC
When Seattle's NBA franchise departed following the 2008 season, Seattle sports fans were lowered into a collective depression. The Sounders, however, proved to be therapeutic: In 2009, the Major League Soccer team—which is owned in part by comedian Drew Carey—sold out every match of its inaugural season, becoming just the second MLS expansion team to win the coveted U.S. Open Cup.

WASHINGTON HUSKIES
The University of Washington is Seattle's school—the purple and gold of the Huskies is worn proudly throughout the city. Husky sports have always been popular here, with football as a strong point: the school won national titles in 1960 and 1991, and has won the Rose Bowl eight times. The Huskies won national championships in men's rowing (2007, 2009), women's softball (2009), and women's cross-country (2008). Basketball is a popular winter draw, with fans flocking to Hec Edmundsen Pavilion.

SEATTLE STORM
After winning a WNBA championship in 2004, the Storm continue to draw good crowds to Key Arena, located at Seattle Center. Led by international superstars Lauren Jackson and Sue Bird, the team hopes to earn another title in the near future. The WNBA season runs from May through August; the team plays at home four to six times a month.

—Nick Horton

7

you (mostly) avoid icy mountain roads. ⊠ *Exit 52 off I–90, Snoqualmie Pass* ☎ *425/434–7669* ⊕ *www.summitatsnoqualmie.com.*

Crystal Mountain. Serious skiers and boarders don't mind the 2½-hour drive here (it's about 75 mi from the city). The slopes are challenging, the snow conditions are usually good, and the views of Mt. Rainier are amazing. Lift tickets cost $55 for a half day and $60 for a full day. Full rental packages run $35. There are only three lodging options on or near the mountain (Crystal Mountain Hotels, Crystal Mountain Lodging Suites, and Alta Crystal Resort). They tend to fill up on busy winter weekends, so book ahead if you want to stay the night. ⊠ *33914 Crystal Mountain Blvd.* ☎ *360/663–2265, 800/695–7623 road conditions, 888/754–6199 snow report* ⊕ *www.skicrystal.com.*

Hurricane Ridge. The cross-country trails here, in Olympic National Park, begin at the lodge and have great views of Mt. Olympus. A small downhill ski and snowboarding area is open weekends and holidays; lift tickets are $10–$25. There's also a tubing/sledding hill. The Hurricane Ridge Visitor Center has a small restaurant, an interpretive center, and restrooms. Admission to the park is $15. Call ahead for road conditions before taking the three-hour drive from Seattle. ⊠ *Olympic National Park, 17 mi south of Port Angeles* ☎ *360/565–3100, 360/565–3131 for road reports* ⊕ *www.hurricaneridge.com.*

★   **The Summit at Snoqualmie.** Chances are good that any local skier you ask took his or her first run at Snoqualmie, the resort closest to the city. With four ski areas—Summit West, Summit Central, Summit East, and the aforementioned Alpental—gentle-to-advanced slopes, rope tows, moseying chairlifts, a snowboard park, and dozens of educational programs, it's the obvious choice for an introduction to the slopes. One-day lift tickets cost $38–$57; equipment packages are $32–$38 a day. The Nordic Center at Summit East is the starting point for 31 mi of cross-country trails. Guided snowshoe hikes are offered here on Friday and weekends. The $17 trail pass includes two rides on the chairlifts. ⊠ *Exit 52 off I–90, Snoqualmie Pass* ☎ *425/434–7669, 206/434–6708 for Nordic center* ⊕ *www.summitatsnoqualmie.com.*

Fodor's Choice   **Whistler.** Whistler, 200 mi north of Seattle, is best done as a three-day ★   weekend trip. (Just make sure your car has chains or snow tires.) And you really can't call yourself a skier here and not go to Whistler at least once. The massive resort is renowned for its nightlife, which is just at the foot of the slopes. You abandon your car outside the village upon arrival and negotiate the entire hotel/dining/ski area on foot. A one-day lift ticket costs about $70 (Canadian), and rental packages are about $32 (Canadian). The area includes more than 17 mi of cross-country trails, usually open November–March. For diehard skiers and boarders who want an extended season, there's summer skiing on Blackcomb Glacier through July. Getting to Whistler has never been easier: The Sea-to-Sky Highway, which connects Whistler to Vancouver, was expanded and improved prior to the 2010 Winter Olympics. ⊠ *Hwy. 99, Whistler, B.C., Canada* ☎ *800/766–0449* ⊕ *www.whistler-blackcomb.com.*

SOCCER

Soccer has always been popular in Seattle, but the sport is soaring to new heights, thanks to the **Seattle Sounders FC**—a Major League Soccer (MLS) franchise. The team played its first season in 2009, and the city went absolutely bonkers. Every single match sold out, and the team went on to win the MLS U.S. Open Cup. The Sounders' matches are held in fan-friendly Qwest Field; the season runs from March through October. Tickets—if you can find them—cost $20–$45 per match. The Seattle Sounders Select women's league team plays at the Starfire Sports Complex in Tukwila, a 15-minute drive south of Downtown. The women's season runs from May through July, and tickets are $10.

SWIMMING

When flying over the suburbs of Seattle, you'll see very few backyard swimming pools. In a city where most people don't own air-conditioners, swimming pools seem an unnecessary luxury. If you're in the city during a summer heat wave, however, you'll be glad to know where the nearest oasis of swimmer-friendly aquamarine water is located. Seattle Parks and Recreation maintains eight indoor pools (Queen Anne, Ballard, Evans, Rainier Beach, Southwest, Medgar Evers, Helene Madison, and Meadowbrook) year-round and two outdoor pools (Colman and Mounger). Entrance to most is $2.75–$3.75. All have lifeguards, lockers, changing rooms, showers, as well as classes and special events. Schedules can change frequently; always call ahead to make sure that a pool is open to the public before heading over. Check out ⊕ *www. seattle.gov/parks* for your nearest neighborhood pool.

In summer months, refresh yourself in Lake Washington instead. ⇨ *Check out the Experience and Neighborhoods chapters in this book for more information.*

TENNIS

There are 151 public tennis courts in Seattle's parks. To reserve a court, call the **Citywide Athletics Office** (☎ *206/684–4062* ⊕ *www.seattle.gov/ PARKS/tennis.asp*). Rates for outdoor courts are $7 per hour.

WALKING TOURS

With an abundance of lush city parks—with anything from meandering paths through old-growth forests to beachside pathways—there's no shortage of great places to walk in Seattle. ⇨ *For complete coverage on parks, see chapters 1 and 2.* Some of our favorite in-city walking paths include those at **Seward Park, Green Lake, Alki Point,** and **Discovery Park**. And, of course, the **Burke-Gilman Trail** meanders through the city, passing many beautiful parks and bodies of water.

Specialized walking tours are a great way to get to know the quirky, historic, or downright zany sides of Seattle.

Bill Speidel's Underground Tour (✉ *608 1st Ave., Pioneer Square* ☎ *206/682–4646* ⊕ *www.undergroundtour.com*) leads guests on fascinating underground tours in the Pioneer Square area. Hear stories of Seattle's pioneering past as you wander subterranean passageways that once were the main roads of old Seattle.

Market Ghost Tours (✉ *1410 Post Alley, Downtown* ☎ *206/322–1218* ⊕ *www.seattleghost.com*) offers weekend tours around the Pike Place Market, weaving in local ghost stories, eerie history, and fun facts about the market and its haunted places.

Savor Seattle Food Tours (✉ *1st Ave. and Pike St., Downtown* ☎ *888/987–2867* ⊕ *www.savorseattletours.com*) serves up two- to three-hour culinary walking tours around town, including a Chocolate Indulgence tour (yum); a Gourmet Seattle tour (which includes stops at fine restaurants to meet chefs, and tasty meals with wine and beer pairings); and a Pike Place Market walking tour led by a local guide.

Side Trips from Seattle

WORD OF MOUTH

"I like the North Cascades—VERY beautiful. Closer [to Seattle], I like Whidbey Island for a weekend. Captain Whidbey Inn is a fun place. I also like going out to the ocean—any of the Pacific Beaches are very nice, about a 3-hour drive from Seattle. Snoqualmie Falls is fun for the day."

—suze

SIDE TRIPS FROM SEATTLE PLANNER

Accessible Beauty

For those who appreciate Mother Nature's more outsize creations—volcanoes, mountains, and glaciers—Mount Rainier National Park beckons. The Park is about 95 mi southeast of the city, making for a lengthy but unforgettable day trip.

Seekers of solitude will appreciate the wild, remote rain forest of Olympic National Park, located 2½ hours west of Seattle.

If you prefer the tranquility of a beautiful shoreline or the artsy vibe of a quaint village, head north to the San Juan Islands. This stunning archipelago is three hours north of Seattle. The drive itself should take an hour and 45 minutes or so, and the ferry ride will take almost as long, depending on which island you visit.

Ferry and Freeway Travel

Traveling in and out of the city—especially during the summer—can be time-consuming. During morning and evening rush hours, traffic on I–5, I–90, and Highway 520 grinds to a halt. It's best to avoid the freeways altogether during these hours, but if you must travel during peak periods, try your best to have more than one person in the car. (H.O.V./carpool lanes, which require a minimum of two occupants, can save you significant time on the interstates.) The **Washington State Department of Transportation** (⊕ www.wsdot.wa.gov) has a wealth of travel information posted on its Web site, including live traffic flow maps.

Likewise, the Washington State Ferry system can become overloaded during peak travel times, leading to lengthy waits, especially during the summer months. Expect delays if you're headed toward the islands on Friday evenings or Saturday mornings. Backups are also likely when returning to the mainland on Sunday evenings. Wait times vary; contact **Washington State Ferries** (☎ 888/808–7977 ⊕ www. wsdot.wa.gov/ferries) for schedules and route information.

Local Food

Seattle is in the midst of a culinary renaissance, and the Puget Sound region is hot on its heels. The islands of Puget Sound are rife with top-notch restaurants serving locally grown produce, seafood, and even island-raised beef. At the head of the pack is Vashon Island. There, small growers like Sea Breeze farm pride themselves on being "beyond organic," and island restaurants serve products from local farms.

WHAT IT COSTS					
	¢	$	$$	$$$	$$$$
Restaurants	under $8	$8–$16	$17–$24	$25–$32	over $32
Hotels	under $100	$100–$150	$151–$200	$201–$250	over $250

Restaurant prices are per person for a main course, excluding tax and tip. Hotel price categories are based on the range between the least and most expensive standard double rooms in high season. Tax (17%) is extra.

Beach or Summit?

Seattle itself is loaded with scenery—its waterways, mountain views, and forested parks will drop your jaw. Repeatedly. But here's a secret: Those jagged peaks on the skyline and those fir-covered islands in Puget Sound look *even better* up close. It's a virtual necessity to dedicate a portion of your visit to Seattle's nearby natural splendors.

Side trips from Seattle can be as brief as an afternoon's ferry ride to Bainbridge Island—or as lengthy as a multiday hike on the flanks of Mt. Rainier. Deciding how much time to spend outside Seattle is just as important as deciding where to venture. If a day is all you've got, consider visiting a nearby island—Bainbridge, Vashon, or Whidbey. All three can be reached via short ferry rides from the Seattle area, and all three have unique pastoral landscapes, scenic beaches, and excellent restaurants.

For a multiday excursion, consider a tour of the Olympic Peninsula and **Olympic National Park** (☎ 800/833–6388 ⊕ www.nps.gov/olym), the jewel of the state's wild areas. Endless coastline, towering rainforests, and jagged peaks can be found throughout the peninsula, and it's best visited over the course of two or three days. Other popular multiday trips include the **San Juan Islands** (☎ 888/468–3701 ⊕ www.visitsanjuans.com) and the Cascade volcanoes—particularly **Mt. Rainier** (☎ 360/569–2211 ⊕ www.nps.gov/mora) and **Mt. St. Helens** (☎ 360/449–7800 ⊕ www.fs.fed.us/gpnf/mshnvm).

What to Do and Where to Do It

Art enthusiasts will find excellent galleries and studios on Bainbridge and Whidbey islands. Antiques shops abound on these isles as well.

Beach walking is a favorite activity on Whidbey, which offers some of the region's most gorgeous strips of sand. Double Bluff and Ebey's Landing, in particular, are can't-miss destinations.

Cycling is particularly popular on the San Juan Islands, though it can be hilly. Consider riding with a tour operator such as **Bicycle Adventures** (☎ 800/443–6060 ⊕ www.bicycleadventures.com).

During the summer, the San Juans are also a can't-miss seakayaking destination. And as for hiking, the state's national parks—Olympic, Mount Rainier, and North Cascades—offer some of the country's greatest trails.

When to Go

Weather in the Puget Sound region is rarely extreme; the area is blessed with a mild, maritime climate. Winter temperatures average in the low 40s, while summer temps average in the low 70s. Summer is by far the most popular time to visit, however, as the sun is far more likely to show its face. Still, spring and fall—particularly September and early October—can be fair and stunningly gorgeous—and far less crowded than June, July, and August.

Festivals

March: In the town of Coupeville on central Whidbey Island, **Penn Cove Mussel Festival** (☎ 360/678–5454 ⊕ www.thepenncovemusselfestival.com) attracts shellfish lovers from around the region.

July: Choochokam Arts Festival (☎ 360/221–6765 ⊕ www.choochokamarts.org) is a Whidbey Island tradition featuring two days of music, arts, crafts, and food. On Bainbridge Island, the **Bainbridge Bluegrass Festival** (☎ 206/842–3185 ⊕ bainbridgebluegrassfestival.com) is a local favorite.

August: The Orcas Island Chamber Music Festival (☎ 866/492–0003 ⊕ www.oicmf.org) is entering its 13th year of "classical music with a view."

8

Updated by
Nick Horton
and Holly S.
Smith

The beauty of Seattle is enough to wow most visitors, but it can't compare to the splendor of the state that surrounds it. You simply must put aside a day or two to venture out to one of the islands of Puget Sound or do a hike or scenic drive in one of the spectacular mountain ranges a few hours outside the city.

If you head west to Olympic National Park, north to North Cascades National Park, or east to the Cascade Range, you can hike, bike, or ski. Two-and-a-half hours southeast of Seattle is majestic Mt. Rainier, the fifth-highest mountain in the contiguous United States. Two hours beyond Rainier, close to the Oregon border, is the Mt. St. Helens National Volcanic Monument. The state-of-the-art visitor centers here show breathtaking views of the crater and lava dome and the spectacular recovery of the areas surrounding the 1980 blast.

You can get a taste of island life on Bainbridge, Whidbey, or Vashon—all easily accessible for day trips—or settle in for a few days on one of the San Juan Islands, where you can hike, kayak, or spot migrating whales and resident sea lions and otters.

Whatever trip you choose to take from Seattle, you'll be amazed at the scenery and wilderness that are immediately evident upon exiting the city. As you leave the city by ferry, the gorgeous Seattle skyline starts to fade as you get closer to craggy, forested islands. As you drive toward your destination, whether into the Cascade National Park or toward Mt. Rainier, you'll encounter huge evergreen trees surrounding the road.

THE ISLANDS OF PUGET SOUND

The islands of Puget Sound—particularly Bainbridge, Vashon, and Whidbey—are the easiest and most popular day trips for Seattle visitors. All three islands offer spectacular scenery (starting with the ferry ride over from Seattle) and a way of life that is even more laid-back than in the city itself—plus, they're easy to get to and easy to get around. Though each island has a smattering of inns and campsites, relatively few people stay the night—it's quite easy to get back to Seattle in time for dinner. Of the three, Whidbey requires the biggest time commitment to get to (it's 30 mi northwest of Seattle), but it has the most spectacular natural attractions. Bainbridge is the most developed island—it's something of a moneyed bedroom community— with a few decent restaurants and even a small winery rounding out its natural attractions. Vashon is the slowest and most pastoral of the islands—if you don't like leisurely strolls and bike rides, you might get bored there quickly.

WORD OF MOUTH

"If you want a multi-day trip, you can go to Olympic National Park (both the coast and the mountains), then take the ferry from Port Angeles to Victoria, B.C. We also like going to Portland, then up the Columbia River Gorge. A great overnight (or super-long one-day trip) is to go to Mt. Rainier National Park, then continue on to Mt. St. Helens before driving home. Of course, at that point, you are almost to Portland, so you could include that as well." —ALF

Bainbridge and Whidbey get tons of visitors in summer. Though you'll usually be able to snag a walk-on spot on the ferry, spaces for cars can fill up, so arrive early. You'll want a car on Whidbey (you can actually drive there, too) and on Bainbridge if you want to tour the entire island. You can also tour Bainbridge on bicycle (just beware the hills), while Vashon is best enjoyed on bicycle.

■ TIP→ For information about transport to nearby islands, tours, and much more, flip to the Travel Smart chapter at the end of this book.

8

BAINBRIDGE ISLAND

35 mins west of Seattle by ferry.

Of the three main islands in Puget Sound, Bainbridge has by far the largest population of Seattle commuters. Certain parts of the island are dense enough to have rush-hour traffic problems, while other areas retain a semi-rural, small-town vibe. Longtime residents work hard to keep parks and protected areas out of the hands of condominium builders, and despite the increasing number of stressed-out commuters, the island still has resident artists, craftspeople, and old-timers who can't be bothered to venture into the big city. Though not as dramatic as Whidbey or as idyllic as Vashon, Bainbridge always makes for a pleasant day trip.

The ferry drops you off in the village of Winslow. Along its compact main street, Winslow Way, it's easy to while away an afternoon among the antiques shops, art galleries, bookstores, and cafés. There are two bike rental shops in Winslow, too, if you plan on touring the island on two wheels. Getting out of town can be a bit nerve-wracking, but you'll soon be on quieter country roads. Be sure to ask for maps at the rental shop, and if you want to avoid the worst of the island's hills, ask the staff to go over your options with you before you set out.

The 150-acre Bloedel Reserve on Bainbridge Island

The **Bainbridge Chamber of Commerce** (☎ 866/805–3700 ⊕ *www.bainbridgechamber.com*) operates a visitor's kiosk close to the ferry terminal as well as a visitor's center at 395 Winslow Way E.

EXPLORING

Bainbridge Island Vineyard and Winery (✉ *8989 Day Rd. E* ☎ *206/842–9463* ⊕ *www.bainbridgevineyards.com*) has 8 acres of grapes that produce small batches of pinot noir, pinot gris, and siegerrebe; fruit wines are made from the seasonal offerings of neighboring farms. It's open for tastings Friday–Sunday 11–5. Tours are offered on Sunday at 2. If you first grab lunch provisions, you can picnic on the pretty grounds.

Twice a year, the island's artists and craftspeople are in the spotlight with the **Bainbridge Island Studio Tour** (☎ *206/842–0504* ⊕ *www.bistudiotour.com*). Participants put their best pieces on display for these three-day events, and you can buy everything from watercolors to furniture directly from the artists. Even if you can't make the official studio tours—held in mid-August and again in late November—check out the Web site, which has maps and information on studios and shops throughout the island, as well as links to artists' Web sites. Many of the shops have regular hours, and you can easily put together your own tour.

Fodor's Choice
★ The 150-acre **Bloedel Reserve** has fine Japanese gardens, a bird refuge, a moss garden, and other gardens planted with island flora. A French Renaissance–style mansion, the estate's showpiece, is surrounded by 2 mi of trails and ponds dotted with trumpeter swans. In 2009, the reserve was nominated as Garden of the Year by *Gardens Illustrated* magazine; it was one of only five gardens worldwide to receive the

nomination. Dazzling rhododendrons and azaleas bloom in spring, and Japanese maples colorfully signal autumn's arrival. You'll want to leave the pooch behind—pets are not allowed on the property, even if they stay in the car. ⊠ *7571 N.E. Dolphin Dr., 6 mi west of Winslow, via Hwy. 305* ☎ *206/842–7631* ⊕ *www.bloedelreserve.org* 🖾 *$12* ☉ *Wed.–Sat. 10–7, Sun. 10–4.*

On the southwest side of the island is the lovely and tranquil 137-acre **Fort Ward State Park.** There are 2 mi of hiking trails through forest, a long stretch of sun-drenched beach, and even a spot for scuba diving. Along with views of the water and the Olympic Mountains, you might be lucky and get a crack view of Mt. Rainier—or of the massive sea lions that frequent the near-shore waters. A loop trail through the park is suitable for all ability levels and will take you past vestiges of the park's previous life as a military installation. There are picnic tables in the park, but no other services are available. ✛ *Take Hwy. 305 out of Winslow; turn west on High School Rd. and follow signs to park.* ☎ *206/842–3931* ⊕ *www.parks.wa.gov* ☉ *Daily 8 AM–dusk.*

WHERE TO EAT

Most of the island's most reliable options are in Winslow—or close to it. You'll also find a major supermarket on the main stretch if you want to pick up some provisions for a picnic, though you can also easily do that in Seattle before you get on the ferry.

¢–$

BAKERY

✕**Blackbird Bakery.** A great place to grab a cup of coffee and a snack before exploring the island, Blackbird serves up rich pastries and cakes along with quiche, soups, and a good selection of teas and espresso drinks. Though there is some nice window seating that allows you to watch the human parade on Winslow Way, the place gets very crowded, especially when the ferries come in, so you might want to take your order to go. ⊠ *210 Winslow Way E, Winslow* ☎ *206/780–1322* ☐ *No credit cards* ☉ *No dinner.*

$$–$$$

BISTRO

✕**Café Nola.** Café Nola is the best option for something a little fancier than pub grub or picnic fare. The bistro setting is pleasant, with pale yellow walls, white tablecloths, and jazz music, and there's a small patio area for alfresco dining. The food is basically American and European comfort cooking with a few modern twists. The lunch menu offers sandwiches, such as an open-faced Dungeness crab melt on foccacia; heartier mains include grilled Alaskan salmon or prawn puttanesca. At dinner, classics like Niman Ranch pork shank and pan-seared scallops steal the show. The restaurant is within walking distance of the main ferry terminal. ⊠ *101 Winslow Way E, Winslow* ☎ *206/842–3822* ⊕ *www.cafenola.com* ☐ *AE, MC, V.*

$

SEAFOOD

✕**Harbor Public House.** An 1881 estate home overlooking Eagle Harbor was renovated to create this casual restaurant at Winslow's public marina. Local seafood—including steamed mussels and clams—pub burgers, and grilled flatiron steak sandwiches are typical fare, and there are 12 beers on tap. This is where the kayaking and pleasure-boating crowds come to dine in a relaxed, waterfront setting. When the sun shines, the harbor-front deck is the place to be, and things get raucous during Tuesday-night open-mike sessions. ⊠ *231 Parfitt Way, Winslow* ☎ *206/842–0969* ⊕ *www.harbourpub.com* ☐ *AE, DC, MC, V.*

8

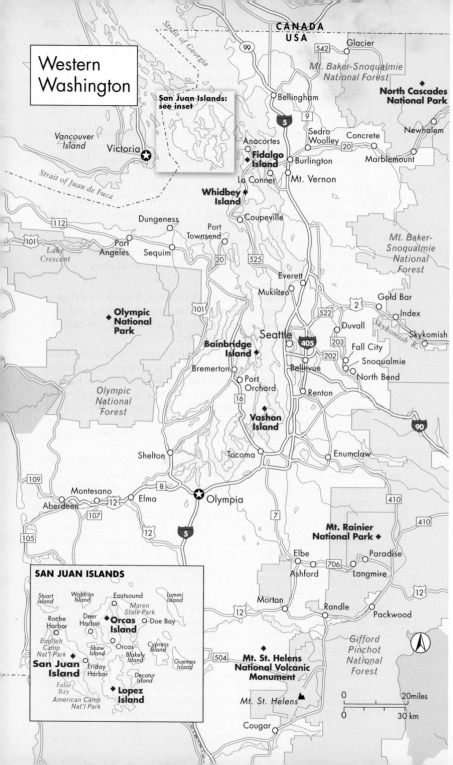

SEATTLE TO WOODINVILLE'S WINERIES

Walla Walla wine country is a bit too far if you've only got a few days, so head to Woodinville, which is roughly 22 mi from Seattle's city center. You'll need a car to get there unless you sign up for a guided tour. Check out ⊕ *www.woodinvillewinecountry.com* for a full list of wineries and touring maps.

WINERIES

There are more than 50 wineries in Woodinville; this list provides good survey:

■ **Chateau Ste. Michelle** (✉ *14111 NE 145th St.* ⊕ *www.ste-michelle.com*) is the grande dame of the Woodinville wine scene, and perhaps the most recognizable name nationwide. Guided tours of the winery are available daily 11:30–4:30. The tasting room is open daily 11–5. Check the Web site for special events like dinners and concerts.

■ **Columbia Winery** (✉ *14030 NE 145th St.* ⊕ *www.columbiawinery.com*) is another major player with a grand house anchoring its winery. Columbia's tasting room is open Sunday–Tuesday 11–6 and Wednesday–Saturday 11–7.

■ **Novelty Hill-Januik** (✉ *14710 Woodinville-Redmond Rd. NE* ⊕ *www.noveltyhilljanuik.com*) is often described as the most Napa-esque experience in Woodinville. The tasting room (open daily 11–5) for these sister wineries is sleek and modern. Themed tastings are $5–$10 per person. Brick-oven pizza is available on weekends.

■ **DeLille Cellars** (✉ *14221 Woodinville-Redmond Rd. NE* ⊕ *www.delillecellars.com*) is on the list of nearly every pricey restaurant in

Seattle. The Carriage House tasting room, slightly north of the winery, is open noon–4:30 daily.

■ **Mark Ryan** (✉ *14810 NE 145th St., #A-1* ⊕ *www.markryanwinery.com*) is an indie winery that has earned praise nationwide for its use of mostly Red Mountain AVA grapes. The winery has a small tasting room open Thursday–Sunday 12–5.

■ **Ross Andrew** (✉ *14810 NE 145th St, #A-2* ⊕ *www.rossandrewwinery.com*) is a newcomer that is already at the top of many enthusiasts' lists for cabs and syrah. The tasting room (next door to Mark Ryan) is open Thursday–Sunday 12–5.

■ **Woodinville Warehouse Wineries** (⊕ *www.woodwarewine.com*) is a collective space for boutique producers who don't have tasting rooms. Tastings are held Friday–Sunday; check the Web site for details.

WHERE TO EAT AND STAY

One of the swankiest hotels in the Puget Sound region, **Willow's Lodge** (⊕ *www.willowslodge.com*), is ideally located for a romantic getaway, only a few minutes away from the major wineries and next door to destination restaurant The Herbfarm.

The Herbfarm (✉ *14590 NE 145th St.* ☎ *425/485-5300* ⊕ *www.theherbfarm.com*) offers a four-hour, nine-course meal (with wine pairings). Menus are planned around themes, depending on seasonal fish, game, and produce. Reservations are essential. Get a simpler meal, but one with an equal focus on wine, at **Purple Café and Wine Bar** (✉ *14459 Woodinville Redmond Rd. NE* ⊕ *www.thepurplecafe.com*).

—Carissa Bluestone

8

VASHON ISLAND

20–35 mins by ferry from West Seattle.

Vashon is the most peaceful and rural of the islands easily reached from the city, home to fruit growers, rat-race dropouts, and a few Seattle commuters.

Biking, strolling, picnicking, and kayaking are the main activities here. A tour of the 13-mi-long island will take you down country lanes and past orchards and lavender farms. There are several artists' studios and galleries on the island, as well as a small commercial district in the center of the island, where a farmers' market is a highlight every Saturday from May to October. The popular Strawberry Festival takes place every July.

GETTING HERE

The car ferry leaves from Fauntleroy in West Seattle for the 20-minute ride. A passenger-only ferry from Pier 50 in Downtown Seattle takes 35 minutes. Note that passenger-only ferries are infrequent, so be sure to plan ahead and double-check the return schedule. Both ferries dock at the northern tip of the island.

VISITOR INFORMATION

The **Vashon-Maury Island Chamber of Commerce** (✉ *17205 Vashon Hwy. SW* ☎ *206/463–6217* ⊕ *www.vashonchamber.com*) is open Tuesday, Wednesday, and Thursday from 9 to 4. The site ⊕ *www.vashonmap. com* is also a good source of information.

EXPLORING

Blue Heron Art Center (✉ *19704 Vashon Hwy.* ☎ *206/463–5131* ⊙ *Tues.– Fri. 11–5, Sat. noon–5*) is the best representative of the island's diverse arts community, presenting monthly exhibits that span all mediums. The gift shop sells smaller items like jewelry.

Vashon has many parks and protected areas. **Jensen Point** has trails, a swimming beach, and boat and kayak rentals. From the ferry terminal, take Vashon Highway SW to S.W. Burton Drive and turn left. Turn left on 97th Avenue SW and follow it around as it becomes S.W. Harbor Drive. You can stroll along the beach at **Point Robinson Park,** which is very picturesque thanks to **Point Robinson Lighthouse** (☎ *206/463–9602* ⊕ *www.vashonparkdistrict.org*). Free tours of the lighthouse are given from noon to 4 on Sunday from mid-May through the summer; call to arrange tours at other times.

WHERE TO EAT

$–$$

AMERICAN

✕ **Hardware Store.** The restaurant's unusual name comes from its former incarnation as a mom-and-pop hardware shop—it occupies the oldest commercial building on Vashon and certainly looks like a relic from the outside. Inside you'll find a charming restaurant that's a cross between a bistro and an upscale diner. Breakfast highlights include rustic French toast and housemade granola. On the lunch menu you'll find simple sandwiches, salads, and burgers; dinner includes hearty old standbys like buttermilk fried chicken, pasta, meat loaf, and grilled salmon. A decent wine list focuses on Northwest and Californian wines. ✉ *17601*

Vashon Hwy. SW ☎ *206/463–1800* ⊕ *www.thsrestaurant.com* ▭ *AE, MC, V.*

$$–$$$ ✕ **La Boucherie.** As the retail and restaurant side of the "beyond organic"
NEW AMERICAN   Sea Breeze Farm, this outpost of ultralocal cuisine serves meats, poultry, and produce grown on or very close to the property. As a result, the menu is highly seasonal, but it always highlights Vashon's growers and farmers. You can order á la carte, but the prix-fixe menu is the way to go. Recent highlights included handmade tagliatelle pasta with Brussels sprouts, bacon, and pine nuts; a grilled lamb chop with celeriac remoulade and lentils; and a grilled Merguez sausage with fingerling mashed potatoes and a fried farm egg. Reservations are essential, and the restaurant serves lunch and dinner on Friday and Saturday only. ✉ *17635 100th Ave. SW* ☎ *206/567–4628* ⊕ *www.seabreezefarm.net* ▭ *MC, V.*

WHIDBEY ISLAND

20 mins by ferry from Mukilteo (5 mi south of Everett) across Possession Sound to Clinton.

Whidbey is a blend of low pastoral hills, evergreen and oak forests, meadows of wildflower (including some endemic species), sandy beaches, dramatic bluffs, with a few pockets of unfortunate suburban sprawl. It's a great place for a scenic drive, for viewing sunsets over the water, for taking ridge hikes that give you uninterrupted views of the Strait of Juan de Fuca, and for boating or kayaking along the protected shorelines of Saratoga Passage, Holmes Harbor, Penn Cove, and Skagit Bay.

The best beaches are on the west side, where wooded and wildflower-bedecked bluffs drop steeply to sand or surf—which can cover the beaches at high tide and can be unexpectedly rough on this exposed shore. Both beaches and bluffs have great views of the shipping lanes and the Olympic Mountains. Maxwelton Beach, with its sand, driftwood, and amazing sunsets, is popular with the locals. Possession Point includes a park and a beach, but it's best known for its popular boat launch. West of Coupeville, Ft. Ebey State Park has a sandy spread and an incredible bluff trail; West Beach is a stormy patch north of the fort with mounds of driftwood.

GETTING HERE

You can reach Whidbey Island by heading north from Seattle on I–5, west on Route 20 onto Fidalgo Island, and south across Deception Pass Bridge. The Deception Pass Bridge links Whidbey to Fidalgo Island. From the bridge it's just a short drive to Anacortes, Fidalgo's main town and the terminus for ferries to the San Juan Islands. It's easier—and more pleasant—to take the 20-minute ferry trip from Mukilteo (30 mi northwest of Seattle) to Clinton, on Whidbey's south end. It's a great way to watch gulls, terns, sailboats, and the occasional orca, gray whale, or bald eagle—not to mention the surrounding scenery, which takes in Camano Island and the North Cascades.

8

LANGLEY
7 mi north of Clinton.

The historic village of Langley is above a 50-foot-high bluff overlooking Saratoga Passage, which separates Whidbey from Camano Island. A grassy terrace just above the beach is a great place for viewing birds that are on the water or in the air. On a clear day, you can see Mt. Baker in the distance. Upscale boutiques selling art, glass, jewelry, books, and clothing line 1st and 2nd streets in the heart of town.

WHERE TO EAT AND STAY

$$–$$$$

BISTRO

✕ **Prima Bistro.** Langley's most popular gathering spot occupies a second-story space on First Street, right above the Star Store Grocery. French cuisine is the headliner here; classic bistro dishes like steak frites, salade niçoise, and confit of duck leg are favorites. But Northwest food—and local, seasonal ingredients—are also present; Penn Cove mussels and oysters are popular. And the wine list is by far the best in town. The bistro's outdoor deck offers views of Saratoga Passage, Camano Island, and beyond, and ample heat lamps ensure that guests enjoy the beauty most of the year. ✉ *201½ 1st St.* ☎ *360/221–4060* ⊕ *www.primabistro. biz* ▭ *MC, V.*

$$$–$$$$

Fodor's Choice
★

▦ **Inn at Langley.** Langley's most elegant inn, the concrete-and-wood Frank Lloyd Wright–inspired structure perches on a bluff above the beach, just steps from the center of town. Elegant, Asian-style guest rooms, all with fireplaces and balconies, have dramatic marine and mountain views. In-room highlights include open Jacuzzi tubs (all with views of Saratoga Passage) and flat-panel televisions. The Inn's restaurant ($$$$; reservations essential), with its double-sided river-rock fireplace and full-view kitchen, is set above a pretty herb garden. In summer it serves sumptuous six-course dinners on Thursday, Friday, and Saturday at 7 and on Sunday at 6. During the off-season—October through May—dinner is served Friday–Sunday. **Pros:** island luxury; lovely views; amazing restaurant. **Cons:** some rooms can be on the small side; decor is starting to feel slightly dated. ✉ *400 1st St.* ☎ *360/221–3033* ⊕ *www. innatlangley.com* ⇲ *28 rooms* ♿ *In-hotel: restaurant, spa, no elevator* ▭ *AE, MC, V* ⧉ *CP.*

$–$$

▦ **Saratoga Inn.** At the edge of Langley, this cedar-shake, Nantucket-style accommodation is a short walk from the town's shops and restaurants, and it overlooks the waters of Saratoga Passage and the stunning North Cascades. Wood-shingle siding, gabled roofs, and wraparound porches lend the inn a neatly blended Euro–Northwest ambience. This theme extends to the interior, with wood floors and fireplaces. The carriage house, which has a deck as well as a bedroom with a king-size bed, a bathroom with a claw-foot tub, and a sitting area with a sleep sofa, offers more privacy. Included in the price is breakfast and a daily wine reception with hors d'oeuvres. **Pros:** breathtaking views; cozy interiors. **Cons:** a bit rustic; some small bathrooms. ✉ *201 Cascade Ave.,* ☎ *360/221–5801 or 800/698–2910* ⊕ *www.saratogainnwhidbeyisland. com* ⇲ *15 rooms, 1 carriage house* ♿ *In-room: no a/c. In-hotel: no-smoking rooms, no elevator* ▭ *AE, D, MC, V* ⧉ *BP.*

This Historic Ferry House is part of Ebey's Landing National Historic Reserve on Whidbey Island.

SHOPPING

At **Brackenwood Gallery** (⊠ *302 1st St.* ☎ *360/221–2978*) you can see pieces by Georgia Gerber, a famed island sculptor whose bronze pieces are regionally famous, and Bruce Morrow, whose Western-themed paintings and prints are popular.

Museo (⊠ *215 1st St.* ☎ *360/221–7737* ⊕ *www.museo.cc*), a gallery and gift shop, carries contemporary art by recognized and emerging artists, including glass artists, of which there are many on Whidbey. **The Wayward Son** (⊠ *107-B 1st St.* ☎ *360/221–3911*) features the creations of local jeweler Sandrajean Wainwright, whose rings, bracelets, and pendants incorporate gemstones of all styles.

COUPEVILLE

On the south shore of Penn Cove, 12 mi north of Greenbank.

Restored Victorian houses grace many of the streets in quiet Coupeville, Washington's second-oldest city. It also has one of the largest national historic districts in the state, and has been used for filming movies depicting 19th-century New England villages. Stores above the waterfront have maintained their old-fashioned character. Captain Thomas Coupe founded the town in 1852. His house was built the following year, and other houses and commercial buildings were built in the late 1800s. Even though Coupeville is the Island County seat, the town has a laid-back, almost 19th-century air.

EXPLORING

Fodor's Choice
★

Ebey's Landing National Historic Reserve encompasses a sand-and-cobble beach, bluffs with dramatic views down the Strait of Juan de Fuca, two state parks, and several privately held pioneer farms homesteaded in the early 1850s. The reserve, the first and largest of its kind, holds nearly 100 nationally registered historic structures, most of them from the 19th century. Miles of trails lead along the beach and through the woods. Cedar Gulch, south of the main entrance to Ft. Ebey, has a lovely picnic area in a wooded ravine above the beach.

Ft. Casey State Park, on a bluff overlooking the Strait of Juan de Fuca and the Port Townsend ferry landing, was one of three forts built after 1890 to protect the entrance to Admiralty Inlet. Look for the concrete gun emplacement and a couple of 8-inch "disappearing" guns. The Admiralty Head Lighthouse Interpretive Center is north of the gunnery emplacements. There are also grassy picnic sites, rocky fishing spots, and a boat launch. ⊠ *2 mi west of Rte. 20* ☎ *360/678–4519* ⊕ *www. parks.wa.gov* ✉ *Free* ⊗ *Daily sunrise–sunset.*

In late May **Ft. Ebey State Park** blazes with native rhododendrons. West of Coupeville on Point Partridge, it has 645 acres of beaches, campsites in the woods, trails to the headlands, World War II gun emplacements, wildflower meadows, spectacular views down the Strait of Juan de Fuca, and a boggy pond. ⊠ *3 mi west of Rte. 20* ☎ *360/678–4636* ⊕ *www. parks.wa.gov* ✉ *Free* ⊗ *Daily sunrise–sunset.*

The **Island County Historical Museum** has exhibits on Whidbey's fishing, timber, and agricultural industries, and conducts tours and walks. The square-timber **Alexander Blockhouse** outside dates from 1855. Note the squared logs and dovetail joints of the corners—no overlapping log ends. This construction technique was favored by many western Washington pioneers. Several old-time canoes are exhibited in an open, roofed shelter. ⊠ *908 NW Alexander St.* ☎ *360/678–3310* ✉ *$3* ⊗ *May–Sept., Mon.–Sat. 10–5, Sun. 11–5; Oct.–Apr., Mon.–Sat. 10–4, Sun. 11–4.*

WHERE TO EAT AND STAY

$$–$$$ ⊠ **The Oystercatcher.** A dining destination for foodies from across the
NEW AMERICAN Northwest, the Oystercatcher is renowned for its local cuisine. The
Fodor's Choice menu is crowded with Whidbey Island produce, seafood, meats, and
★ cheeses, and is heavily influenced by fresh, in-season ingredients. Owners Joe and Jamie Martin have crafted an intimate, romantic dining space in the heart of town, and the restaurant's wine list is stellar. ⊠ *901 Grace St. NW* ☎ *360/678–0683* ⊕ *www.oystercatcherwhidbey.com* ▭ *MC, V* ⊗ *Open Thurs.–Sat. for dinner, Sun. for brunch. No lunch.*

$–$$ ⊠ **Christopher's on Whidbey.** A warm and casual place, Christopher's is in
AMERICAN a house one block from the waterfront. The menu features many Whidbey favorites, including local oysters and mussels, and such flavorful fare as raspberry barbecued salmon, bacon-wrapped pork tenderloin with mushrooms, Penn Cove seafood stew, and linguine with a smoked salmon cream sauce. The wine list is extensive. ⊠ *103 NW Coveland* ☎ *360/678–5480* ▭ *AE, MC, V* ⊗ *No dinner Sun.*

$–$$ ⊡ **Captain Whidbey Inn.** Almost a century old, this venerable madrone lodge on a wooded promontory offers a special kind of hospitality and charm now rarely found. Gleaming fir-paneled rooms and suites, which have pedestal sinks but share bathrooms, are furnished with antiques and modern amenities; quarters on the north side have views of

Penn Cove. More luxurious Lagoon Rooms, in a separate cedar motel, overlook a quiet, marshy expanse. A cluster of small, one-bedroom cabins have stone fireplaces, private baths, and share a hot tub. The on-site Ship of Fools restaurant and tavern are popular with locals. **Pros:** aging elegance; charming; comfortable. **Cons:** interiors a bit tired; some rooms are small. ⊠ *2072 Captain Whidbey Inn Rd., off Madrona Way,* ☎ *360/678–4097 or 800/366–4097* ⊕ *www.captainwhidbey.com* ⇨ *23 rooms, 2 suites, 4 cabins* ♿ *In-room: no a/c (some), no phone (some), no TV. In-hotel: restaurant, bar* ⊟ *D, MC, V.*

$ ⊞ **Compass Rose Bed and Breakfast.** Inside this stately 1890 Queen Anne Victorian, a veritable museum of art, artifacts, and antiques awaits you. The proprietor's naval career carried him and his wife to all corners of the globe, from which they have collected the inn's unique adorn-ments. The innkeepers' friendliness—and the location in the heart of Ebey's Landing National Historical Preserve—will make your stay all the more enjoyable and interesting. **Pros:** sweet service; lovely surround-ings. **Cons:** filled-to-brimming with antiques, making it not terribly child-friendly. ⊠ *508 S. Main St.* ☎ *360/678–5318* ☎ *800/237–3881* ⊕ *www.compassrosebandb.com* ⇨ *2 rooms* ♿ *In-room: no a/c, no phone, no TV. In-hotel: no-smoking rooms, no elevator* ⊟ *No credit cards* ⊺⊙⏐ *BP.*

OAK HARBOR
10 mi north of Coupeville.

Oak Harbor itself is the least attractive and least interesting part of Whidbey—it mainly exists to serve the Whidbey Island Naval Air Sta-tion and therefore has none of the historic or pastoral charm of the rest of the island. It is, however, the largest town on the island and the one closest to Deception Pass State Park. In town, the marina, at the east side of the bay, has a picnic area with views of Saratoga Passage and the entrance of Penn Cove.

EXPLORING

☪   **Deception Pass State Park** has 19 mi of rocky shore and beaches, three
★   freshwater lakes, and more than 38 mi of forest and meadow trails. Located 9 mi north of Oak Harbor, the park occupies the northernmost point of Whidbey Island and the southernmost tip of Fidalgo Island, on both sides of the Deception Pass Bridge. Park on Canoe Island and walk across the bridge for views of two dramatic saltwater gorges, whose tidal whirlpools have been known to swallow large logs. ⊠ *Rte. 20, 9 mi north of Oak Harbor* ☎ *360/675–2417* ⊕ *www.parks.wa.gov* ⊠ *Park free, campsite fees vary* ⊙ *Apr.–Sept., daily 6:30* AM*–dusk; Oct.–Mar., daily 8* AM*–dusk.*

FIDALGO ISLAND

15 mi north of Oak Harbor.

The Deception Pass Bridge links Whidbey to Fidalgo, an island that hardly feels like one. (And it barely is: Fidalgo is separated from the mainland by the narrow waterways of Deception Pass to the south and the Swinomish Channel to the east.) Anacortes, Fidalgo's main town, has some well-preserved brick buildings along the waterfront, several well-maintained old commercial edifices downtown, and many beautiful older homes off the main drag. Still, it's little more than a waypoint for travelers heading to and from the San Juan Islands.

EXPLORING

The frequently changing exhibits at the **Anacortes History Museum** focus on the cultural heritage of Fidalgo and nearby Guemes Island. ✉ *1305 8th St., Anacortes* ☎ *360/293–1915* ⊕ *www.museum.cityofanacortes. org* 🖙 *Free; donations accepted* ⊙ *Thurs.–Sat. 10–4, Sun. 1–4, Mon.– Tues. 10–4. Closed Wed.*

West of Anacortes, near the ferry landing, **Washington Park** has dense forests, sunny meadows, trails, and a boat launch. A narrow loop road winds through woods to overlooks with views of islands and saltwater. You can picnic or camp under tall trees near the shore. ✉ *12th St. and Oakes Ave.* ☎ *360/293–1927* 🖙 *Free, camping $15–$23* ⊙ *Daily sunrise–sunset.*

WHERE TO EAT

$–$$ × **Randy's Pier 61.** The dining room's nautical theme is in keeping with
SEAFOOD   the waterfront setting. From here you can see across the channel to Guemes Island and the San Juans; don't be surprised if a sea lion looks up from the tide rips or if a bald eagle cruises by. Specialties include seafood gumbo, crab cakes, salmon Wellington, crab-stuffed prawns, and a beautifully flavored (and expertly cooked) apples-and-almond salmon. While Randy's is far from haute cuisine, the staff is professional and friendly, and the food is consistently yummy. ✉ *209 T Ave., Anacortes* ☎ *360/293–5108* 🖃 *AE, D, MC, V.*

THE SAN JUAN ISLANDS

In the course of a soggy, gray Northwest winter, Seattleites often dream of an escape, and the vision that fills their minds is usually of the San Juans. Located some 80 mi northwest of Seattle, this group of islands is a romantic's Valhalla. The rolling pastures, rocky shorelines, and thickly forested ridges of these isles are simply breathtaking, and their quaint villages draw art lovers, foodies, and burned out-city folk alike.

There are 176 named islands in the San Juan archipelago, although these and large rocks around them amount to 743 at low tide and 428 at high tide. Sixty are populated (though most have only a house or two), and 10 are state marine parks, some of which are accessible only to kayakers navigating the Cascadia Marine Trail. The three largest islands, Lopez, Orcas, and San Juan, are served regularly by ferries and seaplanes and get packed with visitors in summer. These islands support a little fishing and farming, but tourism generates by far the largest revenues.

Since the 1990s, gray whales have begun to summer here, instead of going north to their arctic breeding grounds; an occasional minke or humpback whale can also be seen frolicking in the kelp.

GETTING HERE

AIR TRAVEL

If traffic and ferry lines *really* aren't your thing, consider hopping aboard a seaplane for the quick flight from Seattle to the San Juan islands. **Kenmore Air** (☎ 866/435–9524 ⊕ *www.kenmoreair.com*) offers several departures from Seattle every day. Sure, the airfare isn't cheap—around $130 each way—but the scenic, hour-long flight is an experience in itself. And the travel time saved is worth a pretty penny. Seaplanes owned by local airlines regularly splash down near the public waterfronts and resort bays around San Juan, Orcas, and Lopez, while charters touch down in private waters away from the crowds.

Air Contacts Island Air (☎ 360/378–2376 ⊕ www.sanjuan-islandair.com). **Northwest Seaplanes** (☎ 800/690–0086 ⊕ www.nwseaplanes.com). **San Juan Airlines** (☎ 800/874–4434 ⊕ www.sanjuanairlines.com).

BOAT AND FERRY TRAVEL

Ferries stop at the four largest islands: Lopez, Shaw, Orcas, and San Juan. Others, many privately owned, can be reached be commuter ferries from Bellingham and Port Townsend.

Washington State ferries depart from Anacortes, about 76 mi north of Seattle, to the San Juan Islands. For walk-on passengers, it's $13.45 from Anacortes to any point in the San Juan Islands. From Anacortes, vehicle and driver fares to the San Juans are $32–$36 to Lopez Island, $40–$44 to Orcas and Shaw islands, $48–$52 to Friday Harbor.

Clipper Navigation operates the passenger-only *Victoria Clipper* jet catamaran service between Pier 69 in Seattle and Friday Harbor. Boats leave daily in season at 7:45 AM; reservations are strongly recommended. The journey costs $47–$52 one way. The *San Juan Island Commuter* has daily scheduled service in season to Orcas Island and Friday Harbor, as well as Lopez Island and a few other smaller islands. Ferries depart at 9:30 AM from the Bellingham Cruise Terminal (about 1½ hours by car from Seattle). One-way fares start at $49.50.

■ TIP➜ Orcas, Lopez, and San Juan islands are extremely popular in high season; securing hotel reservations in advance is essential. Ferry lines are also far more common than in the winter months; contact Washington State Ferries (☎ *888/808–7977* ⊕ *www.wsdot.wa.gov/ferries*) before you travel.

Boat and Ferry Contacts Clipper Navigation (☎ 250/382–8100 in Victoria, 206/448–5000 in Seattle, 800/888–2535 in the U.S. ⊕ www.clippervacations. com). **San Juan Island Commuter** (✉ Bellingham Cruise Terminal, 355 Harris Ave., No. 104, Bellingham ☎ 360/738–8099 or 888/443–4552 ⊕ www.whales. com). **Washington State Ferries** (☎ 206/464–6400, 888/808–7977, 800/843–3779 automated line in WA and BC ⊕ www.wsdot.wa.gov/ferries).

VISITOR INFORMATION

Contacts Lopez Island Chamber of Commerce (☎ 360/468–4664 ⊕ www. lopezisland.com). **Orcas Island Chamber of Commerce** (☎ 360/376–2273 ⊕ www.orcasislandchamber.com). **San Juan Islands Visitors Bureau** (✉ Box 98, Friday Harbor 98250 ☎ 360/468–3701 or 888/468–3701 ⊕ www. visitsanjuans.com).

LOPEZ ISLAND

45 mins by ferry from Anacortes.

Known affectionately as "Slow-pez," the island closest to the main-land is a broad, bay-encircled bit of terrain amid sparkling blue seas, a place where cabinlike homes are tucked into the woods, and boats are moored in lonely coves. Of the three San Juan islands with facilities to accommodate overnight visitors, Lopez has the smallest population (approximately 2,200), and with its old orchards, weathered barns, and rolling green pastures, it's the most rustic and least crowded during high season. Gently sloping roads cut wide curves through golden farmlands and trace the edges of pebbly beaches, while peaceful trails wind through thick patches of forest. Sweeping country views make Lopez a favorite year-round biking locale, and except for the long hill up from the ferry docks, most roads and designated bike paths are easy enough for novices to negotiate.

The only settlement is Lopez Village, really just a cluster of cafés and boutique shops, as well as a summer market and outdoor theater, visitor information center, and grocery store. Other attractions—such as seasonal berry-picking farms, small wineries, kitschy galleries, intimate restaurants, and isolated bed-and-breakfasts—are scattered around the island.

EXPLORING

The **Lopez Island Historical Museum** has artifacts from the region's Native American tribes and early settlers, including some impressive ship and small-boat models and maps of local landmarks. ✉ *28 Washburn Pl., Lopez Village* ☎ *360/468–2049* ⊕ *www.lopezmuseum.org* ✉ *Donations accepted* ⊙ *May–Sept., Wed.–Sun. noon–4, year-round by appointment.*

Lopez Island Vineyard is spread over 6 acres about 1 mi north of Lopez Village. The winery produces estate-grown white wines including Madeleine Angevine and Siegerrebe, as well as dessert wines, such as those made from raspberries, blackberries, and other local fruits. Red wines—including Malbec and cabernet sauvignon—are also made here, albeit with grapes grown in the warmer climates of eastern Washington. ✉ *Fisherman Bay Rd. north of Cross Rd.* ☎ *360/468–3644* ⊕ *www.lopezislandvineyards.com* ✉ *Free* ⊙ *July and Aug., Wed.–Sat. noon–5; May, June, and Sept., Fri. and Sat. noon–5; Apr. and Oct.–Dec., Sat. noon–5.*

★ A quiet forest trail along beautiful **Shark Reef** leads to an isolated headland jutting out above the bay. The sounds of raucous barks and squeals mean you're nearly there, and eventually you may see throngs of seals and seagulls on the rocky islets across from the point. Bring binoculars to spot bald eagles in the trees as you walk, and to view sea otters frolicking in the waves near the shore. The trail starts at the Shark Reef Road parking lot south of Lopez Village, and it's a 15-minute walk to the headland. ✛ *Off Shark Reef Rd., 2 mi south of Lopez Island Airport* ✉ *Free* ⊙ *Daily dawn–dusk.*

Spencer Spit State Park is on former Native American clamming, crabbing, and fishing grounds. The spit is a stop along the Cascadia Marine Trail for kayakers, and it's a good place for summer camping. It's also one of the few Washington beaches where cars are permitted. ⊕ *2 mi northeast of Lopez Village via Port Stanley Rd.* ☎ *360/468–2251* ☒ *Free, camping $14–$28* ⊘ *Mar.–Oct., daily 8–dusk.*

WHERE TO EAT

$$–$$$
AMERICAN

✕ **Bay Café.** Boats dock right outside this pretty waterside mansion at the entrance to Fisherman Bay. In winter, sunlight streams into the window-framed dining room; in summer you can relax on the wraparound porch before a gorgeous sunset panorama. The menu is highlighted by Lopez Island beef and seafood tapas—such as basil prawns with saffron rice and sea scallops with sun-dried tomatoes. Homemade sorbet and a fine crème caramel are among the desserts. Weekend breakfasts draw huge crowds. ☒ *9 Old Post Rd., Lopez Village* ☎ *360/468–3700* ⊕ *www.bay-cafe.com* ▭ *AE, DC, MC, V* ⊘ *Closed Mon.–Wed. Oct.–May. No lunch.*

¢–$
BAKERY
★

✕ **Holly B's Bakery.** Tucked into a small, cabinlike strip of businesses set back from the water, this cozy, wood-paneled dining room is the highlight of daytime dining in the village. Fresh pastries and big homemade breakfasts are the draws. Sunny summer mornings bring diners out onto the patio, where kids play and parents relax. ☒ *Lopez Plaza* ☎ *360/468–2133* ⊕ *www.hollybsbakery.com* ▭ *No credit cards* ⊘ *Closed Dec.–Mar. No dinner.*

WHERE TO STAY

$–$$

▥ **Edenwild.** This large Victorian-style farmhouse, surrounded by gardens and framed by Fisherman's Bay, looks as if it's at least a century old, but it actually dates from 1988. Large rooms, each painted or papered in different pastel shades, are furnished with simple antiques; some have claw-foot tubs and brick fireplaces. The sunny dining room is a cheery breakfast spot. In summer you can sip tea on the wraparound ground-floor veranda or relax with a book on the garden patio. **Pros:** charming touches to each room; spacious quarters; central to town. **Cons:** "central to town" also means that you'll be dealing with town more than some people might like on an island getaway. ☒ *132 Lopez Rd., Lopez Village* ☎ *360/468–3238 or 800/606–0662* ⊕ *www.edenwildinn.com* ⇆ *6 rooms, 2 suites* ⚒ *In-hotel: no kids under 12* ▭ *MC, V* ⊙l *BP.*

SHOPPING

The **Chimera Gallery** (☒ *Village Rd.* ☎ *360/468–3265*), a local artists' cooperative, exhibits and sells crafts, jewelry, and fine art. **Islehaven Books** (☒ *Village Rd.* ☎ *360/468–2132*), which is supervised in part by the owner's pack of five Russian wolfhounds, is stocked with publications on San Juan Islands history and activities, as well as books about the Pacific Northwest. There's also a good selection of mysteries, literary novels, children's books, and craft kits, plus greeting cards, art prints, and maps. Many of the items sold here are the works of local writers, artists, and photographers.

Rosario Point at Rosario Resort on Orcas Island in the San Juans

SPORTS AND THE OUTDOORS

BICYCLING Mountain bike rental rates start at around $5 an hour and $25 a day; tandem, recumbent, and electric bikes are $13–$20 an hour or $42–$65 per day. Reservations are recommended, particularly in summer.

Cascadia Kayak & Bike (✉ *Lopez Village* ☎ *360/468–3008*) makes deliveries to the ferry docks or to your hotel. **Lopez Bicycle Works** (✉ *2847 Fisherman Bay Rd.* ☎ *360/468–2847* ⊕ *www.lopezbicycleworks.com*), at the marina 4 mi from the ferry, can bring bicycles to your door or the ferry.

SEA KAYAKING **Elakah! Expeditions** (☎ *360/734–7270 or 800/434–7270* ⊕ *www.elakah. com*), a family-run sea-kayaking company, leads kayaking clinics on Lopez and two- to five-day trips ($225 to $495) around the San Juans. Specialty trips, such as those for women only, are also organized. **Lopez Kayaks** (☎ *360/468–2847* ⊕ *www.lopezkayaks.com*), open May to October at Fisherman Bay, offers a four-hour tour of the southern end of Lopez for $75 and a two-hour sunset tour for $35. Kayak rentals start at $15 an hour or $40 per day, and the company can deliver kayaks to any point on the island for an additional $10 fee.

ORCAS ISLAND

75 mins by ferry from Anacortes.

Orcas Island, the largest of the San Juans, is blessed with wide, pastoral valleys and scenic ridges that rise high above the neighboring waters. (At 2,409 feet, Orcas' Mt. Constitution is the highest peak in the San Juans.) Spanish explorers set foot here in 1791, and the island is actually

The view of Puget Sound from Mt. Constitution in Orcas Island's Moran State Park

named for their ship—not for the black-and-white whales that frolic in the surrounding waters. The island was also the home of Native American tribes, whose history is reflected in such places as Pole Pass, where the Lummi people used kelp and cedar-bark nets to catch ducks, and Massacre Bay, where in 1858 a tribe from southeast Alaska attacked a Lummi fishing village.

Today, farmers, fishermen, artists, retirees, and summer-home owners make up the population of about 4,500. Houses are spaced far apart, and the island's few towns typically have just one major road running through them. Resorts dotting the island's edges are evidence of the thriving local tourism industry. The beauty of this island is beyond compare; Orcas is a favorite place for weekend getaways from the Seattle area any time of the year, as well as one of the state's top settings for summer weddings.

EXPLORING

Eastsound, the main town, lies at the head of the East Sound channel, which nearly divides the island in two. Small shops here sell jewelry, pottery, and crafts by local artisans. Along Prune Alley is a handful of stores and restaurants.

★ **Moran State Park** comprises 5,000 acres of hilly, old-growth forests dotted with sparkling lakes, in the middle of which rises Mt. Constitution. A drive to the summit affords exhilarating views of the islands, the Cascades, the Olympics, and Vancouver Island. You can explore the terrain along 14 hiking trails and choose from among 151 campsites if you'd like to stay longer. ✣ *Star Rte. 22; head northeast from Eastsound on Horseshoe Hwy. and follow signs* ✦ *Box 22, Eastsound*

98245 ☎ 360/376–2326, 800/452–5678 *for reservations* 🅰 *Camping $21–$28* ⊙ *Daily dawn–dusk.*

WHERE TO STAY

$$
Fodor's Choice
★

🍽 **The Inn at Ship Bay.** This boutique inn is just 1 mi from Eastsound, and the on-site restaurant may be the best dining experience on the island. Tucked into a renovated 1869 farmhouse, the dining room and bar offer a menu that's heavy on local, seasonal ingredients. Island greens, fruits, and seafood are served alongside a regionally focused wine list, and the results are spectacular. An example: during early summer, troll-caught king salmon is accompanied by local spring greens and a bing cherry/sweet herb dressing. Even the bread is memorable; the restaurant serves housemade sourdough from a starter that's more than 100 years old. ✉ *326 Olga Rd., Orcas Island* ☎ *877/276–7296* ⊕ *www.innatshipbay.com* ⊟ *AE, MC, V* ⊙ *Closed Sun.–Mon. Oct.–May. No lunch.*

$–$$$

🍽 **Deer Harbor Inn.** This lodge has eight wood-paneled rooms, each with a balcony and peeled-log furniture. Four cottages—including one with three bedrooms—and the Harborview Suite have whirlpool tubs and propane fireplaces; two houses have kitchens and laundry facilities. The century-old apple orchard is lovely, making it a favorite spot for weddings. **Pros:** shabby-island-chic; B&B furnishings are sweet. **Cons:** too small for some; some areas in needs of updates. ⊕ *5½ mi southwest of West Sound via Deer Harbor Rd.* ☎ *360/376–4110* ⊕ *www.deerharborinn.com* ⤴ *8 rooms, 1 suite, 4 cottages, 2 houses* ⚒ *In-room: no phone, kitchen (some), no TV (some), Wi-Fi. In-hotel: restaurant, laundry facilities, public Wi-Fi* ⊟ *AE, MC, V* 🍽 *CP.*

$
Fodor's Choice
★

🍽 **Turtleback Farm Inn.** Eighty acres of meadow, forest, and farmland in the shadow of Turtleback Mountain surround this forest-green inn. Rooms are divided between the carefully restored late-19th-century green-clapboard farmhouse and the newer cedar Orchard House. All are well lighted and have hardwood floors, wood trim, and colorful curtains and quilts, some of which are made from the fleece of resident sheep. The inn is a favorite place for local weddings. Breakfast is in the dining room or on the deck overlooking Crow Valley, one of the island's most beautiful nooks. **Pros:** knowledgeable owners; intimate, sweet decor. **Cons:** basic breakfasts; rooms vary wildly. ✉ *1981 Crow Valley Rd., Eastsound* ☎ *360/376–3914 or 800/376–4914* ⊕ *www.turtlebackinn.com* ⤴ *11 rooms* ⚒ *In-room: Wi-Fi, no phone, no TV. In-hotel: no elevator* ⊟ *MC, V* 🍽 *BP.*

SHOPPING

Crow Valley Pottery (✉ *2274 Orcas Rd., Eastsound* ☎ *360/376–4260 or 877/512–8184* ⊕ *www.crowvalley.com*) carries ceramics, metalworks, blown glass, and sculptures. **Darvill's Bookstore** (✉ *Eastsound* ☎ *360/376–2135*) specializes in literary fiction, nautical literature, local guidebooks, and more. **Orcas Island Artworks** (✉ *Main St., Olga* ☎ *360/376–4408* ⊕ *www.orcasisland.com/artworks*) displays pottery, sculpture, jewelry, art glass, paintings, and quilts by resident artists.

8

SPORTS AND THE OUTDOORS

BICYCLES AND MOPEDS
Mountain bikes rent for about $30 per day or $100 per week. Tandem, recumbent, and electric bikes rent for about $50 per day. Mopeds rent for $20 to $30 per hour or $60 to $70 per day.

The Boardwalk (⊠ *Orcas Village* ☎ *360/376–2791* ⊕ *www.orcas-islandboardwalk.com*), at the ferry landing, rents road and mountain bikes. **Dolphin Bay Bicycles** (⊠ *Orcas Village* ☎ *360/376–4157 or 360/376–6734* ⊕ *www.rockisland.com/~dolphin*), at the ferry landing, rents road, mountain, and BMX bikes for children and adults. **Orcas Moped Rentals** (⊠ *Orcas Village* ☎ *360/376–5266*), at the ferry landing, rents mopeds and bicycles. **Wildlife Cycles** (⊠ *Eastsound* ☎ *360/376–4708* ⊕ *www.wildlifecycles.com*) rents bikes and can recommend routes all over the island.

BOATING AND SAILING
Amante Sail Tours (⊠ *Deer Harbor* ☎ *360/376–4231*) offers half-day sailing trips for up to six people for $35 per person. **Deer Harbor Charters** (⊠ *Deer Harbor* ☎ *360/376–5989 or 800/544–5758* ⊕ *www.deerharborcharters.com*), an eco-conscious outfitter (they were the first in the San Juans to use biodiesel), has several small sailboats making half-day cruises around the San Juans for marine-wildlife viewing. Rates are $52 to $75 per person. Outboards and skiffs are also available, as is fishing gear. **Orcas Boat Rentals** (⊠ *Deer Harbor* ☎ *360/376–7616* ⊕ *www.orcasboats.com*) has sailboats, outboards, and skiffs for full- and half-day trips. **West Beach Resort** (✛ *3 mi west of Eastsound* ☎ *360/376–2240 or 800/937–8224* ⊕ *www.westbeachresort.com*) rents motorized boats, kayaks and canoes, and fishing gear.

SCUBA DIVING
Island Dive & Water Sports (⊠ *Rosario Resort, Eastsound* ☎ *360/378–2772 or 800/303–8686* ⊕ *www.divesanjuan.com*) has a dive shop with rentals and offers a complete program of services, including instruction, air fills, and charter trips. Two custom dive boats make two-tank dives for $79 with gear; resort packages are available. **West Beach Resort** (⊠ *West Beach* ☎ *360/376–2240 or 877/937–8224*) is a popular dive spot where you can fill your own tanks.

SEA KAYAKING
All equipment is usually included in a rental package or tour. One-hour trips cost around $30; three-hour tours, about $50; day tours, $95–$120; and multiday tours, about $125 per day.

Crescent Beach Kayaks (⊠ *Eastsound* ☎ *360/376–2464* ⊕ *crescentbeach-kayaks.com*) caters to families with free instruction and kayak rentals. **Orcas Outdoors Sea Kayak Tours** (⊠ *Orcas Village* ☎ *360/376–2222* ⊕ *www.orcasoutdoors.com*) has one-, two-, and three-hour journeys, as well as day trips, overnight tours, and rentals. **Shearwater Adventures** (⊠ *Eastsound* ☎ *360/376–4699* ⊕ *www.shearwaterkayaks.com*) holds kayaking classes and runs three-hour, day, and overnight tours from Rosario, Deer Harbor, West Beach, and Doe Bay resorts.

WHALE-WATCHING
Cruises, which run about four hours, are scheduled daily in summer and once or twice weekly at other times. The cost is around $50 per person, and boats hold 20 to 40 people. Wear warm clothing and bring a snack.

Deer Harbor Charters (☎ *360/376–5989 or 800/544–5758 ⊕ www. deerharborcharters.com*) has whale-watching cruises around the island straits. **Eclipse Charters** (☎ *360/376–6566 ⊕ www.orcasislandwhales. com*) searches around Orcas Island for whale pods and other wild-life. **Whale Spirit Adventures** (⊠ *West Sound Marina ☎ 360/376–5052 or 800/376–8018*) offers whale-sighting tours to the accompaniment of new-age chanting or flutes.

SAN JUAN ISLAND

45 mins by ferry from Orcas Island, 75 mins by ferry from Anacortes.

San Juan is the cultural and commercial hub of the archipelago that shares its name. Friday Harbor, the county seat, is larger and more vibrant than any of the towns on Orcas or Lopez, yet San Juan still has miles of rural roads, uncrowded beaches, and rolling woodlands. It's easy to get here, too, making San Juan the preferred destination for travelers who have time to visit only one island.

Lummi Indians were the first settlers on San Juan, with encampments along the north end of the island. North-end beaches were especially busy during the annual salmon migration, when hundreds of tribal members would gather along the shoreline to fish, cook, and exchange news. Many of the Lummi tribe were killed by smallpox and other imported diseases in the 18th and 19th centuries. Smallpox Bay was where tribal members plunged into the icy water to cool the fevers that came with the disease.

The 18th century brought explorers from England and Spain, but the island remained sparsely populated until the mid-1800s. From the 1880s Friday Harbor and its newspaper were controlled by lime-company owner and Republican bigwig John S. McMillin, who virtually ran San Juan Island as a personal fiefdom from 1886 until his death in 1936. The town's main street, rising from the harbor and ferry landing up the slopes of a modest hill, hasn't changed much in the past few decades, though the cafés and shops are snazzier now than they were in the 1960s and '70s. San Juan is the most convenient Pacific Northwest island to visit, since you can take the ferry here and explore the entire island by public transportation or bicycle.

EXPLORING

To watch whales cavorting in Haro Strait, head to **Lime Kiln Point State Park,** on San Juan's western side just 6 mi from Friday Harbor. A rocky coastal trail leads to lookout points and a little white 1914 lighthouse. The best period for sighting whales is from the end of April through August, but a resident pod of orcas regularly cruises past the point. This park is also a beautiful spot to soak in a summer sunset, with expansive views of Vancouver Island and beyond. ⊠ *1567 Westside Rd.* ☎ *360/378–2044* ☜ *Free* ☉ *Daily 8 AM–10 PM; lighthouse tours May–Sept. at 3 and 5.*

It's hard to believe that fashionable **Roche Harbor** at the northern end of San Juan Island was once the most important producer of builder's lime on the West Coast. In 1882 John S. McMillin gained control of the lime company and expanded production. But even in its heyday as a limestone quarrying village, Roche Harbor was known for abundant flowers and welcoming accommodations. McMillin transformed a bunkhouse into private lodgings for his invited guests, who included such notables as Teddy Roosevelt. The guesthouse is now the Hotel de Haro, which displays period photographs and artifacts in its lobby. The staff has maps of the old quarry, kilns, and the Mausoleum, an eerie Greek-inspired memorial to McMillin.

McMillin's heirs operated the quarries and plant until 1956, when they sold the company to the Tarte family. Although the old lime kilns still stand below the bluff, the company town has become a posh resort. Locals say it took two years for the limestone dust to wash off the trees around the harbor. McMillin's former home is now a restaurant, and workers' cottages have been transformed into comfortable visitors' lodgings. With its rose gardens, cobblestone waterfront, and well-manicured lawns, Roche Harbor retains the flavor of its days as a hangout for McMillin's powerful friends—especially since the sheltered harbor is very popular with well-to-do pleasure boaters.

The **San Juan Historical Museum**, in an old farmhouse, presents island life at the turn of the 20th century through historic photography, documents, and buildings. ⊠ *405 Price St.* ☎ *360/378–3949* ⊕ *www.sjmuseum.org* ✉ *$5* ⊙ *Nov.–Mar. by appointment; Apr. and Oct., Sat. 1–4; May–Sept., Wed.–Sat. 10–4, Sun 1–4.*

Ⓒ **San Juan Island National Historic Park** commemorates the Pig War, in which
★ the United States and Great Britain nearly went to war over their respective claims on the San Juan Islands. The dispute began in 1859 when an American settler killed a British soldier's pig, and escalated until roughly 500 American soldiers and 2,200 British soldiers with five warships were poised for battle. Fortunately, no blood was spilled and the disagreement was finally settled in 1872 in the Americans' favor, with Emperor William I of Germany as arbitrator.

The park comprises two separate areas on opposite sides of the island. English Camp, in a sheltered cove of Garrison Bay on the northern end, includes a blockhouse, a commissary, and barracks. A popular (though steep) hike is to the top of Young Hill, from which you can get a great view of northwest side of the island. American Camp, on the southern end, has a visitor center and the remains of fortifications; it stretches along driftwood-strewn beaches. Many of the American Camp's walking trails are through prairie; in the evening, dozens of rabbits emerge from their warrens to nibble in the fields. Great views greet you from the top of the Mt. Finlayson Trail—if you're lucky, you might be able to see Mt. Baker and Mt. Rainier along with the Olympics. From June to August you can take guided hikes and see reenactments of 1860s-era military life. ⊠ *American Camp, 6 mi southeast of Friday Harbor; English Camp, 9 mi northwest of Friday Harbor; park headquarters, 125 Spring St., Friday Harbor* ☎ *360/378–2240* ⊕ *www.nps.gov/sajh* ✉ *Free* ⊙ *American Camp visitor center, June–Sept., daily*

The Whale Museum at Friday Harbor on San Juan Island

8:30–5; Oct.–May, Wed.–Sun. 8:30–4:30. *English Camp visitor center, June–Sept., daily 9–5.*

☾ The **Westcott Bay Institute for Art & Nature** is essentially a 19-acre open-air
★ art gallery within the spectacular Westcott Bay Reserve. You can stroll along winding trails to view more than 100 sculptures spread amid freshwater and saltwater wetlands, open woods, blossoming fields, and rugged terrain. The park is also a haven for birds; more than 120 species nest and breed here. Art workshops and events are scheduled throughout the year in the tented area. ⊠ *Westcott Dr. off Roche Harbor Rd.* ☎ *360/370–5050* ⊕ *www.wbay.org* ✉ *Free* ☾ *Daily dawn–dusk.*

☾ A stairwell painted with a life-size underwater mural leads you to the **Whale Museum.** Models of whales and whale skeletons, recordings of whale sounds, and videos of whales are the attractions. Head around to the back of the first-floor shop to view maps of the latest orca pod trackings in the area. ⊠ *62 1st St. N, Friday Harbor* ☎ *360/378–4710* ⊕ *www.whale-museum.org* ✉ *$6* ☾ *Daily 10–5.*

WHERE TO EAT AND STAY

$–$$ ✕ **Backdoor Kitchen.** This local favorite has finally become known beyond
ECLECTIC San Juan County. As the name might indicate, it's a bit hard to find: The restaurant is tucked in an elegant courtyard a few blocks uphill from the water. The excellent service here complements the star dishes, which include fresh mahimahi baked in tomato-saffron broth, and a Vietnamese-style seared duck breast. Local greens and produce are used often, and the Northwest-heavy wine list cements the Backdoor's status as a regional gem. ⊠ *400-B A St., Friday Harbor* ☎ *360/378–9540*

8

⊕ *backdoorkitchen.com* ▭ *AE, MC, V* ⊘ *No lunch. Dinner hours vary seasonally; call ahead.*

$$$–$$$$

NEW AMERICAN

Fodor's Choice

★

✕ **Duck Soup Inn.** Blossoming vines thread over the cedar-shingled walls of this restaurant. Inside, island-inspired paintings and a flagstone fireplace are the background for creative meals served at comfortable booths. Everything is made from scratch daily, from the sourdough bruschetta to the ice cream. You might start with shrimp- and cheese-stuffed hot chilis, served with a lime-mango sauce and cilantro; or perhaps house-smoked Jones Family Farm oysters from Lopez Island. For a second course, you might have grilled Alaskan sea scallops or a juniper-rubbed filet mignon. Vegetarian options and child portions are available. An excellent selection of Northwest, Californian, and European wines is also on hand. ✉ *50 Duck Soup La.* ☎ *360/378–4878* ⊕ *www. ducksoupinn.com* ▭ *MC, V* ⊘ *Closed Nov.–Mar.; Mon.–Thurs. Oct., Apr., and May; Mon. and Tues. in June; Mon. July–Sept. No lunch.*

$$–$$$

⊡ **Friday Harbor House.** This contemporary hotel takes advantage of its bluff-top location with floor-to-ceiling windows that overlook the marina, ferry landing, and San Juan Channel below. Sleek, modern wood furnishings and fabrics in beige hues fill the rooms, all of which have fireplaces, deep jetted tubs, and at least partial views of the water (be sure to request a marina-view room at booking). The elegant restaurant serves seasonal meals and special wine-tasting dinners, often to a backdrop of glowing sunsets in summer. **Pros:** very comfortable rooms; amazing views. **Cons:** slightly dated decor; tiny lobby. ✉ *130 West St., Friday Harbor* ☎ *360/378–8455* ⊕ *www.fridayharborhouse. com* ⌂ *23 rooms* ⌂ *In-room: refrigerator, Ethernet. In-hotel: restaurant, no-smoking rooms* ▭ *MC, V* ⓘ◎ *CP.*

$–$$

★

⊡ **Kirk House Bed and Breakfast.** Steel magnate Peter Kirk had this Craftsman bungalow built as a summer home in 1907. Rooms are all differently decorated: the Garden Room has a botanical motif, the sunny Trellis Room is done in soft shades of yellow and green, and the Arbor Room has French doors leading out to the garden. You may take breakfast in the parlor—or have it in bed, served on antique Limoges china. Bountiful wicker-basket picnics, with all the trimmings, can be prepared for a day's excursion—but you might not need one after the full breakfast provided each morning. **Pros:** convenient location; yummy breakfasts. **Cons:** tiny bathrooms; two-night minimum stay in high season. ✉ *595 Park St., Friday Harbor* ☎ *360/378–3757 or 800/639–2762* ⊕ *www.kirkhouse.net* ⌂ *4 rooms* ⌂ *In-room: no a/c, no phone, DVD, Wi-Fi. In-hotel: no kids under 10, no-smoking rooms* ▭ *MC, V* ⓘ◎ *BP.*

$–$$

⊡ **Roche Harbor Resort.** First a log trading post built in 1845, and later an 1880s lime-industry complex, including hotel, homes, and offices, this sprawling resort is still centered around the lime deposits that made John S. McMillin his fortune in the late 19th century. Rooms are filled with notable antiques, like the claw-foot tub where actor John Wayne used to soak. Luxury suites in the separate McMillan House have fireplaces, heated bathroom floors, and panoramic water views from a private veranda. The beachside Company Town Cottages, once the homes of lime-company employees, have rustic exteriors but modern interiors.

Elsewhere are contemporary condos with fireplaces; some have lofts and water views. Walking trails thread through the resplendent gardens and the old lime quarries. **Pros:** beautiful grounds; luxurious accommodations. **Cons:** pricey; a bit snooty. ⊠ *4950 Reuben Memorial Dr., 10 mi northwest of Friday Harbor off Roche Harbor Rd., Roche Harbor* ☎ *360/378–2155 or 800/451–8910* ⊕ *www.rocheharbor.com* ⬎ *16 rooms without bath, 14 suites, 9 cottages, 20 condos* ♿ *In-room: kitchen (some), refrigerator (some), DVD (some), no TV (some). In-hotel: 3 restaurants, tennis court, pool, spa* ⊟ *AE, MC, V.*

SHOPPING

Friday Harbor is the main shopping area, with dozens of shops selling a variety of art, crafts, and clothing created by residents, as well as a bounty of island-grown produce. From May to September, the **San Juan Island Farmers' Market** (⊠ *2nd St., Friday Harbor* ☎ *360/378–5240* ⊕ *www.sjifarmersmarket.com*) fills a parking lot two blocks northwest of town on Saturday from 10 to 5.

Arctic Raven Gallery (⊠ *130 S. 1st St.* ☎ *360/378–3433* ⊕ *www.arctic-ravengallery.com*) features a wide variety of Northwest native art, including scrimshaw and wood carvings. **Waterworks Gallery** (⊠ *315 Spring St., Friday Harbor* ☎ *360/378–3060* ⊕ *www.waterworksgallery. com*) represents eclectic, contemporary artists.

Near Friday Harbor, the **San Juan Vineyards** (⊠ *3136 Roche Harbor Rd.* ☎ *360/378–9463* ⊕ *www.sanjuanvineyards.com*), 3 mi north of Friday Harbor, has a winery, tasting room, and gift shop, and organizes such special events as May barrel tastings, "Bottling Day" in July, volunteer grape harvesting in October, and winter wine classes and tastings. Visit **Westcott Bay Sea Farms** (⊠ *904 Westcott Dr., off Roche Harbor Rd.* ☎ *360/378–2489* ⊕ *www.westcottbay.com*), a rustic oyster farm tucked into a small bay 2 mi south of Roche Harbor, for some of the tasty oysters, especially from November through April.

SPORTS AND THE OUTDOORS

BEACHES **American Camp** (✛ *6 mi southeast of Friday Harbor* ☎ *360468–3663*), part of San Juan Island National Historical Park, has 6 mi of public beach on the southern end of the island. **San Juan County Park** (⊠ *380 Westside Rd., Friday Harbor* ☎ *360/378–2992*) has a wide gravel beachfront where orcas often frolic in summer, plus grassy lawns with picnic tables and a small campground.

BICYCLES AND MOPEDS You can rent standard, mountain, and BMX bikes for $30 per day or $100 per week. Tandem, recumbent, and electric bikes rent for about $50 per day. You can rent mopeds for $20 to $30 per hour or $60 to $70 per day. Make sure to reserve bikes and mopeds a few days ahead in summer.

Island Bicycles (⊠ *380 Argyle Ave., Friday Harbor* ☎ *360/378–4941* ⊕ *www.islandbicycles.com*) is a full-service shop that rents bikes. **Island Scooter & Bike Rental** (⊠ *Friday Harbor* ☎ *360/378–8811*) has bikes and scooters for rent. **Susie's Mopeds** (⊠ *125 Nichols, Friday Harbor* ☎ *360/376–5244 or 800/532–0087*) rents mopeds and bicycles. There is another location in Roche Harbor near the airport.

8

A solitary boat in San Juan Island's Friday Harbor

BOATING AND SAILING Fees for moorage at private docks are $8 per night for boats under 26 feet long and $11 per night for larger vessels. Moorage buoys are $5 a night. Fees are paid in cash on-site, while annual permits ($50–$80) are available from shops in Friday Harbor. At public docks, high-season moorage rates are 70¢–$1.75 per foot (of vessel) per night.

Port of Friday Harbor (☎ *360/378–2688* ⊕ *www.portfridayharbor.org*) provides marina services including guest moorage, vessel assistance and repair, bareboat and skippered charters, overnight accommodations, and wildlife and whale-watching cruises. **Roche Harbor Marina** (☎ *360/378–2155* ⊕ *www.rocheharbor.com*) has a fuel dock, pool, grocery, and other guest services. **Snug Harbor Resort Marina** (☎ *360/378–4762*) provides marina services and van service to and from Friday Harbor, including ferry and airport shuttle service, and rents small powerboats.

CHARTERS Charter sailboat cruises start at about $225 per day and run up to $400 per day for deluxe vessels. Charter powerboat trips start at about $150 per day. Extra costs for overnight cruises may include skipper fees ($150–$175), meals ($10–$15 per person daily), preboarding fees ($50–$100), and so on.

Amante Sail Tours (☎ *360/376–4231*) leads morning and afternoon sails for two to six guests. **Cap'n Howard's Sailing Charters** (☎ *360/378–3958 or 360/317–8421* ⊕ *www.capnhoward.com*) hires out full-size vessels for sailing excursions around the islands. **Charters Northwest** (☎ *800/426–2313* ⊕ *www.abcyachtcharters.com*) offers three-day and weeklong full-service sailboat and powerboat charters. **Harmony Charters** (☎ *360/468–3310* ⊕ *www.interisland.com/countess*) conducts daylong

SEATTLE TO SNOQUALMIE FALLS

Spring and summer snowmelt creates a thundering torrent at Snoqualmie Falls: the water pours over a 268-foot rock ledge (100 feet higher than Niagara Falls) to a 65-foot-deep pool. A 2-acre park and observation platform afford views of the falls and the surrounding area, and the 3-mi round-trip River Trail winds through trees and over open slopes to the base of the cascade (⊕ *www. snoqualmiefalls.com*).

Directions from Downtown Seattle: I–5 South to I–90 East. Take the Highway 18 West exit (Exit 25). Turn left onto Highway 18. Turn left onto Railroad Ave. SE (WA-202) for about a mile. Total Time: about 45 min.

The vintage cars of the **Snoqualmie Valley Railroad**, built in the mid-1910s for the Spokane, Portland, and Seattle Railroad, travel between the landmark 1890 Snoqualmie Depot and North Bend. The 110-minute (round-trip) excursion passes through woods, past waterfalls, and around patchwork farmland. ⊠ *38625 S.E. King St., at*

Hwy. 202 ☎ *425/888–3030* ⊕ *www. trainmuseum.org* ☉ *Rides May–Sept.*

For a sublime stay right over Snoqualmie Falls, check into **Salish Lodge** ($$–$$$), a stunning, chalet-style inn. Eight rooms have gorgeous views of the cascades, while others have a river panorama. All the luxurious quarters have featherbeds, fireplaces, whirlpool baths, terry robes, and window seats or balconies. The spa offers relaxing and purifying treatments after a day of kayaking, golfing, or hiking. The elegant Dining Room restaurant serves such eclectic delicacies as wild Scottish partridge, herb-crusted John Dory fillet, and potato-wrapped elk loin; weekend brunches are elaborate. In the cozy and more casual Attic bistro, you can still sample fine Northwest wines. ⊠ *6501 Railroad Ave. SE, Snoqualmie* ☎ *425/888–2556* ⊕ *www. salishlodge.com* ⇨ *81 rooms, 4 suites* ♿ *In-room: safe, DVD (some). In-hotel: 2 restaurants, room service, bar, gym, spa, concierge, laundry service* ⊟ *AE, D, DC, MC, V.*

8

and multiday sailboat charters throughout the San Juan Islands and the Pacific Northwest.

SEA KAYAKING Many experienced kayakers bring their own vessels to the San Juans. But if you're a beginner or didn't bring your own kayak, you'll find many places to rent in Friday Harbor, as well as outfitters providing classes and tours. Be sure to make reservations in summer. One-hour trips start at $30, three-hour tours run about $50, day tours cost $90–$125, and overnight tours cost $100–$125 per day with meals. Equipment is always included in the cost.

A Leisure Kayak Rentals (☎ 360/378–5992 or 800/836–8224) will shuttle you from the ferry to the start of your kayaking class; hourly, daily, and overnight tours are also scheduled. **Crystal Seas Kayaking** (☎ 360/378–4223 or 877/732–7877/625–7245 ⊕ *www.crystalseas.com*) has many trip options including sunset tours and multisport tours that might include biking and camping. **Discovery Sea Kayaks** (☎ 360/378–2559 or 866/461–2559 ⊕ *www.discoveryseakayak.com*) offers both sea-kayaking adventures, including sunset trips and multiday excursions, and whale-watching tours. **San Juan Kayak Expeditions** (☎ *360/378–4436* ⊕ *www.sanjuankayak.com*) runs kayaking and camping tours in two-person kayaks. **Sea Quest** (☎ *360/378–5767 or 888/589–4253* ⊕ *www. sea-quest-kayak.com*) conducts kayak eco-tours with guides who are trained naturalists, biologists, and environmental scientists.

Whale-watching expeditions run three to four hours and around $50 per person. ■TIP→ For the best experience, look for tour companies with small boats that accommodate no more than 20 or 30 people. If booking on a larger vessel, inquire as to whether or not they always fill the boat to capacity or leave a little breathing room. Bring warm clothing even if it's a warm day.

Island Adventures (☎ *360/293–2428 or 800/465–4604* ⊕ *www.island-adventures.com*) has two tours per day from June through August that get you right up next to the orcas. **San Juan Excursions** (☎ *360/378–6636 or 800/809–4253* ⊕ *www.watchwhales.com*) offers daily whale-watching cruises. **Western Prince Cruises** (☎ *360/378–5315 or 800/757–6722* ⊕ *www.orcawhalewatch.com*) operates a four-hour narrated whale-watching tour.

THE PARKS

Washington State's vast wilderness leaves the day-tripper with far too many choices. The closest major parks—Mt. Rainier National Park, Mt. St. Helens National Volcanic Monument, and Olympic National Park—are all spectacular, and very different from each other.

Mt. Rainier is perhaps the most popular destination: it's close enough to Seattle to be an easy day trip; it has plenty of facilities for armchair or novice naturalists, as well as extremely challenging hikes and climbs; and the park is so beautiful that even the drive up to the visitor center is often reward enough for the effort.

Mt. St. Helens, close to Mt. Rainier and once just as popular, is slowly regaining attention as more of its climbing routes and hiking trails reopen. Although viewing the devastation of the 1980 eruption is still a major attraction, witnessing the rebirth underway in many areas of the park is also a major reason to go. If you've seen Mt. Rainier and want something a little different, Mt. St. Helens is a feasible day trip with plenty to offer.

Mt. Rainier, however, is really only rivaled in popularity by the Olympic Peninsula. Wilderness covers much of the rugged peninsula, which is the westernmost corner of the continental United States. Its heart of craggy mountains and a 60-mi stretch of its ocean shore are safeguarded in Olympic National Park. Here, you'll find mythic coastline and dense rain forest, two things not immediately associated with the Seattle area. Many people plan their vacations around camping and hiking in the Olympics, partly because the area is much farther from Seattle than say, Mt. Rainier, and many of its attractions could not be seen during a day trip—unless your "day" started at dawn.

MT. RAINIER NATIONAL PARK

Like a mysterious, white-clad woman, often veiled in clouds even when the surrounding forests and fields are bathed in sunlight, Mt. Rainier is the centerpiece of its namesake park. The impressive volcanic peak stands at an elevation of 14,411 feet, making it the fifth-highest peak in the lower 48 states. More than 2 million visitors a year enjoy spectacular views of the mountain and return home with a lifelong memory of its image.

The mountain holds the largest glacial system in the contiguous United States, with more than two-dozen major glaciers. On the lower slopes you find silent forests made up of cathedral-like groves of Douglas fir, western hemlock, and western red cedar, some more than 1,000 years old. Water and lush greenery are everywhere in the park, and dozens of thundering waterfalls, accessible from the road or by a short hike, fill the air with mist.

GETTING HERE

Drive south on Interstate 5 to State Route 512 (exit 127). Take SR 512 east to SR 7. Then drive south on SR 7 to SR 706 in Elbe. Finally, head east on SR 706 through Ashford to the Nisqually Entrance.

PARK ESSENTIALS

ACCESSIBILITY

The only trail in the park that is fully accessible to those with impaired mobility is Kautz Creek Trail, a ½-mi boardwalk that leads to a splendid view of the mountain. Parts of the Trail of the Shadows at Longmire and the Grove of the Patriarchs at Ohanapecosh are also accessible. Campgrounds at Cougar Rock, Ohanapecosh, and Sunshine Point have several accessible sites. All main visitor centers, as well as National Park Inn at Longmire, are accessible.

ADMISSION FEES AND PERMITS

The entrance fee of $15 per vehicle and $5 for those on foot, motorcycle, or bicycle, is good for seven days. Annual passes are $30. Climbing permits are $30 per person per climb or glacier trek. Wilderness camping permits must be obtained for all backcountry trips, and advance reservations are highly recommended.

ADMISSION HOURS

Mt. Rainier National Park is open 24/7 year-round, but with limited access in winter. Gates at Nisqually (Longmire) are staffed year-round during the day; facilities at Paradise and Ohanapecosh are open daily from late May to mid-October; and Sunrise is open daily July to early October. During off-hours you can buy passes at the gates from machines that accept credit and debit cards. Winter access to the park is limited to the Nisqually entrance, and the Jackson Memorial Visitor Center at Paradise is open on weekends and holidays in winter.

TOURS

Fodor's Choice ★ **Gray Line Bus Tours.** Join a one-day or longer sightseeing tour from Seattle to Mount Rainier and Olympic national parks, Mt. St. Helens, the North Cascades, and the Washington Wine Country (Yakima Valley).

8

✉ *4500 Marginal Way SW, Seattle* ☎ *206/624–5077 or 800/426–7532* ⊕ *www.graylineofseattle.com.*

VISITOR CENTERS

Jackson Memorial Visitor Center. High on the mountain's southern flank, this center houses exhibits on geology, mountaineering, glaciology, and alpine ecology. Multimedia programs are staged in the theater; there's also a snack bar and gift shop. This is the park's most popular visitor destination, and it can be quite crowded in summer. ✉ *Hwy. 706 E, 19 mi. east of the Nisqually park entrance* ☎ *360/569–6036* ☉ *May–mid-Oct., daily 10–6; Nov.–Apr., weekends and holidays 10–5.*

★ **Longmire Museum and Visitor Center.** Glass cases inside this museum preserve plants and animals from the park—including a stuffed cougar—and historical photographs and geographical displays provide a worthwhile overview of the park's history. The adjacent visitor center has some perfunctory exhibits on the surrounding forest and its inhabitants, as well as pamphlets and information about park activities. ✉ *Hwy. 706, 17 mi east of Ashford* ☎ *360/569–2211 Ext. 3314* ▭ *Free* ☉ *July–mid-Oct., daily 9–5; mid-Oct.–June, daily 9–4:30.*

Ohanapecosh Visitor Center. Learn about the region's dense old-growth forests through interpretive displays and videos at this visitor center, near the Grove of the Patriarchs. ✉ *Rte. 123, 11 mi north of Packwood* ☎ *360/569–6046* ☉ *Late May–Oct., daily 9–6.*

Sunrise Visitor Center. Exhibits at this center explain the region's sparser alpine and subalpine ecology. A network of nearby loop trails leads you through alpine meadows and forest to overlooks that have broad views of the Cascades and Rainier. ✉ *Sunrise Rd., 15 mi from the White River park entrance* ☎ *360/663–2425* ☉ *Early July–early Sept, daily 9–6.*

VISITOR INFORMATON

Mount Rainier National Park ✉ *Tahoma Woods, Star Rte., Ashford WA* ☎ *360/569–2211* ⊕ *www.nps.gov/mora.*

SCENIC DRIVES

★ **Chinook Pass Road.** Route 410 (the highway to Yakima) follows the eastern edge of the park to Chinook Pass, where it climbs the steep, 5,432-foot pass via a series of switchbacks. At its top, take in broad views of Rainier and the east slope of the Cascades.

★ **Mowich Lake Road.** In the northwest corner of the park, this 24-mi mountain road begins in Wilkeson and heads up the Rainier foothills to Mowich Lake, traversing beautiful mountain meadows along the way. Mowich Lake is a pleasant spot for a picnic.

Paradise Road. This 9-mi stretch of Highway 706 winds its way up the mountain's southwest flank from Longmire to Paradise, taking you from lowland forest to the ever-expanding vistas of the mountain above. Visit on a weekday if possible, especially in peak summer months, when the road is packed with cars. The route is open year-round.

Sunrise Road. This popular (read: crowded) scenic road carves its way 11 mi up Sunrise Ridge from the White River Valley on the northeast side of the park. As you top the ridge there are sweeping views of the surrounding lowlands. The road is open late June to October.

A walking path through old-growth forest at Mt. Rainier National Park

HISTORIC SITE

National Park Inn. Even if you don't plan to stay overnight, you can stop by year-round to observe the architecture of this 1917 inn, which is on the National Register of Historic Places. While you're here, relax in front of the fireplace in the lounge, stop at the gift shop, or dine at the restaurant. ⊠ *Longmire Visitor Complex, Hwy. 706, 10 mi east of Nisqually entrance, Longmire* ☎ *360/569–2411.*

SCENIC STOPS

Christine Falls. These two-tiered falls were named in honor of Christine Louise Van Trump, who climbed to the 10,000-foot level on Mt. Rainier in 1889 at the age of 9, despite having a crippling nervous-system disorder. ⊠ *Next to Hwy. 706, about 2½ mi east of Cougar Rock Campground.*

Fodor'sChoice ★ **Grove of the Patriarchs.** Protected from the periodic fires that swept through the surrounding areas, this small island of 1,000-year-old trees is one of Mount Rainier National Park's most memorable features. A 1½-mi loop trail heads through the old-growth forest of Douglas fir, cedar, and hemlock. ⊠ *Rte. 123, west of the Stevens Canyon entrance.*

★ **Narada Falls.** A steep but short trail leads to the viewing area for these spectacular 168-foot falls, which expand to a width of 75 feet during peak flow times. In winter the frozen falls are popular with ice climbers. ⊠ *Along Hwy. 706, 1 mi west of the turnoff for Paradise, 6 mi east of Cougar Rock Campground.*

☼ **Tipsoo Lake.** The short, pleasant trail that circles the lake here—ideal for families—provides breathtaking views. Enjoy the subalpine wildflower

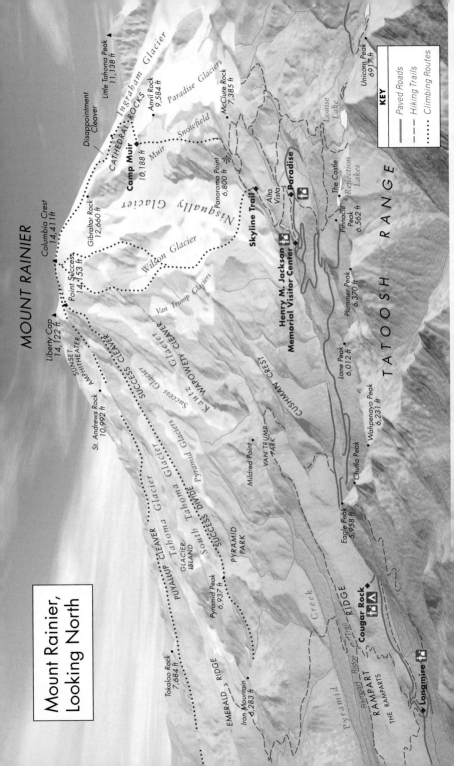

meadows during the summer months; in early fall there is an abundant supply of huckleberries. ⊠ *Off Cayuse Pass east on Hwy. 410.*

SPORTS AND THE OUTDOORS

BIRD-WATCHING

★ Be alert for kestrels, red-tailed hawks, and, occasionally, golden eagles on snags in the lowland forests. Also present at Rainier, but rarely seen, are great horned owls, spotted owls, and screech owls. Iridescent rufous hummingbirds flit from blossom to blossom in the drowsy summer lowlands, and sprightly water ouzels flutter in the many forest creeks. Raucous Steller's jays and gray jays scold passersby from trees, often darting boldly down to steal morsels from unguarded picnic tables. At higher elevations, look for the pure white plumage of the white-tailed ptarmigan as it hunts for seeds and insects in winter. Waxwings, vireos, nuthatches, sapsuckers, warblers, flycatchers, larks, thrushes, siskins, tanagers, and finches are common throughout the park.

HIKING

★ Although the mountain can seem remarkably benign on calm summer days, hiking Rainier is not a city-park stroll. Dozens of hikers and trekkers annually lose their way and must be rescued—and lives are lost on the mountain each year. Weather that approaches cyclonic levels can appear quite suddenly, any month of the year. With the possible exception of the short loop hikes listed here, all visitors venturing far from vehicle access points should carry day packs with warm clothing, food, and other emergency supplies.

EASY **Nisqually Vista Trail.** Equally popular in summer and winter, this trail is a 1¼-mi round-trip through subalpine meadows to an overlook point for Nisqually Glacier. The gradually sloping path is a favorite venue for cross-country skiers in winter; in summer, listen for the shrill alarm calls of the area's marmots. ⊠ *Trailhead at Jackson Memorial Visitor Center, Rte. 123, 1 mi north of Ohanapecosh, at the high point of Hwy. 706.*

Sourdough Ridge Trail. The mile-long loop of this self-guided trail takes you through the delicate subalpine meadows near the Sunrise Visitor Center. A gradual climb to the ridgetop yields magnificent views of Mt. Rainier and the more distant volcanic cones of Mts. Baker, Adams, Glacier, and Hood. ⊠ *Access trail at Sunrise Visitor Center, Sunrise Rd., 15 mi from the White River park entrance.*

Trail of the Shadows. This ½-mi walk is notable for its glimpses of meadowland ecology, its colorful soda springs (don't drink the water), James Longmire's old homestead cabin, and the foundation of the old Longmire Springs Hotel, which was destroyed by fire around 1900. ⊠ *Trailhead at Hwy. 706, 10 mi east of Nisqually entrance.*

MODERATE **Skyline Trail.** This 5-mi loop, one of the highest trails in the park, beck-
Fodor's Choice ons day-trippers with a vista of alpine ridges and, in summer, meadows
★ filled with brilliant flowers and birds. At 6,800 feet, Panorama Point, the spine of the Cascade Range, spreads away to the east, and Nisqually Glacier tumbles downslope. ⊠ *Jackson Memorial Visitor Center, Rte. 123, 1 mi north of Ohanapecosh at the high point of Hwy. 706.*

Van Trump Park Trail. You gain an exhilarating 2,200 feet on this route while hiking through a vast expanse of meadow with views of the

8

southern Puget Sound. The 5-mi track provides good footing, and the average hiker can make it up in three to four hours. ⊠ *Hwy. 706 at Christine Falls, 4.4 mi east of Longmire.*

DIFFICULT

Fodor's Choice

Wonderland Trail. All other Mt. Rainier hikes pale in comparison to this stunning 93-mi trek, which completely encircles the mountain. The trail passes through all the major life zones of the park, from the old-growth forests of the lowlands to the alpine meadows and goat-haunted glaciers of the highlands—pick up a mountain-goat sighting card from a ranger station or visitor center if you want to help in the park's effort to learn more about these elusive animals. Wonderland is a rugged trail; elevation gains and losses totaling 3,500 feet are common in a day's hike, which averages 8 mi. Most hikers start out from Longmire or Sunrise and take 10–14 days to cover the 93-mi route. Snow lingers on the high passes well into June (sometimes July); count on rain any time of the year. Campsites are wilderness areas with pit toilets and water that must be purified before drinking. Only hardy, well-equipped, and experienced wilderness trekkers should attempt this trip, but those who do will be amply rewarded. Wilderness permits are required, and reservations are strongly recommended. △ **Parts of the Wonderland Trail can be severely damaged due to floods. Check with a visitor center for the trail's current status.** For a summer-day hike, it's easiest to explore from Longmire, where a broad, easy section of track climbs through open, wildflower-filled slopes toward a vast panorama of ice-covered ridges. ⊠ *Longmire Visitor Center, Hwy. 706, 17 mi east of Ashford; Sunrise Visitor Center, Sunrise Rd., 15 mi west of the White River park entrance.*

MOUNTAIN CLIMBING

★ Climbing Mt. Rainier is not for amateurs; each year, climbers die on the mountain, and many climbers become lost and must be rescued. Near-catastrophic weather can appear quite suddenly, any month of the year. If you're experienced in technical, high-elevation snow, rock, and ice-field adventuring, Mt. Rainier can be a memorable adventure. Climbers can fill out a climbing card at the Paradise, White River, or Carbon River ranger stations and lead their own groups of two or more. Climbers must register with a ranger before leaving and check out upon return. A $30 annual climbing fee applies to anyone venturing above 10,000 feet or onto one of Rainier's glaciers. During peak season it is recommended that you make a climbing reservation ($20 per group) in advance; reservations are taken by fax beginning in April on a first-come, first-served basis (find the reservation form at ⊕ *www.nps.gov/mora/planyourvisit/climbing.htm*).

For climbing outfitters, ⇨ Multisport Outfitters box.

SKIING AND SNOWSHOEING

Mt. Rainier is a major Nordic ski center for cross-country and telemark skiing. Although trails are not groomed, those around Paradise are extremely popular. If you want to ski with fewer people, try the trails in and around the Ohanapecosh–Stevens Canyon area, which are just as beautiful and, because of their more easterly exposure, slightly less subject to the rains that can douse the Longmire side, even in the dead of winter. You should never ski on the plowed main roads, especially

MULTISPORT OUTFITTER

Rainier Mountaineering Inc.
Reserve a private hiking guide through this highly regarded outfitter, or take part in its one-day mountaineering classes (mid-May through late September), where participants are evaluated on their fitness for the climb and must be able to withstand a 16-mi round-trip hike with a 9,000-foot gain in elevation. The company also arranges private cross-country skiing and snowshoeing guides. ⊠ 30027 Hwy. 706 E, Ashford ☎ 888/892–5462 or 360/569–2227

⊕ www.rmiguides.com ☑ $805 for three-day summit climb package.

Whittaker Mountaineering (⊠ 30027 Hwy. 706 E, Ashford ☎ 800/238–5756 or 360/569–2142 ⊕ www.whittakermountaineering. com). You can rent hiking and climbing gear, skis, snowshoes, snowboards and other outdoor equipment through at this all-purpose Rainier Base Camp outfitter, which also arranges for private cross-country skiing and hiking guides.

in the Paradise area—the snowplow operator can't see you. No rentals are available on the eastern side of the park.

★ Deep snows make Mt. Rainier a snowshoeing pleasure. The Paradise area, with its network of trails, is the best choice. The park's east side roads, routes 123 and 410, are unplowed and provide other good snowshoeing venues, although you must share the main parts of the road with snowmobilers.

Paradise Ski Area. You can cross-country ski or, in the Snowplay Area north of the upper parking lot at Paradise, sled using inner tubes and soft platters from December to April. Check with rangers for any restrictions. In summer, many trails around this side of the mountain are accessible from Paradise. During winter, the easy, 3½-mile Nordic ski route begins at the Paradise parking lot, and follows Paradise Valley/Stevens Canyon Road to Reflection Lakes. Equipment rentals are available at Whittaker Mountaineering in Ashford, or at the National Park Inn's General Store in Longmire. ⊠ Accessible from Nisqually entrance at park's southwest corner and (summer only) from Stevens Canyon entrance at park's southeast corner ☎ 360/569–2211 ⊕ www. nps.gov/mora ☉ May–mid-Oct., daily, sunrise–sunset; mid-Oct.–Apr., weekends sunrise–sunset.

OUTFITTERS AND EXPEDITIONS Adjacent to the National Park Inn, **Rainier Ski Touring Center** (⊠ Hwy. 706, 10 mi east of Nisqually entrance, Longmire ☎ 360/569–2411; 360/569–2271 weekdays) rents cross-country ski equipment and provides lessons from mid-December through Easter, depending on snow conditions. Park rangers lead **Snowshoe Walks** (⊠ 1 mi north of Ohanapecosh on Rte. 123, at the high point of Hwy. 706 ☎ 360/569–2211 Ext. 2328 ☑ Free ☉ Late Dec.–Apr., weekends and holidays) that start at Jackson Memorial Visitor Center at Paradise and cover 1¼ mi in about two hours. Check park publications for exact dates.

WHERE TO EAT

There are a limited number of restaurants inside the park and a few worth checking out beyond its borders. Mount Rainier's picnic areas are justly famous, especially in summer, when wildflowers fill the meadows—resist the urge to feed the yellow pine chipmunks darting about.

IN THE PARK

¢   ✕ **Jackson Memorial Visitor Center.** Traditional grill fare such as hot dogs,
AMERICAN   hamburgers, and soft drinks are served daily from May through early
🖐   October and on weekends and holidays during the rest of the year.
⊠ *Rte. 123, 1 mi north of Ohanapecosh at the high point of Hwy. 706*
☎ *360/569–2211* ⊕ *www.mtrainierguestservices.com* ▤ *No credit cards*
☉ *Closed weekdays early Oct.–Apr.*

$$–$$$ ✕ **National Park Inn.** Photos of Mt. Rainier taken by some of the North-
ECLECTIC   west's top photographers adorn the walls of this inn's large dining
★   room, a bonus on the many days the mountain refuses to show itself.
Meals, served family-style, are simple but tasty: maple hazelnut chicken,
tenderloin tip stir-fry, and grilled red snapper with black bean sauce
and corn relish. For breakfast, don't miss the home-baked cinnamon
rolls with cream-cheese frosting. ⊠ *Hwy. 706, Longmire* ☎ *360/569–
2411* ⊕ *www.mtrainierguestservices.com* ⌣ *Reservations not accepted*
▤ *MC, V.*

$$–$$$ ✕ **Paradise Inn.** Where else can you get a decent Sunday brunch in a his-
CONTINENTAL   toric heavy-timbered lodge halfway up a mountain? Tall, many-paned
★   windows provide terrific views of Rainier, and the warm glow of native
wood permeates the large dining room. The lunch menu is simple and
healthy—grilled salmon, salads, and the like. For dinner, there's nothing like a hearty plate of the inn's signature bourbon buffalo meat loaf.
⊠ *Hwy. 706, Paradise* ☎ *360/569–2413* ⊕ *www.mtrainierguestservices.
com* ⌣ *Reservations not accepted* ▤ *MC, V* ☉ *Closed Oct.–late May.*

¢   ✕ **Sunshine Lodge Food Service.** A cafeteria and grill here serve inexpen-
AMERICAN   sive hamburgers, chili, hot dogs, and snacks from early July to early
🖐   September. ⊠ *Sunrise Rd., 15 mi from the White River park entrance*
☎ *360/663–2425* ⊕ *www.mtrainierguestservices.com* ▤ *No credit cards*
☉ *Closed early Sept.–early July.*

PICNIC AREAS   Park picnic areas are open July through September only.

Paradise Picnic Area. This site has great views on clear days. After picnicking at Paradise, you can take an easy hike to one of the many waterfalls in the area—Sluiskin, Myrtle, or Narada, to name a few. ⊠ *Hwy.
706, 11 mi east of Longmire.*

Sunrise Picnic Area. Set in an alpine meadow that's filled with wildflowers in July and August, this picnic area provides expansive views of the
mountain and surrounding ranges in good weather. ⊠ *Sunrise Rd., 11
mi west of the White River entrance.*

Sunshine Point Picnic Area. A small group of picnic tables at the Sunshine Point Campground sits in an open meadow along the burbling
Nisqually River. ⊠ *Hwy. 706, 1 mi east of the Nisqually entrance.*

OUTSIDE THE PARK

$$–$$$ ✕ **Alexander's Country Inn & Restaurant.** Without a doubt, this classic,
AMERICAN woodsy Northwest country inn built in 1912 serves the best food in
★ the area. Ceiling fans and wooden booths lining the walls make it look
like a country kitchen. Try the steak or trout—freshly caught from
the pond on the grounds. The homemade bread is fantastic, and the
blackberry pie is a must for dessert. Dine inside or outside on a patio
overlooking the trout pond and a waterfall. Box lunches for adventurers
are available upon request. ✉ *37515 Hwy. 706, Ashford* ☎ *360/569–
2323 or 800/654–7615* ⊕ *www.alexanderscountryinn.com* ⊟ *D, MC,
V* ⊗ *Nov.–Apr., no lunch Fri. or weekends.*

¢ ✕ **Scaleburgers.** Once a 1939 logging-truck weigh station, the building
AMERICAN is now a popular restaurant serving homemade hamburgers, fries, milk
☕ shakes. Eat outside on tables overlooking the hills and scenic railroad.
The restaurant is 11 mi west of Ashford. ✉ *54109 Mountain Hwy. E,
Elbe* ☎ *360/569–2247* ⊟ *No credit cards.*

WHERE TO STAY

The Mount Rainier area is remarkably bereft of quality lodging. Rainier's two national park lodges, at Longmire and Paradise, are attractive and well maintained. They exude considerable history and charm, especially Paradise Inn, but unless you've made summer reservations a year in advance, getting a room can be a challenge. Dozens of motels and cabin complexes are near the park entrances, but the vast majority are overpriced and no-frills. With just a few exceptions, you're better off camping.

Five drive-in campgrounds are in the park—Cougar Rock, Ipsut Creek, Ohanapecosh, Sunshine Point, and White River—with almost 700 sites for tents and RVs. None have hot water or RV hookups; showers are available at Jackson Memorial Visitor Center. For backcountry camping, you must obtain a free wilderness permit at one of the visitor centers. Primitive sites are spaced at 7- to 8-mi intervals along the Wonderland Trail. A copy of *Wilderness Trip Planner: A Hiker's Guide to the Wilderness of Mount Rainier National Park,* available from any of the park's visitor centers or through the superintendent's office, is an invaluable guide if you're planning backcountry stays. Reservations for specific wilderness campsites are available from May 1 to September 30 for $20; for details, call the Wilderness Information Center at ☎ *360/569–4453.*

IN THE PARK

$$ 🏨 **National Park Inn.** A large stone fireplace sits prominently in the common room of this country inn, the only one of the park's two inns
★ that's open year-round. Rustic details such as wrought-iron lamps and antique bentwood headboards adorn the rooms. Simple American fare is served in the restaurant *(⇨ Where to Eat).* The inn is operated as a B&B from October through April. **Pros:** classic national park ambience; only lodging inside park open in winter and spring. **Cons:** jam-packed in summer; must book far in advance; some rooms have shared bath. ✉ *Longmire Visitor Complex, Hwy. 706, 10 mi east of Nisqually entrance, Longmire* ☎ *360/569–2275* ⊕ *www.mtrainierguestservices.*

com ✈ *25 rooms, 18 with bath* ♿ *In-room: no a/c, no phone. In-hotel: restaurant* ☰ *MC, V* ⏐◉⏐ *BP.*

$$–$$$

Fodor's Choice
★

▦ **Paradise Inn.** With its hand-carved Alaskan cedar logs, burnished parquet floors, stone fireplaces, Indian rugs, and glorious mountain views, this 1917 inn is a classic example of a national park lodge. German architect Hans Fraehnke designed the decorative woodwork. In addition to the full-service dining room *(⇨ Where to Eat)*, there's a small snack bar and a snug lounge. **Pros:** central to trails; pristine vistas; nature-inspired details. **Cons:** noisy in high season. ✉ *Hwy. 706, Paradise* ⌂ *c/o Mount Rainier Guest Services, Box 108, Star Rte., Ashford 98304* ☎ *360/569–2275* ⊕ *www.mtrainierguestservices.com* ✈ *121 rooms* ♿ *In-room: no phone, no TV. In-hotel: restaurant, bar* ☰ *MC, V* ⊘ *Closed Nov.–mid-May.*

CAMPING

⛺ **Cougar Rock Campground.** A secluded, heavily wooded campground with an amphitheater, Cougar Rock is one of the first to fill up. You can reserve group sites for $3 per person, per night, with a minimum of 12 people per group. Reservations are accepted for summer only. **Pros:** ranger programs; isolated feeling. **Cons:** often crowded. ✉ *2½ mi north of Longmire* ☎ *301/722–1257 or 800/365–2267* ✈ *173 tent/RV sites* ♿ *Flush toilets, dump station, drinking water, fire grates, ranger station* ☰ *AE, D, MC, V* ⊘ *Closed mid-Oct.–Apr.*

¢ ⛺ **Mowich Lake Campground.** This is Rainier's only lakeside campground. At 4,959 feet, it's also peaceful and secluded. Note that the campground is accessible only by 5 mi of convoluted gravel roads, which are subject to weather damage and potential closure at any time. Reservations are not accepted. **Pros:** Mowich Lake setting; isolated. **Cons:** long drive on unpaved roads. ✉ *Mowich Lake Rd., 6 mi east of the park boundary* ☎ *360/568–2211* ✈ *30 tent/RV sites* ♿ *Pit toilets, running water (non-potable), fire grates, picnic tables, ranger station* ⊘ *Closed Nov.–mid-July.*

$ ⛺ **Ohanapecosh Campground.** This lush, green campground in the park's
★ southeast corner has a visitor center, amphitheater, and self-guided trail. It's one of the first campgrounds to open. Reservations are accepted for summer only. **Pros:** great for families; open in early summer. **Cons:** popularity means busy facilities. ✉ *Ohanapecosh Visitor Center, Hwy. 123, 1½ mi north of park boundary* ☎ *301/722–1257 or 800/365–2267* ✈ *188 tent/RV sites* ♿ *Flush toilets, dump station, drinking water, fire grates, ranger station* ☰ *AE, D, MC, V* ⊘ *Closed late Oct.–Apr.*

$ ⛺ **Sunshine Point Campground.** This pleasant, partly wooded campground is near the Nisqually River and the most popular entrance to the park. Sites are first-come, first-served. **Pros:** fewer campers than other spots. **Cons:** subject to spring floods; few amenities. ✉ *5 mi past the Nisqually entrance* ☎ *360/569–2211* ✈ *18 tent/RV sites* ♿ *Pit toilets, drinking water, fire grates* ☰ *AE, D, MC, V.*

$ ⛺ **White River Campground.** At an elevation of 4,400 feet, White River is one of the park's highest and least-wooded campgrounds. Here you can enjoy campfire programs, self-guided trails, and partial views of Mt. Rainier's summit. Sites are first-come, first-served. **Pros:** breathtaking scenery. **Cons:** more exposure to the elements. ✉ *5 mi west of White River entrance* ☎ *360/569–2211* ✈ *112 sites* ♿ *Flush toilets, dump* station, drinking water, fire grates, ranger station

⚐ *Reservations not accepted* ⊘ *Closed mid-Sept.–ea*

OUTSIDE THE PARK

\$\$ ★ 🏨 **Alexander's Country Inn.** Serving guests since 1912, *i* premier lodging just a mile from Mt. Rainier. Antiqu lend the main building romance; there are also two houses. Rates include a hearty breakfast and evening ..... The cozy restaurant (⇨ *Where to Eat;* closed to off-site guests weekdays in winter) is the best place in town for lunch or dinner. Stroll out back to view verdant gardens, or take a dip in a hot tub set over the trout pond. **Pros:** luxury extras; on-site day spa. **Cons:** lots of breakables means it's not great for children. ⊠ *37515 Hwy. 706 E, 4 mi east of Ashford, Ashford* 📠 *360/569–2323 or 800/654–7615* ⊕ *www.alexanderscountryinn. com* 🛏 *12 rooms, 2 3-bedroom houses* ⚐ *In-room: DVD. In-hotel: restaurant, spa* ⊟ *MC, V* ⦿I *BP.*

¢–\$\$ 🏨 **Inn of Packwood.** Cascade mountain peaks tower above this inn, centrally located in the village of Packwood. Pine paneling and furniture lend the rooms rustic charm, and you can swim in an indoor pool beneath skylights or have a picnic beneath a weeping willow. **Pros:** convenient location for exploring; between Mount Rainier and Mount St. Helens. **Cons:** not much privacy. ⊠ *13032 U.S. 12, Packwood,* 📠 *877/496–9666 or 360/494–5500* ⊕ *www.innofpackwood.com* 🛏 *33 rooms* ⚐ *In-room: kitchen (some), refrigerator (some). In-hotel: pool* ⊟ *AE, MC, V* ⦿I *CP.*

\$–\$\$\$ ★ 🏨 **Wellspring.** In the woodlands outside Ashford, the untraditional accommodations here include tastefully designed log cabins, tent cabins, a tree house, and a room in a greenhouse. The Tatoosh lodge, with space for 14, has a huge stone fireplace. Each space is individually decorated: for example, a queen-size feather bed is suspended by ropes beneath a skylight in the Nest Room. This forest-inspired collection of units, the only property of its kind in the area, is the creation of a massage therapist; a variety of spalike amenities are available. **Pros:** unique lodging option; some rooms good for groups or kids; relaxing spa influence. **Cons:** limited amenities. ⊠ *54922 Kernehan Rd., Ashford* 📠 *360/569–2514* 🛏 *1 lodge, 6 cabins, 3 tent cabins, 1 tree house, 1 cottage* ⚐ *In-room: no a/c, no phone, kitchen (some), refrigerator (some), no TV (some). In-hotel: spa* ⊟ *MC, V* ⦿I *EP, CP.*

8

MT. ST. HELENS

Approximately 155 mi southeast of Seattle (about 3 hrs).

It was once a premier camping destination, with a Mt. Fuji–like cone and pristine forest. But the May 18, 1980, eruption blew off its top and stripped its slopes of forest. The 8,365-foot-high mountain, formerly 9,665 feet high, is one of a string of volcanic Cascade Range peaks that runs from British Columbia's Mt. Garibaldi south to California's Mt. Lassen.

The mountain is open to climbers (with permits) after some activity, including a 36,000-foot plume of steam and ash, closed it to climbs in early 2005. Most people come to the park to explore the numerous hiking trails that offer views of the mountain and scenes of devastation and renewal.

The U.S. Forest Service operates the Mt. St. Helens National Volcanic Monument. The user fee is $8 per day for the Johnston Ridge Observatory. You'll also need a Northwest Forest Pass to park at trailheads, visitor centers, and other forest facilities.

Exit 63 going south on I–5 takes you to Highway 505 and onto Highway 504. Highway 504 is the main road through the Mt. St. Helens National Volcanic Monument. The Castle Rock Exit (No. 49) of I–5 is just outside the monument's western entrance. Follow 504 into the park. You can access the park from the north by taking Forest Service Road 25 south from U.S. 12 at the town of Randle. Forest Service Road 25 connects with Forest Service Road 90, which heads east from the town of Cougar. The two forest service roads are closed by snow in winter.

VISITOR INFORMATION

For information on park attractions road and trail conditions, check out the U.S. Forest Service's Mt. St. Helens Web site (⊕ *www.fs.fed. us/gpnf/mshnvm*), as well as the Web site operated by the folks at the area's most popular visitor center, the Forest Learing Center (⊕ *www. mountsthelens.com*).

On the east side of the mountain are two bare-bones visitor centers, Windy Ridge and Ape Cave. The two centers along Highway 504 on the forest's west side—Mt. St. Helens Visitor Center (at Silver Lake) and Johnston Ridge Observatory—are open daily in summer. Johnston Ridge closes from November until May; the other centers remain open daily.

Castle Rock's location on I–5 at the Spirit Lake Highway makes it a major point of entry for the Mt. St. Helens National Monument. The site takes its name from a tree-covered knob that once stood on the banks of the Cowlitz River and served as a navigational landmark for Hudson's Bay Company trappers and traders. The landscape changed dramatically when the 1980 eruption filled the Toutle and Cowlitz rivers with hot volcanic mush.

The original, state-run "SeaQuest" **Mt. St. Helens Visitor Center** (⊠ *Hwy., 5 mi east of I–5, Silver Lake* ☎ *360/274–2100*) doesn't have great views of the mountain, but it has exhibits documenting the eruption and a walk-through volcano.

☾ **Hoffstadt Bluff Visitor Center** (⊠ *Hwy., 27 mi east of I–5* ☎ *360/274–*
★ *5200*) has picnic areas; a helicopter-tour operator; hiking trails; and the Memorial Grove, which honors the 57 people who lost their lives during the 1980 eruption. Admission is free.

☾ The **Forest Learning Center** (⊠ *Hwy. 504, 33 mi east of I–5* ☎ *360/274–*
★ *2140*), a partnership between Weyerhaeuser and Washington state, highlights the recovery and reforestation of the blast zone. Elk viewing, a gift shop, indoor exhibits, and an outdoor play area make this the most popular spot to stop along 504.

Mt. St. Helens appears in the distance as a hiker prepares a meal in the Goat Rocks Wilderness.

The **Johnston Ridge Observatory** (⊠ *Hwy. 504, Milepost 52 [52 mi east of I–5]* ☎ *360/274–2140*) in the heart of the blast zone has spectacular views of the crater and lava dome. Exhibits here interpret the geology of Mt. St. Helens and explain how scientists monitor an active volcano. This is one of the best spots from which to take a great short day hike.

SPORTS AND THE OUTDOORS

CLIMBING Climbing is limited to the south side of the mountain. The most popular route delivers you to the crater's rim. Though this climb is not as technical as Mt. Rainier, making it more accessible to a wider range of visitors, climbers should be in good shape and be comfortable with traversing rugged terrain and rock scrambles. A round-trip climb takes a minimum of seven hours.

Permits (good for one day only) are required year-round. From November to March permits are free and can be obtained at any time at the **Climber's Register** (⊠ *Outside Jack's Restaurant, 13411 Lewis River Rd., Ariel* ☎ *360/231–4276*). Permits for high season, from April to October, must be purchased in advance and cost $22 per person. Permits are sold online only through the **Mt. St. Helens Institute** (⊕ *www.mshinstitute.org*). The Web site also has a good FAQ about climbing the mountain.

HIKING Mt. St. Helens also has plenty of beautiful trails—more than 200 miles' worth—that require less of a commitment than climbing the crater. For a full list of options, check out the Mount St. Helens National Volcano Monument Trail guide, which can be downloaded from the park's Web site or purchased from the park's visitor centers and at other select Forest Service offices.

★ **Ape Cave.** Ape Cave is the longest continuous lava tube in the continental United States, and one of the park's outstanding attractions. Two routes traverse the tube: the lower route is an easy hour-long hike, while the upper route is challenging (expect uneven ground and some scrambles) and takes about three hours. Be sure to bring your own light source and warm clothing—temperatures in the cave don't rise above the mid-40s. In high-season ranger-led walks are sometimes available; inquire at the headquarters. There are several above-ground trails in the area, including the Trail of Two Forests, which includes easy walks to see the remains of a lava-ravaged ancient forest and an optional 45-foot "crawl" through a tree mold. ✚ *Headquarters: From I–5 head east on Hwy. 503 and Forest Service road 90. Turn left on Forest Service road 83, then left again onto Forest Service road 8303, and follow that road to the parking lot.*

OLYMPIC NATIONAL PARK

A spellbinding setting is tucked into the country's far-northwestern corner, within the heart-shaped Olympic Peninsula. Edged on all sides by water, the forested landscape is remote and pristine, and works its way around the sharpened ridges of the snow-capped Olympic Mountains. Big lakes cut pockets of blue in the rugged blanket of pine forests, and hot springs gurgle up from the foothills. Along the coast the sights are even more enchanting: wave-sculpted boulders, tidal pools teeming with sea life, and tree-topped sea stacks.

GETTING HERE

Take a Washington State Ferry from Downtown Seattle's Colman Dock to Bainbridge Island, then drive 13 mi north on SR 305. Travel 7 mi north on SR 3 before heading north on SR 104, across the scenic Hood Canal Bridge. Merge with Highway 101 and drive 35 mi north to Port Angeles and the visitor center. Contact **Washington State Ferries** (☎ 800/843–3779 or 206/464–6400 ⊕ *www.wsdot.wa.gov/ferries*) for information. You can enter the park at a number of points, though access roads do not penetrate far, since the park is 95% wilderness. The best way to get around and to see many of the park's key sites is on foot.

PARK ESSENTIALS

ACCESSIBILITY

There are wheelchair-accessible facilities—including trails, campgrounds, and visitor centers—throughout the park; contact visitor centers for more information.

ADMISSION FEES AND PERMITS

Seven-day vehicle admission fee is $10, plus $5 for each individual; an annual family pass is $30. Parking at Ozette, the trailhead for one of the park's most popular hikes, is $1 per day.

An overnight wilderness permit, available at visitor centers and ranger stations, is $5 (covers registration of your party for up to 14 days), plus $2 per person per night. A frequent-hiker pass, which covers all wilderness use fees, is $30 per year. Fishing in freshwater streams and

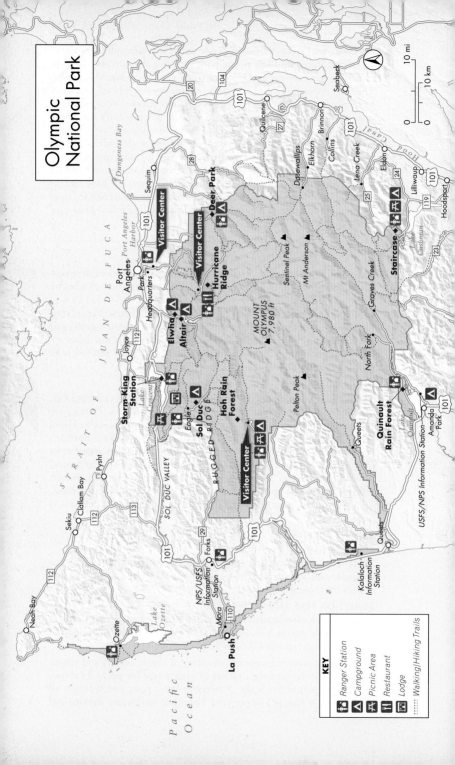

Olympic National Park

KEY

Ranger Station
Campground
Picnic Area
Restaurant
Lodge
Walking/Hiking Trails

10 mi
10 km

Dungeness Bay

Sequim

28

20

104

101

Quilcene

27

Seabeck

Brinnon

101

Hood Canal

Dosewallips

Elkhorn

Collins

Lena Creek

Eldon

24

Lilliwaup

119

101

Hoodsport

25

Port Angeles Harbor

Port Angeles

Park Headquarters

Visitor Center

Visitor Center

Deer Park

Hurricane Ridge

Elwha

Altair

Sentinel Peak

Mt Anderson

23

Lake Cushman

Staircase

MOUNT OLYMPUS 7,980 ft

Pelton Peak

North Fork

Graves Creek

STRAIT OF JUAN DE FUCA

Joyce

112

Storm King Station

Lake Crescent

Sol Duc

Eagle

RUGGED RIDGE

Hoh Rain Forest

Queets

Queets

Quinault Rain Forest

Lake Quinault

Amanda Park

101

USFS/NPS Information Station

Pysht

113

Clallam Bay

Sekiu

112

Neah Bay

112

SOL DUC VALLEY

101

29

Forks

NPS/USFS Information Station

Visitor Center

Lake Ozette

Ozette

Mora

110

La Push

Queets

Kalaloch Information Station

Pacific Ocean

DID YOU KNOW?

Encompassing more than 70 mi of beachfront, Olympic is one of the few national parks of the West with an ocean beach (Redwood, Channel Islands, and some of the Alaskan parks are the others). This rare trait means the park is home to many marine animals, including sea otters, whales, sea lions, and seals.

lakes within Olympic National Park does not require a Washington State fishing license; however, anglers must acquire a salmon-steelhead punch card when fishing for those species. Ocean fishing and harvesting shellfish and seaweed require licenses, which are available at sporting goods and outdoor supply stores.

ADMISSION HOURS

Six park entrances are open 24/7; gate kiosk hours (for buying passes) vary widely according to season and location, but most kiosks are staffed during daylight hours. Olympic National Park is located in the Pacific time zone.

VISITOR CENTERS

Forks Parks and Forest Information Center. The office has park maps and brochures; they also provide permits and rent bear-proof containers. ⊠ *Hwy. 101, Forks* ☎ *No phone* ⊕ *www.forks-web.com* ☼ *June–Aug., daily 9–4; Sept.–May, Fri.–Sun. 9–4.*

Hoh Rain Forest Visitor Center. Pick up park maps and pamphlets, permits, and activities lists in this busy, woodsy chalet; there's also a shop and exhibits on natural history. Several short interpretive trails and longer wilderness treks start from here. ⊠ *Upper Hoh Rd., Forks* ☎ *360/374–6925* ⊕ *www.nps.gov/olym* ☼ *Sept.–June daily 9–6, July and Aug., Fri.–Tues. 9–4.*

Hurricane Ridge Visitor Center. The upper level of this visitor center has exhibits, a gift shop, and a café; the lower level has open seating and nice views. Guided walks and programs start in late June, and you can also get details on the surrounding Winter Use Area ski and sledding slopes. ⊠ *Hurricane Ridge Rd., Port Angeles* ☎ *360/565–3131* ⊕ *www. nps.gov/olym* ☼ *Memorial Day–Labor Day, daily 9–7; late-Dec.–Apr., Fri.–Sun. 10–4.*

Olympic National Park Visitor Center. This modern, well-organized facility, staffed by park rangers, provides everything: maps, trail brochures, campground advice, listings of wildlife sightings, educational programs and exhibits, information on road and trail closures, and weather forecasts. ⊠ *3002 Mount Angeles Rd., Port Angeles* ☎ *360/565–3130* ⊕ *www.nps.gov/olym* ☼ *May–Sept., daily 9–4; Oct.–Apr., daily 10–4.*

South Shore Quinault Ranger Station. This office at the Lake Quinault Lodge has maps, campground information, and program listings. ⊠ *S. Shore Lake Quinault Rd., Lake Quinault* ☎ *360/288–2444* ⊕ *www. nps.gov/olym* ☼ *Memorial Day–Labor Day, weekdays 8–4:30, weekends 9–4.*

Wilderness Information Center (WIC). Located behind Olympic National Park Visitor Center, this facility provides all the information you'll need for a trip in the park, including trail conditions, safety tips, and weather bulletins. The office also issues camping permits, takes campground reservations, and rents bear-proof food canisters for $3. ⊠ *3002 Mount Angeles Rd., Port Angeles* ☎ *360/565–3100* ⊕ *www.nps.gov/olym* ☼ *Late June–Labor Day, Sun.–Thurs. 7:30–6, Fri. and Sat. 7:30–7.*

PARK CONTACT INFORMATION
Olympic National Park. (✉ *600 E. Park Ave., Port Angeles, WA* ☎ *360/565–3130* ⊕ *www.nps.gov/olym*).

SCENIC DRIVE

★ **Port Angeles Visitor Center to Hurricane Ridge.** The premier scenic drive in Olympic National Park is a steep ribbon of curves, which climbs from thickly forested foothills and subalpine meadows into the upper stretches of pine-swathed peaks. At the top, the visitor center at Hurricane Ridge has some truly spectacular views over the heart of the peninsula and across the Strait of Juan de Fuca. (Backpackers note wryly that you have to hike a long way in other parts of the park to get the kinds of views you can drive to here.) Hurricane Ridge also has an uncommonly fine display of wildflowers in spring and summer.

SCENIC STOPS

Fodor'sChoice **Hoh River Rain Forest.** South of Forks, an 18-mi spur road links Highway
★ 101 with this unique temperate rain forest, where spruce and hemlock trees soar to heights of more than 200 feet. Alders and big-leaf maples are so densely covered with mosses they look more like shaggy prehistoric animals than trees, and elk browse in shaded glens. Be prepared for precipitation: the region receives 140 inches or more each year. The visitor center is open daily July through September from 9 to 6, and Friday through Tuesday from 9 to 4 in other months. ✉ *From Hwy. 101, at about 20 mi north of Kalaloch, turn onto Upper Hoh Rd. 18 mi east to Hoh Rain Forest Visitor Center* ☎ *360/374–6925.*

Fodor'sChoice **Hurricane Ridge.** The panoramic view from this 5,200-foot-high ridge
★ encompasses the Olympic range, the Strait of Juan de Fuca, and Vancouver Island. Guided tours are given in summer along the many paved and unpaved trails, where wildflowers and wildlife such as deer and marmots flourish. ✉ *Hurricane Ridge Rd., 17 mi south of Port Angeles* ☎ *360/565–3130 visitor center* ⊙ *Visitor center daily 10–5.*

Kalaloch. With a lodge, a huge campground, miles of coastline, and easy access from the highway, this is another popular spot. Keen-eyed beachcombers may spot sea otters just offshore; they were reintroduced here in 1970. ✉ *Hwy. 101, 32 mi northwest of Lake Quinault* ☎ *360/962–2283 Kalaloch ranger station.*

Lake Crescent. Visitors see Lake Crescent as Highway 101 winds along its southern shore, giving way to gorgeous views of teal waters rippling in a basin formed by Tuscan-like hills. In the evening, low bands of clouds caught between the surrounding mountains often linger over its reflective surface. ✉ *Hwy. 101, 16 mi west of Port Angeles and 28 mi east of Forks* ☎ *360/928–3380 Storm King ranger station.*

★ **Lake Quinault.** This glimmering lake, 4½ mi long and 300 feet deep, is the first landmark you'll reach when driving the west-side loop of U.S. 101. The rain forest is thickest here, with moss-draped maples and alders, and towering spruce, fir, and hemlock. Enchanted Valley, high up near the Quinault River's source, is a deeply glaciated valley that's closer to the Hood Canal than to the Pacific Ocean. A scenic loop drive circles the lake and travels around a section of the Quinault River. ✉ *Hwy. 101,*

8

38 mi north of Hoquiam ☎ *360/288–2444 for Quinault River ranger station* ⊙ *Ranger station May–Sept., daily 8–5.*

Second and Third Beaches. During low tide, the pools here brim with life, and you can walk out to some sea stacks. Gray whales play offshore during their annual spring migration, and most of the year the waves are great for surfing and kayaking (bring a wet suit). ⊠ *Hwy. 101, 32 mi north of Lake Quinault* ☎ *360/374–5460.*

Sol Duc. Sol Duc Valley is one of those magical places where all the Northwest's virtues seem at hand: lush lowland forests, sparkling river scenes, salmon runs, and serene hiking trails. Here, the popular Sol Duc Hot Springs area includes three attractive sulfuric pools ranging in temperature from 98°F to 104°F. ⊠ *Sol Duc Rd. south of U.S. 101, 1 mi past the west end of Lake Crescent* ☎ *360/374–6925 Hoh Rain Forest Visitor Center.*

Staircase. Unlike the forests of the park's south and west sides, Douglas fir is the dominant tree on the east slope of the Olympic Mountains. Fire has played an important role in creating the majestic forest here, as the Staircase Ranger Station explains in interpretive exhibits. ⊠ *At end of Rte. 119, 15 mi from U.S. 101 at Hoodsport* ☎ *360/877–5569 Staircase Ranger Station.*

SPORTS AND THE OUTDOORS

BEACHCOMBING

★ The wild, shell-strewn Pacific coast teems with tide pools and clawed creatures. Crabs, sand dollars, anemones, starfish, and all sorts of shell-fish are exposed at low tide, when flat beaches can stretch out for hundreds of yards. The most easily accessible sand-strolling spots are Rialto, Ruby, First, and Second beaches, near Mora and La Push, and Kalaloch Beach and Fourth Beach in the Kalaloch stretch.

The Wilderness Act and the park's code of ethics instruct visitors to leave all nonliving materials where they are for others to enjoy.

BICYCLING

The rough gravel car tracks to some of the park's remote sites were meant for four-wheel-drive vehicles, but can double as mountain-bike routes. The Quinault Valley, Queets River, Hoh River, and Sol Duc River roads have bike paths through old-growth forest. Graves Creek Road, in the southwest, is a mountain-bike path; Lake Crescent's north side is also edged by the bike-friendly Spruce Railroad Trail. More bike tracks run through the adjacent Olympic National Forest. Note that Highway 101 has heavy traffic and isn't recommended for cycling, although the western side has broad roads with beautiful scenery and can be biked off-season. Bikes are not permitted on foot trails.

OUTFITTERS AND EXPEDITIONS **Bicycle Adventures** (☎ *360/786–0989 or 800/443–6060* ⊕ *www. bicycleadventures.com*), an Olympia bike tour outfit, stages trips in and around the park area, including up Hurricane Ridge. **Mike's Bikes** (⊠ *150 W. Sequim Bay Rd., Sequim* ☎ *360/681–3868* ⊕ *www.mikes-bikes.net*), a bike, gear, and repair shop, is a great resource for advice on routes around the Olympic Peninsula. **Peak 6** (⊠ *4883 Upper Hoh Rd., Forks* ☎ *360/374–5254*), an adventure store on the way to the Hoh Rain

Forest Visitor Center, rents mountain bikes. **Sound Bike & Kayak** (✉ *120 E. Front St., Port Angeles* ☎ *360/457–1240* ⊕ *www.soundbikeskayaks. com*) rents and sells biking equipment.

CLIMBING

At 7,980 feet, Mt. Olympus is the highest peak in the park and the most popular climb in the region. To attempt the summit, participants must register at the Glacier Meadows Ranger Station. Mt. Constance, the third-highest Olympic peak at 7,743 feet, has a well-traversed climbing route that requires technical experience; reservations are recommended for the Lake Constance stop, which is limited to 20 campers. Mt. Deception is another possibility, though tricky snows have caused fatalities and injuries in the last decade. Climbing season runs from late June through September. Note that crevasse skills and self-rescue experience are highly recommended. Climbers must register with park officials and purchase wilderness permits before setting out. The best resource for climbing advice is the Wilderness Information Center in Port Angeles.

OUTFITTERS AND EXPEDITIONS **Alpine Ascents** (✉ *121 Mercer St., Seattle* ☎ *206/378–1927* ⊕ *www. alpineascents.com*) leads tours of the Olympic ranges. **Mountain Madness** (✉ *4218 S.W. Alaska St., Ste. 206, Seattle* ☎ *206/937–8389 or 800/328– 5925* ⊕ *www.mountainmadness.com*) offers adventure trips to summits around the Olympic Peninsula. **Olympic Mountaineering** (✉ *140 W. Front St., Port Angeles* ☎ *360/452–0240* ⊕ *www.olymtn.com*) sells mountaineering gear and organizes climbs and hikes in the park.

FISHING

Bodies of water throughout the park offer numerous fishing possibilities. Lake Crescent is home to cutthroat and rainbow trout, as well as petite kokanee salmon; Lake Cushman, Lake Quinault, and Ozette Lake have trout, salmon, and steelhead; and Lake Mills has three trout varieties. As for rivers, the Bogachiel and Queets have steelhead salmon in season. The glacier-fed Hoh River is home to chinook salmon April to November, and coho salmon from August through November; the Sol Duc River offers all five species of salmon, plus cutthroat and steelhead trout. Rainbow trout are also found in the Dosewallips, Elwha, and Skykomish rivers. Other places to go after salmon and trout include the Duckabush, Quillayute, Quinault, and Salmon rivers. A Washington state punch card is required during salmon-spawning months; fishing regulations vary throughout the park. Licenses are available from sporting goods and outdoor supply stores.

OUTFITTERS AND EXPEDITIONS **Bob's Piscatorial Pursuits** (☎ *866/347–4232* ⊕ *www.piscatorialpursuits. com*), based in Forks, offers year-round fishing trips around Olympic. **Blue Sky Outfitters** (✉ *9674 50th Ave. SW, Seattle* ☎ *8206/938–4030 or 800/228–7238* ⊕ *www.blueskyoutfitters.com*), in Seattle, organizes custom-tailored fishing trips. White-water rafting trips are another specialty. **Kalaloch Lodge** (✉ *157151 U.S. 101, Forks* ☎ *360/962–2271 or 866/525–2562* ⊕ *www.visitkalaloch.com*) organizes guided fishing expeditions around the Olympic Peninsula.

HIKING

Know your tides, or you might be trapped by high water. Tide tables are available at all visitor centers and ranger stations. Remember that a wilderness permit is required for all overnight backcountry visits.

Outfitters and Expeditions Peak 6 (⊠ *4883 Upper Hoh Rd., Forks* ☎ *360/374–5254*) runs guided hiking and camping trips. **Timberline Adventures** (☎ *800/417–2453* ⊕ *www.timbertours.com*) does weeklong excursions around the Olympic Peninsula.

EASY **Hoh Valley Trail.** Leaving from the Hoh Visitor Center, this rain forest jaunt takes you into the Hoh Valley, wending its way alongside Fodor'sChoice the river, through moss-draped maple and alder trees, and past open ★ meadows where elk roam in winter. ⊠ *Hoh Visitor Center, 18 mi east of U.S. 101.*

DIFFICULT **Hurricane Ridge Trail.** A 0.25-mi alpine loop, most of it wheelchair-accessible, leads through wildflower meadows overlooking numerous vistas of the interior Olympic peaks to the south and a panorama of the Strait of Juan de Fuca to the north. ⊠ *Hurricane Ridge Rd., 17 mi south of Port Angeles.*

MODERATE **Boulder Creek Trail.** The 5-mi round-trip walk up Boulder Creek leads to a half-dozen hot spring pools of varying temperatures; some are clothing-optional. ⊠ *End of the Elwha River Rd., 4 mi south of Altair Campground.*

Cape Alva Trail. Beginning at Ozette, this 3-mi trail leads from the forest ★ to wave-tossed headlands. ⊠ *End of the Hoko-Ozette Rd., 26 mi south of Hwy. 112, west of Sekiu.*

Graves Creek Trail. This 6-mi-long moderately strenuous trail climbs from lowland rain forest to alpine territory at Sundown Pass. Due to spring floods, a fjord halfway up is often impassable in May and June. ⊠ *End of S. Quinault Valley Rd., 23 mi east of U.S. 101.*

Sol Duc Trail. The 1.5-mi gravel path off Sol Duc Road winds through Fodor'sChoice thick Douglas fir forests toward the thundering, three-chute Sol Duc ★ Falls. Just 0.1 mi from the road, below a wooden platform over the Sol Duc River, you'll come across the 70-foot Salmon Cascades. In late summer and autumn, thousands of salmon negotiate 50 mi or more of treacherous waters to reach the cascades and the tamer pools near Sol Duc Hot Springs. The popular 6-mi **Lovers Lane Loop Trail** links the Sol Duc falls with the hot springs. You can continue up from the falls 5 mi to the **Appleton Pass Trail**, at 3,100 feet. From there you can hike on to the 8.5-mi mark, where views at the High Divide are from 5,050 feet. ⊠ *Sol Duc Rd., 11 mi south of U.S. 101.*

High Divide Trail. A 9-mi hike in the park's high country defines this trail, which includes some strenuous climbing on its last 4 mi before topping out at a small alpine lake. A return loop along High Divide wends its way an extra mile through alpine territory, with sensational views of Olympic peaks. This trail is only for dedicated, properly equipped hikers who are in good shape. ⊠ *End of Sol Duc River Rd., 13 mi south of U.S. 101.*

Sol Duc Trail

KAYAKING AND CANOEING

Lake Crescent, a serene expanse of teal-colored waters surrounded by deep-green pine forests, is one of the park's best boating areas. Note that the west end is for swimming only; no speedboats are allowed here.

Lake Quinault has boating access from a gravel ramp on the north shore. From U.S. 101, take a right on North Shore Road, another right on Hemlock Way, and a left on Lakeview Drive. There are plank ramps at Falls Creek and Willoughby campgrounds on South Shore Drive, 0.1 mi and 0.2 mi past the Quinault Ranger Station, respectively.

Lake Ozette, with just one access road, is a good place for overnight trips. Only experienced canoe and kayak handlers should travel far from the put-in, since fierce storms occasionally strike—even in summer.

OUTFITTERS AND EXPEDITIONS **Fairholm General Store** (⊠ *U.S. 101, Fairholm* ☎ *360/928–3020* ⊕ *www.fairholmstore.com*) rents rowboats and canoes on Lake Crescent for $10 to $45. It's at the lake's west end, 27 mi west of Port Angeles. **Lake Crescent Lodge** (⊠ *416 Lake Crescent Rd.* ☎ *360/928–3211* ⊕ *www.lakecrescentlodge.com*) rents rowboats for $8.50 per hour and $35 per day. **Log Cabin Resort** (⊠ *Piedmont Rd., off U.S. 101* ☎ *360/928–3325* ⊕ *www.logcabinresort.net*), 17 mi west of Port Angeles, has boat rentals for $10 to $30. The dock provides easy access to Lake Crescent's northeast section. **Rain Forest Paddlers** (⊠ *4882 Upper Hoh Rd., Forks*

A view of meandering Sol Duc Trail

☎ *360/374–5254 or 866/457–8398* ⊕ *www.rainforestpaddlers.com*) takes kayakers down the Lizard Rock and Oxbow sections of the Hoh River.

WHERE TO EAT

The major resorts are your best bets for eating out in the park. Each has a main restaurant, café, and/or kiosk, as well as casually upscale dinner service, with regional seafood, meat, and produce complemented by a range of microbrews and good Washington and international wines. Reservations are either recommended or required.

Outside the park, Port Angeles is the place to go for a truly spectacular meal; several restaurants are internationally renowned by diners and chefs alike, and most are run by famous former chefs. Dozens of small, easygoing eateries offering hearty American-style fare line the main thoroughfares in Forks and Sequim.

IN THE PARK

$$–$$$
AMERICAN
★
✕ **Kalaloch Lodge.** A tranquil country setting and ocean views create the perfect backdrop for savoring local dinner specialties like cedar-planked salmon, fresh shellfish, wild mushrooms, and well-aged beef. Note that seating is every half hour after 5, and reservations are recommended. Hearty breakfasts and sandwich-style lunches are more casual. ✉ *157151 Hwy. 101, Kalaloch* ☎ *866/525–2562* ▭ *AE, MC, V.*

$$–$$$
AMERICAN
★
✕ **Lake Crescent Lodge.** Part of the original 1916 lodge, the fir-paneled dining room overlooks the lake; you also won't find a better spot for a view of the sunset. Entrées include crab cakes, grilled salmon, halibut fish-and-chips, classic American steaks, and elk ribs. A good Northwest wine list complements the menu. Note that meals are only offered

during set hours, but appetizers are served in the lounge—or out on the Sun Porch—from 2 to 10. ✉ *416 Lake Crescent Rd., Port Angeles* ☎ *360/928–3211* ☜ *Reservations essential* ▭ *AE, D, DC, MC, V* ⊙ *Closed mid-Oct.–May.*

$$–$$$
AMERICAN

✗ **The Springs Restaurant.** The main Sol Duc Hot Springs Resort restaurant is a rustic, fir-and-cedar paneled dining room surrounded by trees. Big breakfasts are turned out daily 7:30 to 10; dinner is served daily between 5:30 and 9 (lunch and snacks are available 11 to 4 at the Poolside Deli or Espresso Hut). Evening choices include Northwest seafood and game highlighted by fresh-picked fruits and vegetables. ✉ *12076 Sol Duc Rd., at U.S. 101, Port Angeles* ☎ *360/327–3583* ▭ *AE, D, MC, V* ⊙ *Closed mid-Oct.–mid-May.*

PICNIC AREAS

All Olympic National Park campgrounds have adjacent picnic areas with tables, some shelters, and restrooms, but no cooking facilities. The same is true for major visitor centers, such as Hoh Rain Forest. Drinking water is available at ranger stations, interpretive centers, and inside campgrounds.

East Beach Picnic Area. Set on a grassy meadow overlooking Lake Crescent, this popular swimming spot has six picnic tables and vault toilets. ✉ *At the far east end of Lake Crescent, off Hwy. 101, 17 mi west of Port Angeles.*

La Poel Picnic Area. Tall firs lean over a tiny gravel beach at this small picnic area, which has five picnic tables and a splendid view of Pyramid Mountain across Lake Crescent. ✉ *Off Hwy. 101, 22 mi west of Port Angeles.*

Rialto Beach Picnic Area. Relatively secluded at the end of the road from Forks, this is one of the premier day-use areas in the park's Pacific coast segment. This site has 12 picnic tables, fire grills, and vault toilets. ✉ *Rte. 110, 14 mi west of Forks.*

OUTSIDE THE PARK

$$$–$$$$
FRENCH
Fodor'sChoice
★

✗ **C'est Si Bon.** Far more Euro-savvy than is typical on the Olympic Peninsula, this first-rate restaurant stands out for its decor as well as for its food. The fanciful dining room is done up in bold red hues, with crisp white linens, huge oil paintings, and glittering chandeliers; the spacious solarium takes an equally formal approach. The changing menu highlights homemade onion soup, Cornish hen, Dungeness crab soufflé, and filet mignon. The wine list is superb, with French, Australian, and Northwest choices to pair with everything. ✉ *23 Cedar Park Rd., Port Angeles* ☎ *360/452–8888* ⊕ *www.cestsibon-frenchcuisine.com* ☜ *Reservations essential* ▭ *AE, DC, MC, V* ⊙ *Closed Mon. No lunch.*

$–$$
AMERICAN
★

✗ **Deckside Grill.** With tremendous views of John Wayne Marina and Sequim Bay, this family restaurant is a fun place to watch the ships placidly sail by. The casual menu includes coconut prawns, pasta, grilled chicken, and sandwiches. The kitchen also serves up excellent steak and lamb. ✉ *2577 W. Sequim Bay Rd., Sequim* ☎ *360/683–7510* ▭ *AE, D, MC, V* ⊙ *Closed Mon. and Tues.*

$$–$$$
SEAFOOD
★

✗ **Three Crabs.** An institution since 1958, this large crab shack on the beach, 5 mi north of Sequim, specializes in Dungeness's famed crustacean. Although the clawed creatures are served many ways here, these crabs are so fresh that it's best to simply have them with lemon and but-ter. ⊠ *11 Three Crabs Rd., Sequim* ☎ *360/683–4264* ⊕ *www.the3crabs. com* ⊟ *MC, V* ⊗ *Closed Mon. and Tues.*

WHERE TO STAY

Major park resorts run from good to terrific, with generally comfort-able rooms, excellent facilities, and easy access to trails, beaches, and activity centers. Midsize accommodations, like Sol Duc Hot Springs Resort, are often shockingly rustic—but remember, you're here for the park, not for the rooms.

The towns around the park have motels, hotels, and resorts for every budget. For high-priced stays with lots of perks, base yourself in Port Angeles. Sequim has many attractive, friendly B&Bs, plus lots of inex-pensive chain hotels and motels. Forks is basically a motel town, with a few guesthouses around its fringes.

ABOUT THE CAMP-GROUNDS
Note that only a few places take reservations; if you can't book in advance, you'll have to arrive early to get a place. Each site usually has a picnic table and grill or fire pit, and most campgrounds have water, toilets, and garbage containers; for hookups, showers, and laundry facilities, you'll have to head into the towns. Firewood is available from camp concessions, but if there's no store you can collect dead wood within 1 mi of your campsite. Dogs are allowed in campgrounds, but not on trails or in the backcountry. Trailers should be 21 feet long or less (15 feet or less at Queets Campground). There's a camping limit of two weeks.

If you have a backcountry pass, you can camp virtually anywhere throughout the park's forests and shores. Overnight wilderness permits are $5—plus $2 per person per night—and are available at visitor cen-ters and ranger stations. Note that when you camp in the backcountry, you must choose a site at least ½ mi inside the park boundary.

IN THE PARK

$$$–$$$$
🏠 **Kalaloch Lodge.** A two-story cedar building overlooking the Pacific, Kalaloch has cozy rooms with sea views. The surrounding log cabins have a fireplace or woodstove, knotty-pine furnishings, earth-tone fab-rics, and kitchenettes; the main lodge houses rustic oceanview rooms and suites; and wood-paneled motel-style quarters are in the Seacrest Building. Guests have pool privileges at the Lake Quinault Resort; tow-els are provided. The restaurant's ($$–$$$) menu changes seasonally, but usually includes local oysters, crab, and salmon. **Pros:** ranger tours; clam digging; supreme storm watching in winter. **Cons:** some units are two blocks from main lodge; cabins can smell like pets. ⊠ *157151 U.S. 101* ⌂ *HC 80, Box 1100, Forks 98331* ☎ *360/962–2271 or 866/525–2562* ⊕ *www.visitkalaloch.com* ⇆ *10 lodge rooms, 6 motel rooms, 3 motel suites, 44 cabins* ⌂ *In-room: no phone, kitchen, no TV. In-hotel: restaurant, bar, some pets allowed* ⊟ *AE, D, MC, V.*

$$–$$$
🏠 **Lake Crescent Lodge.** Deep in the forest at the foot of Mt. Storm King, this comfortable 1916 lodge has a wraparound veranda and picture windows that frame the lake's sapphire waters. Rooms in the rustic Roosevelt Cottage have polished wood floors, stone fireplaces, and lake views, while Tavern Cottage quarters resemble modern motel

rooms. The historic lodge has second-floor rooms with shared baths. The lodge's fir-paneled dining room ($$–$$$) overlooks the lake, and the adjacent lounge is often crowded with campers. Seafood dishes like grilled salmon or steamed Quilcene oysters highlight the restaurant menu; reservations are required. **Pros:** gorgeous setting; free wireless access in the wilderness. **Cons:** no laundry; Roosevelt Cottages must be booked a year in advance. ⊠ *416 Lake Crescent Rd., Port Angeles* ☎ *360/928–3211* ⊕ *www.lakecrescentlodge.com* ⟲ *30 motel rooms, 17 cabins, 5 lodge rooms with shared bath* ☼ *In-room: no phone, no TV. In-hotel: 2 restaurants* ⊟ *AE, DC, MC, V* ☽ *Closed Nov.–Apr.*

$$$–$$$$ 🏨 **Lake Quinault Lodge.** On a lovely glacial lake in Olympic National Forest, this beautiful early-20th-century lodge complex is within walking distance of the lakeshore and hiking trails in the spectacular old-growth forest. A towering brick fireplace is the centerpiece of the great room, where antique wicker furnishings sit beneath ceiling beams painted with Native American designs. In the rooms, modern gadgets are traded in for old-fashioned comforts, such as claw-foot tubs, fireplaces, and walking sticks. The lively bar is a good place to unwind after a day outdoors, and the restaurant ($$$–$$$$) serves upscale seafood entrées like baked salmon with capers and onions. **Pros:** hosts summer campfires with s'mores; family-friendly ambience. **Cons:** kayaks and canoes rent out quickly in the summer. ⊠ *South Shore Rd., Box 7, Quinault* ☎ *360/288–2900 or 800/562–6672* ⊕ *www.visitlakequinault.com* ⟲ *92 rooms* ☼ *In-room: no phone, no TV (some). In-hotel: restaurant, bar, pool, some pets allowed* ⊟ *AE, D, MC, V.*

$–$$ 🏨 **Log Cabin Resort.** This rustic hotel has an idyllic setting at the northeast end of Lake Crescent. Settle into one of the A-frame chalet units, standard cabins, small camping cabins, motel units, or RV sites, which include full hookups. Some rooms have full kitchens. Twelve of the units are on the lake. You can rent paddleboats or kayaks to use by the day. **Pros:** bikes and boats available on-site; weekly ranger talks. **Cons:** cabins are very rustic. ⊠ *3183 E. Beach Rd., Port Angeles* ☎ *360/928–3325* ⊕ *www.logcabinresort.net* ⟲ *4 lodge rooms, 24 cabins, 40 RV sites* ☼ *In-room: no a/c, no phone, no TV. In-hotel: restaurant, laundry facilities, Wi-Fi hotspot* ⊟ *D, MC, V* ☽ *Closed Nov.–Mar.*

$$–$$$ 🏨 **Sol Duc Hot Springs Resort.** Deep in the brooding forest along the Sol Duc River, this remote 1910 resort is surrounded by 5,000-foot-tall mountains. The main draw is the pool area, which surrounds a gathering of soothing mineral baths, and has a freshwater swimming pool. Some forest cabins have kitchens, but all are spartan; however, after a day's hike, a dip, and dinner at the Springs Restaurant ($$–$$$), you'll hardly notice. The attractive fir-and-cedar paneled dining room serves unpretentious meals all day, drawing on top Northwest seafood and produce. **Pros:** nearby trails; peaceful setting. **Cons:** steep pool rates. ⊠ *12076 Sol Duc Rd.* ☏ *Box 2168, Port Angeles 98362* ☎ *360/327–3583 or 866/476–5382* ⊕ *www.visitsolduc.com* ⟲ *32 rooms, 6 cabins* ☼ *In-room: no a/c (some), no phone (some), kitchen (some), no TV (some). In-hotel: restaurant, bar, pool* ⊟ *AE, DC, MC, V* ☽ *Closed mid-Oct.–mid-Apr.*

8

CAMPING   ⚠ **Altair Campground.** This small campground sits amid an old-growth
$ forest by the river in the rather narrow Elwha River Valley. The 3-mi
West Elwha Trail leads downstream from the campground. **Pros:** river
views; immediate hiking options. **Cons:** noisy on summer weekends.
⊠ *Elwha River Rd., 8 mi south of U.S. 101, Olympic National Park*
📞 *No phone* 🛏 *30 tent/RV sites* ♿ *Flush toilets, drinking water, fire
grates* ⊗ *Closed Nov.–Mar.*

$ ⚠ **Deer Park Campground.** At 5,400 feet, this is the park's only drive-to
alpine campground. The part-gravel access road is steep and winding; RVs are prohibited. **Pros:** shaded sites; easy access by road. **Cons:**
motor noises. ⊠ *Deer Park (Blue Mountain) Rd., 21 mi south of U.S.
101, Olympic National Park* 📞 *No phone* 🛏 *14 tent sites* ♿ *Pit toilets,
drinking water, fire grates* ⊗ *Closed Oct.–Apr.*

$ ⚠ **Elwha Campground.** The larger of the Elwha Valley's two camp-
grounds, this is one of Olympic's year-round facilities. Two campsite
loops lie in an old-growth forest. **Pros:** spur-of-the-moment camping
opportunity because it's not usually full; amphitheater nearby. **Cons:** no
water in winter. ⊠ *Elwha River Rd., 7 mi south of U.S. 101, Olympic
National Park* 📞 *No phone* 🛏 *40 tent/RV sites* ♿ *Pit toilets, drinking water (summer only), fire grates, public telephone, ranger station*
🚏 *MC, V.*

$ ⚠ **Fairholme Campground.** One of just three lakeside campgrounds in the
★   park, Fairholm is near the Lake Crescent Resort. There is an on-site
boat launch. **Pros:** gorgeous setting; well placed for lakeside explora-
tions. **Cons:** very popular. ⊠ *U.S. 101, 28 mi west of Port Angeles, on
the west end of Lake Crescent, Olympic National Park* 📞 *No phone*
🛏 *88 tent/RV sites* ♿ *Flush toilets, dump station, drinking water, fire
grates, public telephone, swimming (lake)* ⊗ *Closed Nov.–Mar.*

$ ⚠ **Heart O' the Hills Campground.** At the foot of Hurricane Ridge in a
grove of tall firs, this popular year-round campground offers a regular
slate of summer programs. **Pros:** lots of activities; closest campground to
the ridge. **Cons:** only accessible on foot during off-season. ⊠ *Hurricane
Ridge Rd., 4 mi south of the main park visitor center in Port Angeles,
Olympic National Park* 📞 *No phone* 🛏 *105 tent/RV sites (tent-only
in winter)* ♿ *Flush toilets, drinking water, fire grates, public telephone,
ranger station.*

$ ⚠ **Hoh Campground.** Crowds flock to this rain-forest site, near the Hoh
Visitor Center under a canopy of moss-draped maples and towering
spruce trees. **Pros:** kid-friendly day hikes; animal sightings. **Cons:** bears
are sometimes spotted, especially during salmon season. ⊠ *Hoh River
Rd., 17 mi east of U.S. 101, Olympic National Park* 📞 *No phone* 🛏 *88
tent/RV sites* ♿ *Flush toilets, dump station, drinking water, fire grates,
public telephone, ranger station* 🚏 *MC, V.*

$–$$ ⚠ **Kalaloch Campground.** Kalaloch is the biggest and most popular
Olympic campground, and it's open all year. Its vantage of the Pacific
is unmatched on the park's coastal stretch—although the campsites
themselves are set back in the spruce fringe. **Pros:** bluff-top views,
beach access. **Cons:** no reservations taken mid-September–mid-June.
⊠ *U.S. 101, ½ mi north of the Kalaloch Information Station, Olympic
National Park* 📞 *360/962–2271 group bookings* 🛏 *175 tent/RV sites*

⛲ *Flush toilets, dump station, drinking water, fire grates, public telephone, ranger station* = *MC, V.*

$$ ⛰ **Lake Quinault Rain Forest Resort Village Campground.** Stretching along the south shore of Lake Quinault, this RV campground has many recreation facilities, including beaches, canoes, ball fields, and horseshoe pits. Cabins, suites, and apartments are also available. **Pros:** close to Salmon House restaurant; on-site grocery. **Cons:** very busy in summer. ⊠ *3½ mi east of U.S. 101, South Shore Rd., Lake Quinault* ☎ *360/288–2535 or 800/255–6936* ◈ *www.rainforestresort.com* 📥 *31 RV sites* ⛲ *Flush toilets, full hookups, drinking water, showers, grills, picnic tables, electricity, public telephone, general store* = *AE, D, MC, V* ☀ *Closed Nov.–Mar.*

$ ⛰ **Mora Campground.** Along the Quillayute estuary, this campground
★ doubles as a popular staging point for hikes northward along the coast's wilderness stretch. **Pros:** some sites have river views; quick drive to Rialto Beach. **Cons:** throngs of hikers in summer. ⊠ *Rte. 110, 13 mi west of Forks, Olympic National Park* ☎ *No phone* 📥 *94 tent/RV sites (1 walk-in)* ⛲ *Flush toilets, dump station, drinking water, fire grates, public telephone, ranger station.*

$ ⛰ **North Fork Campground.** The park's smallest campground is for self-sufficient travelers who want to enjoy the rain forest in peace. It's deep, wet woods here; RVs are not advised. **Pros:** good place to find solitude. **Cons:** damp setting; primitive. ⊠ *N. Quinault Valley Rd., 19 mi east of U.S. 101, Olympic National Park* ☎ *No phone* 📥 *7 tent sites* ⛲ *Pit toilets, fire grates, ranger station* ☀ *Closed Oct.–Apr.*

$ ⛰ **Ozette Campground.** Hikers heading to Cape Alava, a scenic promontory that is the westernmost point in the lower 48 states, use this lakeshore campground as a jumping-off point. There's a boat launch and a small beach. **Pros:** water activities; stunning panoramas. **Cons:** often closes in winter. ⊠ *Hoko-Ozette Rd., 26 mi south of Hwy. 112, Olympic National Park* ☎ *No phone* 📥 *15 tent/RV sites* ⛲ *Pit toilets, fire grates, ranger station* = *MC, V* ☀ *Call ahead in winter.*

$ ⛰ **Sol Duc Campground.** Sol Duc resembles virtually all Olympic campgrounds save one distinguishing feature—the famed hot springs are a short walk away. **Pros:** easy access to pools; waterfalls close by, too. **Cons:** no water in winter. ⊠ *Sol Duc Rd., 11 mi south of U.S. 101, Olympic National Park* ☎ *360/327–3534* 📥 *82 tent/RV sites* ⛲ *Flush toilets, dump station, drinking water (spring–fall), fire grates, public telephone, ranger station, swimming (hot springs)* ☀ *Closed Nov.–Apr.*

$ ⛰ **Staircase Campground.** In deep woods away from the river, this campground is a popular jumping-off point for hikes into the Skokomish River Valley and the Olympic high country. **Pros:** some sites are next to the river; running water in summer. **Cons:** Staircase Road is closed to vehicles in winter. ⊠ *Rte. 119, 16 mi northwest of U.S. 101, Olympic National Park* ☎ *No phone* 📥 *56 tent/RV sites (tent-only in winter)* ⛲ *Flush toilets, drinking water, fire grates, public telephone, ranger station.*

8

OUTSIDE THE PARK

$$$–$$$$

FodorsChoice

★

☆ **Colette's Bed & Breakfast.** A contemporary mansion curving around 10 acres of gorgeous waterfront property, this B&B offers more space, service, and luxury than any other property in the area. Leather sofas and chairs and a river-rock fireplace make the front room a lovely spot to watch the water through expansive 20-foot windows. The suites, which have such names as Iris, Azalea, and Cedar, also overlook the water and have fireplaces, balconies, CD and DVD players, and two-person hot tubs. A specially made outdoor fireplace means you can enjoy the deck even in winter. Multicourse breakfasts include espresso-based drinks and fresh fruit. **Pros:** water views to Victoria, BC; discreet personal service. **Cons:** does not cater to families. ⌂ *339 Finn Hall Rd., 10 mi east of town, Port Angeles* ☎ *360/457–9197 or 888/457–9777* ⊕ *www.colettes.com* ➪ *5 suites* ⚲ *In-room: refrigerator. In-hotel: restaurant, no kids under 18* ⊟ *MC, V* ⦿ *BP.*

$$$–$$$$

☆ **Quality Inn Uptown.** South of town, at the green edge of the Olympic Mountain foothills, this inn offers a stunning panorama of mountain and harbor scenes. Perks include free wireless Internet and nightly cookies. **Pros:** central location; great views. **Cons:** always busy. ⌂ *101 E. 2nd St., Port Angeles* ☎ *360/457–9434 or 800/858–3812* ⊕ *www.qualityinnportangeles.com* ➪ *51 rooms* ⚲ *In-room: kitchen (some), refrigerator, Wi-Fi. In-hotel: Wi-Fi hotspot* ⊟ *AE, D, DC, MC, V* ⦿ *BP.*

Travel Smart
Seattle

WORD OF MOUTH

"I strongly recommend a Washington State Ferry Ride through the San Juan Islands. Check here for schedules: www.wsdot.wa.gov/ferries. You can also catch the Victoria Clipper for an overnight to Victoria, B.C."

—rolohof_duvall

GETTING HERE AND AROUND

Hemmed in by mountains, hills, and multiple bodies of water, Seattle is anything but a linear, grid-lined city. Twisty, turny, and very long, the city can be baffling to navigate, especially if you delve into its residential neighborhoods—and you should. A good map can help you confidently explore, and you can use the transportation advice in this section to plan your wanderings around the city's sometimes confusing layout. If all else fails, don't hesitate to ask a Seattleite for directions—most residents are friendly and happy to help.

▮ AIR TRAVEL

Nonstop flying time from New York to Seattle is approximately 5 hours; flights from Chicago are about 4–4½ hours; flights between Los Angeles and Seattle take 2½ hours; flights between London and Seattle are about 9½ hours.

Seattle is a hub for regional air service, air service to Alaska, Hawaii, and Canada, as well as for some carriers to Asia. It's also a convenient North American gateway for flights originating in Australia, New Zealand, and the South Pacific. But it's a long westbound flight to Seattle from Europe. Such flights often stop in New York; Washington, D.C.; Boston; or Chicago after crossing the Atlantic, but nonstop flights are definitely available, if a bit pricier.

Airlines and Airports Airline and Airport Links.com (⊕ www.airlineandairportlinks.com) has links to many of the world's airlines and airports.

Airline Security Issues Transportation Security Administration (⊕ www.tsa.gov) has answers for almost every question that might come up. Check here as well for the latest safety regulations. As threat levels ebb and flow, new regulations can pop up overnight. It's best to check the day before your flight for any recent additions to ensure you aren't stuck throwing out any expensive products or scrambling to find the right identification.

AIRPORTS

The major gateway is Seattle–Tacoma International Airport (SEA), known locally as Sea-Tac. The airport is south of the city and reasonably close to it—non-rush-hours trips to Downtown sometimes take less than a half hour. Sea-Tac is a midsize, modern airport that is usually pleasant to navigate through. Our only complaint: inexplicably long waits at the baggage claim, especially at night when they seem to send all flights to one or two carousels.

Sea-Tac has a few restaurants, but no fancy facilities, so don't arrive hours before your flight and expect to be entertained.

Charter flights and small carriers like Kenmore Air that operate shuttle flights between the cities of the Pacific Northwest land at Boeing Field, which is between Sea-Tac and Seattle.

Airport Information Boeing Field (☎ 206/296–7380 ⊕ www.kingcounty.gov/ transportation/kcdot/Airport.aspx). **Seattle– Tacoma International Airport** (☎ 206/787– 5388 ⊕ www.portseattle.org/seatac).

GROUND TRANSPORTATION

Sea-Tac is about 15 mi south of Downtown on I–5 (from the airport, follow the signs to I–5 North, then take the Seneca Street Exit for Downtown). Although it can take as little as 30 minutes to ride between Downtown and the airport, if you're traveling during rush hour, it's best to allow at least an hour for the trip in case of traffic snarls.

Metered cabs cost around $37 (not including tip) between the airport and Downtown, though some taxi companies offer a flat rate to Sea-Tac from select Downtown hotels. Expect to pay $40–$50 to Capitol Hill, Queen Anne or the neighborhoods directly north of the canal. Seattle has a small cab fleet, so expect long waits if a

NAVIGATING SEATTLE

■ Downtown and adjacent Belltown are the easiest neighborhoods to explore and are therefore the one part of the city where you're least likely to need—or want—a car. Also bear the following tips in mind as you navigate the city.

■ Water makes the best landmark. Both Elliott Bay and Lake Union are pretty hard to miss. When you are trying to get your bearings Downtown, Elliott Bay is a much more reliable landmark than the Space Needle.

■ Remember that I-5 literally bisects the city (north–south), and there are limited places at which to cross it (this goes for pedestrians and drivers). From Downtown to Capitol Hill, cross using Pike, Pine, Madison, James, or Yesler; from Lake Union or Seattle Center to Capitol Hill, use Denny; above the Lake Washington Ship Canal (the "canal"), 45th, 50th, and 80th are the major streets running all the way east–west. East–west travel is usually more laborious than north–south trips, so plan accordingly, particularly during rush hour.

■ The major north–south routes connecting the southern part of the city to the northern part are I-5, Aurora Avenue/Hwy. 99, 15th Avenue NW (Ballard Bridge), and Westlake (Fremont Bridge) and Eastlake avenues. With the exception of some difficult on-ramps, I-5 is easy to navigate. Note that Aurora has a limited number of signed exits north of the canal (mostly you just turn directly onto side streets) and a limited number of exits in general Downtown (after the Denny exit if you're heading north to south). Some of the Downtown exits are on the left-hand side, making this road a bit more confusing if you don't know where you're going.

■ Public buses provide a sufficient (if sometimes frustrating) system that's best used to move between Downtown and Capitol Hill or Queen Anne. To get from Downtown to Seattle Center, use the monorail. To get from Downtown to Pioneer Square, walk down 1st Avenue or jump on a south-bound the bus on 1st Avenue. (Note that walking is often the fastest solution around Downtown and Belltown.) Using the bus system to get from Downtown to the neighborhoods above the canal can sometimes be a slow process during non-peak travel times, but trips directly to downtown Ballard and Phinney Ridge/Greenwood are fairly straightforward and efficient.

■ Streets in the Seattle area generally travel east to west, whereas avenues travel north to south. Downtown roads are straightforward: avenues are numbered west to east (starting with 1st Avenue by Elliott Bay and ending with 39th Avenue by Lake Washington), streets are named, and a rough grid pattern can be discerned. Above the Lake Washington Ship Canal, east to west streets are mostly numbered, starting with N. 34th Street in Fremont and going up into the 100s as you head into the northern suburbs. Here, the system for avenues makes much less sense; they're mostly named, but a few are numbered. West of I-5, 1st Avenue NW starts in Fremont, and numbers increase as you go west toward Shilshole Bay, ending with 36th Avenue NW. East of I-5, 1st Avenue NE starts in Wallingford, and the numbers increase as you go toward Lake Washington, ending at 50th Avenue NE.

■ Directionals are often attached to street names. N (north) is for Queen Anne, Seattle Center, and Fremont, Wallingford, and Green Lake. NE (northeast) is for the University District, and NW (northwest) designates Ballard. S (south) marks Downtown streets around Pioneer Square and the International District. SW (southwest) means West Seattle. E (east) designates Capitol Hill and Madison Park, and W (west) means Queen Anne and Magnolia.

lot of flights arrive at the same time, especially late at night.

Shuttle Express has the only 24-hour door-to-door shared van service. Rates vary depending on destination, number of people in your party, and how many bags you have, but a one-way trip to the Downtown hotel area for one adult with two bags is around $32. You can make arrangements at the Shuttle Express counter upon arrival or make advance reservations online or by phone. For trips to the airport, make reservations at least 24 hours in advance. Gray Line Downtown Airporter offers shuttle service to select Downtown hotels for $11 one-way or $18 round-trip. The shuttles run every half hour around the clock. Express Car and Atlas Towncar have limo service to and from the airport. The fare is $45 to Downtown and can be shared by up to four passengers.

■TIP→ Your least expensive transportation option is also probably the best: Sound Transit's Link Light Rail, connected to the 4th floor of the airport parking garage, will take you right to Downtown in 36 minutes for just $2.50 (youth fare is $2 and senior/disabled fare is $1.25). Trains depart every 7½ or 15 minutes, depending on the time of day and run from 5 AM to 1 AM Monday through Saturday and 6 AM to midnight on Sundays. If you don't have a lot of luggage, this is a fantastic option for reaching Downtown cheaply. Take the covered walkway from the airport to the garage, then head up one floor to the 4th floor to find the Link Light Rail station. Once you arrive in Downtown Seattle, you can catch a bus from Westlake Center to other areas of the city, if you're feeling adventurous. Metro Transit's Web site has a great trip planner that provides door-to-door itineraries, explaining any connections you may have to make if you're not staying Downtown; representatives can also help you plan your trip over the phone. Various other shuttle services exist to take passengers directly to surrounding towns and even out to places like the

islands or Mt. Rainier. Check out Sea-Tac's Web site for a list of special shuttles and buses.

Contacts **Atlas Towncar** (☎ 888/646-0606 or 206/860-7777 ⊕ www.atlastowncar.com). **Gray Line Airport Express** (☎ 800/426-7532 recorded schedule info, 206/626-5200 ⊕ www.graylineseattle.com). **Metro Transit** (☎ 206/553-3000 ⊕ tripplanner.kingcounty. gov). **Sound Transit** (☎ 800/201-4900 or 206/398-5000 ⊕ www.soundtransit.org). **Shuttle Express/Express Car** (☎ 425/981-7000 ⊕ www.shuttleexpress.com).

FLIGHTS

American, Continental, Delta, and United are among the many major domestic airlines that fly to Seattle from multiple locations. Alaska Airlines and its affiliate Horizon Air provide service from many states including Alaska and Hawaii, and often have the best fares to and from the city, as Seattle is its hub.

USAirways has flights from Philadelphia, Charlotte, Las Vegas, and Phoenix and connecting routes from most major U.S. cities. Frontier Airlines has flights from Denver, Milwaukee, and Cancun to Seattle. JetBlue has nonstop service to Seattle from New York, Los Angeles, and Boston. Hawaiian Airlines flies daily from points in Hawaii. Southwest Airlines has flights from many cities around the United States. Air Canada flies between Seattle and Vancouver, British Columbia, Calgary, and Toronto. Kenmore Air has scheduled and chartered floatplane flights from Seattle's Lake Union and Lake Washington to the San Juan Islands, Victoria, and the Gulf Islands of British Columbia.

Airline Contacts **Air Canada** (☎ 888/247-2262 ⊕ www.aircanada.com). **Alaska Airlines** (☎ 800/252-7522 ⊕ www.alaskaair.com). **American Airlines** (☎ 800/433-7300 ⊕ www. aa.com). **Continental Airlines** (☎ 800/523-3273 for U.S. and Mexico reservations, 800/231-0856 for international reservations ⊕ www.continental.com). **Delta Airlines** (☎ 800/221-1212 for U.S. reservations, 800/241-4141 for international reservations

⊕ www.delta.com). **Frontier** (☎ 800/432–1359 ⊕ www.frontierairlines.com). **Hawaiian Airlines** (☎ 800/367–5320 ⊕ www.hawaiianair. com). **jetBlue** (☎ 800/538–2583 ⊕ www. jetblue.com). **Kenmore Air** (☎ 866/435–9524 ⊕ www.kenmoreair.com). **Southwest Airlines** (☎ 800/435–9792 ⊕ www.southwest.com). **United Airlines** (☎ 800/864–8331 for U.S. reservations, 800/538–2929 for international reservations ⊕ www.united.com). **USAirways** (☎ 800/428–4322 for U.S. and Canada reservations, 800/622–1015 for international reservations ⊕ www.usairways.com).

■ BUS TRAVEL

ARRIVING AND DEPARTING

Greyhound Lines and Northwest Trailways have regular service to points throughout the Pacific Northwest, the United States, and Canada. The regional Greyhound/Trailways bus terminal at 9th Avenue and Stewart Street is convenient to all Downtown destinations.

Greyhound buses travel several times daily to major towns along I–5 and I–90. Main routes head south from Seattle through Tacoma (45 minutes to 1 hour, $7.70 to $11.75 one way), Olympia (1 hour and 35 to 45 minutes, $12.54 to $18.25 one way), and Portland (3½–4½ hours, $27.28 to $37 one way). Buses going north from Seattle pass through Mt. Vernon (1¼ hours, $11.66 to $17.25 one way), Everett (40 minutes to 1 hour, $9 to $14.25 one way), and Bellingham (2 hours, $14.96 to $21 one way), close to the Canadian border. Eastern routes head to Yakima (3 hours, $29 to $39 one way), Spokane (5½ hours to 8 hours, $39 one way), and many points in between and beyond. Fares are slightly less on weekdays and for round-trip tickets, and discounts are available for U.S. military personnel, veterans, and students. Ask about companion rates, advance purchase savings, and seasonal discounts.

Northwestern Trailways also has daily buses leaving from the Greyhound and Amtrak stations in Seattle that travel within Washington, including from Seattle south through Tacoma ($10 one way), north through Everett ($10 one way), and east through Spokane ($39 one way), as well as long-haul service from points in Idaho.

Long-Haul Bus Info Greyhound Lines (☎ 800/231–2222 or 206/628–5526 ⊕ www. greyhound.com). **Northwestern Trailways** (☎ 800/366–3830 or 206/728–5955 ⊕ www. northwesterntrailways.com).

GETTING AROUND SEATTLE

The Metropolitan Transit's transportation network is inexpensive and fairly comprehensive. So why do so many Seattleites own cars? The most definitive reason is because they can—even though traffic is bad and parking can be tight in many areas of Seattle, the city has yet to meet the level of congestion found in cities like New York and Chicago that really necessitates hanging up the driver's license for a bus pass. The city is also fairly spread out and not overly dense in many parts, allowing a good percentage of the residents to park right outside their homes (or at least the same block) for free. Travelers who come from transit-heavy cities won't be overly thrown by the bus system (although it's not as fast or convenient as a subway system) and may wonder why more Seattleites don't take advantage of the bus system. Residents will tell you that buses still take longer to make most trips, especially if transfers are involved or traffic is particularly bad; and there are long gaps in off-peak schedules—so when you factor in wait time, transit time, and the time it takes to hoof it from your house to the bus stop, a trip that takes 15 minutes by car can take 40 by bus. That said, if you're only using the buses to travel to or from Downtown to the residential neighborhoods, and around Downtown itself, then you'll probably find navigating the system easy and fairly quick. Traveling to the commercial centers of Queen Anne, Capitol Hill, Fremont, the University District, Phinney Ridge/Greenwood, and Ballard by bus from Downtown is relatively easy—from Downtown it takes 10 to 15 minutes to get to Fremont center and 25–35 minutes to get to N.W. Market Street and Ballard Avenue in Ballard. It takes 15 to 30 minutes to get from Westlake Center to the University District.

Most buses, which are wheelchair accessible, run until around midnight or 1 AM; some run all night, though in many cases taking a cab late at night is a much better solution than dealing with sporadic bus service. The visitor center at the Washington State Convention and Trade Center has maps and schedules or you can call Metro Transit directly or, better yet, check online at ⊕ *tripplanner.kingcounty.gov/*: type in your starting point, how far you're willing to walk, and your destination, and it will tell you where and when to catch your bus. If you have a phone with Web access, you can trip-plan on the go with Metro's transit application, and you can check to see if your bus is running on time or late at ⊕ *www.onebusaway.org*. Most bus stops have simple schedules posted telling you when buses arrive; bus stops Downtown often have route maps and more information. Drivers are supposed to announce all major intersections (but feel free to ask them to specifically announce your stop), and you won't have to worry about signaling for a stop at hubs or during peak hours (someone else will probably do it or there will be people waiting at each stop, so the bus will have to pull over). At less-traveled stops in residential neighborhoods and during off-peak hours, you may have to signal for the driver to pull into your stop.

Between 6 AM and 7 PM, city buses are free within the Metro Bus Ride Free Area, bounded by Battery Street to the north, 6th Avenue to the east (and over to 9th Avenue near the convention center), S. Jackson Street to the south, and the waterfront to the west; you'll pay as you disembark if you ride out of this area. Throughout King County, both one-zone fares and two-zone fares at off-peak times are $2 for adults; during peak hours (6 AM–9 AM and 3 PM–6 PM), one-zone fares are $2.25 and two-zone fares $2.75. Unless you travel outside the city limits, you'll pay one-zone fares. Youth ages 6 to 18 are $.75 at all times and up to four children under the age of 5 ride free with a paying adult. Onboard fare-collection boxes have prices posted on them. Transfers between metro buses are free for two hours; if you think you'll need one, make sure you ask the driver for a transfer slip when you get on the bus.

The $4.50 weekend and holiday pass is a bargain if you're doing a lot of touring. Valid for one day, it includes unlimited rides on metro buses and the South Lake Union Trolley. If you're going to be in town for a week or more, consider purchasing either a ticket book or an ORCA card. Ticket books get you a small discount on the overall cost of your bus travels and allow you to pay with a credit card so you don't have to fumble for cash every time you board a bus. ORCA cards are nice if you're going to be in Seattle for a while and want to explore a bit more of the area. ORCA cards are good for trips on King County Metro (Seattle and the Eastside's buses), Community Transit, Everett Transit, Kitsap Transit, Pierce Transit, Sound Transit (Link Light Rail) and the Washington State Ferry system. You can purchase ORCA cards (they cost $5 initially) or ticket books online or at the King Street Station, Westlake Center, or other Metro offices—a complete list is available online.

Fares for city buses are collected in cash or by prepaid tickets and passes *as you board* the bus heading into Downtown, and *as you exit the bus* on the way out of Downtown. There's usually a sign posted on the fare-collection box that tells you when you pay. Fare boxes accept both coins and bills, but drivers won't make change, so don't board the bus with a $5 bill and a hapless grin. If your bus pass has a magnetic strip, just run it through the reader on the fare box; if not, show it to the driver. If you have an ORCA card, simply tap it on the ORCA box. You can buy only bus passes at Metro offices or online, not on the vehicle; cash, debit cards, MasterCard, and Visa are accepted at all offices.

One thing you should prepare yourself for when taking the bus is the overwhelming possibility that there will be at least one crazy or drunk person loudly disturbing the peace. Though Seattleites have countless stories about eventful bus rides, very few of those stories involve actual threats or crimes, so you don't have to worry too much about safety. Just know that commuters rarely want to chat with strangers, so if you respond to that person who's trying a little too hard to get your attention, you're probably in for a 20-minute screed about how the government is spying on them or a way-too-detailed description of a health problem.

Other than that, riding the buses is unpleasant only during rush hours when they're packed with annoyed residents and helmed by frazzled drivers trying to stay on schedule despite the traffic.

City Bus Information Metro Transit
(☎ 206/553–3000 *for customer information, service, and schedules; press 1 for next or current bus time, 206/62–7277 for bus-pass and ticket sales* ⊕ *metro.kingcounty.gov* *and* ⊕ *tripplanner.kingcounty.gov*). **OneBus-Away** (⊕ *www.onebusaway.org*). **ORCA Card** (☎ 888/988–6722 ⊕ *www.orcacard.com*).

▌ CAR TRAVEL

If you aren't staying in a central location, you may find Seattle's transit system frustrating. Access to a car is *almost* a necessity if you want to explore the residential neighborhoods beyond their commercial centers. If you want to do side trips to the Eastside (besides downtown Bellevue, which is easily reached by bus), Mt. Rainier, or pretty much any sight or city outside the Seattle limits (with the exception of Portland, Oregon, which is easily reached by train), you will definitely need a car. Before you book a car for city-

only driving, ask your hotel if they offer car service. Many high-end hotels offer complimentary town-car service around Downtown and the immediate areas.

The best advice about driving in Seattle is to avoid driving during rush hour whenever possible. The worst tangles are on I–5 and I–90, and any street Downtown that has a major on- or off-ramp to I–5. The Fremont Bridge and the 15th Avenue Bridge also get tied up. Aurora Avenue/99 gets very busy but often moves quickly enough. Other than that, you should find driving around Seattle a lot less anxiety-inducing than driving around many other major cities. Though you'll come across the occasional road rager or oblivious driver who assumes driving an SUV makes one invincible, drivers in Seattle are generally courteous and safety-conscious—though you'll want to pay extra attention in the student-heavy areas of Capitol Hill and the U-District.

PARKING

Parking is a headache and a half in many parts of Seattle, but not anywhere as bad as most major cities. Street parking is only guaranteed in the least dense residential areas—even leafy parts of Capitol Hill are crammed full of cars all hours of the day. The north end typically has enough parking, but the central core of Ballard and Fremont can get a little hairy come evenings and weekends. The city has a good share of pay lots and garages in the central core of the city, but even the pay lots can fill up on weekend nights, particularly in Belltown and Capitol Hill. Metered street parking exists in Downtown Seattle and the commercial stretches of Capitol Hill, but consider yourself lucky if you manage to snag a spot. Meter rates and restrictions vary by neighborhood, and cost between $.75 and $2.50 per hour. Downtown only offers short-term parking, but many areas of the city allow long-term parking up to 10 hours in some neighborhoods. Although there are a few old-style coin-only meters left here and there (if you find one that's broken, don't park there or you could face a ticket), most pay stations are electronic and take either coins or debit and credit cards. You get a printed sticker noting the time your parking is up, which you affix to the curbside passenger window. Pay stations are clearly marked by signs with big white Ps in blue circles; there is usually one machine per block of parking spaces. Parking is free Sunday, holidays, and after 6 PM weekdays and Saturday. The maximum meter time is two hours, so if you plan to be Downtown longer and won't be nearby to refill the meter, find a parking lot or garage. ■TIP➔ Make sure you check the signs around your pay station for any additional restrictions—some areas Downtown don't allow street parking during the rush hours of 6 to 9 AM and 3 to 6 PM. You could park and pay and come back to find your car towed.

Street-level pay lots are the next price tier up, though Downtown they are often just as expensive (or more expensive) as garages. Rates vary greatly, but expect to pay at least $5 to $7 before tax for a few hours in Capitol Hill, Downtown, or Belltown, with a cap of around $25 for 24 hours. If a rate looks lower, it might not include tax, so read the fine print if you're on a strict budget. Some pay lots have electronic pay stations similar to metered parking—use bills or a debit or credit card to pay at the station and place the printed ticket on the driver's side dashboard—but some lots still use old-fashioned pay boxes where you shove folded-up bills into a tiny slot with the same number as the space you parked in. So make sure you have some cash on you if you're trolling for pay-lot parking. Very few pay lots have attendants; the ones that do have dedicated pay booths and uniformed employees. Also be aware that most lots don't have in-and-out privileges. Pick a centrally located lot and prepare to walk.

Most Downtown malls and high-rises have garages. Lot and garage rates begin at $5 an hour and cap off around $25 for the day. Park before 9 AM in most lots (some lots are as early as 8 AM, while others allow up to 10 AM) to take advantage of early-bird specials, which typically run $11 to $15 for up to 10 hours of parking. One of the best garages to park in is the Pacific Place mall lot: rates are reasonable, spaces are plentiful, and there's even a valet parking service for a few dollars more. Many merchants in the mall, as well as other local businesses, offer parking validation. Most garages take credit and debit cards.

Evening and weekend parking rates are usually cheaper than those on weekdays, around $10 for parking between 6 (or as early as 4 PM at some lots) and midnight and $5–$12 for parking all day on weekends. Be aware that these lowered rates can go out the window if there are popular events happening near the lots—for example, any lots near Seattle Center will be dramatically higher during a huge happening, like Bumbershoot. After 5 PM, it's just $6 to park at Pacific Place for up to four hours. The Public Market Parking Garage at Pike Place offers free parking after 5 PM for anyone patronizing many of the area's restaurants, including the Alibi Room, Le Pichet, the Pink Door, and Campagne.

A few dozen major Downtown stores, including Nordstrom, participate in the CityPark program, in which shoppers who spend at least $20 at their location get a $1 discount token for use at participating CityPark garages and lots. Tokens may also be used on King County Metro, Community Transit, and Sound Transit buses. A CityPark logo designates shops that are part of the program; garages and lots include those in the Ampco, CPS, Diamond, Imperial, Key Park, Republic, Standard, and U-Park systems, along with the various shopping mall participants' lots. In the International District, look for the dragon parking sign in shop windows; these stores also provide discount parking tokens that can be used in specific neighborhood lots.

Important: No matter where you park, always lock your car and never leave valuables in your vehicle. The city has plenty of problems with break-ins. Don't be fooled by the laid-back suburban feel of some of the residential areas—they all experience waves of car theft and vandalism.

Lastly, you may be tempted to park in large private lots like those belonging to supermarkets. You're really rolling the dice: you may get away with it at small businesses and banks during non-business hours when no one's around to enforce the rules, but large businesses like grocery stores tend to have someone patrolling the lot. If you end up getting a ticket, you'll pay $35, far more money than you'll pay at a garage or pay lot.

RENTAL CARS

Seattle has made some progress with its public transportation options in the last several years, including the addition of the Link Light Rail system, which runs between the airport and Downtown, with future (in-progress) extensions to Capitol Hill and the University of Washington. Unfortunately, the city still has some major catching up to do with cities like New York, Washington, D.C., and San Francisco. The bus is fine for getting around Downtown, Queen Anne, and Capitol Hill, and each neighborhood in itself is very walkable, but the sad truth is that if you want the freedom to fully explore the neighborhoods north of the Lake Washington Ship Canal, off-the-beaten-path destinations, or the Eastside beyond Downtown Bellevue, you'll want to rent a car. If you plan to do side trips to places like Mt. Rainier or the San Juan Islands, a rental car becomes mandatory.

Rates in Seattle vary wildly, beginning at $15 a day (if you snag your deal from an Internet discounter like Hotwire.com or Priceline.com) and up to $70 a day. This does not include the car-rental tax of 18.5%. Hunt around for deals online for the best prices—sometimes you'll get to pick up your car at the airport, or you might have to snag your vehicle from a

city lot. Try to avoid renting a car from the airport, where rental fees, surcharges, and taxes are higher. Most major rental agencies have offices Downtown or along the waterfront, within easy reach of the main hotel area. Of the major agencies at the airport, Thrifty often has the lowest rates because it does not have a counter in the airport.

Booking in advance is always a good idea—and a must on holiday weekends when Seattleites flee the city—but if you're not sure you'll need a car, don't feel compelled to rent one until you're here and you know what your needs are. Last-minute reservations may not yield the best rates, but renting a car only to pay for it to sit in your hotel's parking garage (almost no hotels offer free parking) isn't the greatest of deals either.

Almost no popular hiking trips require special vehicles—the road to Mt. Rainier, for example, is paved the whole way—but if driving 20 mi down a bumpy Forest Service dirt road to reach a remote trailhead sounds like something you want to try, you might want to make sure the vehicle you rent can handle it.

Unless you're hauling around kayaks, rent the smallest car possible, especially if you plan to do a lot of city driving. Downtown has plenty of parking garages, but they're expensive, pay lots are scarcer in other neighborhoods and often have very tight spots that require a lot of maneuvering to get into, and street parking is a headache in all but the quietest residential areas. The smaller the car, the easier it'll be to find a space.

In Washington State you must be 21 and hold a major credit card (many agencies accept debit cards with the MasterCard or Visa logo) to rent a car. Rates may be higher if you're under 25. You'll pay about $12 per day per child seat for children under age 4 or 40 pounds, or per booster seat for children ages 4 to 6 or under 60 pounds, both of which are compulsory in Washington State. You can also rent car seats and baby equipment from local services, such as Tiny Tots Travel (⊕ *www.tinytotstravel.com*).

When you reserve a car, ask about cancellation penalties, taxes, drop-off charges (if you're planning to pick up the car in one city and leave it in another), and surcharges (for being under or over a certain age, for additional drivers, or for driving across state or country borders or beyond a specific distance from your point of rental). All these things can add substantially to your costs. Request car seats and extras such as GPS when you book.

■TIP→ Make sure that a confirmed reservation guarantees you a car. Agencies sometimes overbook, particularly for busy weekends and holiday periods.

■ FERRY TRAVEL

Ferries are a major part of Seattle's transportation network, and they're the only way to reach such points as Vashon Island and the San Juans. Seattle has the largest ferry network in the country and the third largest in the world. Thousands of commuters hop a boat from Bainbridge Island, Bremerton, and other outer towns to their jobs in the city each day—which makes for a gorgeous and unusual commute. For visitors, ferries are one of the best ways to get a feel for the region and its ties to the sea (plus, they're just plain fun). You'll also get outstanding views of the skyline and the elusive Mt. Rainier from the ferry to Bainbridge.

Passenger-only King County Water Taxis depart from Seattle's Pier 50 weekdays during rush hours on runs to Vashon Island and West Seattle. The Vashon Water Taxi is $4.50 each way in cash (discounts for ORCA card users, seniors, and youth). The West Seattle Water Taxi makes a quick, journey from Pier 50 Seacrest Park in West Seattle for $3.50 each way. Pier 50 is served directly by several Metro bus routes—even if you've rented a car, it's a major hassle to park on the waterfront so bussing is the way to go.

■TIP→ Two free Metro DART shuttles take passengers directly from the West Seattle dock to the West Seattle Junction and Admiral neighborhoods. For a great, inexpensive outing, hop on the Water Taxi to West Seattle, take the free shuttle, and spend the afternoon enjoying the great shopping and restaurants in West Seattle.

Clipper Navigation operates the passenger-only *Victoria Clipper* jet catamaran service between Seattle and Victoria year-round and between Seattle and the San Juan Islands, May through September. These longer journeys are a little pricier: $73–$155 round-trip to Victoria, $70–$120 round-trip to the San Juans. Note that *Victoria Clipper* fares are less expensive if booked at least one day in advance, children under 12 are free with select trips (be sure to ask about any promotions or deals), and there are also some great package deals available online.

The Washington State Ferry system serves the Puget Sound and San Juan Islands area. Peak-season fares are charged the first Sunday in May through the second Saturday in October. However, ferry schedules change quarterly, with the summer schedule running mid-June through mid-September. Ferries around Seattle are especially crowded during the city's weekday rush hours and holiday events, while San Juan Islands ferries can be jammed on weekends, holidays, and all of mid-June through September. Be at the ferry, or have your car in line, at least 20 minutes before departure—and prepare to wait several hours during heavily traveled times (on nice days, the ferry lines can take on somewhat of a party feel, and impromptu, multicar Frisbee games are not unheard of). Walk-on space is always available; if possible, leave your car behind.

You can pick up sailing schedules and tickets on board the ferries or at the terminals, and schedules are usually posted in local businesses around the docks. The Washington State Ferry (WSF) automated hotline also provides travel details, including weekly departure and arrival times, wait times, cancellations, and seasonal fare changes. To ask questions or make international reservations for journeys to Sidney, British Columbia, call the regular WSF hotline. Note that schedules often differ from weekdays to weekends and holidays, and departure times may be altered due to ferry or dock maintenance, severe weather or tides, and high traffic volume.

Regular walk-on fares from Seattle are $6.90 to Bainbridge and Bremerton, and from Edmonds to Kingston; $4.45 from Fauntleroy in West Seattle, Point Defiance in Tacoma, or Southworth to Vashon Island; $4.10 from Mukilteo to Clinton, on Whidbey Island; and $2.65 each way between Port Townsend and Keystone, or Fauntleroy to Southworth. Round-trip rates from Anacortes to any point in the San Juan Islands run $10.10 Sunday through Tuesday and $11.20 Wednesday through Saturday. If you'd rather head to Sidney, British Columbia, from Anacortes, it will cost you $16.40 one way; or you can travel to Sidney from the San Juans for $22.55 round-trip. You'll need reservations to visit Sidney. Senior citizens (age 65 and over) and those with disabilities pay half fare; children 5–18 get a 30% discount, and those under age 6 ride free.

Peak-season vehicle fares (including one adult driver) are $11.85 from Seattle to Bainbridge and Bremerton, and from Edmonds to Kingston; $15.20 from Fauntleroy, Point Defiance, or Southworth to Vashon; $9.15 from Port Townsend to Keystone, and from Fauntleroy to Southworth; and $7 from Mukilteo to Clinton. From Anacortes, vehicle and driver fares through the San Juans are $24–$27 to Lopez Island, $29–$33 to Orcas and Shaw islands, $35–$39 to Friday Harbor, and $44 (one way) to Sidney, British Columbia. Peak-season rates are higher, so be sure to check ahead. For all fares, you can pay with cash, major credit cards, and debit cards with MasterCard or Visa logos.

Information Clipper Navigation (☏ 800/888–2535 in the U.S., 250/382–8100 in Victoria, 206/448–5000 in Seattle ⊕ www. clippervacations.com.com). **King County Water Taxi** (☏ 206/684–1551 ⊕ kingcounty. gov/transportation/kcdot/WaterTaxi). **Washington State Ferries** (☏ 800/843–3779 automated line in WA and BC, 888/808–7977, 206/464–6400 ⊕ www.wsdot.wa.gov/ferries).

▎LIGHT-RAIL TRAVEL

The culmination of nearly 50 years of mass-transit debates, Seattle finally unveiled the Central Link Light Rail system in 2009—13 years after area voters approved a tax increase to pay for the project, and six embarrassing years after the Tacoma Link Light Rail opened. So if any residents you talk to seem ridiculously pleased about the rails, you'll know why. The Central line runs between the airport and Downtown, with extensions to Capitol Hill slated to open in 2015 and the University of Washington scheduled for 2014. In 2008, residents approved a ballot measure to extend Link Light Rail Northgate, north of the city, and Lynwood, south to Federal Way, and east to Mercer Island, Bellevue, and Microsoft's main campus in Redmond. Given the area's history, Seattleites aren't counting their Light Rail until it's hatched, but eventually travelers should have a dandy rail route to get them around instead of the hodge-podge of transit options now offered. For now, definitely take advantage of the easy and inexpensive route from Sea-Tac airport to Downtown. Simply head to the Link Light Rail station on the fourth floor of the airport parking garage and arrive in Downtown in 36 minutes for just $2.50 (youth fare is $2 and senior/disabled fare is $1.25). Trains depart every 7½ or 15 minutes, depending on the time of day and run from 5 AM to 1 AM Monday through Saturday and 6 AM to midnight on Sundays.

Information Sound Transit (☏ 800/201/4900 or 206/398–5000 ⊕ www.soundtransit.org)

■ MONORAIL TRAVEL

Built for the 1962 World's Fair, the country's first full-scale commercial monorail is a quick, convenient link for tourists; it travels an extremely short route between the Seattle Center and Downtown's Westlake Mall, located at 4th Avenue and Pike Street. Most travelers could walk the 1-mi route without much of a struggle, but the monorail is nostalgic, retro fun. Making the journey in just 2 minutes, the monorail departs both points every 10 minutes. January through April the monorail runs from 8 to 8 Sunday through Thursday and 9 AM to 11 PM Friday and Saturday; resuming its 9 AM to 11 PM summer schedule May through December. The round-trip fare is $4; youth and senior citizens receive a discount and children age 4 and under ride free.

Information Seattle Center Monorail (☎ 206/905–2620 ⊕ www.seattlemonorail. com).

■ STREETCAR TRAVEL

As if Seattle didn't have enough disparate transit options, the city voted in 2005 to add a cute-as-a-button (if a bit superfluous) trolley to run a mere 11-stop, 2.6-mile route between South Lake Union and Downtown. Coined the "South Lake Union Trolley" by charmingly naive planners who didn't notice the less-than-appealing acronym, it was quickly changed to the South Lake Union Streetcar, but not before Seattleites started sporting "Ride the S.L.U.T." T-shirts en masse. If you'd like to ride the Streetcar, simply wait at any of the designated stops and pay the $2.25 (seniors, disabled, and youth $0.75; children under 5 ride free) fare on the trolley after the driver lets you on. Metro bus passes and transfers may be used. The SLUS runs at 15-minute intervals throughout the day from 6 AM to 9 PM, Monday through Thursday, from 6 AM to 11 PM on Fridays and Saturdays, and 10 to 7 on Sundays and holidays. A First Hill Streetcar was approved by voters in 2008 and is slated to run between Capitol Hill, First Hill, and the International District.

Information Seattle Streetcar (☎ 866/205–5001, 206/553–3000 ⊕ www.seattlestreetcar. org).

■ TAXI TRAVEL

Seattle has a smaller taxi fleet than most major cities; taking a cab is not a major form of transportation in the city, and the number of taxis is highly controlled by the city; accordingly, you'll find that rates run higher here. Most people take cabs only to and from the airport and when they go out partying on weekends. You'll often be able to hail cabs on the street in Downtown, but anywhere else, you'll have to call. Expect long waits on Friday and Saturday nights.

Rides generally run about $2 per mile, and unless you're going a very short distance, the average cost of a cab ride in the city is $10–$25 before tip. The meter drop alone is $2.50, and you'll pay 50¢ per minute stuck in traffic. The nice thing about Seattle metered cabs is that they almost always accept credit cards, and an automated system calls you on your cell phone to let you know that your cab has arrived. All cab companies listed below charge the same rates. Visit ⊕ www. taxifarefinder.com before your trip to see roughly how much the fare will cost, and the best route to tell your driver to take.

Metered cabs are not the best way to visit the Eastside or any destination far outside the city—if you get stuck in traffic, you'll pay dearly for it. Take the bus when possible, and ask your hotel for car-service quotes concerning short side trips outside city limits.

Taxi Companies Orange Cab (☎ 206/905–4212). **Red Top Cab** (☎ 206/789–4949). **Farwest Taxi** (☎ 425/454–5055). **Graytop Cab** (☎ 206/622–4800). **Green Cab** (☎ 206/575–4040). **Yellow Cab** (☎ 206/622–6500).

▌ TRAIN TRAVEL

Amtrak, the U.S. passenger-rail system, has daily service to Seattle from the Midwest and California. The *Empire Builder* takes a northern route from Chicago to Seattle, with a stop in St. Paul. The *Coast Starlight* begins in Southern California, makes stops throughout western Oregon and Washington, including Portland, and terminates its route in Seattle. The *Cascades* travels from Eugene, Oregon, up to Vancouver, British Columbia, with several stops in between. If you want to spend a day or two in Portland, taking the train down instead of driving is a great way to do so. It's fast and comfortable, and the Amtrak station in Portland is centrally located. Sit on the left side of the train on the way down for stunning views of Mt. Rainier. All Amtrak trains to and from Seattle pull into King Street Station off of S. Jackson Street in the International District.

Trains to and from Seattle have regular and business-class compartments. Cars with private bedrooms are available for multiday trips (such as to Chicago), while business-class cars provide more legroom, quieter cars, and complimentary newspapers. Reservations are necessary (you can book up to 11 months in advance), and major credit cards are accepted.

Sounder Trains, run by Sound Transit, are commuter trains that run between Seattle and Everett and Seattle and Tacoma and travel only during peak hours on weekdays. Trains leave Tacoma about every half hour between 4:55 AM and 8 AM, and then twice in the evening rush hour, with stops in Puyallup, Sumner, Auburn, Kent, and Tukwila prior to Seattle. Southbound trains leave Seattle twice during morning rush hour and then every half hour between 3:15 and 6:15 PM. Sounder Trains from Everett have four morning departure times between 5:45 and 7:15 AM, stopping in Mukilteo and Edmonds, and offers four return trips from Seattle between 4:05 and 5:35 PM. (Note that there is daily Amtrak service from most of these cities, offering more departure times.)

Fares are based on distance traveled, starting at $2.75 and running up to $4.75 for the Seattle-to-Tacoma trip; youth, senior citizens, and the disabled receive a discounted fare, and kids under 6 ride free. Tickets can be purchased at machines inside the stations or you can use your ORCA card.

Information Amtrak (☎ *800/872–7245 or 206/382–4125* ⊕ *www.amtrak.com*). **Sound Transit** (☎ *800/201–4900 or 206/398–5000* ⊕ *www.soundtransit.org*).

ESSENTIALS

■ ACCOMMODATIONS

There's a something for everyone, accommodation-wise, in this city, from high-end luxury hotels to clever boutique hotels and environmentally friendly options. You'll find historic properties and brand-new digs to be your home away from home. Seattle also has a number of bed-and-breakfasts, though rooms at them tend to go quickly since they represent the best deals in the city during high season. Many of the favorite B&Bs are in Capitol Hill (although you'll find teeny-tiny ones we don't even list just about anywhere in the city), whereas almost all hotels are Downtown. Though the city does have its share of standard budget chain hotels and motels, most of them are terribly overpriced in high season and in awkward spots in the city. The best rule of thumb to get the room that you want is to book as far in advance as possible.

⇨ *For more information about lodging options and for prices, see Chapter 4, Where to Stay.*

Most hotels and other lodgings require you to give your credit-card details before they will confirm your reservation. If you don't feel comfortable booking your hotel online, call the property to give them this information over the phone or ask if you can fax it. However you book, get confirmation in writing and have a copy of it handy when you check in.

Be sure you understand the hotel's cancellation policy. Some places allow you to cancel without any kind of penalty—even if you prepaid to secure a discounted rate—if you cancel at least 24 hours in advance. Others require you to cancel a week in advance or penalize you the cost of one night. Small inns and B&Bs are most likely to require you to cancel far in advance. Most hotels allow children under a certain age to stay in their parents' room at no extra charge, but others charge for them as extra adults; find out the cutoff age for discounts.

■ TIP → Assume that hotels operate on the European Plan (**EP**, no meals) unless we specify that they use the Breakfast Plan (**BP**, with full breakfast), Continental Plan (**CP**, Continental breakfast), Full American Plan (**FAP**, all meals), Modified American Plan (**MAP**, breakfast and dinner) or are all-inclusive (**AI**, all meals and most activities).

■ CRUISES

Seattle's expanding cruise industry now welcomes some of the world's largest ships to docks on Elliott Bay. The city's strategic location along the West Coast means that it's just a day's journey by water to Canada or California, and you can reach Alaska or Mexico in less than a week. In addition to the six major cruise lines that operate weekly service out of Seattle, you can also sail around Elliott Bay, Lake Union, Lake Washington, or along a combination of local waterways in smaller sightseeing boats like Argosy Cruises (*see Day Tours below*).

Norwegian Cruise Line, Carnival Cruise Line, Celebrity Cruises, Holland America Line, Princess Cruises, and Royal Caribbean all offer seven-day summer cruises from Seattle to Alaska. Princess Cruises and Holland America Line also offer 14-day Alaska excursions, if you have more time to explore The Last Frontier. Travelers looking for shorter trips might enjoy Celebrity Cruises three- and four-day Pacific Northwest excursions. Holland America Line, Princess Cruises, Carnival Cruise Line, and Royal Caribbean leave from the Smith Cove Cruise Terminal on Pier 91; Norwegian Cruise Line and Celebrity Cruises depart from the Bell Street Pier Cruise Terminal at Pier 66.

Cruise Lines Carnival Cruise Line (☎ 800/227–6482 ⊕ www.carnival.com).

Celebrity Cruises (☎ 800/647–2251 ⊕ www. celebritycruises.com). **Holland America Line** (☎ 877/932–4259 ⊕ www.hollandamerica. com). **Norwegian Cruise Line** (☎ 866/234– 7350 or 866/234–0292 ⊕ www.ncl.com). **Princess Cruises** (☎ 800/774–6237 ⊕ www. princess.com). **Royal Caribbean** (☎ 866/562– 7625 ⊕ www.royalcaribbean.com).

▎ DAY TOURS AND GUIDES

BICYCLING
Terrene Tours organizes private day trips for groups of up to five for $580, which includes bike rental, guide, support van, lunch, and drinks. They can also set up overnight tours of the surrounding countryside and islands.

BOAT
Argosy Cruises offers sightseeing cruises, dining cruises, and event cruises around the Puget Sound region. Brunch, lunch, and dinner cruises are available, but of the dining cruises, the Tillicum Village excursion is a favorite with tourists—the four-hour trip takes you to Blake Island, where you'll enjoy steamed clams and alder plank–fired salmon before a performance of dance, song, and storytelling in the tradition of Pacific Northwest Coast Indians ($80 for adults, $30 for youth ages 5–12, children under 5 free). If you just want to see more of the Sound but don't want to shell out the bucks, take a quick narrated sightseeing tour around Elliott Bay with Argosy Cruises (1 hour, from Pier 55, $17–$22 for adults), the Ballard Locks (2½ hours, from Pier 56, $33–$40 for adults), which also offers a cruise between Lake Union and Lake Washington (2 hours, from AGC Marina in South Lake Union, $26–$32). Let's Go Sailing permits passengers to take the helm, trim the sails, or simply enjoy the ride aboard the *Obsession* or the SC70 *Neptune's Car,* both 70-foot ocean racers. May through October, three 1½-hour excursions ($25; $18 kids under 12) depart daily from Pier 54. A 2½-hour sunset sail ($40) is also available. Passengers can bring their own food on board, and catering is available for groups.

BUS TOURS
Gray Line of Seattle operates bus, Segway, and boat tours, including a 6½- hour City Sights/Cruise the Locks Combo tour ($61) that includes a bus tour through the city's many neighborhoods, followed by a cruise from Lake Union to the Ship Canal, the Ballard Locks, and then back to Elliott Bay. The hop-on, hop-off double-decker buses ($21) that do hour-long loops of the city core from the Seattle Center to Pioneer Square are the best bet for travelers who want to experience the city from outside of a bus, too. A fun, environmentally friendly option is their three-hour electric Segway tour, where a personal guide will escort up to six adults around Seattle's downtown landmarks, with stops for coffee along the way. Grayline also does day trips to Mt. Rainier and Mt. St. Helens, though note that these tours stop only at scenic lookouts and visitor centers—you won't actually have the chance to do any hiking or exploring in either park. Aviation buffs might enjoy the four-hour Future of Flight/Boeing tour through the Future of Flight Aviation Center and behind Boeing's hanger doors to watch actual airplane assembly.

CARRIAGE
Sealth Horse Carriages narrated tours ($55 per half hour, $100 per hour) trot away from the waterfront and Westlake Center. This tour is particularly fun in the evening—they provide warm blankets and have weather-proof tops in case the night is chilly or wet.

ORIENTATION
For $44 per person, Show Me Seattle takes up to 14 people in vans on three-hour tours of the major sights. Though they bill the tour as Seattle "as the natives see it," this is an extremely touristy program that makes stops at places like the flagship Eddie Bauer store and the first Starbucks, and the *Sleepless in Seattle* floating home, but it also stops by a few

sites many tourists miss, like the Fremont Troll and the north-end neighborhoods. The tour is comprehensive—it takes in the views at Kerry Park in Queen Anne and heads above the canal to see Fremont, Ballard, and Green Lake—but don't expect this tour to be any more authentic than the others. One nice feature, however, is that they'll pick you up at any downtown hotel.

PLANE

Leaving from Lake Union, Seattle Seaplanes' 20-minute scenic flight for $87.50 per person takes in views of Woodland Park Zoo, Downtown Seattle, the Cascades and Olympics, the Ballard Locks, and Lake Washington. The company also schedules flying lessons, charter trips to places like Mt. Rainier, and dinner flights to the San Juans and area islands. Kenmore Air makes scenic flights over the metro area, as well as to the San Juan Islands, the Skagit Valley Tulip Festival, Port Angeles (*Twilight* fans take note—they offer special packages for this flight), Victoria, British Columbia, and its surrounding areas.

SELF-GUIDED

One way to tour Seattle at your own pace is with the Go Seattle Card, which provides admission to more than 35 of the city's top attractions. The credit-card-style ticket comes with a map and guidebook, and then you're off to explore the Space Needle, Museum of Flight, Museum of Glass, Safeco Field, the Experience Music Project, and other famous sights. Families with kids will enjoy all the kid-friendly attractions, like the Woodland Park Zoo, Indoor Karting, and the Children's Museum, while adult travelers might appreciate the Wine Tour and the included art galleries. Slightly discounted cards are available for children, students, and seniors, and if you're not up for a one-day whirlwind sweep through the city, they also come in two-, three-, five-, and seven-day increments. But before you buy one, think seriously about how many admissions costs you'll encounter each day—the cards start at $45 for one day of sightseeing ($29 for children); the seven-day is probably the best deal at $121 if you're planning to do a lot of the high-admission tours and museums in the area. Unless you're doing a lot of hopping around between museums and major sights like the Space Needle, it may not be worth the price.

WALKING

Chinatown Discovery Tours offers 1½-hour walking tours of the neighborhood and includes admission to the affiliated Wing Luke Asian Museum; tickets are $17. More entertaining might be the Taste of Chinatown private group tour for four to nine people—enjoy a private 90-minute tour, followed by a six-course Chinese lunch for $37 per person. Seattle Walking Tours creates customized, 2½-hour itineraries that cover specific areas of the city. These cost $15 per person for a minimum of three guests.

Tour Companies Argosy Cruises (☎ 888/623–1445 or 206/622–8687 ⊕ www.argosycruises.com). **Chinatown Discovery Tours** (☎ 206/623–5124 ⊕ www.seattlechinatowntour.com). **Go Seattle Card** (☎ 866/628–9029 ⊕ www.goseattlecard.com). **Gray Line of Seattle** (☎ 800/824–8897 or 206/626–5200 ⊕ graylineseattle.com/sightseeingtours.cfm). **Kenmore Air** (☎ 866/435–9524 or 425/486–1257 ⊕ www.kenmoreair.com). **Let's Go Sailing** (☎ 206/624–3931 ⊕ www.sailingseattle.com). **Sealth Horse Carriages** (☎ 206/313–0722 ⊕ www.sealthcarriages.com). **Seattle Seaplanes** (☎ 800/637–5553 or 206/329–9638 ⊕ www.seattleseaplanes.com). **Seattle Tours** (☎ 206/768–1234 ⊕ www.seattlecitytours.com). **Seattle Walking Tours** (☎ 425/885–3173 ⊕ www.seattlewalkingtours.com/walk_tour.htm). **Show Me Seattle** (☎ 206/633–2489 ⊕ www.showmeseattle.com). **Terrene Tours** (☎ 206/325–5569).

▌ MONEY

Almost all businesses and attractions accept debit and credit cards, though small surcharges may apply for charges under $5. The only exceptions are some smaller restaurants and bakeries.

Many metered cabs also accept credit cards or debit cards with the MasterCard or Visa logo.

Prices throughout this guide are given for adults. Substantially reduced fees are almost always available for children, students, and senior citizens.

Throughout this guide, the following abbreviations are used: **AE**, American Express; **D**, Discover; **DC**, Diners Club; **MC**, MasterCard; and **V**, Visa.

▌ ONLINE TRAVEL TOOLS

The tourist boards' sites will no doubt be your first stops. The home page for the Seattle Convention and Visitor's Bureau is ⊕ *www.visitseattle.org*. For insight on the entire state, head to Washington State Tourism's ⊕ *www.experiencewa. com*. Information straight from the city's leaders is at ⊕ *www.cityofseattle.net/ html/visitor*. Forget driving. Take public transportation—including the bus, streetcar, and water taxi. This site tells you how: ⊕ *metro.kingcounty.gov*. OK. So you have to drive. The site ⊕ *www. wsdot.wa.gov/traffic/* will help you navigate Seattle's traffic.

Almost every neighborhood in Seattle has its own Web site, and many have their own blogs, but some are more useful than others. The Downtown Seattle Association offers the very professional-looking ⊕ *www.downtownseattle.com*, with a great calendar page and a helpful "Getting Around" page with good maps. You can learn more about Pioneer Square at ⊕ *www.pioneersquare.org*. The site has excellent maps of the area along with detailed info on parking and on the popular monthly art walks. Ballard's ⊕ *www. inballard.com* has up-to-date listings and reviews of the neighborhood's major businesses and sights, complete with pictures of each. Navigating ⊕ *www.fremont.com* requires some patience, but the calendar and listings are usually kept up to date, and the "Urban Myths" section gives you the back stories on the neighborhood's iconic public art. Find out what's going on in the neighborhood around the University of Washington by logging on to ⊕ *www.udistrictchamber.org*. The site isn't terribly exciting, but it has a good collection of links and a list of merchants that validate parking. Stop by ⊕ *www. greenwood-phinney.com* for the scoop on neighborhood shops and information on their excellent monthly art walk (the second Friday of each month). Surprisingly, Capitol Hill doesn't have its own site, but it has a very popular blog, ⊕ *www.blog. capitolhillseattle.com*. Ignore the crime report-type info on the site (it will scare you unnecessarily, and the neighborhood really is quite safe), and head directly to the blog's maps and calendars. For travelers looking to get off the beaten path, check out ⊕ *www.georgetownneighborhood. com*. "Seattle's Fiesty, Intensely Creative Neighborhood" is worth a look. To learn more about Bellevue, a rapidly growing mini-city in the Eastside suburbs, look to ⊕ *www.bellevuechamber.org*.

NWSource (⊕ *www.nwsource.com*), which is affiliated with the *Seattle Times,* is an easy-to-search database with information on all neighborhoods (and their businesses) in Seattle and the Eastside. It's like a local version of Citysearch—packed with information, at least half of which is up to date. To delve a little too deeply into the daily minutiae of Seattle residents, check out ⊕ *www.seattlest.com*. Among the snark and obsessive commentary on local sports teams, you'll find decent restaurant reviews and the weekly "Get Out" posts, listing the best events in the city from readings at the Elliott Bay Book Company to concerts at Neumo's.

The *Seattle Post-Intelligencer* Web site (⊕ *www.seattlepi.com*) is full of breaking local and national news. The *Seattle Times* daily newspaper is one of the country's largest independently owned. Its Web site (⊕ *www.seattletimes.com*) has frequently updated local news and entertainment information. The site, run by the irreverent free weekly newspaper *The Stranger* (⊕ *www.thestranger.com*), is a good place to find fun things to do—especially at night. The *Seattle Weekly* (⊕ *www.seattleweekly.com*) focuses on local political coverage and entertainment but is a great resource for eating out. Use the site's search tool to narrow your culinary options by type of food, neighborhood, price, and feature (such as outdoor dining).

▌ SAFETY

Seattle is generally safe. The airport, ground transit links, ferries, and popular sights are well monitored by guards and cameras, and the city's knowledgeable travel personnel are on hand to help set visitors in the right direction. Tight rules apply as to what you can bring into stadiums, arenas, and performance venues; expect bag searches, X-ray machines, and/or metal detectors.

Use common sense and you'll avoid trouble. Always lock your car (there are plenty of break-ins, especially in residential areas), don't leave valuables in your vehicle, and park in lighted areas after dark; be careful when walking alone Downtown during late hours; don't flash cash or valuables in heavily touristed areas where petty theft might occur. Keep your laptop in the hotel safe when it's not in use.

Panhandlers tend to frequent Pioneer Square, Belltown, Capitol Hill, the U-District, and some area parks. Even visitors and transplants who come from other major cities with large homeless populations are surprised by how aggressive (and at times, verbally abusive) Seattle's panhandlers can be. You may pass your entire vacation without incident, but don't be surprised if someone curses you out after you refuse to give them money.

▌ TAXES

There is a 15.6% hotel tax in Seattle for hotels with more than 60 rooms, 9.5% for properties with fewer than 20 rooms; in Bellevue the rates are 9.5% and 12%, respectively. Renting a car in Seattle will set you back with a 19.2% tax, and there are additional taxes for renting cars at the airport.

The sales tax in Seattle is 9.5% and is applied to all purchases except groceries and prescription drugs. At restaurants you'll pay a 10% food and beverage tax.

▌ TIME

Washington State is in the Pacific Standard Time zone, which is 2 hours earlier than Chicago, 3 hours earlier than New York, 8 hours earlier than London, and 18 hours earlier than Sydney.

▌ TIPPING

Tips and service charges are usually not automatically added to a bill in the United States (except when your party is over six people). If service is satisfactory, customers generally give wait staff, taxi drivers, barbers, hairdressers, and so forth, a tip of from 15% to 20% of the total bill (Be aware that tipping wait staff less than 15% is considered a sign that service was bad). Bellhops, doormen, and porters at airports and railway stations are generally tipped $1 for each item of luggage. In Seattle there is no recognized system for tipping concierges. A gratuity of $2–$5 is suggested if you have the concierge arrange for a service such as restaurant reservations, theater tickets, or a town car, and $10–$20 if the service is more extensive or unusual, such as having a large bouquet of roses delivered on a Sunday.

▌ VACATION PACKAGES

Packages *are not* guided excursions. Packages combine airfare, accommodations, and perhaps a rental car or other extras (theater tickets, guided excursions, boat trips, reserved entry to popular museums, transit passes), but they let you do your own thing. During busy periods packages may be your only option, as flights and rooms may be sold out otherwise.

Packages will definitely save you time. They can also save you money, particularly in peak seasons, but—and this is a really big "but"—you should price each part of the package separately to be sure. And be aware that prices advertised on Web sites and in newspapers rarely include service charges or taxes, which can up your costs by hundreds of dollars.

■ TIP → Some packages and cruises are sold only through travel agents. Don't always assume that you can get the best deal by booking everything yourself.

Each year consumers are stranded or lose their money when packagers—even large ones with excellent reputations—go out of business. How can you protect yourself?

First, always pay with a credit card; if you have a problem, your credit-card company may help you resolve it. Second, buy trip insurance that covers default. Third, choose a company that belongs to the United States Tour Operators Association, whose members must set aside funds to cover defaults. Finally, choose a company that also participates in the Tour Operator Program of the American Society of Travel Agents (ASTA), which will act as mediator in any disputes.

You can also check on the tour operator's reputation among travelers by posting an inquiry on one of the Fodors.com forums.

Organizations American Society of Travel Agents (*ASTA* ⊕ *www.travelsense.org*).
United States Tour Operators Association (*USTOA* ⊕ *www.ustoa.com*). ■ TIP → Local tourism boards can provide information about lesser-known and small-niche operators that sell packages to only a few destinations.

▌ VISITOR INFORMATION

The Seattle Convention and Visitors Bureau is really pulling out all the stops these days. Not only have they coined a new slightly cringe-worthy yet oddly appropriate tagline for Seattle—"Metronatural"—but they have rebranded their visitor center as the "Citywide Concierge Center." The service, which has an office in the Washington State Trade and Convention Center on Pike Street (between 7th and 8th avenues), can help you plan all aspects of your trip from securing events tickets to making accommodations and restaurant reservations to arranging ground transportation and other services. They're set up to accept drop-ins (open weekdays 9 to 5 daily in the summer and during the winter months), and you can also contact them before your trip with questions and requests. They have a second information location at 1st and Pike, open daily from 10 to 6. This location isn't as full service as the 7th and Pike center, but they'll still be able to answer many questions, offer suggestions, and load you up with maps and brochures.

If you're having trouble planning a side trip out of the city, call Washington State Tourism; you can request brochures or speak with a travel planner weekdays from 8 to 5 PST (closed on major holidays).

Contacts Seattle Convention and Visitors Bureau (☎ *206/461–5840* ⊕ *www.visitseattle. org*). **Washington State Tourism** (☎ *800/544– 1800* ⊕ *www.experiencewa.com*).

INDEX

PHOTO CREDITS

1, Jeremy Edwards/iStockphoto. 2, SuperStock/age fotostock. 3, SuperStock/age fotostock. 5, Mark B. Bauschke/Shutterstock. **Chapter 1: Experience Seattle:** 8-9, Patrick Bennett/Alamy. 10, Liem Bahneman/ Shutterstock. 11 (left), Bitman/Flickr. 11 (right), Arthur S. Aubry. 12, Steve Whiston/Burke Museum. 13 (left), Tes de Luna. 13 (right), Stephen Finn/Shutterstock. 16, Victrola Coffee/Kent Colony. 17, George Ostertag/age fotostock. 18, Justin Gollmer. 19 (left), Natalia Bratslavsky/Shutterstock. 19 (right), Geoffrey Smith. 20 (left), Lara Swimmer Photography. 20 (top right), HeyRocker/Flickr. 20 (bottom right), Anita Elder/iStockphoto. 21 (top left), Tim Thompson. 21 (bottom left), KingWu/iStockphoto. 21 (top right), Vladimir Menkov/wikipedia.org. 21 (bottom right), Arbotetum Foundation/Joy Spurr. 22, Justin Gollmer. 23(left), dizfunkshinal/Flickr. 23(right), neelsky/Shutterstock. 24, razvan.orendovici/Flickr. 25, Seattle Municipal Archives/Flickr. 26, Pacific Science Center. 27, quaziefoto/Flickr. 28, iotae/Flickr. 29, Mark Windom / age fotostock. 30, Arboretum Foundation/Joy Spurr. 31 (left), Greg Vaughn. 31 (top right), mikeledray/Shutterstock. 31 (bottom), Charles Finkel. 32 (all), Victrola Coffee/Kent Colony. 33 (left), LWY/Flickr. 33 (top), mtcarlson/Flickr. 33 (bottom), Victrola Coffee/Kent Colony. 34 (top), Vaclav Mach/Shutterstock. 34 (bottom), Elysian Brewing Company. 35 (top), David Blaine/ Flickr. 35 (bottom), Charles Finkel. 35 (right), Patrick Wright Photography. 36 (left), Greg Vaughn. 36 (right), Chateau Ste. Michelle. 37 (left), Kevin Cruff. 37 (right), Chateau Ste. Michelle. 38, Greg Vaughn. **Chapter 2: Seattle Neighborhoods:.** 39, José Fuste Raga/age fotostock. 42, Lara Swimmer Photography. 43, Mariusz S. Jurgielewicz/Shutterstock. 45, Lara Swimmer Photography. 47, RonGreer. Com/Shutterstock. 48, jeffwilcox/Flickr. 50, Joseph Calev/Shutterstock. 53, Caitlin Mirra/Shutterstock. 54, Anita Elder/iStockphoto. 56, Caitlin Mirra/Shutterstock. 57, Gregory Olsen/iStockphoto. 59, Poul Costinsky/Shutterstock. 61, Chris Cheadle/age fotostock. 63, Laura Komada. 65, Richard Cummins/ age fotostock. 67, Wing Luke Museum. 69, moochida/Flickr. 70, Wing Luke Museum . 71, rutlo/ Flickr. 73, Sue Elias/Flickr. 75, Jill Hardy. 76, neelsky/Shutterstock. 79, wikipedia.org. 81, Glenn R. McGloughlin/Shutterstock. 82, dherrera_96/Flickr. 83, Theo Chocolate, Inc. 85, Harry Hu/Shutterstock. 86, Danita Delimont/Alamy. 88, Anita Elder/iStockphoto. 89, L.L.Masseth/Shutterstock. 91, Wildcat Dunny/Flickr. 92, Danita Delimont/Alamy. 94, RonGreer.Com/Shutterstock. 97, dk/Alamy. 98, Wonderlane/Flickr. 99 and 101, Andrew Waits/Burke Museum. 102, DVD R W/wikipedia.org. 104, L.L.Masseth/Shutterstock. 105, Tim Thompson. 107, Meredith Blache/iStockphoto. 109, Tammy Wolfe/iStockphoto. 110, Kevin Cruff. 113, Joseph Calev/Shutterstock. 114, Sayaka Ito. 116, joaquinuy/ Flickr. **Chapter 3: Where to Eat:** 117-18, Geoffrey Smith. 120, John Granen. 122-23, Chas Redmond/ Flickr. 124 (top), Geoffrey Smith. 124 (bottom), Nick Jurich of flashpd.com. 125 (top and bottom), Geoffrey Smith. 127, Nick Jurich of flashpd.com. 134 and 141, Geoffrey Smith. 143, Thomas M. Barwick. 146, 2008 John Granen. 157, joaquinuy/Flickr. 160, Geoffrey Smith. 161, Thomas M. Barwick. **Chapter 4: Where to Stay:** 171, Peter Vitale. 172, Benjamin Benschneider. 174, Steve Sanacore. 176 (left), Fairmont Hotels & Resorts. 176 (right), Pan Pacific Hotel Seattle. 182 (top), Fairmont Hotels & Resorts. 182 (bottom), Benjamin Benschneider. 188 (top), Mark Bauschke. 188 (left), Pan Pacific Hotel Seattle. 188 (right), Hotel 1000. **Chapter 5: Nightlife and the Arts:** 203, HeyRocker/Flickr. 206, p_a_h/ Flickr. 215, Elysian Brewing Company. 222, Richard Cummins/age fotostock. 225, HeyRocker/Flickr. 227, Dcoetzee/wikipedia.org. **Chapter 6: Shopping:** 237, Pike Place Market. 239-40, MACSURAK/ Flickr. 241 (left), SheriW/Flickr. 241 (right), thebittenword.com/Flickr. 242, Vérité Ventures. 243 (left), ChrisDag/Flickr. 243 (right), Hunters Capital. 252, Chris Howes/Wild Places Photography/Alamy. 256, Chuck Pefley/Alamy. 258, Mark B. Bauschke/Shutterstock. 258 (bottom), Charles Amundson/Shutterstock. 260 (left), piroshky bakery. 260 (top), The Tasting Room. 260 (right), Beecherís Handmade Cheese. 261 (left), Phillie Casablanca/Flickr. 261 (top), Nick Jurich of flashpd.com. 261 (right), eng1ne/ Flickr. 262 (top left), Liem Bahneman/Shutterstock. 262 (bottom), Pike Place Market PDA. 262 (right), World Pictures/Phot/age fotostock. 263 (left), Stephen Power/Alamy. 263 (right), Rootology/wikipedia. org. 270, Tes de Luna. **Chapter 7: Sports and Activities:** 277, Agua Verde Paddle Club. 278, fotofriends/Shutterstock. 280, ebis50/Flickr. 283, rob casey/Alamy. 284, Joe Mabel/wikipedia.org. 285 (left), Nathan Fabro/iStockphoto. 285 (right), Wolfgang Kaehler/Alamy. 286 (top), Visions of America, LLC/Alamy. 286 (bottom), wikipedia.org. 287, Chris Howes/Wild Places Photography/Alamy. 289 (left), Danita Delimont/Alamy. 289 (center), jeffwilcox/Flickr. 289 (right), Chad Davis. 290, Agua Verde Paddle Club. 296-97, Peter Arnold, Inc./Alamy. **Chapter 8: Side Trips from Seattle:** 303, Christina T. Mallet/age fotostock. 304, mike harrison/iStockphoto. 306, yel02/Flickr. 308, LegalAdmin/Flickr. 315, Richard Cummins/age fotostock. 316, Joe Becker/age fotostock. 323, Hauke Dressler/age fotostock. 324, UnGePhoto/Shutterstock. 329, Danita Delimont/Alamy. 332, Bill Stevenson/age fotostock. 337, Paula Borchardt/age fotostock. 338-39, zschnepf/Shutterstock. 349, Danny Warren/Shutterstock. 350, Joop Snijder/iStockphoto. 353, Lindsay Douglas/Shutterstock. 360, Steve Bower/Shutterstock.

NOTES

NOTES

NOTES

NOTES

NOTES

NOTES

ABOUT OUR WRITERS

Former Fodor's editor Carissa Bluestone is a Seattle-based freelance writer and editor. She's written about the Emerald City for Fodor's *Pacific Northwest*, TravelandLeisure.com, and Concierge.com; explored the future of sustainable tourism for Worldchanging.com; and updated several other Fodor's guides, including *Mexico* and *Alaska*. She has edited numerous books on subjects ranging from sustainability to martial arts.

Cedar Burnett sometimes finds herself "sleep-packing" in the night for whatever travel adventure she's been dreaming about and is training her toddler to say, "Where is the bathroom?" in 17 different languages. A Seattle native, Cedar can usually be found hiking around the city when she's not writing. She updated this edition's Where to Stay, Shopping, and Travel Smart chapters.

Seattle-based freelancer Nick Horton has been writing about the Pacific Northwest for six years. In addition to his Fodor's assignments, he has written for *Seattle Magazine, Seattle Business, Alaska Airlines Magazine,* and the late, great *Seattle Post-Intelligencer*. Nick's interests include cycling, running, and the wide worlds of food and wine, and he is constantly exploring the many corners of his beloved Washington State.

Heidi Johansen edited and wrote for this edition. A native Seattleite, she relished the opportunity to explore and write about the museums, parks, restaurants, and coffeehouses that lured her back to the Emerald City from New York.